Lecture Notes in Artificial Intelligence   8876

Subseries of Lecture Notes in Computer Science

LNAI Series Editors

Randy Goebel
  University of Alberta, Edmonton, Canada
Yuzuru Tanaka
  Hokkaido University, Sapporo, Japan
Wolfgang Wahlster
  DFKI and Saarland University, Saarbrücken, Germany

LNAI Founding Series Editor

Joerg Siekmann
  DFKI and Saarland University, Saarbrücken, Germany

T0234444

Krzysztof Janowicz   Stefan Schlobach
Patrick Lambrix   Eero Hyvönen (Eds.)

Knowledge Engineering and Knowledge Management

19th International Conference, EKAW 2014
Linköping, Sweden, November 24-28, 2014
Proceedings

 Springer

Volume Editors

Krzysztof Janowicz
University of California, Santa Barbara, CA, USA
E-mail: janowicz@ucsb.edu

Stefan Schlobach
VU University Amsterdam, The Netherlands
E-mail: k.s.schlobach@vu.nl

Patrick Lambrix
University of Linköping, Sweden
E-mail: patrick.lambrix@liu.se

Eero Hyvönen
Aalto University, Finland
E-mail: eero.hyvonen@aalto.fi

ISSN 0302-9743   e-ISSN 1611-3349
ISBN 978-3-319-13703-2   e-ISBN 978-3-319-13704-9
DOI 10.1007/978-3-319-13704-9
Springer Cham Heidelberg New York Dordrecht London

Library of Congress Control Number: 2014955256

LNCS Sublibrary: SL 7 – Artificial Intelligence

Typesetting: Camera-ready by author, data conversion by Scientific Publishing Services, Chennai, India

Printed on acid-free paper

Springer is part of Springer Science+Business Media (www.springer.com)

Preface

This volume contains the proceedings of the 19th International Conference on Knowledge Engineering and Knowledge Management (EKAW 2014), held in Linköping, Sweden, during November 24–28, 2014. This was the first EKAW conference in a Nordic country. It was concerned with all aspects of eliciting, acquiring, modeling, and managing knowledge, the construction of knowledge-intensive systems and services for the Semantic Web, knowledge management, e-business, natural language processing, intelligent information integration, personal digital assistance systems, and a variety of other related topics.

The special focus of EKAW 2014 was *Diversity*. Today, multi-thematic, multi-perspective, multi-cultural, multi-media, and multi-dimensional data are available at an ever-increasing spatial, temporal, and thematic resolution. This allows us to gain a more holistic understanding of complex physical and social processes that cannot be explained from within one domain alone. While scale and complexity of information has always attracted attention, its heterogeneity in nature and usage are only now being investigated more systematically. To publish, retrieve, clean, reuse, and integrate these data requires novel knowledge engineering and management methods. Thus, EKAW 2014 put a special emphasis on this diversity of knowledge and its usage.

For the main conference we invited submissions for research papers that present novel methods, techniques, or analysis with appropriate empirical or other types of evaluation, as well as in-use papers describing applications of knowledge management and engineering in real environments. We also invited submissions of position papers describing novel and innovative ideas that are still in an early stage. In addition to the regular conference submission, we established a combined conference/journal submission track. Papers accepted for the combined track were published as regular research papers in this EKAW 2014 Springer conference proceedings and authors were also invited to submit an extended version of their manuscript for a fast-track in the *Semantic Web* journal (SWJ) published by IOS Press. The journal follows an open review process. All submitted papers were publicly available during the review phase and the reviews and final decisions were posted online, thereby making the review process more transparent.

Overall, we received 168 abstract submissions, 138 which were submitted as papers. We are very glad to report that 45 author teams decided to submit to the combined track, thus making their papers and reviews publicly available. These papers were either accepted for the conference and journal, for the conference only, or rejected for both. In total, 45 submissions were accepted by the Program Committee: seven for the combined EKAW/SWJ track, 17 full papers for the conference only, 17 as short(er) papers, and four position papers.

To complement the program, we invited three distinguished keynote speakers:

- Pascal Hitzler (Wright State University, Dayton, Ohio, USA) presented a talk on "Ontology Design Patterns for Large-Scale Data Interchange and Discovery."
- Arianna Betti (University of Amsterdam, The Netherlands) gave a talk on "Concepts in Motion."
- Oscar Corcho (Universidad Politecnica de Madrid, Spain) discussed the question "Ontology Engineering for and by the Masses: Are We Already There?"

The program chairs of EKAW 2014 were Krzysztof Janowicz from the University of California, Santa Barbara, USA, and Stefan Schlobach from the Vrije Universiteit Amsterdam, The Netherlands.

The EKAW 2014 program included a Doctoral Consortium that provided PhD students an opportunity to present their research ideas and results in a stimulating environment, to get feedback from mentors who are experienced research scientists in the community, to explore issues related to academic and research careers, and to build relationships with other PhD students from around the world. The Doctoral Consortium was intended for students at each stage of their PhD. All accepted presenters had an opportunity to present their work to an international audience, to be paired with a mentor, and to discuss their work with experienced scientists from the research community. The Doctoral Consortium was organized by Ying Ding from the Indiana University Bloomington, USA, and Chiara Ghidini from The Fondazione Bruno Kessler in Italy.

In addition to the main research track, EKAW 2014 hosted four satellite workshops and two tutorials:

Workshops

1. *VISUAL2014.* International Workshop on Visualizations and User Interfaces for Knowledge Engineering and Linked Data Analytics
2. *EKM1.* The First International Workshop on Educational Knowledge Management
3. *ARCOE-Logic 2014.* The 6th International Workshop on Acquisition, Representation and Reasoning about Context with Logic
4. *WaSABi2014.* The Third International Workshop on Semantic Web Enterprise Adoption and Best Practice

Tutorials

1. *K4D*: Managing and Sharing Knowledge in Rural Parts of the World. By Stefan Schlobach, Victor de Boer, Christophe Guret, Stéphane Boyera, and Philippe Cudré-Mauroux.
2. *Language Resources and Linked Data.* By Jorge Gracia, Asuncion Gomez-Perez, Sebastian Hellmann, John McCrae, Roberto Navigli, and Daniel Vila-Suero.

The workshop and tutorial programs were chaired by Eva Blomqvist from Linköping University, Sweden, as well as Valentina Presutti from STLab ISTC-CNR, Italy.

Finally, EKAW 2014 also featured a demo and poster session. We encouraged contributions that were likely to stimulate critical or controversial discussions about any of the areas of the EKAW conference series. We also invited developers to showcase their systems and the benefit they can bring to a particular application. The demo and poster programs of EKAW 2014 were chaired by Guilin Qi from the Southeast University, China, and Uli Sattler from the University of Manchester, UK.

The conference organization also included Axel-Cyrille Ngonga Ngomo from the Universität Leipzig, Germany, as the sponsorship chair, Henrik Eriksson and Patrick Lambrix both from Linköping University, Sweden, took care of local arrangements, and Zlatan Dragisic and Valentina Ivanova from Linköping University, Sweden, acted as Web presence chairs. Eero Hyvönen from Aalto University, Finland, and Patrick Lambrix from Linköping University, Sweden, were the general chairs of EKAW 2014.

Thanks to everybody, including attendees at the conference, for making EKAW 2014 a successful event.

November 2014

Patrick Lambrix
Eero Hyvönen
Krzysztof Janowicz
Stefan Schlobach

Organization

The 19th EKAW 2014 conference in Linköping was organized by the following team.

Executive Committee

General Chairs

Patrick Lambrix	Linköping University, Sweden
Eero Hyvönen	Aalto University, Finland

Program Chairs

Krzysztof Janowicz	University of California, Santa Barbara, USA
Stefan Schlobach	VU University, The Netherlands

Workshop and Tutorial Chairs

Eva Blomqvist	Linköping University, Sweden
Valentina Presutti	STLab ISTC-CNR, Italy

Demo and Poster Chairs

Guilin Qi	Southeast University, China
Uli Sattler	University of Manchester, UK

Sponsorship Chair

Axel-Cyrille Ngomo	Leipzig University, Germany

Doctoral Consortium Chairs

Ying Ding	Indiana University Bloomington, USA
Chiara Ghidini	FBK, Italy

Local Organization Chairs

Patrick Lambrix	Linköping University, Sweden
Henrik Eriksson	Linköping University, Sweden

Web Presence Chairs

Zlatan Dragisic	Linköping University, Sweden
Valentina Ivanova	Linköping University, Sweden

Program Committee

Benjamin Adams	The University of Auckland, Australia
Lora Aroyo	VU University Amsterdam, The Netherlands
Sören Auer	University of Bonn and Fraunhofer IAIS, Germany
Nathalie Aussenac-Gilles	IRIT Toulouse, France
Andrea Ballatore	UCD Dublin, Ireland
Wouter Beek	VU University Amsterdam, The Netherlands
Olivier Bodenreider	US National Library of Medicine, USA
Joost Breuker	University of Amsterdam, The Netherlands
Christopher Brewster	Aston University, Birmingham, UK
Liliana Cabral	CSIRO, Australia
Vinay Chaudhri	SRI International, USA
Michelle Cheatham	Wright State University in Dayton, Ohio, USA
Paolo Ciancarini	University of Bologna, Italy
Philipp Cimiano	University of Bielefeld, Germany
Paul Compton	The University of New South Wales, Australia
Olivier Corby	Inria, France
Ronald Cornet	AMC - Universiteit van Amsterdam, The Netherlands
Claudia D'Amato	University of Bari. Italy
Mathieu D'Aquin	The Open University, UK
Aba-Sah Dadzie	University of Birmingham, UK
Victor de Boer	VU Amsterdam, The Netherlands
Stefan Decker	DERI Galway, Ireland
Daniele Dell'Aglio	DEI, Politecnico di Milano, Italy
Emanuele Della Valle	DEI, Politecnico di Milano, Italy
Klaas Dellschaft	University Koblenz-Landau, Germany
Zlatan Dragisic	Linköping University, Sweden
Henrik Eriksson	Linköping University, Sweden
Dieter Fensel	University of Innsbruck, Austria
Jesualdo Tomás Fernández-Breis	Universidad de Murcia, Spain
Antske Fokkens	VU Amsterdam, The Netherlands
Aldo Gangemi	Université Paris 13 and CNR-ISTC, France
Serge Garlatti	Telecom Bretagne, France
Dragan Gasevic	Athabasca University, Canada
Chiara Ghidini	FBK-irst, Italy
Luca Gilardoni	Quinary
Paul Groth	VU University Amsterdam, The Netherlands
Michael Gruninger	University of Toronto, Canada
Jon Atle Gulla	Norwegian University of Science and Technology, Norway

Christophe Guéret	Data Archiving and Networked Services (DANS)
Asunción Gómez-Pérez	Universidad Politécnica de Madrid, Spain
Peter Haase	fluid Operations
Harry Halpin	World Wide Web Consortium
Tom Heath	Open Data Institute
Martin Hepp	Bundeswehr University of Munich, Germany
Jesper Hoeksema	VU University Amsterdam, The Netherlands
Rinke Hoekstra	University of Amsterdam/VU University Amsterdam, The Netherlands
Aidan Hogan	Universidad de Chile, Chile
Matthew Horridge	Stanford University, USA
Andreas Hotho	University of Würzburg, Germany
Yingjie Hu	University of California, Santa Barbara, USA
Zhisheng Huang	Vrije University Amsterdam, The Netherlands
Antoine Isaac	Europeana and VU University Amsterdam, The Netherlands
Valentina Ivanova	Linköping University, Sweden
C. Maria Keet	University of Cape Town, South Africa
Adila A. Krisnadhi	Wright State University, USA, and Universitas Indonesia
Wolfgang Maass	Saarland University, Germany
Grant McKenzie	University of California, Santa Barbara, USA
Albert Meroño Peñuela	VU University Amsterdam, DANS, KNAW, The Netherlands
Peter Mika	Yahoo! Research
Michele Missikoff	IASI-CNR
Riichiro Mizoguchi	Japan Advanced Institute of Science and Technology
Dunja Mladenic	Jozef Stefan Institute, Slovenia
Andrea Moro	Sapienza, Università di Roma, Italy
Enrico Motta	Knowledge Media Institute, The Open University, UK
Raghavan Mutharaju	Kno.e.sis Center, Wright State University, USA
Axel-Cyrille Ngonga Ngomo	University of Leipzig, Germany
Vit Novacek	DERI, National University of Ireland, Galway
Jens Ortmann	Softplant GmbH
Matteo Palmonari	University of Milano-Bicocca, Italy
Viktoria Pammer	Know-Center Graz, Austria
Maryam Panahiazar	Kno.e.sis Center, Wright State University, USA
Sujan Perera	Kno.e.sis Center, Wright State University, USA
Wim Peters	University of Sheffield, UK
Mohammad Taher Pilevar	Student University
H. Sofia Pinto	Instituto Superior Tecnico

Additional Reviewers

Abu Helou, Mamoun
Bozzato, Loris
Costabello, Luca
Ell, Basil
Faerber, Michael
Fensel, Anna
Fleischhacker, Daniel
García, José María
Gentile, Anna Lisa
Hentschel, Christian
Huan, Gao
Kapanipathi, Pavan
Knuth, Magnus
Lasierra Beamonte, Nelia
Mosso, Pierluigi

Muñoz, Emir
Neidhardt, Julia
Nuzzolese, Andrea Giovanni
Petrucci, Giulio
Pinkel, Christoph
Pobiedina, Nataliia
Schreiber, Guus
Taglino, Francesco
Thalhammer, Andreas
Thomas, Christopher
Waitelonis, Joerg
Wijeratne, Sanjaya
Wu, Tianxing
Zhang, Lei

Keynote Papers

Concepts in Motion

Arianna Betti

Universiteit van Amsterdam
ariannabetti@gmail.com

Abstract. The history of ideas traces the development of ideas such as evolution, liberty, or science in human thought as represented in texts. Recent contributions [2] suggest that the increasing quantities of digitally available historical data can be of invaluable help to historians of ideas.

However, these and similar contributions usually apply generic computer methods, simple n-gram analyses and shallow NLP tools to historical textual material. This practice contrasts strikingly with the reality of research in the history of ideas and related fields such as history of science. Researchers in this area typically apply painstakingly fine-grained analyses to diverse textual material of extremely high conceptual density. Can these opposites be reconciled? In other words: Is a digital history of ideas possible?

Yes, I argue, but only by requiring historians of ideas to provide explicitly structured semantic framing of domain knowledge before investigating texts computationally (models in the sense of [1]), and to constantly re-input findings from the interpretive point of view in a process of semi-automatic ontology extraction.

This is joint work with Hein van den Berg.

References

1. Betti, A., van den Berg, H.: Modeling the History of Ideas. British Journal for the History of Philosophy 22(3) (2014) (forthcoming)
2. Michel, J.B., Yuan Kui, S., Aviva Presser, A., Veres, A., Gray, M.K., Pickett, J.P., Hoiberg, D.: Quantitative analysis of culture using millions of digitized books. Science 331(6014), 176–182 (2011)

Ontology Engineering for and by the Masses: Are We Already There?

Oscar Corcho

Universidad Politecnica de Madrid

Abstract. We can assume that most of the attendees to this conference have created or contributed to the development of at least one ontology, and many of them have several years of experience in ontology development. The area of ontology engineering is already quite mature, hence creating ontologies should not be a very difficult task. We have methodologies that guide us in the process of ontology development; we have plenty of techniques that we can use, from the knowledge acquisition stages to ontology usage; we have tools that facilitate the transition from our ontology conceptualizations to actual implementations, including support for tasks like debugging, documenting, modularising, reasoning, and a large etcétera. However, how many ontology developers are there now in the world? Are they hundreds, thousands, tens of thousands maybe? Not as many as we may like... In fact, whenever I setup an heterogeneous ontology development team in a domain, I still find lots of difficulties to get the team running at full speed and with high quality results. In this talk I will share some of my most recent experiences on the setup of several small ontology development teams, composed of a combination of city managers, policy makers and computer scientists, for the development of a set of ontologies for an upcoming technical norm on "Open Data for Smart Cities", and will discuss on the main success factors as well as threats and weaknesses of the process, with the hope that this can give some light towards making ontology engineering more accessible to all.

Ontology Design Patterns for Large-Scale Data Interchange and Discovery

Pascal Hitzler

Data Semantics (DaSe) Laboratory, Wright State University, USA
pascal.hitzler@wright.edu
http://www.pascal-hitzler.de

Abstract. Data and information integration remains a major challenge for our modern information-driven society whereby people and organizations often have to deal with large data volumes coming from semantically heterogeneous sources featuring significant variety between them. In this context, data integration aims to provide a unified view over data residing at different sources through a global schema, which can be formalized as an ontology. From the end-users perspective, the data integration problem can be seen as a data access problem whereby the emphasis is on how such a unified view should help the nontechnical end-users in accessing the data from such heterogeneous sources. Early efforts to solve these problems led to a number of relational database integration approaches which have been very useful in specific situations. Unfortunately, they still require very significant manual efforts in creating and maintaining the mappings between the global and local schema, as the resulting integrations are often rigid and not transferable to new application scenarios without investing even more human expert resources, and furthermore, the global schema expressivity is limited which makes it difficult for the end-users to pose ad-hoc queries for their information needs.

Ontology design patterns have been conceived as modular and reusable building blocks for ontology modeling. We argue that a principled use of ontology design patterns also improve large-scale data integration under heterogeneity, as compared to the use of a monolithic ontology as global schema. In particular, the adoption of ontology design patterns can simplify several key aspects of the ontology application life cycle, including knowledge acquisition from experts, collaborative modeling and updates, incorporation of different perspectives, data-model alignment, and social barriers to adoption.

We report on recent progress we have made with this approach as part of our work on improving data discovery in the Earth Sciences, and point out key challenges on the road ahead.

Acknowledgments. This work was supported by the National Science Foundation awards 1017225 III: Small: TROn – Tractable Reasoning with Ontologies, 1354778 EAGER: Collaborative Research: EarthCube Building Blocks, Leveraging Semantics and Linked Data for Geoscience Data Sharing and Discovery

(OceanLink), and 1440202 EarthCube Building Blocks: Collaborative Research: GeoLink – Leveraging Semantics and Linked Data for Data Sharing and Discovery in the Geosciences. Any opinions, findings, and conclusions or recommendations expressed in this material are those of the author and do not necessarily reflect the views of the National Science Foundation.

References

1. Cheatham, M., Hitzler, P.: String similarity metrics for ontology alignment. In: Alani, H., Kagal, L., Fokoue, A., Groth, P., Biemann, C., Parreira, J.X., Aroyo, L., Noy, N., Welty, C., Janowicz, K. (eds.) ISWC 2013, Part II. LNCS, vol. 8219, pp. 294–309. Springer, Heidelberg (2013)
2. Cheatham, M., Hitzler, P.: The properties of property alignment. In: Proceedings OM-2014, The Ninth International Workshop on Ontology Matching, at the 13th International Semantic Web Conference, ISWC 2014, Riva del Garda, Trentino, Italy (to appear, October 2014)
3. Hitzler, P., Janowicz, K.: Linked Data, Big Data, and the 4th Paradigm. Semantic Web 4(3), 233–235 (2013)
4. Hitzler, P., Krötzsch, M., Rudolph, S.: Foundations of Semantic Web Technologies. Chapman & Hall/CRC (2010)
5. Jain, P., Hitzler, P., Sheth, A.P., Verma, K., Yeh, P.Z.: Ontology 'alignment for linked open data. In: Patel-Schneider, P.F., Pan, Y., Hitzler, P., Mika, P., Zhang, L., Pan, J.Z., Horrocks, I., Glimm, B. (eds.) ISWC 2010, Part I. LNCS, vol. 6496, pp. 402–417. Springer, Heidelberg (2010)
6. Jain, P., Hitzler, P., Yeh, P.Z., Verma, K., Sheth, A.P.: Linked Data is Merely More Data. In: Brickley, D., Chaudhri, V.K., Halpin, H., McGuinness, D. (eds.) Linked Data Meets Artificial Intelligence, pp. 82–86. AAAI Press, Menlo Park (2010)
7. Janowicz, K., van Harmelen, F., Hendler, J.A., Hitzler, P.: Why the data train needs semantic rails. AI Magazine (to appear, 2014)
8. Janowicz, K., Hitzler, P.: The Digital Earth as knowledge engine. Semantic Web 3(3), 213–221 (2012)
9. Krisnadhi, A., Arko, R., Carbotte, S., Chandler, C., Cheatham, M., Finin, T., Hitzler, P., Janowicz, K., Narock, T., Raymond, L., Shepherd, A., Wiebe, P.: An ontology pattern for oceanograhic cruises: Towards an oceanograhper's dream of integrated knowledge discovery. Tech. Rep. 2014.1, OceanLink Technical Report (2014), http://pascal-hitzler.de/

Table of Contents

Automatic Ontology Population from Product Catalogs.............. 1
*Céline Alec, Chantal Reynaud-Delaître, Brigitte Safar, Zied Sellami,
and Uriel Berdugo*

Measuring Similarity in Ontologies: A New Family of Measures 13
Tahani Alsubait, Bijan Parsia, and Uli Sattler

Relation Extraction from the Web Using Distant Supervision 26
Isabelle Augenstein, Diana Maynard, and Fabio Ciravegna

Inductive Lexical Learning of Class Expressions..................... 42
*Lorenz Bühmann, Daniel Fleischhacker, Jens Lehmann,
Andre Melo, and Johanna Völker*

Question Generation from a Knowledge Base 54
*Vinay K. Chaudhri, Peter E. Clark, Adam Overholtzer,
and Aaron Spaulding*

Inconsistency Monitoring in a Large Scientific Knowledge Base 66
*Vinay K. Chaudhri, Rahul Katragadda, Jeff Shrager,
and Michael Wessel*

Pay-As-You-Go Multi-user Feedback Model for Ontology Matching 80
*Isabel F. Cruz, Francesco Loprete, Matteo Palmonari, Cosmin Stroe,
and Aynaz Taheri*

Information Flow within Relational Multi-context Systems 97
Luís Cruz-Filipe, Graça Gaspar, and Isabel Nunes

Using Linked Data to Diversify Search Results a Case Study in Cultural
Heritage 109
*Chris Dijkshoorn, Lora Aroyo, Guus Schreiber, Jan Wielemaker,
and Lizzy Jongma*

Personalised Access to Linked Data 121
Milan Dojchinovski and Tomas Vitvar

Roadmapping and Navigating in the Ontology Visualization
Landscape 137
Marek Dudáš, Ondřej Zamazal, and Vojtěch Svátek

aLDEAS: A Language to Define Epiphytic Assistance Systems   153
    Blandine Ginon, Stéphanie Jean-Daubias, Pierre-Antoine Champin,
    and Marie Lefevre

Ontology Design Pattern Property Specialisation Strategies   165
    Karl Hammar

The uComp Protégé Plugin: Crowdsourcing Enabled Ontology
Engineering   181
    Florian Hanika, Gerhard Wohlgenannt, and Marta Sabou

Futures Studies Methods for Knowledge Management in Academic
Research   197
    Sabine Kadlubek, Stella Schulte-Cörne, Florian Welter,
    Anja Richert, and Sabina Jeschke

Adaptive Concept Vector Space Representation Using Markov Chain
Model   203
    Zenun Kastrati and Ali Shariq Imran

A Core Ontology of Macroscopic Stuff   209
    C. Maria Keet

Feasibility of Automated Foundational Ontology Interchangeability   225
    Zubeida Casmod Khan and C. Maria Keet

Automating Cross-Disciplinary Defect Detection in Multi-disciplinary
Engineering Environments   238
    Olga Kovalenko, Estefanía Serral, Marta Sabou, Fajar J. Ekaputra,
    Dietmar Winkler, and Stefan Biffl

Querying the Global Cube: Integration of Multidimensional Datasets
from the Web   250
    Benedikt Kämpgen, Steffen Stadtmüller, and Andreas Harth

VOWL 2: User-Oriented Visualization of Ontologies   266
    Steffen Lohmann, Stefan Negru, Florian Haag, and Thomas Ertl

What Is Linked Historical Data?   282
    Albert Meroño-Peñuela and Rinke Hoekstra

A Quality Assurance Workflow for Ontologies Based on Semantic
Regularities   288
    Eleni Mikroyannidi, Manuel Quesada-Martínez,
    Dmitry Tsarkov, Jesualdo Tomás Fernández Breis, Robert Stevens,
    and Ignazio Palmisano

Adaptive Knowledge Propagation in Web Ontologies   304
    Pasquale Minervini, Claudia d'Amato, Nicola Fanizzi,
    and Floriana Esposito

Using Event Spaces, Setting and Theme to Assist the Interpretation
and Development of Museum Stories 320
  Paul Mulholland, Annika Wolff, Eoin Kilfeather, and Evin McCarthy

Functional-Logic Programming for Web Knowledge Representation,
Sharing and Querying 333
  Matthias Nickles

Inferring Semantic Relations by User Feedback 339
  Francesco Osborne and Enrico Motta

A Hybrid Semantic Approach to Building Dynamic Maps of Research
Communities 356
  Francesco Osborne, Giuseppe Scavo, and Enrico Motta

Logical Detection of Invalid SameAs Statements in RDF Data 373
  Laura Papaleo, Nathalie Pernelle, Fatiha Saïs, and Cyril Dumont

Integrating Know-How into the Linked Data Cloud 385
  *Paolo Pareti, Benoit Testu, Ryutaro Ichise, Ewan Klein,
  and Adam Barker*

A Dialectical Approach to Selectively Reusing Ontological
Correspondences 397
  Terry R. Payne and Valentina Tamma

Uncovering the Semantics of Wikipedia Pagelinks 413
  *Valentina Presutti, Sergio Consoli, Andrea Giovanni Nuzzolese,
  Diego Reforgiato Recupero, Aldo Gangemi, Ines Bannour,
  and Haïfa Zargayouna*

Closed-World Concept Induction for Learning in OWL Knowledge
Bases 429
  David Ratcliffe and Kerry Taylor

YASGUI: Feeling the Pulse of Linked Data 441
  Laurens Rietveld and Rinke Hoekstra

Tackling the Class-Imbalance Learning Problem in Semantic Web
Knowledge Bases 453
  *Giuseppe Rizzo, Claudia d'Amato, Nicola Fanizzi,
  and Floriana Esposito*

On the Collaborative Development of Application Ontologies:
A Practical Case Study with a SME 469
  *Marco Rospocher, Elena Cardillo, Ivan Donadello,
  and Luciano Serafini*

Relationship-Based Top-K Concept Retrieval for Ontology Search 485
  Anila Sahar Butt, Armin Haller, and Lexing Xie

A Knowledge Driven Approach towards the Validation of Externally
Acquired Traceability Datasets in Supply Chain Business Processes   503
    Monika Solanki and Christopher Brewster

Testing OWL Axioms against RDF Facts: A Possibilistic Approach.   519
    Andrea G.B. Tettamanzi, Catherine Faron-Zucker,
    and Fabien Gandon

Quantifying the Bias in Data Links.   531
    Ilaria Tiddi, Mathieu d'Aquin, and Enrico Motta

Using Neural Networks to Aggregate Linked Data Rules   547
    Ilaria Tiddi, Mathieu d'Aquin, and Enrico Motta

Temporal Semantics: Time-Varying Hashtag Sense Clustering.   563
    Giovanni Stilo and Paola Velardi

Using Ontologies: Understanding the User Experience   579
    Paul Warren, Paul Mulholland, Trevor Collins, and Enrico Motta

A Conceptual Model for Detecting Interactions among Medical
Recommendations in Clinical Guidelines: A Case-Study
on Multimorbidity   591
    Veruska Zamborlini, Rinke Hoekstra, Marcos da Silveira,
    Cédric Pruski, Annette ten Teije, and Frank van Harmelen

Learning with Partial Data for Semantic Table Interpretation.   607
    Ziqi Zhang

Author Index.   619

Automatic Ontology Population
from Product Catalogs

Céline Alec[1], Chantal Reynaud-Delaître[1], Brigitte Safar[1], Zied Sellami[2],
and Uriel Berdugo[2]

[1] LRI, CNRS UMR 8623, Université Paris-Sud, France
{celine.alec,chantal.reynaud,brigitte.safar}@lri.fr
[2] Wepingo, 6 Cour Saint Eloi, Paris, France
{zied.sellami,uriel.berdugo}@wepingo.com

Abstract. In this paper we present an approach for ontology population based on heterogeneous documents describing commercial products with various descriptions and diverse styles. The originality is the generation and progressive refinement of semantic annotations leading to identify the types of the products and their features whereas the initial information is very poor quality. Documents are annotated using an ontology. The annotation process is based on an initial set of known instances, this set being built from terminological elements added in the ontology. Our approach first uses semi-automated annotation techniques on a small dataset and then applies machine learning techniques in order to fully annotate the entire dataset. This work was motivated by specific application needs. Experimentations were conducted on real-world datasets in the toys domain.

Keywords: ontology population, semantic annotation, B2C application.

1   Introduction

Today in B2C (Business to Consumer) applications many products and information are available to users over the Internet, but the volume and the variety of the sources make it difficult to find the right product quickly and easily. In a typical 3-tier architecture the business layer is devoted to extracting and organizing the data and the information to be later presented to the users. Ontologies can help to analyze data and understand them, acting in fact as intermediaries between end-users' requirements and suppliers' products. An ontology is a conceptualization of a particular domain [6]. It represents concepts, attributes and relations between concepts.

In this paper, we will use a specific ontology in which each concept denotes a category of products and has properties defined according to the users' searching requirements. Given a description of a product extracted from a supplier catalog, our approach will find the concepts in the ontology for which the product should be an instance. The problem of matching an item from a catalog across multiple

K. Janowicz et al. (Eds.): EKAW 2014, LNAI 8876, pp. 1–12, 2014.

product categories in an ontology is related to ontology population in ontology engineering. Although multiple approaches have been proposed [10], to the best of our knowledge none have been evaluated on instances with very poor and non contextualized descriptions and coming from heterogeneous sources. In our case, we need to look for concepts in an ontology based on the values of very few facets. We propose an approach to annotate products in an automated way, then these annotated products will be introduced as individuals in the ontology making them accessible to the end-users. The originality of our approach relies on its capability to generate and progressively refine annotations even starting from short and not precise descriptions. Once a certain amount of instances have been semi-automatically annotated, we use machine learning techniques to identify concepts that can be associated with new instances in order to fully annotate the catalog. This approach is catalog- and domain-independent but more particularly suitable to be used with ontologies that are classifications of products and features.

Our work is motivated by specific application needs, in the context of a collaboration with the Wepingo start-up[1] which aims at using semantic web technologies with B2C applications. We show our results on the basis of a domain ontology and product catalogs provided by the company.

The remainder of this paper is structured as follows. Section 2 exposes the domain and the data. Section 3 presents existing research work that relates to ours. In Section 4 we detail our approach. Experiments are presented in Section 5. Finally, Section 6 concludes the presentation and outlines future work.

2 Domain and Data

In this section we present both the ontology in the toys domain and the documents to be annotated. Both the ontology and the catalogs are in French but have been translated into English in the examples described in this paper.

2.1 The *ESAR* Ontology

The *ESAR* ontology (cf. Figure 1) describes the knowledge related to the toys domain in accordance with the ESAR standard defined by psychologists [5]. This standard identifies toys' categories and features into two independent classifications. Toys' categories refer to the types of toys such as Building kit or Game of chance, while features refer to educational values transmitted by a toy such as Concentration or Dexterity, or to its general purpose such as Cooperative game or Associative game. An example of category is presented in Table 1.

The *ESAR* ontology is defined as $O_{ESAR} = (C_{ESAR}, L_{ESAR}, H_{ESAR}, Att_{ESAR}, A_{ESAR})$. C_{ESAR} consists of a set of concepts composed of 33 categories and 129 features which are not interrelated. The lexicon L_{ESAR} consists of a set of lexical entries for the concepts and is provided with a reference function $F : 2^L \rightarrow 2^C$,

---

[1] www.wepingo.com

which maps sets of lexical units to sets of concepts. The lexicon is composed of two subsets of terms: *Label* and *Ex*. Each concept $c \in C_{\text{ESAR}}$ is associated with at least one label in *Label*. *Ex* consists of examples for some leaf concepts (cf. Table 1). $L_{ESAR}(c)$ is the set of terms of L_{ESAR} denoting the concept c. H_{ESAR} is a small set of subsumption relationships between concepts. Att_{ESAR} is the set of attributes defining the concepts, restricted in this ontology to the attribute $Definition$. Furthermore, the set of axioms is denoted as A_{ESAR}. This set is initially empty. Our approach enables to complete it.

Fig. 1. The *ESAR* ontology

Table 1. The Staging game concept

Label	Staging game
Definition	Pretend game in which the player is the director. He creates scenarios developed to reproduce specific topics, specific scenes, events, jobs, etc. These types of games require to be able to stage the relevant accessories to the context or the shown situation.
Ex	playmobil, puppet, figurine, ...

2.2   Documents to Be Annotated

The documents, denoted in this work as *Corpus*, are sheets from several catalogs describing a toy by its label, its brand, its description which is short and not contextualized, and its category. Note that the category here is not the same as in O_{ESAR}. It varies widely depending on the supplier. It can be very general as Toy or Games, as very specific as HABA cubes and beads to assemble or Brick, and sometimes difficult to interpret as Bosch or United Colors. The form and content of the descriptions are far away from the concept definitions in O_{ESAR}. An example of a toy specification is shown in Figure 2a.

3   Related Work

Ontology population methods differ according to whether the ontology is rich or light-weight. Here, we will focus on methods suitable for light-weight ontologies. The reader can learn more on methods working with rich ontologies, for example in [10]. With light-weight ontologies, population methods largely depend on the analysis of texts present in properties of the input data. Text analysis approaches can be classified into two fundamental types: linguistic and statistical approaches. Linguistic approaches rely on formulations in texts in order to identify knowledge-rich contexts [1], they try to extract named entities or other elements by eventually using additional semantic resources such as glossaries, dictionaries or knowledge bases. On the other hand, statistical approaches [9] treat a text as a whole and take advantage of redundancy, regularities, co-occurrences, or other linguistic trend behaviours.

Ontology population methods use text analysis techniques to find mentions in the documents referring to concepts in the ontology. This corresponds to a semantic annotation process. Semantic annotation methods can be classified into two primary categories [11], (1) *pattern-based* with either patterns automatically discovered or manually defined and (2) *machine learning-based* which use either statistical models to predict the location of entities within texts or induction.

All the works cited so far refer directly to the information extraction and semantic annotation domain. They consist in looking for textual fragments in documents that mention concepts or instances of concepts belonging to the ontology and linking these fragments to the concepts which are referred to. However, our objective is slightly different, original and challenging. We are seeking to understand whether a whole document, such as a specification of a product, fits into the description of a concept in the ontology. If it is, the product will be represented in the ontology as an instance of that concept. Consequently, our research goal is closer to [8] and [2]. Their similar aim is to evaluate proximity between the description of a general element (e.g. a job or an ontology concept) and more specific elements (e.g. applications or concept instances). In [8] the authors focus on matching job candidates through their CV, cover letters and job offers. Documents having to be compared are represented with vectors and their proximity is computed using combinations of various similarity measures (Cosine, Minkowski, and so on). By contrast, in [2] where the goal is to automatically populate a concept hierarchy describing hotel services, the approach relies on an initial set of instances given by an expert. Each hotel service, defined by hotelkeepers with their own vocabulary, is compared to these initial instances. A service is considered as an instance of the concept corresponding to the closest instance following similarity calculation based on n-grams. These two approaches are interesting but they do not deal with very short, heterogeneous and unstructured documents, especially with product catalogs created for trade purposes. Under these conditions, the use of similarity measures is inappropriate. Thus, our approach does not use similarity measures but, instead, it enables to annotate documents based on an initial set of known instances, this set being built from terminological elements added in the ontology [12].

4   Ontology Population: Methodology

The ontology populating approach consists in generating a knowledge base $BC(O, I, W)$ from the ontology O with $W : 2^I \rightarrow 2^C$, a *member* function which maps sets of instances belonging to I to sets of concepts belonging to C.

The workflow of our methodology is the following. It first enhances O_{ESAR} by adding terminological knowledge. This step can be viewed as a pre-processing phase. The enriched ontology is used to annotate a sample of documents in a semi-automatic way. These annotations are then exploited by machine learning techniques applied to all documents in the *Corpus* to be annotated. These various phases applied to toys' domain are detailed in the following sections.

4.1   Ontology Enrichment

O_{ESAR} is enriched by adding two types of elements thanks to domain experts intervention. We added new terms associated with concepts to L_{ESAR} and statements about concepts represented as axioms in A_{ESAR}.

Completing L_{ESAR} is like enriching the terminological part of the ontology. Examples extracted from external resources have been added to Ex. These additions are names of toys or games extracted from a website[2] using the ESAR classification and names of sport games extracted from Wikipedia. We also added new terminological elements: linguistic signs and complex linguistic signs. Linguistic signs, called LS, are terms or expressions denoting a concept. Musical or speaking are examples of linguistic signs associated with the concept Sound game. Complex linguistic signs, called $CompLS$, in the form "term AND [NO] term AND [NO] term ..." help to make each concept different from the others. For instance, there are two types of dominoes game. A domino game can be an Association game with numbered dominoes to be connected or it can be a Construction game with dominoes placed in order to build a path, a bridge or other structures. The use of complex signs allows to distinguish these two types of games. The Construction game will be evoked by the joint presence of the terms domino and construction while the Association game will be evoked by the presence of the term domino and the absence of the term construction. Due to the fact that examples and linguistic signs are very different, we choose to keep them separated but the annotation process exploits them in the same way. After enrichment L_{ESAR} will be in the form $L_{ESAR} = \{Label \cup Ex \cup LS \cup CompLS\}$.

Axioms added in A_{ESAR} are of two types:

1) Reliable knowledge having a very high degree of accuracy. These axioms are represented with propositional rules of two types. Incompatibility rules between concepts give priority to one of them. They are in the form: IF concept$_A$ AND concept$_B$ THEN NO concept$_A$. Dependency rules represent either inclusions or missing relations between concepts. They are in the form: IF concept$_A$ THEN concept$_B$.

2) Heuristic knowledge allowing potential features to be inferred from categories, those features that seem to be associated with a category. These rules are automatically generated, based on examples and linguistic signs which are common to categories and features, respectively denoted Cat and $Feat$, as follows:

$\forall\ cat_i \in Cat,\ \forall\ feat_k \in Feat,$
If $\exists v \in L_{ESAR}(cat_i)$ such as $v \in L_{ESAR}(feat_k)$,
then $create\ the\ rule$: $cat_i \underset{potentially}{\Rightarrow} feat_k$.

In this way, for example, Skill game potentially implies Eye-hand coordination and this is deduced since both elements in the rule share the same example spinning-top. The set of rules was then manually completed.

---

[2] http://www.jeuxrigole.com/liste-des-jeux.html

4.2 Annotation of a Representative Sample of the Domain

The annotation process aims at finding as many relevant candidate annotations as possible for a given product. It proceeds in four steps:

1. Generate an initial set: the construction of an initial set of candidate annotations defining the interpretation context of a product;
2. Find inconsistencies: the identification of inconsistencies that correspond to incompatible annotations in the interpretation context;
3. Imply concepts: the completion of the candidate annotations by adding implied concepts;
4. Manually validate the set of candidate annotations.

4.2.1. Generate an Initial Set

The annotation generation process of the toy sheets is based on the set $lemme(c)$ of each concept c, $lemme(c)$ being a set of lemmas of the lexicon L_{ESAR}. Lemmas of available information on toys, e.g. their name, brand, category and description, are stored in $info(t)$ for each toy t described in the $Corpus$.

$$\forall c \in C_{ESAR}, lemme(c) = lemmatisation(L_{ESAR}(c))$$
$$\forall t \in Corpus, info(t) = lemmatisation\{Name(t) \cup Brand(t) \cup Cat(t) \cup Desc(t)\}$$

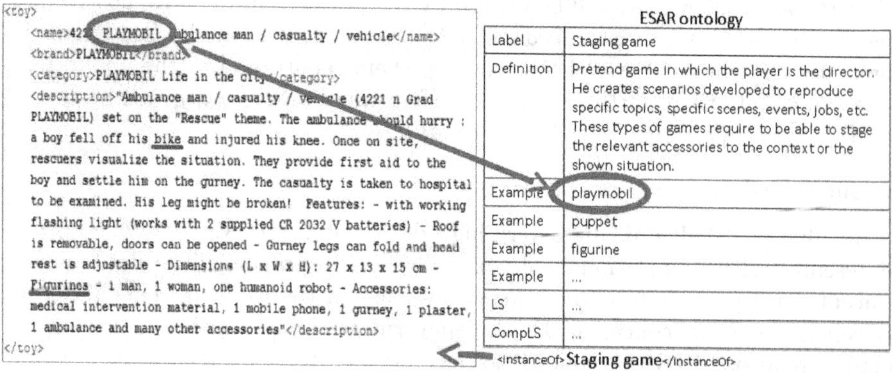

(a) An example of a toy specification   (b) The Staging game concept

Fig. 2. An example of an annotation

The annotation generation process is a search of word inclusions. For a concept c, it detects if information about a toy t includes an element of $lemme(c)$. If it is, the toy t is annoted with the concept c, as a category or a feature.

$\forall t \in Corpus, \forall c \in C_{ESAR}$,

If $\exists v \in lemme(c)$ such as $v \in info(t)$ then t `instanceOf` c.

In complex linguistic signs, terms preceded by the word NO are referred to as *negative terms* and the others as *positive terms*. We consider that a toy t contains a complex linguistic sign cls if:

$\forall \, pt \, \in PositiveTerms(cls), \forall \, nt \, \in NegativeTerms(cls)$,
$pt \in info(t)$ and $nt \notin info(t)$

The first annotations generated in this step form the interpretation context of a toy t defined as follows: $Ctxt(t) = \{c \mid t \text{ instanceOf } c\}$.

For instance, the toy' specification in Figure 2a contains the playmobil term which is an example of the Staging game concept. Therefore this toy is annotated by the Staging game concept. Similarly the bike term leads to annotate it with Motor game and the figurine term allows to add the Expressive creativity, Reproduction of roles and Reproduction of events features.

Analyzing such a context is easier than analyzing unstructured textual documents. The next steps require sets of rules applicable to the results obtained at the previous step. These steps are described hereafter.

4.2.2. Find Inconsistencies

Searching inconsistencies is a refinement process aiming at detecting and eliminating erroneous concepts from the interpretation context of a toy. The objective is to enhance the precision of the results. Incompatibility rules introduced during the enrichment step are applied to contexts. Indeed, contexts may include several concepts and some of them have to be removed in the presence of others. The result is A_1, a set of annotations such as $A_1(t) \subset Ctxt(t)$. For instance, the toy in figure 2a has been annotated as Motor game in step 1 because the bike term is included into the description, when it is not a real bike but a miniature. In that particular context, the Motor game annotation is not suitable. This inconsistency is easier to detect by checking it against the other annotations in the context than by seeking to finely understand the toy description. Applying the r_1 incompatibility rule: IF Staging game AND Motor game THEN NO Motor game, allows to remove the unsuitable annotation.

4.2.3. Imply Concepts

As the aim of the previous step is to detect inconsistencies, the precision of the annotations is enhanced. This step aims to improve the annotations. We enhance recall by taking advantage of all the accurate implications between concepts, represented in the initial or in the enriched ontology. Additional annotations can be identified. At the end of this step, we obtain A_2, a set of annotations such as $A_1(t) \subset A_2(t)$. For instance, based on the two dependency rules, IF Endurance THEN Sport game and IF Sport game THEN Motor game, a toy already annotated with the concept Endurance will also be, as a result, annotated by the two concepts Sport game and Motor game.

Figure 3 is an illustration of the search of inconsistencies and then of the completion phase related to the example in Figure 2a. Searching inconsistencies leads to remove Motor game by applying the r_1 rule. The completion step adds the following concepts: Inventive creation and Differed imitation.

These three steps can be equally applied to category or feature concepts although, in practice, very few feature annotations are found in our scenario. The reason is that our features are abstract notions denoted by limited linguistic signs. Consequently, additional reasoning steps are necessary in order to discover more feature annotations, from the category annotations found before.

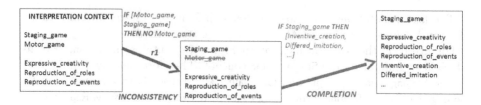

Fig. 3. Illustration of searching inconsistencies and completion steps

This process is based on two heuristics relying on already recognized category annotations.

The first heuristic is the identification of features which are common to toys already annotated and validated by users and belonging to the same category as the toy under study. The result is A_p, a set of annotations such as $A_2(t) \subset A_\mathrm{p}(t)$. A_p is the set of default **proposed annotations**.

The second heuristic is the application of potential implication rules. They are not accurate rules. However, given a toy t, their application allows to obtain a set of additional features annotations, called A_s for **suggested annotations**. This set of suggested annotations can be seen as a filter to remove features which are not related to the considered toy for sure.

The confidence is higher for proposed annotations than for suggested annotations, this is why we separate them into two sets. The user interface for the manual validation process exploits this distinction.

4.2.4. Manually Validate the Set of Candidate Annotations

Validating annotations is important because a solid basis with correct annotations is needed for the machine learning part. The software which generates the annotations is implemented with a user graphical interface. For each toy, the interface displays the proposed annotations and, in a different way, the suggested ones. It allows a user to confirm or modify annotations of a toy and to add missing annotations. The interface is dynamic: if the user adds or deletes annotations, the implied concepts are automatically added, and the suggested features are modified. The user's work is then reduced to a minimum. Once the annotations have been validated, toys are added to I_{ESAR}.

4.3 Annotation of the Complete Corpus by Sample-Based Learning

Thanks to the tool presented in the previous sections, 316 toys have been annotated, represented the initial and representative sample of toys. This section presents the phase related to a supervised learning model which operates on the sample in order to annotate new toys. These new toys will be added in I_{ESAR}.

The linear classifier LIBLINEAR [4], based on SVM [3] and especially advisable for document classification [7] has been used. We built a classifier SVM for each concept c_i predicting if a toy has to be annotated or not by c_i. We have therefore built 162 SVM models, one per concept in the ontology.

Several bag-of-words models [13] (binary and tf-idf) have been tested to represent toys as vectors. The world is described using a dictionary composed of lemmas collected from toys specifications. Several parameters can be fixed (See Section 5.2). The representation in vectors of the toys and the construction of the SVM models are completely automatic. Once the parameters have been definitively established, all the toys from the catalog are automatically annotated by the different SVM models and added to I_{ESAR}.

5   Evaluation of the Approach

In this section, we evaluate the semi-automatic annotation and the machine-learning phases, in a separate way. In addition, we defined an experimental protocol in order to evaluate the precision of the instances introduced in I_{ESAR} using our approach.

5.1   Evaluation of the Quality of the Proposed Annotations (semi-automatic phase)

Experimental protocol. In order to evaluate the quality of proposed annotations in the annotation tool, we formed a gold standard with a sample of 100 toys randomly built and manually annotated. Only toys categories are considered in this evaluation. Feature annotations are not evaluated because they are difficult to establish, either manually or automatically. We then compared the proposed annotations with the manual ones.

Table 2. Precision, Recall and F-measure for the annotation process

Step	Precision	Recall	F-measure
Initial ontology	0.38	0.20	0.26
+ Examples + linguistic signs	0.87	0.55	0.68
+ Complex linguistic signs	0.88	0.59	0.71
+ Searching inconsistencies (+ completion)	0.94	0.64	0.76

Results. Table 2 shows that precision and recall have improved with the enrichment and refinement steps. The most significant improvement results from the new examples and linguistic signs. A toy annotated with several categories, at least one of which is non relevant, has been considered as false when comparing the results with manual annotations. By contrast, a partial but correct annotation has been considered as acceptable. That way, dependency rules did not modify the results when in fact they introduced a lot of annotations. An analysis of the results shows that the precision is satisfactory even if recall is relatively low. Having a high precision for proposed annotations is very important. That means that the work of the expert will be minimized. Fewer annotations will have to be removed among the proposed ones. Recall remains low. This reflects that even if the terminological part of the ontology was complemented by examples and linguistic signs, such an enrichment is still not sufficient.

5.2   Evaluation of the Machine Learning Phase

Experimental Protocol. The machine learning part of our approach has been evaluated on the Staging game concept. We constructed a SVM model on a sample of toys extracted from a catalog: the training set was composed of 316 toys coming from the Toys'R'Us catalog and having been annotated with our tool. We noted the error rate on the other toys of the catalog: the test set was composed of 595 toys annotated using our tool but only with the Staging game concept. We tested 36 models and chose the model which generates the lowest error rate (model 12b obtained with parameters in bold italics on Table 3 and an error rate of 2.52%). The same set of parameters has been applied in the 162 SVM models that have been built (one per concept in the ontology).

Results. Table 3 shows an extract of the error rates of the Staging game classifier on the Toys'R'Us test set. The parameter C represents the cost for violation of constraints. In other words, the higher C, the more the data have to be correct and not noisy. Specification corresponds to the elements considered in the vector from the different attributes of a toy: label L, brand B, category C, description D. Representation is the vector representation that has been used, either binary or tf-idf. Experiments have been conducted with two *stop-lists*, a basis *stop-list* which eliminates words like numbers, pronouns, prepositions, determinants, abbreviations and conjunctions, and one that eliminates also adverbs (columns (a) and (b) in Table 3 respectively). The training set is representative of the whole Toys'R'US catalog and thus also of the test set. That is to say, toys of the test set are similar to at least one toy of the training set. This explains the fact that the error rate is low.

Table 3. Error rates for the annotation of the test set for Staging games

				Error rates	
№	C	Specification	Representation	Basis stop-list (a)	*Basis stop-list + without adverbs (b)*
...	...	...	...	...	...
10	10	LBC	TF-IDF	6.72%	6.72%
11	10	LBCD	Binary	3.87%	4.87%
12	*10*	*LBCD*	*TF-IDF*	3.03%	*2.52%*
13	100	LB	Binary	9.41%	9.41%
14	100	LB	TF-IDF	9.75%	9.75%
...	...	...	...	...	...

5.3   Population Evaluation

Experimental Protocol. We need to validate the annotations provided by the machine learning phase. We attempted to annotate, using the SVM model that has been previously found, a set of 100 toys coming from another catalog named Jeux et jouets en Folie and being the most heterogeneous as possible. Let us note that these toys are very different from those contained in the Toys'R'US catalog.

The two catalogs have no common toys. Consequently, the learning model, only based on a representative sample of the Toys'R'US catalog, may be less effective of the data coming from the Jeux et jouets en Folie catalog.

Results. We saw in 5.2 that when training set is representative of test set, we got an error rate of 2.52% which is very low. The 100 toys extracted from Jeux et jouets en Folie are very different from toys of the training set. We cannot expect to get such a low error rate. Table 4 shows the results obtained with model 12b applied on these 100 Jeux et jouets en Folie toys. 15 toys have been properly annotated out of 31 of Staging game type. No toys have been annotated with Staging game when, in fact, they were not. Error rate is higher: 16%. We can see that errors come from false negatives because precision is 100% but recall is almost 50%. As we said, it is a low recall because the training set, extracted from the Toys'R'Us catalog, is not representative of the toys coming from Jeux et jouets en Folie. That seems perfectly satisfactory and we can assume to obtain a higher recall with a SVM model built from a larger training set including a representative subset of Jeux et jouets en Folie toys.

Table 4. Results on 100 toys from Jeux et Jouets en folie catalog

Results	
Error rates	16%
Precision	100%
Recall	48.39%
F-Measure	65.22%

6   Conclusion and Future Work

This paper proposed an original approach able to establish links between catalog products and concepts in a domain ontology. It allows to populate an ontology in a semi-automatic way. Its originality is twofold. First, it generates annotations in an iterative way. Second, it is a good illustration of a joint approach combining both automatic and semi-automatic steps and optimizing the work of the user. The approach consisted in developing the most generic techniques as possible. The first results of the annotation process with categories are promising. The machine learning part worked quite well with toys of the type Staging game while these kinds of toys are difficult to identify.

Future work will be done in several directions. First, we want to investigate an alternative approach more appropriate to features. Second, we will focus on the effort to complete linguistic signs and define axioms, and try to reduce this effort by using automated techniques. The automatic part could also be improved by testing other machine learning approaches (Naive Bayes method, Multi-Layer Perceptron, etc.) and other forms of representations which consider synonyms, for instance. Finally the approach is domain independent to some extent. It is repeatable on corpus describing e-commerce products with appropriate knowledge. It would be of interest to apply it to other fields, as the gift field or travel and tourism areas which are of great interest to the Wepingo company.

References

1. Barriere, C., Agbago, A.: Terminoweb: a software environment for term study in rich contexts. In: Proceedings of the 2005 International Conference on Terminology, Standardization and Technology Transfer, pp. 103–113 (2006)
2. Béchet, N., Aufaure, M.A., Lechevallier, Y.: Construction et peuplement de structures hiérarchiques de concepts dans le domaine du e-tourisme. In: IC, pp. 475–490 (2011)
3. Cortes, C., Vapnik, V.: Support-vector networks. In: Machine Learning, pp. 273–297 (1995)
4. Fan, R.E., Chang, K.W., Hsieh, C.J., Wang, X.R., Lin, C.J.: LIBLINEAR: A library for large linear classification. Journal of Machine Learning Research 9, 1871–1874 (2008)
5. Garon, D., Filion, R., Chiasson, R.: Le système ESAR: guide d'analyse, de classification et d'organisation d'une collection de jeux et jouets. Editions ASTED (2002)
6. Gruber, T.R.: A translation approach to portable ontology specifications. Knowledge Acquisition 5(2), 199–220 (1993)
7. Hsu, C.W., Chang, C.C., Lin, C.J.: A practical guide to support vector classification. Tech. rep., Dept. of Computer Science, National Taiwan University (2003)
8. Kessler, R., Béchet, N., Roche, M., Moreno, J.M.T., El-Bèze, M.: A hybrid approach to managing job offers and candidates. Information Processing and Management 48(6), 1124–1135 (2012)
9. Manning, C.D., Schütze, H.: Foundations of Statistical Natural Language Processing. The MIT Press, Cambridge (1999)
10. Petasis, G., Karkaletsis, V., Paliouras, G., Krithara, A., Zavitsanos, E.: Ontology population and enrichment: State of the art. In: Knowledge-Driven Multimedia Information Extraction and Ontology Evolution, pp. 134–166 (2011)
11. Reeve, L.: Survey of semantic annotation platforms. In: Proceedings of the 2005 ACM Symposium on Applied Computing, pp. 1634–1638. ACM Press (2005)
12. Reymonet, A., Thomas, J., Aussenac-Gilles, N.: Modelling ontological and terminological resources in OWL DL. In: Proceedings of ISWC (2007)
13. Salton, G., McGill, M.J.: Introduction to Modern Information Retrieval. McGraw-Hill, Inc., New York (1986)

Measuring Similarity in Ontologies:
A New Family of Measures

Tahani Alsubait, Bijan Parsia, and Uli Sattler

School of Computer Science, The University of Manchester, United Kingdom
{alsubait,bparsia,sattler}@cs.man.ac.uk

Abstract. Several attempts have been already made to develop similarity measures for ontologies. We noticed that some existing similarity measures are ad-hoc and unprincipled. In addition, there is still a need for similarity measures which are applicable to expressive Description Logics and which are terminological. To address these requirements, we have developed a new family of similarity measures. Two separate empirical studies have been carried out to evaluate the new measures. First, we compare the new measures along with some existing measures against a gold-standard. Second, we examine the practicality of using the new measures over an independently motivated corpus of ontologies.

1 Introduction

The process of assigning a numerical value reflecting the degree of resemblance between two ontology concepts or the so called conceptual similarity measurement is important for numerous applications (e.g., classical information retrieval, ontology matching [6], ontology learning [3]). It is also known that similarity measurement is difficult. This can be easily seen by looking at the several attempts that have been made to develop similarity measures, see for example [5,16,22,17,10]. The problem is also well-founded in psychology and a number of psychological models of similarity have been already developed, see for example [14,21,7]. Rather than adopting a psychological model for similarity as a foundation, we noticed that some existing similarity measures for ontologies are ad-hoc and unprincipled. In addition, there is still a need for similarity measures which are applicable to expressive Description Logics (DLs) (i.e., beyond $\mathcal{EL}$) and which are terminological (i.e., do not require an *ABox*). To address these requirements, we have developed a new family of similarity measures which are founded on the feature-based psychological model [21]. The individual measures vary in their accuracy/computational cost based on which *features* they consider.

Two separate empirical studies have been carried out to evaluate the new measures. First, we compare the new measures along with some existing measures against a gold-standard. Second, we examine the practicality of using the new measures over an independently motivated corpus of ontologies (BioPortal[1] library) which contains over 300 ontologies. In addition, we examine whether

---

[1] http://bioportal.bioontology.org/

K. Janowicz et al. (Eds.): EKAW 2014, LNAI 8876, pp. 13–25, 2014.

cheap measures can be an approximation of some more computationally expensive measures.

To understand the major differences between similarity measures w.r.t. the task in which they are involved in, consider, for example, the following three tasks:

- Task1: Given a concept C, retrieve all concepts D s.t. Similarity$(C, D) > 0$.
- Task2: Given a concept C, retrieve the N most similar concepts.
- Task3: Given a concept C and some threshold Δ, retrieve all concepts D s.t. Similarity$(C, D) > \Delta$.

We expect most similarity measures to behave similarly in Task 1 because we are not interested in the particular similarity values nor any particular ordering among the similar concepts. However, the Task 2 gets harder as N gets smaller. In this case, a similarity measure that underestimates the similarity of some very similar concepts and overestimates the similarity of others can fail the task. In Task 3, the actual similarity values matter. Hence, using the most accurate similarity measure is essential.

2   Preliminaries

We assume the reader to be familiar with DL ontologies. In what follows, we briefly introduce the relevant terminology. For a detailed overview, the reader is referred to [1]. The set of terms, i.e., concept, individual and role names, in an ontology $\mathcal{O}$ is referred to as its signature, denoted $\tilde{\mathcal{O}}$. Throughout the paper, we use N_C, N_R for the sets of concept and role names respectively and $C_{\mathcal{L}}$ to denote a set of possibly complex concepts of a concept language $\mathcal{L}(\Sigma)$ over a signature Σ and we use the usual entailment operator $\models$.

3   Desired Properties for Similarity Measures

Various psychological models for similarity have been developed (e.g., Geometric [14], Transformational [7] and Features [21] models). Due to the richness of ontologies, not all models can be adopted when considering conceptual similarity in ontologies. This is because many things are associated with a concept in an ontology (e.g., atomic subsumers/subsumees, complex subsumers/subsumees, instances, referencing axioms). Looking at existing approaches for measuring similarity in DL ontologies, one can notice that approaches which aim at providing a numerical value as a result of the similarity measurement process are mainly founded on feature-based models [21], although they might disagree on which features to consider.

In what follows, we concentrate on feature-based notions of similarity where the degree of similarity S_{CD} between objects C, D depends on features common to C and D, unique features of C and unique features of D. Considering both common and distinguishing features is a vital property of the features model.

Looking at existing approaches for measuring similarity in ontologies, we find that some of these approaches consider common xor unique features (rather than both) and that some approaches consider features that some instances (rather than all) of the compared concepts have. To account for all the features of a concept, we need to look at all (possibly complex) entailed subsumers of that concept. To understand this issue, we present the following example:

Example 1. *Consider the ontology:*
$\{Animal \sqsubseteq Organism \sqcap \exists eats.\top,$ $Plant \sqsubseteq Organism,$
$Carnivore \sqsubseteq Animal \sqcap \forall eats.Animal,$ $Herbivore \sqsubseteq Animal \sqcap \forall eats.Plant,$
$Omnivore \sqsubseteq Animal \sqcap \exists eats.Animal \sqcap \exists eats.Plant\}$

Please note that our "Carnivore" is also known as *obligate* carnivore. A good similarity function $Sim(\cdot)$ is expected to derive that Sim(Carnivore, Omnivore) > Sim(Carnivore, Herbivore) because the first pair share more **common** subsumers and have fewer **distinguishing** subsumers. On the one hand *Carnivore*, *Herbivore* and *Omnivore* are all subsumed by the following **common** subsumers (abbreviated for readability): $\{\top, Org, A, \exists e.\top\}$. In addition, *Carnivore* and *Omnivore* share the following **common** subsumer: $\{\exists e.A\}$. On the other hand, they have the following **distinguishing** subsumer: $\{\exists e.P\}$ while *Carnivore* and *Herbivore* have the following **distinguishing** subsumers: $\{\exists e.P, \forall e.P, \exists e.A, \forall e.A\}$. Here, we have made a choice to ignore (infinitely) many subsumers and only consider a select few. Clearly, this choice has an impact on $Sim(\cdot)$. Details on such design choices are discussed later.

4   Overview of Existing Approaches

We classify existing similarity measures according into two dimensions as follows.

Taxonomy vs. Ontology Based Measures. Taxonomy-based measures [16,22,17,13,11] only consider the taxonomic representation of the ontology (e.g., for DLs, we *could use* the inferred class hierarchy); hence only atomic subsumptions are considered (e.g., $Carnivore \sqsubseteq Animal$). In fact, this can be considered an approximated solution to the problem which might be sufficient in some cases. However, the user must be aware of the limitations of such approaches. For example, direct siblings are always considered equi-similar although some siblings might share more features/subsumers than others.

Ontology-based measures [5,10,12] take into account more of the knowledge in the underlying ontology (e.g., $Carnivore \sqsubseteq \forall eats.Animal$). These measures can be further classified into (a) structural measures, (b) interpretation-based measures or (c) hybrid. Structural measures [10,12] first transform the compared concepts into a normal form (e.g., $\mathcal{EL}$ normal form or $\mathcal{ALCN}$ disjunctive normal form) and then compare the syntax of their descriptions. To avoid being purely syntactic, they first unfold the concepts w.r.t. the *TBox* which limits the applicability of such measures to cyclic terminologies. Some structural measures [12] are applicable only to inexpressive DLs (e.g., $\mathcal{EL}$) and it is unclear how they can be extended to more expressive DLs. Interpretation-based measures mainly depend on the notion of canonical models (e.g., in [5] the canonical model based on the *ABox* is utilised) which do not always exist (e.g., consider disjunctions).

Intensional vs. Extensional Measures. Intensional measures [16,22,10,12] exploit the terminological part of the ontology while extensional measures [17,13,11,5] utilise the set of individual names in an *ABox* or instances in an external corpus. Extensional measures are very sensitive to the content under consideration; thus, adding/removing an individual name would change similarity measurements. These measures might be suitable for specific content-based applications but might lead to unintuitive results in other applications because they do not take concept definitions into account. Moreover, extensional measures cannot be used with pure terminological ontologies and always require representative data.

5   Detailed Inspection of Some Existing Approaches

After presenting a general overview of existing measures, we examine in detail some measures that can be considered "cheap" options and explore their possible problems. In what follows, we use $S_{\text{Atomic}}(C)$ to denote the set of atomic subsumers for concept C. We also use $\text{Com}_{\text{Atomic}}(C, D), \text{Diff}_{\text{Atomic}}(C, D)$ to denote the sets of common and distinguishing atomic subsumers respectively.

5.1   Rada et al.

This measure utilises the length of the shortest path [16] between the compared concepts in the inferred class hierarchy. The essential problem here is that the measure takes only distinguishing features into account and ignores any possible common features.

5.2   Wu and Palmer

To account for both common and distinguishing features, Wu & Palmer [22] presented a different formula for measuring similarity, as follows:

$$S_{\text{Wu \& Palmer}}(C, D) = \frac{2 \cdot |\text{Com}_{\text{Atomic}}(C,D)|}{2 \cdot |\text{Com}_{\text{Atomic}}(C,D)| + |\text{Diff}_{\text{Atomic}}(C,D)|}$$

Although this measure accounts for both common and distinguishing features, it only considers atomic concepts and it is more sensitive to commonalties.

5.3   Resnik and other IC Measures

In information theoretic notions of similarity, the information content $IC_C = -logP_C$ of a concept C is computed based on the probability (P_C) of encountering an instance of that concept. For example, $P_\top = 1$ and $IC_\top = 0$ since $\top$ is not informative. Accordingly, Resnik [17] defines similarity $S_{\text{Resnik}}(C, D)$ as:

$$S_{\text{Resnik}}(C, D) = IC_{LCS}$$

where LCS is the least common subsumer of C and D (i.e., the most specific concept that subsumes both C and D). IC measures take into account features that some instances of C and D have, which are not necessarily neither common nor distinguishing features of all instances of C and D. In addition, Resnik's measure in particular does not take into account how far the compared concepts are from their least common subsumer. To overcome this problem, two [13,11] other IC-measures have been proposed:

$$S_{\text{Lin}}(C, D) = \frac{2 \cdot IC_{LCS}}{IC_C + IC_D}$$

$$S_{\text{Jiang\&Conrath}}(C, D) = 1 - IC_C + IC_D - 2 \cdot IC_{LCS}$$

6   A New Family of Similarity Measures

Following our exploration of existing measures and their associated problems, we present a new family of similarity measures that addresses these problems. The new measures adopt the features model where the features under consideration are the subsumers of the concepts being compared. The new measures are based on Jaccard's similarity coefficient [9] which has been proved to be a proper metric (i.e., satisfies the properties: equivalence closure, symmetry and triangle inequality). Jaccard's coefficient, which maps similarity to a value in the range [0,1], is defined as follows (for sets of "features" A', B' of A, B, i.e., subsumers of A and B):

$$J(A, B) = \frac{|(A' \cap B')|}{|(A' \cup B')|}$$

We aim at similarity measures for general OWL ontologies and thus a naive implementation of this approach would be trivialised because a concept has infinitely many subsumers. To overcome this issue, we present some refinements for the similarity function in which we do not simply count all subsumers but consider subsumers from a set of (possibly complex) concepts of a concept language $\mathcal{L}$. Let C and D be concepts, let $\mathcal{O}$ be an ontology and let $\mathcal{L}$ be a concept language defined over the signature of $\mathcal{O}$. We set:

$$S(C, \mathcal{O}, \mathcal{L}) = \{D \in \mathcal{L}(\widetilde{\mathcal{O}}) \mid \mathcal{O} \models C \sqsubseteq D\}$$

$$\text{Com}(C, D, \mathcal{O}, \mathcal{L}) = S(C, \mathcal{O}, \mathcal{L}) \cap S(D, \mathcal{O}, \mathcal{L})$$

$$\text{Union}(C, D, \mathcal{O}, \mathcal{L}) = S(C, \mathcal{O}, \mathcal{L}) \cup S(D, \mathcal{O}, \mathcal{L})$$

$$\text{Sim}(C, D, \mathcal{O}, \mathcal{L}) = \frac{|Com(C, D, \mathcal{O}, \mathcal{L})|}{|Union(C, D, \mathcal{O}, \mathcal{L})|}$$

To design a new measure, it remains to specify the set $\mathcal{L}$. In what follows, we present some examples:

$$AtomicSim(C, D) = Sim(C, D, \mathcal{O}, \mathcal{L}_{\text{Atomic}}(\widetilde{\mathcal{O}})), \text{ and } \mathcal{L}_{\text{Atomic}}(\widetilde{\mathcal{O}}) = \widetilde{\mathcal{O}} \cap N_C.$$

$$SubSim(C, D) = Sim(C, D, \mathcal{O}, \mathcal{L}_{\text{Sub}}(\widetilde{\mathcal{O}})), \text{ and } \mathcal{L}_{\text{Sub}}(\widetilde{\mathcal{O}}) = Sub(\mathcal{O}).$$

$$GrSim(C, D) = Sim(C, D, \mathcal{O}, \mathcal{L}_{\text{G}}(\widetilde{\mathcal{O}})), \text{ and } \mathcal{L}_{\text{G}}(\widetilde{\mathcal{O}}) = \{E \mid E \in Sub(\mathcal{O})$$

$$\text{or } E = \exists r.F, \text{ for some } r \in \widetilde{\mathcal{O}} \cap N_R \text{ and } F \in Sub(\mathcal{O})\}.$$

where $Sub(\mathcal{O})$ is the set of concept expressions in $\mathcal{O}$. $AtomicSim(\cdot)$ captures taxonomy-based measures since it considers atomic concepts only. The rationale of $SubSim(\cdot)$ is that it provides similarity measurements that are sensitive to the modeller's focus which is captured in the subconcepts of the ontology. It also provides a cheap (yet principled) way for measuring similarity in expressive DLs since the number of candidates is linear in the size of the ontology. To capture more possible subsumers, one can use the grammar-based measure $GrSim(\cdot)$. We have chosen to include only grammar concepts which are subconcepts or which take the form $\exists r.F$ to make the following experiments more manageable. However, the grammar can be extended easily.

7   Approximations of Similarity Measures

Some of the presented examples for similarity measures might be practically inefficient due to the large number of candidate subsumers. For this reason, it would be nice if we can explore and understand whether a "cheap" measure can be a good approximation for a more expensive one. We start by characterising the properties of an approximation in the following definition.

Definition 1. *Given two similarity functions $Sim(\cdot)$, $Sim'(\cdot)$, and an ontology $\mathcal{O}$, we say that:*

- *$Sim'(\cdot)$ preserves the order of $Sim(\cdot)$ if $\forall A_1, B_1, A_2, B_2 \in \widetilde{\mathcal{O}}: Sim(A_1, B_1) \leq Sim(A_2, B_2) \implies Sim'(A_1, B_1) \leq Sim'(A_2, B_2)$.*
- *$Sim'(\cdot)$ approximates $Sim(\cdot)$ from above if $\forall A, B \in \widetilde{\mathcal{O}}: Sim(A, B) \leq Sim'(A, B)$.*
- *$Sim'(\cdot)$ approximates $Sim(\cdot)$ from below if $\forall A, B \in \widetilde{\mathcal{O}}: Sim(A, B) \geq Sim'(A, B)$.*

Consider $AtomicSim(\cdot)$ and $SubSim(\cdot)$. The first thing to notice is that the set of candidate subsumers for the first measure is actually a subset of the set of candidate subsumers for the second measure ($\widetilde{\mathcal{O}} \cap N_C \subseteq Sub(\mathcal{O})$). However, we need to notice also that the number of entailed subsumers in the two cases need not be proportionally related. For example, if the number of atomic candidate subsumers is n and two compared concepts share $\frac{n}{2}$ common subsumers, we cannot conclude that they will also share half of the subconcept subsumers. They could actually share all or none of the complex subsumers. Therefore, the order-preserving property need not be always satisfied. A similar argument can be made to show that entailed subconcept subsumers are not necessarily proportionally related to the number of entailed grammar-based subsumers. We conclude that the above examples of similarity measures are, theoretically, non-approximations of each other.

8   Empirical Evaluation

The empirical evaluation constitutes two parts. In Experiment 1, we carry out a comparison between the three measures $GrSim(\cdot)$, $SubSim(\cdot)$ and $AtomicSim(\cdot)$

against human experts-based similarity judgments. In [15], IC-measures along with Rada measure [16] has been compared against human judgements using the same data set which is used in the current study. The previous study [15] has found that IC-measures are worse than Rada measure so we only include Rada measure in our comparison and exclude IC-measures. We also include another path-based measure with is Wu & Palmer [22]. In Experiment 2, we further study in detail the behaviour of our new family of measures in practice. $GrSim(\cdot)$ is considered as the expensive and most precise measure in this study. We use $AtomicSim(\cdot)$ as the cheap measure as it only considers atomic concepts as candidate subsumers. Studying this measure can allow us to understand the problems associated with taxonomy-based measures as they all consider atomic subsumers only. Recall that taxonomy-based measures suffer from other problems that were presented in the conceptual inspection section. Hence, $AtomicSim(\cdot)$ can be considered the best candidate in its class since it does not suffer from these problems. We also consider $SubSim(\cdot)$ as a cheaper measure than $GrSim(\cdot)$ and more precise than $AtomicSim(\cdot)$ and we expect it to be a better approximation for $GrSim(\cdot)$ compared to $AtomicSim(\cdot)$. We excluded from the study instance-based measures since they require representative data which is not guaranteed to be present in our corpus of ontologies.

We have shown in the previous section that the above three measures are not approximations of each other. However, this might not be the case in practice as we will explore in the following experiment. We study the relation between $AtomicSim(\cdot)$ and $SubSim(\cdot)$ and refer to this as AS, the relation between $AtomicSim(\cdot)$ and $GrSim(\cdot)$ and refer to this as AG, the relation between $SubSim(\cdot)$ and $GrSim(\cdot)$ and refer to this as SG. For each relation, we examine the following properties: (1) order-preservation, (2-3) approximation from above/below, (4) correlation and (5) closeness. Properties 1-3 are defined in Definition 1. For correlations, we calculate Pearson's coefficient for the relation between each pair of measures. Finally, two measures are considered close if the following property holds: $|Sim_1(C, D) - Sim_2(C, D)| \leq \Delta$ where $\Delta = 0.1$ in the following experiment.

8.1 Infrastructure

With respect to hardware, we used the following machine: Intel Quad-core i7 2.4GHz processor, 4 GB 1333 MHz DDR3 RAM, running Mac OS X 10.7.5. As for the software, firstly, the OWL API v3.4.4 [8] is used. To avoid runtime errors caused by using some reasoners with some ontologies, a stack of freely available reasoners were utilised: FaCT++ [20], HermiT [18], JFact [2], and Pellet [19].

8.2 Test Data

Experiment 1. For the purposes of our comparison study, we use the 2010 version of SNOMED CT. This ontology has been described as the most complete

---

[2] http://jfact.sourceforge.net/

reference terminology in existence for the clinical environment [2]. It provides comprehensive coverage of diseases, clinical findings, therapies, body structures and procedures. As in February 2014, the ontology has 397,924 concepts.

The reason for choosing this particular ontology is the availability of test data that shows the degree of similarity between some concepts from that ontology as rated by medical experts. Pedersen et al. [15] introduced a test set consisting of 30 pairs of clinical terms. The similarity between each pair is rated by two groups of medical experts: physicians and coders. For details regarding the construction of this dataset, the reader is referred to [15]. We consider the average of physicians and coders similarity values in the comparison. We include in our study 19 pairs out of the 30 pairs after excluding pairs that have at least one concept that has been described as an ambiguous concept in the ontology (i.e., is assigned as a subclass of the concept ambiguous_concept) or not found in the ontology.

Experiment 2. The BioPortal library of biomedical ontologies was used to evaluate the new measures. The corpus contains 365 user contributed ontologies (as in October 2013) with varying characteristics such as axiom count, concept name count and expressivity.

A snapshot of the BioPortal corpus from November 2012 was used. It contains a total of 293 ontologies. We excluded 86 ontologies which have only atomic subsumptions as for such ontologies the behaviour of the considered measures will be identical, i.e., we already know that $AtomicSim(\cdot)$ is good and cheap. We also excluded 38 more ontologies due to having no concept names or due to run time errors. This has left us with a total of 169 ontologies.

Due to the large number of concept names (565,661) and difficulty of spotting interesting patterns by eye, we calculated the pairwise similarity for a sample of concept names from the corpus. The size of the sample is 1,843 concept names with 99% confidence level. To ensure that the sample encompasses concepts with different characteristics, we picked 14 concepts from each ontology. The selection was not purely random. Instead, we picked 2 random concept names and for each random concept name we picked some neighbour concept names (i.e., 3 random siblings, atomic subsumer, atomic subsumee, sibling of direct subsumer). This choice was made to allow us to examine the behaviour of the considered similarity measures even with special cases such as measuring similarity among direct siblings.

8.3 Experiment Workflow

Experiment 1. The similarity of 19 SNOMED CT concept pairs was calculated using the three methods along with Rada [16] and Wu & Palmer [22] measures. We compare these similarities to human judgements taken from the Pedersen et al.[15] test set.

Experiment 2.
Module Extraction: For optimisation, rather than working on the whole ontology, the next steps are performed on a $\perp$-module [4] with the set of 14 concept names as seed signature. One of the important properties of $\perp$-modules

is that they preserve almost all the seed signature's subsumers. There are 3 cases in which a $\perp$-module would miss some subsumers. The first case occurs when $\mathcal{O} \models C \sqsubseteq \forall s.X$ and $\mathcal{O} \models C \sqsubseteq \forall s.\perp$. The second case occurs when $\mathcal{O} \models C \sqsubseteq \forall s.X$ and $\mathcal{O} \models \forall s.X \equiv \top$. The third case occurs when $\mathcal{O} \models C \sqsubseteq \forall s.X$ and $\mathcal{O} \not\models C \sqsubseteq \exists s.X$. Since in all three cases $\forall s.X$ is a vacuous subsumer of C, we chose to ignore these, i.e., use $\perp$-modules without taking special measures to account for them.

Candidate Subsumers Extraction: In addition to extracting all atomic concepts in the $\perp$-module we recursively use the method getNestedClassExpressions() to extract all subconcepts from all axioms in the $\perp$-module. The extracted subconcepts are used to generate grammar-based concepts. For practical reasons, we only generate concepts taking the form $\exists r.D$ s.t. $D \in Sub(\mathcal{O})$ and r a role name in the signature of the extracted $\perp$-module. Focusing on existential restrictions is justifiable by the fact that they are dominant in our corpus (77.89% of subconcepts) compared to other complex expression types (e.g., universal restrictions: 2.57%, complements: 0.14%, intersections: 13.89, unions: 2.05%).

Testing for Subsumption Entailments: For each concept C_i in our sample and each candidate subsumer S_j, we test whether the ontology entails that $C_i \sqsubseteq S_j$. If the entailment holds, subsumer S_j is added to the set of C_i's subsumers.

Calculating pairwise similarities: The similarity of each distinct pair in our sample is calculated using the three measures.

8.4   Results and Discussion

Experiment 1 (How good are the new measures?). $GrSim$ and $SubSim$ had the highest correlation values with experts' similarity (Pearson's correlation coefficient $r = 0.87, p < 0.001$). Secondly comes $AtomicSim$ with $r = 0.86$. Finally comes Wu & Palmer then Rada with $r = 0.81$ and $r = 0.64$ respectively. Clearly, the new expensive measures are more correlated with human judgements which is expected as they consider more of the information in the ontology. The differences in correlation values might seem to be small but this is expected as SNOMED is an $\mathcal{EL}$ ontology and we expect the differences to grow as the expressivity increases. Figure 1 shows the similarity curves for the 6 measures used in this comparison. As we can see in the figure, the new measures along with Wu & Palmer measure preserve the order of human similarity more often than the Rada measure. And, they mostly underestimated the similarity whereas the Rada measure was mostly overestimating the human similarity.

Experiment 2 Cost of the new measures. One of the main issues we want to explore in this study is the cost (in terms of time) for similarity measurement in general and the cost of the most expensive similarity measure in particular.

The average time per ontology taken to calculate grammar-based pairwise similarities was 2.3 minutes (standard deviation $\sigma = 10.6$ minutes, median $m = 0.9$ seconds) and the maximum time was 93 minutes for the Neglected Tropical Disease Ontology which is a $\mathcal{SRIQ}$ ontology with 1237 logical axioms, 252 concepts and 99 roles. For this ontology, the cost of $AtomicSim(\cdot)$ was only 15.545 sec and 15.549 sec for $SubSim(\cdot)$. 9 out of 196 ontologies took over 1 hour to be

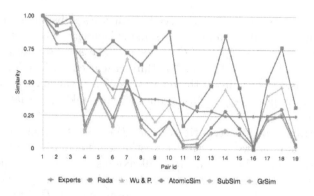

Fig. 1. 6 Curves of similarity for 19 SNOMED clinical terms

processed. One thing to note about these ontologies is the high number of logical axioms and roles. However, these are not necessary conditions for long processing times. For example, the Family Health History Ontology has 431 roles and 1103 logical axioms and was processed in less than 13 sec. Clearly, $GrSim(\cdot)$ is far more costly than the other two measures. This is why we want to know how good/bad a cheaper measure can be.

Approximations and correlations. Regarding the relations (AS, AG, SG) between the three measures, we want to find out how frequently a cheap measure can be a good approximation for/have a strong correlation with a more expensive measure. Recall that we have excluded all ontologies with only atomic subsumptions from the study. However, in 21 ontologies (12%), the three measures were perfectly correlated ($r = 1, p < 0.001$) mostly due to having only atomic subsumptions in the extracted module (except for three ontologies which have more than atomic subsumptions). In addition to these perfect correlations for all the three measures, in 11 more ontologies the relation SG was a perfect correlation ($r = 1, p < 0.001$) and AS and AG were very highly correlated ($r \geq 0.99, p < 0.001$). These perfect correlations indicate that, in some cases, the benefit of using an expensive measure is totally neglectable.

In about a fifth of the ontologies (21%), the relation SG shows a very high correlation ($1 > r \geq 0.99, p < 0.001$). Among these, 5 ontologies were 100% order-preserving and approximating from below. In this category, in 22 ontologies the relation SG was 100% close. As for the relation AG, in only 14 ontologies (8%) the correlation was very high.

In nearly half of the ontologies (49%), the correlation for SG was considered medium ($0.99 > r \geq 0.90, p < 0.001$). And in 19 ontologies (11%), the correlation for SG was considered low ($r < 0.90, p < 0.001$) with ($r = 0.63$) as the lowest correlation value. In comparison, the correlation for AG was considered medium in 64 ontologies (38%) and low in 55 ontologies (32.5%).

As for the order-preservations, approximations from above/below and closeness for the relations AG and SG, we summarise our findings in the following table. Not surprisingly, $SubSim(\cdot)$ is more frequently a better approximation to $GrSim(\cdot)$ compared to $AtomicSim(\cdot)$. Although one would expect that the

Table 1. Ontologies satisfying properties of approximation

	Order-preservations	Approx. from below	Approx. from above	Closeness
AG	32	32	37	28
SG	44	49	42	56

properties of an ontology have an impact on the relation between the different measures used to compute the ontology's pairwise similarities, we found no indicators. With regard to this, we categorised the ontologies according to the degree of correlation (i.e., perfect, high, medium and low correlations) for the SG relation. For each category, we studied the following properties of the ontologies in that category: expressivity, number of logical axioms, number of concepts, number of roles, length of the longest axiom, number of subconcepts. For ontologies in the perfect correlation category, the important factor was having a low number of subconcepts. In this category, the length of the longest axiom was also low (≤ 11, compared to 53 which is the maximum length of the longest axiom in all the extracted modules from all ontologies). In addition, the expressivity of most ontologies in this category was $\mathcal{AL}$. Apart from this category, there were no obvious factors related to the other categories.

How bad is a cheap measure?. To explore how likely it is for a cheap measure to encounter problems (e.g., fail one of the tasks presented in the introduction), we examine the cases in which a cheap measure was not an approximation for the expensive measure. AG and SG were not order-preserving in 80% and 73% of the ontologies respectively. Also, they were not approximations from above nor from below in 72% and 64% of the ontologies respectively and were not close in 83% and 66% of the ontologies respectively.

If we take a closer look at the African Traditional Medicine ontology for which the similarity curves are presented in Figure 2, we find that the SG is 100% order-preserving while AG is only 99% order-preserving. Note that for presentation purposes, only part of the curve is shown. Both relations were 100% approximations from below. As for closeness, SG was 100% close while AG was only 12% close. In order to determine how bad are $AtomicSim(\cdot)$ and $SubSim(\cdot)$ as cheap approximations for $GrSim(\cdot)$, we study the behaviour of these measures w.r.t. the Tasks 1-3 presented in the introduction.

Both cheap measures would succeed in performing Task 1 while only $SubSim(\cdot)$ can succeed in Task 2 (1% failure chance for $AtomicSim(\cdot)$). For Task 3, there is a higher failure chance for $AtomicSim(\cdot)$ since closeness is low (12%).

As another example, we examine the Platynereis Stage Ontology for which the similarity curves are presented in Figure 3. In this ontology, both AG and SG are 75% order-preserving. However, AG was 100% approximating from above while SG was 85% approximating from below (note the highlighted red spots). In this case, both $AtomicSim(\cdot)$ and $SubSim(\cdot)$ can succeed in Task 1 but not always in Tasks 2 & 3 with $SubSim(\cdot)$ being worse as it can be overestimating in some cases and underestimating in other cases.

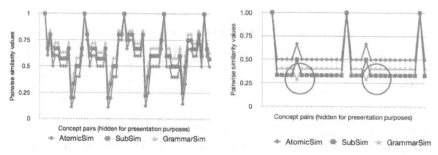

Fig. 2. African Traditional Medicine

Fig. 3. Platynereis Stage Ontology

In general, both measures are good cheap alternatives w.r.t. Task 1. However, $AtomicSim(\cdot)$ would fail more often than $SubSim(\cdot)$ when performing Tasks 2-3.

9   Conclusion and Future Research Directions

In conclusion, no obvious indicators were found to inform the decision of choosing between a cheap or expensive measure based on the properties of an ontology. However, the task under consideration and the error rate allowed in the intended application can help. In general, $SubSim(\cdot)$ seems to be a good alternative to the expensive $GrSim(\cdot)$. First, it is restricted in a principled way to the modeller's focus. Second, it has less failure chance in practise compared to $AtomicSim(\cdot)$.

As for our future research directions, we aim to extend the study by looking at different notions of similarity and relatedness (e.g., similarity between pairs of concepts usually referred to as relational similarity). Finally, we would like to apply and evaluate the presented measures in a real ontology-based application.

References

1. Baader, F., Calvanese, D., McGuinness, D.L., Nardi, D., Patel-Schneider, P.: The Description Logic Handbook: Theory, Implementation and Applications, 2nd edn. Cambridge University Press (2007)
2. Campbell, J.R., Carpenter, P., Sneiderman, C., Cohn, S., Chute, C.G., Warren, J.: Phase ii evaluation of clinical coding schemes: completeness, taxonomy, mapping, definitions, and clarity. Journal of the American Medical Informatics Association 4, 238–251 (1997)
3. Cohen, T., Widdows, D.: Empirical distributional semantics: Methods and biomedical applications. Journal of Biomedical Informatics 42(2), 390–405 (2010)
4. Cuenca Grau, B., Horrocks, I., Kazakov, Y., Sattler, U.: Modular reuse of ontologies: Theory and practice. J. of Artificial Intelligence Research 31, 273–318 (2008)
5. d'Amato, C., Staab, S., Fanizzi, N.: On the Influence of Description Logics Ontologies on Conceptual Similarity. In: EKAW 2008 Proceedings of the 16th International Conference on Knowledge Engineering: Practice and Patterns (2008)
6. Euzenat, J., Shvaiko, P.: Ontology matching. Springer (2007)
7. Hahn, U., Chater, N., Richardson, L.B.: Similarity as transformation. COGNITION 87 (1), 1–32 (2003)

8. Horridge, M., Bechhofer, S.: The OWL API: A Java API for working with OWL 2 ontologies. In: Proceedings of the 6th International Workshop on OWL: Experiences and Directions, OWLED (2009)
9. Jaccard, P.: Etude comparative de la distribution florale dans une portion des alpes et du jura. Bulletin de la Societe Vaudoise des Sciences Naturelles 37, 547–579 (1901)
10. Janowicz, K.: Sim-dl: Towards a semantic similarity measurement theory for the description logic ALCNR in geographic information retrieval. In: SeBGIS 2006, OTM Workshops 2006, pp. 1681–1692 (2006)
11. Jiang, J., Conrath, D.: Semantic similarity based on corpus statistics and lexical taxonomy. In: Proc. of the 10th International Conference on Research on Computational Linguistics, Taiwan (1997)
12. Lehmann, K., Turhan, A.-Y.: A framework for semantic-based similarity measures for $\mathcal{ELH}$-concepts. In: del Cerro, L.F., Herzig, A., Mengin, J. (eds.) JELIA 2012. LNCS, vol. 7519, pp. 307–319. Springer, Heidelberg (2012)
13. Lin, D.: An information-theoretic definition of similarity. In: Proc. of the 15th International Conference on Machine Learning, Morgan Kaufmann, San Francisco (1998)
14. Nosofsky, R.M.: Similarity scaling and cognitive process models. Annual Review of Psychology 43, 25–53 (1992)
15. Pedersen, T., Pakhomov, S., Patwardhan, S., Chute, C.: Measures of semantic similarity and relatedness in the biomedical domain. Journal of Biomedical Informatics 30(3), 288–299 (2007)
16. Rada, R., Mili, H., Bicknell, E., Blettner, M.: Development and application of a metric on semantic nets. IEEE Transaction on Systems, Man, and Cybernetics 19, 17–30 (1989)
17. Resnik, P.: Using information content to evaluate semantic similarity in a taxonomy. In: Proceedings of the 14th International Joint Conference on Artificial Intelligence (IJCAI 1995), vol. 1, pp. 448–453 (1995)
18. Shearer, R., Motik, B., Horrocks, I.: HermiT: A highly-efficient OWL reasoner. In: Proceedings of the 5th International Workshop on OWL: Experiences and Directions, OWLED-08EU (2008)
19. Sirin, E., Parsia, B., Grau, B.C., Kalyanpur, A., Katz, Y.: Pellet: A practical OWL-DL reasoner. Journal of Web Semantics 5(2) (2007)
20. Tsarkov, D., Horrocks, I.: faCT++ description logic reasoner: System description. In: Furbach, U., Shankar, N. (eds.) IJCAR 2006. LNCS (LNAI), vol. 4130, pp. 292–297. Springer, Heidelberg (2006)
21. Tversky, A.: Features of similarity. Psycological Review 84(4) (Jully 1977)
22. Wu, Z., Palmer, M.: Verb semantics and lexical selection. In: Proceedings of the 32nd Annual Meeting of the Association for Computational Linguistics (ACL 1994), pp. 133–138 (1994)

Relation Extraction from the Web Using Distant Supervision

Isabelle Augenstein, Diana Maynard, and Fabio Ciravegna

Department of Computer Science, The University of Sheffield, UK
{i.augenstein,d.maynard,f.ciravegna}@dcs.shef.ac.uk

Abstract. Extracting information from Web pages requires the ability to work at Web scale in terms of the number of documents, the number of domains and domain complexity. Recent approaches have used existing knowledge bases to learn to extract information with promising results. In this paper we propose the use of distant supervision for relation extraction from the Web. Distant supervision is a method which uses background information from the Linking Open Data cloud to automatically label sentences with relations to create training data for relation classifiers. Although the method is promising, existing approaches are still not suitable for Web extraction as they suffer from three main issues: data sparsity, noise and lexical ambiguity. Our approach reduces the impact of data sparsity by making entity recognition tools more robust across domains, as well as extracting relations across sentence boundaries. We reduce the noise caused by lexical ambiguity by employing statistical methods to strategically select training data. Our experiments show that using a more robust entity recognition approach and expanding the scope of relation extraction results in about 8 times the number of extractions, and that strategically selecting training data can result in an error reduction of about 30%.

1 Introduction

Almost all of the big name Web companies are currently engaged in building 'knowledge graphs' and these are showing significant results in improving search, email, calendaring, etc. Even the largest openly-accessible ones, such as Freebase [5] and Wikidata [31], are however far from complete. Most of the missing information is available in the form of free text on Web pages. To access that knowledge and populate knowledge bases, text processing methods such as relation extraction are necessitated. In this paper, we understand relation extraction as the problem of extracting relations, e.g. origin(musical artist, location), for entities, e.g. "The Beatles" of certain classes (e.g. musical artist). One important aspect to every relation extraction approach is how to annotate training and test data for learning classifiers. In the past, four groups of approaches have been proposed (see also Section 2).

Supervised aproaches use manually labelled training and test data. Those approaches are often specific for, or biased towards a certain domain or type of text. This is because information extraction approaches tend to have a higher performance if training and test data is restricted to the same narrow domain. In addition, developing supervised approaches for different domains requires even more manual effort.

K. Janowicz et al. (Eds.): EKAW 2014, LNAI 8876, pp. 26–41, 2014.

Unsupervised approaches do not need any annotated data for training and instead extract words between entity mentions, then cluster similar word sequences and generalise them to relations. Although unsupervised aproaches can process very large amounts of data, the resulting relations are hard to map to ontologies. In addition, it has been documented that these approaches often produce uninformative as well as incoherent extractions [11].

Semi-supervised methods only require a small number of seed instances. The hand-crafted seeds are used to extract patterns from a large corpus, which are then used to extract more instances and those again to extract new patterns in an iterative way. The selection of initial seeds is very challenging - if they do not accurately reflect the knowledge contained in the corpus, the quality of extractions might be low. In addition, since many iterations are needed, these methods are prone to semantic drift, i.e. an unwanted shift of meaning. This means these methods require a certain amount of human effort - to create seeds initially and also to help keep systems "on track" to prevent them from semantic drift.

A fourth group of approaches are *distant supervision* or *self-supervised* learning approaches. The idea is to exploit large knowledge bases (such as Freebase [5]) to automatically label entities in text and use the annotated text to extract features and train a classifier. Unlike supervised systems, these approaches do not require manual effort to label data and can be applied to large corpora. Since they extract relations which are defined by vocabularies, these approaches are less likely to produce uninformative or incoherent relations.

Although promising, distant supervision approaches have so far ignored issues arising in the context of Web extraction and thus still have limitations that require further research. Note that some of those issues are not specific to distant supervision and have been researched for supervised, semi-supervised or unsupervised approaches. To illustrate those limitations, consider the following example:

"*Let It Be* is the twelfth and final album by *The Beatles* which contains their hit single '*Let it Be*'. The band broke up in 1974."

Unrecognised Entities: Distant supervision approaches use named entity classifiers that recognise entities that were trained for the news domain. When applying those approaches to heterogenous Web pages, types of entities which do not exist in that domain are not recognised. Two of those types are *MusicalArtist:track* and *MusicalArtist:album*, i.e. *Let It Be* would not be recognised.

Restrictive assumption: Existing distant supervision systems only learn to extract relations which do not cross sentences boundaries, i.e. sentences which contain an explicit mention of the name of both the subject and the object of a relation. This results in data sparsity. In the example above, the second sentence does not contain two named entities, but rather a pronoun representing an entity and a NE. While coreference resolution tools could be applied to detect the NE the pronoun refers to, those tools have a low performance on heterogeneous Web pages, where formatting is often used to convey coreferences and linguistic anomalies occur, and because they are based on recognising the NE in the first place.

Ambiguity: In the first sentence, the first mention of *Let It Be* is an example for the *MusicalArtist:album* relation, whereas the second mention is an example of the

MusicalArtist:track relation. If both mentions are used as positive training data for both relations, this impairs the learning of weights of the relation classifiers. This aspect has already been partly researched by existing distant supervision approaches.

Setting: The general setting of existing distant supervision approaches is to assume that every text might contain information about any possible property. Making this assumption means that the classifier has to learn to distinguish between all possible properties, which is unfeasable with a large domain and a big corpus.

This paper aims to improve the state of the art in distant supervision for Web extraction by: (1) recognising named entities across domains on heterogeneous Web pages by using Web-based heuristics; (2) to report results for extracting relations across sentence boundaries by relaxing the distant supervision assumption; (3) to propose statistical measures for increasing the precision of distantly supervised systems by filtering ambiguous training data; and (4) to document an entity-centric approach for Web relation extraction using distant supervision.

2 Related Work

There are have been several different approaches for information extraction from text for populating knowledge bases which try to minimise manual effort in the recent past. *Semi-supervised bootstrapping approaches* such as KnowItAll [10], NELL [7], PROSPERA [19] and BOA [13] start with a set of seed natural language patterns, then employ an iterative approach to both extract information for those patterns and learn new patterns. For KnowItAll, NELL and PROPERA, the patterns and underlying schema are created manually, whereas they are created automically for BOA by using knowlege contained in DBpedia.

Ontology-based question answering systems often use patterns learned by semi-supervised information extraction approaches as part of their approach, Unger et al. [29], for instance, use patterns produced by BOA.

Open information extraction (Open IE) approaches such as TextRunner [36], Kylin [32], StatSnowball [37], Reverb [11], WOE [33], OLLIE [16] and ClausIE [9] are unsupervised approaches, which discover relation-independent extraction patterns from text. Although they can process very large amounts of data, the resulting relations are hard to map to desired ontologies or user needs, and can often produce uninformative or incoherent extractions, as mentioned in Section 1.

Bootstrapping and Open IE approaches differ from our approach in the respect that they learn extraction rules or patterns, not weights for features for a machine learning model. The difference between them is that statistical approaches take more different factors into account to make 'soft' judgements, whereas rule- and pattern-based approaches merge observed contexts to patterns, then only keep the most prominent patterns and make hard judgments based on those. Because information is lost in the pattern merging and selection process, statistical methods are generally more robust to unseen information, i.e. if the training and test data are drawn from different domains, or if unseen words or sentence contructions occur. We opt for a statistical approach, since we aim at extracting information from heterogenous Web pages.

Automatic ontology learning and population approaches such as FRED [21] and LODifier [4] extract an ontology schema from text, map it to existing schemas and extract information for that schema. Unlike bootstrapping approaches, they do not employ an iterative approach. However, they rely on several existing natural language processing tools trained on newswire and are thus not robust enough for Web information extraction.

Finally, *distantly supervised or self-supervised approaches* aim at exploiting background knowledge for relation extraction, most of them for extracting relations from Wikipedia. Mintz et al. [18] aim at extracting relations between entities in Wikipedia for the most frequent relations in Freebase. They report precision of about 0.68 for their highest ranked 10% of results depending what features they used. In contrast to our approach, Mintz et al. do not experiment with changing the distant supervision assumption or removing ambiguous training data, they also do not use fine-grained relations and their approach is not class-based. Nguyen et al. [20]'s approach is very similar to that of Mintz et al. [18], except that they use a different knowledge base, YAGO [26]. They use a Wikipedia-based named entity recogniser and classifier (NERC), which, like the Stanford NERC classifies entities into persons, relations and organisations. They report a precision of 0.914 for their whole test set, however, those results might be skewed by the fact that YAGO is a knowledge base derived from Wikipedia. In addition to Wikipedia, distant supervision has also used to extract relations from newswire [22,23], to extract relations for the biomedical domain [8,24] and the architecture domain [30]. Bunescu and Mooney [6] document a minimal supervision approach for extracting relations from Web pages, but only apply it to the two relations *company-bought-company* and *person-bornIn-place*. Distant supervision has also been used as a pre-processing step for learning patterns for bootstrapping and Open IE approaches, e.g. Kylin, WOE and BOA annotate text with DBpedia relations to learn patterns.

A few strategies for seed selection for distant supervision have already been investigated: at-least-one models [14,27,22,35,17], hierarchical topic models [1,25], pattern correlations [28], and an information retrieval approach [34]. At-least-one models [14,27,22,35,17] are based on the idea that "if two entities participate in a relation, at least one sentence that mentions these two entities might express that relation" [22]. While positive results have been reported for those models, Riedel et al. [22] argues that it is challenging to train those models because they are quite complex. Hierarchical topic models [1,25] assume that the context of a relation is either specific for the pair of entities, the relation, or neither. Min et al. [17] further propose a 4-layer hierarchical model to only learn from positive examples to address the problem of incomplete negative training data. Pattern correlations [28] are also based on the idea of examining the context of pairs of entities, but instead of using a topic model as a pre-processing step for learning extraction patterns, they first learn patterns and then use a probabilistic graphical model to group extraction patterns. Xu et al. [34] propose a two-step model based on the idea of pseudo-relevance feedback which first ranks extractions, then only uses the highest ranked ones to re-train their model.

Our research is based on a different assumption: Instead of trying to address the problem of noisy training data by using more complicated multi-stage machine learning models, we want to examine how background data can be even further exploited by testing if simple statistical methods based on data already present in the knowledge base can help to filter unreliable training data. Preliminary results for this have already been reported in Augenstein [3]. The benefit of this approach compared with other approaches is that it does not result in an increase of run-time during testing and is thus more suited towards Web-scale extraction than approaches which aim at resolving ambiguity during both training and testing. To the best of our knowledge, our approach is the first distant supervision approach to address the issue of adapting distant supervision to relation extraction from heterogeneous Web pages and to address the issue of data sparsity by relaxing the distant supervision assumption.

3   Distantly Supervised Relation Extraction

Distantly supervised relation extraction is defined as automatically labelling a corpus with properties, P and resources, R, where resources stand for entities from a knowledge base, KB to train a classifier to learn to predict binary relations. The distant supervision paradigm is defined as follows: [18]:

> If two entities participate in a relation, any sentence that contains those two entities might express that relation.

In general relations are of the form $(s, p, o) \in R \times P \times R$, consisting of a subject, a predicate and an object; during training, we only consider statements, which are contained in a knowledge base, i.e. $(s, p, o) \in KB \subset R \times P \times R$. In any single extraction we consider only those subjects in a particular class $C \subset R$, i.e. $(s, p, o) \in KB \cap C \times P \times R$. Each resource $r \in R$ has a set of lexicalisations, $L_r \subset L$. Lexicalisations are retrieved from the KB, where they are represented as the name or alias, i.e. less frequent name of a resource.

3.1   Seed Selection

Before using the automatically labelled corpus to train a classifier, we detect and discard examples containing highly ambiguous lexicalisations. We measure the degree to which a lexicalisation $l \in L_o$ of an object o is ambiguous by the number of senses the lexicalisation has. We measure the number of senses by the number of unique resources representing a lexicalisation.

Ambiguity Within an Entity. Our first approach is to discard lexicalisations of objects if they are ambiguous for the subject entity, i.e. if a subject is related to two different objects which have the same lexicalisation, and express two different relations. To illustrate this, let us consider the problem outlined in the introduction again: *Let It Be* can be both an *album* and a *track* of the subject entity *The Beatles*, therefore we would like to discard *Let It Be* as a seed for the class *Musical Artist*.**Unam**: For a given subject s, if we discover a lexicalisation for a related entity o, i.e. $(s, p, o) \in KB$ and $l \in L_o$, then, since it may be the case that $l \in L_r$ for some $R \ni r \neq o$, where also $(s, q, r) \in KB$ for some $q \in P$, we say in this case that l has a "sense" o and r, giving rise to ambiguity. We then define A_l^s, the ambiguity of a lexicalisation with respect to the subject as follows: $A_l^s = |\{r \mid l \in L_o \cap L_w \wedge (s, p, o) \in KB \wedge (s, v, w) \in KB \wedge w \neq o\}|$.

Ambiguity across Classes. In addition to being ambiguous for a subject of a specific class, lexicalisations of objects can be ambiguous across classes. Our assumption is that the more senses an object lexicalisation has, the more likely it is that that object occurence is confused with an object lexicalisation of a different property of any class. An example for this are common names of book authors or common genres as in the sentence "*Jack* mentioned that he read *On the Road*", in which *Jack* is falsely recognised as the author Jack Kerouac.

Stop: One type of very ambiguous words with many senses are stop words. Since some objects of relations in our training set might have lexicalisations which are stop words, we discard those lexicalisations if they appear in a stop word list. We use the one described in Lewis et al. [15], which was originally created for the purpose of information retrieval and contains 571 highly frequent words.

Stat: For other highly ambiguous lexicalisations of object entities our approach is to estimate cross-class ambiguity, i.e. to estimate how ambiguous a lexicalisation of an object is compared with other lexicalisations of objects of the same relation. If its ambiguity is comparatively low, we consider it a reliable seed, otherwise we want to discard it. For the set of classes under consideration, we know the set of properties that apply, $D \subset P$ and can retrieve the set $\{o \mid (s, p, o) \in KB \wedge p \in D\}$, and retrieve the set of lexicalisations for each member, L_o. We then compute A_o, the number of senses for every lexicalisation of an object L_o, where $A_o = |\{o \mid l \in L_o\}|$.

We view the number of senses of each lexicalisation of an object per relation as a frequency distribution. We then compute min, max, median ($Q2$), the lower ($Q1$) and the upper quartile ($Q3$) of those frequency distributions and compare it to the number of senses of each lexicalisation of an object. If $A_l > Q$, where Q is either $Q1$, $Q2$ or $Q3$ depending on the model, we discard the lexicalisation of the object.

3.2 Relaxed Setting

In addition to increasing the precision of distantly supervised systems by filtering seed data, we also experiment with increasing recall by changing the method for creating test data. Instead of testing, for every sentence, if the sentence contains a lexicalisation of the subject and one additional entity, we relax the former restriction. We make the assumption that the subject of the sentence is mostly consistent within one paragraph as the use of paragraphs usually implies a unit of meaning, i.e. that sentences in one paragraph often have the same subject. In practice this means that we first train classifiers using the original assumption and then, for testing, instead of only extracting information from sentences which contain a lexicalisation of the subject, we also extract information from sentences which are in the same paragraph as a sentence which contains a lexicalisation of the subject. Our new relaxed distant supervision assumption is then:

> If two entities participate in a relation, any *paragraph* that contains those two entities might express that relation, even if not in the same sentence, provided that another sentence in the paragraph in itself contains a relationship for the same subject.

Table 1. Freebase classes and properties used

Class	Property	Class	Property
Book	author	Film	release date
	characters		director
	publication date		producer
	genre		language
	ISBN		genre
	original language		actor
			character
Musical Artist	album	Politician	birthdate
	active (start)		birthplace
	active (end)		educational institution
	genre		nationality
	record label		party
	origin		religion
	track		spouses

This means, however, that we have to resolve the subject in a different way, e.g. by searching for a pronoun which is coreferent with the subject mention in a different sentence. We use a simpler, less expensive approach: we do not attempt to find the subject of the sentence at all, but instead disregard all features which require the position of the subject mention to be known. Features used in both the relaxed setting and the normal setting are documented in Section 4.6.

4 System

4.1 Corpus

To create a corpus for Web relation extraction using background knowledge from Linked Data, four Freebase classes and their six to seven most prominent properties are selected, as shown in Table 1. To avoid noisy training data, we only use entities which have values for all of those properties and retrieve them using the Freebase API. This resulted in 1800 to 2200 entities per class. For each entity, at most 10 Web pages were retrieved via the Google Search API using the search pattern "*subject_entity*" *class_name relation_name*', e.g. '"The Beatles" Musical Artist Origin'. By adding the class name, we expect the retrieved Web pages to be more relevant to our extraction task. Although subject entities can have multiple lexicalisations, Freebase distinguishes between the most prominant lexicalisation (the entity name) and other lexicalisations (entity aliases). We use the entity name for all of the search patterns. In total, the corpus consists of 560,000 pages drawn from 45,000 different websites. An overview of the distribution of websites per class is given in Table 2.

Table 2. Distribution of websites per class in the Web corpus sorted by frequency

Class	%	Website	Class	%	Website
Book	20%	en.wikipedia.org	Film	15%	en.wikipedia.org
	15%	www.goodreads.com		15%	www.imdb.com
	12%	www.amazon.com		3%	www.amazon.com
	9%	www.amazon.co.uk		3%	www.rottentomatoes.com
	4%	www.barnesandnoble.com		1%	www.amazon.co.uk
	3%	www.abebooks.co.uk		1%	www.tcm.com
	2%	www.abebooks.com		1%	www.nytimes.com
	28%	Others		61%	Others
Musical	21%	en.wikipedia.org	Politician	17%	en.wikipedia.org
Artist	6%	itunes.apple.com		4%	www.huffingtonpost.com
	5%	www.allmusic.com		3%	votesmart.org
	4%	www.last.fm		3%	www.washingtonpost.com
	3%	www.amazon.com		2%	www.nndb.com
	2%	www.debate.org		2%	www.evi.com
	2%	www.reverbnation.com		2%	www.answers.com
	57%	Others		67%	Others

4.2 NLP Pipeline

Text content is extracted from HTML pages using the Jsoup API, [1] which strips text from each element recursively. Each paragraph is then processed with Stanford CoreNLP [2] to split the text into sentences, tokenise it, annotate it with part of speech (POS) tags and normalise time expressions. Named entities are classified using the 7 class (time, location, organisation, person, money, percent, date) named entity model.

4.3 Relation Candidate Identification

Some of the relations we want to extract values for cannot be categorised according to the 7 classes detected by the Stanford NERC and are therefore not recognised. An example for this is *MusicalArtist:album*, *MusicalArtist:track* or *MusicalArtist:genre*. Therefore, as well as recognising named entities with Stanford NERC as relation candidates, we also implement our own NER, which only recognises entity boundaries, but does not classify them.

To detect entity boundaries, we recognise sequences of nouns and sequences of capitalised words and apply both greedy and non-greedy matching. The reason to do greedy as well as non-greedy matching is because the lexicalisation of an object does not always span a whole noun phrase, e.g. while 'science fiction' is a lexicalisation of an object of *Book:genre*, 'science fiction book' is not. However, for *MusicalArtist:genre*, 'pop music' would be a valid lexicalisation of an object. For greedy matching, we consider whole noun phrases and for non-greedy matching all subsequences starting with

---

[1] http://jsoup.org
[2] http://nlp.stanford.edu/software/corenlp.shtml

the first word of the those phrases, i.e. for 'science fiction book', we would consider 'science fiction book', 'science fiction' and 'book' as candidates. We also recognise short sequences of words in quotes. This is because lexicalisation of objects of *MusicalArtist:track* and *MusicalArtist:album* often appear in quotes, but are not necessarily noun phrases.

4.4 Annotating Sentences

The next step is to identify which sentences express relations. We only use sentences from Web pages which were retrieved using a query which contains the subject of the relation. To annotate sentences, we retrieve all lexicalisations L_s, L_o for subjects and objects related under properties P for the subject's class C from Freebase. We then check, for each sentence, if it contains at least two entities recognised using either the Stanford NERC or our own entity recogniser (Section 4.3), one of which having a lexicalisation of a subject and the other a lexicalisation of an object of a relation. If it does, we use this sentence as training data for that property. All sentences which contain a subject lexicalisation and one other entity that is not a lexicalisation of an object of any property of that subject are used as negative training data for the classifier. Mintz et al. [18] only use 1% of their negative training data, but we choose to deviate from this setting because we have less training data overall and have observed that using more negative training data increases precision and recall of the system. For testing we use all sentences that contain at least two entities recognised by either entity recogniser, one of which must be a lexicalisation of the subject. For our relaxed setting (Section 3.2) only the paragraph the sentence is in must contain a lexicalisation of the subject.

4.5 Seed Selection

After training data is retrieved by automatically annotating sentences, we select seeds from it, or rather discard some of the training data, according to the different methods outlined in Section 3.1. Our baseline models do not discard any training seeds.

4.6 Features

Given a relation candidate as described in Section 4.3, our system then extracts the following lexical features and named entity features, some of them also used by Mintz et al. [18]. Features marked with (*) are only used in the normal setting, but not in the relaxed setting(Section 3.2).

- The object occurrence
- The bag of words of the occurrence
- The number of words of the occurrence
- The named entity class of the occurrence assigned by the 7-class Stanford NERC
- A flag indicating if the object or the subject entity came first in the sentence (*)
- The sequence of POS tags of the words between the subject and the occurrence (*)
- The bag of words between the subject and the occurrence (*)

- The pattern of words between the subject entity and the occurrence (all words except for nouns, verbs, adjectives and adverbs are replaced with their POS tag, nouns are replaced with their named entity class if a named entity class is available) (*)
- Any nouns, verbs, adjectives, adverbs or named entities in a 3-word window to the left of the occurrence
- Any nouns, verbs, adjectives, adverbs or named entities in a 3-word window to the right of the occurrence

Compared with the system we use a baseline [18] we use richer feature set, specifically more bag of words features, patterns, a numerical feature and a different, more fine-grained named entity classifier.

We experiment both with predicting properties for relations, as in Mintz et al. [18], and with predicting properties for relation mentions. Predicting relations means that feature vectors are aggregated for relation tuples, i.e. for tuples with the same subject and object, for training a classifier. In contrast, predicting relation mentions means that feature vectors are not aggregated for relation tuples. While predicting relations is sufficient if the goal is only to retrieve a list of values for a certain property, and not to annotate text with relations, combining feature vectors for distant supervision approaches can introduce additional noise for ambiguous subject and object occurrences.

4.7 Models

Our models differ with respect to how sentences are annotated for training, how positive training data is selected, how negative training data is selected, which features are used, how and if features are combined, and how sentences are selected for testing.

Mintz: This group of models follows the setting of the model which only uses lexical features described in Mintz et al. [18]. Sentences are annotated using the Stanford NERC [12] to recognise subjects and objects of relations, 1% of unrelated entities are used as negative training data and a basic set of lexical features is used. If the same relation tuple is found in several sentences, feature vectors extracted for those tuples are aggregated. For testing, all sentences containing two entities recognised by the Stanford NERC are used.

Comb: This group of models follows the setting described in Section 4. It uses sentences annotated with both Stanford NERC and our NER (Section 4.3). All negative training data is used and feature vectors for the same relation tuples are aggregated. For testing, all sentences containing two entities recognised by both Stanford NERC and our NER are used.

Sing: The setting for Sing is the same as the setting for Comb apart from that for Sing we do not aggregate feature vectors. This means we predict labels for relation mentions instead of for relations.

Unam, Stop, Stat: Those models select seed data according to the different strategies outlined in Section 3.1.

NoSub: This group of models uses the relaxed setting described in Section 3.2 which does not require sentences to explicitly contain subjects.

4.8 Classifier

In order to be able to compare our results, we choose the same classifier as in Mintz et al. [18], a multi-class logistic regression classifier. We train one classifier per class and model. The models are then used to classify each relation value candidate into one of the relations of the class or NONE (no relation).

5 Evaluation

To evaluate our models we carried out a hold-out evaluation on 50% of our corpus, i.e. for both training and testing we use relations already present in Freebase to annotate our Web corpus. We then conduct an evaluation using those labels for the whole evaluation set and an additional manual evaluation of the highest ranked 10% of predictions per property [3]. We use the three metrics: number of predictions (number of occurrences which are predicted to be a value of one of the properties for an entity), precision and relative recall. Ideally, we would like to report recall, which is defined as the number of detected true positives devided by the number of positive instances. However, this would mean having to manually examine the whole corpus for every positive instance. Our respective models are restricted as to how many positive predictions they can make by the distant supervision assumption or the relaxed distant supervision assumption. Therefore, we report relative recall for which the number of positive instances equals the number of positive instances, also called *hits*, identified by automatic labelling.

5.1 Evaluation Method

We compute the number of predictions, precision and relative recall for the whole evaluation set and different model combinations using the automatic labels. While this does not allow us to compute exact results for every model, it is a close estimate and is helpful for feature tuning. Results for different models detailed in Section 4.7 averaged over all properties of each class are listed in Table 3. Model settings are incremental, i.e. the row Mintz lists results for the model Mintz, the row after that, + Stop lists results for the model Mintz using the seed selection method Stop, the row after that lists results for the seed selection methods Stop and Unam, and so forth.

For our manual evaluation, we rank all predictions by probability per property and manually annotate and compare from the top 10%, then average results over all properties per class, as shown in Table 4.

5.2 Results

From our automatic evaluation (Table 3) results we can observe that there is a significant difference in terms of performance between the different model groups.

The **Mintz** baseline model we re-implemented has the highest relative recall out of all models. This is because, for candidate identification, only entities recognised by

---

[3] Our evaluation data is available via www.dcs.shef.ac.uk/~Isabelle/EKAW2014/

Table 3. Automatic evaluation results: Number of positive predictions (N), relative recall (R) and precision (P) for all models and Freebase classes

Model	Book			Musical Artist			Film			Politician		
	N	P	R	N	P	R	N	P	R	N	P	R
Mintz	1248	0.205	**0.844**	2522	0.217	0.716	1599	0.237	**0.722**	1498	0.165	**0.865**
+ Stop	1248	0.204	0.842	2513	0.222	**0.691**	1597	0.236	0.72	1491	0.184	0.764
+ Unam	1258	0.204	0.842	2512	0.230	0.678	1597	0.236	0.72	1490	**0.185**	0.767
+ Stat75	1224	0.234	0.62	2409	0.220	0.277	1582	**0.241**	0.43	1462	0.144	0.514
+ Stat50	1221	**0.240**	0.627	2407	0.232	0.262	1549	0.24	0.4	1459	0.146	0.517
+ Stat25	1205	**0.240**	0.623	2398	**0.250**	0.244	1510	0.22	0.34	1455	0.153	0.515
Comb	1647	0.736	**0.326**	5541	0.619	**0.328**	2506	0.726	**0.403**	1608	**0.809**	0.513
+ Stop	1648	0.736	0.311	5516	0.652	0.281	2514	0.723	0.388	1688	0.81	0.476
+ Unam	1648	0.732	0.308	5505	0.65	0.262	2514	0.723	0.388	1674	0.806	0.464
+ Stat75	1622	**0.784**	0.206	5133	0.664	0.136	2505	**0.736**	0.27	1646	0.8	0.3
+ Stat50	1627	0.781	0.204	5130	0.668	0.126	2490	0.735	0.262	1661	0.8	0.29
+ Stat25	1610	0.777	0.182	5053	**0.679**	0.107	2482	0.735	0.241	1662	0.8	0.27
Sing	16242	0.813	**0.476**	19479	0.619	**0.298**	12139	0.726	**0.435**	4970	0.851	**0.653**
+ Stop	16188	0.814	0.46	19213	0.64	0.271	12139	0.726	**0.435**	4952	**0.856**	0.628
+ Unam	16188	0.814	0.46	19162	0.657	0.264	12139	0.726	**0.435**	4952	**0.856**	0.628
+ Stat75	15182	**0.849**	0.288	17204	0.723	0.118	12056	**0.738**	0.321	4896	0.791	0.185
+ Stat50	19072	0.837	0.26	16996	0.729	0.113	12042	0.736	0.302	4897	0.794	0.182
+ Stat25	19239	0.84	0.226	16705	**0.738**	0.101	12003	0.735	0.38	4896	0.795	0.174
Comb NoSub	7523	0.661	0.237	24587	0.595	0.371	10563	0.574	**0.427**	4035	0.633	**0.375**
Sing NoSub	43906	**0.747**	**0.438**	96012	**0.643**	**0.479**	29214	**0.665**	0.359	40848	**0.683**	0.193

Stanford NERC are used. For other models we also use our own NER, which does not assign a NE label to instances. As a result, the NE class feature for the relation extractor is missing for all those NEs only detected by our own NER, which makes it much more difficult to predict a label. However, the Mintz baseline model also has the lowest precision and the Mintz group of models has the lowest number of positive predictions. The low number of positive predictions is directly related to the low number of relation candidates because the Stanford NERC fails to recognise some of the NEs in the text.

The **Comb** group of models has a much higher precision than the Mintz group of models. This difference can be explained by the difference in features, but mostly the fact that the Mintz group of models only uses 1% of available negative training data. The absolute number of correctly recognised property values in the text is about 5 times as high as the Mintz group of features which, again, is due to the fact that Stanford NERC fails to recognise some of the relevant entities in the text. However, this also means that the relative recall is lower because those entities are harder to recognise.

We achieve the highest precision overall, though only by a small margin compared to Comb models and dependent on the class, with our **Sing** group of models, which do not combine feature vectors for relation mentions with the same lexicalisation. Because lexicalisations are ambiguous, merging them can lead to noisy feature vectors and a lower precision. On the other hand, rich feature vectors can provide an advantage over sparse feature vectors if they are not noisy.

For the **Unam, Stop and Stat** models, we observe that removing some of the ambiguities helps to improve the precision of models. However, removing too many positive

Table 4. Manual evaluation results: Number of true positives (N) and precision (P) for all Free-base classes

Model	Book		Musical Artist		Film		Politician	
	N	P	N	P	N	P	N	P
Mintz	105	0.236	216	0.255	110	0.343	103	0.241
Comb	168	0.739	510	0.672	283	0.764	150	0.863
Sing	1546	0.855	2060	0.586	1574	0.766	488	0.868
Sing Stop-Unam	1539	0.857	2032	0.620	1574	0.766	485	**0.874**
Sing Stop-Unam-Stat75	1360	**0.948**	1148	**0.694**	303	**0.775**	474	0.82
Comb NoSub	705	0.653	2363	0.619	973	0.623	363	0.687
Sing NoSub	4948	0.663	11286	0.547	2887	0.673	3970	0.703

training instances hurts precision. Further, while Stop-Unam improves results for all classes, Stop-Unam-Stat75 does not improve precision for Politician. This model works better for some properties than others due to the original motivation: to improve precision for n-ary properties which on average have multiple values for a property per entity. Although we examine n-ary properties for Politician, all of those have on average just one or two values per property. Therefore, removing positive training examples does not improve precision. For other classes, we achieve the highest precision with the Unam-Stop-Stat75 models, though this comes at the expense of recall, which might not be desirable for some scenarios.

Our **NoSub** models, which are based on a relaxed distant supervision assumption, show a surprisingly high precision. In addition, the total number of positive predictions for the models based on the relaxed assumption is three times as much as for the same models which are based on the original distant supervision assumption. Results based on automatically generated labels for this group of models have to viewed with caution though: automatic labelling is more prone to false positives than for other models.

Our manual evaluation of the highest ranked 10% of results per property (Section 4) confirm the general tendency we already observed for our automatic evaluation. In addition, we can observe that there is a sizable difference in precision for different properties and classes. It is easiest to classify numerical values correctly, followed by people. Overall, we achieve the lowest precision for *Musical Artist* and the highest for *Book*.

When examining the training set we further observe that there seems to be a strong correlation between the number of training instances and the precision for that property. This is also an explanation as to why removing possibly ambiguous training instances only improves precision up to a certain point: the classifier is better at dealing with noisy training data than too little training data.

We also analyse the test data to try to identify patterns of errors. The two biggest groups of errors are entity boundary recognition and subject identification errors. An example for the first group is the following sentence:

"\<s>The Hunt for Red October\</s> remains a masterpiece of military \<o>fiction\</o>."

Although "fiction" would be correct result in general, the correct property value for this specific sentence would be "military fiction". Our NER suggests both as possible candidates (since we employ both greedy and non-greedy matching), but the classifier should only classify the complete noun phrase as a value of *Book:genre*. There are several reasons for this: "military fiction" is more specific than "fiction", and since Freebase often contains the general category ("fiction") in addition to more fine-grained categories, we have more property values for abstract categories to use as seeds for training than for more specific categories. Second, our Web corpus also contains more mentions for broader categories than for more specific ones. Third, when annotating training data, we do not restrict positive candidates to whole noun phrases, as explained in Section 4.2. As a result, if none of the lexicalisations of the entity match the whole noun phrase, but there is a lexicalisation which matches part of the phrase, we use that for training and the classifier learns wrong entity boundaries. The second big group of errors is that occurrences are classified for the correct relation, but the wrong subject.

"<s>Anna Karenina</s> is also mentioned in <o>R. L. Stine</o>'s Goosebumps series Don't Go To Sleep."

In that example, "R. L. Stine" is predicted to be a property value for *Book:author* for the entity "Anna Karenina". This happens because, at the moment, we do not take into consideration that two entities can be in *more than one* relation. Therefore, the classifier learns wrong, positive weights for certain contexts.

6 Discussion and Future Work

In this paper, we have documented and evaluated a distantly supervised class-based approach for relation extraction from the Web which strategically selects seeds for training using simple, statistical methods. Previous distantly supervised approaches have been tailored towards extraction from narrow domains, such as news and Wikipedia, and are therefore not fit for Web relation extraction: they fail to identify named entities correctly, they suffer from data sparsity, and they either do not try to resolve noise caused by ambiguity or do so at a significant increase of runtime. They further assume that every sentence may contain any entity in the knowledge base, which is very costly.

Our research has made made a first step towards achieving those goals. We experiment with a simple NER, which we use in addition to a NERC trained for the news domain and find that can especially improve on the number of extractions for non-standard named entity classes such as *MusicalArtist:track* and *MusicalArtist:album*. At the moment, our NER only recognises, but does not classify NEs. In future work, we aim to research distantly supervised named entity classification methods to assist relation extraction.

To overcome data sparsity and increase the number of extractions, we experiment with relaxing the distant supervision assumption to extract relations across sentence boundaries. This results in about six times the number of extractions at a still fairly reasonable precision. Our future work plans are to improve our strategy by adding constraints on subjects of relations and to experiment with unsupervised coreference resolution methods. One additional resource we want to exploit for this is semi-structured information contained on Web pages, since it is much easier to interpret than text.

We further show that simple, statistical methods to select seeds for training can help to improve the precision of distantly supervised Web relation extractors. The performance of those methods is dependent on the type of relation it is applied to and on how many seeds there are available for training. Removing too many seeds tends to hurt performance rather than improve it. In future work, we aim at refining our seed selection methods and apply them dependent on the relation type and number of available seeds, and also evaluate them for more different classes and relations. A detailed description of future work goals is also documented in Augenstein [2].

Acknowledgements. We thank the anonymous reviewers for their valuable feedback. This research was partly supported by the EPSRC funded project LODIE: Linked Open Data for Information Extraction, EP/J019488/1.

References

1. Alfonseca, E., Filippova, K., Delort, J.Y., Garrido, G.: Pattern Learning for Relation Extraction with a Hierarchical Topic Model. In: Proceedings of ACL (2012)
2. Augenstein, I.: Joint information extraction from the web using linked data. In: Janowicz, K., et al. (eds.) ISWC 2014, Part II. LNCS, vol. 8797, pp. 505–512. Springer, Heidelberg (2014)
3. Augenstein, I.: Seed Selection for Distantly Supervised Web-Based Relation Extraction. In: Proceedings of the COLING Workshop on Semantic Web and Information Extraction (2014)
4. Augenstein, I., Padó, S., Rudolph, S.: LODifier: Generating Linked Data from Unstructured Text. In: Proceedings of ESWC, pp. 210–224 (2012)
5. Bollacker, K., Evans, C., Paritosh, P., Sturge, T., Taylor, J.: Freebase: A Collaboratively Created Graph Database For Structuring Human Knowledge. In: Proceedings of ACM SIGMOD, pp. 1247–1250 (2008)
6. Bunescu, R.C., Mooney, R.J.: Learning to Extract Relations from the Web using Minimal Supervision. In: Proceedings of ACL (2007)
7. Carlson, A., Betteridge, J., Kisiel, B., Settles, B., Hruschka, E.R., Mitchell, T.M.: Toward an Architecture for Never-Ending Language Learning. In: Proceedings of AAAI (2010)
8. Craven, M., Kumlien, J.: Constructing Biological Knowledge Bases by Extracting Information from Text Sources. In: Proceedings of ISMB (1999)
9. Del Corro, L., Gemulla, R.: ClausIE: Clause-Based Open Information Extraction. In: Proceedings of WWW, pp. 355–366 (2013)
10. Etzioni, O., Cafarella, M., Downey, D., Kok, S., Popescu, A., Shaked, T., Soderland, S., Weld, D.S., Yates, A.: Web-scale Information Extraction in KnowItAll. In: Proceedings of WWW, pp. 100–110 (2004)
11. Fader, A., Soderland, S., Etzioni, O.: Identifying relations for open information extraction. In: Proceedings of EMNLP, pp. 1535–1545 (2011)
12. Finkel, J.R., Grenager, T., Manning, C.D.: Incorporating Non-local Information into Information Extraction Systems by Gibbs Sampling. In: Proceedings of ACL (2005)
13. Gerber, D., Ngomo, A.C.N., Gerber, D., Ngomo, A.C.N., Unger, C., Bühmann, L., Lehmann, J., Ngomo, A.C.N., Gerber, D., Cimiano, P.: Extracting Multilingual Natural-Language Patterns for RDF Predicates. In: Proceedings of EKAW, pp. 87–96 (2012)
14. Hoffmann, R., Zhang, C., Ling, X., Zettlemoyer, L.S., Weld, D.S.: Knowledge-Based Weak Supervision for Information Extraction of Overlapping Relations. In: Proceedings of ACL, pp. 541–550 (2011)
15. Lewis, D.D., Yang, Y., Rose, T.G., Li, F.: RCV1: A New Benchmark Collection for Text Categorization Research. Journal of Machine Learning Research 5, 361–397 (2004)
16. Mausam, S.M., Soderland, S., Bart, R., Etzioni, O.: Open Language Learning for Information Extraction. In: Proceedings of EMNLP-CoNLL, pp. 523–534 (2012)

17. Mintz, M., Bills, S., Snow, R., Jurafsky, D.: Distant Supervision for Relation Extraction with an Incomplete Knowledge Base. In: Proceedings of HLT-NAACL, pp. 777–782 (2013)
18. Mintz, M., Bills, S., Snow, R., Jurafsky, D.: Distant supervision for relation extraction without labeled data. In: Proceedings of ACL, vol. 2, pp. 1003–1011 (2009)
19. Nakashole, U., Theobald, M., Weikum, G.: Scalable Knowledge Harvesting with High Precision and High Recall. In: Proceedings of WSDM, pp. 227–236 (2011)
20. Nguyen, T.V.T., Moschitti, A.: End-to-End Relation Extraction Using Distant Supervision from External Semantic Repositories. In: Proceedings of ACL (Short Papers), pp. 277–282 (2011)
21. Presutti, V., Draicchio, F., Gangemi, A.: Knowledge Extraction Based on Discourse Representation Theory and Linguistic Frames. In: Proceedings of EKAW, pp. 114–129 (2012)
22. Riedel, S., Yao, L., McCallum, A.: Modeling relations and their mentions without labeled text. In: Balcázar, J.L., Bonchi, F., Gionis, A., Sebag, M. (eds.) ECML PKDD 2010, Part III. LNCS, vol. 6323, pp. 148–163. Springer, Heidelberg (2010)
23. Riedel, S., Yao, L., McCallum, A., Marlin, B.M.: Relation Extraction with Matrix Factorization and Universal Schemas. In: Proceedings of HLT-NAACL, pp. 74–84 (2013)
24. Roller, R., Stevenson, M.: Self-supervised relation extraction using UMLS. In: Kanoulas, E., Lupu, M., Clough, P., Sanderson, M., Hall, M., Hanbury, A., Toms, E. (eds.) CLEF 2014. LNCS, vol. 8685, pp. 116–127. Springer, Heidelberg (2014)
25. Roth, B., Klakow, D.: Combining Generative and Discriminative Model Scores for Distant Supervision. In: Proceedings of ACL-EMNLP, pp. 24–29 (2013)
26. Suchanek, F.M., Kasneci, G., Weikum, G.: YAGO: A Large Ontology from Wikipedia and WordNet. Web Semantics: Science, Services and Agents on the World Wide Web 6(3), 203–217 (2008)
27. Surdeanu, M., Tibshirani, J., Nallapati, R., Manning, C.D.: Multi-instance Multi-label Learning for Relation Extraction. In: Proceedings of EMNLP-CoNLL, pp. 455–465 (2012)
28. Takamatsu, S., Sato, I., Nakagawa, H.: Reducing Wrong Labels in Distant Supervision for Relation Extraction. In: Proceedings of ACL, pp. 721–729 (2012)
29. Unger, C., Bühmann, L., Lehmann, J., Ngonga Ngomo, A.C., Gerber, D., Cimiano, P.: Template-Based Question Answering over RDF Data. In: Proceedings of WWW, pp. 639–648 (2012)
30. Vlachos, A., Clark, S.: Application-Driven Relation Extraction with Limited Distant Supervision. In: Proceedings of the COLING Workshop on Information Discovery in Text (2014)
31. Vrandečić, D., Krötzsch, M.: Wikidata: A Free Collaborative Knowledge Base. Communications of the ACM (2014)
32. Wu, F., Weld, D.S.: Autonomously Semantifying Wikipedia. In: Proceedings of the CIKM, pp. 41–50 (2007)
33. Wu, F., Weld, D.S.: Open Information Extraction Using Wikipedia. In: Proceedings of ACL, pp. 118–127 (2010)
34. Xu, W., Hoffmann, R., Zhao, L., Grishman, R.: Filling Knowledge Base Gaps for Distant Supervision of Relation Extraction. In: Proceedings of ACL, pp. 665–670 (2013)
35. Yao, L., Riedel, S., McCallum, A.: Collective Cross-document Relation Extraction Without Labelled Data. In: Proceedings of EMNLP, pp. 1013–1023 (2010)
36. Yates, A., Cafarella, M., Banko, M., Etzioni, O., Broadhead, M., Soderland, S.: TextRunner: Open Information Extraction on the Web. In: Proceedings of HLT-NAACL: Demonstrations, pp. 25–26 (2007)
37. Zhu, J., Nie, Z., Liu, X., Zhang, B., Wen, J.R.: StatSnowball: a Statistical Approach to Extracting Entity Relationships. In: Proceedings of WWW, pp. 101–110 (2009)

Inductive Lexical Learning of Class Expressions

Lorenz Bühmann[1], Daniel Fleischhacker[2], Jens Lehmann[1],
Andre Melo[2], and Johanna Völker[2]

[1] AKSW Research Group, University of Leipzig, Germany
{buehmann,lehmann}@informatik.uni-leipzig.de
[2] Data & Web Science Research Group, University of Mannheim, Germany
{daniel,andre,johanna}@informatik.uni-mannheim.de

Abstract. Despite an increase in the number of knowledge bases published according to Semantic Web W3C standards, many of those consist primarily of instance data and lack sophisticated schemata, although the availability of such schemata would allow more powerful querying, consistency checking and debugging as well as improved inference. One of the reasons why schemata are still rare is the effort required to create them. Consequently, numerous ontology learning approaches have been developed to simplify the creation of schemata. Those approaches usually either learn structures from text or existing RDF data. In this submission, we present the first approach combining both sources of evidence, in particular we combine an existing logical learning approach with statistical relevance measures applied on textual resources. We perform an experiment involving a manual evaluation on 100 classes of the DBpedia 3.9 dataset and show that the inclusion of relevance measures leads to a significant improvement of the accuracy over the baseline algorithm.

1 Introduction

There has recently been an increase in the number and size of RDF knowledge bases, in particular in the context of the Linked Open Data initiative. However, there is still a lack of knowledge bases that use expressive ontologies and instance data structured according to those ontologies. Many datasets focus on instance data and give less attention to the ontological layer. One of the reasons for this is the effort required to build up an ontology. To address this problem, a multitude of approaches have been devised using a plethora of methods [24]. In particular, there have been two main branches of research: On the one hand, lexical ontology learning approaches aim at constructing ontologies from textual input [25] and, on the other hand, logical learning approaches use existing RDF data as input to construct ontologies [15,3]. In this work, we present the first algorithm, we are aware of, which combines lexical and logical ontology learning. This constitutes the first step on a larger research agenda aiming to improve ontology learning algorithms to a state in which they achieve sufficient precision and recall to be employed in practice. Previous studies have shown that current algorithms have not yet achieved this goal (see e.g. [20]) and ontology learning remains an extremely challenging problem.

Using a short example, we briefly want to illustrate how schemata improvements can enable more powerful reasoning, consistency checking, and improved querying

K. Janowicz et al. (Eds.): EKAW 2014, LNAI 8876, pp. 42–53, 2014.

possibilities. In particular, in this article we are concerned with learning $\mathcal{EL}$ description logic concepts for definitions.

Example 1. The following definition in description logic syntax was learned by our approach for the class `Astronaut`[1] in DBpedia [23].

$$\texttt{Astronaut} \equiv \texttt{Person} \sqcap \exists\texttt{mission.SpaceMission}$$
$$\sqcap \exists\texttt{timeInSpace.minute}$$

The definition states that a person who was on a space mission and spent time in space is an astronaut and vice versa. Adding this definition to an ontology can have the following benefits: 1.) It can be used to detect inconsistencies and quality problems. For instance, when using the Pellet Constraint Validator[2] on a knowledge base with the above axiom, it would report astronauts without an associated space mission as violation.[3] 2.) Additional implicit information can be inferred, e.g., in the above example each person, who was on a space mission and spent time in space can be inferred to belong to the class `Astronaut`, which means that an explicit assignment to that class is no longer necessary. 3.) It can serve as documentation for the purpose and correct usage of schema elements. For instance, in the above example it can be argued that someone is an astronaut if he is trained for a space mission, whereas the definition requires to actually take part in such a mission. The definition clarifies the intended usage. Overall, we make the following contributions:

- first approach to combining logical and lexical ontology learning
- analysis of statistical relevance measures for learning class expressions
- a manual evaluation on a realistic large scale data set

The adapted algorithm is called *ELTL* ($\mathcal{EL}$ Tree Learner) and part of the open-source framework DL-Learner[4] [19] for concept learning in description logics (DLs). The remainder of the paper is structured as follows: In Section 2 we present related work. Section 3 covers preliminaries such as a definition of the learning problem in logical ontology learning and a description of the base algorithm we use. Subsequently, in Section 4, we describe how statistical relevance measures applied on textual resources can be integrated into the logical learning framework. Section 5 describes experiments and insights obtained from them and we conclude in Section 6.

2 Related Work

Since we presented the first approach towards unifying logical (data-based) and lexical (text-based) ontology learning, we describe related work in both areas.

Ontology Learning from Structured Data. Early work on the application of machine learning to Description Logics (DLs) essentially focused on demonstrating the PAC-learnability for various terminological languages derived from CLASSIC. In particular,

---

[1] We omit the namespace http://dbpedia.org/ontology/ for readability.
[2] http://clarkparsia.com/pellet/icv/
[3] Under OWL semantics, this is not a violation, due to the Open World Assumption, unless we can infer from other knowledge that the person cannot have taken part in a mission.
[4] http://dl-learner.org

Cohen and Hirsh investigate the CORECLASSIC DL proving that it is not PAC-learnable [5] as well as demonstrating the PAC-learnability of its sub-languages, such as C-CLASSIC [6], through the bottom-up LCSLEARN algorithm. These approaches tend to cast supervised concept learning to a structural generalizing operator working on equivalent graph representations of the concept descriptions. Recently, many approaches have been proposed that adopt the idea of *generalization as search* [26] performed through suitable operators that are specifically designed for DL languages [2,15,21] on the grounds of the previous experience in the context of ILP. There is a body of research around the analysis of such operators [22,18] and studies on the practical scalability of algorithms using them [14]. Supervised learning systems, such as YINYANG [15] and DL-Learner [19] have been implemented and adoptions implemented for the ontology learning use case [20,3]. Also techniques from the area of data mining have been used for unsupervised ontology learning [31]. As an alternative model, a new version of the FOIL algorithm [29] has been implemented, resulting in the DL-FOIL system [8]. The general framework has been extended to cope with logical representations designed for formal Web ontologies [9].

Ontology Learning from Text. Unlike logical approaches which have been developed to generate ontologies from structured data, lexical or NLP-based methods [32] draw upon the huge amounts of unstructured text available, e.g., on the web. Many of these methods combine lexico-syntactic patterns (e.g., Hearst patterns [13]) and linguistic resources like WordNet with machine learning techniques. While a growing number of ontology learning methods also leverages linked data or ontologies (e.g. FRED [28]), the results are mostly limited to atomic entities and simple axioms. An exception to this are pattern-based approaches to translating natural language definitions into class expressions such as LExO [30].

Altogether, we can see that attempts have been made to integrate semantic web data and logical inference into lexical approaches to ontology learning. However, there has been little if any work on integrating lexical evidence into logics-based ontology learning algorithms so far.

3 Preliminaries

For an introduction to OWL and description logics, we refer to [1]. In this section, we focus on giving an overview of the base learning algorithm we draw on. The task we investigate resembles *Inductive Logic Programming* [27] using a description logic knowledge base as background knowledge and $\mathcal{EL}$ concepts as target language. In the ontology learning problem we consider, we learn a definition of a class A, which has (inferred or asserted) instances in the considered ontology. To define the class learning problem, we need the notion of a *retrieval* reasoner operation $R_{\mathcal{K}}(C)$, which returns the set of all instances of C in a knowledge base $\mathcal{K}$.

Definition 1 (class learning problem). *Let an existing named class A in a knowledge base $\mathcal{K}$ be given. Analogous to standard information retrieval, the F-Score of an $\mathcal{EL}$ concept C is computed based on precision on recall where the precision is defined as $\frac{|R_{\mathcal{K}}(C) \cap R_{\mathcal{K}}(A)|}{|R_{\mathcal{K}}(C)|}$ and recall as $\frac{|R_{\mathcal{K}}(C) \cap R_{\mathcal{K}}(A)|}{|R_{\mathcal{K}}(A)|}$. The goal of the* class learning problem *is to maximize F-Score wrt. A.*

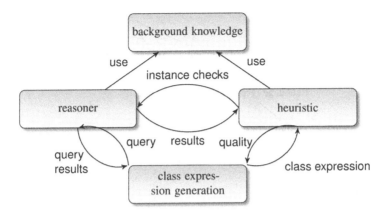

Fig. 1. Outline of the general learning approach in ELTL: Class expressions taking the available background knowledge into account are generated and evaluated in a heuristic with respect to the target learning problem. Figure adapted from [14].

Figure 1 gives a brief overview of our base algorithm *ELTL* ($\mathcal{EL}$ Tree Learner), which follows the common "generate and test" approach in ILP. This means that learning is seen as a search process and several class expressions are generated and tested against a background knowledge base. Each of those class expressions is evaluated using a heuristic, which we will analyze later in more detail.

Definition 2 (refinement operator). *A* quasi-ordering *is a reflexive and transitive relation. In a quasi-ordered space* $(S, \preceq)$ *a* downward (upward) refinement operator ρ *is a mapping from* S *to* 2^S, *such that for any* $C \in S$ *we have that* $C' \in \rho(C)$ *implies* $C' \preceq C$ $(C \preceq C')$. C' *is called a* specialization *(*generalization*) of* C.

Refinement operators can be used for searching in the space of expressions. As ordering we can use subsumption ($\sqsubseteq$), which is a quasi-ordering relation. If an expression C subsumes an expression D ($D \sqsubseteq C$), then C will cover all examples which are covered by D. This makes subsumption a suitable order for searching in expressions as it allows to prune parts of the search space without losing possible solutions.

The approach we used is a top-down algorithm based on refinement operators as illustrated in Figure 2. This means that the first class expression which will be tested is the most general expression ($\top$), which is then mapped to a set of more specific expressions by means of a downward refinement operator. Naturally, the refinement operator can be applied to the obtained expressions again, thereby spanning a *search tree*. The search tree can be pruned when an expression does not cover sufficiently many instances of the class A we want to describe.

The heart of such a learning strategy is to define a suitable refinement operator and an appropriate search heuristics for deciding which nodes in the search tree should be expanded. The refinement operator in the ELTL algorithm is defined and evaluated in [21] and has several beneficial theoretical properties not further detailed here.

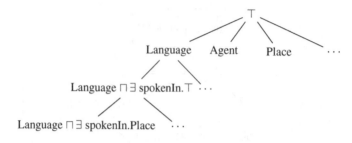

Fig. 2. Illustration of a search tree in ELTL

4   Approach

The learning algorithms in the DL-Learner framework are designed by combining a refinement operator with a search heuristic. While the operator itself is *ideal* with respect to a set of beneficial theoretical properties as shown in [21], we are investigating and improving the learning algorithm by incorporating a more intelligent search heuristic.

Learning concepts in Description Logics is a search process. The refinement operator is used for building the search tree, while a heuristic decides which nodes to expand. This decision can be done based on different criteria like the number of positive and/or negative examples covered by the class expression or the length of the concept represented by the node. While the existing heuristics basically rely on scores based on metrics according to coverage of the examples obtained via logical inference, we have observed in previous experiments [20,3] that best coverage does not always result in the most intuitive class expressions, and the search process can be improved by taking into account information contained in textual resources. Therefore, we extract statistical information out of given text, which might give some insights on the relevance of other ontology entities for the class we want to describe. This idea is substantiated by the assumption that words which are more related to each other tend to co-occur more often in texts as also expressed in the famous statement to "know a word by the company it keeps" [10] as frequently quoted throughout the linguistics community. This relevance score can then be combined with the other metrics in the heuristic and, thus, influence the navigation in the search tree, which in the end can result in better class descriptions.

Apart from the novel idea of including those relevance measures, one of our main goals was to evaluate which measure is suitable. In order to measure the relevance of entities for the definition of a given entity, we use popular co-occurrence based association measures [4]. The measures employed in this paper are Jaccard, Dice, Semi-conditional Information (SCI), Pointwise Mutual Information (PMI), Log Likelihood Ratio (LLR), Chi-Square (χ^2), T-test, and Significant PMI (sPMI) [7]. The first two measures have the advantage of being simple to compute and their values always fall into the $[0, 1]$ interval. The latter five measures incorporate some notion of statistical significance, by considering the ratio of observed ($f(x, y)$) and expected frequency assuming independence $Ef(x, y)$ of an entity pair x, y. PMI takes into account only the occurrence probabilities, ignoring the absolute frequency, which results in a tendency to yield high score values for low frequency pairs. sPMI solves this problem by incorporating corpus level significance, which considers the probability of observing a given deviation between $f(x, y)$ and its expected value $Ef(x, y)$. SCI multiplies PMI by the conditional probability $p(y|x)$, which tends to favor highly frequent pairs, therefore compensating the PMI's problem. LLR and χ^2 are the only ones which have the null addition property [4], which means that the measure is affected by the addition of data containing neither x not y.

Apart from influencing the search process in the learning algorithm, the textual evidence included by relevance measures can also influence the final ranking of class expressions. Actually, we have two possibilities of how the learning process can benefit from information contained in texts related to the knowledge base:

External Text Corpus. The first option relies on an external text corpus $\mathcal{C}$. We treat each document d in the corpus as a separate context and get information about the occurrence of the class c we want to describe, the occurrences of each other schema entity (a class or property) e_i, as well as the joint occurrences of c with each e_i. The retrieved information is then processed by the chosen relevance measures. The computation of the relevance score for each e_i is done in advance before the learning algorithm starts, because we have to normalize the values (we're doing a min-max normalisation), especially when we're using more than one relevance measure. In the current approach, we check the occurrence of an entity in a text by just taking a human-readable name for the entity[5] and check if it occurs syntactically in the text, i.e., we do not perform any kind of disambiguation which is planned to be integrated in a future version.

Local Textual Information. The second option uses textual resources which are contained in the underlying knowledge base, e.g., the individuals could be accompanied by textual descriptions summarizing important facts about them like the birth place of a person or that an astronaut participated in a particular space mission. This information can be used to get the relevance of the schema entities e_i by checking for the occurrences of its labels in the descriptions of instances of the class we want to describe.

5   Evaluation

5.1   Experimental Setup

We performed our experiments on the English DBpedia data set in version 3.9 accessible via a local mirror. The DBpedia data set was extracted from Wikipedia and at its core consists of resources corresponding to Wikipedia articles and facts extracted from article pages. DBpedia provides a lightweight OWL ontology, which defines the different classes and properties used throughout the data set. The DBpedia ontology contained a total of 529 classes of which 423 are leaf classes, i.e., classes not having any non-trivial subclasses. Furthermore, the ontology contained 927 object and 1,406 datatype properties. The ontology is also used for extracting the data from Wikipedia using mappings between infobox templates and ontology classes as described in [23]. The extraction process based on this mapping results in the so-called mapping-based data set which we use in our experiments. Overall, our experiments data set contained about 63.5 million triples describing 3,243,481 instances.

---

[5] Usually we use `rdfs:label`, but it's of course possible to use any other property.

On this data set, we used DL-Learner (specifically ELTL) enhanced with the relevance metrics as described above to learn class expressions for the classes contained in the DBpedia ontology. As a corpus for the relevance metrics the abstracts of all Wikipedia articles which described concepts modeled by an ontology class were crawled and then provided for retrieval using a SOLR[6] instance. This corresponds to the "External Text Corpus" scenario described in the Section 4. Though we also implemented the second scenario, we opted to only evaluate the first one which is more generally usable because it does not rely on greater amounts of textual descriptions in the data set itself.

We generated class expressions for all leaf classes of the DBpedia ontology which had at least 3 instances (288 out of 423). We then computed a sample set of at most 100 positive examples (instances belonging to the class) and 200 negative examples. For the negative examples, 100 instances belonging to the sibling classes and 100 instances of super classes which were not contained in the class to describe were randomly chosen. After applying DL-Learner, we performed a manual evaluation to find the combination of relatedness measures which resembles the human perception of intuitiveness of a class expression best. To do this, we randomly chose 100 of the classes with at least 10 alternative class expressions generated. For each class with more than 50 class expressions, we picked the top-50 expressions ranked by F-score. We handed the generated lists to four human annotators (two researchers not involved in the research presented in this submission from the Universities of Mannheim and Leipzig, respectively) along with the instruction to mark the class expressions which they consider most suitable for being added to the DBpedia ontology as definitions of the class. Additionally, we explicitly highlighted the possibility of marking multiple class expressions in cases where they are equally suitable or no expression if there was no expression close to an acceptable definition. The evaluation process took two hours per annotator on average. An example of evaluated class expressions for the class Astronaut is shown in Table 1.

In the second part of the evaluation, we applied several classification approaches to the F-score and relevance measures values to find a combination which is suited to reproduce the human assessment of intuitiveness. For this purpose, we employed the implementations provided by the Weka toolkit [12] in version 3.6.6.

5.2   Results

First, we computed the inter-rater agreement using the Fleiss' Kappa [11] statistical measure to get a score of how much homogeneity, or consensus, there is in the ratings given by judges. We evaluated the agreement on two different levels in terms of granularity. On the class level we expect to have an agreement if the evaluators selected at least one class expression to be useful as definition for the corresponding class. Here we got a Fleiss' Kappa value of 0.51 which can be interpreted as "moderate agreement" [17]. On the more fine-grained class expression level, we assume to have an agreement if the same class expression was selected as an appropriate class definition. The Fleiss' Kappa value was approximately 0.28 which can be seen as a "fair agreement". For the 288 classes processed by DL-Learner on average 51 class expressions have been generated. The average length of the expressions, which is defined in a straightforward way,

---

[6] https://lucene.apache.org/solr/, version 4.1.0

Table 1. Excerpt of the 50 class expressions that have been evaluated for the class `Astronaut`. The first column denotes the rank of the DL-Learner output without taking statistical measures into account

# class expression	F-score	PMI	sPMI
1 Person ⊓ ∃ selection.⊤	0.977	0.662	0.529
3 Person ⊓ ∃ selection.⊤ ⊓ ∃ birthPlace.PopulatedPlace	0.960	0.797	0.549
4 Person ⊓ ∃ selection.⊤ ⊓ ∃ birthPlace.Place	0.960	0.716	0.518
5 Person ⊓ ∃ mission.SpaceMission	0.950	0.493	0.664
8 Person ⊓ ∃ selection.⊤ ⊓ ∃ nationality.Country	0.947	0.707	0.498
12 Person ⊓ ∃ nationality.Country	0.937	0.697	0.489
13 Person ⊓ ∃ selection.⊤ ⊓ ∃ occupation.PersonFunction	0.937	0.672	0.487
15 Person ⊓ ∃ timeInSpace.minute	0.933	0.771	0.571
17 Person ⊓ ∃ mission.SpaceMission ⊓ ∃ timeInSpace.minute	0.933	0.620	0.643
19 Person ⊓ ∃ selection.⊤ ⊓ ∃ mission.SpaceMission	0.933	0.584	0.603
21 Person ⊓ ∃ mission.SpaceMission ⊓ ∃ birthPlace.Place	0.933	0.615	0.599
22 Person ⊓ ∃ selection.⊤ ⊓ ∃ nationality.Country ⊓ ∃ birthPlace.Place	0.933	0.733	0.499
29 Person ⊓ ∃ selection.⊤ ⊓ ∃ birthDate.date	0.923	0.553	0.466
30 Person ⊓ ∃ mission.SpaceMission ⊓ ∃ occupation.PersonFunction	0.923	0.571	0.568
31 Person ⊓ ∃ mission.SpaceMission ⊓ ∃ nationality.Country	0.923	0.605	0.579
41 Person ⊓ ∃ selection.⊤ ⊓ ∃ birthPlace.PopulatedPlace ⊓ ∃ mission.SpaceMission	0.920	0.703	0.596
48 Person ⊓ ∃ selection.⊤ ⊓ ∃ nationality.Country ⊓ ∃ occupation.PersonFunction	0.917	0.701	0.477

namely as the sum of the numbers of concept, role, quantifier, and connective symbols occurring in the expression was ≈ 10.

Our experiments address the following research questions:

1.) Which relevance measures are particular suitable, and how should they be combined?

2.) Can a combination of statistical relevance measures improve the results of logical ontology learning?

In order to answer the first question, we cast this task as a supervised machine learning problem itself in which F-score and the presented relevance measures are features of a learned definition. A definition is then considered to be a positive example if an evaluator selected it in our experiment and negative otherwise. Since this leads to a skewed distribution with more negative examples, we applied random subsampling on the negative examples. This results in an equal distribution of 302 positive and negative examples. In a first step, we used these to obtain a suitable classifier. We ran different types of classifiers (see Table 2a), i.e., support vector machines, decision trees, rules and probabilistic classifiers, as implemented in the Weka toolkit[7], with their default settings and used 10-fold cross-validation. As a baseline, we used an optimal threshold for the F-Score, which was determined by the Weka threshold selector meta classifier. An interesting insight is that the inclusion of relevance measures indeed significantly improves the standard approach of computing F-Score on the underlying RDF data, which allows us to positively answer the first research question.

The C4.5 decision tree algorithm performed best, so we used it as a base for feature analysis. This analysis was performed by using standard wrappers for feature subset

---

[7] http://www.cs.waikato.ac.nz/ml/weka/

Table 2. Results of relevance measure analysis

(a) Results of 10-fold cross-validation for different classifiers.

algorithm	accuracy	F-score	AUC
C4.5	77.5%	77.1%	79.6%
SVM	73.3%	74.6%	73.3%
Logistic Regression	72.8%	73.3%	79.9%
Conjunctive Rule	69.5%	67.9%	72.5%
Naive Bayes	64.1%	54.3%	75.6%
ELTL Baseline	59.4%	61.7%	63.8%

(b) Accuracy gain for features using C4.5.

feature added	accuracy
T-test	61.3%
+ F-score	73.5%
+ LLR	77.3%
+ Jaccard	77.0%
+ PMI	78.0%
+ χ^2	78.1%
+ SCI	78.5%

selection [16]. In this case, we could exhaustively run all combinations of features in C4.5 via 10-fold cross-validation and optimizing for predictive accuracy. The best performing feature subset is {F-score, PMI, χ^2, Jaccard, LLR, SCI, T-test}. We used this subset and iteratively removed the feature which caused the least loss in predictive accuracy. This allows us to observe the increase in accuracy obtained by adding features as shown in Table 2b:

The first three features led to significant improvements in the ability to detect promising definitions whereas the other features showed only small contributions (even negative in one case). We also analyzed the weights of normalized features in the SVM classifier:

$$3.6477 \times \text{F-score} \quad -2.2027 \times \text{PMI} \quad -0.1476 \times \chi^2$$
$$+0.7601 \times \text{Dice} \quad +0.8325 \times \text{Jaccard} \quad -0.4517 \times \text{LLR}$$
$$+0.2963 \times \text{SCI} \quad +3.7772 \times \text{sPMI} \quad +1.1387 \times \text{T-test} \quad -4.5916$$

It is notable here that PMI indeed has a negative weight. We believe this is due to high PMI values for low frequency entity pairs, so the negative weight along with the high positive weight of sPMI essentially acts as a noise filter. χ^2 and LLR also have negative weights, which might be related to their null addition property. We also noted that some metrics have very low values close to zero in the majority of cases and are essentially only used a tie breaker in the SVM classifier whereas the C4.5 decision tree can make better use of those values.

5.3 Discussion

During the manual annotation of the created class expressions, the annotators did not find suitable definitions for the classes in a number of cases. Based on the comments provided by the annotators and manual inspection of the affected classes, we were able to find patterns helping to categorize the problems. In the following, we describe the categories and give examples for each.

Limited Ontology Vocabulary. This problem arises due to relying on the classes and properties defined in the DBpedia ontology. In these cases, the ontology does not provide any entities which could be used to describe the class both accurately and exhaustively. For example, the expressions generated for describing the class `Bodybuilder` contained properties as `height` together with the class `Athlete`. Obviously, this is a correct description of a bodybuilder but it also matches all other athletes since the "restrictions" are actually properties of the parent class. However, DL-Learner was unable to choose a better definition since the ontology did not contain single properties or combinations of these specifically able to describe a body builder. This type of problems could only be solved by manually adding more specific properties or classes.

Limited Usage of Vocabulary. A related problem arose when the ontology contained an entity usable to describe a class fully which was not created by DL-Learner. For instance, when describing the concept `CanadianFootballLeague`, DL-Learner created definitions like `SportsLeague ⊓ ∃team.SportsTeam` that describes a sports league but is not specific enough to exclude sport leagues other than Canadian football league. Replacing `SportsTeam` in the definition by `CanadianFootballTeam` would lead to a flawless definition but is not proposed by DL-Learner. This is because the positive examples do not contain a significant number of assignments of teams to a Canadian football league that are also asserted to be Canadian football teams.[8] Again, this problem is hardly solvable when learning expressions but only at the data level.

Superfluous Restrictions. Some class expressions were also not chosen by the annotators because they contained superfluous restrictions. This is most often the case when defining subclasses of `Person` like `Writer` and including restrictions on, e.g., `birthPlace`. Clearly, this is not a restricting property for writers all being persons. Thus, some of these definitions were not chosen by the annotators who tried to choose the definitions as compact as possible. Most probably, this problem is also caused by the missing vocabulary to describe some classes suitably. We could try to prevent the generation of such definitions by considering the domain and ranges of properties and filtering restrictions if properties are defined for super classes of the currently considered class. However, then we would depend more strongly on the correctness of the schema whose quality showed to be doubtful in many cases throughout our experiments.

Another interesting example is the definition of an `Architect`, which uses the property `significantBuilding` though from the word meaning this would not be a definition covering all architects but only the more renowned ones which not only have regular buildings but also significant ones. DBpedia, as it is derived from Wikipedia, contains only few data on architects which are not famous for their buildings. A different but less general problem was discovered for classes belonging to the biological taxonomy in DBpedia. Here, some generated wrong definitions pointed to flaws in the usage of biology-specific properties like `kingdom`.

In summary, we discovered a combination of measures for generating more intuitive class expressions. From the inclusion of textual information, we were able to complement the purely logical information employed by DL-Learner with additional knowledge about how related specific properties are evaluated by humans. Most problems detected during the manual annotation can be traced back to missing or underspecified input data.

---

[8] Only 2 of 10 teams are assigned to be a Canadian football team.

6   Conclusion

In this paper, we presented first steps towards combining the previously distinct logical and lexical ontology learning areas. By extending a formerly pure logic based approach with statistical methods which can be used on text corpora, we were able to foster the generation of more intuitive class expressions. An extensive manual evaluation with four human annotators showed that the integration of relevance measures can significantly improve results. Nevertheless, we also discovered and analyzed several problems for which we were partially able to trace them back to data quality issues.

In the near future work, we plan to closely integrate the output of the lexical analysis into the refinement process. This might positively influence the search in the hypotheses space, thus, might result in a faster generation of more intuitive solutions first. Additionally, we are going to extend our approach by more sophisticated word sense disambiguation techniques, which will help us to more accurately identify mentions of ontology entities in the text. We will also include WordNet and other lexical resources that can facilitate the detection of words which are synonymous to ontology entity labels. Furthermore, we are going to apply our novel combined logical and statistical approach on more datasets to examine its performance in other domains and use cases.

Acknowledgment. This research was partially funded by the DFG project GOLD (*Generating Ontologies from Linked Data*). Johanna Völker is supported by a Margarete-von-Wrangell scholarship of the European Social Fund (ESF) and the Ministry of Science, Research and the Arts Baden-Württemberg.

References

1. Baader, F., Calvanese, D., McGuinness, D., Nardi, D., Patel-Schneider, P. (eds.): The Description Logic Handbook. Cambridge University Press (2003)
2. Badea, L., Nienhuys-Cheng, S.-H.: A refinement operator for description logics. In: Cussens, J., Frisch, A.M. (eds.) ILP 2000. LNCS (LNAI), vol. 1866, pp. 40–59. Springer, Heidelberg (2000)
3. Bühmann, L., Lehmann, J.: Pattern based knowledge base enrichment. In: 2th International Semantic Web Conference, Sydney, Australia, October 21-25 (2013)
4. Chaudhari, D., Damani, O.P., Laxman, S.: Lexical co-occurrence, statistical significance, and word association. In: EMNLP, pp. 1058–1068. ACL (2011)
5. Cohen, W.W., Hirsh, H.: Learnability of description logics. In: Proceedings of the Fourth Annual Workshop on Computational Learning Theory. ACM Press (1992)
6. Cohen, W.W., Hirsh, H.: Learning the CLASSIC description logic. In: Proc. of the Int. Conf. on Principles of Knowledge Representation and Reasoning, pp. 121–133. Morgan Kaufmann (1994)
7. Damani, O.P.: Improving pointwise mutual information (pmi) by incorporating significant co-occurrence. CoRR, abs/1307.0596 (2013)
8. Fanizzi, N., d'Amato, C., Esposito, F.: DL-FOIL concept learning in description logics. In: Železný, F., Lavrač, N. (eds.) ILP 2008. LNCS (LNAI), vol. 5194, pp. 107–121. Springer, Heidelberg (2008)
9. Fanizzi, N., d'Amato, C., Esposito, F.: Induction of concepts in web ontologies through terminological decision trees. In: Balcázar, J.L., Bonchi, F., Gionis, A., Sebag, M. (eds.) ECML PKDD 2010, Part I. LNCS, vol. 6321, pp. 442–457. Springer, Heidelberg (2010)

10. Firth, J.R.: A synopsis of linguistic theory 1930-1955. Studies in linguistic analysis, 1–32 (1957)
11. Fleiss, J.L., et al.: Measuring nominal scale agreement among many raters. Psychological Bulletin 76(5), 378–382 (1971)
12. Hall, M., Frank, E., Holmes, G., Pfahringer, B., Reutemann, P., Witten, I.H.: The WEKA data mining software: an update. SIGKDD Explorations 11(1), 10–18 (2009)
13. Hearst, M.A.: Automatic acquisition of hyponyms from large text corpora. In: COLING, pp. 539–545 (1992)
14. Hellmann, S., Lehmann, J., Auer, S.: Learning of OWL class descriptions on very large knowledge bases. International Journal on Semantic Web and Information Systems 5(2), 25–48 (2009)
15. Iannone, L., Palmisano, I., Fanizzi, N.: An algorithm based on counterfactuals for concept learning in the semantic web. Applied Intelligence 26(2), 139–159 (2007)
16. Kohavi, R., John, G.H.: Wrappers for feature subset selection. Artificial Intelligence 97(1), 273–324 (1997)
17. Landis, J.R., Koch, G.G.: The measurement of observer agreement for categorical data. Biometrics 33(1), 159–174 (1977)
18. Lehmann, J.: Hybrid learning of ontology classes. In: Perner, P. (ed.) MLDM 2007. LNCS (LNAI), vol. 4571, pp. 883–898. Springer, Heidelberg (2007)
19. Lehmann, J.: DL-Learner: learning concepts in description logics. Journal of Machine Learning Research (JMLR) 10, 2639–2642 (2009)
20. Lehmann, J., Auer, S., Bühmann, L., Tramp, S.: Class expression learning for ontology engineering. Journal of Web Semantics 9, 71–81 (2011)
21. Lehmann, J., Haase, C.: Ideal Downward Refinement in the $\mathcal{EL}$ Description Logic. In: De Raedt, L. (ed.) ILP 2009. LNCS, vol. 5989, pp. 73–87. Springer, Heidelberg (2010)
22. Lehmann, J., Hitzler, P.: Concept learning in description logics using refinement operators. Machine Learning Journal 78(1-2), 203–250 (2010)
23. Lehmann, J., Isele, R., Jakob, M., Jentzsch, A., Kontokostas, D., Mendes, P.N., Hellmann, S., Morsey, M., Kleef, P.v., Auer, S., Bizer, C.: DBpedia – A large-scale, multilingual knowledge base extracted from Wikipedia. Semantic Web Journal (2014)
24. Lehmann, J., Völker, J. (eds.): Perspectives on Ontology Learning. Studies on the Semantic Web. AKA Heidelberg (2014)
25. Maedche, A., Staab, S.: Ontology learning for the semantic web. IEEE Intelligent systems 16(2), 72–79 (2001)
26. Mitchell, T.M.: Generalization as search. Artificial Intelligence 18(2), 203–226 (1982)
27. Nienhuys-Cheng, S.-H., de Wolf, R.: Foundations of Inductive Logic Programming. LNCS, vol. 1228. Springer, Heidelberg (1997)
28. Presutti, V., Draicchio, F., Gangemi, A.: Knowledge Extraction Based on Discourse Representation Theory and Linguistic Frames. In: ten Teije, A., Völker, J., Handschuh, S., Stuckenschmidt, H., d'Acquin, M., Nikolov, A., Aussenac-Gilles, N., Hernandez, N. (eds.) EKAW 2012. LNCS, vol. 7603, pp. 114–129. Springer, Heidelberg (2012)
29. Quinlan, J.R.: Learning logical definitions from relations. Machine Learning 5, 239–266 (1990)
30. Völker, J., Hitzler, P., Cimiano, P.: Acquisition of OWL DL axioms from lexical resources. In: Franconi, E., Kifer, M., May, W. (eds.) ESWC 2007. LNCS, vol. 4519, pp. 670–685. Springer, Heidelberg (2007)
31. Völker, J., Niepert, M.: Statistical schema induction. In: Antoniou, G., Grobelnik, M., Simperl, E., Parsia, B., Plexousakis, D., De Leenheer, P., Pan, J. (eds.) ESWC 2011, Part I. LNCS, vol. 6643, pp. 124–138. Springer, Heidelberg (2011)
32. Wong, W., Liu, W., Bennamoun, M.: Ontology learning from text: A look back and into the future. ACM Comput. Surv. 44(4), 20 (2012)

Question Generation from a Knowledge Base

Vinay K. Chaudhri[1], Peter E. Clark[2], Adam Overholtzer[1], and Aaron Spaulding[1]

[1] Artificial Intelligence Center, SRI International, Menlo Park, CA, 94025
[2] Vulcan Inc., 505 Fifth Ave S., Suite 900, Seattle, WA, 98104

Abstract. When designing the natural language question asking interface for a formal knowledge base, managing and scoping the user expectations regarding what questions the system can answer is a key challenge. Allowing users to type ask arbitrary English questions will likely result in user frustration, because the system may be unable to answer many questions even if it correctly understands the natural language phrasing. We present a technique for responding to natural language questions, by suggesting a series of questions that the system can actually answer. We also show that the suggested questions are useful in a variety of ways in an intelligent textbook to improve student learning.

1 Introduction

Creating natural language interfaces for knowledge bases and databases is an actively studied problem for knowledge acquisition systems [9,10,11,13,14]. The design choices for these interfaces range from supporting a full-fledged natural language interface to using a formal query language such as SPARQL. In between lie options such as using a controlled natural language interface [10] or an interface guided by the ontology [14]. Using a full natural language interface is compelling, as it requires no training, but creates the obvious problem of the system not always being able to understand the question. Moreover, even if the system correctly understood the question, the knowledge base may be unable to answer the question. In this paper we describe a suggested question (SQ) facility that in response to the user's natural language questions, suggests questions that the system can actually answer. Such a facility both scopes the user's expectations, and minimizes the training requirements.

The context of our work is an intelligent textbook called Inquire Biology [3] that helps students to learn better. Inquire includes a curated biology knowledge base [8] and a reasoning system [15] for answering questions. This application required that the training for its users, who are students, be close to zero. Several studies with students have found both Inquire and the SQ facility reported here to be effective in practice [3].

We begin this paper by giving examples of different ways in which SQs are used in Inquire. We then give background on the knowledge base and the questions that can be answered by using it. Next, we describe our approach to question generation. Finally, we consider lessons learned and conclude with a summary.

2 Suggested Questions in Inquire

First and foremost, the SQs are used to auto-complete and suggest alternative questions in response to a user's natural language question input. In Figure 1, we show the

K. Janowicz et al. (Eds.): EKAW 2014, LNAI 8876, pp. 54–65, 2014.
© Springer International Publishing Switzerland 2014

question answering dialog box which also illustrates the questions that are suggested in response to a user's input. In this example, the user's question is well-formed and will be answered as it is, but in many cases, the question as typed cannot be answered. The suggested questions provide alternative questions that are closely related to the concepts in the user's questions and that are known to be answerable by the system.

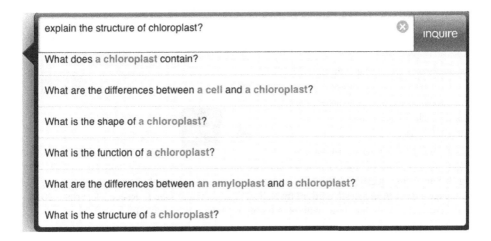

Fig. 1. Suggesting questions in response to a user's questions

Second, as the user is reading the textbook, and creates a highlight, the system will generate questions that relate to the highlighted text. This feature is illustrated in Figure 2 in which the user highlighted the word *Mitochondrion*. In response to this highlight, the system automatically generated questions that are shown in the right margin.

Finally, when the user views the answer to a question, or views the summary of a concept, we embed a set of SQs that can provide further information. In Figure 3, we show the concept of Mitochondrion, and the suggested follow-up questions in the bottom right hand corner.

3   Knowledge Base and Question Answering Capability

Our system uses a knowledge representation that has many of the standard features such as classes, individuals, class-subclass hierarchy, disjointness, slots, slot hierarchy, necessary and sufficient properties, and Horn rules [5]. Although knowledge engineers can edit any portion of the KB, domain experts author only existential rules [1] through a graphical user interface. An example of a rule authored by the domain experts is shown in Figure 4. In this graph, the root node is Mitochondria and is shown in white background and is universally quantified. Every other node in the graph is existentially quantified. For example, this graph asserts that for every instance of a Mitochondria, there exists an Enzyme and a Mitochondrial-Matrix such that Mitochondria has-part

Mitochondria: Chemical Energy Conversion

Mitochondria are found in nearly all eukaryotic cells, including those of plants, animals, fungi, and most protists. Some cells have a single large mitochondrion, but more often a cell has hundreds or even thousands of mitochondria; the number correlates with the cell's level of metabolic activity. For example, cells that move or contract have proportionally more mitochondria per volume than less active cells.

What is the relationship between a mitochondrion and a eukaryotic cell?

Are mitochondrions part of eukaryotic cells?

In a mitochondrion, what do protein enzymes produce?

What is located at a eukaryotic cell,

| NOTES | QUESTIONS | *i* |

The mitochondrion is enclosed by two membranes, each a phospholipid bilayer with a unique collection of embedded proteins (Figure 6.17). The outer membrane is smooth, but the

FIGURE 6.17 *The mitochondrion, site of cellular respiration.*

Fig. 2. Suggesting questions while the student is reading the textbook. The textbook content is from page 110 of *Biology* (9th edition) by Neil A. Campbell and Jane B. Reece, Copyright 2011 by Pearson Education, Inc. Used with permission of Pearson Education, Inc.

Mitochondrion

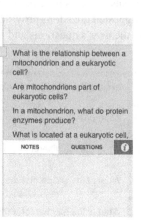

An organelle in eukaryotic cells that serves as the site of cellular respiration; uses oxygen to to break down organic molecules and synthesize ATP.

Mitochondrion is a type of: semiautonomous organelle .

Properties of a mitochondrion

▫ *Quantity:*
The quantity of the mitochondrion is directly proportional to the rate of energy transformation by organism.

Structure of a mitochondrion

▫ *Length:* between 1 and 10 micrometers

▫ *Shape:* oval like

▫ *Has region:*

  ▫ mitochondrial matrix

▫ *Has part:* SHOW ALL 6

  ▫ mitochondrial membrane

How is a mitochondrion created?

What is the function of a mitochondrion?

What is the shape of a mitochondrion?

What is the structure of a mitochondrion?

SHOW ALL 10

Fig. 3. Suggesting follow up questions. The images 6.17, 6.16 and 10.17 are from *Biology* (9th edition) by Neil A. Campbell and Jane B. Reece, Copyright 2011 by Pearson Education, Inc. Used with permission of Pearson Education, Inc.

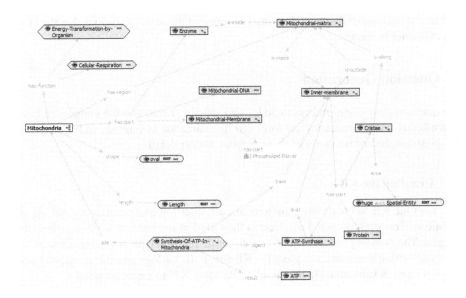

Fig. 4. Existential rule for Mitochondria

an Enzyme, and that Mitochondria has-region Mitochondrial-Matrix, and further that the Enzyme is-inside the Mitochondrial-Matrix.

Our current knowledge base (KB) covers more than 5500 concepts. By the time, the project concluded and the funding stopped, approximately 2000 had been well developed. A team of biologists performed the curation and also extensively tested the KB by posing a large set of questions. An encoding effort of approximately 12 person years was invested by the biologists in creating this KB.

Each question answered by the system can be viewed as an abstract question template, and we currently have more than 30 such question templates. Instead of enumerating all the question templates, we consider a few salient ones below. For each question template, we first give a phrase identifying it, followed by its abstract formulation, and then an example. (1) Definitional questions. What is X? What is an RNA? (2) Find a value question. What is the R of X? What are the parts of a nucleus? (3) Yes-No question. Is it true that Y is R of X? Is it true that DNA is part of chloroplast? (4) Identification question. What X has the following specific properties? What cells have a nucleus? (5) Relationship question. What is the relationship between X and Y? What is the relation between Chromosome and Protein? (6) Comparison questions: What are the [similarities/differences] between X and Y? What are the [similarities/differences] between Chromatin and Gene? (7) How many questions. How many Ys are R of X? How many chromosomes does a human cell have? (8) Event relations. What is the R of an event X? What does DNA transfer?

Reasoning processes underlying these questions have been previously published [7,6,4]. For the purpose of this paper, we will primarily be concerned with the problem of automatically generating instantiations of the above questions that the system can actually answer.

4 Question Generation

The question generation process includes two steps: (1) crawling the knowledge base to synthesize a question in logical form and its realization in English, and (2) ranking the questions. Below we consider these steps in greater detail.

4.1 Crawling the KB

We crawl the KB to create instantiations of each question and generate a database of questions. This pre-computed database is then used at run-time to select questions to suggest. The crawling process is different for each question type as we explain next.

For definition questions, we query the KB for all the biology specific concepts. Each concept name is substituted in the template "What is X?" to create a question.

For the *find a value question*, we process the graph corresponding to each existential rule. The questions are generated based on the length of the path from the root node which can be controlled as a parameter. For example, for the concept shown in Figure 4, the root node is Mitochondria. For a concept with root node X, if a relation R has more than one value, (e.g., has-part), we generate the question: What are the parts of X? (Here, has-part is realized as "parts" in the English version of the question.) For a concept with root node X, if a relation R has only one value, we generate the question: What is the R of X? This process can be recursively repeated by traversing the graph to a greater depth. For example, for a depth two, we would get questions of the form: What is R1 of Y that is R2 of X? This question is realized in English as "What are the parts of the mitochondrial membrane that are also a part of a mitochondrion?"

For a *yes-no question*, the process is very similar to the *find a value* question type except that for such questions instead of querying for a value of a relation, we are interested in testing whether a specific value is in a given relationship to the concept. An example of such a question is "Is it true that an enzyme is a part of mitochondrion?" If we wish to generate a question that has a negative answer, we can switch the correct relationship with another relationship. For example, we could produce "Is it true that an enzyme is a region of a mitochondrion?"

The *identification questions* are generated for concepts that have sufficient properties defined for them. An example of such a question is: What cells have a nucleus? This question is generated from the sufficient property for being a Eukaryotic-Cell which is that any cell with a nucleus is a Eukaryotic-Cell. One challenge in generating such questions is that if a concept has a complex sufficient property, generating good English sentences corresponding to it can be very hard.

For generating a *relationship question*, we pick two concepts. We choose the first concept based on the context in which the question is to be generated. For example, if the question is in response to a highlighting of the text, one of the concepts must appear in the highlight. If the question will be generated for a concept summary page, then that concept is chosen as one of the two concepts. We choose the second concept based on the following criteria: (a) the second concept must have either a direct or indirect relationship to the first concept in some concept graph; and (2) the second concept could be a sibling of the first concept in the class taxonomy. An example of such a question is "What is the relationship between a mitochondrion and chloroplast?"

For generating a *comparison question*, we must choose two concepts. The first concept is chosen based on the context as it was done for the relationship question. The second concept is chosen based on the following criteria: (a) the second concept is a sibling of the first concept in the class taxonomy (b) the second concept is disjoint from the first concept (c) the second concept is related to the first concept using the same relationship such as has-part. An example of such a question is: "What is the difference between a glycolipid and a glycoprotein?" Here, both glycolipid and glycoprotein are sibling subclasses of an Amphipathic-Molecule, and are also related to a Biomembrane by a has-part relationship.

We generate a *how many question* based on the cardinality constraints in the KB. For every qualified number constraint present in the KB, we generate the following question: How many Ys are R of X? An example of such a question is "how many chromosomes does a human cell have?"

The *event centered questions* require a slightly different crawling of the KB as these questions are based on the participants of an event. Thus, the crawling of the KB can be viewed as breadth-first search. For example, for an event E, if we have two relations $R1$ and $R2$ with respective values of X and Y, we can generate a question using E and X such that Y is the answer. Suppose we have a process representing virus infection in which the agent is Virus and the object is a Cell. For this representation, we can generate a question such as "What does a Virus infect?"

4.2   Ranking the Questions

Using the methods described in the previous section, we populate a question database. Our question database contains more than 20,000 questions; for any given situation, several hundred questions could be relevant. Because we do not wish to overwhelm the user, we must select most interesting questions and display them in some ranked order.

The first step in selecting the relevant questions is identifying the relevant concepts and relations that should serve as the trigger point for selecting questions from the SQs database. For suggesting questions in response to a question typed in by the user (as in Figure 1), we determine the concept names that the user has already typed in the question. For suggesting questions in response to a user highlight (as in Figure 2), we identify all the concept mentions in the selected region of the text. For suggesting follow up questions (as in Figure 3), we use the concepts in the questions, but we make sure that we do not suggest the question that the user has already asked. The identification of concepts based on the question or selected region of text, as well as identification of relevant questions based on the concept names, is done by a semantic search that considers lexical mappings between the text and the concept names. Based on the concepts identified for each situation, we search the SQ database to determine all the relevant questions. The questions selected during this step are used for further ranking as we explain next.

The ranking function should rank questions based on their quality, importance and relevance to the input paragraph. Another ranking criterion should be the diversity in question types and KB content. Even if some question types are more interesting than others, or some concepts are more important, that does not mean the system should always rank those types of questions at the top of the list. Students should be given a broader landscape of questions they could potentially ask the system. Ranking should assure diversity in question types and concepts for which the questions are generated. Whenever no clear motive exists for ranking a question higher or lower, one can rank based on the length of the question. Short questions should be given higher preference over longer questions. Because if a question is too long, then either it is quite likely too complex, or the SQ system may fail to properly phrase the question.

Our approach for ranking based on question types was to associate a numeric score with each question type. Our ranking scheme and the rationale for it is summarized in Table 4.2. A lower numeric score indicates higher interest. These rankings were provided by the biology teachers on our development team.

Table 1. Ranking question types

Question type	Rank	Rationale
Event centered	0.3	They are complex and short, and therefore, considered interesting
Identification	0.4	Very small in number and important for the definition of a concept
How many	0.8	Very small in number, so wherever they exist, we use them
Comparison	1	Very important for learning and education
Find a value	2	These questions are important, but there are too many of them
Relationship	4	Overall a good question but there can be too many all of which are not interesting
Yes/No	6	The answer to these questions is not very interesting, and there are too many of these
Definitional	8	Definitions are easily available through user interface

With each question we associate two ranking values: (1) The first ranking value is referred to as rank within a concept, and is a rank of that question within all the questions that are generated for that concept and an ordering based on the length of question. For a given concept, we expect that multiple questions of each type exist; (2) The second rank referred to as rank within a question type, and is a rank of a question within the questions for a concept that are of the system type. We compute the overall score of a question as a product of rank within the concept, rank within a question type and the overall rank of a question type based on the ranking in Table 4.2.

5 Evaluation

There are two kinds of evaluations of interest: (1) Given a paragraph, to what extent does the SQ facility generate questions that are educationally useful? (2) For the questions generated by the SQ facility, how many of the questions are educationally useful and ranked in the order of interest? To evaluate each of these aspects, we designed two separate evaluations that we discuss next.

5.1 Testing Coverage of Educationally Useful Questions

We selected a page with six paragraphs from the biology textbook. We chose the page in a way that its content was adequately represented in the KB to provide a good basis for question generation. We asked two biology teachers to generate questions that they thought were important for each of the six paragraphs. We asked them to generate as many important questions as they could findl; however, a minimum of three questions per paragraph was expected. The questions were to be asked from the perspective of a student who wants to learn, or who is curious about some new information that is not present in the current paragraph, but is related to it. Further analysis of these questions revealed what makes a good and interesting question in the given contexts.

After the first task was completed, we computed how many of the questions generated during this process were also present in the questions generated by the SQ facility. The following table summarizes those results.

Table 2. Coverage of educationally useful questions

Questions that can be generated and answered	29
Questions that could be potentially generated and answered	35
Questions that are too complex to generate	27
Questions that are too vague	8
Total number of questions	99

The above data show that of 99 questions authored by biologists, 8 questions were too vague. An example of a vague question is: "Is there anything else in nucleus besides genes?". This question was considered too vague as it is too open ended about what is being asked. Thus, 91 questions were deemed of good quality. The SQ system's current capability could generate 29 of these questions. An example of such a question is: "What is the difference between a nuclear matrix and a nuclear lamina?" This is a comparison question and can be easily generated and answered by the system. The system could potentially generate 35 more questions by minor extensions to the current capability. An example of such a question is: "During what phase of the cell cycle does chromatin condense into chromosomes?" This is an event-oriented question that specifies the context of the cell cycle and that requires an extension to the current SQ facility. Some questions produced by the biologists were too difficult to generate and to answer by the system. An example of such a question is: "During transcription, what is the advantage in synthesizing RNA instead of DNA?" Our system does not currently represent such information. Thus, of the 91 good-quality questions, 64 questions (i.e., 70%) were in an easy reach of the current SQ capability, making it a viable way to formulate questions in this domain. The remaining questions would not be answerable by the system even if they could be properly formulated and understood by the system.

5.2 Evaluating the Quality of Generated Questions

For the selected page, we computed the questions produced by the SQ facility. Each question was labeled by the system as relevant or not relevant for each paragraph. The biology teachers were asked to rate questions for each paragraph that the system deemed relevant on a three-point scale: (1) The question is definitely important. (This question is useful and could be presented to the student.) (2) This is a mediocre question. (This question might have a good answer but is probably not very relevant information. This question may also have good content but is a poorly formed question.) (3) This is not a good question. (This question should be thrown out because the answer is irrelevant information to a student.) Further, from the set of questions that were rated a "1", the raters were asked to select the top three questions for each paragraph.

The system found 38 concepts in the selected page, for which it generated a set of 376 unique questions. For these questions, we asked two different raters to give rating data points. Their ratings were aggregated, and the overall scores were as follows: 28.7% questions received a score of 1; 43.6% of questions received a score of 2; and 27.7% of questions received a score of 3. Because the total number of questions was 376, this gave us 108 questions for this page that received a score of 1. This set provided a good starting point for questions that we could use in our system right away and also left ample room for further improvement.

Let us consider examples of questions from each category. As an example of a question rated "1" by both biologists, consider "What is the relationship between a chromosome and a DNA?" This question gets at the deep knowledge associated with the structural relationship between these two entities. As an example of a question rated "2" by both biologists, consider: "What is the relationship between a DNA and deoxyribose?" This question was rated a "2" because the biologists felt that it questioned two very closely related entities. As an example of question rated as "3", consider: "Is it true that translation termination is a sub step of termination?" This question was not considered particularly deep and educationally useful by the biologists.

6 Related Work

Considerable recent interest has been shown in generating questions for intelligent tutoring systems (For example, see http://www.questiongeneration.org). As we have seen in our work, question generation has two distinct aspects: (1)generating the question and (2) identifying which question is most useful to a user in a given situation. A key difference between our work and these related efforts is that in our system, the questions are generated only from a curated knowledge base, while most question generation systems attempt question generation starting from English text [19,20]. Our goals differ in that we strive to provide a natural querying interface to a knowledge base that scopes user expectations about what the system can do. Perhaps, the work closest in spirit to ours is a recent effort to generate questions from linked data [12]. The approaches to ranking the SQs range from purely lexical criteria for the quality of the generated questions [16,20] to ranking based on pedagogical goals [18]. Our work on ranking falls somewhere in between these two approaches as we determine the ranking of questions based on the current capabilities of our knowledge based system and the empirical feedback from teachers and students.

Although users would prefer having a full natural language interface for accessing a knowledge base [17], few deployed system have seen a high degree of success. The work we reported here builds on our previous work [10] to provide a controlled natural language interface to a knowledge base. Although the previous interface was effective for users who could be given 4-6 hours of training, it still resulted in frequent awkward question formulations. In many cases, even when the system correctly understood the question, the reasoning system could not answer the question, causing significant frustration to the user. In an approach based on question generation, we are guaranteed that the system can indeed answer the question. Because the user is relieved of formulating the question into a controlled English, the system requires no training. A major disadvantage of this approach is that it is criticized for being too limited because it does not handle the full natural language statement of questions.

7   Recent Work

Since the initial design and evaluation reported here, the suggested question facility has been substantially enhanced. The system now generates all the questions that were previously marked as *could be generated with minor extension*. We achieved this by substantially enhancing the number of question templates in the system. The current system contains over 90 question templates. In spite of the substantial enhancements, the basic design of the question generation mechanism that has been described eariler in this paper has remained the same.

We have also conducted a study with end-user students that suggested that the SQ capabilities were well used and liked by students. A complete description of this study has been published previously [3], and therefore, we only summarize the salient points here.

We recruited current community-college biology students (n=25) who were studying Biology and trained them on the use of Inquire, including strategies for using the question answering features. The students were given one hour to read a section of the text, 90 minutes to answer a series of questions representative of a typical homework assignment, and 20 minutes to complete a closed book quiz on the content they had just read.

Compared to control groups with a print text book (n=24) or a version of *Inquire* without suggested questions and the question answering capability (n=24), the participants with the full SQ and QA functionality scored significantly better on the quiz (full *Inquire* vs. Ablated *Inquire*: 0.0015 p-value from a 2 tailed t-test; Full *Inquire* vs. Textbook: 0.0535) and homework (Full *Inquire* vs. Textbook: 0.0187). In the course of the study, the 25 students in the Full *Inquire* condition made heavy use of the SQ/QA capabilities, with Inquire answering 363 questions, with 194 unique questions. 61 questions were asked from the "blue card suggestions, and 60 from the related questions. During a post session debrief, all participants remarked that they relied on the autocomplete capability when asking questions, largely as a way of insuring that a question was properly formed.

8   Future Work and Summary

The SQ facility must evolve with the question answering facility of the system. As new question types are added, the question types for the SQ facility should be accordingly expanded. Although the current system always generates the same set of questions for a given highlight, one can imagine a generalization of this capability in which different sets of questions are suggested for different purposes. For example, the questions suggested when the user is reading the book for the first time could be different from the questions that are suggested when the user is studying for an exam. The questions suggested at the time of reading can serve both to review previously read information or as a self-test tool to assess whether the student has understood the material. More generally, there is a tremendous potential to devise novel interactive dialogs based on these questions which are sensitive to the current knowledge and learning goals, and are also designed to be instructive to the student by teaching them what are the right questions to ask. Although the current system produces reasonable English sentences, the quality of the English can be further improved by using a good natural language generation system [2]. The current system restricts itself to only a single sentence question; generating multi-sentence questions is open for future research. The ranking function can also be further tuned to specific pedagogical goals. Finally, we need to ensure the scalability of these methods when the size of the KB increases to the scope of full textbook, and the number of question templates is expanded by an order of magnitude.

In summary, we have described a practical approach for constructing a natural language query front end for a knowledge base. This work was conducted in the context of an intelligent textbook application that was required to be a walk up and use system. Our approach was based on generating the questions by crawling the knowledge base. In response to a free form question typed by the user, the system suggests most closely matching question that it can actually answer. Our evaluation results showed that the resulting capability provides good coverage of educationally useful questions and produces good quality questions. We believe an approach based on SQs is a deployable method for querying complex information that strikes an ideal balance between ease of use, user expectations, and implementation feasibility.

Acknowledgments. This work has been funded by Vulcan Inc. and SRI International. We thank the members of the AURA development team for their contributions to this work. We are grateful to Mihai Lintean whose summer project with us provided the foundation for this work.

References

1. Baget, J.-F., Leclère, M., Mugnier, M.-L., Salvat, E.: On rules with existential variables: Walking the decidability line. Artificial Intelligence 175(9), 1620–1654 (2011)
2. Banik, E., Kow, E., Chaudhri, V.K.: User-Controlled, Robust Natural Language Generation from an Evolving Knowledge Base. In: ENLG 2013: 14th European Workshop on Natural Language Generation (2013)
3. Chaudhri, V.K., Cheng, B., Overholtzer, A., Roschelle, J., Spaulding, A., Clark, P., Greaves, M., Gunning, D.: Inquire Biology: A Textbook that Answers Questions. AI Magazine 34(3) (September 2013)
4. Vinay, K.: Chaudhri, Nikhil Dinesh, and Craig Heller. Conceptual Models of Structure and Function. Technical report, SRI International (2013)

5. Chaudhri, V.K., Heymans, S., Wessel, S.C.T.M.: Object-Oriented Knowledge Bases in Logic Programming. In: Technical Communication of International Conference in Logic Programming (2013)

6. Chaudhri, V.K., Heymans, S., Overholtzer, A., Spaulding, A., Wessel, M.: Large-scale analogical reasoning. In: Proceedings of AAAI-2014 Conference (2014)

7. Chaudhri, V.K., Heymans, S., Wessel, M., Tran, S.C.: Query Answering in Object Oriented Knowledge Bases in Logic Programming. In: Workshop on ASP and Other Computing Paradigms (2013)

8. Chaudhri, V.K., Wessel, M.A., Heymans, S.: KB_Bio_101: A challenge for OWL reasoners. In: The OWL Reasoner Evaluation Workshop (2013)

9. Cimiano, P., Haase, P., Heizmann, J., Mantel, M., Studer, R.: Towards portable natural language interfaces to knowledge bases–the case of the ORAKEL System. Data & Knowledge Engineering 65(2), 325–354 (2008)

10. Clark, P., Chaw, K.B.J., Chaudhri, V.K., Harrison, P., Fan, J., John, B., Porter, B., Spaulding, A., Thompson, J., Yeh, P.: Capturing and answering questions posed to a knowledge-based system. In: Proceedings of the Fourth International Conference on Knowledge Capture, K-CAP (October 2007)

11. Damljanović, D., Bontcheva, K.: Towards enhanced usability of natural language interfaces to knowledge bases. In: Web 2.0 & Semantic Web, pp. 105–133. Springer (2009)

12. d'Aquin, M., Motta, E.: Extracting relevant questions to an rdf dataset using formal concept analysis. In: Proceedings of the Sixth International Conference on Knowledge Capture, pp. 121–128. ACM (2011)

13. Distelhorst, G., Srivastava, V., Rosse, C., Brinkley, J.F.: A prototype natural language interface to a large complex knowledge base, the foundational model of anatomy. In: AMIA Annual Symposium Proceedings, vol. 2003, p. 200. American Medical Informatics Association (2003)

14. Franconi, E., Guagliardo, P., Trevisan, M.: An intelligent query interface based on ontology navigation. In: Proceedings of the Workshop on Visual Interfaces to the Social and Semantic Web (VISSW 2010), vol. 565, Citeseer (2010)

15. Gunning, D., Chaudhri, V.K., Clark, P., Barker, K., Chaw, S.-Y., Greaves, M., Grosof, B., Leung, A., McDonald, D., Mishra, S., Pacheco, J., Porter, B., Spaulding, A., Tecuci, D., Tien, J.: Project Halo update: Progress toward Digital Aristotle. AI Magazine (Fall 2010)

16. Heilman, M., Smith, N.A.: Good question! Statistical ranking for question generation. In: Human Language Technologies: The 2010 Annual Conference of the North American Chapter of the Association for Computational Linguistics, pp. 609–617. Association for Computational Linguistics (2010)

17. Kaufmann, E., Bernstein, A.: How useful are natural language interfaces to the semantic web for casual end-users? In: The Semantic Web, pp. 281–294. Springer (2007)

18. Liu, M., Calvo, R.A., Rus, V.: Automatic question generation for literature review writing support. In: Intelligent Tutoring Systems, pp. 45–54. Springer (2010)

19. Olney, A.M., Graesser, A.C., Person, N.K.: Question generation from concept maps. Dialogue & Discourse 3(2), 75–99 (2012)

20. Yao, X., Bouma, G., Zhang, Y.: Semantics-based question generation and implementation. Dialogue & Discourse 3(2), 11–42 (2012)

Inconsistency Monitoring in a Large Scientific Knowledge Base

Vinay K. Chaudhri[1], Rahul Katragadda[2], Jeff Shrager[1], and Michael Wessel[1]

[1] Artificial Intelligence Center, SRI International, Menlo Park, CA, 94025
[2] Evalueserve Private Limited, Gurgaon - 122001, Haryana, India

Abstract. Large scientific knowledge bases (KBs) are bound to contain inconsistencies and under-specified knowledge. Inconsistencies are inherent because the approach to modeling certain phenomena evolves over time, and at any given time, contradictory approaches to modeling a piece of domain knowledge may simultaneously exist in the KB. Underspecification is inherent because a large, complex KB is rarely fully specified, especially when authored by domain experts who are not formally trained in knowledge representation. We describe our approach for inconsistency monitoring in a large biology KB. We use a combination of anti-patterns that are indicative of poor modeling and inconsistencies due to underspecification. We draw the following lessons from this experience: (1) knowledge authoring must include an intermediate step between authoring and run time inference to identify errors and inconsistencies; (2) underspecification can ease knowledge encoding but requires appropriate user control; and (3) since *real-life* KBs are rarely consistent, a scheme to derive useful conclusions in spite of inconsistencies is essential.

1 Introduction

We describe how we monitored and resolved inconsistencies in KB_Bio_101[7,10], a biology knowledge base (KB), developed as part of Project Halo [12]. Any large KB inherently faces issues of inconsistency and underspecification that result from complex knowledge engineering processes. What we call "underspecification" is especially crucial if the KB is to be authored by domain experts who are unable to provide rigorous and complete knowledge representation. We refer to such issues as "process problems". In addition, scientific knowledge bases will *of necessity* be both inconsistent and underspecified because any interesting science is itself, to some extent, inconsistent and underspecified. We refer to these issues as "actual" inconsistency and underspecification. Although this paper's focus is on "process problems", many of the same techniques are applicable to dealing with actual inconsistency and underspecification.

To create KB_Bio_101, domain experts used a state-of-the-art knowledge-authoring system called AURA [17] to encode a significant subset of a popular biology textbook [23]. The team relied on a knowledge factory process and a set of guidelines that specified a systematic process to encode textbook sentences [4,6]. The knowledge engineering team was based in India at a commercial organization called Evalueserve, and thus, was at an arms length from the research team that created AURA. The AURA team

K. Janowicz et al. (Eds.): EKAW 2014, LNAI 8876, pp. 66–79, 2014.

trained two knowledge engineers from Evalueserve by bringing them to SRI, who were in turn, responsible for training the biologists based in India. At its peak, the knowledge encoding team consisted of 8 biologists and 2 knowledge engineers. The biologists had no prior training in knowledge representation. They were selected through an aptitude test designed to test their conceptual abilities, and were put through a 20 hour AURA training.

The KB_Bio_101 contains more than 5000 classes, and over 100,000 axioms, and is a central component of an electronic textbook called *Inquire Biology* [3]. Inquire was extensively tested in pilot studies with college students. The pilot experiment had 74 students. Thus, not only was the KB encoded in a large scale knowledge engineering effort, it was subjected to actual use in the context of an end-user application. Inquire is not, however, available as a commercial product for sale in the market place.

The representation used in KB_Bio_101 has many standard features, such as an ability to define classes, class hierarchies, relations, relation hierarchies, inverse relations, and domain and range constraints [8]. KB_Bio_101 also explicitly permits underspecification [9]. For example, we may have a statement in the KB the following statements: every car has an engine; a Subaru is a subclass of car; and that its engine is large. These statements introduce under-specification in that they do not make it explicit whether the engine of Subaru that is large is the same engine that it inherits from Car. AURA deals with underspecification by using a heuristic reasoning module to make default inference that lets it conclude that the engine of Subaru must be the same as the engine it inherits from its super class car. Underspecification tolerance facilitates knowledge encoding by biologists who have limited training in knowledge representation. KB_Bio_101uses existential rules which can be structured as graphs [10]. Graph structured rules are crucial for representing knowledge in a biology textbook. KB_Bio_101 is the first effort to put this level of expressiveness in the hands of biologists.

Considerable prior work focuses on tools for testing and debugging KBs [27,20,22,24,28]. Most appropriate debugging tools should be used to address problems in the KB, and yet, a strategy in which the KB should neither have underspecification nor inconsistency before deployment is too constrained. Therefore, instead of taking a "debugging" stance in which all inconsistencies must be repaired immediately, a much better view is one of *monitoring* and *continuous improvement*.

We report on the monitoring and continuous improvement of KB_Bio_101 as it evolved during a period of approximately one year. The reported monitoring focused on detecting the inconsistencies due to modeling choices as well as the inconsistencies due to underspecification. Our work is experimental in that instead of focusing on new tools and techniques, we report on our practical experience of monitoring the KB for inconsistencies and of making ongoing improvements. We based our monitoring process on anti-patterns [11] which suggest potentially poor modeling, and on the inconsistencies reported by the reasoning engine or as observed by domain experts. We do not claim to have invented new techniques. We hope that our experience report on applying known techniques in the context of a large scale project could be illustrative to others to show what it takes to engineer a complex knowledge base.

We give concrete examples of ontology patterns that we used to monitor the quality of the KB. We also present a real-life example of the problems in an underspecified KB due to ambiguities caused by multiple inheritance. We begin the paper with a discussion of our approach to KB testing. We then describe the anti-patterns and then consider an example problem caused by KB underspecification. We conclude the paper with a discussion and a summary of the lessons learned. While we reference substantial prior work that is the basis of our work, this paper is self-contained so that it can be understood and appreciated without reading any of the prior papers.

2   Approach to Knowledge Base Monitoring

Our approach to monitoring the knowledge base was based on two kinds of tests: tests based on anti-patterns, and based on systematically querying every relation for a sample instance of every class in the KB. The knowledge engineers execute both of these tests programmatically. After an initial error analysis, the test results are passed to the domain experts so that they can address the representation errors in the KB. We will explain these tests in more detail below.

2.1   Anti-Patterns

An anti-pattern is an axiom schema that is indicative of poor modeling choices or captures some inconsistency in the KB. It is a first-order logic formula of the form

$$\exists v.[Pre(v) \Rightarrow conclusion\_predicate(v, \ldots)]$$

We say that the axiom is applicable if $KB \models \exists v.[Pre(v)]$, where v is a vector of variables, $conclusion\_predicate$ is some error or warning predicate name. We did not use the anti-patterns to capture inconsistencies caused due to under-specification.

We used the anti-patterns in a three phased approach: detect, fix and prevent. First, we defined an anti-pattern and identified the undesirable content in the KB. Knowledge engineers performed this first step. Second, once the problematic content was *detected*, we scheduled a revision to the KB to *fix* it. Domain experts performed the revisions. Third, after the revision was completed, the anti-pattern was added to the KB as an integrity constraint to *prevent* new inconsistencies at the time of the authoring. Knowledge engineers performed this final step. Not all anti-patterns need to be added to the KB as integrity constraints. Some patterns only indicate a potential problem that the encoder should review. We refer to such patterns as warning patterns. We now consider examples of anti-patterns in three categories: (a) dealing with changing guidelines (b) dealing with lazy inference; and (c) warning patterns.

2.2   Dealing with Changing Guidelines

Two commonly used relationships to capture the structure of entities are *has-part* and *has-region* [2,14,26]. Our starting guidelines on the use of these relations did not clearly address: Should an entity be allowed to be a direct part of more than one other entity? Can an entity be both a direct part and a direct region of another entity? Our initial ontology allowed users to create a representation in which an entity could be a direct part of more than one other entity, and an entity could be both a direct part and a region of another entity. This modeling approach caused confusion among the encoders. For example, should an organic skeleton be both a part and a region of an organic molecule? Based on extensive study of prior research [15,16], we now disallow such usage. A region is only defined in relation to other entities, and therefore, an entity cannot be both a part and a region of another entity [5]. We further require that an entity can be a direct part of only one other entity. We capture these two new guidelines using the following patterns:

$$\exists x, y, z.[has\text{-}part(y, x) \wedge has\text{-}part(z, x), y \neq z \Rightarrow \\ error(bad\text{-}has\text{-}part, x, y, z)] \tag{1}$$

$$\exists x, y.[has\text{-}part(x, y) \wedge has\text{-}region(x, y) \Rightarrow \\ error(bad\text{-}has\text{-}part\text{-}and\text{-}region, x, y)] \tag{2}$$

When we initially introduced tests based on these two patterns, several hundred assertions in the KB violated them. Automatically addressing some of the violations was possible. For example, if A has parts B and C, and C is already known to be a part of B, we can automatically remove the assertion that A has part C which can be inferred by the system. But, automatic determination was impossible in numerous cases, and the domain experts needed to manually repair these instances. After all such errors were repaired, we implemented these patterns as integrity constraints in the KB so that the encoders could no longer encode knowledge violating them.

2.3 Dealing with Lazy Inference

Inference using the representation in KB_Bio_101 is, in full generality, undecidable [8]. Lazy inference is a technique to bound computation time (i.e., the user is allowed to add assertions to the KB, but their complete consequences are not computed until certain inferences are requested). In the pattern shown in axiom 3, we check for violation of disjointness axioms. In axiom 4, we show a check that looks for violation of the *ir-reflexive* constraint on *has-part* relationship. Although these axioms are already incorporated in the inference engine, they are not fully enforced until needed. For example, while editing the KB, a domain expert cannot create a class that is a subclass of two disjoint classes, or make an assertion such that an entity is a part of itself. But, there are situations that that may lead to a conclusion that some instance belongs to two disjoint classes, or an entity is inferred to be a part of itself. Using anti-patterns gives us the best of both worlds: disjointness axioms are enforced in a lazy manner at the time of editing but in an eager manner during offline testing of the KB.

$$\exists x.[instance\text{-}of(x, \mathsf{C}) \wedge instance\text{-}of(x, \mathsf{D}) \wedge \\ disjoint(\mathsf{C}, \mathsf{D}) \Rightarrow \\ error(violated\text{-}disjointness, \mathsf{C}, \mathsf{D}, x)] \tag{3}$$

$$\exists x.[has\text{-}part(x, x) \Rightarrow \\ error(bad\text{-}reflexive\text{-}has\text{-}part, x)] \tag{4}$$

In the axioms above, C and D are classes, and the relation *disjoint*(A,B) has the standard meaning that the classes A and B have no instances in common [8].

2.4   Warning Patterns

Some axiom patterns in the KB could be indicative of a problem, but in other cases, could capture legitimate knowledge. For example, if a process has multiple steps, but none of those steps is defined to be its first step, it could indicate incompleteness in the representation. But, in some cases, such information may not be available, and it could be a legitimate representation. We can capture this by using the pattern shown in rule 5. Such patterns should not be added to the KB as hard integrity constraints.

$$\exists x, y.[subevent(x, y) \wedge \\ \not\exists z.[first\text{-}subevent(x, z)] \Rightarrow \\ warning(missing\text{-}first\text{-}subevent, x)] \tag{5}$$

The above pattern is implemented as a test during the editing process so that a domain expert is alerted whenever such a situation is encountered.

2.5   Discussion

New comers to our project, and especially our academic colleagues with no experience in engineering a large KB, frequently question why do we need anti-patterns at all. Why could we not simply represent them using integrity constraints to start with? An anti-pattern cannot be immediately represented as an integrity constraint because the KB is constantly evolving, and some anti-patterns are not known ahead of time. KB_Bio_101 evolved over a period of time, and we revised many modeling decisions as we went along. (The evolving decisions are documented in a knowledge engineering manual [4].) When a new modeling decision is instituted, a large number of axioms that contradict that decision may exist. Simply adding an integrity constraint to the KB reflecting the new modeling decision will invalidate those pre-existing axioms. Because an authoring tool should prevent a user from writing invalid axioms, the concepts that contain such axioms can no longer be edited and saved if the integrity constraints are present in the KB. The revisions to axioms are scheduled over a period of weeks to months. The insertion of the newly defined anti-pattern as an integrity constraint must wait until the axioms violating it have been updated and revised. Some inconsistencies and errors in the KB are detected only during the testing process. This can happen due to two reasons: (1) unexpected inference is not seen until the test is performed; and (2) due to lazy inference some inferences are delayed only until requested. The lazy inference is a standard editing model used by editors such as Protégé [21]. As the inconsistencies are only detected during the testing process, the appropriate constraints cannot be anticipated ahead of time. As we detect such inconsistencies, we first formalize them using anti-patterns so that they can be proactively monitored. Our current test suite contains a total of 20 such patterns.

Let us consider if we could have avoided these problems by better training? Our project has been an effort to industrialize knowledge construction. We used well-designed aptitude tests and training methods to recruit and train staff members. Through these processes, our encoding team became proficient in knowledge entry. Therefore, we do not believe more training would have made any difference. In fact, in controlled experiments conducted in prior work, we have shown that the domain experts entering knowledge using AURA are as effective as the knowledge engineers [17]. The issues we faced are inherent to a large scale knowledge engineering effort, and others undertaking similar endeavors will need to adopt methods such as anti-patterns.

A related question is how to determine good anti patterns? An anti pattern can either follow from ontology design or could be developed through empirical testing of the KB. An example of our approach for developing ontology design patterns can be found elsewhere [5]. Our ontology design is driven by a set of competency questions that dictate the distinctions that should be captured in the ontology. As noted earlier, some patterns are determined empirically as the KB is tested, and problematic inferences are identified. Each problematic inference can serve the basis for specifying an anti-pattern.

3   Underspecification in the KB

We begin this section by first defining what we mean by underspecification. We follow that by giving a pathological example where the automated method for dealing with underspecification that is currently supported in AURA breaks down. The novelty of our method and its relationship to other techniques has been previously published [9]. The discussion of pathological examples, and monitoring of inconsistencies caused by such cases extends the prior work which was purely theoretical [9].

3.1   Definition (Underspecification)

A large and complex KB that models some aspect of the real world can rarely be fully specified. Two examples of such underspecification are (1) some of the cardinality constraints are omitted and (2) some properties of all individual instances of a class are specialized across a class hierarchy, but specific references to which particular values are specialized are omitted. Let us consider the statement: "Every Car has an engine and a tank connected to the engine." We can represent this statement in first-order logic as follows.

$$\forall x.[instance\text{-}of(x, \mathsf{Car}) \Rightarrow$$
$$\exists e, t.[instance\text{-}of(e, \mathsf{Engine}) \land$$
$$instance\text{-}of(t, \mathsf{Tank}) \land has\text{-}engine(x, e) \land$$
$$has\text{-}tank(x, t) \land connected\text{-}to(e, t)]]$$
(6)

This axiom applies to all individual instances of the class Car and defines two slots *has-engine* and *has-tank*. The slot *has-engine* (resp. *has-tank*) associates an instance x of Car, with and instance of Engine (resp. Tank). The instance t of Tank has a further slot *connected-to* that has a value that is the same as e which is an instance of Engine and is the value of the *has-engine* slot.

While constructing a KB, specializing properties of classes along the class hierarchy is common. While doing so, one may need to refer to a value that was introduced in one of the super classes. For example, assume that we add the following axioms:

$$\forall x.[instance\text{-}of(x, \mathsf{Suburban}) \Rightarrow$$
$$instance\text{-}of(x, \mathsf{Car})]$$
(7)

$$\forall x.[instance\text{-}of(x, \mathsf{Suburban}) \Rightarrow$$
$$\exists e.[instance\text{-}of(e, \mathsf{Engine}) \wedge \tag{8}$$
$$has\text{-}engine(x, e) \wedge size(e, Large)]]$$

These axioms state that Suburban is a subclass of Car, and every Suburban has a large engine. Axioms (6)-(8) are an example of an underspecified KB in the sense that they omit the relationship between an Engine introduced in axiom (6) and the Engine introduced in axiom (8). In one possible interpretation, the engines mentioned in axioms (6) and (8) refer to the same individual and in another interpretation they refer to different individuals. A system can handle such underspecification in the following ways:

1. While writing (8), provide a mechanism that a user can use to explicitly state that the engine in axiom (8) is a specialization of the engine introduced in (6). We refer to this approach as *explicit coreference*. For example, formulas (6) and (8) should be given as:

$$\forall x.[instance\text{-}of(x, \mathsf{Car}) \Rightarrow$$
$$[instance\text{-}of(f_1(x), \mathsf{Engine}) \wedge$$
$$instance\text{-}of(f_2(x), \mathsf{Tank}) \wedge$$
$$has\text{-}engine(x, f_1(x)) \wedge \tag{9}$$
$$has\text{-}tank(x, f_2(x)) \wedge$$
$$connected\text{-}to(f_1(x), f_2(x))]]$$

$$\forall x.[instance\text{-}of(x, \mathsf{Suburban}) \Rightarrow \tag{10}$$
$$size(f_1(x), Large)]$$

2. Add a cardinality constraint to the KB saying that cars have exactly one engine. We refer to this approach as the *cardinality constraint*.
3. Support a default reasoning mechanism that can draw intuitive conclusions with axioms 6- 8. We refer to this approach as the *underspecified KB*.

The explicit co-reference approach has the advantage that it leaves no ambiguity, but it has a major disadvantage: it breaks the modularity of axioms in that while writing one axiom, we must refer to other axioms. While creating the class Suburban, we must refer to its super class Car, and explicitly say which specific engine value we are specializing. If after creating Car and Suburban, we introduce a super class Vehicle and we want this class to also have a value for *has-engine*, we must refer to its subclasses and make sure all of them now specialize the Engine value introduced in Vehicle. In the case of multiple inheritance, for example, if a Car were to be a subclass of Vehicle and Gas-driven objects each of which provides an Engine, the KB author must resolve how the multiple inheritance must be handled while defining Car. The approach breaks down completely when we need to answer a novel question about an object that must be an instance of multiple classes, and no pre-existing class exists that specifies how values from those multiple parents must be combined. The disadvantage of the explicit co-reference approach is especially a limiting factor when the KB is to be authored by a domain expert who is not well-versed in logical knowledge representation, and when the knowledge base must evolve over a period of time.

In the cardinality constraint approach we can deductively conclude that axioms (6) and (8) must refer to the same Engine value. This approach can work for many situations, but in some cases, using such constraints is incorrect. For example, race cars may have more than one engine, and adding a constraint that every car has exactly one engine is too strong.

In an underspecified KB approach, we assume that the inherited and locally defined engines must be the same unless there is a reason to believe otherwise. Thus, the class definitions for Car, Suburban, Vehicle, and Gas-driven objects could be written without making any reference to each other. For example, axiom 10 will be written as follows:

$$\forall x.[instance\text{-}of(x, \text{Suburban}) \Rightarrow \\ size(f_3(x), Large)] \tag{11}$$

The task of the default reasoning system is to conclude that $f_1(x) = f_3(x)$ unless conflicting knowledge exists in the KB. Such inferences can be made at the time of question answering. If the KB contained knowledge to the contrary, for example, for a RaceCar, we introduce a new engine such as TurboDieselEngine, and we had a statement in the KB saying that the class TurboEngine is disjoint from GasEngine, then the system will assume that an inherited Gas-driven engine could not be the same as a TurboEngine. By supporting such reasoning with an underspecified KB, we retain the modularity of class definitions. The users can write their KB in a modular fashion, and be confident that any obvious missing details will be filled in by the reasoning mechanism at the time of answering questions. AURA implements heuristic unification to do such default reasoning with an underspecified KB [9]. A formalization of this reasoning was previously published. Practical experience in using this facility that is described next is novel.

3.2   A Pathological Example of Underspecification

Reasoning to determine which inherited value is being specialized works effectively as long as each slot has only one value of a particular type, or if multiple values of the same type exist, but that they can be distinguished based on their slot values. Such reasoning breaks down whenever slot values exist that are indeed different but cannot be distinguished. We illustrate this with an example.

We have three classes: Amino-Acid, Polar-Molecule and Polar-Amino-Acid. The Polar-Amino-Acid is a subclass of both Amino-Acid and Polar-Molecule, thus, introducing multiple inheritance in the class hierarchy. Next, we will introduce the axioms for these concepts. We have purposefully omitted complete definitions for these concepts to focus only on those aspects that led to problematic inferences.

$$\forall x.[instance\text{-}of(x, \text{Polar-Molecule}) \Rightarrow \\ \exists a1, a2, p.[instance\text{-}of(p, \text{Polar-Covalent-Bond}) \land \\ instance\text{-}of(a1, \text{Atom}) \land \\ instance\text{-}of(a2, \text{Atom}) \land \\ possesses(x, p) \land \\ has\text{-}part(x, a1) \land has\text{-}part(x, a2) \\ is\text{-}between(p, a1, a2)]] \tag{12}$$

$$\forall x.[instance\text{-}of(x, \text{Amino-Acid}) \Rightarrow$$
$$\exists h, n, c, o, b1, b2.[instance\text{-}of(b1, \text{Single-Bond}) \wedge$$
$$instance\text{-}of(b2, \text{Double-Bond}) \wedge$$
$$instance\text{-}of(h, \text{Hydrogen}) \wedge$$
$$instance\text{-}of(n, \text{Nitrogen}) \wedge$$
$$instance\text{-}of(c, \text{Carbon}) \wedge \tag{13}$$
$$instance\text{-}of(o, \text{Oxygen}) \wedge$$
$$possesses(x, b1) \wedge possesses(x, b2) \wedge$$
$$has\text{-}part(x, h) \wedge has\text{-}part(x, n)$$
$$has\text{-}part(x, o) \wedge has\text{-}part(x, c)$$
$$is\text{-}between(b1, h, n) \wedge is\text{-}between(b2, c, o)]]$$

Axiom 12 states that a Polar-Molecule has two atoms as its parts, possesses a Polar-Covalent-Bond that is between those two atoms. Axiom 13 states that an Amino-Acid has parts Hydrogen, Oxygen, Nitrogen and Carbon, and that it possesses a Single-Bond between the Hydrogen and the Nitrogen, and a Double-Bond between a Carbon and Oxygen. Because a Polar-Amino-Acid is a subclass of both Polar-Molecule and Amino-Acid, it will inherit two atoms from Polar-Molecule and four atoms (a Carbon, a Hydrogen, a Oxygen and a Nitrogen) from Amino-Acid. Further, it will inherit a Polar-Covalent-Bond from Polar-Molecule and a Single-Bond and a Double-Bond from the Amino-Acid. Because Polar-Covalent-Bond, Single-Bond, and Double-Bond are all sibling classes in the class hierarchy, they could not all be referring to the same bond is apparent and therefore, they will be inherited as separate individuals. But, because Carbon, Hydrogen, Oxygen and Nitrogen are all subclasses of Atom, the two atoms inherited from the Polar-Molecule could possibly be referring to two of the four atoms being inherited from Amino-Acid. In the current system, two of the atoms inherited from Polar-Molecule would get equated with two of the atoms from Polar-Amino-Acid giving an incorrect behavior. The domain experts observed this behavior, as they were not able to override the automatic conclusions derived by the system. In many other examples, such ambiguous multiple inheritance leads to violations of integrity constraints in the system which are reported as errors by the inference engine.

One can add additional rules for such inferences to work correctly. For example, in this case one could add a default rule that prevents atoms from participating in two different bonds, but that will conflict with the Chemistry knowledge. Getting such default rules to work well across variety of situations is extremely difficult in practice.

3.3 Monitoring Errors due to Underspecification

We monitored the errors due to underspecification using two methods. First, each concept was visually inspected to check for quality, and any erroneous inferences made by the system were spotted by the domain experts. The example we considered above illustrates such a situation. Second, we created a systematic test as follows. We created a sample instance of each concept and queried all of its relations. In this process, the system must inherit information, and any errors detected during this process are reported by the reasoner.

4   Experimental Results

We begin by describing our approach for implementing the KB tests. To implement the tests for anti-patterns, we created an augmented KB, called KB_A which contained an instance of each concept in the KB. For each instance in the KB_A, we queried all of its relations so that all the rules applicable to that instance were exercised at least once. This process created many more individuals, which were added to KB_A. For example, for the concept Polar-Molecule and axiom 12, the KB_A would contain an individual x that is an instance of Polar-Molecule, and individuals p, $a1$ and $a2$ that are respectively instances of classes Polar-Covalent-Bond, Atom and Atom. Further, KB_A would contain the assertions

$$possesses(x, p) \land is\text{-}between(p, a1, a2) \land$$
$$has\text{-}part(x, a1) \land has\text{-}part(x, a2) \tag{14}$$

We formulated each anti-pattern test as a conjunctive query. For example, the test shown in axiom 1 could be formulated as the following query: $y \neq z \land has\text{-}part(y, x) \land has\text{-}part(z, x)$. All bindings to x would then help identify the assertions in the KB that violate this ontology pattern.

AURA's implementation for dealing with inconsistencies is based on the intuition that any time an inconsistency is discovered during the reasoning process, the assertions involved in the inconsistency can no longer be used for any further inference. This approach is very close to what has been proposed by others [18].

For the rest of the section, we present data that shows the evolution of the KB as errors were detected and resolved during a period of February 2012 through April 2013. During this period, the knowledge entry team worked on chapters 2-12, 36 and 41 from the textbook [23].

As we can see in Figure 1, when the test based on the anti-patterns for multiple incoming *has-part* relationship was initially implemented, more than 400 assertions violated this test. The number of such assertions grew for a few months. With improved training of the encoding team, and the resolution of errors, these errors started reducing to zero. After the KB was free from such errors, we instituted an integrity constraint to enforce this error so that this error did not occur again. We continue to monitor the KB for such errors even after the integrity constraints had been instituted.

In Figure 2, we show the trend of the inconsistency errors in the KB. These are the inconsistencies reported by the systematic tests for under-specification. The fluctuation in the number of errors also corresponds to the amount of knowledge being entered. The knowledge entry ramped up during 2012. No new substantial knowledge entry occurred during January 2013 through April 2013, allowing the team to eliminate most of the errors from the KB. Each of the spikes corresponds to some major event in the encoding process (for example, a change in upper ontology, the addition of a new constraint that invalidates some KB knowledge, etc.).

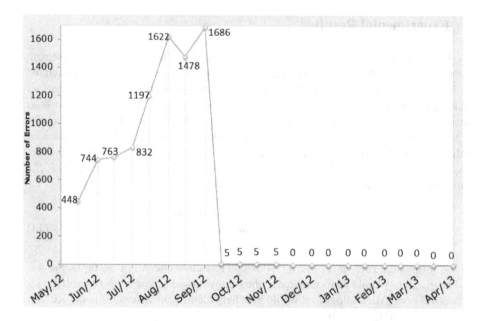

Fig. 1. Violations of multiple incoming *has-part* pattern

5 Lessons Learned

Three general lessons can be drawn from the experience of the monitoring and continuous improvement of KB_Bio_101: (1) a need for managing the separation between authoring and reasoning; (2) a need for user control over under-specified reasoning; and (3) a need to derive useful conclusions in face of inconsistency.

The activity of authoring a KB can be compared to the authoring of a computer program. For a computer program, when using editors such as Emacs or vi, a clear separation exists between a program and the results of its execution. After a program is authored, it can be compiled, the errors detected, and the source code updated to fix the errors. Further debugging requires executing the program and checking for run time errors. Similar steps exist for knowledge authoring, where the axioms are first authored and then the errors checked at the execution time when questions are answered. But, for knowledge authoring, having a program compilation stage is uncommon. In AURA, as well as in other common KB editors such as Protégé [21], correct syntax is ensured by performing minimal reasoning when the axioms are authored. Our experience suggests an intermediate step between authoring and run time execution. Such a step should contain both consistency tests and tests based on ontology patterns. We found such tests to be cheaper to execute than checking for similar problems through run time testing of the overall system.

Because domain experts with little training in knowledge representation could create KB_Bio_101, which is of non-trivial size and complexity, we can conclude that an authoring environment based on underspecification was extremely effective in practice.

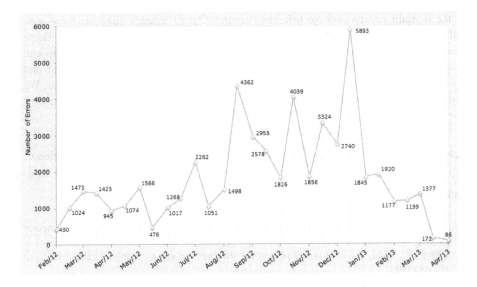

Fig. 2. Trend of inconsistency errors in the KB

For those situations, where the underspecification in the representation is too ambiguous for the system to resolve automatically, a lack of user control became problematic. This result is indicated by a pathological example that we discussed, and by the numerous inconsistencies that we had to address. Tools are needed to warn users about such ambiguous cases of underspecification, so that the users could guide the system in resolving them. A question for future research is to determine whether such a facility could be built that is usable by domain experts.

An evolving KB is almost never error free. A reasoner should be able to produce useful results in the face of inconsistencies. Several techniques have been researched to achieve this objective [1,19], however, they are not yet common place in leading reasoners [25,13]. With AURA's reasoning model, we can perform functional system testing by posing questions in parallel to addressing inconsistencies.

6   Summary and Conclusions

KB_Bio_101 is the first effort to put high levels of expressiveness in the hands of domain experts who have limited training in knowledge representation and reasoning. Due to domain complexity, KB evolution over time, and the likelihood of domain-inherent actual inconsistency and underspecification, enabling KB development in the presence of inconsistencies and underspecification is crucial. The KB developers should continuously monitor and correct the inconsistencies.

We described the evolution of KB_Bio_101 over a period of one year as we monitored it for inconsistencies and underspecification, and continuously improved it. Our monitoring approach utilized a suite of anti-patterns, and the inconsistencies reported by the domain experts and the inference engine. Our experience suggests three general principles / features for the design of future knowledge-authoring systems. These principles are: (1) an intermediate phase between knowledge authoring and end-to-end system testing that can help detect errors, (2) user control over under-specification, and (3) support for deriving useful conclusions with an inconsistent knowledge base. We hope that this experience report will help guide the construction of next generation of knowledge systems.

Acknowledgments. This work has been funded by Vulcan Inc. and SRI International.

References

1. Blair, H.A., Subrahmanian, V.: Paraconsistent logic programming. Theoretical Computer Science 68(2), 135–154 (1989)
2. Casati, R., Varzi, A.C.: Parts and places: the structures of spatial representations. Bradford Books (1999)
3. Chaudhri, V.K., Cheng, B., Overholtzer, A., Roschelle, J., Spaulding, A., Clark, P., Greaves, M., Gunning, D.: Inquire Biology: A textbook that answers questions. AI Magazine 34(3) (September 2013)
4. Chaudhri, V.K., Dinesh, N.: AURA knowledge engineering manual. Technical report, SRI International (2013)
5. Chaudhri, V.K., Dinesh, N., Heller, C.: Conceptual models of structure and function. In: Second Annual Conference on Advances in Cognitive Systems (2013)
6. Chaudhri, V.K., Dinesh, N., Inclezan, D.: Three lessons in creating a knowledge base to enable explanation, reasoning and dialog. In: Second Annual Conference on Cognitive Systems (December 2013)
7. Chaudhri, V.K., Heymans, S., Wessel, M., Tran, S.C.: Large object oriented knowledge bases: A challenge for reasoning engines. In: Newsletter of Association of Logic Programming (October 2013)
8. Chaudhri, V.K., Heymans, S., Wessel, M., Tran, S.C.: Object-oriented knowledge bases in logic programming. In: Technical Communication of International Conference in Logic Programming (2013)
9. Chaudhri, V.K., Tran, S.C.: Specifying and reasoning with under-specified knowledge bases. In: International Conference on Knowledge Representation and Reasoning (2012)
10. Chaudhri, V.K., Wessel, M.A., Heymans, S.: KB_Bio_101: A challenge for OWL reasoners. In: The OWL Reasoner Evaluation Workshop (2013)
11. Corcho, O., Roussey, C., Vilches-Blázquez, L., Dominguez, I.P.: Pattern-based OWL ontology debugging guidelines. In: CEUR Workshop Proceedings (2009)
12. Friedland, N., Allen, P., Mathews, G., Whitbrock, M., Baxter, D., Curtis, J., Shepard, B., Miraglia, P., Angele, J., Staab, S., Moench, E., Opperman, H., Wenke, D., Israel, D., Chaudhri, V., Porter, B., Barker, K., Fan, J., Chaw, S.Y., Yeh, P., Tecuci, D., Clark, P.: Project Halo: Towards a digital Aristotle. AI Magazine (2004)
13. Gebser, M., Kaufmann, B., Neumann, A., Schaub, T.: Conflict-driven answer set solving. IJCAI, 386–392 (2007)
14. Guizzardi, G.: Ontological foundations for structural conceptual models. CTIT, Centre for Telematics and Information Technology (2005)
15. Guizzardi, G.: On the representation of quantities and their parts in conceptual modeling. In: FOIS, pp. 103–116 (2010)

16. Guizzardi, G.: Ontological foundations for conceptual part-whole relations: the case of collectives and their parts. In: Advanced Information Systems Engineering, pp. 138–153. Springer (2011)
17. Gunning, D., Chaudhri, V.K., Clark, P., Barker, K., Chaw, S.-Y., Greaves, M., Grosof, B., Leung, A., McDonald, D., Mishra, S., Pacheco, J., Porter, B., Spaulding, A., Tecuci, D., Tien, J.: Project Halo update: Progress toward digital Aristotle. In: AI Magazine (Fall 2010)
18. Kassoff, M., Genesereth, M.R.: Paraconsistent inference from data using existential Ω-entailment. International Journal of Semantic Computing 5(03), 257–269 (2011)
19. Maier, F., Ma, Y., Hitzler, P.: Paraconsistent OWL and related logics. Semantic Web (2012)
20. McGuinness, D.L., Fikes, R., Rice, J., Wilder, S.: The Chimaera ontology environment. In: AAAI/IAAI 2000, pp. 1123–1124 (2000)
21. Noy, N.F., Sintek, M., Decker, S., Crubézy, M., Fergerson, R.W., Musen, M.A.: Creating semantic web contents with Protege-2000. IEEE Intelligent Systems 16(2), 60–71 (2001)
22. Parsia, B., Sirin, E., Kalyanpur, A.: Debugging OWL ontologies. In: Proceedings of the 14th International Conference on World Wide Web, pp. 633–640. ACM (2005)
23. Reece, J.B., Urry, L.A., Cain, M.L., Wasserman, S.A., Minorsky, P.V., Jackson, R.B.: Campbell Biology. Benjamin Cummings imprint of Pearson, Boston (2011)
24. Schlobach, S., Cornet, R.: Non-standard reasoning services for the debugging of description logic terminologies. In: IJCAI, vol. 3, pp. 355–362 (2003)
25. Shearer, R., Motik, B., Horrocks, I.: Hermit: A highly-efficient OWL reasoner. In: OWLED, vol. 432 (2008)
26. Spear, A.D.: Ontology for the twenty first century: An introduction with recommendations. Institute for Formal Ontology and Medical Information Science: Saarbrucken, Germany (2006)
27. Suwa, M., Scott, A.C., Shortliffe, E.H.: An approach to verifying completeness and consistency in a rule-based expert system. AI Magazine 3(4), 16 (1982)
28. Wang, H., Horridge, M., Rector, A.L., Drummond, N., Seidenberg, J.: Debugging OWL-DL ontologies: A heuristic approach. In: Gil, Y., Motta, E., Benjamins, V.R., Musen, M.A. (eds.) ISWC 2005. LNCS, vol. 3729, pp. 745–757. Springer, Heidelberg (2005)

Pay-As-You-Go Multi-user Feedback Model for Ontology Matching

Isabel F. Cruz[1], Francesco Loprete[2], Matteo Palmonari[2],
Cosmin Stroe[1], and Aynaz Taheri[1]

[1] University of Illinois at Chicago
{ifc,cstroe1,ataher2}@cs.uic.edu
[2] Università di Milano-Bicocca
f.loprete@campus.unimib.it, matteo.palmonari@disco.unimib.it

Abstract. Using our multi-user model, a community of users provides
feedback in a pay-as-you-go fashion to the ontology matching process by
validating the mappings found by automatic methods, with the following
advantages over having a single user: the effort required from each user is
reduced, user errors are corrected, and consensus is reached. We propose
strategies that dynamically determine the order in which the candidate
mappings are presented to the users for validation. These strategies are
based on mapping quality measures that we define. Further, we use a
propagation method to leverage the validation of one mapping to other
mappings. We use an extension of the AgreementMaker ontology matching system and the Ontology Alignment Evaluation Initiative (OAEI)
Benchmarks track to evaluate our approach. Our results show how F-
measure and robustness vary as a function of the number of user validations. We consider different user error and revalidation rates (the latter
measures the number of times that the same mapping is validated). Our
results highlight complex trade-offs and point to the benefits of dynamically adjusting the revalidation rate.

1 Introduction

The ontology matching problem consists of mapping concepts in a *source* ontology to semantically related concepts in a *target* ontology. The resulting set
of mappings is called an *alignment* [1], which is a subset of the set of all possible mappings, which we call the *mapping space*. As ontologies increase in size,
automatic matching methods, which we call *matchers*, become necessary. The
matching process also requires feedback provided by users: in real-world scenarios, and even in the systematic ontology matching benchmarks of the Ontology
Alignment Evaluation Initiative (OAEI), alignments are neither correct nor exhaustive when compared against a *gold standard*, also called *reference alignment*.
An important consideration is that domain experts such as those with whom we
collaborated in the geospatial domain [2], require the ability to verify the correctness of a subset of the mappings. In this paper we propose a semi-automatic
ontology matching strategy that supports feedback provided by multiple domain

K. Janowicz et al. (Eds.): EKAW 2014, LNAI 8876, pp. 80–96, 2014.
© Springer International Publishing Switzerland 2014

experts to match two ontologies. Our strategy first computes an alignment using automatic matching methods and then allows for the domain experts to request a mapping to validate. In the rest of the paper, the term *users* refers to the domain experts, not to casual users often called *workers* in crowdsourcing terminology. The fact that our users are domain experts will influence some of our assumptions.

Our approach works in the following way: once a user posts a request, one of the candidate mappings is *selected* and presented to the user who can label the mapping as correct or incorrect. Our strategy assumes that mappings labeled as correct (resp. incorrect) by a majority of users are correct (resp. incorrect), thus allowing for mislabeling by users. The result of this validation can be *propagated* to "similar" mappings thus saving users' effort while ensuring, if such propagation is effectively performed, the quality of the resulting alignment. The matching process continues iteratively by selecting new candidate mappings and presenting them to users for validation. Our method is designed in such a way that at each iteration the mapping that is perceived to be of less quality is the one selected for validation. Therefore, our quality ranking functions are intrinsically dynamic as the quality-based ranking of the mappings changes from iteration to iteration, to take into account each user-provided validation. This approach, which not only allows for the system to quickly adjust, is also devised to run in a pay-as-you-go fashion, where we may stop the iterative process at any stage. Our pay-as-you-go strategy is in opposition to first collecting a predetermined number of validations n for each mapping, considering the majority vote after that, and only then propagating the user-provided feedback. During those n iterations, we would only be progressing on a single mapping. Following our approach, during n iterations we will be making progress on as many as n mappings and propagating the user-provided feedback at each iteration.

Previous approaches to ontology matching assume that feedback is given by individual users or that users always validate a mapping correctly [3,4,5]. However, errors must be taken into account in feedback mechanisms for information integration systems [6]. Therefore, we want to show that a high-quality alignment can be attained by involving multiple users so as to reduce the effort required by each individual user while allowing for user error. To this end, we need to ensure coverage of the mapping space, while not demanding that each user validate all the mappings. Because of user errors, some mappings may need to be validated several times.

We consider two important rates: one measures the errors made by the users, which we call the *error rate*, and the other measures the proportion of mappings presented to the users for validation that have been already validated in previous iterations, which we call the *revalidation rate*. We conduct experiments with the OAEI Benchmarks track to evaluate the gain in quality (measured in terms of F-measure) and the robustness (defined as the ratio between the quality of the alignment for a given error rate and the quality of the alignment when no errors are made) as a function of the number of validations for different error and revalidation rates. Our results highlight complex trade-offs and point to the benefits of adjusting the revalidation rate.

In Section 2, we describe the architecture of the multi-user feedback ontology matching system and give an overview of the combined automatic and manual process. In Section 3, we describe the key elements of the proposed approach: a model for the evaluation of the quality of the mappings, the ranking functions used for candidate mapping selection, and the method used for feedback propagation. In Section 4, we present the results of our experiments conducted on the OAEI Benchmarks track. In Section 5, we describe related work. Finally, in Section 6, we draw some conclusions and describe future work.

2   Assumptions and Approach Overview

We assume that as members of a community, domain users are committed to an ontology matching task and are reliable. Therefore we do not deal with problems such as the engagement of users or the assessment of their reliability, which have been investigated in crowdsourcing approaches [7]. Even if we consider possible errors in validating mappings, thus causing inconsistency among users, we assume consistency for the same user, thus we do not present the same mapping more than once to the same user. We also do not distinguish among users although some users may make fewer errors than others. Instead we consider an overall error rate associated with a sequence of validated mappings. We assume that given a group of users whose reliability is known (or can be estimated), we can determine the corresponding error rate.

The validation of a mapping m by a user assigns a label l to that mapping. We define the homonymous function *label*, such that *label(m)* has value 1 or 0 depending on whether the user considers that m is or is not part of the alignment, respectively. When more than one user is involved, we use a consensus-based approach to decide whether a mapping belongs to an alignment. Consensus models include a simple majority vote, a sophisticated weighted majority vote, or more complex models such as tournament selection [8]. In this paper, we consider a simple majority vote, where *Val* is an odd number of validations considered sufficient to decide by majority (we do not require that all the users vote on each mapping); thus, *minimum consensus*, $MinCon = \lfloor (Val/2) + 1 \rfloor$, is the minimum number of similar labels that is needed to make a correct decision on a mapping.

We restrict our focus to equivalence mappings. Differently from other interactive techniques for ontology matching [9], our approach is independent from the cardinality of the alignment, because the desired cardinality can be set at the end of feedback loop.

The architecture of our multi-user ontology matching strategy can be built around any ontology matching system. In our case we use AgreementMaker [10,11]. We list the steps of the feedback loop workflow:

Step 1: Initial Matching. During the first iteration, before feedback is provided, all data structures are created. A set of k matchers is run, each one creating a *local similarity matrix* where the value of each element (i, j) is the similarity score associated with mapping $m_{i,j}$ of element i of the source ontology to element j of the target ontology. For each mapping we can then define a *signature vector* with the k similarity scores computed for that mapping by the k individual matchers [5]. The results of the individual matchers are combined into a *global similarity matrix* where the value of each element represents the similarity between two concepts, which is computed by aggregating the scores of individual matchers into a final score [10]. An optimization algorithm is run to select the final alignment so as to maximize the overall similarity [11] and satisfy the mapping cardinality.

Step 2: Validation Request. A user asks for a mapping to validate, triggering the feedback loop.

Step 3: Candidate Selection. For each user who requests a mapping to validate, a mapping is chosen using two different candidate selection strategies combined by one meta-strategy (explained in detail in Section 3.2). Each strategy uses quality criteria to rank the mappings. The highest ranked mappings are those mappings that are estimated to have lowest quality, the expectation being that they are the more likely to be incorrect. The mapping quality is assessed at each iteration. When a user requests a mapping for validation, the meta-strategy selects one candidate selection strategy and presents the highest-ranked mapping to the user. Our approach is inspired by active learning methods and aims to present to the users those mappings that are most informative for the ontology matching problem. Mappings that are wrongly classified by the system at a current iteration are considered to be informative, because the result can be improved as long as the error is corrected [4,5].

Step 4: User Validation. The selected mapping is validated by the user. The user can label a mapping as being correct or incorrect but can also skip that particular mapping when unsure of the label to assign to the mapping.

Step 5: Feedback Aggregation. A *feedback aggregation matrix* keeps track of the feedback collected for each mapping and of the users who provided that feedback. The data in this matrix are used to compute mapping quality measures in the candidate selection and feedback propagation steps.

Step 6: Feedback Propagation. This method updates the *global similarity matrix* by changing the similarity score for the validated mapping and for the mappings whose signature vector is close to the signature vector of the mapping that was just validated, according to a distance measure.

Step 7: Alignment Selection. An optimization algorithm [11] used in **Step 1**, is run on the updated *similarity matrix* as input, and a refined alignment is selected. At the end of this step, we loop through the same steps, starting from **Step 2**.

3   Quality-Based Multi-User Feedback

In this section we describe the Candidate Selection and Feedback Propagation steps, which play a major role in our model. First, we explain the Mapping Quality Model, which is used by both steps.

3.1   Mapping Quality Model

We use a mapping quality model to estimate the quality of the candidate mapping, which uses five different mapping quality measures:

Automatic Matcher Agreement (AMA). This measure ranks mappings in increasing order of quality. It measures the agreement of the similarity scores assigned to a mapping by different automatic matchers and is defined as $AMA(m) = 1 - DIS(m)$, where $DIS(m)$ is the *Disagreement* associated with mapping m. It is defined as the variance of the similarity scores in the signature vector and is normalized to the range $[0.0, 1.0]$ [5].

Cross Sum Quality (CSQ). This measure ranks mappings in increasing order of quality. Given a source ontology with n concepts, a target ontology with p concepts, and a matrix Σ of the similarity scores between the two ontologies, for each mapping $m_{i,j}$ the *cross sum quality* (1) sums all the similarity scores σ_{ij} in the same ith row and jth column of Σ. The sum is normalized by the maximum sum of the scores per column and row in the whole matrix.

$$CSQ(m_{ij}) = 1 - \frac{\sum_{v=1}^{p} \sigma_{iv} + \sum_{k=1}^{n} \sigma_{kj}}{MaxRowSum(\Sigma) + MaxColumnSum(\Sigma)} \tag{1}$$

This measure assigns a higher quality score to a mapping that does not conflict with other mappings, a conflict occurring when there exists another mapping for the same source or target concept. This measure takes into account the similarity score of the mappings, assigning a lower quality to mappings that conflict with mappings of higher similarity.

Table 1. An example of a similarity matrix. Empty cells have value 0.

i \ j	0	1	2	3	4	5
0	0.45					0.70
1					0.30	
2			0.60			
3		0.50			0.90	
4				0.80		
5	0.40		0.10			0.90

Table 2. Examples for the *Consensus (CON)* and *Propagation Impact (PI)* quality measures with $MinCon = 3$

Mapping	$Corr(m_i)$	$Inc(m_i)$	$CON(m_i)$	$PI(m_i)$
m_1	1	1	0.00	1.00
m_2	1	0	0.33	0.66
m_3	2	1	0.33	0.5

For the matrix of Table 1, the values of $CSQ(m_{3,4})$ and $CSQ(m_{2,2})$ are:

$$CSQ(m_{3,4}) = 1 - \frac{1.2 + 1.4}{1.4 + 1.6} = 0.13 \qquad CSQ(m_{2,2}) = 1 - \frac{0.6 + 0.7}{1.4 + 1.6} = 0.57$$

Mapping $m_{2,2}$ has higher quality than $m_{3,4}$ because $m_{2,2}$ has only one conflict with $m_{5,2}$ while $m_{3,4}$ has two conflicts, $m_{1,4}$ and $m_{3,1}$. Also, the conflicting mapping $m_{5,2}$ has lower similarity than the conflicting mappings $m_{1,4}$ and $m_{3,1}$, further contributing to the difference in quality between $m_{3,4}$ and $m_{2,2}$.

Similarity Score Definiteness (SSD). This measure ranks mappings in increasing order of quality. It evaluates how close the similarity σ_m associated with a mapping m is to the similarity scores' upper and lower bounds (respectively 1.0 and 0.0) using the following formula:

$$SSD(m) = |\sigma_m - 0.5| * 2$$

SSD will assign higher quality to the mappings considered more definite in their similarity score. The least definite similarity score is 0.5.

Consensus (CON). This measure ranks mappings in increasing order of quality. In the multi-user ontology matching scenario, a candidate mapping may be labeled as correct by some users and as incorrect by others. In our approach we assume that the majority of users are able to make the correct decision. The *consensus (CON)* quality measure uses the concept of minimum consensus $MinCon$, as defined in Section 2 to capture the user consensus gathered on a mapping at a given iteration. Given a mapping m, $CON(m)$ is maximum when the mapping is labeled at least $MinCon$ times as correct, denoted by $Corr(m)$, or as incorrect, denoted by $Inc(m)$:

$$CON(m) = \begin{cases} 1 & \text{if } Corr(m) \geq MinCon \text{ or } Inc(m) \geq MinCon \\ \frac{|Corr(m) - Inc(m)|}{MinCon} & \text{otherwise} \end{cases}$$

Three examples of CON quality evaluation are shown in Table 2. According to the consensus gathered among the users, the quality of mappings m_2 and m_3 is higher than the quality of mapping m_1.

Propagation Impact (PI). This measure ranks mappings in decreasing order of quality. Given the current set of user validations received by the system at some iteration, PI estimates the impact of future user validations on the similarity evaluation in the feedback propagation step of the loop. Using the concept of *minimum consensus ($MinCon$)*, PI tries to identify the mappings for which a new validation will bring more information into the system. Intuitively, the mappings that will introduce more information when validated are the ones that have the same number of correct and incorrect validations. Because of the "tie" in user validations, we have the least information about these mappings, thus by breaking that tie the system makes a decision. Defining $\Delta Corr(m) = MinCon - Corr(m)$ and $\Delta Inc(m) = MinCon - Inc(m)$, then:

$$PI(m) = \begin{cases} 0 & \text{if } Corr(m) = MinCon \text{ or } Inc(m) = MinCon \\ \frac{min(\Delta Corr(m), \Delta Inc(m))}{max(\Delta Corr(m), \Delta Inc(m))} & \text{otherwise} \end{cases}$$

Considering the examples in Table 2, mapping m_3 has the lowest PI score (highest quality) because the number of times it was labeled as correct is close to $MinCon$. Mapping m_1 has the highest PI score (lowest quality) because we are in a tie situation and new feedback on that mapping is required. Mapping m_2 has medium PI because one validation has been propagated but because it is potentially incorrect, another validation is needed to improve the confidence of the system about this mapping.

As can be seen from the example in Table 2, the intuition captured by PI is slightly different from the one captured by CON. While $CON(m_2) = CON(m_3) = 1/3$, m_2 and m_3 have different PI scores.

3.2   Quality-Based Candidate Selection

Every measure in our mapping quality model returns a quality score in the range $[0.0, 1.0]$. In AMA, CSQ, SSD, and CON, a higher score represents a higher mapping quality. Because we want to select the lowest quality, we subtract each of these quality measures from 1. This quantity is represented using a $^-$ superscript. We combine these quantities using well-known aggregation functions, e.g., maximum or average, to define different candidate selection strategies. We further combine individual candidate selection strategies into a *candidate selection meta-strategy*, which combines two candidate selection strategies: *Disagreement and Indefiniteness Average (DIA)*, which is used to select unlabeled mappings (mappings that have not been validated by any user in previous iterations) and *Revalidation (REV)*, which is used to select already labeled mappings (mappings that have been validated in previous iterations). Both strategies use quality measures that change over time and rank mappings at each iteration.

The DIA strategy uses the function $DIA(m) = AVG(DIS(m), SSD^-(m))$. It favors mappings that are at the same time the most disagreed upon by the automatic matchers and have the most indefinite similarity values. The two measures CON and PI cannot be used in this strategy because they consider previous validations. After an experimental evaluation of different combinations of the other quality measures, we found that the combination of DIS and SSD (without CSQ) is the best combination of measures to find those mappings that were misclassified by the automatic matchers. The limited effectiveness of CSQ for ranking labeled mappings can be explained by the limited number of mappings that are misclassified due to conflicts with other mappings. Our mapping selection algorithm uses the similarity values generated by automatic matchers to solve many of these potential conflicts in a correct way [11].

The second strategy, *Revalidation (REV)*, ranks mappings using the function:

$$REV(m) = AVG(CSQ^-(m), CON^-(m), PI(m))$$

This strategy favors mappings with lower consensus and that could have changed significantly, and harmfully, the quality of the current alignment. The analysis of the users' activity, which is explicitly captured by CON and PI, is crucial to this strategy. In addition, since several mappings might have similar CON and PI in the first iterations, REV favors also mappings with potential conflicts with other mappings leveraging the CSQ measure. In this strategy, CSQ is preferred to DIS and DSS because: i) to rank already labeled mappings, disagreement among users, measured with CON and PI, is more informative than disagreement among automatic matchers, measured by DIS, ii) labeled mappings will

have very definite similarity scores, and, therefore, very similar DSS scores, and
iii) more potential conflicts can emerge as more feedback is collected.

This meta-strategy uses two probabilities, p_{DIA} and p_{REV}, such that $p_{DIA} + p_{REV} = 1$, which are associated respectively to the DIA and REV strategies. The
parameter p_{REV} is called *revalidation rate* and is used to specify the proportion of
mappings presented to the users for validation that have been already validated
in previous iterations. We consider a constant revalidation rate, because we do
not have empirical data that shows whether the users make more (or fewer)
errors as the matching process unfolds. If such evidence is found, the revalidation
rate can be changed accordingly. The meta-strategy verifies also that the same
mapping (chosen from the REV list) is not presented for validation to the same
user more than once.

3.3   Quality-Based Feedback Propagation

When the selected mapping is validated by a user, the feedback is propagated by
updating a subset of the Similarity Matrix. We experimentally evaluated several
feedback propagation methods, including a method used in our previous work [5],
a method based on learning similarity scores with a logistic regression model,
and a method based on our user quality measures. For our experiments, we use
this last method, which we call *Quality Agreement (QA) Propagation*, because
it achieves the best trade-off between speed and robustness.

In QA Propagation, the similarity of the validated mapping is set to 1 or 0
depending on the label assigned by the user. To propagate the similarity to other
mappings, we compute the Euclidean distance between the signature vectors of
the validated mapping, denoted by m_v, and the signature vectors of all the
mappings for which consensus has not been reached. A distance threshold th_P
is used to identify the class of mappings most similar to the mapping labeled
by the user. The mappings in this class have their similarity increased if the
validated mapping is labeled as correct, and decreased otherwise. The change is
proportional to: 1) the quality of the labeled mapping and of the mappings in
the similarity class, measured respectively by two quality measures Q and Q',
and 2) a *propagation gain* defined by a constant g such that $0 \leq g \leq 1$, which
regulates the magnitude of the update. This constant will determine how much
the quality of the labeled mapping will affect the quality of the mappings in the
similarity class. After the propagation of a validation $label(m_v)$, the similarity
$\sigma_t(m_c)$ of a mapping m_c in the similarity class at an iteration t is defined by:

$$\sigma_t(m_c) = \begin{cases} \sigma_{t-1}(m_c) + min\left(Q(m_v) * Q'(m_c) * g, 1 - \sigma_{t-1}(m_c)\right) & \text{if } label(m_v) = 1 \\ \sigma_{t-1}(m_c) - min\left(Q(m_v) * Q'(m_c) * g, \sigma_{t-1}(m_c)\right) & \text{if } label(m_v) = 0 \end{cases}$$

We adopt a conservative approach to propagation to make the system more
robust to erroneous feedback. We define $Q(m_v) = CON(m_v)$ and $Q'(m_c) = AVG(AMA(m_c), SSD(m_c))$. Thus, the similarity of the mappings in this class is
increased/decreased proportionally to: i) the consensus on the labeled mapping,
and ii) the quality of the mappings in the similarity class. For example, for
$CON(m_v) = 0$, the similarity of other mappings in the class is not updated. In

addition, when $g = 0$, the propagation function changes the similarity of the validated mapping but not the similarity of other mappings in the class.

4   Experiments

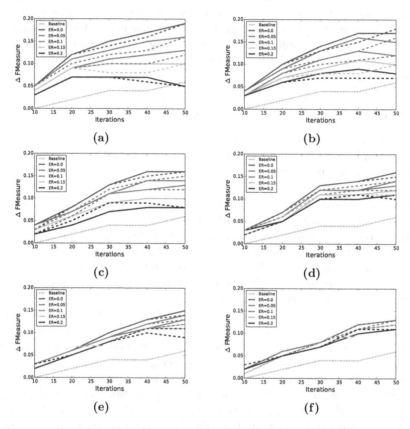

Fig. 1. Each chart presents the results obtained with a different revalidation rate (RR): (a) RR = 0.0; (b) RR = 0.1; (c) RR = 0.2; (d) RR = 0.3; (e) RR = 0.4; (f) RR = 0.5. The dashed lines represent a propagation gain equal to zero.

Experimental Setup. Our experiments are conducted using four matching tasks in the Benchmarks track of OAEI 2010, which consist of real-world bibliographic reference ontologies that include BibTeX/MIT, BibTeX/UMBC, Karlsruhe and INRIA, and their reference alignments. We chose these ontologies because they have been used in related studies [3,4,5,7]. In the evaluation we use two measures based on F-Measure:

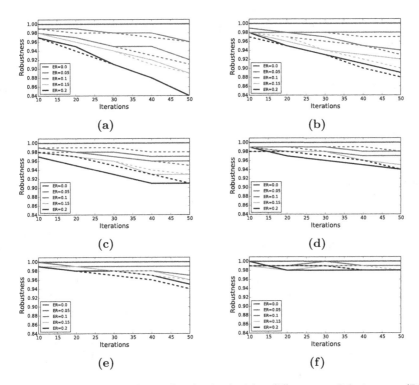

Fig. 2. Each chart presents the results obtained with a different revalidation rate (RR): (a) RR = 0.0; (b) RR = 0.1; (c) RR = 0.2; (d) RR = 0.3; (e) RR = 0.4; (f) RR = 0.5. Dashed lines represent a propagation gain equal to zero.

Gain at iteration t, ΔF-Measure(t), is the difference between the F-Measure at iteration t as evaluated after the Candidate Selection Step and the F-Measure at the Initial Matching Step (see Section 2).

Robustness at iteration t, Robustness(t), is the ratio at iteration t of the F-Measure obtained under error rate er, $FM_{ER=er}(t)$, and the F-Measure obtained with zero error rate, $FM_{ER=0}(t)$, for the same configuration. A robustness of 1.0 means that the system is impervious to error.

We conduct our experiments by simulating the feedback provided by the users. Our focus is on the evaluation of methods that minimize the users' overall effort and make the system robust against users' errors. This kind of simulation is needed to comparatively assess the effectiveness of different candidate selection and propagation methods before performing experiments with real users, where presentation issues play a major role. We consider a community of 10 users, and simulate their validation at each iteration using the reference alignment. We note that we have made two assumptions that can be revised as they do not alter the substance of the method. The first reflects the fact that we do not distinguish among users as mentioned in Section 2 and therefore consider a constant error rate for each sequence of validated mappings. The study of a community of users might uncover an appropriate probability distribution function for the error (e.g., Gaussian). The second assumption is related to the choice of *Val*, which following Section 2 we set to 5, and therefore *MinCon* = 3. Studying the users could lead to setting *Val* so as to guarantee a desired upper bound for the error rate. Without this knowledge, we considered several error rates while keeping *Val* constant.

In the Initial Matching Step we use a configuration of AgreementMaker that runs five lexical matchers in parallel. The LWC matcher [11] is used to combine the results of five lexical matchers, and two structural matchers are used to propagate the similarity scores. The similarity scores returned by these matchers are used to compute the signature vectors. In our experiments we compute the gain and robustness at every iteration t from 1 to 100, with four different error rates (ER) (0.05, 0.1, 0.15, 0.2) and twelve different system configurations. The configurations stem from six different revalidation rates (RR) (0.0, 0.1, 0.2, 0.3, 0.4, 0.5) used in the candidate selection strategy, and two different feedback propagation gains, $g = 0$ and $g = 0.5$. When $g = 0$, the propagation step affects only the mapping validated by the user, that is, it does not change the similarity of other mappings. We set the threshold used for cluster selection at $th_P = 0.03$. This value is half the average Euclidean distance between the signature vectors of the first 100 validated mappings and the remaining mappings with a non-zero signature vector. Remarkably, this value was found to be approximately the same for all matching tasks, thus being a good choice. In the Alignment Selection Step we set the cardinality of the alignment to 1:1. The evaluation randomly simulates the labels assigned by the users according to different error rates. Every experiment is therefore repeated twenty times to eliminate the bias intrinsic in the randomization of error generation. In the analysis of the results we will report the average of the values obtained in each run of the experiments.

We also want to compare the results obtained with our model, which propagates the user feedback at each iteration in a pay-as-you-go fashion, with a model that adopts an *Optimally Robust Feedback Loop (ORFL)* workflow, inspired by CrowdMap, a crowdsourcing approach to ontology matching [7]. In their approach, similarity is updated only when consensus is reached on a mapping, which happens after five iterations when *Val* = 5. To simulate their approach we modify our feedback loop in such a way that a correct validation is generated every five iterations (it is our assumption that the majority decision is correct). CrowdMap does not use a candidate selection strategy because all the mappings are sent in parallel to the users. We therefore use our candidate selection strategy with *RR* = 0 to define the priority with which mappings are validated and do not propagate the similarity to other mappings.

Result Analysis. We ran our first experiment on two of the OAEI Benchmarks ontologies, 101 and 303. We chose these ontologies because their matching produced the lowest initial F-Measure (0.73) when compared with the results for the other matching tasks 101-301 (0.92), 101-302 (0.86) and 101-304 (0.93). Thus we expect to see a higher gain for 101-303 than for the others. Table 3 shows for each matching task the number of correct mappings, false positives, false negatives, and the initial F-Measure.

Table 3. Results after the Initial Matching Step

Matching Task	# Correct Mappings	# False Positives	# False Negatives	F-Measure
101-301	50	6	2	92.31
101-302	36	5	5	86.11
101-303	40	23	4	72.73
101-304	74	9	2	92.90

Figure 1 shows the gain in F-Measure after several iterations using different configurations of our model and the ORFL approach. Each chart presents results for a candidate selection strategy that uses a specific revalidation rate (RR). Solid lines represent configurations with propagation gain $g = 0.5$, while dashed lines represent configurations with zero propagation gain. Different colors are associated with different error rates. The dotted line represent the results obtained with the ORFL approach. In the charts, the steeper a curve segment between two iterations, the faster the F-measure gain between those iterations. It can be observed that our approach is capable of improving the quality of the alignment over time. However, it is also the case that as time increases the quality can decrease especially for lower revalidation rates, that is, primarily for charts (a), (b), (c) of Figure 1. As the revalidation rate increases, $\Delta F\text{-}Measure(t)$ always increases when the propagation gain is different from zero.

Figure 2 shows the robustness of different configurations evaluated at different iterations, varying both the error and the revalidation rates. Each chart presents results for a candidate selection strategy that uses a specific revalidation rate (RR). Solid lines represent configurations with propagation gain $g = 0.5$, while dashed lines represent configurations with zero propagation gain. Different colors represent results obtained with different error rates. Robustness decreases as time increases and error rate increases, more noticeably for low revalidation rates and for zero propagation gain. However, as revalidation rates increase, we see a sharp increase in robustness.

We ran further experiments with three other matching tasks of the OAEI 2010 Benchmarks track. Table 4 contains the results for the three other tasks (101-301, 101-302, 101-304) and shows $\Delta F\text{-}Measure(t)$ at different iterations under two different error rates (0.0 and 0.1), two different revalidation rates (0.2 and 0.3), in different configurations with or without gain (Gain or NoGain), for our pay-as-you-go workflow, together with a comparison with ORFL. We discuss the results for an error rate up to 0.1 because the initial F-Measure in these matching tasks is high (0.92, 0.86, and 0.93, respectively), therefore we do not expect that users will make more errors than automatic matchers. In the absence of error, our model always improves the quality of the alignment for the three tasks faster than ORFL (except for iteration 100 of 101-304 where both methods have the same gain of 0.05). For an error rate of 0.1, our model performs better than ORFL for $t = 10$ for every matching task, and for $t = 25$ in two of them. For $t = 50$ it performs worse than ORFL for two of the tasks and better for one of the tasks. For $t = 100$, ORFL always performs better.

Table 4. ΔF-*Measure*(t) for the matching tasks with higher initial F-Measure

ER	RR	CONF	101-301(0.92)				101-302(0.86)				101-304(0.92)			
			@10	@25	@50	@100	@10	@25	@50	@100	@10	@25	@50	@100
0.0	0.2	NoGain	0.03	0.05	0.05	0.05	0.03	0.05	0.06	0.08	0.0	0.05	0.05	0.05
0.0	0.2	Gain	0.03	0.04	0.04	0.05	0.03	0.06	0.06	0.08	0.0	0.05	0.05	0.05
0.0	0.3	NoGain	0.02	0.05	0.05	0.05	0.03	0.05	0.06	0.08	0.0	0.04	0.05	0.05
0.0	0.3	Gain	0.02	0.04	0.04	0.05	0.03	0.05	0.06	0.08	0.0	0.03	0.05	0.05
0.1	0.2	NoGain	0.03	0.04	0.01	-0.01	0.02	0.01	0.0	-0.02	0.0	0.03	0.03	0.0
0.1	0.2	Gain	0.03	0.03	0.01	0.0	0.02	0.03	0.01	0.01	0.0	0.03	0.03	0.00
0.1	0.3	NoGain	0.02	0.04	0.02	0.0	0.03	0.02	0.00	0.01	0.0	0.03	0.04	0.02
0.1	0.3	Gain	0.02	0.03	0.01	0.0	0.03	0.03	0.01	0.01	0.0	0.03	0.04	0.01
-	0.0	ORFL	0.0	0.02	0.04	0.05	0.01	0.03	0.05	0.05	0.0	0.0	0.0	0.05

Finally, we establish a comparison between our multi-user approach, which relies heavily on a quality model, and the single user approach of Shi et al. [4]. We want to determine which quality model performs better in our feedback loop workflow. The candidate selection strategy used by Shi et al. uses three measures, *Contention Point*, *Multi-Matcher Confidence*, and *Similarity Distance*, whose intent is close to that of our quality measures *CSC*, *AMA*, and *SSD*. We ran an experiment with the same ontologies, 101-303, that were used in Section 4 in an error-free setting (like the one considered by Shi et al.), comparing two candidate selection strategies with no propagation gain: one uses the best combination of their three measures, while the other uses our approach with revalidation rate equal to zero, as shown in Table 5. For the candidate selection strategy that uses our measures, we obtain a ΔF-*Measure*(50) that is on average 3.8 times higher than the ΔF-*Measure*(50) obtained with their measures.

Table 5. Comparison with selection strategy of Shi et al. [4], showing F-measure(0), F-measure(100), and ΔF-*Measure*(t), for $t = 10, 20, 30, 40, 50, 100$

Quality Measures	F-Measure(0)	@10	@20	@30	@40	@50	@100	F-Measure(100)
Active Learning [4]	0.73	0.01	0.02	0.05	0.08	0.12	0.15	0.88
$AVG(DIS, SSD^-)$	0.73	0.05	0.12	0.14	0.16	0.19	0.26	0.99

Conclusions. From our experiments with four different matching tasks characterized by different initial F-Measure values, we draw the following conclusions:

1. When users do not make errors, our method improves the quality of the alignment much faster in every matching task than an optimally robust feedback loop (ORFL) method that labels a mapping only after having collected from the users every validation needed to reach consensus.
2. An increasing error rate can be counteracted by an increasing revalidation rate, still obtaining very good results for an error rate as high as 0.2 and a revalidation rate of 0.5.

3. In the presence of errors, our approach is particularly effective when the initial alignment has lower quality and includes a higher number of false positives (see Table 3). In the matching task with lower initial F-Measure, every configuration of our method improves the quality of the alignment much faster than the optimally robust feedback loop method, even when error rates are as high as 0.2. Propagating the feedback to mappings other than the mapping labeled by the user at the current iteration shows a higher gain in F-Measure in several of the experiments.

4. In the presence of errors, the F-Measure gain decreases after a certain number of iterations, unless a high revalidation rate is used. The number of iterations after which the gain in F-Measure decreases, which is clearly correlated with the error rate, appears to also be correlated with the quality of the initial alignment and, in particular, with the number of false positives (see Table 3). For example, using a revalidation rate of 0.3 and an error rate of 0.1, the F-Measure gain starts to decrease after 25 iterations in matching tasks with at most six false positives in the initial alignment (101-301, 101-302), and does not decrease before the 50th iteration in matching tasks where the initial alignment contains at least nine false positives (101-303, 101-304).

5. When the error rate is unknown, a revalidation rate equal to 0.3 achieves a good trade-off between F-measure gain and robustness because of the "stability" of the results as displayed in the (d) charts of Figures 1 and 2. We note that propagation leads to better results for the F-measure gain than for robustness.

6. Propagation leads in general to better results (F-measure gain and robustness) than no propagation. There are however, a few exceptions. The most notorious is for ER=0.2 and RR=0.2. In this case, it appears that errors get propagated, without being sufficiently counteracted by revalidation. When revalidation increases to RR=0.3 then the results with propagation and without propagation are very close but propagation wins for RR=0.4 and 0.5.

7. According to our results, the revalidation rate should be changed over time, starting with a lower revalidation rate and then switching to a higher revalidation rate. The higher the error, the sooner the switch should occur.

5 Related Work

Leveraging the contribution of multiple users has been recognized as a fundamental step in making user feedback a first class-citizen in data integration systems, such as those for schema and ontology matching [6,7]. Ontology matching approaches relying on the feedback provided by a single user are a precursor to multi-user systems. They include the work of Shi et al. [4], Duan et al. [3], and Cruz et al. [5]. Shi et al. use an active learning approach to determine an optimal threshold for mapping selection and propagate the user feedback using a graph-based structural propagation algorithm. Duan et al. use a supervised method to learn an optimal combination of both lexical and structural similarity metrics. Cruz et al. use signature vectors that identify the mappings for which the system is less confident and propagate the validated mappings based on the similarity of signature vectors; the overall goal is to reduce the uncertainty of the mappings. Shi et al. and Cruz et al. use a (static) candidate selection strategy.

In multi-user scenarios, several opportunities arise, such as the possibility of gathering consensus on mappings, as well as challenges, such as the need to deal with noisy feedback [6,7]. Many multi-user scenarios use crowdsourcing on a web platform: for example, CrowdMap [7] for ontology matching and ZenCrowd [12] for data linking. As in our multi-user feedback approach, both CrowdMap and ZenCrowd engage multiple workers to solve a semantic-based matching task and use revalidation. However, CrowdMap does not integrate automatic matching methods with user feedback and does not investigate methods for candidate mapping selection nor feedback propagation.

Workers may not have specific skills nor a specific interest in the task that they perform other than the monetary reward that they get. Therefore, strategies are needed to assess their performance. For example, McCann et al. [13] classify workers as trusted or untrusted. Another example is provided by Osorno-Gutierrez et al. [14], who investigate the use of crowdsourcing for mapping database tuples. They address the workers' reliability, identifying both workers whose answers may contradict their own or others'. Meilicke et al. [9] propose a reasoning approach to identify the inconsistencies after manual mapping revision by human experts. One of their strategies is to remove some mappings from the search space based on the cardinality of the alignment (e.g., using the 1:1 cardinality assumption). Our feedback model works prominently on the similarity matrix: a desired cardinality constraint can be specified by configuring the alignment selection algorithm (Step 7).

Similarly to some single-user feedback strategies, the recent crowdsourcing approach of Zhang et al., aims to reduce the uncertainty of database schema matching [15] measured in terms of the entropy computed using the probabilities associated with sets of tuple correspondences, called matchings. They proposed two algorithms that generate questions to the crowd. Best candidates are those that can obtain highest certainty with lowest cost. In comparison with our approach, they do not obtain consensus on a mapping and each mapping is only validated once.

6   Conclusions and Future Work

A multi-user approach needs to manage inconsistent user validations dynamically and continuously throughout the matching task, while aiming to reduce the number of mapping validations so as to minimize user effort. In this paper, we presented a mapping model that uses quality measures in the two main steps of the system: the Candidate Mapping Selection and the Feedback Propagation steps. In the first step, a dynamic mechanism ranks the candidate mappings according to those quality measures so that the mappings with lower quality are the first to be presented for validation, thus accelerating the gain in quality. In the second step similarity among mappings is used to validate mappings automatically without direct user feedback, so as to cover the mapping space faster.

Our experiments brought clarity on the trade-offs among error and revalidation rates required to minimize time and maximize robustness and F-measure. Our strategies show under which circumstances we can afford to be "aggressive" by propagating results from the very first iterations, instead of waiting for a consensus to be built.

Future work may consider user profiling, so that there is a weight associated with the user validations and how they are propagated depending on the feedback quality. In this paper we tested different constant error rates to model a variety of users' behavior as an aggregate. Other models may take into account the possibility that users' engagement decreases along time due to the repetitiveness of the validation task, thus leading to an increasing error rate, or that in certain situations users learn with experience and make fewer errors, thus leading to a decreasing error rate. We therefore plan to perform studies to determine the impact of users' behavior along time on the error distribution so as to change the candidate selection meta-strategy accordingly. Our overall strategy could also be modified to present one mapping together with several mapping alternatives. In this case, the visualization of the context for those alternatives could prove beneficial. This visualization can be included in a visual analytics strategy for ontology matching [5] modified for multiple users.

Acknowledgments. This work was supported in part by NSF Awards CCF-1331800, IIS-1213013, IIS-1143926, and IIS-0812258, by a UIC-IPCE Civic Engagement Research Fund Award, and by the EU FP7-ICT-611358 COMSODE Project.

References

1. Euzenat, J., Shvaiko, P.: Ontology Matching. Springer, Heidelberg (2007)
2. Cruz, I.F., Sunna, W.: Structural Alignment Methods with Applications to Geospatial Ontologies. Transactions in GIS, Special Issue on Semantic Similarity Measurement and Geospatial Applications 12, 683–711 (2008)
3. Duan, S., Fokoue, A., Srinivas, K.: One Size Does Not Fit All: Customizing Ontology Alignment Using User Feedback. In: Patel-Schneider, P.F., Pan, Y., Hitzler, P., Mika, P., Zhang, L., Pan, J.Z., Horrocks, I., Glimm, B. (eds.) ISWC 2010, Part I. LNCS, vol. 6496, pp. 177–192. Springer, Heidelberg (2010)
4. Shi, F., Li, J., Tang, J., Xie, G., Li, H.: Actively Learning Ontology Matching via User Interaction. In: Bernstein, A., Karger, D.R., Heath, T., Feigenbaum, L., Maynard, D., Motta, E., Thirunarayan, K. (eds.) ISWC 2009. LNCS, vol. 5823, pp. 585–600. Springer, Heidelberg (2009)
5. Cruz, I.F., Stroe, C., Palmonari, M.: Interactive User Feedback in Ontology Matching Using Signature Vectors. In: IEEE International Conference on Data Engineering (ICDE), pp. 1321–1324. IEEE (2012)
6. Belhajjame, K., Paton, N.W., Fernandes, A.A.A., Hedeler, C., Embury, S.M.: User Feedback as a First Class Citizen in Information Integration Systems. In: Conference on Innovative Data Systems Research (CIDR), pp. 175–183 (2011)

7. Sarasua, C., Simperl, E., Noy, N.F.: CROWDMAP: Crowdsourcing Ontology Alignment with Microtasks. In: Cudré-Mauroux, P., Heflin, J., Sirin, E., Tudorache, T., Euzenat, J., Hauswirth, M., Parreira, J.X., Hendler, J., Schreiber, G., Bernstein, A., Blomqvist, E. (eds.) ISWC 2012, Part I. LNCS, vol. 7649, pp. 525–541. Springer, Heidelberg (2012)

8. Bourdaillet, J., Roy, S., Jung, G., Sun, Y.: Crowdsourcing Translation by Leveraging Tournament Selection and Lattice-Based String Alignment. In: AAAI Conference on Human Computation and Crowdsourcing (HCOMP), vol. WS-13-18. AAAI (2013)

9. Meilicke, C., Stuckenschmidt, H., Tamilin, A.: Supporting Manual Mapping Revision Using Logical Reasoning. In: National Conference on Artificial Intelligence (AAAI), pp. 1213–1218. AAAI Press (2008)

10. Cruz, I.F., Palandri Antonelli, F., Stroe, C.: AgreementMaker: Efficient Matching for Large Real-World Schemas and Ontologies. PVLDB 2(2), 1586–1589 (2009)

11. Cruz, I.F., Palandri Antonelli, F., Stroe, C.: Efficient Selection of Mappings and Automatic Quality-driven Combination of Matching Methods. In: ISWC International Workshop on Ontology Matching (OM). CEUR Workshop Proceedings, vol. 551, pp. 49–60 (2009)

12. Demartini, G., Difallah, D.E., Cudré-Mauroux, P.: ZenCrowd: Leveraging Probabilistic Reasoning and Crowdsourcing Techniques for Large-scale Entity Linking. In: International World Wide Web Conference (WWW), pp. 469–478. ACM, New York (2012)

13. McCann, R., Shen, W., Doan, A.: Matching Schemas in Online Communities: A Web 2.0 Approach. In: IEEE International Conference on Data Engineering (ICDE), pp. 110–119. IEEE (2008)

14. Osorno-Gutierrez, F., Paton, N.W., Fernandes, A.A.A.: Crowdsourcing Feedback for Pay-As-You-Go Data Integration. In: VLDB Workshop on Databases and Crowdsourcing (DBCrowd), vol. 1025, pp. 32–37 (2013)

15. Zhang, C.J., Chen, L., Jagadish, H.V., Cao, C.C.: Reducing Uncertainty of Schema Matching via Crowdsourcing. PVLDB 6(9), 757–768 (2013)

Information Flow within Relational Multi-context Systems[*]

Luís Cruz-Filipe[1], Graça Gaspar[2], and Isabel Nunes[2]

[1] Dept. of Mathematics and Computer Science, University of Southern Denmark
[2] LabMAg, Faculdade de Ciências, Universidade de Lisboa, Portugal

Abstract. Multi-context systems (MCSs) are an important framework for heterogeneous combinations of systems within the Semantic Web. In this paper, we propose generic constructions to achieve specific forms of interaction in a principled way, and systematize some useful techniques to work with ontologies within an MCS. All these mechanisms are presented in the form of general-purpose design patterns. Their study also suggests new ways in which this framework can be further extended.

1 Introduction

In parallel with the proliferation of different reasoning systems, larger and larger bodies of knowledge are being built in several fields, each with its expressiveness and efficiency, that can benefit enormously from adequate frameworks allowing to reason with information coming from different sources. Integrating several knowledge sources in a modular and flexible way is nowadays a growing need, and there has been significant growth in the research and development of this kind of heterogenous systems. As such, best practices should be devised as early as possible to guide the design and implementation of these systems, as has been done for other frameworks [2,26].

A particular class of heterogeneous combinations is that of non-monotonic multi-context systems (MCSs) [3], which consist of several independent systems ("contexts") interacting through Datalog-style "bridge rules", controlling the flow of information by means of knowledge added to a context whenever some information is inferred in other contexts. MCSs have been a topic of active research recently, and several variants of MCSs have been proposed to deal with particular situations. Of particular interest are *relational* MCSs [15], where each context has a first-order sublanguage. These generalize MCSs, since one can take the first-order sublanguage to be empty. However, they allow bridge rules with actual first-order variables, instead of seeing such rules simply as meta-level notation for the (potentially very large) set of all their closed instances. This is useful to express information flow between logic-based systems, as a single rule can "transport" all instances of a predicate from one context to another.

---

[*] This work was supported by: Danish Council for Independent Research, Natural Sciences; and Fund. Ciência e Tecnologia under contract PEst-OE/EEI/UI0434/2011.

K. Janowicz et al. (Eds.): EKAW 2014, LNAI 8876, pp. 97–108, 2014.

Most example MCSs presented so far were designed to illustrate the potential of this formalism, but to our knowledge there has not been much effort in the development of systematic techniques to write MCSs. This is the main achievement of this paper: we propose generic mechanisms, in the form of general-purpose design patterns, that achieve specific forms of interaction between contexts within an MCS in a principled way – e.g. extending a context by means of a definition in the language of another context, giving closed-world semantics for particular predicates in a context with open-world semantics, or reasoning within the merge of two contexts while keeping them separate. The study of these design patterns not only facilitates the development of future MCSs, but also suggests new ways in which their language can be extended. Our departure point was the study of design patterns for multi dl-programs [10] – a generalization of dl-programs [13] with multiple knowledge bases –, which can be seen as a subclass of MCSs by means of a systematic translation [9]. The present study is however much more general than the combination of the work in those two publications.

The paper is organized as follows. Section 2 summarizes previous research relevant to this work. Section 3 recalls the formal definition of relational MCS and introduces an elementary communication pattern for MCSs. Section 4 discusses more general interaction patterns, and Section 5 explores particular applications to MCSs using ontologies. Section 6 discusses future directions for this work.

2   Related Work

Software design patterns enhance software quality by establishing best practices together with a "common language" between development teams that substantially enriches their communication, and hence the whole design process. From very basic, abstract, patterns that can be used as building blocks of several more complex ones, to business-specific patterns and frameworks, dozens of design patterns have been proposed in e.g. [16,17]. Although most of the work around design patterns focuses on the object-oriented paradigm, several patterns are fundamental enough to be independent of the modeling and programming paradigms used. Thus, effort has also been made in adapting these best practices to other paradigms and in finding new paradigm-specific patterns [2,26]. In this line, we proposed a set of design patterns for Mdl-programs [10] – a formalism to join description logics with rules [9], generalizing the original dl-programs [13].

Multi-context systems [3] (MCSs) are heterogeneous non-monotonic systems whose components (called *contexts*) are knowledge bases that can be expressed in different logics (e.g., a theory in classical logic, a description logic knowledge base, a set of temporal logic formulas, a logic program under answer set semantics, or a set of default logic rules). Unlike Mdl-programs, the communication between the components is not centralized, but rather distributed among them via sets of (non-monotonic) *bridge rules*. Since they were originally proposed, several variations of MCSs have been studied that add to their potential fields of application. Examples are managed MCS [4], whose bridge rules allow arbitrary operations (e.g. deletion or revision operators) on context knowledge bases to be defined; relational MCSs [15], which introduce variables and aggregate expressions in bridge rules, extending the semantics of MCSs accordingly; or dynamic MCSs [11], designed to cope with situations where knowledge sources and their contents may change over time and are not known *a priori*. We will work within relational MCSs and discuss a possible generalization of dynamic MCSs.

There are other formalisms to combine different reasoning systems. HEX-programs [14] are higher-order logic programs with external atoms, and they are also heterogeneous since these external atoms may query systems that use different languages. The homogenous approach is exemplified by hybrid MKNF knowledge bases [23], which however are not modular. (Partial) translations between these formalisms have been studied to compare their expressive power and to allow transfer of technology from one formalism into another [4,9,19].

Yet another way of combining reasoning systems is ontology mediation, which facilitates the interoperability of different ontologies by allowing exchange of instance data through the identification of alignments or the merging of overlapping ontologies. An *alignment* between two distinct ontologies establishes relationships between pairs of entities, one from each ontology. These relationships are then made concrete in the form of ontology mappings, with some tools [6,12] resorting to "bridge axioms" or even an ontology of generic bridges [21] whose instances define mappings between the original ones. Alignments are also sometimes used as a first step towards defining a single ontology that merges the original ones. However, merging ontologies requires solving the inconsistencies or incoherences that might arise, which are difficult problems for which several distinct theoretic approaches have been proposed [7], and much effort has been put on the development of tools to assist with ontology merging [20].

Ontology alignment patterns [25] help designers to identify alignments by looking at common patterns of ontology mismatches. Both these and the definition of an ontology of generic mappings are complementary to the construction in Section 5, which translates a previously identified alignment into MCS bridge rules and shows how to emulate partial ontology merging within an MCS. These patterns are a complement of, rather than an alternative to, ontology design patterns [18].

3   Information Flow in Relational Multi-context Systems

We begin this section with a quick summary of the notion of relational MCS [15].

A *relational logic* L is a quadruple $\langle \mathsf{KB}_L, \mathsf{BS}_L, \mathsf{ACC}_L, \Sigma_L \rangle$, where KB_L is the set of well-formed logic bases of L, BS_L is a set of possible belief sets, $\mathsf{ACC}_L :$ $\mathsf{KB}_L \to 2^{\mathsf{BS}_L}$ is a function assigning to each knowledge base a set of acceptable sets of beliefs, and Σ_L is a signature consisting of sets P_L^{KB} and P_L^{BS} of predicate names (with associated arity) and a universe U_L of object constants, such that $U_L \cap (P_L^{\mathsf{KB}} \cup P_L^{\mathsf{BS}}) = \emptyset$. If $p \in P_L^{\mathsf{KB}}$ (resp. $p \in P_L^{\mathsf{BS}}$) has arity k and $c_1, \ldots, c_k \in U_L$ then $p(c_1, \ldots, c_k)$ must be an element of some knowledge base (resp. belief set). These elements are called *relational ground elements*, while other elements of knowledge bases or belief sets are called *ordinary*. This notion generalizes that of logic in a general MCS, where all elements are ordinary (so $P_L^{KB} = P_L^{BS} = U_L = \emptyset$).

Let $\mathfrak{I}$ be a finite set of indices, $\{L_i\}_{i \in \mathfrak{I}}$ be a set of relational logics, and V be a set of variables distinct from predicate and constant names in any L_i. A *relational element* of L_i has the form $p(t_1, \ldots, t_k)$ where $p \in P_{L_i}^{KB} \cup P_{L_i}^{BS}$ has arity k and each t_j is a term from $V \cup U_{L_i}$, for $1 \leq j \leq k$. A *relational k-bridge rule* over $\{L_i\}_{i \in \mathfrak{I}}$ and V is a rule of the form

$$(k : s) \leftarrow (c_1 : p_1), \ldots, (c_q : p_q), \mathsf{not}(c_{q+1} : p_{q+1}), \ldots, \mathsf{not}(c_m : p_m) \qquad (1)$$

such that $k, c_i \in \mathfrak{I}$, s is a knowledge base element of L_k and $p_1, \ldots, p_m$ are beliefs of L_{c_i}.

A *relational multi-context system* is a collection $M = \{C_i\}_{i \in \mathfrak{I}}$ of contexts $C_i = \langle L_i, kb_i, br_i, D_i \rangle$, where L_i is a relational logic, $kb_i \in KB_{L_i}$ is a knowledge base, br_i is a set of relational i-bridge rules, and D_i is a set of import domains $D_{i,j}$, with $j \in \mathfrak{I}$, such that $D_{i,j} \subseteq U_j$. Unless otherwise stated, $D_{i,j}$ is assumed to be the finite domain consisting of the constants appearing in kb_j or in the head of a rule in br_j.

The semantics of relational MCSs is defined in terms of ground instances of bridge rules, obtained from each rule $r \in br_i$ by uniform substitution of each variable X in r by a constant in $\bigcap D_{i,j}$, with j ranging over the indices of the contexts to which queries containing X are made in r. A *belief state* for M is a collection $S = \{S_i\}_{i \in \mathfrak{I}}$ where $S_i \in BS_{\mathcal{L}_i}$ for each $i \in \mathfrak{I}$. Rule (1) is *applicable* w.r.t. belief state S if $p_i \in S_{c_i}$ for $1 \leq i \leq q$ and $p_i \notin S_{c_i}$ for $q < i \leq m$. The set of the heads of all applicable rules in br_i w.r.t. S is denoted by $\mathsf{app}_i(S)$. An *equilibrium* is a belief state S such that $S_i \in ACC_i(kb_i \cup \mathsf{app}_i(S))$. Particular types of equilibria originally defined for MCSs [3] transfer to relational MCSs, but we will not use them.

From this point onwards we will only consider relational MCSs, and omit the adjective "relational" for brevity. The discussion below takes place within the setting of an MCS $M = \{C_i\}_{i \in \mathfrak{I}}$ unless otherwise stated.

The basic communication structure of MCSs can be embodied in a very simple design pattern, which is useful as a building block for more elaborate patterns, and we can state its soundness. The proof of this and subsequent results can be found in the extended version of this paper [8].

Pattern *Observer*.

Problem. The semantics of $p \in P_i^{KB}$ should include all instances of $p_j \in P_{\varphi(j)}^{KB}$, with $1 \leq j \leq \ell$ and $\varphi(j) \in \mathfrak{I}$, of the same arity.

Solution. Add the bridge rules $(i : p(\boldsymbol{X})) \leftarrow (\varphi(j) : p_j(\boldsymbol{X}))$ to br_i, with $\boldsymbol{X} = X_1, \ldots, X_k$ and $1 \leq j \leq \ell$.

Proposition 1. *Let $M = \{C_i\}_{i \in \mathfrak{I}}$ be an MCS such that $kb \subseteq ACC_i(kb)$ for every $kb \in KB_i$, and let $p \in P_i^{KB}$ be defined from $p_j \in P_{\varphi(j)}^{KB}$ for $j = 1, \ldots, \ell$ by application of **Observer**. Let $S = \{S_i\}_{i \in \mathfrak{I}}$ be an equilibrium for M. For each j, if $p_j(t) \in S_{\varphi(j)}$ for some t, then $p(t) \in S_i$.*

4 Extending Expressiveness of Contexts

An MCS's information flow capabilities can be applied to extend the language of one context using syntactic means available in another. As an example, suppose that we want to define the transitive closure of a binary relation in a context that has no primitives for this. At the semantic level, this can be achieved for named individuals by means of an auxiliary context that can define transitive closures. We introduce two patterns to deal with this situation; the first one is a particular case of the second, but it is important enough to discuss on its own.

Pattern *Fixpoint definition*.

Problem. In context C_i we want to define a predicate p from other predicates by means of a logic program.

Solution. (i) Add a logic programming context C_θ, i.e. a context such that $\mathsf{ACC}_\theta(\mathsf{kb})$ contains only the minimal model of kb over the constants in U_i, and $D_{i,\theta} = D_{\theta,i} = D_{i,i}$. (ii) Apply *Observer* to import from C_i to C_θ all instances of the predicates necessary to define p. (iii) Take kb_θ to be the definition of p. (iv) Apply *Observer* to export p from C_θ to C_i.

Proposition 2. *Let predicate p be defined in context C_θ by application of **Fixpoint definition** and $S = \{S_j\}_{j \in \mathfrak{I}}$ be an equilibrium of the corresponding MCS. Define I to be the restriction of S_i to the Herbrand base of kb_θ (with constants in U_i). Then $S_\theta \subseteq I$.*

In particular, this pattern allows us to view deductive databases as MCSs – context C_i is the database, context C_θ is the view, and bridge rules connect them.

In general, it can happen that I contains more information about p; this can be avoided by applying *Observer* to both p and $\neg p$ in the last step, but this can easily lead to inconsistency if C_i proves some $p(t)$ that is not derived by C_θ.

This construction works at the level of the instances – we cannot reason abstractly about properties of defined concepts, as individuals outside the import domain are never "carried over" by bridge rules. This is a necessary evil – otherwise, one easily gets undecidability of reasoning in the resulting MCS.

Example 1. Let C_1 be a context for a decidable fragment of first-order logic where there are binary predicates R, Rt and S, $\mathsf{ACC}_1(\mathsf{kb})$ is the set of logical consequences of kb, and kb_1 contains the axiom $\forall x, y (\mathsf{R}(x,y) \rightarrow \mathsf{S}(x,y))$ together with some instances of R (but none of Rt). The goal is to have Rt be the transitive closure of R, but this is not first-order definable. Application of *Fixpoint definition* defines a logic programming context C_2, where kb_2 defines Rt as the transitive closure of R in the usual way, and contains no other rules. Then we add the two bridge rules $(2 : \mathsf{R}(X,Y)) \leftarrow (1 : \mathsf{R}(X,Y))$ and $(1 : \mathsf{Rt}(X,Y)) \leftarrow (2 : \mathsf{Rt}(X,Y))$ to the resulting MCS. In this way, in every equilibrium $\{S_1, S_2\}$ of $\{C_1, C_2\}$ the semantics of Rt in S_1 will coincide with the transitive closure of R in S_1 on named individuals. However, S_1 does not necessarily satisfy $\forall x, y(R(x, y) \rightarrow S(x, y))$: it can happen that $R(c_1, c_2)$ holds for individuals c_1 and c_2 that are not interpretations of constants in C_1's (syntactic) domain, and the semantics of the bridge rules can not guarantee that $Rt(c_1, c_2)$, and hence $S(c_1, c_2)$, holds.

A generalization of this mechanism is the more encompassing problem of defining a predicate in one context by means of a construct only available in other contexts. Typical examples include: description logic contexts, where concept/role constructors are restricted to guarantee decidability and complexity bounds on reasoning; relational databases, where no definitional mechanisms exist; or impredicative definitions in first-order contexts. We can achieve this by means of a similar construction: export the instances of the predicates required for the definition into a context with the desired ability, write the definition in that context, and import the instances of the defined predicate back to the original context. Whether negations of predicates should be observed depends on the particular application.

Pattern *External definition*.

Problem. In context C_i, we want to define a predicate p by means of a construct that is only available in context C_j.

Solution. (i) Extend $D_{i,j}$ and $D_{j,i}$ with $D_{j,j}$. (ii) Apply ***Observer*** to import all instances of the necessary predicates [and their (default) negations] from C_i to C_j. (iii) Define p in kb_j. (iv) Apply ***Observer*** to export p [and $\neg p$] from C_j to C_i.

Proposition 3. *Let predicate p be defined in context C_i by application of **External definition** and S be an equilibrium of the corresponding MCS. Define I and J to be the restrictions of S_i to the language of C_j and of S_j to the language of C_i, respectively. Then $p(t) \in I$ whenever $p(t) \in J$, with the converse implication holding if all negations are also being observed.*

These two patterns fit well with terminological knowledge bases, where concepts are defined in terms of other concepts whose definitions (or instances) may be provided by an external entity. This construction works very nicely if C_i does not allow individuals outside the import domain, namely if C_i is a relational or deductive database, or a logic program.

Another important concern when designing systems is that of querying a context or group of contexts subject to variation minimizing the necessary changes to the contexts querying them. This variation can happen either because that context's contents are expected to change often, or because one does not want to know explicitly which context is being queried when writing bridge rules. (A concrete example will be presented in the next section.) This encapsulation can be achieved by means of the following pattern, which generalizes ***Observer***.

Pattern *Group encapsulation.*

Problem. Contexts $C_1, \ldots, C_k$ should be encapsulated, i.e. other contexts should not include queries $(i : p)$ in the bodies of their bridge rules, for $i = 1, \ldots, k$.

Solution. (i) Define functions $\sigma_i : \Sigma_i \to \Sigma_I$ and create a new interface context C_I with $U_I = \bigcup_{i=1}^{k} U_i$, $\mathsf{KB}_I = \left\{ \bigcup_{i=1}^{k} \sigma_i(\mathsf{kb}_i) \mid \mathsf{kb}_i \in \mathsf{KB}_i \right\}$, $\mathsf{kb}_I = \emptyset$, $\mathsf{BS}_I = \mathsf{KB}_I$, $\mathsf{ACC}_I(\mathsf{kb}) = \{\mathsf{kb}\}$, and $D_{I,i} = U_i$ for $i = 1, \ldots, k$. (ii) For every relational symbol $p \in \Sigma_i$, apply *Observer* to make $\sigma_i(p)$ in C_I an observer of p. (iii) In every other context, instead of writing $(i : p)$ in the body of a bridge rule, write $(I : \sigma_i(p))$.

Proposition 4. *Let M be an MCS where C_I is defined by application of* **Group encapsulation.** *Define M' by removing C_I from M and replacing every rule r with all rules obtained from r by replacing each query $(I : q)$ with a query $(i : p)$ for which $\sigma_i(p) = q$. Then:*

1. *If S is an equilibrium of M, then $S_I = \bigcup_{i=1}^{k} \{\sigma_i(p)(t) \mid p(t) \in S_i\}$.*
2. *S is an equilibrium of M iff $S \setminus S_I$ is an equilibrium of M'.*

This pattern can be made more general by also considering queries of the form $\mathsf{not}(i : p)$. Removing the restriction $\mathsf{kb}_I = \emptyset$ we obtain a more powerful design pattern where the interface context can implement algorithms to decide which contexts to query on what. A more interesting possibility would be to allow a limited form of second-order bridge rules, so that other contexts can query C_I and use the result to know which context to query on which symbol.

This kind of approach has been tackled in [19], but the second-order notation therein is an abbreviation for all closed instances of a rule – solving the presentation problem, but not the practical one. Higher-order variables in bridge rules are considered in the schematic contexts of [11], but within a more general setting where they are used as placeholders for contexts that are not known *a priori* and may change over time. Our tentative proposal is to let bridge rules use higher-order variables that serve as predicate names or context identifiers (formally numbers, but in practice URLs), with a requirement that their first occurrence in the body of a rule must be positive and in an argument position. This would allow implementation of indirection-style techniques, with interface contexts serving as mediators indicating what queries to pose to which contexts.

Pattern *Indirection.*

Problem. We want to protect an MCS from variations in bridge rules that include atoms where both the context being queried and the predicate in the query may change with time.

Solution. (i) Create an interface context C_I implementing the algorithm to decide which contexts should be queried and what the predicate names in actual queries should be. (ii) In every rule with expectable variations, include a query to C_I whose answer provides all required information, and use the result in subsequent literals in the body of the rule.

The proposal of having higher-order variables in bridge rules as first-class citizens would allow us to have the best of both worlds: the number of actual rules would be kept small, and the configuration algorithm of [11] can be seen as a particular implementation of the interface context. We will return to this issue at the end of the next section.

5   Applications to Ontology Manipulation

This section discusses specific mechanisms to deal with MCSs that contain ontologies as contexts. Due to their open-world semantics, this kind of knowledge bases brings specific challenges. We consider an ontology to be a particular knowledge base whose underlying logic is a description logic.

Definition 1. *An ontology $\mathcal{O}$ based on description logic $\mathcal{L}$ induces the context* $\mathsf{Ctx}(\mathcal{O}) = \langle L, \mathcal{O}, \emptyset, U_{\mathcal{L}} \rangle$, *with* $L = \langle \mathsf{KB}_{\mathcal{L}}, \mathsf{BS}_{\mathcal{L}}, \mathsf{ACC}_{\mathcal{L}}, \Sigma_{\mathcal{L}} \rangle$ *defined as follows:* $\mathsf{KB}_{\mathcal{L}}$ *contains all well-formed knowledge bases of $\mathcal{L}$; $\mathsf{BS}_{\mathcal{L}}$ contains all sets of literals in the language of $\mathcal{L}$; $\mathsf{ACC}_{\mathcal{L}}(\mathsf{kb})$ is the singleton set containing the set of kb's known consequences (positive and negative); and $\Sigma_{\mathcal{L}}$ is the signature underlying $\mathcal{L}$.*

Belief sets (the elements of $\mathsf{BS}_{\mathcal{L}}$) need not be categorical: they may contain neither $\mathsf{C}(\mathsf{a})$ nor $\neg\mathsf{C}(\mathsf{a})$ for particular C and a. This gives ontologies their typical open-world semantics. For this reason, the only element of $\mathsf{ACC}_{\mathcal{L}}(\mathsf{kb})$ may not be a model of kb. This is in contrast with [3], where $\mathsf{ACC}_{\mathcal{L}}(\mathsf{kb})$ contains all models of kb (see Example 2 below).

Default reasoning. Default rules can be encoded in dl-programs [13]. This construction can be simplified in the framework of MCSs.

A default rule r has the form $\alpha_1, \ldots, \alpha_k : \beta_1, \ldots, \beta_n / \gamma$, where all α_i, β_j and γ are literals, with semantics: if, for some instantiation θ of the free variables in r, all $\alpha_i \theta$ hold and it is consistent to assume that all $\beta_j \theta$ hold, then $\gamma \theta$ is inferred. Besides Reiter's original semantics [24] based on *extensions* – theories that are fixpoints w.r.t. default rules – many other semantics have been proposed [1].

Pattern *Default rule*.

Problem. Context C_i should include default rule $\alpha_1, \ldots, \alpha_k : \beta_1, \ldots, \beta_n / \gamma$.
Solution. Include $(i : \gamma) \leftarrow (i : \alpha_1), \ldots, (i : \alpha_k), \mathsf{not}(i : \beta_1), \ldots, \mathsf{not}(i : \beta_n)$ in br_i.

The standard default semantics corresponds to *minimal* equilibria – equilibria whose belief sets are not proper supersets of those in any other equilibria.

Proposition 5. *Let $\mathcal{O}$ be an ontology and Γ be a set of default rules in the language of $\mathcal{O}$. Let M be the MCS with a single context $\mathsf{Ctx}(\mathcal{O})$ and bridge rules obtained by applying **Default rule** to the rules in Γ. Then S is a minimal equilibrium of M iff S is an extension of $\mathcal{O}$ and Γ.*

Corollary 1. *If: for every extension E and rule $\alpha_1, \ldots, \alpha_k : \beta_1, \ldots, \beta_n / \gamma \in \Gamma$, $\alpha_i \in E$ iff $\mathcal{O}$ proves α_i; then all equilibria of M are extensions of $\mathcal{O}$ and Γ.*

In particular, if the rules in Γ are *prerequisite free* [5] (i.e. $k = 0$), then every equilibrium of M corresponds to an extension of $\mathcal{O}$ and Γ, and conversely. This is interesting in practice, as it corresponds to many useful applications such as the modeling of closed-world reasoning by means of default rules [5]. For this correspondence to hold, however, it is essential that $\mathsf{Ctx}(\mathcal{O})$ be defined as above, and not by having the usual models-as-belief-sets construction of [3].

Example 2. Suppose that $\mathcal{O}$ is the ontology consisting of the single formula $\mathsf{C(a)} \sqcup \mathsf{C(b)}$. Then $\mathcal{O}$'s models contain at least one of $\mathsf{C(a)}$ or $\mathsf{C(b)}$. Since none of these is guaranteed to hold in all models, $\mathsf{ACC}_\mathcal{L}(\mathcal{O}) = \emptyset$. Adding closed-world semantics to C by means of the translated default rule $(1 : \neg \mathsf{C}(X)) \leftarrow \mathsf{not}(1 : \mathsf{C}(X))$ yields two equilibria, corresponding to the two extensions of the corresponding default rule: $\{\mathsf{C(a)}, \neg \mathsf{C(b)}\}$ and $\{\mathsf{C(b)}, \neg \mathsf{C(a)}\}$. With the approach from [3], $\mathsf{ACC}_\mathcal{L}(\mathcal{O})$ contains the three models $\{\mathsf{C(a)}, \neg \mathsf{C(b)}\}$, $\{\mathsf{C(b)}, \neg \mathsf{C(a)}\}$ and $\{\mathsf{C(a)}, \mathsf{C(b)}\}$. The bridge rule above has no effect, and adding it to the corresponding MCS still yields three equilibria, one of which does not correspond to an extension.

The pattern **Default rule** generalizes default rules to MCSs not generated from an ontology. Furthermore, allowing literals from other contexts in the body of rules we can encode more general default rules. We can then see minimal equilibria for MCSs with applications of this pattern as generalized default extensions, systematically approximating closed-world reasoning in a standard way.

To obtain *true* closed-world reasoning (so that the MCS in Example 2 would be inconsistent, as $\mathcal{O}$ is inconsistent with the closed-world assumption) one could define ACC_i as a binary operator, allowing different treatment of the original belief state and the conclusions derived from the application of bridge rules.

Working with alignments. Another problem that occurs quite often in practice is that of reasoning within the merge of two ontologies without actually constructing the merged ontology. An *alignment* [25] between two ontologies $\mathcal{O}_1$ and $\mathcal{O}_2$ is a set $\mathcal{A}$ of atoms $t(P, Q)$ where P is a concept (or role) from $\mathcal{O}_1$, Q is a concept (resp. role) from $\mathcal{O}_2$, and $t \in \{\mathsf{subsumed}, \mathsf{subsumes}, \mathsf{equivalent}, \mathsf{disjoint}\}$.

Definition 2. *Let $\mathcal{O}_1$ and $\mathcal{O}_2$ be two ontologies and $\mathcal{A}$ be an alignment between them. The MCS induced by $\mathcal{A}$ is $M(\mathcal{O}_1, \mathcal{O}_2, \mathcal{A})$, containing $\mathsf{Ctx}(\mathcal{O}_1)$ and $\mathsf{Ctx}(\mathcal{O}_2)$ with the following bridge rules: for each triple $\mathsf{subsumed}(P, Q) \in \mathcal{A}$,*

$$(2 : Q(X)) \leftarrow (1 : P(X)) \qquad and \qquad (1 : \neg P(X)) \leftarrow (2 : \neg Q(X)) \qquad (2)$$

if P, Q are concepts; for each triple $\mathsf{disjoint}(P, Q) \in \mathcal{A}$,

$$(2 : \neg Q(X)) \leftarrow (1 : P(X)) \qquad and \qquad (1 : \neg P(X)) \leftarrow (2 : Q(X)) \qquad (3)$$

if P, Q are concepts; or the binary counterparts of these, if P, Q are roles. The triple $\mathsf{subsumes}(P, Q)$ is treated as $\mathsf{subsumed}(Q, P)$, and $\mathsf{equivalent}(P, Q)$ is seen as the conjunction of $\mathsf{subsumed}(P, Q)$ and $\mathsf{subsumed}(Q, P)$.

Again this achieves a merge of $\mathcal{O}_1$ and $\mathcal{O}_2$ at the level of the individuals in the import domain – we cannot reason e.g. about the potential subsumption of a concept from $\mathcal{O}_1$ by a concept from $\mathcal{O}_2$. Still, this construction is useful as it avoids the extra step of constructing a new ontology.

There is a more practical aspect of this approach that we can ameliorate: when querying $M(\mathcal{O}_1, \mathcal{O}_2, \mathcal{A})$, one must know where the concept or role in the query originates from. This issue can be bypassed by applying **Group Encapsulation** to hide the two contexts in this MCS.

Pattern *Alignment*.

Problem. We want to reason about the instances in the merge of two ontologies $\mathcal{O}_1$ and $\mathcal{O}_2$ w.r.t. a given (consistent) alignment $\mathcal{A}$, without building the merged ontology.

Solution. Apply **Group Encapsulation** to $M(\mathcal{O}_1, \mathcal{O}_2, \mathcal{A})$.

This design pattern assumes that $\mathcal{A}$ is consistent; however, it may happen that $\mathcal{A}$ is not guaranteed to be consistent. To avoid inconsistencies at the level of the instances, we may use the more robust technique from [22], taking the maximal consistent merge of $\mathcal{O}_1$ and $\mathcal{O}_2$ by writing the alignment triples as default rules. This translates to constructing $M'(\mathcal{O}_1, \mathcal{O}_2, \mathcal{A})$ as $M(\mathcal{O}_1, \mathcal{O}_2, \mathcal{A})$ but replacing the bridge rules with those obtained by **Default Rule**, protecting the context from the introduction of (explicit) inconsistencies. For example, if C and D are concepts, then subsumed(C, D) would yield

$$(2 : D(X)) \leftarrow (1 : C(X)), \text{not } (2 : \neg D(X))$$
$$(1 : \neg C(X)) \leftarrow (2 : \neg D(X)), \text{not } (1 : C(X))$$

Example 3. Suppose $\mathcal{O}_1$ has the instance axioms $\mathsf{C(a)}$ and $\mathsf{C(b)}$, $\mathcal{O}_2$ only has the axiom $\neg\mathsf{D(a)} \sqcup \neg\mathsf{D(b)}$, and $\mathcal{A}$ contains subsumed(C, D). Then $M'(\mathcal{O}_1, \mathcal{O}_2, \mathcal{A})$ has two equilibria: $\langle\{\mathsf{C(a)}, \mathsf{C(b)}\}, \{\mathsf{D(a)}, \neg\mathsf{D(b)}\}\rangle$ and $\langle\{\mathsf{C(a)}, \mathsf{C(b)}\}, \{\neg\mathsf{D(a)}, \mathsf{D(b)}\}\rangle$. In both, the semantics of D is maximal (it includes as many instances of C as it may consistently do), but none satisfies the alignment axiom $\mathsf{C} \sqsubseteq \mathsf{D}$ since $\mathcal{A}$ is inconsistent with $\mathcal{O}_1$ and $\mathcal{O}_2$.

There is a drawback to this construction: the number of bridge rules grows with the number of concepts and roles in $\mathcal{O}_1$ and $\mathcal{O}_2$. It would be useful to be able to write these bridge rules in a second-order language, e.g. the first rule in (2) would become $(2 : D(X)) \leftarrow (0 : \mathsf{subsumes}(C, D)), (1 : C(X))$ where context C_0 is simply $\mathcal{A}$. The interesting aspect is that context C_0 can be seen as a relational (first-order) context – it is the usage of its "constants" as predicate names in the bridge rules that gives them a higher-order nature. We are currently developing a formal theory of MCSs with higher-order rules.

6   Conclusions

In this paper we addressed several issues related to the flow of information between the several components of a relational MCS, presenting general-purpose design patterns that systematize the constructs supporting this communication.

Due to the specific semantics of bridge rules, these constructions only affect the individuals in the import domains of the contexts where new predicates are defined. This apparent limitation is essential to avoid fundamental inconsistency and undecidability problems: the main advantage of these design patterns is precisely allowing one to mimic extending the expressiveness of a context for one particular definition in a way that, in its full generality, would render the context inconsistent or undecidable.

We also discuss constructions adapted to working with ontologies, introducing a new definition of context generated from an ontology, fundamentally different from previous work [3], capturing the nature of the open- vs closed-world semantics in the form required to allow fine-tuning of the particular interpretation for specific predicates.

The development of these design patterns also suggests syntactic extensions to MCSs: making the consequence operator binary, allowing different treatment of data from the knowledge base and data inferred from application of bridge rules, in order to have true closed-world reasoning; and higher-order bridge rules, where the result of queries to one context can be used to decide *which* predicates to use on subsequent queries to other contexts, or even *to which* context those queries should be made. The last construct has been used in the form of meta-level notation, as an abbreviation for a set of rules, in previous work [11,19]. We are currently working on making these two constructions first-class citizens of MCSs, allowing them in the syntax of bridge rules and studying their semantics.

References

1. Antoniou, G.: A tutorial on default logics. ACM Computing Surveys 31(3), 337–359 (1999)
2. Antoy, S., Hanus, M.: Functional logic design patterns. In: Hu, Z., Rodríguez-Artalejo, M. (eds.) FLOPS 2002. LNCS, vol. 2441, pp. 67–87. Springer, Heidelberg (2002)
3. Brewka, G., Eiter, T.: Equilibria in heterogeneous nonmonotonic multi-context systems. In: AAAI 2007, pp. 385–390. AAAI Press (2007)
4. Brewka, G., Eiter, T., Fink, M., Weinzierl, A.: Managed multi-context systems. In: Walsh, T. (ed.) IJCAI, pp. 786–791. IJCAI/AAAI (2011)
5. Brewka, G., Niemelä, I., Truszczyński, M.: Nonmonotonic reasoning. In: van Harmelen, F., Lifschitz, V., Porter, B. (eds.) Handbook of Knowledge Representation, ch. 6, pp. 239–284. Elsevier (2008)
6. de Bruijn, J., Ehrig, M., Feier, C., Martíns-Recuerda, F., Scharffe, F., Weiten, M.: Ontology mediation, merging, and aligning. In: Davies, J., Studer, R., Warren, P. (eds.) Semantic Web Technologies: Trends and Research in Ontology-based Systems, John Wiley & Sons, Ltd., Chichester (2006)
7. Cóbe, R., Wassermann, R.: Ontology merging and conflict resolution: Inconsistency and incoherence solving approaches. In: Workshop on Belief change, Nonmonotonic reasoning and Conflict Resolution, BNC (2012)
8. Cruz-Filipe, L., Gaspar, G., Nunes, I.: Information flow within relational multi-context systems. Technical Report 2014;03, Faculty of Sciences of the University of Lisbon (September 2014), http://hdl.handle.net/10455/6900

9. Cruz-Filipe, L., Henriques, R., Nunes, I.: Description logics, rules and multi-context systems. In: McMillan, K., Middeldorp, A., Voronkov, A. (eds.) LPAR-19 2013. LNCS, vol. 8312, pp. 243–257. Springer, Heidelberg (2013)
10. Cruz-Filipe, L., Nunes, I., Gaspar, G.: Patterns for interfacing between logic programs and multiple ontologies. In: Filipe, J., Dietz, J. (eds.) KEOD 2013, pp. 58–69. INSTICC (2013)
11. Dao-Tran, M., Eiter, T., Fink, M., Krennwallner, T.: Dynamic distributed nonmonotonic multi-context systems. In: Brewka, G., Marek, V., Truszczynski, M. (eds.) Nonmonotonic Reasoning, Essays Celebrating its 30th Anniversary. Studies in Logic, vol. 31. College Publications (2011)
12. Dou, D., McDermott, D., Qi, P.: Ontology translation by ontology merging and automated reasoning. In: Ontologies for Agents: Theory and Experiences, pp. 73–94. Springer (2005)
13. Eiter, T., Ianni, G., Lukasiewicz, T., Schindlauer, R.: Well-founded semantics for description logic programs in the semantic Web. ACM Transactions on Computational Logic 12(2) (2011) Article Nr 11
14. Eiter, T., Ianni, G., Schindlauer, R., Tompits, H.: A uniform integration of higher-order reasoning and external evaluations in answer-set programming. In: Kaelbling, L.P., Saffiotti, A. (eds.) IJCAI 2005, pp. 90–96. Professional Book Center (2005)
15. Fink, M., Ghionna, L., Weinzierl, A.: Relational information exchange and aggregation in multi-context systems. In: Delgrande, J.P., Faber, W. (eds.) LPNMR 2011. LNCS, vol. 6645, pp. 120–133. Springer, Heidelberg (2011)
16. Fowler, M.: Patterns of Enterprise Application Architecture. Addison–Wesley (2002)
17. Gamma, E., Helm, R., Johnson, R., Vlissides, J.: Design Patterns: Elements of Reusable Object-Oriented Software. Addison–Wesley (1995)
18. Gangemi, A., Presutti, V.: Ontology design patterns. In: Staab, S., Studer, R. (eds.) Handbook on Ontologies, 2nd edn. International Handbooks on Information Systems, pp. 221–243. Springer (2009)
19. Homola, M., Knorr, M., Leite, J., Slota, M.: MKNF knowledge bases in multi-context systems. In: Fisher, M., van der Torre, L., Dastani, M., Governatori, G. (eds.) CLIMA XIII 2012. LNCS, vol. 7486, pp. 146–162. Springer, Heidelberg (2012)
20. Kim, J., Jang, M., Ha, Y.-g., Sohn, J.-C., Lee, S.J.: MoA: OWL ontology merging and alignment tool for the semantic web. In: Ali, M., Esposito, F. (eds.) IEA/AIE 2005. LNCS (LNAI), vol. 3533, pp. 722–731. Springer, Heidelberg (2005)
21. Maedche, A., Motik, B., Silva, N., Volz, R.: MAFRA – A mApping fRAmework for distributed ontologies. In: Gómez-Pérez, A., Benjamins, V.R. (eds.) EKAW 2002. LNCS (LNAI), vol. 2473, pp. 235–250. Springer, Heidelberg (2002)
22. Meyer, T.A., Lee, K., Booth, R.: Knowledge integration for description logics. In: Veloso, M.M., Kambhampati, S. (eds.) AAAI 2005, pp. 645–650. AAAI Press / The MIT Press (2005)
23. Motik, B., Rosati, R.: Reconciling description logics and rules. Journal of the ACM 57 (June 2010) Article Nr 30
24. Reiter, R.: A logic for default reasoning. Artificial Intelligence 13, 81–132 (1980)
25. Scharffe, F., Zamazal, O., Fensel, D.: Ontology alignment design patterns. Knowledge and Information Systems, 1–28 (April 2013)
26. Sterling, L.: Patterns for Prolog programming. In: Kakas, A.C., Sadri, F. (eds.) Computational Logic: Logic Programming and Beyond. LNCS (LNAI), vol. 2407, pp. 374–401. Springer, Heidelberg (2002)

Using Linked Data to Diversify Search Results a Case Study in Cultural Heritage

Chris Dijkshoorn[1], Lora Aroyo[1], Guus Schreiber[1],
Jan Wielemaker[1], and Lizzy Jongma[2]

[1] Computer Science, The Network Institute, VU University Amsterdam
{c.r.dijkshoorn,lora.aroyo,guus.schreiber,jan.wielemaker}@vu.nl
[2] Rijksmuseum Amsterdam, The Netherlands
l.jongma@rijksmuseum.nl

Abstract. In this study we consider wether, and to what extent, additional semantics in the form of Linked Data can help diversifying search results. We undertake this study in the domain of cultural heritage. The data consists of collection data of the Rijksmuseum Amsterdam together with a number of relevant external vocabularies, which are all published as Linked Data. We apply an existing graph search algorithm to this data, using entries from the museum query log as test set. The results show that in this domain an increase in diversity can be achieved through adding external vocabularies. We also analyse why some vocabularies have a significant effect, while others influence the results only marginally.

Keywords: Linked Data, Diversity, Semantic Search, Cultural Heritage.

1 Introduction

One of the promises of Linked Data is that it can be used to achieve richer, more diverse search results. This paper reports on a case study on diversifying search results that we performed in the domain of cultural heritage. Cultural heritage is a knowledge-rich domain, in which many external vocabularies are available, often as Linked Data. Also, we expect that, given the nature of the domain, a significant group of users would be interested in retrieving a more diverse palette of search results than the standard ones. For example, searching for "Rembrandt" should provide you with much more insights and related artworks than just his master pieces.

As data for this study we used the collection data of the Rijksmuseum Amsterdam. We enriched the collection metadata with a number of external vocabularies that have been published as Linked Data, such as the Art & Architecture Thesaurus, WordNet and Iconclass. We employ an existing graph search algorithm to find search results [13]. This algorithm finds paths in the graph from the search term to target objects, in this case artworks. The algorithm also clusters the results by classifying paths and grouping the results with similar path classes. Two example clusters for the search term "rembrandt" would be works with as creator 'rembrandt' and works in a location labelled with "rembrandt"

K. Janowicz et al. (Eds.): EKAW 2014, LNAI 8876, pp. 109–120, 2014.

(e.g., the Rembrandt House). In this study we use the number of resulting clusters and the path length as indicators of diversity. As sample queries we collected the terms in the museum's query log for the duration of one month. We see this study as a step towards showing how Linked Data could be used to create a richer search experience. Showing this might help to make institutions aware of the potential added value of investing in Linked Data.

This paper is structured as follows. In the next section we discuss related work. Section 3 describes the collection data and Linked Data used in the study. In Section 4 we discuss the experimental setup, including the test set and the graph search algorithm. Results are discussed in Section 5. In Section 6 we reflect on the results and consider future directions.

2   Related Work

A lot of work has been done on integrating cultural heritage collections and linking them to external sources. Hyvonen et al. created a portal to integrated collections of Finnish museums, using semantic web techniques [5]. Europeana is an initiative which supports the integration of European cultural heritage collections [6]. It comprises over 26 million metadata records, originating from more than 2,000 cultural heritage institutions. The aggregation comes at a cost, the collections have to adhere to the Europeana Data Model, which can result in a loss of semantic relations.

De Boer et. al. describe a methodology of publishing collections as Linked Data while preserving the rich semantics [2]. Similar methodology is applied by Szekely et al. in [9]. They stress the importance of high data quality for museums. By integrating collections and linking them to external vocabularies the amount of available data increases, giving rise to the need for structured means to access the information [3].

Researchers at Europeana clustered artworks at different granularities to create an overall picture and provide users with related objects [11]. The clustering approach is useful for identifying duplicate records, although at lower granularities users had difficulties explaining why artworks were clustered together. Regularities in the Linked Data cloud can be used to cluster, while still being able to explain how the objects are related. Hollink et al. use predefined patterns to improve image search [4] and similar paths are successfully used in a content based-recommender system [12].

There is a growing interest in the diversification of search results in the field of information science. Introducing more diverse results is used to address the ambiguity of keyword queries. Agrawal et al. assign topics to the user intent and documents and optimise the chance that the user is satisfied by the results [1].

An increasing number of systems use Linked Data to support users. Mismuseos[1] lets you search in integrated Spanish art collections and refine results using filters and facets. Constitute includes RDF representations of over 700

---

[1] http://www.mismuseos.net/

constitutions and lets users search and compare them[2]. Seevl uses semantic web techniques to provide search and discovery services over musical entities [7]. The BBC is developing a system to open up their radio archives, automatically annotating audio fragments and using crowdsourcing mechanisms to refine the data [8].

3 Data

In this section we describe the characteristics of the collection data of the Rijksmuseum and its links to external vocabularies. An overview of the datasets and how these are connected is given in Figure 1.

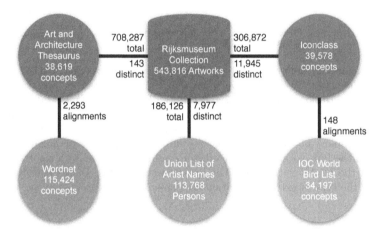

Fig. 1. Overview of Rijksmuseum collection data and links to external vocabularies

The **Rijksmuseum collection** consists of around 1,000,000 artworks. Around 25% of the collection is available in a digital form: some 180,000 prints and 70,000 other works have been digitised. Catalogers have added annotations to the records, when possible originating from structured vocabularies.

The Rijksmuseum provides through a non-public API access to 550,000 collection objects. This server provides data in the format of the RDF-based Europeana Data Model (EDM) [6]. Figure 2 shows an example of an object represented in EDM. The format makes a distinction between the unique "work" and (possibly multiple) digital representations and metadata descriptions of the work. EDM thus caters for alternative representations of the same object in different (sub)collections.

The **Iconclass vocabulary**[3] is designed to be used to annotate subjects, themes and motifs in Western art. Iconclass is available as linked data since

---

[2] https://www.constituteproject.org/
[3] http://www.iconclass.org/help/lod

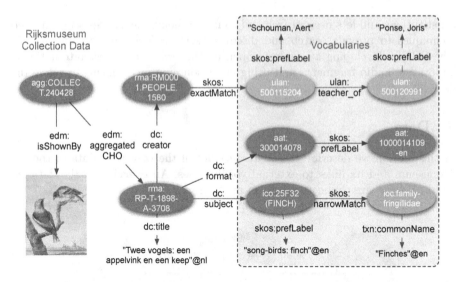

Fig. 2. Rijksmuseum artwork "Two birds". The top-left resource (`agg:COLLECT.240428`) represents the actual "work". The work has a digital representation (bottom-left) and a metadata description (`rma:RP-T-1898-A-3708`)[5]. Four pieces of metadata are shown: the title is represented as a literal, the subject is an Iconclass category, the format points to an AAT concept, and the creator of the work is represented with a resource from an in-house vocabulary of artists. The Iconclass subject category has an alignment with a bird class in the IOC vocabulary. The creator resource is aligned with a corresponding resource in the ULAN vocabulary. The link between the two ULAN concepts is one example of the type of extra information accessible through this alignment.

2012, containing almost 40,000 resources. Iconclass categories are defined using a code grammar. For example, the top-level category *Nature* has code 2; the category *song birds* has code 25F32. The category hierarchy is modelled using `skos:broader` and `skos:narrower` predicates. In this study we use some 300,000 links from collection objects to Iconclass categories.

The Getty research institute compiles, maintains and distributes vocabularies that focus on visual arts and architecture, in particular (i) the **Union List of Artist Names** (ULAN), (ii) the **Art & Architecture Thesaurus** (AAT), and (iii) the **Thesaurus of Geographic Names** (TGN). For this study we chose to link the Rijksmuseum collection to AAT and ULAN. AAT has 77,470 resources describing techniques, materials and styles which artworks can have in common. In this experiment we use the recently released Linked Data version of AAT[4]. ULAN includes biographic information about 113,768 artists and is in addition a valuable source of relations between persons, such as "collaborated with" and "teacher of". We use the XML version of ULAN converted to RDF and create links with the collection based on string matching.

---

[4] http://www.getty.edu/research/tools/vocabularies/lod/

WordNet is a source of lexical information about the English language. It provides short descriptions of words, groups words with the same meaning into synsets and defines the semantic relations between those sets. We use the Word-Net 2.0 version published by W3C [6], comprising over 79,000 nouns, 13,000 verbs and 3,000 adverbs. We reuse the 2,293 alignments made between AAT and Word-Net by Tordai et al. [10].

The International Ornithologists Union maintains a comprehensive list of bird names. We convert the XML version of this **IOC World Bird**[7] to RDF, adding labels from the multilingual version. This results in a taxonomy of 34,197 concepts describing the orders, families, genera, species and subspecies of birds and the corresponding structure. We manually align the bird concepts of Iconclass to matching concepts in the IOC vocabulary.

4   Methods

4.1   Experimental Setup

Firstly, we investigated how many query terms have matches in the dataset. For this purpose we collected query terms on the Rijksmuseum website during one month (see Section 4.2 below). The terms are then matched with the literal index of the triple store containing the collection data and the five external vocabularies. As the frequency of the query term might be a factor influencing the number of matches, we split the list of query terms into three sublists, containing respectively the high, medium and low-frequency query terms. The query terms are split in such a way that the three sums of the number of times, that the queries in a sublist are used, are equal for each split.

Secondly, we explore to what extent the external semantics improve semantic search results. To this end we use an existing semantic search algorithm (see Section 4.3 below for details) to perform a search on all query terms. We do this five times, each time with a different dataset configuration: (i) only collection data, (ii) AAT and WodNet added, (iii) Iconclass and IOC added, (iv) ULAN added, and (v) all vocabularies added. The reason for combining AAT with WordNet and Iconclass with IOC stems from the dependencies between these vocabularies, as shown in Figure 1.

The graph search algorithm delivers the results in clusters of semantically similar results. Per obtained cluster we analyse the path length in the graph as well as the number of clusters. This gives us per query information about the average path length, average number of clusters and average number of results. The results of this analysis are again split in three parts according to the query frequencies (high, medium, low).

The code developed for these experiments as well as the resulting data are available online[8].

---

[6] http://www.w3.org/TR/wordnet-rdf/

[7] http://www.worldbirdnames.org/ioc-lists/

[8] https://github.com/rasvaan/cluster_search_experimental_data

4.2   Query Logs

We used the query logs of January 2014 of the Rijksmuseum. From these logs we extracted all distinct query terms used plus their frequency. This provided us with 48,733 unique query terms. We filtered out 4,074 terms because they were either object IDs[9] or were in some other way erroneous. The resulting set of 44,659 query terms was used in the experiments. The split into frequency groups of query terms resulted in 2,393 terms in the high split (high frequency), 16,963 query terms in the medium split (medium frequency), and 25,303 terms in the low split (low frequency).

It should be noted that these queries were made against the collection data without the external vocabularies. This causes a bias because the collection data contain mainly Dutch terms and therefore users who have used the search interface before are likely to refrain from using English search terms, knowing that these are of limited value.

4.3   Graph Search

We developed a semantic search system that enables the exploration of collections by using a keyword query to produce clusters of semantically related objects[10]. We use the graph search algorithm as described in [13]. The algorithm matches the query term with literals in the triplestore, using stemming. When the match exceeds a given threshold it is added to a list. The literals in this list are used as a starting point to traverse the graph structured data. This traversal continues registering the times a specified target class is found, all the while recoding the steps it makes. The starting literal and successive properties and resources used as steps, form the path in the graph which serves as the basis for clustering. For clustering the properties in the path are abstracted to their root properties when possible. In addition resources are abstracted to their class, unless they are a concept. This allows to merge clusters based on similar semantics.

5   Results

We have collected data of four types:

- The number of query terms in the test set that have, in principle, matches in the dataset.
- The number of search results for each of the query terms in the dataset with and without the external Linked Data.
- The number of clusters of search results for each of the query terms in the dataset with and without the external Linked Data.
- The distribution of path lengths of search results for each of the query terms in the dataset with and without subsets of the external Linked Data.

---

[9] Some problems with the existing query interface can be circumvented by entering directly an object ID of an artwork, e.g. SK-A-4979. For the purposes of this study we left out the query terms resulting from this practice.

[10] http://sealinc.ops.few.vu.nl/clustersearch/

Matches between Query Terms and Dataset. In Figure 3 can be seen that 94% of the query terms in the high frequency split match literals in the collection data. ULAN and AAT match over 50% and continue to match many query terms in the lower splits. WordNet, Iconclass and IOC have less matches, with the IOC percentage on all splits below 12%. There is a decrease between the query frequency splits, were in the low split all the matches in external vocabularies are less than 23%.

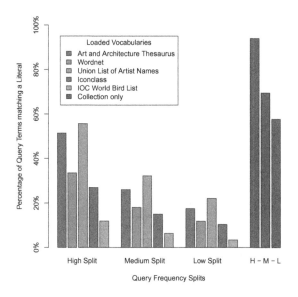

Fig. 3. Bar chart showing the percentage of query terms that match with a label in the vocabularies

To illustrate, the query term "rembrandt" matches in AAT, ULAN, and the collection data. Where in the collection and ULAN labels of "Rembrandt van Rijn" are matched, AAT matches "Rembrandt frames". The query term "watercolor" has no match in the collection data, but does match in AAT, ULAN, and WordNet. In AAT it matches materials and a technique, in ULAN descriptions of painters and in WordNet the type of paint in addition to the watercolour painting as an object.

The numbers above give an indication of the potential in the data to be used for search. It depends on actual links between resources in the dataset on whether these can actually be used during search.

Search Results Per Query. Figure 4 shows the overall increase of search results when the external vocabularies are loaded. The increase is marked but moderate. The increase is highest in the third quartile of the high split; the quartile raises from 214.0 to 268.8. The mean increases from 81.5 to 104.5 search results. To give an example, when the external vocabularies are loaded the query term "rembrandt" has 674 instead of 636 results. Instead of no results, "watercolor" increases to 9 results. It should be pointed out that the number of clusters (not shown here, see below) influences the maximum number of results, as the algorithm imposes a maximum of 100 search results per cluster.

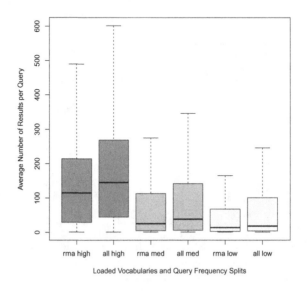

Fig. 4. Overall number of search of results per query term. The boxes marked as "rma" represent the baseline (collection data only); the boxes marked with "all" represent the search results with all vocabularies loaded.

Clusters Per Query. Figure 5 shows how the number of clusters of search results increases when the external vocabularies are loaded. The median increases with one for the medium and high splits. There is also a marked increase in the range: some queries apparently lead to a large number of clusters. Thus, the external vocabularies not only lead to more results, but also more diversified results.

The number of clusters for the query term "rembrandt" increases from 12 to 15, adding for example a cluster of paintings of "Pieter Lastman" who was a teacher of Rembrandt and paintings of "Salomon Koninck" who was, according to ULAN, an ardent follower of Rembrandt. One cluster is found for "watercolor", containing water colour paintings by "Pieter Withoos", based on the descriptive note "He specialized in watercolors of insects and flowers.". An example of a query term leading to a large number of clusters is "rubens": 8 clusters are created

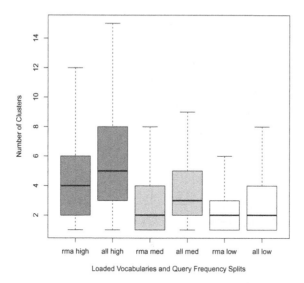

Fig. 5. Box plot of the number of clusters per query. The boxes marked as "rma" represent the baseline (collection data only); the boxes marked with "all" represent the search results with all vocabularies loaded.

with the collection data loaded, 15 with the external vocabularies loaded, adding among others clusters about students and assistants of Peter Paul Rubens.

Path Length Per Query. Finally, we look at the path length of search results. A longer path length suggests a diversification of results. For path length we have looked at the contribution that the different vocabularies give to the path length. This can provide us an indication which vocabularies are most useful.

Figure 6 shows how the path length of the search results changes when particular vocabularies are loaded. The first column shows the baseline, where the path length is either 1 or 2. We see that adding AAT plus WordNet or Iconclass plus IOC has hardly any effect on the path length. The Union List of Artist Names (ULAN) has a significant effect on the path length. ULAN leads to 22% of the paths being longer than 2, up to paths of length 15.

ULAN is actually responsible for almost the complete path length diversity (see last column). We can see an example of this phenomenon when we look again at the keyword query "rubens". The following path generated a cluster with artworks of a student of Peter Paul Rubens:

Rubens, Peter Paul → teacher of → Dyck, Anthony van
Dyck, Anthony van → creator → <several artworks>

Why does only ULAN contribute significantly to the diversity of path lengths? If we look at Figure 1 we see that ULAN has the highest number of links from the

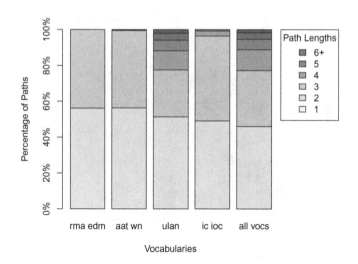

Fig. 6. Path lengths of search results, shown as percentage of all search results. The first column shows the baseline (only collection data); columns 2-4 depicts the three (groups of) vocabularies separately; column 5 shows the situation when all external vocabularies are loaded.

collection data to distinct resources in ULAN. Also, the structure of ULAN (with many crosslinks such as "teacher" and "collaborator") makes it suitable for search diversification. In contrast, the links to AAT involve only a limited number of AAT resources, and are possibly not of much interest to users (typically things like "canvas", "oil paint" and "print").

Iconclass does have, like ULAN, many links from the collection data to distinct Iconclass resources and also interesting internal links. The likely reason why this does not lead to more search results is probably that Iconclass does not have Dutch labels. The test set of query terms came from the current search facility which works only with Dutch-language metadata. Assuming this has led to a limited usage of other languages for search, Iconclass resources were of little use for this test set. So, this part of the results is likely to be biased by the test set.

6   Discussion

This case study suggests that Linked Data in the form of vocabularies can indeed be used to diversify search results to meet the needs of a significant group of users, e.g. general audience and humanities scholars, that would be interested in retrieving a more diverse palette of search results beyond just the standard and popular ones. Moreover, diversifying search results helps also the collection owners in promoting specific parts of their collection.

The results show that for this application domain we can achieve (i) an increase in number of results, and (ii) indirectly through the number of clusters and the path length, an increase in the semantic variety of search results. However, not all vocabularies appear to be equally useful. Thus, it is important for collection owners to know the influence of each vocabulary on the accessibility of their collections, and further integrate this in the strategies for collection annotation. Based on this study we hypothesise that the usefulness of vocabularies for diversification of search results depends on the following two factors:

1. the number of links between distinct vocabulary resources and the metadata of target search objects;
2. the richness of the internal links between vocabulary objects;

Results clearly show that vocabularies, such as ULAN and Iconclass, which provide rich semantics for additional context (e.g. relation between people and their roles) have significant influence on the diversity of the results. In previous studies [12] and related work [11], [4] we also show that these vocabularies are a valuable source of context and relevance for end users.

This study has a number of limitations. Firstly, our test set is a set of query terms (44.5K) that came from logs of the existing search log of the institution involved. People, who use a search interface multiple times, are likely to limit their search to terms that work well with this interface. Therefore, the fact that the Iconclass vocabulary did not contribute a lot to diversity, may be a result of this bias. Secondly, there is not yet a set of standard semantic-search algorithms. It could well be the case that other algorithms lead to different results with the same data and test set. Also, clusters and path length are indirect indicators of diversity. More studies are needed to show how valuable these indicators are and how they compare to diversity measures as introduced in [1]. Thirdly, the data set we used is limited in nature. It would be good to perform studies like these also in large, more heterogeneous datasets.

With this study we show the promise and added-value of Linked Data for diversifying search results. We plan on extending this work by adding additional external vocabularies and investigating ways of increasing the density of the links between the collection and vocabularies.

Acknowledgements. This publication was supported by the Dutch national program COMMIT/. We are grateful to all our project colleagues for the discussions on this subject.

References

1. Agrawal, R., Gollapudi, S., Halverson, A., Ieong, S.: Diversifying search results. In: Proceedings of the Second ACM International Conference on Web Search and Data Mining, WSDM 2009, pp. 5–14. ACM, New York (2009)

2. de Boer, V., Wielemaker, J., van Gent, J., Hildebrand, M., Isaac, A., van Ossenbruggen, J., Schreiber, G.: Supporting Linked Data Production for Cultural Heritage Institutes: The Amsterdam Museum Case Study. In: Simperl, E., Cimiano, P., Polleres, A., Corcho, O., Presutti, V. (eds.) ESWC 2012. LNCS, vol. 7295, pp. 733–747. Springer, Heidelberg (2012)

3. Grimnes, G.A., Edwards, P., Preece, A.D.: Instance based clustering of semantic web resources. In: Bechhofer, S., Hauswirth, M., Hoffmann, J., Koubarakis, M. (eds.) ESWC 2008. LNCS, vol. 5021, pp. 303–317. Springer, Heidelberg (2008)

4. Hollink, L., Schreiber, G., Wielinga, B.: Patterns of semantic relations to improve image content search. Web Semantics Science Services and Agents on the World Wide Web 5(3), 195–203 (2007)

5. Hyvönen, E., Mäkelä, E., Salminen, M., Valo, A., Viljanen, K., Saarela, S., Junnila, M., Kettula, S.: Finnish museums on the semantic web. Web Semantics: Science, Services and Agents on the World Wide Web 3(2-3), 224–241 (2005)

6. Isaac, A., Haslhofer, B.: Europeana linked open data – data.europeana.eu. Semantic Web Journal 4(3), 291–297 (2013)

7. Passant, A.: seevl: mining music connections to bring context, search and discovery to the music you like. Semantic Web Challenge 2011 (2011)

8. Raimond, Y., Ferne, T.: The bbc world service archive prototype. Semantic Web Challenge 2013 (2013)

9. Szekely, P., Knoblock, C.A., Yang, F., Zhu, X., Fink, E.E., Allen, R., Goodlander, G.: Connecting the smithsonian american art museum to the linked data cloud. In: Cimiano, P., Corcho, O., Presutti, V., Hollink, L., Rudolph, S. (eds.) ESWC 2013. LNCS, vol. 7882, pp. 593–607. Springer, Heidelberg (2013)

10. Tordai, A., van Ossenbruggen, J., Schreiber, G., Wielinga, B.: Aligning large SKOS-like vocabularies: Two case studies. In: Aroyo, L., Antoniou, G., Hyvönen, E., ten Teije, A., Stuckenschmidt, H., Cabral, L., Tudorache, T. (eds.) ESWC 2010, Part I. LNCS, vol. 6088, pp. 198–212. Springer, Heidelberg (2010)

11. Wang, S., Isaac, A., Charles, V., Koopman, R., Agoropoulou, A., van der Werf, T.: Hierarchical structuring of cultural heritage objects within large aggregations. CoRR (2013)

12. Wang, Y., Stash, N., Aroyo, L., Gorgels, P., Rutledge, L., Schreiber, G.: Recommendations based on semantically enriched museum collections. Web Semantics: Science, Services and Agents on the World Wide Web 6(4), 283–290 (2008)

13. Wielemaker, J., Hildebrand, M., van Ossenbruggen, J., Schreiber, G.: Thesaurus-Based Search in Large Heterogeneous Collections. In: Sheth, A.P., Staab, S., Dean, M., Paolucci, M., Maynard, D., Finin, T., Thirunarayan, K. (eds.) ISWC 2008. LNCS, vol. 5318, pp. 695–708. Springer, Heidelberg (2008)

Personalised Access to Linked Data

Milan Dojchinovski and Tomas Vitvar

Web Intelligence Research Group
Faculty of Information Technology
Czech Technical University in Prague
`firstname.lastname@fit.cvut.cz`

Abstract. Recent efforts in the Semantic Web community have been primarily focused on developing technical infrastructure and technologies for efficient Linked Data acquisition, publishing and interlinking. Nevertheless, due to the huge and diverse amount of information, the actual access to a piece of information in the LOD cloud still demands significant amount of effort. In this paper, we present a novel configurable method for personalised access to Linked Data. The method recommends resources of interest from users with similar tastes. To measure the similarity between the users we introduce a novel resource semantic similarity metric, which takes into account the *commonalities* and *informativeness* of the resources. We validate and evaluate the method on a real-world dataset from the Web services domain. The results show that our method outperforms the other baseline methods in terms of accuracy, serendipity and diversity.

Keywords: personalisation, recommendation, Linked Data, semantic distance, similarity metric.

1 Introduction

In the past years, the Semantic Web community has been primarily focused on developing technical infrastructure and technologies to make the Web of Data feasible [3]. Consequently, these efforts led the development of various methods for Linked Data acquisition, publishing and interlinking, which gave birth to $1,091$ Linked Datasets (as of April 2014 [11]), which is an overall growth of 271% compared to only 294 datasets published in September 2011. Along with these efforts, many end-user applications that *consume* and *deliver* Linked Data have been developed. Between the most studied applications which leverage Linked Data are recommender systems. In a nutshell, Linked Data based recommender systems produce recommendations of Linked Data resources representing items of interest. To predict the resources of interest, they exploit the relations and interactions of the users with the resources. The problem of recommendation of Linked Data resources has been addressed in several recent methods [9,10,14,1,7,5,8]. However, proposed methods are primarily developed for a specific domain, they require manual pre-processing of the datasets and

K. Janowicz et al. (Eds.): EKAW 2014, LNAI 8876, pp. 121–136, 2014.

they can hardly be adapted to new datasets. Thus, there is a need of new sophisticated methods which will be enough robust to process Linked Data from different domains and provide accurate, while at the same time serendipitous and diverse Linked Data resource recommendations.

In this paper, we present a method for personalised access to Linked Data. The method recommends resources of interest for a user. It relies on the assumption that *if a person A and person B have interest in similar resources, then person A is likely to have interest in similar resources in the future, as person B*. To predict resources of interest, the method first measures the similarity between resources representing users, and then recommends resources from similar users. To measure the similarity between two resources in a Linked Data dataset, we propose a novel similarity measure which primarily relies on the shared information of the resources in an RDF graph. The similarity of the resources we compute based on their shared context (i.e., overlap of the surrounding RDF sub-graphs), which we call *resource context graphs*. When computing the similarity of the resources, our method takes into consideration 1) *the size of shared context*–the amount of common resources, 2) *the connectivity of each shared resource*–how well are the context resources connected with the users' resources, and 3) *the informativeness of each shared resource*–less probable resources are considered to be more specific, and consequently more informative than the more common ones. The resources' informativeness is primarily incorporated to differentiate informative shared resources from non-informative, such as resources of type *owl:Thing* or *skos:Concept*. A prototype of the method was implemented on top of the neo4j[1] graph database and we show a resource recommendation use case in the Web services domain. We evaluate the method on several experiments showing that the method produces highly accurate, serendipitous and diverse recommendations compared to the traditional recommendation techniques. For the evaluation we use a real-world dataset, the Linked Web APIs dataset, which is an RDF representation of the ProgrammableWeb[2], the largest Web service and mashup repository.

The reminder of the paper is as follows. Section 2 describes the method, its definitions and algorithms. Section 3 describes several experiments we run to validate and evaluate the method. Section 4 reports on existing methods that relate to ours. Section 5 provide discussions and future directions. Finally, Section 6 concludes the paper.

2   Personalised Resource Recommendation

We formulate the problem of personalised recommendation of resources as problem of ranking and recommending top-N most relevant resources. We base our method on the collaborative filtering technique: it estimates the similarity between users, and produces resource recommendations from users with similar tastes. To this end, we develop two novel graph-based metrics: 1) for measuring

---

[1] http://www.neo4j.org/

[2] http://www.programmableweb.com/

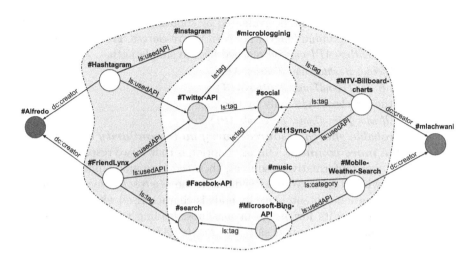

Fig. 1. Excerpt from the Linked Web APIs dataset with resource context graphs with context distance of 3

semantic resource similarity, and 2) for measuring *semantic resource relevance*. The first, we use to compute similarity between users represented as RDF resources. The second, uses the computed user similarities to estimate the relevance for each resource candidate.

The metric for measuring semantic resource similarity we develop based on a set of assumptions. The set of assumptions is as follows.

(i) **The more information two resources share, the more similar they are.** The first assumption is that if two resources share some information, then they are similar to each other. Considering an RDF graph, a shared information, as described in [1], might be an object of triples where subjects are the resources in question. In this case, only shared information in distance of one will be taken into consideration, when estimating their similarity. However, depending on the way the RDF data is modelled, similar resources might share information in any distance. Thus, in our method we allow adjustment of the context distance as required. Figure 1 shows an excerpt of the Linked Web APIs dataset (see Section 3.1 for more information about the dataset). In the figure, we present two context graphs with a distance of 3, for the users *Alfredo* and *mlachwani*. Considering the figure, the users have 6 resources in common. Note that if we choose a lower distance values, 1 or 2, no shared information will be evidenced.

(ii) **Better connected shared resources carry more similarity information.** According to the assumption, for the user *Alfredo*, the *Twitter-API* carries more similarity information than the *Facebook-API* or the *search* tag, since the *Twitter-API* is better connected to the resource representing the user *Alfredo*. This can be evaluated by counting the simple paths[3] with a pre-defined maximum length, between the resources. From the *Alfredo's* node the *Twitter-API* can be reached by two simple paths

$p_1 = \{Alfredo,\ Hashtagram,\ Twitter\text{-}API\}$

$p_2 = \{Alfredo,\ FriendLynx,\ Twitter\text{-}API\}$

, while the *Facebook-API* only by one

$p_3 = \{Alfredo,\ FriendLynx,\ Facebook\text{-}API\}$

(iii) **Less probable shared resources carry more similarity information than the more common.** Our assumption is that if two resources have in common more informative resources, then they are more similar. Considering the whole Linked Web APIs dataset, the *Microsoft-Bing-API* carries more information content, since its node is characterised with a low degree value 40 (due to its low usage in mashups, leading to a low number of incident links). On the other side, the *Twitter-API* and *Facebook-API* are popular Web APIs and extensively used in mashups, and their node degree values are 799 and 418, respectively. To conclude, the *Microsoft-Bing-API* is more informative than the *Twitter-API* and *Facebook-API* and will carry more similarity information.

Based on these assumptions, we develop our method for personalised resources recommendation. First, we propose a theoretical definition of Linked Data, followed by several definitions that we use to ground our metrics for computation of resource similarity and relevance. We present the algorithm that we use to compute the semantic similarity between resources, and the algorithm that uses the computed resource similarity to recommend relevant resources from similar users.

2.1   Definitions

Definition 1. *Let $\mathcal{G}$ be a Linked Data dataset defined as a graph $\mathcal{G} = (\mathcal{R}, \mathcal{L})$ in which $\mathcal{R} = \{r_1, r_2, ..., r_n\}$ is a set of resources identified with their URIs, and $\mathcal{L} = \{l_1, l_2, ..., l_m\}$ is a set of links (predicates) between those resources, where $l_i = (r_j, r_k)$ is a concrete link between two resources.*

While this definition describes one dataset, the LOD cloud can be described as union of all G_i datasets. Note that ontologies are not excluded from the definition, and they can be also modelled.

Definition 2. *Let $\mathcal{G}_{r_i,d} = (\mathcal{R}_i, \mathcal{L}_i)$ be a sub-graph of a Linked Data dataset graph $\mathcal{G}$ whose resources ($\mathcal{R}_i$) and links ($\mathcal{L}_i$) sets are subset of those of $\mathcal{G}$ with restriction that only nodes within maximum distance d from the resource r_i are included. We will further refer to this sub-graph as a **resource context graph**.*

Definition 3. *Let $\mathcal{C}_{r_i,r_j}$ be a set of resources shared by context graphs of the resources r_i and r_j. We will refer to this set of resources as a **shared context**.*

---

[3] Note that by *simple path* we mean a path without repeating vertices, as it is defined in the graph theory.

According to the assumption (iii), in order to give less impact to the less informative resources, we perform weightening of the resources based on the information content (IC) they convey. In the information theory [12], the information content of a concept is defined as the logarithm (i.e., with base 2) of the inverse of its probability

$$IC(c) = -\log(\pi(c)), \tag{1}$$

where $\pi(c)$ is the probability of occurrence of the concept c. The probability $\pi(c)$ is calculated as the quotient of the frequency of occurrence of c and the total number of concepts in the corpus. In the following definition we adopt the general definition of IC to be applicable in Linked Data.

Definition 4. *Let $RIC(r_i)$ be a function which computes the IC carried by a resource (RIC) defined as*

$$RIC(r_i) = -\log(\frac{deg(r_i)}{max\{deg(r_k) : r_k \in \mathcal{R}\}}) \tag{2}$$

where the probability of occurrence of a resource is computed as the quotient of $deg(r_i)$ – resource degree computed as the total number of incident links, and $max\{deg(r_k) : r_k \in \mathcal{R}\}$ – the degree of the resource with the highest degree. Computed resource information content is within the interval [0,1]. See Section 3.2 for actual computed information content of the resources in the Linked Web APIs dataset.

Definition 5. *Let $gain(p)$ be a function which computes the gain of information from one end to another in a simple path $p = \{r_1, r_2, ..., r_n\}$ where r_i is the i-th resource in the list of resources visited in the path from r_1 to r_n. We define the function for computing the information gain as*

$$gain(p) = \prod_{i=1}^{n} RIC(r_i) \tag{3}$$

Note that the gain function is a multiplicative function of RIC weights with values between 0 and 1, and computed gain for longer paths will be lower than for shorter paths. We use the function to compute the connectivity of a shared resource with a user's resource. For a closer shared resource (shorter path) the computed gain will be higher, than for the more distant shared resource (longer path).

2.2 Algorithm: *"Computing Resource Similarity"*

The similarity between two resources r_i and r_j we compute according to the following algorithm.

Inputs:
- Graph $\mathcal{G}$ representing a Linked Data dataset.

- A context graph $\mathcal{G}_{r_i,d_i} = (\mathcal{R}_i, \mathcal{L}_i)$ for r_i with context distance d_i.
- A context graph $\mathcal{G}_{r_j,d_j} = (\mathcal{R}_j, \mathcal{L}_j)$ for r_j with context distance d_j.
- A shared context set $\mathcal{C} = \{c_1, c_2, ..., c_n\}$ of the context graphs $\mathcal{G}_{r_i,d_i}$ and $\mathcal{G}_{r_j,d_j}$.

Output:

- A computed similarity sim_{ij} for the resources r_i and r_j.

Uses:

- A function $paths(r_i, r_j, d)$ that returns a set of all simple paths (with a maximum length d) between two resources.
- A function $gain(p)$ that computes the gain of information in a path p.

Algorithm:

1: *// compute the amount of similarity between the two resources*
2: *// as a sum of the similarity carried by each shared resource in $\mathcal{C}$*
3: $sim_{ij} \leftarrow 0$
4: **for all** $c_k \in \mathcal{C}$ **do**
5:    *// sum the information gained in all simple paths between*
6:    *// the resource r_i and the shared context resource c_k*
7:    $\mathcal{P}_i \leftarrow paths(r_i, c_k, d_i)$, $s_{r_i} \leftarrow 0$
8:    $s_{r_i} \leftarrow s_{r_i} + \sum_{p \in \mathcal{P}_i} gain(p)$
9:    *// sum the information gained in all simple paths between*
10:    *// the resource r_j and the shared context resource c_k*
11:    $\mathcal{P}_j \leftarrow paths(r_j, c_k, d_j)$, $s_{r_j} \leftarrow 0$
12:    $s_{r_j} \leftarrow s_{r_j} + \sum_{p \in \mathcal{P}_j} gain(p)$
13:    $sim_{ij} \leftarrow sim_{ij} + \frac{s_{r_i} + s_{r_j}}{2}$
14: **end for**

For each shared context resource c_k, the algorithm first retrieves all simple paths (lines 7 and 11) between the shared context resource c_k and the resources we compute similarity for (r_i and r_j). Next, In lines 8 and 12, the algorithm computes the gained information for each simple path taking into account the pre-computed resource informativeness. The algorithm independently computes the semantic similarity of the shared context resource c_k to the both resources (r_i and r_j). Finally, in line 13, the algorithm computes the semantic similarity carried by a single context resource, as an arithmetic mean of the computed similarity to the both resources (r_i and r_j). The final similarity score is computed as sum of the similarity information carried by each context resource.

2.3 Algorithm: *"Computing Resource Relevance"*

The computed resource similarity using the previous algorithm, is then used to compute the relevance of a resource candidate for a given user. The relevance of the resource for a user we compute according to the following algorithm.

Inputs:

- Graph $\mathcal{G}$ representing a Linked Data dataset.

- Resources r_u - a user requester, and r_c - a resource candidate.
- A set of users' resources $\mathcal{R}' = \{r_1, r_2, ..., r_n\}$, where $r_k \in \mathcal{R} \setminus r_u$.
- A set of user similarity scores $S = \{s_{u1}, s_{u2}, ..., s_{un}\}$, where s_{uk} is a semantic similarity computed with Alg 2.2 for the resource r_u and $r_k \in \mathcal{R}'$.

Output:
- A computed relevance score for the resource candidate r_c and the user r_i.

Uses:
- A function C that returns a resource context graph for a given resource.
- A function $paths(r_i, r_j, d)$ that returns a set of all simple paths (with a maximum length d) between two resources.
- A function $gain(p)$ that computes the gain of information in a path p.

Algorithm:
1:   $rel \leftarrow 0$
2: **for all** $r_k \in \mathcal{R}'$ **do**
3:    // create a resource context graph
4:    $\mathcal{G}_{r_k} \leftarrow C(r_k, d, \mathcal{G})$
5:    // check presence of the resource r_c in the context graph
6:    **if** $r_c \in \mathcal{G}_{r_k}$ **then**
7:     // sum the gain of information for all simple paths between
8:     // the user and the resource candidate
9:     $\mathcal{P} \leftarrow paths(r_c, r_k, d)$
10:     $rel \leftarrow rel + s_{uk} * \sum_{p_i \in \mathcal{P}} gain(p_i)$
11:    **end if**
12: **end for**

First, the algorithm creates a context graph for each user similar with the user r_u (line 4). Next, the algorithm checks whether the resource candidate is present in the context graph (line 6). If yes, the algorithm computes the connectivity of the similar user and the resource candidate r_c (lines 9–10). The connectivity is computed as sum of the gained information for all the simple paths between the user and the resource candidate r_c. In line 10, the algorithm also takes into account the pre–computed similarity score s_{uk} between the users. The final score is a sum of the relevance values computed from each similar user.

3   Experimental Evaluation

In this section, we describe the dataset used for validation and evaluation of the method. We present a resource recommendation use case and we report on the results from several experiments. In the experiments we addressed following set of questions:

- *What is the quality of the recommendations provided by our method in comparison with the other traditional methods?*
- *How the resource information content (RIC) influences the quality of the recommendations?*
- *How surprising and diverse recommendations generates the method?*

3.1 Dataset Description

In order to validate and evaluate the method, we opted for the Linked Web APIs dataset [2]. The Linked Web APIs dataset is an RDF dataset representing the ProgrammableWeb service repository. It consists of information about developers, mashups they have developed, Web APIs used for the mashups, tags and categories associated with the mashups and the Web APIs. Moreover, the dataset also contains technical information about the Web APIs, such as supported protocols and data formats.

The Linked Web APIs dataset re-uses several well-known ontologies developed by the community. We use concepts from the FOAF[4] ontology (prefix foaf) to represent the mashup developers (*foaf:Person*), concepts from the WSMO-lite[5] [15] ontology (prefix wl) to represent the Web APIs (*wl:Service*), and terms such as *dc:title* and *dc:creator* from the Dublin Core[6] vocabulary (prefix dc). Further, we create new concepts (*ls:Mashup, ls:Tag, ls:Category, ls:DataFormat*) and properties (*ls:format, ls:tag, ls:category, ls:usedAPI*) for which we use the ls prefix.

The dataset represents the information of the ProgrammableWeb repository as of April 24th 2014, and it contains over 170K RDF triples describing 11,339 APIs, 7,415 mashups and 5,907 users. Figure 1 shows an excerpt of the dataset.

3.2 Use-case: Resources Recommendations

In order to validate and demonstrate our method, we developed a resource recommendation use case for the Web services domain: recommendation of resources representing Web APIs. For this purpose we used the Linked Web APIs dataset. After loading the dataset, for each resource we compute its information content (see definition 4). Table 1 shows the top 5 resources with highest and lowest information content.

Table 1. Top 5 resources with highest (left) and lowest RIC (right)

Resource ID	Label	RIC (bits)	Resource ID	Label	RIC (bits)
27766	Paigeadele user	1.00000	7	Service class	0.00000
27871	retouching tag	0.92576	13	Mashup class	0.04550
28017	Pbwiki API	0.88233	34	Person class	0.06985
28015	Usefulbytes API	0.85151	39	Tag class	0.13267
28014	Philly add API	0.82761	12	mapping tag	0.13273

As expected, resources which are more distinctive, have higher RIC, and will have higher influence in the similarity computation, while the most probable resources, are less informative, and will have less influence in the similarity computation. For example, the resources representing ontological classes, such as the

---

[4] http://xmlns.com/foaf/0.1/

[5] http://www.w3.org/Submission/WSMO-Lite/

[6] http://dublincore.org/documents/dcmi-terms/

wl:Service or *ls:Mashup* class, carry less RIC due to their high degree value in the RDF graph. On the other side, sharing resource representing the tag *retouching* or the *Usefulbytes API*, will carry more RIC due to their low degree value.

Next, using the Algorithm 2.2 we compute the similarity between the resources representing users. In the Linked Web APIs dataset those are instances of the *foaf:Person* class. When computing the resource similarity it is necessary to set the context distance of resource context graphs (see definition 2). We experimentally set the context distance to 2, thus only resources within distance of 2 will be taken into account when creating the resource context graphs. In this case, only resources representing mashups, Web APIs and assigned tags will be present in the context graphs. See Section 5 for discussion on setting the resource context distance.

Finally, using the Algorithm 2.3 we compute the relevance between each user and each resource candidate. Here, we focused on computation of relevance only for instances of the class *wl:Service*, however, the relevance can be be computed for any other resources, e.g., categories, mashups and even users. Table 2 shows the top 5 most similar users with the user *Alfredo* and the top 5 Web APIs with highest relevance score, also for the user *Alfredo*.

Table 2. Top 5 most similar users with the user *Alfredo* (left) and the top 5 most relevant Web APIs (right)

Resource ID	Username	Similarity score	Resource ID	API Name	Relevance score
511	Avishai	2.11250	245	Twitter API	49.78257
731	Frogcologne	1.79806	10	Google Maps API	36.32023
20130	Nobosh	1.69410	129	Facebook API	33.34930
2505	Tripsailor	1.64018	331	Box API	27.85667
1407	Rakfl	1.63710	165	Flickr API	24.60448

3.3 Evaluation

In order to evaluate the quality of our method in terms of *accuracy* and *usefulness* of the recommendations, we followed standard evaluation protocols for recommender systems. For the evaluation we used the Linked Web APIs dataset and we randomly created training (80%) and testing partition (20%). This led to creation of 3,089 test cases.

For the evaluation of the accuracy we focused on several standard well-known metrics used for evaluation of recommender systems [4]. The metrics used for the evaluation of the accuracy are as follows.

- *Precision and Recall.* A classical evaluation metrics where precision is defined as a fraction of the retrieved items that are relevant, and recall is defined as a fraction of the relevant documents that are retrieved.
- *Area Under the Curve (AUC).* Measures the quality of a list of ranked items. The AUC is equivalent to the probability that the recommender will rank a randomly chosen positive instance higher than a randomly chosen negative

instance. For a random recommender it can be expected to get half the positives and half the negatives correct with an AUC value close to 0.5.

- *Normalized Discounted Cumulative Gain (NDCG).* Measures the quality of a list of ranked items taking into account the position of each item. It gives higher weight to items with higher rank.
- *Mean Average Precision (MAP).* Measures the quality of the list of ranked items as mean of the average precision for a set of test queries.
- *Mean Reciprocal Rank (MRR).* Considers the rank position of the items in the ranking list. A reciprocal rank for a single query is computed as a reciprocal of the rank at which the relevant item is retrieved.

In order to evaluate how the information content influences the accuracy, we evaluated the accuracy on two variants of our method. One which takes into account the informativeness of the resources, and one which does not. For the latter, we experimentally set the informativeness for all the resources at a fixed value of 0.9. Note that choosing any value in the interval between 0 and 1 will have same effect on the final results. We also performed a comparison of our method with the traditional personalised collaborative filtering methods (*User-KNN* and *Item-KNN*)[7] and non-personalised methods (*Random*[8] and *Most popular*[9]), which we consider as baseline. The evaluation was conducted using the evaluation environment MyMediaLite[10] v3.10, which also provides implemen-

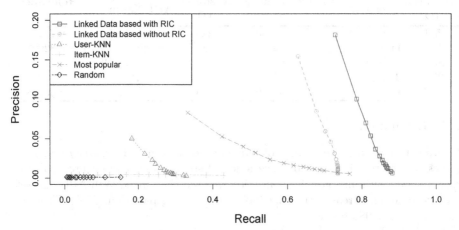

Fig. 2. Precision and Recall curves obtained for different methods.[11]

---

[7] For the UserKNN and ItemKNN baseline methods, was used a cosine similarity function with the default neighbourhood size experimentally set to k=80.

[8] Random recommender - randomly recommends items from a given set.

[9] Most popular recommender - recommends items weighted by the number of times they have been seen in the past.

[10] MyMediaLite evaluation environment - http://mymedialite.net/

[11] The precision/recall curves were obtained looking @topN, with N set to [5;10;15;20;30;40;50;60;70;80;90;100;150;200].

The results show that our method outperforms the traditional personalised *User-KNN* and *Item-KNN* recommendation methods, as well as the simple *Random* and *Most popular* recommendation methods. The results also show that our method achieves better results when taking into account the resource information content. From all the evaluated methods, the lowest results were achieved for the *Random* recommender. Slightly better results were achieved by the *Item-KNN*, followed by the *User-KNN*. It is interesting the fact that the *Most popular* method achieved better results compared to the other baseline methods. Most likely it is due to the long-tail distribution of the Web API usage in mashups, where small number of Web APIs enjoy significantly greater popularity than the others [13,16].

The results for the *AUC, NDCG, MAP* and *MRR* metrics are summarized in Table 3.

Table 3. Evaluation results for: Area Under the Curve (AUC), Normalized Discounted Cumulative Gain (NDCG), Mean Average Precision (MAP), Mean Reciprocal Rank (MRR)

	Random	Most popular	User-KNN	Item-KNN	Linked Data based without RIC	Linked Data based with RIC
AUC	0.50831	0.89072	0.64023	0.71038	0.89162	**0.95093**
NDCG	0.11608	0.38547	0.22278	0.11273	0.59401	**0.69486**
MAP	0.0064	0.26235	0.14506	0.02114	0.53442	**0.62358**
MRR	0.00742	0.2946	0.17653	0.02355	0.57835	**0.66882**

It can be observed that also for the other metrics our method outperforms the baseline methods. Here we can again see that the variant of our method, which takes into account the informativeness of the resources achieves better results over the variant which does not. An improvement of 6.65% was achieved for AUC, 16.98% for NDCG, 16.68% for MRR, and 15.64% for MRR.

Apart from the accuracy, another important dimension of the recommender system, as argued in [4], is the usefulness of the recommendations in terms of *"how surprising and diverse the recommendations are"*. Since in our case the user requester and the recommended items are represented as nodes in graph, we define the *serendipity* as the length of the shortest path between the requester's resource (r_u) and the recommended resource (r_i). A larger value of the shortest path indicates greater surprise. The overall serendipity of a set of resources (set C) is the average serendipity of the resources in the set.

$$Serendipity(r_u, C) = \frac{\sum_{r_i \in C} shortest\text{-}path(r_u, r_i)}{|C|} \qquad (4)$$

The *diversity* of a set of recommended resources we compute as the average dissimilarity among all resource pairs. The formula used for computation of diversity is as follows.

$$Diversity(C) = \frac{\sum_{r_i \in C} \sum_{r_j \in C - r_i} (1 - similiarity(r_i, r_j))}{\frac{|C| * (|C| - 1)}{2}} \qquad (5)$$

Here, the similarity between the resources we compute as the Jaccard coefficient of the context graphs of the resources (each r_i and r_j) in the set of recommendations C. Computed diversity score is in the [0, 1] interval, where values close to 0 indicates very similar set of recommended resource, and close to 1 very diverse resource recommendations. In the Web services recommendation use case, diverse recommendations can be considered those recommendations where the Web APIs belong to different category, have assigned different tags, support different protocols or data formats, or have been used by different users.

We evaluate the serendipity and diversity looking at the top 5, 10, 15 and 20 recommendations. The results from the evaluation of the serendipity and diversity are summarised in Table 4.

Table 4. Results from the evaluation of serendipity and diversity

	@top-N	Random	Most Popular	User-KNN	Item-KNN	Linked Data based without RIC	Linked Data based with RIC
Serendipity	@top-5	2.97752	2.66810	2.59197	2.68006	3.18881	3.03271
	@top-10	2.98455	2.67465	2.65514	2.70402	3.54821	3.26700
	@top-15	2.98364	2.65816	2.68101	2.71267	3.73117	3.36509
	@top-20	2.98455	2.65184	2.69780	2.70968	**3.84142**	**3.42444**
Diversity	@top-5	0.65339	0.58347	0.62092	0.63349	0.83417	0.81949
	@top-10	0.65317	0.61354	0.62411	0.64392	0.86044	0.82912
	@top-15	0.65370	0.60374	0.63159	0.64558	0.87511	0.82884
	@top-20	0.65347	0.60719	0.63276	0.64287	**0.88435**	**0.83114**

The results from the evaluation of serendipity and diversity show that our method outperforms the other methods. It can be also observed that the variant of our method which does not consider the informativeness of the resources produce more serendipitous and diverse recommendations compared to the variant which considers the informativeness. We can conclude that there is a trade-off between accuracy and serendipity/diversity which is directly influenced by the resource informativeness. In other words, when considering the resource informativeness our method provides more accurate but less serendipitous and diverse recommendations.

We also studied the optimal trade-off between the precision/recall and serendipity/diversity. Figure 3.3 depicts the obtained trade-off curves for our method.

The results show that the optimal values are: i) precision 0.12, recall 0.77 and serendipity 3.2, ii) precision 0.13, recall 0.763 and diversity 0.825. It can be also observed that the optimal precision/recall and serendipity/diversity is achieved when recommending between the top 5 and top 10 most relevant resources.

4 Related Work

A particular method that relates to ours is the *DBrec* presented in [10]. The method is supported by a semantic distance measure for measuring relatedness

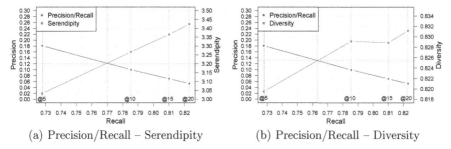

(a) Precision/Recall – Serendipity   (b) Precision/Recall – Diversity

Fig. 3. Trade-off between serendipity and accuracy studied @top 5, 10, 15 and 20

between resources. The measure is defined as a function of the direct and indirect links between resources. One limitation of this measure is that similarity between resources can be measured only if the graph distance between the resources is not more than two. Since the smallest distance between the users in the Linked Web APIs dataset is four (i.e., *foaf:Person* → *ls:Mashup* → *wl:Service* → *ls:Mashup* → *foaf:Person*) the measure will fail to produce recommendations for the Linked Web APIs dataset. In comparison, our method can be easily adapted to any dataset by setting the resource context distance parameter. Although the *DBrec* method has been validated on different domains found in DBpedia it demands manual pre-processing of the dataset. The *DBrec* uses only subsets of the DBpedia dump, which needs to be defined in advance for the particular domain. In contrast, our method is not domain or dataset specific and does not require any manual pre-processing of the datasets – it exploits RDF datasets in their original form.

The authors in [1] propose a Linked Data enabled content-based movie recommender, which uses a vector space model to compute similarities between the movies. The approach is not suitable for computation of similarities of resources in datasets (i.e., Linked Web APIs) where the graph distance between the resources is more than two. Moreover, the approach has been developed for the movies domain [9] and its adaptation to other domains requires manual pre-processing. In [14] the authors also use the vector space model to compute similarities between entities for ontology alignment, however, only similarities between directly linked resources can be computed.

In [7] authors propose a *Lookup Explore Discovery* (LED) exploratory search system, which recommends DBpedia resources related to the named entities recognized in the query. The resources are ranked by exploiting i) the co-occurrence of the resources' labels in DBpedia abstracts and ii) the wikilinks information. Moreover, external information sources are queried (Google, Yahoo! and Bing) and their co-occurrence in the returned pages is also evaluated. The system exploits small portion from a single Linked Data dataset, which is DBpedia.

Discovery Hub [5] is an exploratory search engine which recommends resources from the DBpedia namespace. It uses an adapted version of the spreading activation algorithm over typed graphs. The system exploits only small portion of the available information in DBpedia – triples with properties *dcterms:subject* and *rdf:type*, and the DBpedia Pagelinks partition.

Aemoo [8] is another exploratory search system which provides a summary of knowledge about entities. It uses fixed of Encyclopedic Knowledge Patterns (EKPs) to filter out valuable knowledge about the entities. It uses DBpedia as primary source of knowledge

The only existing approach which considers the resource informativeness can be found in [6]. The informativeness of the resources is computed as sum of the information content of its features (directly linked resources). Thus, a resource linked to another resource with high information content, will result also in a high informative resource. In comparison, in our approach we compute the informativeness of the resources based on the number of in-out links incident with the resource. Therefore, the information content of the directly linked resources does not have influence on the resource informativeness.

5   Discussion and Future Work

Setting the Resource Context Distance. The resource context distance allows us to control the amount of context used when computing the resource similarity. The larger context distance we set, the more context is considered. For example, with distance set to 1, only directly linked resources will be used as context. In datasets, where users in an RDF graph are close to each other, will require setting lower distance, while in datasets, where users are far, will require higher distance. Choosing small context distance in datasets where the users are far from each other, can lead to possibly no overlap of the resource context graphs, and consequently no similarity computed. In our experiments, we set the distance to two, and thus, the context of the user resources will contain resources representing the mashups the user created, the Web APIs used in the mashups and the assigned tags. Also, it is obvious that the size of the context directly influences the time required for computation of the resource similarity. In our future work, we would like to explore methods for automatic determination of optimal context distance for a given dataset.

Resource Similarity Computation in Multi-Domain Datasets. When computing resource similarity our method uses the shared resource context. While the Linked Web APIs is a single-domain dataset, in a multi-domain datasets, such as DBpedia, the shared contexts might contain resources from various domains, which might have direct influence on the recommendations. For illustration, two users being similar in the music domain, does not mean they are similar also in the Web service domain. In our future work, we would like to explore such situations, assess their impact on the quality of the recommendations and appropriately adapt our method. Last but not least we want to evaluate the method on other benchmark datasets with different characteristics and from other domains. This includes, for example, the MovieLens, the DBLP dataset, and the ACM DL dataset.

6   Conclusions

A growing number of published datasets in the LOD cloud require new methods that can provide more efficient access to Linked Data. In this paper, we have presented a novel configurable method for personalised access to Linked Data. The method can be easily adapted to a dataset from any domain and make use of it. It relies on the collaborative filtering approach and it recommends resources from users with similar resource interests. The method is supported with two novel metrics for computing resource similarity and relevance. When computing the similarity between the users the method primarily takes into account the *commonalities*, the *informativeness* and the *connectiviteness* of the shared resources. We validated the method on a resource recommendation use case from the Web services domain and we presented its capabilities. We also evaluated the method on a real-world dataset and the results show that the method outperforms the traditional personalised collaborative filtering and non-personalised methods in terms of accuracy, serendipity and diversity. The results also show that considering the informativeness of the resources improves the quality of the recommendations.

Acknowledgement. This work was supported by the Grant Agency of the Czech Technical University in Prague, grant No. SGS14/104/OHK3/1T/18. We also thank to Programmableweb.com for supporting this research.

References

1. Di Noia, T., et al.: Linked open data to support content-based recommender systems. In: Proceedings of the 8th International Conference on Semantic Systems, I-SEMANTICS 2012, pp. 1–8. ACM, New York (2012)
2. Dojchinovski, M., Kuchar, J., Vitvar, T., Zaremba, M.: Personalised graph-based selection of web aPIs. In: Cudré-Mauroux, P., Heflin, J., Sirin, E., Tudorache, T., Euzenat, J., Hauswirth, M., Parreira, J.X., Hendler, J., Schreiber, G., Bernstein, A., Blomqvist, E. (eds.) ISWC 2012, Part I. LNCS, vol. 7649, pp. 34–48. Springer, Heidelberg (2012)
3. Heath, T.: How will we interact with the web of data? IEEE Internet Computing 12(5), 88–91 (2008)
4. Herlocker, J.L., Konstan, J.A., Terveen, L.G., Riedl, J.T.: Evaluating collaborative filtering recommender systems. ACM Trans. Inf. Syst. 22(1), 5–53 (2004)
5. Marie, N., Gandon, F., Ribière, M., Rodio, F.: Discovery hub: On-the-fly linked data exploratory search. In: Proceedings of the 9th International Conference on Semantic Systems, I-SEMANTICS 2013, pp. 17–24. ACM, New York (2013)
6. Meymandpour, R., Davis, J.G.: Linked data informativeness. In: Ishikawa, Y., Li, J., Wang, W., Zhang, R., Zhang, W. (eds.) APWeb 2013. LNCS, vol. 7808, pp. 629–637. Springer, Heidelberg (2013)
7. Mirizzi, R., Di Noia, T.: From exploratory search to web search and back. In: Proceedings of the 3rd Workshop on Ph.D. Students in Information and Knowledge Management, PIKM 2010, pp. 39–46. ACM, New York (2010)
8. Musetti, A., et al.: Aemoo: Exploratory search based on knowledge patterns over the semantic web. Semantic Web Challenge (2012)

9. Ostuni, V.C., et al.: Cinemappy: a context-aware mobile app for movie recommendations boosted by dbpedia. In: de Gemmis, M., et al. (eds.) SeRSy. CEUR Workshop Proceedings, vol. 919, pp. 37–48. CEUR-WS.org (2012)
10. Passant, A.: dbrec — music recommendations using dBpedia. In: Patel-Schneider, P.F., Pan, Y., Hitzler, P., Mika, P., Zhang, L., Pan, J.Z., Horrocks, I., Glimm, B. (eds.) ISWC 2010, Part II. LNCS, vol. 6497, pp. 209–224. Springer, Heidelberg (2010)
11. Schmachtenberg, M., Bizer, C., Paulheim, H.: Adoption of the linked data best practices in different topical domains. In: Janowicz, K., et al. (eds.) ISWC 2014. LNCS, vol. 8796, pp. 245–260. Springer, Heidelberg (2014)
12. Sheldon, R.: A First Course in Probability. Macmillan, New York (1976)
13. Tapia, B., Torres, R., Astudillo, H.: Simplifying mashup component selection with a combined similarity- and social-based technique. In: Proceedings of the 5th International Workshop on Web APIs and Service Mashups, Mashups 2011, pp. 8–14. ACM, New York (2011)
14. Tous, R., Delgado, J.: A vector space model for semantic similarity calculation and OWL ontology alignment. In: Bressan, S., Küng, J., Wagner, R. (eds.) DEXA 2006. LNCS, vol. 4080, pp. 307–316. Springer, Heidelberg (2006)
15. Vitvar, T., Kopecký, J., Viskova, J., Fensel, D.: WSMO-lite annotations for web services. In: Bechhofer, S., Hauswirth, M., Hoffmann, J., Koubarakis, M. (eds.) ESWC 2008. LNCS, vol. 5021, pp. 674–689. Springer, Heidelberg (2008)
16. Weiss, M., Gangadharan, G.R.: Modeling the mashup ecosystem: structure and growth. R&D Management 40(1), 40–49 (2010), http://dx.doi.org/10.1111/j.1467-9310.2009.00582.x, doi:10.1111/j.1467-9310.2009.00582.x

Roadmapping and Navigating in the Ontology Visualization Landscape

Marek Dudáš, Ondřej Zamazal, and Vojtěch Svátek

Department of Information and Knowledge Engineering,
University of Economics, W. Churchill Sq.4, 130 67 Prague 3, Czech Republic
{marek.dudas,ondrej.zamazal,svatek}@vse.cz

Abstract. Proper visualization is essential for ontology development, sharing and usage; various use cases however pose specific requirements on visualization features. We analyzed several visualization tools from the perspective of use case categories as well as low-level functional features and OWL expressiveness. A rule-based recommender was subsequently developed to help the user choose a suitable visualizer. Both the analysis results and the recommender were evaluated via a questionnaire.

1 Introduction

Numerous visualization methods have been proposed for OWL ontologies and many software tools implementing them appeared in the past decade, ranging from semantic-web-specific approaches to proposals of UML[1] profiles [4,14,16] leveraging on the similarity with software engineering models. However, so far no visualization method has been accepted by the majority of the semantic web community as de facto standard. One reason clearly is that different use cases require different ontology visualization methods.

The goal of this paper is, first, to *survey* existing software tools from the use case perspective ('roadmapping' aspect of the paper), and, second, to build a prototype *ontology visualization tools recommender* based on our insights ('navigation' aspect of the paper). We believe that such a recommendation tool could find a broad audience of ontology/vocabulary users within the semantic web and linked data realms.

Section 2 provides a classification of ontology visualization use cases based on existing literature. Section 3 surveys existing visualization tools and evaluates them with respect to use case categories. Section 4 briefly presents our recommender, both structurally and in use. Section 5 overviews the outcomes of a questionnaire survey over both the findings from our analysis and the recommender. Section 6 summarizes related work. Finally, Section 7 wraps up the paper with conclusions and future work.

---

[1] http://www.omg.org/spec/UML/2.4.1/

K. Janowicz et al. (Eds.): EKAW 2014, LNAI 8876, pp. 137–152, 2014.
© Springer International Publishing Switzerland 2014

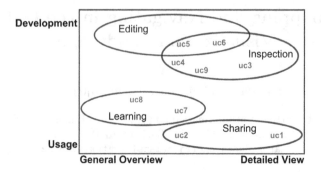

Fig. 1. Ontology visualization use case categories

2   Visualization Use Case Categories and Tool Features

Based on ad hoc analyses of literature and own experience, we collected nine possible *use cases* of ontology visualization: making screenshots of selected parts of an ontology *(uc1)* or of its overall structure *(uc2)*; structural error detection *(uc3)*; checking the model adequacy (how well the ontology covers its domain) *(uc4)*; building a new ontology *(uc5)*; adapting an existing ontology, e.g., adding entities or transforming the style, to fit specific usage *(uc6)*; analyzing an ontology in order to annotate data with (or create instances of) its entities *(uc7)*; deciding about the ontology suitability for a specific use case *(uc8)*; analyzing an ontology in view of mapping its entities to those from another ontology *(uc9)*.

We then aggregated the use cases to four *categories*, named *Editing, Inspection, Learning* and *Sharing*, positioned in a 2-dimensional space. The first dimension distinguishes whether the user actively 'develops' the ontology or just 'uses' it. The second dimension is the required level of detail, i.e. whether an overview (e.g., class hierarchy) is enough or a detailed view (e.g., axioms related to a class) is needed. The categorization, incl. use cases,[2] is shown in Fig. 1. *Editing* is a 'development' category that needs both a general and detailed view, while *Inspection* focuses on a detailed view. Within visualization for 'usage', *Learning* tends to use the general overview and *Sharing* tends to use the detailed view. The categories are not completely disjoint: *Inspection* overlaps with *Editing*, since the user usually needs to inspect the impact of her/his edits.

Inspired by categorization of tasks that should be supported by an information visualization application as defined in [19] (and adapted in [13]) and evaluation criteria classes described in [7], we further identified seventeen relevant *features* implemented in ontology visualization tools:

F1. *Zoom-Out Overview*: zooming out to get a summary view of the ontology.
F2. *Radar View*: displaying a small 'minimap' of the displayed ontology.
F3. *Graphical Zoom*: enlarging the displayed graphical elements.

---

[2] The positions of use cases are merely w.r.t. their categories and not in terms of quantitative coordinates. E.g., *uc3* may not need a more detailed view than *uc4*.

F4. *Focus on Selected Entity*: centering the view on a selected entity and its surroundings and hiding other parts of the ontology.

F5. *History*: keeping the history of navigation steps performed by the user, thus allowing for undo/redo actions.

F6. *Pop-Up Window*: displaying details on a chosen entity in a separate window.

F7. *Incremental Exploration*: starting by a small part of the ontology and gradually expanding the nodes selected by the user (as detailed in [9]).

F8. *Search*: text-based search leading to highlighting the matched entities.

F9. *Hide Selected Entity*: hiding parts of the ontology the user is currently not interested in, thus avoiding a cluttered view.

F10. *Filter Specific Entity Type*: e.g., hiding all object properties at once.

F11. *Fisheye Distortion*: zooming in for a part of the graph and zooming out for the rest; focuses on a detail but keeps the context, see, e.g., [18].

F12. *Edge Bundles*: grouping edges with similar paths, thus alleviating the clutter; implemented, e.g., in GLOW [10].

F13. *Drag&Drop Navigation*: moving a graph that is bigger than the screen around by dragging it with the mouse.

F14. *Drag&Drop User Layout*: allowing to move the individual nodes around.

F15. *Clustering*: 'intelligent' grouping of nodes or displaying a subset of 'important' nodes, as in KC-Viz [15].

F16. *Integration with Editing*: the user can select a visualized node or edge and edit its properties in, e.g., a pop-up window.

F17. *Graphical Editing*: the tool supports creating new entities by, e.g., drawing edges between the displayed nodes.

Referring to [7], F1–F5 are associated with a criteria class called *Help and User Orientation*, F6–F8 with *Navigation and Browsing*, F9–F10 with *Dataset Reduction*, F11–F14 with *Spatial Organization*, and F15 with *Information Coding*. F16 and F17 have no corresponding class in [7]. In each use case category most of the 17 features should ideally be supported; however, their importance varies. The alignment between the categories and tool features is, mostly, intuitive:

Editing ranges from developing a new ontology to merely changing a property value. Usually, the purpose of visualization is to find the entity to be changed or to become parent of a new entity. Important features are *Pop-Up Window* (to see detailed properties of a selected entity), *Search* (to easily find entities to be edited) and obviously *Integration with Editing* and *Graphical Editing*.

Inspection needs a detailed view of the ontology to see errors or deficiencies. It is often implied by *Editing*, as the user needs to see the state of the ontology before and after an edit. *Pop-Up Window* and *Search* are thus important here as well (while *Integration with Editing* and *Graphical Editing* not so). Additionally, *Hide Selected Entity*, *Filter Specific Entity Type* and *Focus on Selected Entity* are useful, as it is easier to spot errors after hiding the previously checked elements and/or focusing on the unchecked ones.

Learning means gaining knowledge about the *domain* the ontology covers or learning about the ontology *itself* so as to use it. The view need not be as detailed as for discovering errors (in *Inspection*). The user often only needs to see the available classes and properties, their hierarchy and their domain/range relationships; especially non-technical users who only want to learn the *domain* are unlikely to understand complex axioms anyway. Important features are thus *Zoom-Out Overview*, *Radar View* (to see an overview of the ontology) and *Incremental Exploration* (for user-friendly exploration of the ontology in more – but not too much – detail).

Sharing is similar to *Learning*, except for one more actor to whom the ontology is to be explained and shared with. The visualization should thus support displaying a part of the ontology; e.g., a picture of it can be made for an article describing the ontology. *Hide Selected Entity* is important for displaying the desired part only, and *Drag&Drop User Layout* is useful for achieving an appropriate layout, e.g., placing important entities into the center.

3   Multi-aspect Analysis of Visualization Tools

3.1   Analysis Overview

Initially we identified 21 visualization tools. For the 11 we considered as 'usable', we then characterized their supported features and language constructs. In Table 1, the "Plugin for" column specifies if the tool is a plugin for an ontology development environment (otherwise it is a standalone application). "Editor" is ticked if the tool supports editing of the visualized ontology. "Method" lists available visualization methods as defined in [13].[3] "Supports" contains "RDFS" if the tool only visualizes RDFS constructs and "OWL" if it visualizes at least some constructs from OWL. Finally and most important, in "State" we specify if we consider, by our hands-on experience, the tool as stable enough to be used in real use cases ("Usable"), still in early state of development ("Devel.") or not publicly available for download ("N/A"). The eleven 'usable' tools have been both evaluated in detail and included into the knowledge base of our recommender. The detailed analysis aimed to find out what features the tools implement (and how well), what language constructs they visualize and how they deal with larger ontologies. To test the last aspect we applied them on SUMO[4] (with several thousands of classes) and Biochemistry[5] (with several hundred classes).

3.2   Analysis of Selected Tools: Summaries

Table 2 shows the features (from Section 2) we found as supported in each tool. The number indicates the support level as evaluated by us: "1" means "only implemented partially and/or in a rather user-unfriendly way"; "2" means "fully implemented"; empty cell means "not implemented". The reasons for evaluating some of the features for certain tools with "1" are discussed in Section 3.3. Table 3 shows the language-level expressiveness of the tools, i.e. which OWL constructs can be visualized in it. Finally, Table 4 (left part) shows the 'suitability scores'

---

[3] Due to space we omit a mapping of these methods to our list of tool features.

[4] http://www.ontologyportal.org/

[5] http://ontology.dumontierlab.com/biochemistry-complex

Table 1. Ontology visualization tools overview

Tool	Plugin for	Editor	Method	Supports	State
CmapTools		x	Concept maps	OWL	N/A
CropCircles	SWOOP		Euler diagrams	RDFS	N/A
Entity Browser	Protégé 3/4	x	Indented list	RDFS	Usable
GLOW	Protégé 4.x		Node-link	RDFS	Devel.
Jambalaya	Protégé 3.x	x	Node-link, Space-filling	OWL	Usable
KC-Viz	Neon-Toolkit		Node-link	RDFS	Usable
Knoocks		x	Space-filling, Node-link	RDFS	Devel.
Navigowl	Protégé 4.x		Node-link	RDFS	Devel.
Ontograf	Protégé 4.x		Node-link	OWL	Usable
Ont. Visualizer	Neon-Toolkit		Node-link	RDFS	Usable
Ontoself			3D Node-link	RDFS	N/A
Ontosphere			3D Node-link	RDFS	Devel.
Ontoviewer			2.5D Node-link	RDFS	N/A
Ontoviz	Protégé 3.x		UML	RDFS	Usable
OWL VisMod		x	Space-filling, Node-link	RDFS	N/A
OWLeasyViz		x	Euler diagrams	RDFS	N/A
OWLGrEd		x	UML	OWL	Usable
OWLViz	Protégé 3.x		UML	RDFS	Usable
SOVA	Protégé 4.x		Node-link	OWL	Usable
TGVizTab	Protégé 3.x		Node-link	RDFS	Usable
TopBraid		x	Node-link	OWL	Usable

(ss) of each tool for each of the *use case categories*. The scores are calculated from the values in Table 2 using the following simple formula:

$$ss = \sum ImportantFeatureScores \cdot \alpha + \sum OtherFeatureScores \cdot \beta$$

Important features for each use case category are specified in Section 2. 'Other features' are all features which are not specified as important for the given use case category, with the exception of *Integration with Editing* and *Graphical Editing*, which are only taken into account for *Editing*. The feature score is 0, 1 or 2 as shown in Table 2. The multiplication coefficients α and β were set to 3 and 0.5, respectively, since these values provided good discriminatory ability in our initial test with the recommender system. The suitability scores are normalized to interval <-3;3> in the recommender (Section 4) and used as weights for the appropriate rules.

For the purposes of further evaluation using a questionnaire, we generalized the findings from the analysis into Table 4 (right part). It shows the performance of each tool in several aspects expressed on a scale of "very weak" ($--$), "weak" ($-$), "strong" ($+$) and "very strong" ($++$). The "OWL" aspect means how complete the visualization is: whether the tool only displays classes or also object properties, datatype properties etc. The "C. Classes" column shows how well the tool displays complex classes. The remaining columns show the performance of the tool in each category (based on the suitability scores and our experience

Table 2. Features implemented in each tool

Tool	Zoom-out Overview	Radar View	Graphical Zoom	Focus on Selected Entity	History (undo/redo)	Pop-up Window / Tooltip	Incremental Exploration	Search	Hide selected entity	Filter Specific Entity Type	Fisheye Distortion	Edge Bundles	Drag&Drop Navigation	Drag&Drop User Layout	Clustering	Integration with Editing	Graphical Editing
Entity Browser	2					2	2	2								2	
Jambalaya	1	1	1			2	1	2	2	2	1			2		2	
KC-Viz	2	2		2	2	2	1	2	2				2	2	2		
Ontograf		2	2			2	2	2		1			2	2		1	
Ontology Visualizer	2	2	2	2		2	2							2			
Ontoviz		2							2				2				
OWLGrEd	1	2	1			2	2					1		2		2	2
OWLViz	2	1	2			2	2	1	2							2	
SOVA	1	2						2		2			2	2			
TGVizTab	1	1	2				2	2	2	2	1		2				
TopBraid		2	1						2					2			2

Table 3. Types of language constructs visualized by each tool

Tool	Classes	Object Prop.	Datatype Prop.	Instances	Annotations	Univ./Exist. Rest.	Cardinality	Enumeration	Intersection	Union	Complement	equivalentClass	disjointWith	subClassOf	Property Char.
Entity Browser	x	x	x	x											
Jambalaya	x	x		x	x							x		x	
KC-Viz	x	x		x					x					x	
Ontograf	x	x		x	x			x	x	x	x	x		x	
Ontology Visualizer	x													x	
Ontoviz	x	x	x	x			x	x	x	x	x	x			
OWLGrEd	x	x	x	x	x	x	x	x	x	x	x	x	x	x	x
OWLViz	x														
SOVA	x	x		x		x	x	x	x	x	x	x	x	x	x
TGVizTab	x	x												x	
TopBraid	x	x	x	x	x	x	x	x	x	x	x	x	x	x	x

Table 4. Suitability scores and generalized performance of each tool in various aspects

Tool	Suitability Scores				Strong/weak aspects					
	Editing	Inspection	Learning	Sharing	OWL	C. Classes	Inspection	Editing	Learning	Sharing
Entity Browser	20,0	14,0	14,0	4,0	−	−−	−	+	+	−−
Jambalaya	23,5	30,0	12,5	17,5	−	−	++	++	−	++
KC-Viz	18,0	28,0	20,5	20,5	−	−	++	−	++	++
Ontograf	20,5	25,0	12,5	12,5	+	+	++	+	−	+
Ontology Vizualizer	12,0	17,0	17,0	12,0	−−	−−	−	−−	+	+
Ontoviz	3,0	8,0	3,0	8,0	+	++	−−	−−	−−	−−
OwlGrEd	22,5	10,5	13,0	10,5	++	++	−−	++	−	−
OWLViz	19,5	23,5	16,0	11,0	−−	−−	++	+	+	−
SOVA	10,5	15,5	8,0	10,5	++	++	−	−−	−−	−
TGVizTab	12,5	27,5	15,0	12,5	−−	−−	++	−	+	+
TopBraid	9,5	8,5	8,5	13,5	++	++	−−	−−	−−	+

with the tools). The performance of the tools regarding large ontologies is only discussed verbally in the next subsection.

3.3   Analysis of Selected Tools: Details

Jambalaya [21] can load and display large ontologies thanks to the treemap view. It can perform *Zoom-Out Overview*, but too many edges crossing other edges and nodes, as well as node overlap in the node-link view and hard-to-read labels in the treemap view makes it less useful in comparison with other tools. To use *Graphical Zoom*, the user has to first switch to 'zooming mode' – intuitive zooming with mousewheel is not supported. Nodes can be retracted/expanded, but Jambalaya displays the whole ontology by default – incremental exploration cannot be started from a selected node. *Fisheye-distortion* is applied only on the selected node and does not include its surroundings.

The strong feature of **KC-Viz** is the automated selection of 'most important classes' called 'key concepts'. This makes it very suitable for large ontologies. It offers a large number of well implemented features which makes it suitable for most of the use case categories.

Ontograf[6] can only be used for smaller ontologies and is limited to RDFS expressiveness.

Although **Ontology Visualizer**[7] only displays the class hierarchy and its range of features is limited, it is quite suitable for *Learning* thanks to its implementation of incremental exploration, and it can deal with larger ontologies.

---

[6] http://protegewiki.stanford.edu/wiki/OntoGraf
[7] http://neon-toolkit.org/wiki/Main_Page

Ontoviz[8] displays the most detailed view by default and it is incapable of displaying an *overview* of the whole ontology. It can visualize a larger ontology if the user wants to see only a small part of it at once: the user can select exactly what part of the ontology should be displayed.

The main advantage of **OWLGrEd** [2] is its large coverage of OWL constructs. Its use for *Editing* is supported, e.g., by the possibility to directly draw relationships as edges between the nodes. The *Zoom-out Overview* is possible but not very usable: the labels are hard to read and the view is cluttered. It implements some sort of edge bundles but not as well as, e.g., GLOW [11]. As in the case of Ontograf, larger ontologies are not supported well: OWLGrEd was not capable to load SUMO, and for Biochemistry the ontology was loaded correctly but the result was an extremely cluttered visualization without any chance to determine which nodes the edges are connecting.

As **OWLViz**[9] was able to load the SUMO ontology, it can be considered for visualizing large ontologies. However, it displays only classes and their hierarchy.

Protégé[10] contains the indented list ontology visualization, **Entity Browser**, as an integral part of its GUI. As the Neon-Toolkit[11] and TopBraid Composer[12] offer almost identical implementations of indented-list-based entity browsers, we rather provide a generic analysis of this method that applies to all three. It offers a sort of *Zoom-Out Overview* by default (the simple list of entities), while the features related to node-link visualization are obviously unsupported. *Editing* is inherent, and even very large ontologies can be visualized without problems.

SOVA is the only tool in this survey that displays all OWL constructs (but datatype properties) as graphical elements in one view. Large ontologies can be displayed in a simplified alternative view similar to OWLViz (classes-only).

TGVizTab [1] offers a few advanced, but imperfectly implemented, features like fisheye-distortion. Its main disadvantage is that it is available only as a plugin for the older Protégé 3.

The node-link visualization of **TopBraid Composer**[13] shows all types of entities as nodes and properties as edges connecting them. The visualization is rather provided at the RDF level, so even `owl:Class` is shown as a separate node and every class is connected to it through an `rdf:type` edge. While good for learning the OWL language, this feature does not contribute to clearness of the visualization. Even if such redundant elements are hidden, the visualization gets cluttered quite quickly and thus it is not suitable for large ontologies.

---

[8] http://protegewiki.stanford.edu/wiki/OntoViz
[9] http://www.co-ode.org/downloads/owlviz/
[10] http://protege.stanford.edu
[11] http://neon-toolkit.org
[12] Discussed below with respect to its node-link method.
[13] http://www.topquadrant.com/products/TB_Composer.html

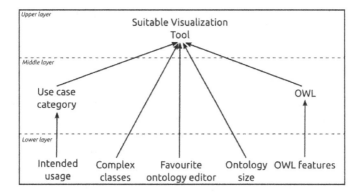

Fig. 2. Abstracted inference network for the recommendation knowledge base

4   Ontology Visualization Tools Recommender

The recommender[14] is built as a knowledge base (KB) for the NEST expert system shell [3]. NEST covers the functionality of compositional rule-based expert systems (with uncertainty handling), non-compositional (Prolog-like) expert systems, and case-based reasoning systems. NEST employs a combination of backward and forward chaining and it processes uncertainty according to the algebraic theory of Hajek [8]. In order to capture (task-specific) domain knowledge for rule-based reasoning, we employed the following apparatus of NEST:

- *Attributes and propositions.* Attributes are used to describe the features of the consulted case, and propositions are derived from the values of attributes. There are four types of attributes: binary, single nominal, multiple nominal, and numeric. *Fuzzy intervals*, for a numeric attribute, allow to express vague information such as *high body temperature.*
- *Rules* having a *condition* (disjunction of literal[15] conjunctions) and *conclusion* (list of literals) component. There are three types of rules. A *compositional* rule has its conclusion equipped with a weight expressing the degree of uncertainty of the conclusion if the condition holds with certainty. Furthermore, to evaluate the ultimate weight of a proposition, all contributions having this proposition in its conclusion are evaluated and combined. An *apriori* rule is a compositional rule without condition. Finally, a *logical* rule is a non-compositional rule without weights.

Our KB contains 8 attributes, 36 propositions, 32 compositional rules and 1 apriori rule. An abstraction of its inference network is in Fig. 2. Directed edges indicate groups of compositional rules connecting the attributes (shown as texts); the grouping is based on the corresponding propositions.[16] The KB consists of

---

[14] The recommender is available at `http://owl.vse.cz:8080/OVTR/`.

[15] 'Literal' is not meant here in the RDF sense but as 'attribute-value pair'.

[16] The full inference network is at `http://owl.vse.cz:8080/OntoVisualTool/`.

three layers. The top layer only contains one node, representing the *recommendation of visualization tool*. The middle layer contains two nodes, which aggregate the relevant answers from the user: *Use case category* (editing, inspection, learning and sharing) and *OWL* (the importance of particular OWL features). The bottom layer represents possible user answers to questions:

- *Complex classes*: importance of anonymous classes based on various OWL constructs such as union, complement, intersection etc.
- *Intended usage*: the nine use cases from Section 2.
- *Ontology size*: fuzzy intervals for 'small', 'medium' and 'large' ontologies.
- *OWL features*: importance of particular OWL features (object properties, interclass relationships, datatype properties and property characteristics), aiming to infer the overall importance of OWL support in the visualization.
- *Favorite ontology editor*: the user's preference for some (freely available) ontology editor: Protégé 3, Protégé 4 or Neon Toolkit.

This KB thus encompasses the main insights we gained from 'roadmapping the ontology visualization landscape' as presented in the first part of the paper.

4.1   Recommender Usage Example

We include an example of usage of the recommender. The particular source case refers to paper [17], where *Ontoviz* is used to show (as screenshots) parts of the ontology that is being described in the paper. We tried to emulate the hypothetical entering of information about the ontology into the recommender by the paper authors. Technically, this consisted in answering the above mentioned questions with Likert-scale answers (represented by numbers from the interval <-3;3> where 3 means "Certainly yes" and -3 means "Certainly no"), or with exact numbers for numeric questions, as follows: *Complex classes*: 3; *Intended usage*: Screenshots: 3; *Ontology size*: 91; *OWL features*: Object Properties: 1, Interclass Relationships: 3, Datatype Properties: 1, Property Characteristics: -1;[17] *Favorite ontology editor*: Protégé 3: 3,[18] Protégé 4: -2, Neon Toolkit: -3.

The recommendation is in Fig. 3 (a). The tool indeed recommends *Ontoviz* with the weight of 1.671 (of the maximum of 3). The next most suitable tool is *TopBraid*. Least suitable, in turn, are *Ontology Visualizer* and *OWLViz*.

The final weight of the proposition supporting *Ontoviz* has been inferred as indicated in Fig. 3 (b), where the rule hierarchy is shown. Rules marked as green by the explanation component[19] of NEST (and annotated with a circled-plus sign for the sake of B/W readability, in the screenshot only) positively contribute to the weight of their superordinate rule; rules marked as red (circled-minus sign in the screenshot) contribute negatively; rules in grey are indifferent in this

---

[17] The questions regarding OWL properties have been answered with lower weights since there are only 7 properties in the ontology. Property Characteristics are not mentioned in the paper, so we consider them as unimportant.

[18] Protégé 3 is mentioned in the paper as the tool used for the ontology development.

[19] Currently only in the desktop version, http://sorry.vse.cz/~berka/NEST/.

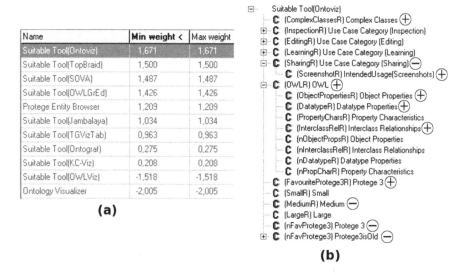

Fig. 3. (a) The recommendation results. (b) The inference explanation.

particular inference. *Ontoviz* scores high in this case since it visualizes all the required types of OWL entities including complex classes and it is a plugin for Protégé 3, which is used (i.e. preferred) by the authors of the paper. The score is lowered by the "SharingR" rule, as Ontoviz is not very suitable for the *Sharing* use case category, by the "MediumR" rule, as *Ontoviz* can only clearly display a small number of entities, and by the two rules at the bottom of the list, which are built-in rules slightly lowering the score of Protégé 3 plugins, as it has been meanwhile replaced by the newer version (4) and is not supported anymore.

5 Evaluation

As the evaluation of both the overall analysis and the recommender requires human expertise,[20] we prepared a web-based *anonymous questionnaire*,[21] sent invitations to participate in it to several relevant mailing lists, and also asked several people from the area of ontology engineering, including authors of the surveyed visualization tools, directly. The respondents were asked about their level of expertise in ontologies and their experience with ontology visualization tools: which they used, in what use case (out of the 9 use cases described in Section 2) and whether they were satisfied with it. Then, they were asked whether they agree with the categorization of their use case, with the weak and strong aspects of the visualization tool as inferred from our analysis and with our categorization system itself. Finally, a consultation with the recommender was offered

---

[20] Yet, we also made a literature-based evaluation, available at `http://bit.ly/1phLBdm` along with additional details about the evaluation described in this section.

[21] Available at `http://owl.vse.cz:8080/OVQuestionnaire/`

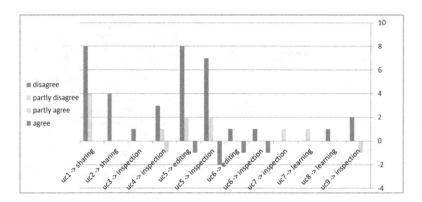

Fig. 4. Counts of respondent opinions to each use case → category mapping

and if they ran through it, they were asked to express their satisfaction with the resulting recommendation. During the consultation, the respondents could describe either a real visualization scenario or a hypothetical one. We gathered answers from 32 respondents, out of which 3 skipped the consultation.

Agreement with the Categorization System. When introduced to a brief description of the use case categories (as described in Section 2), 13 respondents answered that the categorization makes "perfect sense", the same number of respondents stated that it makes "more or less sense", 5 replied that it "does not make much sense", and no one chose "does not make sense at all"; 1 respondent did not answer this question. To sum up, about 84% of respondents partly or fully agreed with the categorization.

Agreement with the Categorizations of Use Cases. Figure 4 shows the counts of respondent opinions about specific use case mappings to category (partial and full disagreement counts are shown as negative values). Each respondent could describe up to three different use cases. We gathered 40 opinions. Agreement clearly prevailed, with the exception of *uc6, Adapting an existing ontology*, where one respondent agreed and one disagreed with the mappings to both editing and inspection.

Agreement with Strong/Weak Aspects of the Tools. When the respondent stated s/he has experience about some visualization tool, s/he was asked about his/her opinions about each of the strong/weak aspects of the tool as shown in the right part of Table 4. We mapped the answers to numerical values as follows: "agree" → "1", "partly agree" → "0.5", "partly disagree" → "-0.5", and "disagree" → "-1". The average of the numerical values of all 141 answers from 27 respondents was approx. 0.34. If we look at the average agreement on each aspect of each tool separately, only the weak and very weak aspects of SOVA and OwlGrEd had averages below 0 (i.e. the respondents rather disagreed).

Satisfaction with the Consultation. 29 respondents ran the consultation, of which 14 (48%) were satisfied and 7 (24%) partly satisfied with the resulting recommendation, i.e. 72% of respondents were partly or fully satisfied. In 23 (79%) cases, KC-Viz was recommended as the most suitable tool. Such a high percentage of one tool was mainly caused by the fact that most of the respondents (approx. 66%) entered an ontology size larger than 120 entities, which is considered by the recommender as 'large', and KC-Viz is considered as the most suitable tool for large ontologies. These results suggest that we should reconsider the rules in the KB related to the size of the ontology (the risk of clutter when a larger ontology is visualized might be over-estimated for some tools).

6   Related Work

We are unaware of a recent analysis with as large coverage of visualization tools as in this paper, nor of an implemented system for tool recommendation. Our questionnaire was inspired by a survey [6] done several years ago aimed at discovering which visualization tools are used by whom and for what tasks. The options offered to the respondents regarding the usage of the tool partially agree with our use case categories: "Check for inconsistencies or errors" is our *Inspection*, "Present reports to others" is *Sharing* and "Help with understanding new ontologies" is *Learning*. We consider the remaining three options either too specific ("Show hidden relationships" and "Show areas of interest") or too general ("Assist with navigating information space"). [12] describes the results of a comparative evaluation of (Protégé) Entity Browser, Jambalaya, TGViz and Ontoviz done with a group of test users. Time needed to perform a set of several predefined tasks in each tool by each user was measured and the users were also asked to fill in a questionnaire after using the tools. The users achieved the best performance with Entity Browser, which also received the best score regarding questions about perceived effectiveness. The tasks were aimed at finding specific information about instances, which would be classified as *Learning*. Our results agree with those from [12] in that Entity Browser is slightly better for *Learning* than Jambalaya and that Ontoviz is the worst of the four tools. The difference is in the evaluation of TGVizTab, which performed worse than Entity Browser in [12] but has a higher suitability score for *Learning* in our study. However, [12] compares the tools using a single ontology and a specific use case, while our analysis is aimed at comparing the tools regarding different ontologies and use cases. A subsequent paper by the same group, [13], defines a categorization of visualization methods and tasks, and includes a thorough (but ageing) survey of ontology visualization tools. An approach similar to [12] has been chosen in [22] for a comparative evaluation of Ontograf, OWL2Query and DLQuery: a group of users was asked to perform a set of predefined tasks aimed at finding information about instances and the time to complete each task was measured. A review of Protégé Entity Browser, Ontoviz, OntoSphere, Jambalaya and TGVizTab is available in [20]. The review includes a comparison of features and types of OWL entities supported by each visualization tool similar to our

Table 2 and Table 3. While it is less detailed and lacks evaluation of the quality of implementation of the features, it includes a review of support of 'Animated Transactions',[22] which we considered unimportant. Finally, [5] proposes rough guidelines for visualization tool design.

7   Conclusions and Future Work

We overviewed and analyzed the current ontology visualization tools by taking into account newly formed (aggregated) *use case categories*, *visualization tool features*, *language constructs*, and *scalability* with respect to ontology size. For selecting a suitable visualizer we designed a simple *recommender*. We also performed a *questionnaire-based evaluation* of the recommender and of our analytical findings. The respondents generally agreed with the proposed use case categorization and with the strong and weak aspects we identified for the tools, and they were mostly satisfied with the recommender suggestions.

In the future we plan to improve the recommender according to the feedback from the questionnaire, in particular, the rules concerning the size of the ontology to be visualized. Moreover, since our analysis of the ability of the tools to display large ontologies is rather subjective, we plan to arrange for a more exact assessment in this respect. We will also continuously monitor the visualization 'landscape' so as to include new tools, such as VOWL[23] and OLSViz,[24] and reflect them in the KB. Furthermore, a next release of the KB will directly consume input from automatic analysis of ontology structure.[25] Finally, we are aware that our treatment of visualization use cases is so far only based on experience in the semantic web area. Insights from the broader human-computer interaction research, such as [23], should also be exploited.

Acknowledgement. The research is supported by VŠE IGA grant F4/34/2014 (IG407024). Ondřej Zamazal is supported by the CSF grant 14-14076P, "COSOL – Categorization of Ontologies in Support of Ontology Life Cycle". We thank to Vladimír Laš for help with setting up our KB for the web variant of NEST, and to the anonymous respondents of the survey.

References

1. Alani, H.: TGVizTab: An ontology visualisation extension for Protege. In: K-CAP 2003 Workshop on Visualization Information in Knowledge Engineering (2003)
2. Bardzins, J., et al.: OWLGrEd: A UML Style Graphical Editor for OWL. In: Ontology Repositories and Editors for the Semantic Web, Hersonissos (2010)

---

[22] Animation of the transition between different states of the visualization.

[23] http://vowl.visualdataweb.org/

[24] http://ols.wordvis.com/

[25] A preliminary implementation of such an analysis is at http://owl.vse.cz:8080/MetricsExploration/, but not yet integrated with the recommender.

3. Berka, P.: NEST: A Compositional Approach to Rule-Based and Case-Based Reasoning. In: Advances in Artificial Intelligence, 15 p. (2011), http://www.hindawi.com/journals/aai/2011/374250/
4. Brockmans, S., Volz, R., Eberhart, A., Löffler, P.: Visual modeling of OWL DL ontologies using UML. In: McIlraith, S.A., Plexousakis, D., van Harmelen, F. (eds.) ISWC 2004. LNCS, vol. 3298, pp. 198–213. Springer, Heidelberg (2004)
5. Da Silva, I.C.S., Freitas, C.M.D.S., Santucci, G.: An integrated approach for evaluating the visualization of intensional and extensional levels of ontologies. In: Proceedings of the 2012 BELIV Workshop: Beyond Time and Errors-Novel Evaluation Methods for Visualization, p. 2. ACM (2012)
6. Ernst, N.A., Storey, M.-A.: A Preliminary Analysis of Visualization Requirements in Knowledge Engineering Tools. University of Victoria (2003)
7. Freitas, C.M.D.S., et al.: On evaluating information visualization techniques. In: Proceedings of the Working Conference on Advanced Visual Interfaces, pp. 373–374. ACM, New York (2002)
8. Hajek, P.: Combining functions for certainty degrees in consulting systems. International Journal of Man-Machine Studies 22(1), 59–76 (1985)
9. Herman, I., Melanon, G., Marshal, M.S.: Graph visualization and navigation in information visualization: A survey. IEEE Transactions on Visualization and Computer Graphics 6(1), 24–43 (2000)
10. Hop, W., et al.: Using Hierarchical Edge Bundles to visualize complex ontologies in GLOW. In: Proceedings of the 27th Annual ACM Symposium on Applied Computing, pp. 304–311. ACM (2012)
11. Howse, J., Stapleton, G., Taylor, K., Chapman, P.: Visualizing ontologies: A case study. In: Aroyo, L., Welty, C., Alani, H., Taylor, J., Bernstein, A., Kagal, L., Noy, N., Blomqvist, E. (eds.) ISWC 2011, Part I. LNCS, vol. 7031, pp. 257–272. Springer, Heidelberg (2011)
12. Katifori, A., et al.: A comparative study of four ontology visualization techniques in protege: Experiment setup and preliminary results. In: IEEE Information Visualization 2006, pp. 417–423 (2006)
13. Katifori, A., et al.: Ontology visualization methods – a survey. ACM Computing Surveys (CSUR) 39(4), 10 (2007)
14. Kendall, E.F., Bell, R., Burkhart, R., Dutra, M., Wallace, E.K.: Towards a Graphical Notation for OWL 2. In: OWLED 2009 (2009)
15. Motta, E., Mulholland, P., Peroni, S., d'Aquin, M., Gomez-Perez, J.M., Mendez, V., Zablith, F.: A novel approach to visualizing and navigating ontologies. In: Aroyo, L., Welty, C., Alani, H., Taylor, J., Bernstein, A., Kagal, L., Noy, N., Blomqvist, E. (eds.) ISWC 2011, Part I. LNCS, vol. 7031, pp. 470–486. Springer, Heidelberg (2011)
16. Parreiras, F.S., Walter, T., Gröner, G.: Visualizing ontologies with UML-like notation. In: Ontology-Driven Software Engineering. ACM (2010)
17. Rene Robin, C.R., Uma, G.V.: Development of educational ontology for software risk analysis. In: Proceedings of the 2011 International Conference on Communication, Computing & Security, ICCCS 2011, pp. 610-615. ACM (2011)
18. Sarkar, M., Brown, M.H.: Graphical fisheye views of graphs. In: Proceedings of the SIGCHI Conference on Human Factors in Computing Systems, pp. 83–91. ACM (June 1992)
19. Shneiderman, B.: The eyes have it: A task by data type taxonomy for information visualizations. In: Proceedings of the IEEE Symposium on Visual Languages, pp. 336–343. IEEE (1996)

20. Sivakumar, R., Arivoli, P.V.: Ontology Visualization Protege Tools: A Review. International Journal of Advanced Information Technology 1(4) (2011), http://airccse.org/journal/IJAIT/papers/0811ijait01.pdf
21. Storey, M., et al.: Jambalaya: Interactive visualization to enhance ontology authoring and knowledge acquisition in Protégé. In: Workshop on Interactive Tools for Knowledge Capture, K-CAP-2001 (2001)
22. Swaminathan, V., Sivakumar, R.: A Comparative Study of Recent Ontology Visualization Tools With a Case of Diabetes Data. International Journal of Research in Computer Science 2(3), 31 (2012)
23. Weidong, H. (ed.): Handbook of Human Centric Visualization. Springer (2014)

aLDEAS: A Language to Define Epiphytic Assistance Systems

Blandine Ginon[1,2], Stéphanie Jean-Daubias[1,3], Pierre-Antoine Champin[1,3], and Marie Lefevre[1,3]

[1] Université de Lyon, CNRS
[2] INSA-Lyon, LIRIS, UMR5205, F-69621, France
[3] Université Lyon 1, LIRIS, UMR5205, F-69622, France
{name.surname}@liris.cnrs.fr

Abstract. We propose a graphical language that enables the specification of assistance systems for a given application, by means of a set of rules. This language is completed by several assistance actions patterns. We implemented these propositions through an assistance editor aimed at assistance designers, and a generic assistance engine able to execute the specified assistance for the target-application end users, without a need to modify this application. We performed several experimentations both with assistance designers and with target-applications end users.

Keywords: Language, user assistance, rule-based system, epiphytic tools.

1 Introduction

User assistance is one solution to overcome the difficulties of handling and using software applications. It helps preventing the user from under-exploiting or even rejecting those applications.

We define assistance as the set of means facilitating the handling and use of an application, in a way suitable to the user and to the use context. The assistance aims at enabling the user to exploit fully all the possibilities of an application, and it facilitates the appropriation of the knowledge and competencies required to use this application. It includes the four assistance types defined by [3]: supplementation, support, assistance and substitution.

The development of an assistance system suitable to an application is a complex and expensive task, often neglected by applications designers. A person other than the application designer may then wish to plug an assistance system to an application that has no assistance or an incomplete one. For instance, in the context of a user community, an expert may wish to design an assistance system to make novice users benefit from his/her experience. In the case where the assistance designer is not the target-application designer, the source code of the target-application is most of the time not available; it is then not possible to integrate an assistance system directly in the application. What's more, as in our example, the potential assistance designer is not always

K. Janowicz et al. (Eds.): EKAW 2014, LNAI 8876, pp. 153–164, 2014.

a programmer. An alternative to the classical approach of development of an assistance system integrated into the application consists in adopting an epiphytic approach to make possible the *a posteriori* specification and execution of an assistance system in an existing application without the need to modify it. An epiphytic assistance, that we call an *epi-assistant*, is an assistant able to perform actions in an external target-application, without disturbing its functioning [6].

The work presented in this paper takes place in the context of the AGATE project that aims to propose generic models and unified tools to make possible the setup of assistance systems in any existing application, that we call the target-application. For this purpose, we proposed an adjunction process of epi-assistance system in a target-application in two phases (cf. Fig. 1). The first phase involves an assistance designer: an expert of the target-application who wishes to design an assistance system. This phase enables the assistance designer to specify the assistance that he/she wishes for the target-application, by defining a set of assistance rules. The second phase involves the target-application end users. It consists in the execution of the assistance specified by the designer. This phase occurs at each use of the target-application by an end user; it is composed of three processes. The monitoring of the target-application exploits a set of epi-detectors [4] that enable the continuous observation and the tracing of all interactions between the user and the target-application interface. In parallel, the process identifying assistance needs exploits the assistance rules defined by the designer and triggers the process elaborating an answer to the identified assistance need. The answer is executed as one or several assistance actions, performed by an epi-assistant in the target-application.

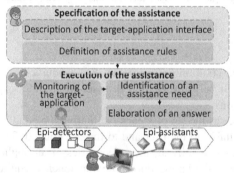

Fig. 1. Adjunction process of an epi-assistance system in a target-application

During the specification phase, the assistance designers need to elicit their knowledge about how to use the target application, in order to specify the assistance system. This phase must be accessible to an assistance designer that can be neither non-computer scientist nor knowledge engineering expert. Then the specified assistance is executed automatically during the execution phase. As a consequence, the assistance needs to be formalized enough. A solution to make these two points possible is to use a pivot language: we proposed aLDEAS, a graphical language to help assistance designers designing assistance rules. Moreover, we propose a set of patterns to guide them in defining complex assistance actions. We then present the implementation of these patterns in the SEPIA system. Finally, we describe the experimentations that we performed in order to evaluate the usability of aLDEAS and its implementation in the SEPIA system.

2   Related Work

Several authors have studied the *a posteriori* specification of assistance systems for existing target-applications. The approaches of [7] and [1] allow to plug an advisor system in a scenario from the environments Telos and ExploraGraph. These advisor systems are defined by an assistance designer through a set of rules of the form <trigger event, trigger condition, assistance action, end event>. The trigger condition can include a consultation of the user profile and of the assistance history in order to personalize and contextualize the assistance. The proposed assistance actions are textual messages displayed in a pop-up for Telos, and animations or messages conveyed by an animated agent for ExploraGraph. The approach proposed by [8] allows to plug an advisor system in a Web application, in order to trigger assistance actions when the end user clicks on a link. The proposed actions are textual messages displayed in a pop-up, which can contain links to a Web page or to resources related to the assistance. The provided assistance can be personalized according to a browsing history. The assistance provided by these advisor systems can also be expressed by rules with the form <trigger event: click on a link, trigger condition: browsing history, assistance action>. The CAMELEON model [2] allows to plug an animated agent able to move, perform animations and display messages in a Web application, thanks to tags inserted in an epiphytic way in the page.

Assistance rules seem to be suited to represent epiphytic assistance systems. Nevertheless, these different approaches cannot be used in any application. Indeed, they are specific to a given environment or to the Web. We are interested in the *a posteriori* plugging of assistance systems to very diverse existing target-applications. What's more, we would like to allow a fine-grained personalization of the assistance, according to the user profile and to the assistance history, like in Telos and ExploraGraph, but also according to the user's past actions, not only the browsing history as in [8], and according to the state of the target-application. Finally, to make possible a wider personalization of the assistance, we would like to propose a large choice of assistance actions: if the same assistance action can be performed in different ways, like pop-up or animated agent, it will be easier for the assistance designer to specify assistance suited to the user's specificities and to the context.

3   The aLDEAS Language

We propose aLDEAS (a Language to Define Epi-Assistance Systems), a graphical rule language aimed at assistance designers for defining assistance systems. We choose to propose a graphical language, very suitable to the representation by a set of simple rules of assistance systems, in particular epiphytic assistance systems. Its different components (cf. Fig. 2) are presented in detail in this section. We will show thereafter how these components can be combined to create assistance actions addressing assistance needs that will then be executed by our system SEPIA on top of the target-application. An aLDEAS block is a labelled direct graph, with nodes and edges taken from Fig. 2. It must have exactly one source, which must be a "block start", and one or several sinks, which must all be "block end". It is executed by walking the graph; the effect of walking each type of node is described in the following.

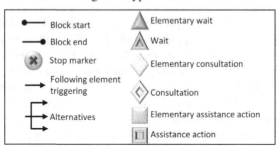

Fig. 2. Components of aLDEAS

3.1   Waits

Waits are nodes that cause the execution to pause until the occurrence of a given event. Elementary waits, represented in the language by the symbol △, can expect a specific user's action, like a click on a given button, they can expect an event of the assistance system, like the triggering of a given assistance action, or they can wait for the end of a timer. A timer is associated to a duration and can be triggered after any event linked to the user's action or to the assistance system. For instance, a timer can be used to trigger an assistance action after two minutes without any user's action.

Several elementary waits can be combined to create a complex wait, represented by ▲. Thus, such elements can wait for a given succession of elementary events making up a higher level event, for instance an action of red eyes correction on a photo.

3.2   Consultations

Consultations are nodes that fetch information, in order to personalize and contextualize the assistance. The aLDEAS language proposes several types of elementary consultations, represented in the language by ◇. It makes possible the direct consultation of the user, to make him choose between several options for instance. It is also possible to consult the target-application state, in order for instance to know the content of a text field, or which item is selected in a combo box. Finally, aLDEAS makes possible the consultation of resources linked to the assistance, such as the user's profile (that contains notably information on the user's preferences regarding assistance, or his skills in the target-application), the assistance history (that contains information relative to the rules and actions triggered for the user), and the user's traces (that contains information about all the interactions between the user and the target-application interface). Elementary consultations can be combined by a logical formula to create a complex consultation represented by ◇. A consultation, either elementary or complex, returns a value which can have different types: Boolean, text or number. For instance, a consultation of the assistance history can return a number indicating how many times an assistance action has been trigger.

Consultation nodes typically have several outgoing edges, represented as ⊨ (alternative branching), where each edge is labeled with a Boolean expression. The execution of the block will continue only along the edge(s) with the expression of which is satisfied by the returned value. If several edges are satisfied, the corresponding paths will be executed in parallel. An example of alternative is given in the rule R0 in Fig. 7.

3.3   Assistance Actions

Our language proposes two categories of elementary assistance actions, represented by ▦: integrated actions and actions external to the target-application interface. The grayed actions on Fig. 3 and Fig. 4 that are the only aLDEAS actions that are not implemented in the current version of SEPIA (cf. section 5).

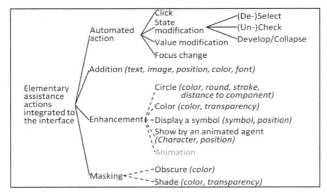

Fig. 3. Elementary assistance actions integrated to the target-application interface

The *integrated actions* act directly on a given component of the target-application interface, like a button or a text field. aLDEAS proposes four types of such actions on a component (cf. Fig. 3): automated actions, to act on behalf of the user; addition of component, to enrich the target-application interface (for instance by a new button enabling the user to ask for help); enhancement, to guide the user and attract his attention on a component; and masking, to simplify the target-application interface to the user's eyes. An action integrated to the target-application interface can be associated to several optional parameters, indicated by dotted line in Fig. 3. For instance, for an enhancement, a component of the target-application interface can be shown by an animated agent or circled by a stroke with a given color and size.

On the other hand, *actions external* to the target-application interface are not specifically linked to a component. aLDEAS proposes three types of such actions (cf. Fig. 4): messages, associated to a text that can be displayed and/or read; animations, for instance an animated agent applauding; and resources that can be proposed to the user, for instance a demonstration video, a forum or an application like the calculator.

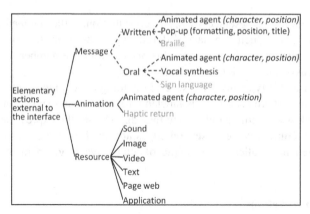

Fig. 4. Elementary assistance actions external to the target-application interface

Whenever an elementary action node is encountered, the corresponding action is launched, and the execution walks immediately to the next node; this allows several actions to be active at the same time (such as a message and an enhancement). Actions can stop on their own (e.g. playing a sound), be stopped by the user (e.g. by closing a message box), but some actions need to be explicitly stopped. This can be specified with the stop marker ✖: this node causes all the actions started in the current block to stop. Fig. 5 gives the example of a block composed of two elementary assistance actions: a message and an enhancement. The action also contains an end event: the message and the enhancement will disappear after 30 seconds.

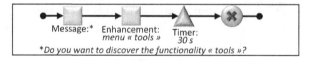

Fig. 5. Example of a block with a stop marker

3.4   Complex Assistance Actions

Any aLDEAS block can be invoked in another block as a complex assistance action, represented by the symbol ▯. This node causes the execution of the invoking block to stall until the execution of the invoked block finishes.

A complex assistance action can return a value, which must be indicated under the corresponding end marker (cf. examples Fig. 9 and Fig. 10). In the blocks invoking this action, the corresponding node will be followed by an alternative branching, as described in the end of Section 3.2.

4   aLDEAS Patterns

In order to facilitate the definition in aLDEAS of complex assistance actions, we propose a set of patterns. For that purpose, we enrich our language with two structures: "or" branching and optional elements preceded by a "?". These structures do not describe the assistance execution; they represent a choice to be made by the assistance designer at the time of the pattern instantiation.

4.1   Assistance Rules Pattern

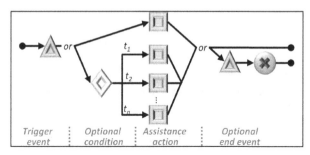

Fig. 6. Assistance rules pattern

The aim of our language is to enable assistance designers to specify the assistance that they wish for a target-application, by means of a set of rules. In aLDEAS, we define an assistance rule as a complex action that complies with the pattern given in Fig. 6. A rule starts with a trigger event that corresponds to the waiting of an event. A rule then contains an assistance action or a consultation with an alternative branching followed by as many assistance actions. A rule can be associated with an end event that corresponds to a wait for that event followed by the stop marker. If a rule has no end event, it will leave all its actions to stop on their own (or be stopped by the user). Fig. 7 gives the example of two assistance rules created for the target-application PhotoScape, a freeware for photo correction. Rule R0 contains a trigger event (the assistance launch) and a consultation of the user asking if he/she wishes help. R1 will be triggered if the user chooses the option "yes, I want help". The rule R7 is triggered by a click on component 228 (the "tools" menu of PhotoScape). R7 triggers an assistance action made up of two elementary assistance actions: the enhancement of component 210 (the "red eyes" button of PhotoScape), and a message suggesting the user to click on this button. The click on the "red eyes" button will put an end to the rule R7 and thus delete both the enhancement and the message.

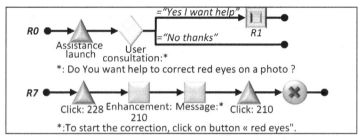

Fig. 7. Example of the assistance rules R0 and R7 for PhotoScape

4.2   Complex Assistance Actions Pattern

The aLDEAS language makes possible the definition of complex assistance actions, combining several elementary elements. The definition of such actions can be difficult. For this reason, we defined complex assistance actions patterns associated with our language, in order to facilitate the definition of some complex actions frequently encountered in existing assistance systems: animated agents actions, guided presentation and step-by-step. In this section, only the patterns relative to step-by-step actions are given.

An **animated agent action** makes possible the combination of several elementary actions for a given character: messages, animation (show a component, applaud, greet…), and moving on the screen. For instance: the animated agent places itself next to the "e-mail" field, it displays the message "don't forget to fill your e-mail address", and it shows the field until the user modifies the value of this field.

A **guided presentation** is made of several steps, in which a component is enhanced and possibly presented by a message. We frequently find this kind of assistance actions in existing applications, notably when an application is launched for the first time, or after an update. The instantiation of the guided presentation pattern is a way for the assistance designer to representation his knowledge on the target-application functionalities.

A **step-by-step** aims at facilitating the achievement of a given task by detailing it in several elementary steps. Each step corresponds to an action to perform on a component of the target-application interface. We call **automated step-by-step** a step-by-step in which the assistance system will perform the actions on behalf of the user. We call **guided step-by-step** a step-by-step in which the assistance system will ask the user to perform the required actions. The patterns of a step for automated step-by-step and for guided step-by-step are given respectively in Fig. 9 and Fig. 10: these two step patterns are used by the step-by-step pattern (cf. Fig. 8), on which the step are represented by ⊡. The instantiation of the step-to-step pattern is a way for the assistance designer to representation his knowledge on the different actions to do in order to perform a given task in the target-application.

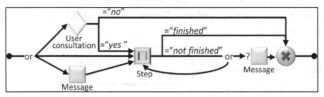

Fig. 8. Step-by-step pattern

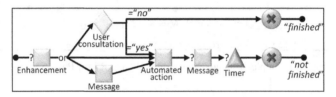

Fig. 9. Step for automated step-by-step pattern

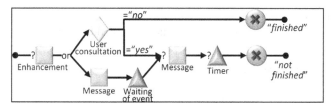

Fig. 10. Step for guided step-by-step pattern

5 Implementation in SEPIA

We implemented aLDEAS and the patterns that complete it in the SEPIA environment (Specification and Execution of Personalized Intelligent Assistance).

The **assistance editor** is a tool aimed at assistance designers. It implements aLDEAS and makes possible the specification, for any given target-application, of an assistance system described by a set of assistance rules complying with the rule pattern (cf. Fig. 6). The assistance editor provides an interface for the definition the elementary assistance action presented in Section 3.3 (except the grayed actions on Fig. 3 and Fig. 4), and for the definition of action that instantiate the pattern proposed in Section 4.2. No knowledge on aLDEAS is required to use the assistance editor.

We developed a set of **epi-assistants**, able to perform in a target-application the elementary assistance actions proposed by aLDEAS and defined thanks to our assistance editor. The *automated actions* are available on any web application, on Windows native and Java applications, and on Linux GKT and Qt applications. Our epi-assistants performing these actions use a user script for web applications and different accessibility libraries for desktop applications: UIAutomation, JavaAccessibility and ATK-SPI [4]. *Enhancement* and *masking* actions are available for the same categories of applications as they need the same technology to find the bounding rectangle of the component that must be enhanced or masked. *Animated agent actions* are available on any Windows web or desktop application. *Messages* and *resource launch* are available for any application.

We developed a **generic assistant engine** able to execute the assistance specified by the assistance designer in the editor. To perform elementary assistance actions, the engine invokes one of our epi-assistants. Regarding complex assistance actions instantiating one of our patterns, the engine ensures their management and invokes an epi-assistant when necessary.

6 Evaluations

The propositions presented in this paper have already been evaluated in several ways. Regarding the feasibility of our approach, it is demonstrated by its implementation in SEPIA, through the editor and the engine, completed by our epi-detectors and epi-assistants. In this section, we present the studies lead to evaluate the usability of aLDEAS. We also performed several studies to evaluate the utility and acceptation of the assistance provided to end users that are not presented here [5].

6.1   Usability of aLDEAS

We made two experiments that aimed at evaluating the usability of aLDEAS language by assistance designers, with both computer-scientists and non-computer scientists.

Use of aLDEAS by Computer Scientists

In the context of a computer science master degree, students have developed in pairs simple ILE (Interactive Learning Environment), without any assistance system. We asked to the 29 students the create assistance system for the 14 ILE developed in order to demonstrate that aLDEAS can help assistance designers to specify an assistance system. First, each pair has been separated in two rooms, during 90 minutes. In the first rooms, 14 assistance designers have to define "on paper" an assistance system for their ILE, without any formalism. In the other room, 15 assistance designers have to define an assistance system in aLDEAS. They previously received explanations on aLDEAS. Each pair was then gathered during 90 minutes in order to share their work, and to define their final assistance system in aLDEAS. In a second time, the assistance designers had to use the SEPIA system during 3 hours, in order to define their assistance system, and to test it in their ILE.

Each pair succeeded in creating an assistance system with aLDEAS. A satisfaction questionnaire showed that 93% of the assistance designers found aLDEAS easy to use, and 76% thought that aLDEAS helped them to define their assistance system. 63% of the assistance designers thought that the use of aLDEAS facilitates the specification of the assistance with the SEPIA system and 67% found it easy to use to define assistance rules. Several assistance designers also noticed in their comment to the satisfaction questionnaire that aLDEAS helped them to work in pair and to formalize their ideas.

Use of aLDEAS by Non-computer Scientists

We ask five non-computer scientists to use aLDEAS in order to represent an assistance system for the red eyes correction on a photo with PhotoScape. These five assistance designers were between 11 to 68 years old. The assistance designers received explanations on aLDEAS during 5 minutes, and they had examples of aLDEAS rules, coming from another assistance system.

First, the assistance designer used successfully aLDEAS language to define "on paper" between 7 to 9 assistance rules complying with aLDEAS pattern. This work lasted between 30 to 45 minutes. In a second time, they used the SEPIA system to create and test their assistance system, after a short presentation of the SEPIA assistance editor. This work lasted between 55 to 95 minutes.

Four assistance designers on five found aLDEAS easy to use, and all of them declared that aLDEAS helped them a lot to create their assistance system. What's more, they found that the definition of rules with the SEPIA editor is easy once the rules are defined in aLDEAS. These encouraging results seem to show that the aLDEAS language and its implementation in the SEPIA system can be used by assistance designers without any knowledge in programming. It has to be confirmed by a wider experiment with non-computer scientists, with other target-applications than PhotoScape.

7   Discussion

In order to evaluate the coverage of the language that we propose, we used it to model various existing assistance systems, representative of the assistance types that are the most frequently found. Thus, aLDEAS makes possible the modeling of assistance systems frequently used in Web applications that contain a form: for instance, theses assistance systems explain to the user where to find information to fill a field, or advise the user when a field is not filled. Guided presentation of a software or functionality, a typical assistance system, can also be modeled in our language. Otherwise, there are many tutorials proposed by expert users in order to guide a user step-by-step to achieve a task, thanks to annotated screen shots and messages. Our language allows to model such assistance systems, with the advantage that they will be integrated in the target-application. Thus, instead of annotated screen shots, the assistance system can directly enhance the target-application user interface. Nevertheless, some assistance systems cannot be modeled with our language: it is the case for assistance systems very specific to an application and that require information not available from outside the application. For instance, some recommender systems integrated in online sale applications use information relative to all the articles consulted or bought by all users. aLDEAS does not make possible the consultation of this kind of information.

We also evaluated aLDEAS language by comparing it to existing approach for *a posteriori* specification of assistance for a target-application. Compared to the approach proposed by [8], aLDEAS can model such assistance action, as a wait for a click event on a given link, optionally followed by a consultation of the browsing history, then by an assistance action of type message (that can contain link towards another web page or resource). aLDEAS also proposes elementary assistance action to launch resources directly without a need use a link in a message. Compared to the approach proposed by [2], aLDEAS allows to define assistance actions involving animated agents able to move themselves in a web page, to express themselves orally or textually, and by gestures and animations. We also facilitate the definition of such actions by proposing a pattern of animated agent actions. Finally, our language allows to define rules of the form <trigger event, trigger condition, assistance action, end event> (cf. Section 4.1) equivalent to the rules used in the approaches of [7] and [1]. What's more aLDEAS allows to define more complex and varied assistance rules. aLDEAS also proposes a larger choice of elementary assistance actions, and patterns facilitating the definition of assistance actions composed of several elements.

8   Conclusion and Perspectives

The aLDEAS language and the complex assistance action patterns that we presented allow to define assistance systems suitable to their target-application. By adopting a fully epiphytic approach, we make possible the *a posteriori* plugging of assistance systems in existing applications. These applications have not to be specifically designed for the integration of assistance, any access to its source code is necessary and any programming skills are required of the assistance designer. The experimentation that we performed showed that aLDEAS can be used to define assistance systems "on paper", by assistance designers with or without programming skills. Moreover, aLDEAS seem to help assistance designers to represents the assistance that they wish for the target-application.

The aLDEAS language is implemented in the SEPIA system. The experimentation that we performed showed that SEPIA can be used by assistance designers, with or without programming skills. What's more, SEPIA can be used to provide end users with efficient assistance, in order to help them to achieve a given task, in particular in the context of the discovery or occasional use of the target-application.

We now work on a method to help the assistance designer to identify the assistance needs of an application, in order to help him/her to define an efficient assistance system. This method will also make possible the end users to provide the assistance designer with feedback, in order to help him/her to improve the assistance system.

References

1. Dufresne, A., Paquette, G.: ExploraGraph: a flexible and adaptive interface to support distance learning. In: Ed-Media, Victoria, Canada, pp. 304–309 (2000)
2. Carlier, F., Renault, F.: Educational webportals augmented by mobile devices with iFrimousse architecture. In: ICALT, Sousse, Tunisia, pp. 236–240 (2010)
3. Gapenne, O., Lenay, C., Boullier, D.: Defining categories of the human/technology coupling: theoretical and methodological issues. In: ERCIM Workshop on User Interface for All, Paris, France, pp. 197–198 (2002)
4. Ginon, B., Champin, P.-A., Jean-Daubias, S.: Collecting fine-grained use traces in any application without modifying it. In: Workshop EXPPORT of ICCBR, New-York, USA (2013)
5. Ginon, B., Thai, L.V., Jean-Daubias, S., Lefevre, M., Champin, P.-A.: Adding epiphytic assistance systems in learning applications using the SEPIA system. In: Ec-Tel, Graz, Austria (2014)
6. Paquette, G., Pachet, F., Giroux, S., Girard, J.: EpiTalk, a generic tool for the development of advisor systems. In: IJAIED, pp. 349–370 (1996)
7. Paquette, G., Rosca, I., Mihaila, S., Masmoudi, A.: TELOS: A Service-Oriented Framework to Support Learning and Knowledge Management. In: Pierre, S. (ed.) E-Learning Networked Environments and Architectures, pp. 79–109 (2007)
8. Richard, B., Tchounikine, P.: Enhancing the adaptivity of an existing Website with an epiphyte recommender system. New Review of Hypermedia and Multimedia 10, 31–52 (2004)

Ontology Design Pattern Property Specialisation Strategies

Karl Hammar[1,2]

[1] Information Engineering Group, Jönköping University, Sweden
[2] Department of Computer and Information Science, Linköping University, Sweden
karl.hammar@jth.hj.se

Abstract. Ontology Design Patterns (ODPs) show potential in enabling simpler, faster, and more correct Ontology Engineering by laymen and experts. For ODP adoption to take off, improved tool support for ODP use in Ontology Engineering is required. This paper studies and evaluates the effects of strategies for object property specialisation in ODPs, and suggests tool improvements based on those strategies. Results indicate the existence of three previously unstudied strategies for ODP specialisation, the uses of which affect reasoning performance and integration complexity of resulting ontologies.

1 Introduction

Content Ontology Design Patterns (hereafter ODPs) were introduced by Gangemi [7] and Blomqvist & Sandkuhl [3] in 2005 (extending upon ideas by the W3C Semantic Web Best Practices and Deployment Working Group[1]), as a means of facilitating practical ontology development. These patterns are intended to help guide ontology engineering work by non-expert users, by packaging best practices into small reusable blocks of ontology functionality, to be adapted and specialised by those users in their individual ontology development use cases. Studies indicate that ODP usage can help lower the number of modelling errors and inconsistencies in ontologies, and that they are by the users perceived as useful and helpful [2,5].

This idea has gained some traction within the academic community, as evidenced by the Workshop on Ontology Patterns series of workshops. However, the adoption of ODPs among practitioners is still quite limited. In order to support increased adoption and use of ODPs (and potentially, as a result thereof, increased adoption and use of Semantic Web technologies and ontologies in general), methods and tooling supporting their usage are required. While there are available tools for ODP use (e.g., the XD Tools for NeOn Toolkit), the functionality of these tools is limited; they are based on their authors' largely intuitive understanding of ODP usage and practices at the time when ODPs were first proposed. In order to improve tooling to support today's users, an empirically founded understanding of how ODPs are actually used today is needed.

---

[1] http://www.w3.org/2001/sw/BestPractices/

K. Janowicz et al. (Eds.): EKAW 2014, LNAI 8876, pp. 165–180, 2014.

The author's present research concerns the development of such improved ODP tooling based on published ODPs and ontologies. In this paper, the focus is on the choices that users face when specialising an ODP, and the potential consequences those choices may give rise to. The work was initiated using the following research question:

- How are Content Ontology Design Patterns used or specialised in Ontology Engineering projects for the Semantic Web, and what are the effects of such usage?

In studying this rather generally expressed question, as further described in Section 3.1, several ODP application strategies were observed (listed and discussed in Section 3.2). The discovery of these strategies gave rise to more specific research questions on their usages and effects:

1. To what degree are the class-oriented, property-oriented, or hybrid ODP specialisation strategies used in published ODPs and ontologies?
2. What are the reasoning performance effects of specialising ODPs and ontologies in accordance with the class-oriented or property-oriented strategies?

The main contributions of this paper are a classification of three different strategies for ODP specialisation based on the semantics of object property domains and ranges, and a partial understanding of the consequences of employing two of these specialisation strategies. Additionally, the paper contributes suggestions on how to implement tooling supporting users in specialising ODPs based on a strategy that is consistent with their preferences and goals.

The paper is structured as follows: Section 2 introduces the background and some related work in the area. Section 3 describes the ODP specialisation strategies and the method by which they were discovered. Section 4 details a study on the use of these strategies in published ontologies, and the effects of such uses. Section 5 discusses the consequences of these findings for the development of ODP support tools. Section 6 concludes the paper by summarising the answers to the posed research questions.

2   Background and Related Work

Ontology Design Patterns were introduced at around the same time independently by Gangemi [7] and Blomqvist and Sandkuhl [3]. The former define such patterns by way of a number of characteristics that they display, including examples such as *"[an ODP] is a template to represent, and possibly solve, a modelling problem"* [7, p. 267] and *"[an ODP] can/should be used to describe a 'best practice' of modelling"* [7, p. 268]. The latter describes ODPs as generic descriptions of recurring constructs in ontologies, which can be used to construct components or modules of an ontology. Both approaches emphasise that patterns, in order to be easily reusable, need to include not only textual descriptions of the modelling issue or best practice, but also some formal encoding of the proposed solution.

The understanding of Ontology Design Patterns has been heavily influenced by the work taking place in the NeOn Project, the results of which include a pattern typology [13]. This typology is based on the uses to which patterns are put, whether they represent best practices in reasoning, naming, transformation, content modelling, etc. This paper focuses exclusively on Content patterns (the most common type of patterns). Content patterns represent some content in the domain of discourse, and their formal representations are typically packaged as reusable mini-ontologies in OWL format.

Ontology Design Patterns have also been studied within the CO-ODE project [1,6], the results of which include a repository of patterns[2] and an Ontology Pre-Processing Language (OPPL)[3]. The patterns proposed and developed in these works are also Content ODPs, but they are generally more abstract or foundational in nature than those developed within the NeOn project. These patterns also double as transformation patterns, since they can be used in conjunction with the OPPL macro language to enable rapid transformation of large ontologies.

2.1   eXtreme Design

The eXtreme Design (XD) collaborative ontology development method, developed within the NeOn Project, is based on the use of Ontology Design Patterns [4]. XD is defined as *"a family of methods and associated tools, based on the application, exploitation, and definition of Ontology Design Patterns (ODPs) for solving ontology development issues"* [12, p. 83]. The method is influenced by the eXtreme Programming (XP) agile software development method, and like it, emphasises incremental development and continuous requirements management. Like XP it also recommends pair development, test driven development, refactoring, and a divide-and-conquer approach to problem-solving [11].

The XD method consists of a number of tasks, illustrated in Figure 1. The main development tasks are performed in iterating loops; these tasks are in the figure enclosed in a grey box. The "Reuse and integrate ODPs" task is where the developer specialises a selected ODP (representing a general reusable solution) to the specific modelling scenario. It is the choices that the developer need to make when performing this task, which are explored in the scope of this paper.

2.2   XD Tools

The XD method is supported by the XD Plugin for the Eclipse-based NeOn Toolkit[4]. The XD Plugin provides a number of components that simplify pattern browsing, selection, and specialisation. The specialisation component provides a wizard interface for specialising ODPs, consisting of three steps:

1. Specialising leaf classes of the class hierarchy by defining subclasses

---

[2] http://odps.sourceforge.net/odp/html/index.html
[3] http://oppl2.sourceforge.net/
[4] http://neon-toolkit.org/

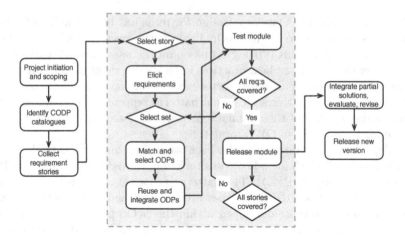

Fig. 1. XD Workflow (adapted from [12])

2. Specialising leaf properties of the property hierarchy by defining subproperties
3. Defining domains and ranges of newly defined subproperties to correspond with the new subclasses

The specialisation wizard also provides a certain degree of validation of the generated specialisations, by presenting the user with a list of generated axioms, expressed in natural language, for the user to reject or accept. Unfortunately, the XD Tools plugin's dependence on the NeOn Toolkit (which is no longer developed or maintained) means that ontology engineers who want to use newer tools and standards are unable to use XD Tools. Instead, they have to do their ODP-based ontology engineering without adequate tool support.

3   Understanding ODP Specialisation

In order to answer the initial research question, a two-part method was employed. Initially, a set of ODP-using ontologies were studied in order to extract commonalities or strategies regarding how ODPs were specialised. The following two subsections describe this process, and the ODP specialisation strategies discovered by it. Subsequently, the usage of those specialisation strategies among ontologies and the consequences of such use, were evaluated. These latter evaluations are described in section 4.

3.1   Study Setup

Ontologies making use of ODPs first had to be located and downloaded. For this purpose, a method combining several different sources of ontologies was employed. The initial set of ODP-using patterns was retrieved using the Google Custom Search API[5]. This API was queried repeatedly, using all known ODP URIs; the results were downloaded, filtered based on type, and only such results that held both one or more instances of *owl:Ontology* and one or more references to known ODP namespaces were kept. Additionally, the LODStats[6] list of RDF dataset vocabularies, the Linked Open Vocabularies[7] dataset, and the known uses and instantiations of ODPs from OntologyDesignPatterns.org[8] were added to this set (the same criteria for filtering were employed). This resulted in 22 ODP-using OWL ontologies being found and downloaded. Additionally, a set of 19 such ontologies originating with the IKS[9] project were added to the set[10].

From these 41 ontologies, 107 *specialisation mapping axioms*, that is, subsumption or equivalence axioms linking a class or property defined in the ontology to a class or property defined in a known ODP, were extracted. These mapping axioms were analysed for recurring patterns based on the features of the ODP class or property being specialised, and based on the type of mapping properties used. An excerpt of the set of extracted mapping axioms is displayed in Table 1.

Table 1. Excerpt from the set of extracted ODP specialisation mapping axioms

ODP Class/Property	Role in specialisation	Occurrences
place.owl#Place	superclass	4
parameter.owl#Parameter	superclass	2
collectionentity.owl#hasMember	superproperty	1
bag.owl#hasItem	superproperty	1
bag.owl#hasItem	used in property restriction	4

Table 2 summarises the type of mappings used in the gathered data. As the table shows, simple mapping using *rdfs:subClassOf* and *rdfs:subPropertyOf* predicates against ODP named classes is the most common, together accounting for 85 % of all specialisation axioms. In all but a handful of these uses, ODP classes and properties act as superclasses and superproperties to specialised classes and properties. Equivalency mappings against named ODP concepts are used less often; no uses of *owl:equivalentProperty* are observed at all, and *owl:equivalentClass* is only used in a few cases.

The use of existential or universal quantification restrictions involving ODP classes and properties is worth noting. In the studied set of ontologies, such

---

[5] https://developers.google.com/custom-search/
[6] http://stats.lod2.eu/
[7] http://lov.okfn.org/
[8] http://ontologydesignpatterns.org/
[9] http://www.iks-project.eu/
[10] Ontologies and scripts used in this paper are available via http://goo.gl/jjU9OE

Table 2. ODP Specialisation Mapping Axioms Summary

Mapping axiom type	Occurrences
rdfs:subClassOf against named ODP class	32
rdfs:subPropertyOf against named ODP property	59
owl:equivalentClass against named ODP class	3
owl:equivalentProperty against named ODP property	0
rdfs:subClassOf against value constraint over ODP property	7
owl:equivalentClass against value constraint over ODP property	2
rdfs:subClassOf against value constraint over ODP class	4
owl:equivalentClass against value constraint over ODP class	0

restrictions are used to constrain the uses of ODP object properties, locally emulating domain or range axioms; for instance, a WeatherForecast is defined as being equivalent to the union of two restrictions, one using a project-defined vocabulary, and one on the WeatherForecast being an information realisation (i.e., EquivalentClass (WeatherForecast objectSomeValuesFrom(informationRealization:realizes WeatherInformation))).

Such a use of restrictions to constrain the local semantics of object properties can be seen as a form of specialisation of a more general model, or ODP, for a particular modelling case. This observation leads us to consider how this type of specialisation strategy differs from the more common strategy of specialising subproperties with defined domains and ranges, as supported by the existing XD Tools. In order to develop tool support for the use of property restrictions in ODP specialisation, the consequences of applying this type of modelling need be studied, such that users can be informed of the potential effects of applying either the traditional (hereafter denoted *"property-oriented"*, due to the use of subproperties) strategy for ODP specialisation, or the alternative restriction-based strategy (hereafter denoted *"class-oriented"*, due to the use of property restrictions on subclasses).

3.2   Study Results

The following section discusses and exemplifies the two initially discovered strategies of ODP specialisation. The possibilities of and the consequences of combining the two strategies in a third, hybrid strategy, are also discussed. Two things are important to note. Firstly, an *ODP specialisation* is here defined as the set of specialisation mapping axioms that together specialise a single ODP for use in a target ontology. In most cases each ODP specialisation will consist of several specialisation mapping axioms, each specialising different classes or properties of the ODP. Often this set of axioms will be held in an ontology module imported into the target ontology, an *ODP specialisation module*. Secondly, in discussing the relative usage frequency of the strategies, we here only compare those specialisations that modify the semantics of object properties defined in the original ODP (simple class taxonomies without any object property specialisation have been filtered out), and we also include specialisations of ODP specialisations; as OWL imports are transitive, this type of layered structure is not uncommon. This gives a total of 20 ODP specialisations, the distributions of which over the specialisation strategies are summarised in Table 3.

Table 3. ODP Specialisation Strategy Use

Specialisation strategy	Occurrences
Property-oriented	9
Class-oriented	6
Hybrid	5

Property-Oriented Strategy. The property-oriented strategy is the most common type of ODP specialisation seen in the originally studied set of ODP specialisations, being used in 9 out of 20 cases. This may be due to the fact that OWL tools and tutorials tend to emphasize properties as basic language features, and the construction of property subsumption hierarchies specialising those properties as fundamental modelling tasks.

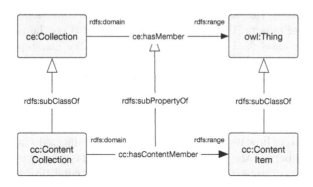

Fig. 2. Property-oriented ODP Specialisation Strategy

The process by which an ODP is specialised in accordance with the property-oriented strategy is illustrated and exemplified in Figure 2 (the example is taken from an ontology developed in the IKS project). In the figure, the *ce:* namespace prefix indicates that classes or properties are defined within the CollectionEntity ODP[11], whereas the *cc* namespace prefix indicates that classes or properties are

---

[11] http://ontologydesignpatterns.org/wiki/Submissions:CollectionEntity

defined within the ODP specialisation module ContentCollection. We see that the higher level class definitions defined in the ODP or OWL language itself (*ce:Collection*, *owl:Thing*) are specialised for the modelling problem at hand using newly defined subclasses (*cc:ContentCollection*, *cc:ContentItem*), and that the usage of *ce:hasMember* is specialised to apply to these new class definitions via a new subproperty *cc:hasContentMember* with corresponding domain and range declarations. As shown by [10], the *rdfs:subPropertyOf* definition implies that domains and ranges of subproperties must be subsets of the domains and ranges of their superproperties.

It should be noted that this specialisation strategy does not necessarily need to be fully instantiated in all parts; there are several cases where only one subclass is created, and where either the domain or range of the created subproperty are therefore defined over a more general term. Indeed, that is the way in which the CollectionEntity ODP itself is structured in Figure 2, with *ce:hasMember* having a range of *owl:Thing*. The important thing about this strategy, and the key differentiator against the class-oriented strategy, is the definition of a subproperty.

Class-Oriented Strategy. The class-oriented strategy is a little less common in the studied set of ODP specialisations, being seen in 6 of 20 cases. The fundamental idea of this strategy is to avoid creating specialised subproperties, by instead reusing the object properties of the original ODP, and locally constraining the usage of those properties by way of property restrictions on specialised classes. As shown by Horridge et al. [8] the definitions SubClassOf(A ObjectAllValuesFrom(someProperty B)) imposes a local range of B on the property *someProperty* for the class A. Using the same approach, we can represent a local domain of A over the property *someProperty* where the target of that property is B, by defining EquivalentClass(A ObjectSomeValuesFrom(someProperty B)).

The concept is illustrated in Figure 3. The namespaces used in the figure are *ir:*, denoting the Information Realization ODP[12], and *wf:*, denoting the Weather Forecast ODP specialisation module. In this example a *wf:WeatherForecast* class is defined in terms of how its member individuals are connected via the *ir:realizes* property to members of the *wf:WeatherInformation* class. In layman terms, the *owl:equivalentClass* property restriction imposes the condition that any individual which is connected via *ir:realizes* to some other individual that is a *wf:WeatherInformation*, must itself be a *wf:WeatherForecast*; this restriction corresponds to the use of a *rdfs:domain* definition over a specialised property in the property-oriented strategy. Similarly, the *rdfs:subClassOf* property restriction imposes the condition that only individuals that are *wf:WeatherInformation* may be linked via *ir:realizes* from an individual that is a *wf:WeatherForecast*; this corresponds to a rdfs:range axiom in the property-oriented strategy.

Note that the use of the term *corresponds to* above does not imply that the described uses of property restriction axioms are logically equivalent to the

---

[12] http://ontologydesignpatterns.org/wiki/Submissions:Information_realization

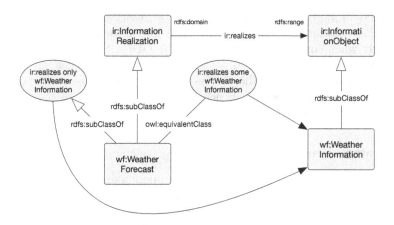

Fig. 3. Class-oriented ODP Specialisation Strategy (rounded rectangles denote named classes, ovals denote property restriction axioms)

use of domain or range axioms; merely that both modelling strategies allow for describing similar phenomena, via expressing constraints on which types of entities that object properties can connect.

Hybrid Strategy. In addition to the pure property-oriented or pure class-oriented strategies for ODP specialisation, the combination of the two in a hybrid strategy approach also occurs in the set of ODP specialisations: 5 of the 20 ODP specialisations use such a hybrid strategy. In these specialisations, subproperties with domain and range declarations are defined, and the classes involved are also defined using universal and/or existential quantification restrictions ranging over the newly created subproperties. The latter restriction axioms are possibly redundant if they are in this manner defined over properties that have themselves got domains and ranges. They could however be helpful from a usability perspective, in a large ontology of taxonomic nature, i.e. with a large class subsumption hierarchy, where one wants readers of said ontology to be able to easily grasp how classes are intended to be interconnected without having to study the property subsumption hierarchy.

4 Strategy Usage and Effects

As seen in Section 3.1, the number of published ODP specialisations in which object property specialisation takes place is limited; only 20 such cases were found. This is too small a dataset to base conclusions on. This section broadens the scope from just ODP specialisations to ontologies in general. If the same strategies are also observed in a larger set of ontologies, this strengthens the notion that ontology engineers need tool support for these strategies. Similarly, if the effects of applying these strategies can be observed on ontologies in general, ODP specialisation tooling need take this into account, and guide the user accordingly when constructing ontologies using ODPs. Section 4.1 describes a study on to what extent the strategies are employed in ontologies published on the web. Section 4.2 discusses the effects of using the property-oriented or class-oriented strategies, and details a benchmark-based evaluation of the reasoning performance effects of such use.

4.1 Strategy Use

The ontologies studied were gathered in the same manner as described in Section 3.1. While we previously selected only those downloaded RDF files that held instances of *owl:Ontology* and that had references to known ODP namespaces, in this case the latter selection filter was dropped, and all downloaded graphs containing OWL ontologies were kept. This resulted in 423 ontologies for study.

```
Input: graph = An RDF graph containing an owl:Ontology
1  restrictionProperties = List();
2  hasDomainOrRange = List();
3  for subProperty defined in graph do
4  |    if hasDomain(subProperty) then
5  |    |    Append(hasDomainOrRange,subProperty);
6  |    if hasRange(subProperty) then
7  |    |    Append(hasDomainOrRange,subProperty);
8  for class defined in graph do
9  |    for superClass in getSuperClass(class) do
10 |    |    if hasPredicate(superClass, owl:allValuesFrom) then
11 |    |    |    restrictionProperty = getObject(superClass,owl:onProperty);
12 |    |    |    Append(restrictionProperties,restrictionProperty);
13 |    for equivalentClass in getEquivalentClass(class) do
14 |    |    if hasPredicate(equivalentClass, owl:someValuesFrom) then
15 |    |    |    restrictionProperty = getObject(equivalentClass,owl:onProperty);
16 |    |    |    Append(restrictionProperties,restrictionProperty);
17 if Overlap(Set(hasDomainOrRange),Set(restrictionProperties)) > 0 then
18 |    Return(Hybrid strategy);
19 if Size(hasDomainOrRange) == 0 AND Size(restrictionProperties) == 0 then
20 |    Return(No property specialisation occurring);
21 if Size(hasDomainOrRange) > Size(restrictionProperties) then
22 |    Return(Property-oriented strategy);
23 else
24 |    Return(Class-oriented strategy);
```

Algorithm 1. Detects ontology property specialisation strategy

---

Algorithm 1 was then executed over the ontology set. Per the algorithm, the number of specialised object properties that have domain or range definitions are compared against the number of properties that occur in a restriction emulating a local domain or range, and the ontology as a whole is classified based on the most commonly occurring type of structure. In the case that an overlap exists between these two sets, that is, that there are individual object properties that are specialised in both ways, the ontology is classified as employing the hybrid strategy. The results of this classification are summarised in Table 4 (simple taxonomies and alignment ontologies not defining any own OWL constructs have been filtered out of the results).

Table 4. Ontology Specialisation Strategy Use

Specialisation strategy	Occurrences
Property-oriented	193
Class-oriented	33
Hybrid	23
No property specialisation occurring	98

These results indicate that all three object property specialisation strategies discovered in Section 3.2 to some extent also occur in ontology engineering where ODPs are not used. The results also indicate that the property-oriented strategy is by a significant margin the most commonly used strategy. Comparing against the previously studied ODP specialisations (Table 3), we see that the class-oriented and hybrid strategies are used less frequently in ontologies (13 % vs 30 % of cases for the former, 9 % vs 25 % of cases for the latter). This suggests there may be a difference in how ontology engineering is performed when using ODPs as compared to in the general case.

4.2   Strategy Effects

An advantage of the property-oriented strategy is that it creates new subproperties, which can themselves be dereferenced and annotated or typed as needed. For instance, such a specialised subproperty could be defined to be transitive or functional, without this definition affecting the parent property. Another advantage is that this type of modelling is accessible from a usability perspective; the simple tree view of the property subsumption hierarchy as used in many tools enables the ontology engineer or end-user to get an at-a-glance understanding of how the properties are organised and intended to be used. Yet another advantage is that, given that domains and ranges are defined, inferring the type of individuals connected via the property is a relatively fast operation, when compared to the class-oriented strategy.

The main advantage of the class-oriented specialisation strategy is that no subproperties are created, but rather that the original parent properties are reused. This allows RDF datasets that are expressed in accordance with an ontology using this strategy to be natively interoperable with other datasets using the same property, without the need for reasoning. This is particularly relevant in an ODP context, where the ODP and its properties are intended be reused extensively. Such interoperability can have many advantages, including in querying, where SPARQL triple patterns will often define only the predicate used and leave subject and object variables unbound. Further, this strategy allows for modelling typing based on property links, much like *duck typing* in programming; such an approach can have advantages in situations where the ontology engineer does not control the predicates used in data creation or extraction, but rather has to deal with what they are given.

There are also downsides to this strategy, most noticeably in terms of reasoning performance. As pointed out by Horridge et al. [8], universal quantification axioms, used in this strategy to emulate *rdfs:range* definitions, are disallowed in the computationally friendly OWL 2 EL profile. As illustrated by Urbani et al. [15], using property restrictions to infer typing requires multiple joins between large sets of candidate entities, greatly complicating reasoning, particularly when dealing with large datasets. The results of Kang et al. [9] also indicate that there may be performance penalties associated with this type of reasoning. Their predictive model for reasoning performance includes eight ontology metrics categorised as impacting or strongly impacting reasoning performance; of these, three (the number of existential quantifications, average class out-degree, and subsumption tree impurity) are increased by employing the class-oriented strategy, as opposed to the property-oriented one. The strongest impact factor of any metric in their model is the number of existential quantification axioms, which are heavily used in this modelling strategy.

Reasoning Performance Evaluation. In order to evaluate the reasoning performance effects of the class-oriented and property-oriented specialisation strategies, an experiment was set up using the well known LUBM[13] and BSBM benchmarks[14]. The hypothesis was that, due to the above mentioned characteristics of the two strategies, the execution of reasoning tasks on datasets using ontologies adhering to the property-oriented strategy would be faster than on the same datasets using ontologies adhering to the class-oriented strategy.

Each of the two benchmark suite ontologies were adapted to both the property-oriented and class-oriented strategies, via replacing domain and range axioms by universal and existential quantification restrictions or vice versa (in the case of BSBM, as an OWL ontology is not provided, said ontology first had to be created from scratch using the BSBM Dataset Specification). Datasets of non-trivial size (LUBM: 1053084 triples, BSBM: 334479 triples) were then generated using each benchmark suite's data generator. In order to make the performance evaluation tasks which include inferring typing axioms non-trivial, RDF typing axioms generated by the benchmark data generators were removed.

The datasets were then used together with the property- and class-oriented benchmark ontologies as input for two leading OWL reasoners, Pellet (version

---

[13] http://swat.cse.lehigh.edu/projects/lubm/

[14] http://wifo5-03.informatik.uni-mannheim.de/bizer/berlinsparqlbenchmark/

2.3.1) and HermIT (version 1.3.8). The operations performed were consistency checking (ensuring that no contradictory axioms exist in the datasets and ontologies), and realization (finding the most specific class that a named individual belongs to). As the HermiT reasoner does not support performing realization from the command line, it was only used to perform consistency checking over the two datasets. The experiments were executed on a quad-core 2.6 GHz Intel Core i7 machine with an 8 GB Java heap size, running Mac OS X 10.9.3.

Table 5. Specialisation strategy realisation performance effects

Reasoning task	Benchmark	Reasoner	PO time	CO time
Consistency checking	BSBM	Pellet	1.274 s	1.897 s
Consistency checking	BSBM	HermiT	1.984 s	27.193 s
Consistency checking	LUBM	Pellet	8.230 s	42.887 s
Consistency checking	LUBM	HermiT	10.097 s	46 min, 17 s
Realising individuals	BSBM	Pellet	2.389 s	9.482 s
Realising individuals	LUBM	Pellet	1.801 s	4+ hours

As illustrated in Table 5, the hypothesis holds for the generated datasets. In all of the reasoning tasks performed, the use of class-oriented ontologies resulted in slower execution than the use of property-oriented ontologies. In most cases the effects were severe; in one case execution of the reasoning task was halted when no results were reported after 4 hours of continuous execution. It should be noted that the inferred axioms of the reasoning tasks were equivalent, regardless of which strategy the ontology in question used.

5   Discussion

As shown above, the different strategies for object property specialisation are used both in the specialisation of ODPs and in specialisation of ontologies. The consequences of selecting one or the other of the strategies can be significant, and there is a trade-off to make: the class-oriented strategy can reduce the complexity of RDF data integration via the use of shared RDF predicates, but is very slow to reason with, while on the other hand the property-oriented strategy is far more efficient for reasoning but requires the use of new properties. This tradeoff is not common knowledge in the ontology engineering community, and consequently, methods and tools that aid engineers in understanding it, would be beneficial. Furthermore, it seems that the usages of the two strategies differ such that the class-oriented strategy is more commonly used in ODP specialisation than in ontologies in general. If this is the case, and if this more common use of the class-oriented strategy is a consequence of the design or use of ODPs, then tooling for ODP specialisation needs to support ontology engineers in applying this to them unfamiliar type of modelling.

Such improved ODP specialisation tooling needs to support at least three different tasks: applying a strategy when specialising an ODP, visualising strategy use in an ODP-based ontology in a user-friendly manner, and refactoring an ODP-based ontology from using one strategy to another.

The first task requires updating the ODP specialisation wizard from the existing XD Tools to be strategy-aware. Upon initiating said wizard, the user needs to be given the choice of by which strategy the ODP is to be specialised. This choice needs to be supported by both information on known effects of strategy use (e.g., guidance texts regarding the trade-offs) and by information on existing strategy use in the ontology project under development and/or the ODP itself. In the case that the user selects the class-oriented or hybrid strategies, the second and third steps of the existing XD tools specialisation wizard (specialising leaf properties, and defining domains and ranges) would need be either replaced or modified, to support the implementation of said strategy.

The second task concerns how to display strategy use in an accessible manner, such that an ontology engineer can quickly ascertain the suitability of an ODP-based ontology for different purposes. For this purpose, the existing Protégé ontology metrics view could be extended with metrics indicating specialisation strategy. In order to simplify the use of ontologies built using a class-oriented strategy, displaying the "emulated" domains and ranges of specialised properties in proximity to those properties' definitions would be helpful.

The third task concerns refactoring an ontology from using one strategy to another, and also harmonising strategy use in the case that different strategies are employed in different parts of an ontology. This appears to be a good use case for the OPPL (Ontology Pre-Processing Language) macro language for ontology transformation discussed in Section 2.

In addition to improved ODP tools, the discovery of these specialisation strategies may also warrant updates to ODP repositories; these repositories would need to provide examples of ODPs specialised per the different strategies. This may necessitate new visual representations for representing universal and existential restrictions in an accessible and user-friendly manner; the work of Stapleton et al.[14] in this direction appears very promising.

5.1 Delimitations and Future Work

This is, to the author's best knowledge, the first work on specialisation strategies for object properties. Consequently, there are many limitations in place, and many opportunities for further work. To begin with, the numbers of ODP specialisations initially studied, benchmarks used for reasoning performance evaluation, and reasoners used for that testing, is limited. Validation of these results on larger datasets and other benchmarks and reasoners would be welcome.

It is likely that the strategies discovered here have more effects and tradeoffs associated with them than just those discussed in this paper. For instance, we note that using the class-oriented strategy, typing is inferred from the typing of related individuals; from this we see that the degree of interconnectedness of individuals in a knowledge base expressed according to the class-oriented strategy will have an impact on reasoning performance over that knowledge base; the strategy used may give rise to different effects across different datasets.

Two other areas that the author aims to explore further in the near future are the effects of applying the hybrid strategy, and if, and in that case how, these strategies can be applied to datatype properties.

6   Conclusions

In this paper we have studied how Content Ontology Design Patterns (ODPs) are used and specialised in practical Ontology Engineering tasks, with an eye towards improving tooling for such engineering work. The main contributions of this work are a classification of three different strategies for ODP specialisation, and an initial understanding of some consequences of employing these strategies. We have shown that these strategies are being used in modelling of publicly released ontologies, both ODP-based and non ODP-based ones. We have noted the trade-off that an ontology engineer may need to make between reasoning performance efficiency on the one hand, and data integration simplicity on the other. Finally, we have suggested and are in the process of implementing tooling improvements to better support Ontology Engineers in understanding and using these strategies.

References

1. Aranguren, M.E., Antezana, E., Kuiper, M., Stevens, R.: Ontology Design Patterns for Bio-ontologies: A Case Study on the Cell Cycle Ontology. BMC Bioinformatics 9(suppl 5) (2008)
2. Blomqvist, E., Gangemi, A., Presutti, V.: Experiments on Pattern-based Ontology Design. In: Proceedings of the Fifth International Conference on Knowledge Capture, pp. 41–48 (2009)
3. Blomqvist, E., Sandkuhl, K.: Patterns in Ontology Engineering: Classification of Ontology Patterns. In: Proceedings of the 7th International Conference on Enterprise Information Systems, pp. 413–416 (2005)
4. Daga, E., Blomqvist, E., Gangemi, A., Montiel, E., Nikitina, N., Presutti, V., Villazon-Terrazas, B.: D2.5.2: Pattern Based Ontology Design: Methodology and Software Support. Tech. rep., NeOn Project (2007)
5. Dzbor, M., Suárez-Figueroa, M.C., Blomqvist, E., Lewen, H., Espinoza, M., Gómez-Pérez, A., Palma, R.: D5.6.2 Experimentation and Evaluation of the NeOn Methodology. Tech. rep., NeOn Project (2007)
6. Egaña, M., Rector, A.L., Stevens, R., Antezana, E.: Applying ontology design patterns in bio-ontologies. In: Gangemi, A., Euzenat, J. (eds.) EKAW 2008. LNCS (LNAI), vol. 5268, pp. 7–16. Springer, Heidelberg (2008)
7. Gangemi, A.: Ontology Design Patterns for Semantic Web Content. In: Gil, Y., Motta, E., Benjamins, V.R., Musen, M.A. (eds.) ISWC 2005. LNCS, vol. 3729, pp. 262–276. Springer, Heidelberg (2005)
8. Horridge, M., Aranguren, M.E., Mortensen, J., Musen, M.A., Noy, N.F.: Ontology Design Pattern Language Expressivity Requirements. In: Proceedings of the 3rd Workshop on Ontology Patterns (2012)

9. Kang, Y.-B., Li, Y.-F., Krishnaswamy, S.: Predicting reasoning performance using ontology metrics. In: Cudré-Mauroux, P., et al. (eds.) ISWC 2012, Part I. LNCS, vol. 7649, pp. 198–214. Springer, Heidelberg (2012)
10. Keet, C.M.: Detecting and revising flaws in OWL object property expressions. In: ten Teije, A., Völker, J., Handschuh, S., Stuckenschmidt, H., d'Acquin, M., Nikolov, A., Aussenac-Gilles, N., Hernandez, N. (eds.) EKAW 2012. LNCS, vol. 7603, pp. 252–266. Springer, Heidelberg (2012)
11. Presutti, V., Blomqvist, E., Daga, E., Gangemi, A.: Pattern-Based Ontology Design. In: Ontology Engineering in a Networked World, pp. 35–64. Springer (2012)
12. Presutti, V., Daga, E., Gangemi, A., Blomqvist, E.: eXtreme Design with Content Ontology Design Patterns. In: Proceedings of the Workshop on Ontology Patterns (WOP), p. 83 (2009)
13. Presutti, V., Gangemi, A., David, S., Aguado de Cea, G., Suárez-Figueroa, M.C., Montiel-Ponsoda, E., Poveda, M.: D2.5.1: A Library of Ontology Design Patterns: Reusable Solutions for Collaborative Design of Networked Ontologies. Tech. rep., NeOn Project (2007)
14. Stapleton, G., Howse, J., Taylor, K., Delaney, A., Burton, J., Chapman, P.: Towards diagrammatic ontology patterns. In: Proceedings of the 4th Workshop on Ontology and Semantic Web Patterns (2014)
15. Urbani, J., Kotoulas, S., Maassen, J., van Harmelen, F., Bal, H.: OWL reasoning with webPIE: Calculating the closure of 100 billion triples. In: Aroyo, L., Antoniou, G., Hyvönen, E., ten Teije, A., Stuckenschmidt, H., Cabral, L., Tudorache, T. (eds.) ESWC 2010, Part I. LNCS, vol. 6088, pp. 213–227. Springer, Heidelberg (2010)

The uComp Protégé Plugin:
Crowdsourcing Enabled Ontology Engineering

Florian Hanika[1], Gerhard Wohlgenannt[1], and Marta Sabou[2]

[1] WU Vienna
{florian.hanika,gerhard.wohlgenannt}@wu.ac.at
[2] MODUL University Vienna
marta.sabou@modul.ac.at

Abstract. Crowdsourcing techniques have been shown to provide effective means for solving a variety of ontology engineering problems. Yet, they are mainly being used as external means to ontology engineering, without being closely integrated into the work of ontology engineers. In this paper we investigate how to closely integrate crowdsourcing into ontology engineering practices. Firstly, we show that a set of basic crowdsourcing tasks are used recurrently to solve a range of ontology engineering problems. Secondly, we present the *uComp Protégé plugin* that facilitates the integration of such typical crowdsourcing tasks into ontology engineering work from within the Protégé ontology editing environment. An evaluation of the plugin in a typical ontology engineering scenario where ontologies are built from automatically learned semantic structures, shows that its use reduces the working times for the ontology engineers 11 times, lowers the overall task costs with 40% to 83% depending on the crowdsourcing settings used and leads to data quality comparable with that of tasks performed by ontology engineers.

Keywords: crowdsourcing, ontology engineering, ontology learning, Protégé plugin.

1 Introduction

Ontology engineering consists of a collection of knowledge acquisition and management techniques for creating and maintaining ontologies during their entire life-cycle. Ontology engineering tasks tend to be complex, costly and, above all, time-consuming processes.

Let's consider the task of ontology creation. To reduce its complexity, ontology construction is often bootstrapped by re-using existing or automatically derived ontologies. Ontology learning methods, for example, automatically extract ontologies from (a combination of) unstructured and structured resources. Although the extracted ontologies already provide a good basis for building the ontology, they typically contain questionable or wrong ontological elements and require a phase of verification and redesign (especially pruning) by the ontology engineer. The ontology verification phase involves, among others, checking

K. Janowicz et al. (Eds.): EKAW 2014, LNAI 8876, pp. 181–196, 2014.

that the ontology concepts are relevant to the domain of interest and that the extracted subsumption relations are correct.

Crowdsourcing methods provide effective means to solve such ontology verification tasks by outsourcing these to "an undefined, generally large group of people in the form of an open call" [5]. As detailed in Section 2, crowdsourcing has been used effectively to solve a range of ontology engineering tasks. However, crowdsourcing techniques require high upfront investments (understanding the techniques, creating appropriate tasks) and therefore, despite their proven usefulness, these techniques remain outside the reach of most ontology engineers.

In this paper we investigate how to more closely embed crowdsourcing into ontology engineering. In the area of Natural Language Processing (NLP), where the use of crowdsourcing is highly popular [12], there already exists an effort towards supporting easy integration of crowdsourcing methods into linguists' work: the GATE Crowdsourcing Plugin is a new component in the popular GATE NLP platform that allows inserting crowdsourcing tasks into larger NLP workflows, from within GATE's user interface [1]. Noy and colleagues [10] introduce a vision for similar tool support to facilitate the integration of crowdsourcing into ontology engineering. To achieve our goal we seek answer to two research questions:

Which tasks can be crowdsourced? We distill a set of crowdsourcing tasks that are likely to be common to solving a variety of ontology engineering problems and which should be implemented by the desired tool support (Section 2).

How to implement crowdsourcing enabled ontology engineering? We present a tool, the uComp Protégé plugin, which allows ontology engineers to crowdsource tasks directly from within the popular ontology engineering tool and as part of their ontology engineering work (Section 3).

We evaluate some of the functionality of the plugin to estimate the improvements made possible over manually solving a set of tasks in terms of time and cost reductions, while maintaining good data quality (Section 4). Our findings show that, in a scenario where automatically extracted ontologies are verified and pruned, the use of the plugin significantly reduces the time spent by the ontology engineer (11 times) and leads to important cost reductions (40% to 83% depending on the crowdsourcing settings used) without a loss of quality with respect to a manual process.

2   Use of Crowdsourcing for Knowledge Acquisition

Crowdsourcing methods are usually classified in three major genres depending on the motivation of the human contributors (i.e., payment vs. fun vs. altruism). Mechanised labour (MLab) is a type of paid-for crowdsourcing, where contributors choose to carry out small tasks (or micro-tasks) and are paid a small amount of money in return. Popular crowdsourcing marketplaces include Amazon's Mechanical Turk (MTurk) and CrowdFlower (CF). Games with a purpose (GWAPs) enable human contributors to carry out computation tasks as a side effect of playing online games [20]. Finally, in altruistic crowdsourcing a task is carried out by a large number of volunteer contributors. Crowdsourcing methods have been used to support several knowledge acquisition and, more specifically, ontology engineering tasks. To provide an overview of these methods we will group them along the three major stages of the Semantic Life-cycle as identified by Siorpaes in [17] and sum them up in Table 1.

Stage 1: Build and Maintain Semantic Web Vocabularies. Eckert and colleagues [4] relied on MTurk micro-workers to build a concept hierarchy in the philosophy domain. Crowdsourcing complemented the output of an automatic hierarchy learning method in: a) judging the relatedness of concept pairs and b) specifying the level of generality between two terms (more/less specific than). Noy and colleagues [10] focused on verifying the correctness of taxonomic relations. As for GWAPs, the OntoPronto game [17] aims to support the creation and extension of Semantic Web vocabularies. Players are presented with a Wikipedia page of an entity and they have to (1) judge whether this entity denotes a concept or an instance; and then (2) relate it to the most specific concept of the PROTON ontology, therefore extending PROTON with new classes and instances. Climate Quiz [16] is a Facebook game where players evaluate whether two concepts are related (e.g. environmental activism, activism), and which label is the most appropriate to describe their relation. The possible relation set contains both generic (is a sub-category of, is identical to, is the opposite of) and domain-specific (opposes, supports, threatens, influences, works on/with) relations. Guess What?! [9] goes beyond eliciting or verifying relations between concepts to creating complex concept definitions. Players (1) assign a class name to a complex class description (e.g., assign *Banana* to *fruit&yellow&grows on trees*) and (2) verify such class definitions.

Stage 2: Align Semantic Web Vocabularies. The CrowdMap system enlists micro-workers to solve the ontology alignment task [15] by asking them to 1) verify whether a given relation is correct (e.g., "Is conceptA the same as conceptB? yes/no ") and 2) specify how two given terms are related, in particular by choosing between sameAs, isAKindOf and notRelated. SpotTheLink has been instantiated to align the eCl@ss and UNSWPC [17] as well as the DBpedia and PROTON ontologies [18]. The final version of the game solves ontology alignment through two atomic tasks: (1) choosing a related concept – given a DBpedia concept players choose and agree upon a related PROTON concept; (2) specifying the type of relation between two concepts.

Stage 3: Annotate Content and Maintain Annotations. In ZenCrowd [3] crowd-workers verify the output of automatic entity linking algorithms. Concretely, given a named entity, e.g., "Berlin", and a set of DBpedia URLs generated automatically, crowd-workers choose all the URLs that represent that entity or "None of the above" if no URL is suitable. In essence, this is an annotation task. WhoKnows? [21] and RISQ! [23] are GWAPs which rely on similar mechanisms: they use LOD facts to generate questions and use the answers to (1) evaluate property rankings (which property of an instance is the most important/relevant); (2) detect inconsistencies; and (3) find doubtful facts. While WhoKnows?! uses a classroom paradigm and aims towards being an educational game, RISQ! is a Jeopardy-style quiz game.

Table 1. Overview of approaches addressing problems in various stages of the Semantic Web life-cycle [17], their genres and the type of crowdsourcing tasks that they employ

SW Life-cycle Stage	Approach	Genre	Solved Task
Stage 1: Build and maintain Semantic Web vocabularies	InPho [4]	MLab	(T3) Specification of Relation Type (subs)
			(T1) Specification of Term Relatedness
	Noy [10]	MLab	(T2) Verification of Relation Correctness (subs)
	OntoPronto [17]	GWAP	Class vs. instance decisions
			(T3) Specification of Relation Type (subs/instOf)
	Climate Quiz [16]	GWAP	(T3) Specification of Relation Type (8 relations)
	Guess What?! [9]	GWAP	Verify complex class definitions
			Generate class names for complex defs
Stage 2: Align Semantic Web vocabularies	CrowdMap [15]	MLab	(T2) Verification of Relation Correctness (subs/eqv)
			(T3) Specification of Relation Type (subs/eqv)
	SpotTheLink [18]	GWAP	(T1) Specification of Term Relatedness
			(T3) Specification of Relation Type (subs/eqv)
Stage 3: Annotate content, maintain annotations	ZenCrowd [3]	MLab	Text to URL mapping (annotation)
	WhoKnows? [21]	GWAP	Answering quiz questions
	RISQ! [23]	GWAP	Answering quiz questions

2.1 Typical Crowdsourcing Tasks in Ontology Engineering

Based on the analysis above, we distill a set of recurrent basic crowdsourcing task types used to solve a variety of ontology engineering problems, as follows.

T1. Specification of Term Relatedness. Crowd-workers judge whether two terms (typically representing ontology concepts) are related. In some cases they are presented with pairs of terms [4] while in others they might need to choose a most related term from a set of given terms [18]. This type of crowdsourcing task is suitable both in ontology creation [4] and in ontology alignment scenarios [18].

T2. Verification of Relation Correctness. Presented with a pair of terms (typically representing ontology concepts) and a relation between these terms, crowd-workers judge whether the suggested relation holds. Frequently verified relations include generic ontology relations such as equivalence [15] and subsumption [10,15], which are relevant both in ontology evaluation [10] and ontology alignment scenarios [15].

T3. Specification of Relation Type. In these tasks, crowd-workers are presented with two terms (typically corresponding to ontology concepts) and choose an appropriate relation from a set of given relations. Most efforts focus on the specification of generic ontology relations such as equivalence [16,15,18], subsumption [16,4,17,15,18], disjointness [16] or instanceOf [17,16]. The verification of domain-specific named relations such as performed by Climate Quiz [16] is less frequent.

T4. Verification of Domain Relevance. For this task, the crowdworkers confirm whether a given term is relevant for a domain of discourse. This task is mostly needed to support scenarios where ontologies are extracted using automatic methods, for example, through ontology learning.

The core crowdsourcing tasks above have been used by several approaches and across diverse stages of ontology engineering, thus being of interest in a wide range of ontology engineering scenarios. As such, they guided the development of our plugin, which currently supports tasks T2, T4, and partially T3.

3   The uComp Protégé Plugin

In order to support ontology engineers to easily and flexibly integrate crowd-sourcing tasks within their work, we implemented a plugin in Protégé, one of the most widely used ontology editors. The typical workflow of using the plugin involves the following main stages (as also depicted in Figure 1).

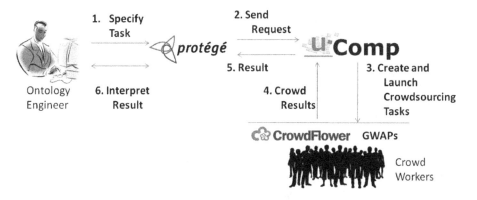

Fig. 1. Main stages when using the uComp plugin

1. Task Specification. An ontology engineer using Protégé can invoke the functionalities of the plugin from within the ontology editor at any time within his current work. The plugin allows specifying some well defined ontology engineering tasks, such as those discussed in Section 3.2 above. The view of the plugin that is appropriate for the task at hand is added to the editor's user interface via the *Window → Views* menu. The ontology engineer then specifies the part of the ontology to verify (eg. a specific class or all classes in the ontology), provides additional information and options in the plugin view and then starts the evaluation. Crowdsourced tasks can be canceled (or paused) anytime during the crowdsourcing process. We further detail the plugin's functionality in Section 3.1.

2. **Task Request.** The plugin uses the uComp API[1] to request the processing of the task by the crowd.

3. **Creation of Crowdsourcing Tasks.** The crowdsourcing process happens through the uComp platform[2], a hybrid-genre crowdsourcing platform which facilitates various knowledge acquisition tasks by flexibly allocating the received tasks to GWAPs and/or mechanised labour platforms alike (in particular, CrowdFlower) [14] depending on user settings.

4. **Collection of Crowd Results.** The uComp platform collects crowd-work harvested by individual genres (GWAPs and micro-task crowdsourcing).

5. **Combination of Crowd Results.** When all crowdsourcing tasks of a job have completed, the platform combines the results and provides them to the plugin.

6. **Result Presentation and Interpretation.** As soon as available, the plugin presents the results to the ontology engineer and saves them in the ontology. All data collected by the plugin is stored in the ontology in `rdfs:comment` fields, for example information about the ontology domain, the crowdsourcing job ID, and the crowd-created results. Depending on the result, the ontology engineer will perform further actions such as deleting parts of the ontology which have been validated as non-relevant.

3.1   Plugin Functionality

The plugin provides a set of views for crowdsourcing the following tasks:

- Verification of Domain Relevance (T4)
- Verification of Relation Correctness - Subsumption (T2)
- Verification of Relation Correctness - InstanceOf (T2) - the verification of *instanceOf* relations between an individual and a class.
- Specification of Relation Type (T3) is a Protégé view component that collects suggestions for labeling unlabeled relations by assigning to them a relation type from a set of relation types specified by the ontology engineer.
- Verification of Domain and Range where crowd-workers validate whether a property's *domain* and *range* axioms are correct.

In this paper we focus on the first two functionalities, which we now describe in more detail.

Verification of Domain Relevance (T4) is supported by the "uComp Class Validation" view of the plugin and crowdsources the decision of whether a concept (class) is relevant for a domain. Figure 2 shows the screenshot of this view for the class "carbon" before initiating the verification. The plugin view's interface contains the following information:

---

[1] `http://tinyurl.com/uCompAPI`

[2] The platform is being developed in the uComp project (`http://www.ucomp.eu/`)

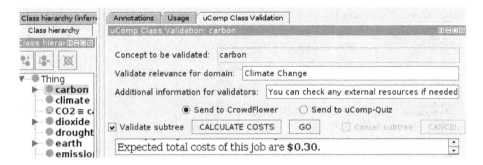

Fig. 2. The interface of the uComp Class Validation view used to create a Verification of Domain Relevance (T4) task

Task Specific Information such as the concept selected by the user for validation. This part of the view is diverse among different plugin functionalities.

Generic information such as the *domain* of the ontology, i.e., the field of knowledge which the ontology covers, is present in all views of the plugin. If entered once, the domain will be stored in the ontology (as `rdfs:comment`) and be pre-filled subsequently, but it can also be changed at any time.

Additional information For every task, the plugin contains a predefined task description (typically including examples) which is presented to the crowdworker. If the ontology engineer wants to extend this task description, (s)he can provide more guidelines in the *additional information* field. This functionality is present in all the views of the plugin.

Recursive control allows performing a task (e.g., domain relevance validation) not only for the current class, but for a larger part of or even the entire ontology. If the *Validate subtree* option is selected, the plugin crowdsources the specified task for the current concept and all its subconcepts recursively. To apply the functionality to the entire ontology, the plugin is invoked from the uppermost class, i.e., (*Thing*).

GO button to start the crowdsourcing process.

Verification of Relation Correctness - Subsumption (T2). is achieved with the *uComp SubClass Validation*. When selecting a class in Protégé, the plugin automatically detects its superclasses (if any) and fills the boxes in the plugin UI. As with any plugin functionality, the elements of the user interface are described in the plugin documentation, and additional information is also given interactively as mouse-over overlays. As soon as results are available these are presented in the UI, as shown in Figure 3. The screenshot gives an example with one evaluator, who rated the *IS-A* relation between "education" and "business" as invalid. If the majority of judgements is negative, a button to remove the relation is displayed.

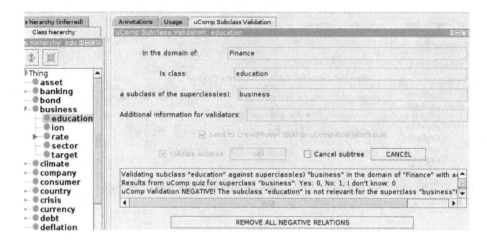

Fig. 3. Screenshot showing the interface for subClassOf relation validation, including the display of results

3.2 Crowdsourcing Task Interfaces

Upon receiving the request from the Protégé plugin, the uComp API selects the appropriate crowdsourcing genre and creates the relevant crowd-jobs. Currently the platform can crowdsource tasks either to GWAPs such as Climate Quiz [16] or to CrowdFlower, with a hybrid-genre strategy currently being developed. In this paper, we test the plugin by crowdsourcing only through CrowdFlower.

Figure 4 depicts the crowdsourcing interfaces created automatically by the uComp platform for the two tasks discussed above, namely the verification of domain relevance (part a) and the validation of subsumption relations (part b) . The uComp platform requires only the task data from the Protégé plugin and it provides relevant instructions as well as gold units to all tasks. Additionally, each crowdsourcing interface is extended with straightforward verification questions (i.e., typing some letters of the input terms). It has been shown experimentally (e.g. [6,8]), that extending task interfaces with explicitly verifiable questions forces workers to process the content of the task and also signals to them that their answers are being scrutinized.

To ensure a good quality output, by default all created jobs are assigned to Level 3 CrowdFlower contributors which are the contributors delivering, on average, the highest quality work. Also, for the moment we assume that the verified ontologies will be in English and therefore we restrict contributors to the main English speaking countries: Australia, United Kingdom and United States. In each created job we present 5 units per page and for each unit we collect 5 individual judgements. A price per task of $0.05 was specified for all jobs. A task is complete when all requested judgments have been collected.

The plugin is available from Protégé's central registry as the *uComp Crowd-sourcing Validation plugin*. The plugin has been tested with Protégé versions 4.2 and 4.3, as well as the recent version 5.0 (beta). A local configuration file

Fig. 4. Generated CrowdFlower job interface for (a) the Verification of Domain Relevance (T4) and (b) the Verification of Relation Correctness (T2) tasks

contains the uComp-API key[3] and various adaptable settings (e.g., judgements per unit, price per unit).

4   Evaluation

We evaluate the Plugin in the context of an ontology learning scenario as described in the introduction because i) bootstrapping ontology engineering by extracting an initial ontology automatically is a feasible and frequent ontology engineering approach and ii) automatically generated ontologies present errors that are best solved through human intervention. After the verification step with the uComp plugin, the resulting ontologies are used as part of a media monitoring tool[4] with the purpose of visualising information extracted from text corpora in a way that is meaningful to the web (i.e., non-specialised) audience. Therefore, agreement on the elements of these ontologies by the general public is, in this particular use case scenario, very important.

The goal of the evaluation is to assess the improvements that the uComp Plugin could enable in an ontology engineering scenario in terms of typical project completion aspects such as time, cost and quality of output. Concretely, the evaluation goals can be summarised into the following questions:

Time. *How does the use of the plugin affect the time needed to perform ontology engineering tasks?* We distinguish the total task time (T_{tt}) as the time taken from the start of the ontology engineering task until its finalisation; and the time of the ontology engineer spent actively in the task (T_{oe}). In a crowdsourced scenario, $T_{oe} < T_{tt}$, because the ontology engineer is only actively working during the outsourcing of the task. In contrast, in a traditional scenario $T_{oe} = T_{tt}$.

Cost. *Are there cost benefits associated with the use of the plugin?* We compute costs related to payments for the involved work-force, that is payments to ontology experts (C_{oe}) and payments to crowd-workers (C_{cs}). Ontology engineer costs are computed by multiplying the time they spend on the task (T_{oe})

---

[3] Request a key from the uComp team, see http://tinyurl.com/uCompAPI
[4] http://www.ecoresearch.net/climate/

with an average monthly wage. To allow comparison to other studies [11], the wage of a research scientist was assumed to be $54,000 per annum.

Quality. *What are the implications on the quality of the resulting output when using the Plugin?* Several studies have shown that the quality of various knowledge acquisition tasks performed by crowd-workers is, in general, similar to (or even better than) the quality of tasks performed by ontology engineers [19,10,13]. While the quality of the obtained data is not the core focus of our evaluation, we expect to obtain similar results to previous studies.

Usability. *Is the plugin usable?* As any end-user tool, the plugin should be easy to understand and use by the average ontology engineer already familiar with the Protégé environment.

4.1 Evaluation Setup

The setup involves a group of 8 ontology engineers which perform the same tasks over the same datasets but using two different approaches. In the first setting (S_Manual), all ontology engineers used the traditional (that is manual) approach to perform the ontology engineering tasks. In the second setting (S_Crowd), four of the eight ontology engineers used the Plugin to crowdsource (that is, create and launch) the same ontology engineering tasks, after being given a brief tutorial about the plugin (30 minutes). The two settings were then compared along the time, cost and quality dimensions. Time was measured as number of minutes to complete the task. Regarding the evaluators, four were experienced Protégé users, the other four work in the Semantic Web area but have limited knowledge of Protégé and were shortly trained in Protégé. None of the ontology engineers involved had any strong expertise in a particular domain.

Evaluation Data. The input to all evaluation tasks are ontologies generated by the ontology learning algorithm described in [22] (primarily) from textual sources. We evaluate the plugin over two ontologies covering two diverse domains (climate change and finance). We chose a general knowledge domain (finance) and a domain which requires domain familiarity or interest (climate change). More specialised domains will be evaluated as future research, but earlier work has already [10] investigated crowd-worker performance across ontologies of different domains/generality. The ontologies tested are of small to medium size, large ontologies would have made the manual evaluation stage unfeasible. The Climate Change ontology has 101 classes and 61 relations (out of which 43 are taxonomic relations) while the Finance ontology has 77 classes and 50 relations (20 of which are taxonomic relations). The ontologies were used as generated. The ontologies used in the evaluation process, the instructions given to the manual evaluators, and the results, are found online[5].

---

[5] http://tinyurl.com/ucomp

Evaluation Tasks. We perform the evaluation of the plugin over two different ontology engineering tasks in order to 1) test different functionalities of the plugin; and 2) obtain evaluation results over a range of tasks. These tasks are:

T_DomRel :Verification of Domain Relevance (T4). For each concept of the ontology decide whether it is relevant for the domain in question (in our case, climate change and finance). In S_Manual, evaluators were asked to perform this task by assigning True/False values to a class level annotation property that we created for the purposes of our experiments (named *uComp_class_relevance*).

T_SubsCorr: Verification of Relation Correctness – Subsumption (T2). For all subsumption relations in the ontology evaluators verified whether they were correct. In S_Manual, evaluators recorded their judgements in an annotation property at the relation level created for the purpose of the experiments (*uComp_subclassof_check*).

4.2   Evaluation Results

Task Duration. Table 2 lists the task duration for the two ontologies and the two settings, detailed in terms of the average time intervals spent by the ontology engineer (T_{oe}), by using crowdsourcing (T_{cs}) and the total time of the task ($T_{tt} = T_{oe} + T_{cs}$). In the case of S_Crowd, the time needed for the ontology engineers to create and launch the crowdsourcing task was on average between 1 and 2 minutes. To simplify calculations, we chose to take the average time as 2 minutes across all tasks. We notice that the time reduction ratio for the ontology engineer across the two settings (computed as the ratio of the ontology engineering time in Setting 1 and Setting 2) is significant and ranges from a 13.7 fold reduction to a 7.5 fold reduction, with an overall average of 11: thus ontology engineers need to spend 11 times less time on the task when using the Plugin than in the manual scenario. The duration of the overall task increases and varies between 2.4 and 4.7 hours. Note however, that the current evaluation setup maximizes quality rather than speed. Faster completion rates (possibly at the expense of data quality) could have been obtained by not restricting the geographical location and previous achievements of the crowd-workers.

Table 2. Task duration in minutes per ontology, evaluation task and setting

	Climate Change Ontology						Finance Ontology					
	T_DomRel			T_SubsCorr			T_DomRel			T_SubsCorr		
	T_{oe}	T_{cs}	T_{tt}	T_{oe}	T_{cs}	T_{tt}	T_{oe}	T_{cs}	T_{tt}	T_{oe}	T_{cs}	T_{tt}
S_Manual (Avg)	27.4	0	27.4	23.0	0	23.0	21.3	0	21.3	15.0	0	15.0
S_Manual (StdDev)	5	0	5	6.2	0	6.2	7.1	0	7.1	5.6	0	5.6
S_Crowd (Avg)	2	240	242	2	280	282	2	140	142	2	200	202
S_Manual/S_Crowd	13.7	-	0.11	12.5	-	0.08	10.65	-	0.15	7.5	-	0.07

Costs. For the cost analysis, we compute average costs for the total task (C_{tt}) as the sum of the average cost of the ontology engineer (C_{oe}) and the average cost of the crowd-sourced tasks (C_{cs}) as detailed in Table 3. Considering an annual salary of \$54,000 and a corresponding \$26 hourly wage[6], average ontology engineering costs were computed based on the average times shown in Table 2. Cost savings were then computed for each cost category.

Table 3. Average costs (in \$) for the ontology engineer (C_{oe}), crowd-workers (C_{cs}) and the entire task (C_{tt}) across ontologies and settings

	Climate Change Ontology						Finance Ontology					
	T_DomRel			T_SubsCorr			T_DomRel			T_SubsCorr		
	C_{oe}	C_{cs}	C_{tt}	C_{oe}	C_{cs}	C_{tt}	C_{oe}	C_{cs}	C_{tt}	C_{oe}	C_{cs}	C_{tt}
S_Manual (Avg)	11.9	0	11.9	9.9	0	9.9	9.2	0	9.2	6.5	0	6.5
S_Crowd (Avg)	0.9	8.48	9.38	0.9	3.58	4.48	0.9	6.49	7.39	0.9	1.67	2.57
Cost Savings (%)	92.4	-	21.2	90.1	-	54.7	90.2	-	19.7	86.15	-	60.5
S_CrowdCheap (Avg)	0.9	1.02	2.1	0.9	0.43	1.33	0.9	0.78	1.68	0.9	0.2	1.1
Cost Savings (%)	92.4	-	82.3	90.1	-	86.5	90.2	-	81.7	86.15	-	83

Ontology engineer cost savings are high and range from 92.4% to 86.15%, averaged at 89.9%. For the entire task, cost savings are moderate (19.7% - 60.5%, Avg = 39%), with Setting 2 reducing S_Manual costs with 40%. Note, however, that task level cost savings will ultimately depend on the cost that ontology engineers decide to pay to crowd-workers. For example, choosing a cheaper task setting than currently (i.e., 3 judgements, with \$0.01 per task vs. the current 5 judgements and \$0.05 per task) will lead to average cost savings of 83.3% for the total task (S_CrowdCheap in Table 3). From the plugin's perspective, the major goal is reducing ontology engineering costs, as crowdsourcing costs will depend on the constraints of the ontology engineer and are hard to generalise.

Data Quality. Lower completion times and costs should not have a negative effect on the quality of the crowdsourced data. Since we do not possess a baseline for either of the two tasks, we will perform a comparative evaluation and contrast inter-rater agreement levels between ontology engineers with those of crowdworkers. We have measured inter-rater agreement with Fleiss' Kappa which is used to assess reliability of agreement with a fixed number of raters and categorical ratings assigned to a number of items.

Table 4 presents inter-rater agreement per task and per setting, with the number of raters per task given in parentheses. According to the interpretation of Landis and Koch [7] the inter-rater agreement among manual expert evaluators (S_Manual) is moderate. Agreement among the four groups of Crowd-Flower workers is substantial (S_Crowd). The combined agreement (manual ex-

---

[6] In practice, considering benefits, overhead and vacation, the actual costs for a productive hour are likely to be higher than \$26. Nevertheless, we decided to keep \$26 in order to be able to compare our findings to similar studies.

Table 4. Fleiss' Kappa values of inter-rater agreement per setting and when combining the data of the two settings

	Climate Change Ontology		Finance Ontology	
	T_DomRel	T_SubsCorr	T_DomRel	T_SubsCorr
S_Manual	0.338 (8)	0.502 (8)	0.496 (8)	0.419 (8)
S_Crowd	0.633 (4)	0.841 (4)	0.520 (4)	0.826 (4)
S_ManualCrowd	0.392 (12)	0.582 (12)	0.505 (12)	0.508 (12)

pert and crowdworkers) is always higher than for manual evaluators alone. A detailed inspection of results reveals that judgement is difficult on some questions, for example relevance of given concepts for the climate change domain often depends on the point of view and granularity of the domain model. But in general, crowdworkers have a higher inter-rater agreement, which often corresponds with the majority opinion of manual experts, thereby raising Fleiss' kappa (S_ManualCrowd). Also, the agreement between the crowd and experts is higher than among experts, possibly because crowdsourcing data is the majority view derived from 5 judgements as compared to a single expert judgement.

Plugin Usability was assessed by means of the System Usability Scale (SUS), the most used questionnaire for measuring perceptions of usability [2]. Based on data collected from the entire test population (i.e., all 8 ontology engineers), we obtained a SUS score of 85, which corresponds to the 90th percentile rank and positions the plugin in the class of "A" type system, that is systems with maximal usability. All evaluators agreed that (a) they would prefer using the plugin instead of performing the tasks manually and that (b) the use of the plugin saved a lot of their time. They considered the recursive task verification particularly useful when focusing on large (parts of the) ontologies. One suggested making the plugin data and results more visually appealing, and showing the anticipated cost before crowdsourcing – both of which have been implemented in the meantime. Given the small scale of the usability evaluation, we consider it only as indicative that the Plugin has a good usability.

5   Summary and Future Work

In this paper we investigated the idea of closely embedding crowdsourcing techniques into ontology engineering. Through an analysis of previous works using crowdsourcing for ontology engineering, we concluded that a set of basic crowdsourcing tasks are repeatedly used to achieve a range of ontology engineering processes across various stages of the ontology life-cycle. We then presented a novel tool, a Protégé plugin, that allows ontology engineers to use these basic crowdsourcing tasks from within their ontology engineering working context in Protégé. An evaluation of the plugin in an ontology engineering scenario where automatically learned ontologies in two different domains are assessed for domain relevance and subsumption correctness, revealed that the use of the plugin reduced overall project costs, lowered the time spent by the ontology engineer (without extending the time of the overall tasks to over 4 hours) and returned good quality data that was in high agreement with ontology engineers. Finally, our evaluators have provided positive feedback about the usability of the plugin.

Our evaluation focused on assessing the concept of a crowdsourcing plugin. Although we plan to make use of the uComp platform, this particular evaluation forwarded all tasks directly to CrowdFlower and therefore is not influenced by the particularities of the uComp framework. As a first evaluation of the plugin, we focused on small-scale ontologies and therefore cannot offer insights, at this stage, about how the plugin scales to large-scale ontologies. Another important question to address is whether crowd-workers can replace domain experts for application scenarios where domain specific meaning must be conveyed by the domain models. Both of these issues are important for our future work.

We consider our work as a first step towards the wide adoption of crowd-sourcing by the ontology engineering community, and therefore, we see ample opportunities for future work. Firstly, since the use of crowdsourcing has matured enough, it is a good time to move on from isolated approaches towards a methodology of where and how crowdsourcing can efficiently support ontology engineers. Such methodological guidelines should inform tools such as our own plugin while our plugin could offer a means to build and test these guidelines. Secondly, in terms of the plugin development, we plan further extending its functionality (1) to support additional HC tasks; (2) to allow greater control over job settings as well as (3) to permit monitoring of the results as they become available from within Protégé. Thirdly, the scalability of the proposed approach remains to be investigated - while the current evaluation did not focus on this aspect, we expect that the automatic distribution of tasks for parallel processing will make this approach feasible for dealing with large ontologies as well. We also plan to evaluate the plugin in other ontology engineering scenarios (e.g., ontology matching) and to conduct larger scale usability studies. Future work will also reveal best use cases of the plugin identifying those cases when it can be used to collect generic knowledge as opposed to application areas where it should be used to support the work of a distributed group of domain experts.

Acknowledgments. The work presented in this paper was developed within project uComp, which receives the funding support of EPSRC EP/K017896/1, FWF 1097-N23, and ANR-12-CHRI-0003-03, in the framework of the CHIST-ERA ERA-NET.

References

1. Bontcheva, K., Roberts, I., Derczynski, L., Rout, D.: The GATE Crowdsourcing Plugin: Crowdsourcing Annotated Corpora Made Easy. In: Proc. of the 14th Conference of the European Chapter of the Association for Computational Linguistics (EACL). ACL (2014)
2. Brooke, J.: SUS: a quick and dirty usability scale. Taylor & Francis, London (1996)

3. Demartini, G., Difallah, D.E., Cudré-Mauroux, P.: ZenCrowd: Leveraging Probabilistic Reasoning and Crowdsourcing Techniques for Large-scale Entity Linking. In: Proceedings of the 21st International Conference on World Wide Web, pp. 469–478. ACM (2012)

4. Eckert, K., Niepert, M., Niemann, C., Buckner, C., Allen, C., Stuckenschmidt, H.: Crowdsourcing the Assembly of Concept Hierarchies. In: Proc. of the 10th Annual Joint Conference on Digital Libraries, JCDL 2010, pp. 139–148. ACM (2010)

5. Howe, J.: Crowdsourcing: Why the Power of the Crowd is Driving the Future of Business (2009), http://crowdsourcing.typepad.com/

6. Kittur, A., Chi, E.H., Suh, B.: Crowdsourcing User Studies with Mechanical Turk. In: Proc. of the 26th Conference on Human Factors in Computing Systems, pp. 453–456 (2008)

7. Landis, J., Koch, G.: The measurement of observer agreement for categorical data. Biometrics 33(1), 159–174 (1977)

8. Laws, F., Scheible, C., Schütze, H.: Active Learning with Amazon Mechanical Turk. In: Proc. of the Conf. on Empirical Methods in NLP, pp. 1546–1556 (2011)

9. Markotschi, T., Völker, J.: Guess What?! Human Intelligence for Mining Linked Data. In: Proc. of the Workshop on Knowledge Injection into and Extraction from Linked Data at the International Conference on Knowledge Engineering and Knowledge Management, EKAW-2010 (2010)

10. Noy, N.F., Mortensen, J., Musen, M.A., Alexander, P.R.: Mechanical Turk As an Ontology Engineer?: Using Microtasks As a Component of an Ontology-engineering Workflow. In: Proceedings of the 5th Annual ACM Web Science Conference, WebSci 2013, pp. 262–271. ACM (2013)

11. Poesio, M., Kruschwitz, U., Chamberlain, J., Robaldo, L., Ducceschi, L.: Phrase Detectives: Utilizing Collective Intelligence for Internet-Scale Language Resource Creation. Transactions on Interactive Intelligent Systems 3(1), 1–44 (2013)

12. Sabou, M., Bontcheva, K., Scharl, A.: Crowdsourcing Research Opportunities: Lessons from Natural Language Processing. In: Proc. of the 12th International Conference on Knowledge Management and Knowledge Technologies (iKNOW). Special Track on Research 2.0 (2012)

13. Sabou, M., Bontcheva, K., Scharl, A., Föls, M.: Games with a Purpose or Mechanised Labour?: A Comparative Study. In: Proc. of the 13th International Conference on Knowledge Management and Knowledge Technologies, i-Know 2013, pp. 1–8. ACM (2013)

14. Sabou, M., Scharl, A., Föls, M.: Crowdsourced Knowledge Acquisition: Towards Hybrid-genre Workflows. International Journal of Semantic Web and Information Systems 9(3), 14–41 (2013)

15. Sarasua, C., Simperl, E., Noy, N.F.: CROWDMAP: Crowdsourcing Ontology Alignment with Microtasks. In: Cudré-Mauroux, P., et al. (eds.) ISWC 2012, Part I. LNCS, vol. 7649, pp. 525–541. Springer, Heidelberg (2012)

16. Scharl, A., Sabou, M., Föls, M.: Climate Quiz: a Web Application for Eliciting and Validating Knowledge from Social Networks. In: Proceedings of the 18th Brazilian Symposium on Multimedia and the Web, WebMedia 2012, pp. 189–192. ACM (2012)

17. Siorpaes, K., Hepp, M.: Games with a Purpose for the Semantic Web. IEEE Intelligent Systems 23(3), 50–60 (2008)

18. Thaler, S., Simperl, E., Siorpaes, K.: SpotTheLink: Playful Alignment of Ontologies. In: Proceedings of the 2011 ACM Symposium on Applied Computing, pp. 1711–1712. ACM (2011)

19. Thaler, S., Simperl, E., Wölger, S.: An Experiment in Comparing Human-Computation Techniques. IEEE Internet Computing 16(5), 52–58 (2012)

20. von Ahn, L., Dabbish, L.: Designing games with a purpose. ACM Commun. 51(8), 58–67 (2008)

21. Waitelonis, J., Ludwig, N., Knuth, M., Sack, H.: WhoKnows? Evaluating Linked Data Heuristics with a Quiz that Cleans Up DBpedia. Interact. Techn. Smart Edu. 8(4), 236–248 (2011)

22. Wohlgenannt, G., Weichselbraun, A., Scharl, A., Sabou, M.: Dynamic Integration of Multiple Evidence Sources for Ontology Learning. Journal of Information and Data Management 3(3), 243–254 (2012)

23. Wolf, L., Knuth, M., Osterhoff, J., Sack, H.: RISQ! Renowned Individuals Semantic Quiz - a Jeopardy like Quiz Game for Ranking Facts. In: Proc. of the 7th International Conference on Semantic Systems, I-Semantics 2011, pp. 71–78. ACM (2011)

Futures Studies Methods for Knowledge Management in Academic Research

Sabine Kadlubek, Stella Schulte-Cörne, Florian Welter,
Anja Richert, and Sabina Jeschke

Institute of Information Management in Mechanical Engineering (IMA)/ Center for Learning
and Knowledge Management (ZLW) & Assoc. Institute for Management Cybernetics e.V.
(IfU) RWTH Aachen University, Aachen, Germany
{Sabine.Kadlubek,Stella.Schulte-Coerne,Florian.Welter,
Anja.Richert,Sabina.Jeschke}@ima-zlw-ifu.rwth-aachen.de

Abstract. The management of academic knowledge is a relatively young area of attention. Higher education entities accumulate a great deal of knowledge and the management of this asset is more than ever crucial for the strategic alignment. Hence, this paper aims at showing that knowledge management in academic research should work hand in hand with futures studies to develop and foster a strategic orientation. For this purpose the knowledge management model by Probst et al. (1998) with its eight building blocks serves as a framework. The focus of this paper lies on the processes of *knowledge goals* and *knowledge identification* and it is suggested that the futures studies methods monitoring, scenario technique and forecasting are suitable to complement knowledge management methods within academic research due to their ability to identify and concentrate information and knowledge relevant to the future.

Keywords: Futures Studies· Knowledge Management· Academic Research· Monitoring· Forecasting· Scenario Technique

1   Introduction

The assumption that science and research are independent from material incentives [1] is out-of-date for universities. These and other higher education institutions are increasingly exposed to market pressures caused by the demand to become more productive and competitive [2]. Hence, academic entities rely on external funding to realize innovative scientific and technological projects and ideas. Additionally, knowledge – especially novel knowledge – is the main capital of these entities. In order to manage this asset, the implementation of knowledge management in academia appears to become increasingly important [3]. Therefore it is necessary that knowledge management includes a future orientation to align a strategy well in advance in order to grant public research funds. In that respect knowledge management and futures studies are predestined to work hand in hand to develop and foster a strategic orientation in terms of targeted investments and the forward-looking identification of funding opportunities.

K. Janowicz et al. (Eds.): EKAW 2014, LNAI 8876, pp. 197–202, 2014.

A central knowledge management model in German literature is the eight building blocks model by Gilbert Probst et al. (1998) [4]. It serves here as a framework due to its broad popularity in research and practice. These building blocks "provide an outline of the areas where active knowledge management is possible" [ibid]. Considering that in research the pivotal interest foremost lays in future requirements and challenges, the creation of yet unknown knowledge is fundamental. Hence, the focus lies on the building blocks *knowledge goals* and *knowledge identification* due to their future orientation with respect to novel knowledge. In the course of this paper the integration of the futures studies methods *monitoring, scenario technique* and *forecasting* to the knowledge management of these two building blocks is suggested in order to continuously monitor and evaluate the performance (monitoring), identify diverse future challenges (scenario technique, forecasting) and thus develop plans of action for the desired future state.

2   New Challenges for Knowledge Management in Academia

Since several decades the generation, exchange as well as diffusion of knowledge depicts a major field of research in various scientific communities. With regard to the growing research community of knowledge management, a couple of authors developed principles and models that are dealing with normative, strategic, tactic and operative knowledge management elements. Nonaka and Takeuchi (1995) [5] e. g. focus on the entire knowledge creation in companies and Bhatt (2000) [6] considers the organization of knowledge by describing a knowledge (management) cycle. A further framework for knowledge management, which is worth mentioning here, is provided by Wiig et al. (1997) [7]. It describes four activities of knowledge management – Review, Conceptualize, Reflect and Act – which are performed sequentially (ibid). In contrast, Probst et al. (1998) [4] do not consider knowledge management as a sequential process but rather a recursive one. The authors stress that the model was firstly developed to connect results of action research and organizational learning with real problems of managers in companies (ibid). The model comprises eight so called "building blocks"– integrating strategic and operative management levels – that are connected by an iteration loop (fig.1).

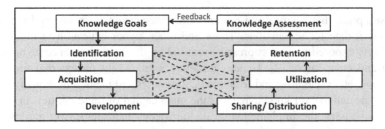

Fig. 1. Eight building blocks of knowledge management by Probst et al. (1998)

On a strategic level the iteration loop of the model begins with the building block *knowledge goals*. This is followed by the building blocks: *knowledge identification, knowledge acquisition, knowledge development, knowledge sharing/distribution, knowledge utilization* and *knowledge retention* on an operative level. In this operative level systemic interconnections and cause-effect-relations of core processes are suggested by the authors (ibid). Ending with the building block *knowledge assessment* on the strategic level, the iteration loop is completed (fig.1).

Considering the expansion of different forms in new public management, such as a more entrepreneurial alignment of universities in single federal states of Germany (Hochschulfreiheitsgesetz NRW 2006) [8], a reflection of the model in terms of its transferability from business environments to academia can be a promising next step. However, there are obvious differences between an economic and an academic system with regard to knowledge [9]. A business organization usually faces the problem that knowledge assets are rarely visible. Hence, the detection, distribution and utilization of knowledge are the crucial tasks and building blocks. In contrast, the focus of academia lies on the constant generation of novel knowledge (ibid).

3   Knowledge Goals and Knowledge Identification

"Agreement on strategic goals is the core element in strategic planning, which in turn provides the basis for implementation and monitoring" [4]. In the case of a university, for example, it has become crucial to focus on future funding opportunities. Consequently, strategic research goals have to be set in order to identify future spheres of competence. In doing so it is important that the forecast and therefore the generated knowledge is reliable, i.e. it needs to be related to concrete research objectives. Already applied knowledge management methods, which support the process of goal setting, are "Strategic Knowledge Assets" [10] or knowledge-based "SWOT Analysis" [7]. The more detailed it is known, which knowledge is actually available, the more precise is the definition of the unknown. Therefore, the building block *knowledge identification* is highly linked to the previously introduced building block *knowledge goals*. "Our knowledge goals will point us towards the areas and sources of knowledge which we need in order to strengthen our existing competencies or create new ones" [4]. The challenge within academic research is to identify the boundaries of already existing knowledge in order to excel. Knowledge management methods such as "Competence Mining", which is based on data mining techniques to identify the staff's competences based on their publications, support the identification of individual competences [11] and enhance the transparency required to attain the previously set goals.

In the following the integration of futures studies methods in knowledge management is suggested as it comprises a potential and promising added value for new forms of knowledge management in academic research environments.

4   Integration of Futures Studies in Knowledge Management

4.1   Futures Studies and Its Methods: Why and Wherefore?

"Studying the future is not simply economic projections or sociological analysis or technological forecasting, but a multi-disciplinary examination of change in all major areas of life to find the interacting dynamics that are creating the next age." [12]. Futures studies and its methods provide a long-range view and thus relevant knowledge to different facets of futures. Considering the remarks about the features of the building blocks *knowledge goals* and *knowledge identification* it is clear that they are future orientated. Society or nature is not deterministic but rather incoherent. Since the future cannot be predicted it is important to plan within the context of alternative futures. Futures studies can identify future spheres of competence and create knowledge, assured through structured and methodical procedures that are able to support decision-making processes. Futures studies methods are as heterogeneous as their object and thus combine qualitative and quantitative approaches. They identify and concentrate information and knowledge relevant to the future, and thus serve for the administrative work at educational providers [13]. That is why futures studies are able to support knowledge management processes not only in businesses but also in science.

4.2   Monitoring, Scenario Technique and Forecasting

The methods *monitoring*, *scenario technique* and *forecasting* are characterized by the fact that they are used variably for different time scales and thus are qualified for different requests in knowledge management processes.

Monitoring can be defined as a directed observation of key indicators relevant in a special field and is usually coupled with an undirected search for clues and evidence linked to the indicators. Special information about processes and findings are collected to stimulate activities that are able to enhance their efficiency and effectiveness. The purpose of monitoring-activities and processes is to steadily observe a particular object based on relevant information, to reflect it and to initiate change. With regard to *knowledge goals* and *knowledge identification* a continuous monitoring supports detecting concrete and possible developments in (academic) research. If an adjustment or reorientation in research is opted, a next step is the detection of the necessary know-how to pursue the new path successfully. Thus monitoring rather serves to assess developments over time descriptively and on the basis of reliable and regularly collected data [14] to develop plans of action. In the monitoring project 'International Monitoring', funded by the German Federal Ministry of Education and Research from 2007 to 2013, the monitoring method was exemplarily used and adapted to establish a continuous observation of fields of future action on the topic of innovative ability and thus to foster the sustainable competitiveness of Germany and Europe in the global market (http://www.internationalmonitoring.com/home.html).

Forecasting is likely to be understood as the prediction respectively the projection of future developments on the basis of both earlier developmental stages and the actual situation [15]. As it is usually aimed to find strategies suitable to influence the future developments in a positive, economically and socially responsible way, the statements carried out take the form of conditional statements [13]. Forecasts can be short-term, intermediate and long-term orientated. They can support the knowledge management building blocks by generating relatively assured data about future developments and therefore provide a reliable basis for decision making about future research developments. As an example within the meta project 'DemoScreen', funded by the German Federal Ministry of Education and Research, expert workshops were taking place in order to elaborate future needs for research in terms of social innovation (http://demoscreen.de/).

Through *scenarios* future developments or states of a forecasting object under certain and alternative conditions will be investigated and an aggregated picture for a certain prognostic time horizon will be designed. Thus, scenarios are based on information, opinions, views and valuations which determine their probability of occurrence. Questions like "What can happen?" or "How can a specific target be reached?" define the range in which different types of scenarios can be classified [16]. Thus, goals, role models, options of action, recommendations and measures can be developed to shape the future as well as the journey towards it. In academic research scenarios allow to identify research desiderata and to anticipate possible developments. They help to detect interferences and support strategy development as well as the definition of research respectively knowledge goals. The scenario technique allows developing a long-term strategy which also includes unprecedented phenomena and developments. This aspect is interesting for research since it aims at finding out the yet unknown and increasingly depends on funding. Thus the main benefit deriving from the scenario technique method with regard to the building blocks *knowledge goals* and *knowledge identification* is the set of alternative futures which offers a plausible and consistent framework for the development of a strategy concerning required future knowledge.

5   Conclusion

In the present paper three selected methods of futures studies were discussed in terms of their added value to knowledge management of academia with a special focus on their value for the building blocks *knowledge goals* and *knowledge identification* by Probst et al. (1998). This knowledge management model provides several development options when applied for academic research, whereby this paper focused on two out of eight building blocks due to their importance for the definition of an academic strategy. The proposed integration of the three above mentioned futures studies methods into this model illustrates a useful and promising support for detecting future challenges and demands such as exemplarily highlighted for monitoring and meta projects, funded by the German Federal Ministry of Education and Research. The selected methods complement knowledge management and enhance the research strategy by examining future developments and their completion – an important aspect for academic research e.g. in terms of external funding opportunities. Hence, a current strategy can be adapted if profound future changes are detected and thus decisions for future research projects can be shaped. The strengths of the foregoing methods in the present case lay in thinking more systematically, anticipating a long-term perspective, considering alternatives when thinking about the future and improving the quality of decision-making. This paper aimed to introduce the idea of conducting knowledge management together with futures studies. There are many more suitable methods available and a further investigation of combinations and benefits is a promising next step.

References

1. Ma, T., Liu, S., Nakamori, Y.: Roadmapping as a Way of Knowledge Management for Supporting Scientific Research in Academia. Systems Research and Behavioral Science 23(6), 743–755 (2006)
2. Rowley, J.: Is Higher Education Ready for Knowledge Management? The International Journal of Educational Management 14(7), 325–333 (2000)
3. Sousa, C.A., Hendriks, P.H.: Connecting Knowledge to Management. The Case of Academic Research. Organization 15(6), 811–830 (2008)
4. Probst, G., Raub, S., Romhardt, K.: Managing Knowledge. Building Blocks for Success. John Wiley & Sons, Chichester (1998)
5. Nonaka, I., Takeuchi, H.: The Knowledge-Creating Company. Oxford University Press, New York (1995)
6. Bhatt, G.D.: Organizing knowledge in the knowledge development cycle. Journal of Knowledge Mangement 4(1), 15–26 (2000)
7. Wiig, K., De Hoog, R., Van Der Spek, R.: Supporting Knowledge Management: A Selection of Methods and Techniques. Expert Systems with Applications 13(1), 15–27 (1997)
8. Ministerium für Inneres und Kommunales des Landes Nordrhein-Westfalen, https://recht.nrw.de/lmi/owa/br_vbl_detail_text?anw_nr=6&vd_id=1460&menu=1&sg=0&keyword=Hochschulfreiheitsgesetz
9. Kölbel, M.: Wissensmanagement in der Wissenschaft. In: Fuchs-Kittowski, K., Umstätter, W., Wagner-Döbler, R. (eds.) Wissensmanagement in der Wissenschaft: Wissenschaftsforschung Jahrbuch, pp. 89–101. Gesellschaft für Wissenschaftsforschung, Berlin (2004)
10. Remus, U.: Prozessorientiertes Wissensmanagement. Konzepte und Modellierung. Dissertation. Universität Regensburg, Wirtschaftswissenschaftliche Fakultät (2002)
11. Rodrigues, S., Oliveira, J., de Souza, J.M.: Competence Mining for Team Formation and Virtual Community Recommendation. In: Proceedings of the 9th Conference on Computer Supported Work in Design, Conventry, UK, May 24-26, vol. 1, pp. 44–49. IEEE Computer Society (2005)
12. Glenn, J.C.: Introduction to the Futures Research Methods Series. In: Glenn, J.C., Gordon, T.J. (eds.) Futures Research Methodology – V2.0. AC/UNU Millennium Project (2003)
13. Tiberius, V.: Hochschuldidaktik der Zukunftsforschung. VS Verlag, Wiesbaden (2011)
14. Stockmann, R.: Qualitätsmanagement und Evaluation – Konkurrierende oder sich ergänzende Konzepte. CEval Arbeitspapiere No. 3. CEval. Saarbrücken (2002)
15. Löchtefeld, S.: Backcasting – Ein Instrument zur Zukunftsgestaltung. In: Rietmann, S., Hensen, G. (eds.) Werkstattbuch Familienzentrum, pp. 109–117. Methoden für die erfolgreiche Praxis. VS Verlag, Wiesbaden (2009)
16. Börjesona, L., Höjera, M., Dreborgb, K., Ekvallc, T., Finnvedena, G.: Scenario types and techniques: Towards a user's guide. Futures 38(7), 723–739 (2006)

Adaptive Concept Vector Space Representation Using Markov Chain Model

Zenun Kastrati and Ali Shariq Imran

Norwegian Information Security Lab, Gjøvik University College, Norway
{zenun.kastrati,ali.imran}@hig.no

Abstract. This paper proposes an adaptive document representation (concept vector space model) using Markov Chain model. The vector space representation is one of the most common models for representing documents in classification process. The document classification based on ontology classification approach is represented as a vector, whose components are ontology concepts and their relevance. The relevance is represented the by frequency of concepts' occurrence. These concepts make various contributions in classification process. The contributions depend on the position of concepts where they are depicted in the ontology hierarchy. The hierarchy such as classes, subclasses and instances may have different values to represent the concepts' importance. The weights to define concepts' importance are generally selected by empirical analysis and are usually kept fixed. Thus, making it less effective and time consuming. We therefore propose a new model to automatically estimate weights of concepts within the ontology. This model initially maps the ontology to a Markov chain model and then calculates the transition probability matrix for this Markov chain. Further, the transition probability matrix is used to compute the probability of steady states based on left eigenvectors. Finally, the importance is calculated for each ontology concept. And, an enhanced concept vector space representation is created with concepts' importance and concepts' relevance. The concept vector space representation can be adapted for new ontology concepts.

Keywords: document classification, concept vector space, document representation model, Markov chain model.

1 Introduction

Today, the web is the main source of information which is consistently increasing. The information is usually kept in unstructured and semi-structured format. More than 80 % of the information of an organization is stored in an unstructured format (reports, email, views, news, etc), and the rest is stored in structured format [1]. Therefore, discovering and extracting useful information from these resources is difficult without organization and summarization of text documents, and this is an extremely vital and tedious process in today's digital world [2]. An automatic classification in this regard plays a key role in organizing these massive sources of unstructured text information into an organized format.

K. Janowicz et al. (Eds.): EKAW 2014, LNAI 8876, pp. 203–208, 2014.

Automatic text document classification is a process of automatically assigning a text document in a given domain to one or more class labels from a finite set of predefined categories. The first step in classification process is the preprocessing of the text documents and storing the information in a data structure, which is more appropriate for further processing. This can be achieved by a vector space model. The vector space model is one of the most common models for representing text documents and it is widely used in text document classification [3].

There are two major approaches for a text document representation into vector space model - machine learning approach and ontology based approach. The machine learning approach, which is based on the idea that a text document can be represented by a set of words known as bag-of-words representation, and the ontology approach which follows the idea that text document can be represented by a set of concepts known as bag-of-concepts representation. Ontology based approach represents semantic aspects of the text documents through entities defined within the domain ontology. A text document using the domain ontology is represented as a vector, whose components are concepts and their relevance. Concepts are extracted from a domain ontology and the relevance is calculated using frequency of concepts' occurrence in the corpus which makes this domain.

It is argued in [4,5] that contribution of ontology concepts in classification process depends on the position of concepts where they are depicted in the hierarchy and this contribution is indicated by a weight. The hierarchy consists of classes, subclasses and instances that may have different weights to represent the concepts' importance. These weights are usually calculated either manually or empirically through trial and error by conducting experiments. Researchers in [5] calculate weights of ontology concepts by performing experiments. They experimented many times to adjust the parameters which denote the importance of the concepts in ontology. After the experiment was conducted several times, they proposed to set the parameter value 0.2 when the concepts were classes, 0.5 when concepts were subclasses and 0.8 when concepts were instances in ontology. The approach implemented in [4,6] proposed to use layers of ontology tree to indicate the abstract degree of concepts. Researchers used layers to represent the position of concepts in ontology and the weight of a concept is calculated by counting the length of path from the root node. The same approach of using layers for calculating concepts' weight values were used in [7]. They proposed the idea to consider only the leaf concepts of an ontology, in contrast of using all concepts, presuming that leaf concept are the most important elements in the ontology. The leaf concepts can be any subset of ontology that forms a set of mutually independent concepts. They assume that more general concepts, such as super-classes, are implicitly taken into account through the leaf concepts by distributing their importance to all of their sub-classes down to the leaf concepts in equal proportion. The drawback of these approaches is that they do not calculate the weights of concepts in ontology automatically. In fact, they tune it empirically through trial and error by conducting experiments thus keeping these weights fixed. We therefore address these issues in this paper by proposing

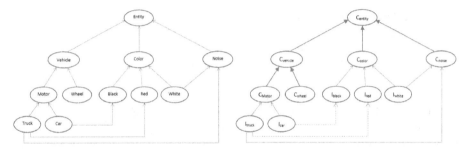

Fig. 1. Mapping of entity ontology to Markov chain model

a new approach for automatically calculating weights of concepts in an ontology and then using these weights to enhance the concept vector space representation model.

The rest of the paper is organized as follows. Section 2 describes our proposed method in detail while section 3 concludes the paper.

2 Proposed Model and Methodology

The following section describes the proposed model which is inspired from [8]. The proposed model consists of three subtasks; mapping the domain ontology into a Markov chain model, calculation of the transition probability matrix for Markov chain model and calculation of the importance for each concept in ontology. The final step is building a concept vector space model.

2.1 Modelling of Markov Model by a Domain Ontology

Following the formal definition of the domain ontology, we will adopt a model where the ontology will be presented as a directed acyclic graph in which classes and their instances are structured in a hierarchy. This definition will be represented by the tuple $O = (C, H, I, type(i), rel(i))$ [8], where:

- C is a non-empty set class identifiers;
- H is a set of taxonomy relationship of C;
- I is a potentially empty set I of instance identifiers;
- $type(i)$ is an instance to class relation;
- $rel(i)$ is an instance to instance relation.

The graphical representation of the domain ontology will be implemented using the Markov chain model. The Markov chain model is adopted because of its ability to deal with flexible relationships, such as inter-instance relationships and non-hierarchical relationships between classes.

To be consistent with the ontology definition we partitioned the set of Markov chain states into two disjoint subsets; S_C, which contains the states corresponding to ontology classes, and S_I, which contains the states corresponding to ontology instances.

The Markov chain modelling is an equivalent mapping which means that classes (*entity, vehicle, motor*) in the ontology and the instances of those classes (*truck, car, red*) are mapped to states (C_{entity}, $C_{vehicle}$, C_{motor}, I_{truck}, I_{car}, I_{red}) in the Markov chain. Whereas, all instance-to-instance relations, instance-to-class relations and non-hierarchical relations between instances, and classes are mapped to state transitions. As can be seen from the figure 1, three types of state transitions are identified as a result of mapping of ontology to Markov chain: concept-to-concept state transitions (C_{entity}, $C_{vehicle}$) indicated with bold line arrows, concept-to-instance state transitions (C_{motor}, I_{truck}) indicated with lines with open arrows and instance-to-instance state transitions (I_{truck}, I_{red}) indicated with dash line arrows.

2.2   Calculation of Transition Probability Matrix and Calculation of Concepts' Importance

The transition probability matrix for Markov chain model will be calculated based on the Page Rank algorithm [9]. We can employ this algorithm since our Markov chain model meets the so called irreducible property. This means that graph is finite and from every state it is possible to go to every other state, and the probability of transition from a state i to a state j is only dependent on the state i and not on the path to arrive at state j. The irreducible property is very important because it guarantees the convergence of the algorithm.

The page rank algorithm will be adjusted with a new parameter called the probability distribution weight (ω)[8]. This parameter determines how probabilities are distributed between states representing classes (S_C), and states representing instances (S_I), following each random jump. If $\omega = 0$, random jump probability is distributed only among instance states, and if $\omega = 1$, random jump probability is distributed only among class states.

Once we get the transition probability matrix, then we can calculate the importance of each concept in a given ontology. The importance (Imp) is calculated using equation 1.

$$Imp(c) = -\log_2\left(\frac{\vec{e}_{state(c)}}{\sum_{s \in S_c} \vec{e}_s}\right) \tag{1}$$

where $\vec{e}_{state(c)}$ indicates the principal left eigenvector component calculated from transition probability matrix for the Markov chain state S_c.

2.3   Building the Concept Vector Space Representation Model

The final step of the proposed model is building a concept vector space representation model. The Concept vector space model is created using the relevance of ontology concepts (frequency of occurrence of concepts), and the importance of ontology concepts calculated as described in section 2.2.

The concept vector space representation model will be employed as a tool in the classification process in order to organize text documents in a structured form. As a result, every new unlabeled text document will be assigned to a predefined category. This will be done by calculating the similarity between the concept vector space representation created by the ontology and the concept vector space representation created by the unlabeled text document. Then, the text document will be assigned to a category having the highest similarity value with respect to that text document.

To evaluate the performance of the proposed model an experiment will be conducted. The aim is to evaluate and compare the classification results, in terms of accuracy (precision/recall), obtained using the enhanced concept vector space representation with results obtained using the traditional concept vector space representational model.

3   Conclusion

In this paper, an adaptive concept vector space representation model using Markov Chain model is proposed. The vector space model is one of the most common models for representing text documents in classification process and it can be represented by terms or concepts. The concept representation uses the domain ontology where the document is represented by ontology concepts and their relevance. These concepts make various contributions in classification process and this depends on the position of concepts where they are depicted in the ontology hierarchy. The existing techniques build the concept vector space model calculating the actual position of the concepts in an ontology hierarchy, either manually or empirically through trial and error. We proposed a new approach to automatically estimate the importance indicated by weights of ontology concepts, and to enhance the concept vector space model using automatically estimated weights. Further research is required on implementation of the proposed model on real domain ontology in order to have a reliable comparison and evaluation of performance with the existing approaches. We also plan to conduct further studies to examine how the proposed model can improve the performance of text document classification process.

References

1. Raghavan, P.: Extracting and Exploiting Structure in Text Search. In: SIGMOD Conference, p. 635 (2003)
2. Al-Azmi, A.-A.R.: Data, Text, and Web Mining for Business Intellegence: A Survey. International Journal of Data Mining & Knowledge Management Process (IJDKP) 3(2) (2013)
3. Keikha, M., Khonsari, A., Oroumchian, F.: Rich document representation and classification: An analysis. Knowledge-Based Systems 22(1), 67–71 (2009)
4. Gu, H., Zhou, K.: Text Classification Based on Domain Ontology. Journal of Communication and Computer 3(5) (2006)
5. Yang, X., Sun, N., Zhang, Y., Kong, D.: General Framework for Text Classification based on Domain Ontology. In: 3rd International Workshop on Semantic Media Adaptation and Personalization (2008)

6. Fang, J., Guo, L., Wang, X., Yang, N.: Ontology-Based Automatic Classification and Ranking for Web Documents. In: Proceedings the Fourth International Conference on Fuzzy Systems and Knowlede Discovery, China, (2007)

7. da Costa Pereira, C., Tettamanzi, A.G.B.: An Evolutionary Approach to Ontology-Based User Model Acquisition. In: Di Gesú, V., Masulli, F., Petrosino, A. (eds.) WILF 2003. LNCS (LNAI), vol. 2955, pp. 25–32. Springer, Heidelberg (2006)

8. Frost, H.R., McCray, A.: Markov Chain Ontology Analysis (MCOA). BMC Bioinformatics 13(14), 23 (2012)

9. Brin, S., Page, L.: The anatomy of a large-scale hypertextual Web search engine. In: Proceedings of the 7th International Conference on World Wide Web, vol. 7 (1998)

A Core Ontology of Macroscopic Stuff

C. Maria Keet

Department of Computer Science, University of Cape Town, South Africa
mkeet@cs.uct.ac.za

Abstract. Domain ontologies contain representations of types of stuff (matter, mass, or substance), such as milk, alcohol, and mud, which are represented in a myriad of ways that are neither compatible with each other nor do they follow a structured approach within the domain ontology. Foundational ontologies and Ontology distinguish between pure stuff and mixtures only, if it contains stuff. We aim to fill this gap between foundational and domain ontologies by applying the notion of a 'bridging' core ontology, being an ontology of categories of stuff that is formalised in OWL. This core ontology both refines the DOLCE and BFO foundational ontologies and resolves the main type of interoperability issues with stuffs in domain ontologies, thereby also contributing to better ontology quality. Modelling guidelines are provided to facilitate the Stuff Ontology's use.

1 Introduction

Stuffs, or, depending on one's background, also called matter, mass, or substance, and normally denoted with mass nouns in natural language, are generally considered to deserve their own ontological category distinct from countable objects. They are entities such as wood, milk, water, honey, and whipped cream, that can be counted only in specific quantities. They are important in many subject domains, such as the environment (e.g., soil, air in the environment ontology EnvO [7]), medicine with the various body substances (blood and fat in SNOMED CT [29], and in manufacturing (an amount of oil greasing the machine, steel [18]). A more elaborate ongoing use case is that of traceability of food and its ingredients [11], concerning handling bulk goods [31], such as soybean, flour, and breakfast cereals: the flow of the ingredients have to be monitored in the food production chain for food safety and swift and adequate response in case of problems. This requires a way to track parts and portions of the bulk, and mixing them with other portions of stuff. From a modelling viewpoint, this requires representing the stuffs adequately, how the stuffs relate, and their temporal dimension; we focus on the first topic in this paper.

Related works about stuff can be divided roughly into philosophy, foundational ontologies, and domain ontologies. Discourses in Ontology (philosophy) concern portions, quantities, constitution, and distinguishing stuff from object [2,5,9,12] and the nature of stuff and it representation [9,24,32], which, if it accepts stuff, remains at a very basic distinction between 'pure' stuff that has

K. Janowicz et al. (Eds.): EKAW 2014, LNAI 8876, pp. 209–224, 2014.

one kind of basis or granule (e.g., gold, water) and 'mixed' stuff (e.g., lemonade, milk), and the philosophy of chemistry [6,25,24], that concerns itself with, among others, deuterium in water and historical interpretations of the nature of stuff. The former is too generic and the latter too detailed for most domain ontologies. Foundational ontologies, such as DOLCE [23], BFO [4], and GFO [17], have no or one stuff category, hence do not provide any modelling guidance in that regard. Contrast this with domain ontologies, which have from several (BioTop [3]) to very many (SNOMED CT) kinds of stuff. For instance, SNOMED CT's Body substance has as direct subclasses, among others, Nervous system hormone-like substance (pure stuff), and Regurgitated food and Breath (mixtures), and EnvO's Environmental material has as direct subclasses Anthropogenic environmental material, Clay, and Foam. The main issue for handling stuff consistently is due to the gap between Ontology and foundational ontologies on the one hand, and domain ontologies on the other, and in particular the absence of methodological guidance where the former may be applicable to, and beneficial for, the latter. A recent overview of methodologies [15] notes the absence of foundational ontology use in all surveyed methodologies.

Thus, there is a disconnect between the foundational ontologies on the one hand, and domain ontologies on the other, yet there is a pressing need for adequate representation of stuffs in domain ontologies. To address this issue, we apply the notion of a bridging *core ontology* that connects the very general contents of a foundational ontology to the entities represented in domain ontologies. Core ontologies have been developed elsewhere for, among others, events and multimedia entities, and has some general guidelines for its development [27]. Here we describe the Stuff Ontology, which functions as such a core ontology. To address this comprehensively, one has to consider the essential features of stuff compared to other categories, which stuff categories have to be added to suffice for its application in domain ontology development, and find a way to formalise it adequately. We focus on the latter two, and assume that stuff exists and deserves its own category. We describe the modelling decisions, including the refinement of the notion of 'pure' stuff and specialisation of mixtures into homogeneous and heterogeneous mixtures, and several subcategories, and several roles and basic relationships have to be introduced, such as the 'basis' type (granule) a stuff is made up of and what sub (part) stuffs it has. A most precise formalisation requires either second order logic or a sorted logic, but to keep usability in mind, we formalise this ontology in OWL so that it can be imported easily into extant ontologies and actually be used in comparatively widely used software infrastructure for ontologies. We evaluate the core ontology against the set of desirable features specified in [27] and add (potential) usability to it, including a decision diagram, linking the stuff ontology to DOLCE and BFO, and illustrating how stuff can be represented more accurately in domain ontologies for interoperability by availing of this core ontology, using the nature of the stuff as modelling criterion rather than the various roles it may play.

In the remainder of the paper, we discuss other ontologies (Section 2) and present the stuff ontology in Section 3. This is followed by implementation aspects and evaluation of the core ontology in Section 4, and we close in Section 5.

2   Related Works: Ontology and Ontologies

Davis [9] identified five options how to represent stuff—particles, fields, two for continuous matter, and a hybrid model—where a hybrid one with portions and particles is the only one used in both the literature and ontologies. Among the hybrids, distinctions are drawn regarding shareability of parts, with sums for 'pure' kinds of stuff and rigid embodiments for mixtures [2], therewith distinguishing stuff with instances of a single element or molecule as part from those that have instance of more than one different type of molecule with a stuff-forming relation between them [2,12], inclusion of time and modality [12,25], and interaction of quantities of stuff and spatial character of mereological relations [25]. First, we grant stuff its own ontological category distinct from objects, and we agree with a hybrid model. Second, we restrict it here to the categories and kinds of stuff and an a-temporal view, because most ontologies and related computational infrastructure are only for atemporal logical theories.

Let us assess several foundational ontologies on their inclusion of stuff. DOLCE's Amount of matter has examples such as gold, wood, sand, and meat with as commonality "that they are endurants with no unity ... [and] are mereologically invariant" [23]; it has no subcategories. GFO has Mass_entity ≡ Amount of substrate, which is a "special persistant whose instances are distinct amounts at certain timepoints" [17]; it has no subcategories either. BFO v1.1 does not have stuff, though object aggregate leans in that direction (a mereological sum of its members, alike a fleet); pedantically, it means that according to the philosophical commitments of BFO, stuff does not exist. The most recent SUMO ([30] cf. [26]) has Substance, which is something "in which every part is *similar* to every other in every relevant respect...any *parts* have *properties* which are *similar* to those of the *whole*" (emphasis added). Its subclass PureSubstance covers both the elements and compounds and has subclasses such as GreenhouseGas (indeed a stuff) and HydrophilicLipidHead (part of a molecule, i.e., and object), whereas Mixture is "two or more pure substances, combined in varying proportions - each retaining its own specific properties.", with direct subclasses, e.g., Glass ($\geq$1 pure stuff) and Sewage ($>$1 pure and mixed stuffs). It has a partition into natural and synthetic substances, and with direct subclasses including Beverage, Electricity, and Juice. Thus, SUMO has categories and kinds of stuff, and, as we shall see, useful informal definitions, but the modelling criteria for the domain stuffs are too limited and not uniform. Cyc [8] has an undefined StuffType with subclasses TemporalStuffType and ExistingStuffType, and a relationship granuleOf-Stuff that has StuffType as domain and ObjType as range. Its hierarchy contains EdibleStuff as a direct instance of ExistingStuffType, which is a direct generalisation of FoodOrDrink, Nutrient, CerealFood, FruitAndVegetableFood, and so on. Aside from the instantiation issue, they are *roles* that both objects (e.g., apple) and stuffs (e.g., vitamin A) play from the anthropocentric viewpoint, not that they rigidly are those things.

Regarding domain ontologies, we could find only one that addresses stuff explicitly, being the ontology for maintenance actions of industrial objects [18]. It has at least seven subcategories of stuff, distinguishing between pure and mixed stuff (with further division in solution and emulsion, but not other colloids) and state-based divisions (solid, liquid, and gas); its KIF3.0 version is not available, however. BioPortal lists many ontologies that include stuff and 4 were selected randomly. The loggerhead nesting ontology [22] has Stuff with four subclasses: air, mucus, sand, water. EnvO's environmental material has direct subclasses such as clay and water (particular kinds of stuff) and foam (a type/category of stuff). Its food product—potentially overlapping with SUMO's food classes—contains stuffs, such as sugar (the sucrose, 'table sugar'), meat, milk, and so on organised mostly by source (animal, fish, plant) but mixed with other criteria (e.g., nonfat dry milk). In [2,12]'s viewpoint, however, sugar is an unstructured or discrete stuff, and milk and meat are structured/nondiscrete, and of which it is already known that they require different constraints to handle portions in time [12]. SNOMED CT has many kinds of stuff. Considering even just its direct subclasses, they include Allergen class (with subclasses), oil, materials (with subclasses surgical material, adhesive agent, culture medium, body material (with subclass, among others, fat and crystal)), substance of abuse, chemical, biological substance, and body substance. However, crystal is a solid state, adhesive agent is function-oriented, and substance of abuse is contextual.

Thus, there is no set of modelling criteria within and throughout the ontologies, and a gap exists on guidance from Ontology and foundational ontologies for modelling stuffs, and its consequent diverse use in domain ontologies.

3   Overview of the Stuff Ontology

Typical examples of stuffs in the Ontology literature are Water and Gold versus Lemonade, Oil, Milk, and Wood, where the first two are called unstructured, discrete, or pure kinds of stuff and the latter structured, non-discrete, or mixed stuffs [2,5,12] without further refinements, which is insufficient to categorise stuffs in domain ontologies. The philosophy of chemistry concerning stuff, notably [6,25], goes into more detail than is necessary for the current scope of macroscopic stuff (such as element decay, heavy water, the structure of solids, categorisation of crystals, whether Water is the same as H_2O). We will use the very same principles, however, as considered in those works:

- a granule, grain, or basis type of the stuff, which is at one finer-grained level than the stuff itself (see also [20]);
- a so-called stuff-forming relation between the entities 'in' the stuff, i.e., that it is made of at that adjacent finer-grained level;
- homogeneous versus heterogeneous matter;
- we concur with Brakel's conclusion that the focus has to be on "macroscopic sameness" [6] and Barnett's notion of "least portion" [2]: the least portion is the smallest portion that still exhibits the macroscopic properties of that kind of stuff.

The chemistry discussed in this section can be found in any chemistry textbook; we used [19,28] and IUPAC's Gold Book [http://goldbook.iupac.org/] to cross-check the chemistry information, and more details, explanations, and examples can be found there (the author's prior education in food science and its lecture notes aided in devising the food examples).

We introduce several categories of stuff, and define most of them in the next two sections; the taxonomy is depicted in Fig. 1, where each of the direct subclasses are disjoint, except Bulk. To make this practically useful for ontology development, a representation in OWL 2 DL is preferred thanks to its expressiveness, computational infrastructure, and relatively wide uptake, which can be slimmed to one of its less expressive profiles if needed. This extensively annotated stuff ontology is available online (see Section 4), and some key definitions are included in this paper in DL notation. It required an adjustment due to expressivity limitations, but it is outweighed by the usability argument: using a second order logic, a many-sorted logic, or variable n-ary predicate, relegates the ontology to a paper-based exercise only that would still not be practically usable in ontology development and ontology-driven information systems for, among others, food processing.

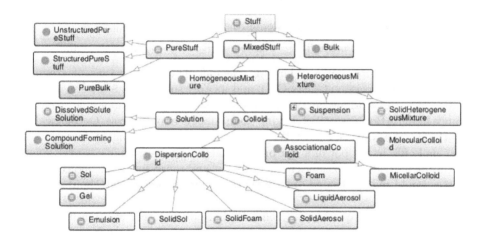

Fig. 1. Taxonomy of main categories of stuff (Ontograf rendering)

3.1 Pure Stuff

Really pure stuff occurs very rarely in nature and is not interesting practically, depending on what one categorises under pure stuff, if anything, and if so, how. What is widely agreed upon is that there is pure stuff that consists of objects that instantiate only one most specific single type of granule: H_2O *molecules* in the case of water, Au *atoms* in the case of gold (one can go further down into isotopes, which is beyond the scope), but also the individual soybean, as *multi-molecular particle* (MMP) in the soybean storage silo handled as bulk. Molecules have as parts atoms and can be separated into the element or molecule form of the element and are created by putting together an amount of molecules such that each component portion loses its properties and become something else that has other properties than its constituent atoms or molecules. This is not the case for gold. There is a difference between an amount of stuff made up of instances of one of the elements as listed in the periodic table of elements, like Au, and pure stuffs that consist of molecules. They are both PureStuff, though, as the instances—some amount of that stuff—consist of instances of one type of 'basis', 'grain', or 'granule' only. Because 'grain' has specific connotations as individual entity and 'base' is a bit vague, we will use hasGranuleType to relate to the kind of entity at that next finer-grained level of analysis, which is a partial representation of the "constant basis principle" [12] and a generalisation of BioTop's and Cyc's granular parts, and is typed as in Eqs. 1-2, where MultiMolecularParticle is abbreviated as MMP. We will use hasSubStuff to relate a stuff playing the whole role with its part-stuff, in line with the taxonomy of part-whole relations [21] (Eqs. 3-4). This results in the definition for PureStuff in Eq. 5.

$$\exists\, hasGranuleType.\top \sqsubseteq Stuff \tag{1}$$

$$\top \sqsubseteq \forall hasGranuleType.(Atom \sqcup Molecule \sqcup MMP) \tag{2}$$

$$\exists\, hasSubStuff.\top \sqsubseteq Stuff \tag{3}$$

$$\top \sqsubseteq \forall hasSubStuff.Stuff \tag{4}$$

$$PureStuff \equiv Stuff \sqcap\, = 1\, hasSubStuff.(PureBulk \sqcup StructuredPureStuff \sqcup$$
$$UnstructuredPureStuff) \sqcap\, = 1\, hasGranuleType.(Atom \sqcup Molecule \sqcup MMP) \tag{5}$$

For instance, TableSugar is a kind of PureStuff that has one type of granule, Molecule (more precisely: $C_{12}H_{22}O_{11}$), and its only sub-stuff is Sucrose. The only way to have this working in OWL, is to represent each kind of molecule as an instance in the ABox, instead of making them subclasses of Molecule. Ontologically, $C_{12}H_{22}O_{11}$ is a universal (or: OWL class) and there are very many instances of that molecule in the pot of sugar on your table. However, no-one is ever going to encode individual molecules in an ontology, and representing the molecules as classes would require second order logic regarding the knowledge about granule types.

PureStuff has three subtypes, being UnstructuredPureStuff, StructuredPureStuff, and PureBulk. The first one has as granule *one type of element*, such as a amount of gold consisting of instances of the element Au. The second one has as granule type *one type of molecule* (and the atoms are part of the molecules in a specific configuration), like water (H_2O), ethanol (C_2H_5OH), vitamin A, and so on; existing resources that contain such molecules are the Chemical Entities of Biological Interest (CHeBi) ontology [10] and the Chemical thesaurus [http://www.chemthes.com]. In chemistry, these entities are called *compounds*. The reasons for this distinction are the differences in granule and divisibility with compound formation and destruction in the right situation. One cannot simply put the right amount of C, H, and O atoms together and have as mereological sum ethanol, and ethanol can be destroyed by, among others, the enzyme alcohol dehydrogenase, such that the constituent atoms survive but not the molecule. Unlike the unstructured pure stuff, there is, in philosophy terminology, a so-called *stuff-forming relation* [2] for structured pure stuff, restricted to one that concerns covalent chemical bonds, which we denote with compoundFormingRelation and to which one can attach properties like the ratio and environmental parameters (not pursued here). This does not hold for unstructured pure stuffs. While it is the case, as with StructuredPureStuff, that dividing an amount of, say, gold to the smallest portion and down to an instance of the granule always remains gold, and no matter how we combine or sum different amounts of gold, it always remains gold (setting aside the ion formation to Au^{3+}), the compound formation with ratio of components to form the compound and right conditions is not applicable for its atoms are not bound covalently to atoms of another type, hence, it is not a compound. One could argue that elements are formed as well and therefore should be considered 'compounds' of protons, neutrons, and electrons, but this occurs at many orders of magnitude less than compound formation, and is one step more fine-grained than the next level of analysis, and therefore can be ignored. Third, and finally, PureBulk is pure stuff at the macroscopic level, where some bulk goods fit, such as an amount of tea biscuits or soybeans with as granule type the multi-molecular object TeaBiscuit (resp., Soybean). They are the macroscopic equivalent of the molecule and there is only one granule type; hence, with respect to the chosen granule type, an amount of tea biscuits with granules the multi-molecular particles as instances of TeaBiscuit is then just as much structured pure stuff. Because of the different single granule type, we shall categorise these under PureBulk.

In sum, PureStuff's subtypes differ in granule type they have, which is either one type of Atom (element), Molecule, or MultiMoleculeParticle (MMP), which are subtypes of Physical Object (represented in any of one's preferred foundational ontology); see Eqs. 6-8 for the simplified OWL version in DL rendering.

$$UnstructuredPureStuff \equiv PureStuf \sqcap \forall hasGranuleType.Atom \sqcap$$
$$= 1\, hasGranuleType.Atom \tag{6}$$
$$StructuredPureStuff \equiv PureStuf \sqcap \forall hasGranuleType.Molecule \sqcap$$
$$= 1hasGranuleType.Molecule \tag{7}$$
$$PureBulk \equiv PureStuf \sqcap \forall hasGranuleType.MMP \sqcap\, = 1\, hasGranuleType.MMP \tag{8}$$

Once it is determined the type of granule is of one kind, then there is a sameness in summation, i.e., two amounts of the same kind of pure stuff is still of that kind of pure stuff.

3.2 Mixed Stuff

Mixtures, also called "structured stuff" [12] or "nondiscrete stuff" [2], are illustrated in the philosophy literature with entities such as lemonade, oil, milk, and wood. While they are indeed all 'structured' in some way, what is meant is that they are mixed stuffs consisting of different stuffs related with a stuff-forming relation [2,12] both when considered from the viewpoint of stuffs and as a collection of the chosen granule type. What holds for all individual mixtures is that they are composed of at least two amounts of stuff that instantiate distinct kinds of stuff (hence, have also distinct granules) that are mixed. To formalise this, we face the same issue as with pure stuff (second order logic, which is 'pushed down' into first order here as well), and that it is not possible to express that the two stuffs are distinct. For the latter reason, we use $\sqsubseteq$ instead of $\equiv$:

$$\text{MixedStuff} \sqsubseteq \text{Stuff} \sqcap \ge 2 \text{ hasSubStuff.Stuff} \tag{9}$$

For instance, the mixture lemonade has water, sugar, and lemon juice as sub-stuffs. Thus, mixtures are indeed different from pure stuff. However, they are not all of the same kind or not all in the same way to the extent that those differences have an effect on portions and parts. Informally, Sprite soda drink is a true *solution*, consisting of water, carbon dioxide, and sugar, whereas milk is an *emulsion* of protein and fat globules dispersed evenly in water, wood is yet again different, being a solid heterogeneous mixture, whereas mud is a *suspension* of unevenly distributed sand in water. The former two examples are kinds of homogeneously mixed stuffs and the latter is an example of heterogeneously mixed stuff, which we elaborate on in the next two subsections.

Heterogeneous Mixed Stuff. HeterogeneousMixture is a combination of different stuffs, of which at least one has a fairly large particle size, that do not react chemically, and the stuffs that the mixed stuff is composed of can be separated by purely physical means (filtration, etc.). This can be sub-divided into a solid, liquid, and a gaseous version. The liquid version with solid particles (usually >1 μm) is called Suspension, which has as characteristics that the substance naturally separates, with separation due to sedimentation, creaming, flocculation, or coalescence unless they are 'stabilized' by some other stuff, as regularly happens in the production process; e.g., tomato juice, mud. A SolidHeterogeneousMixture is the solid version of a suspension; e.g., wood has a compartmentalisation of the components into cellulose, hemicellulose, lignin, and other stuffs like waxes. The interesting aspect here, is that the *state* of the stuffs become relevant for describing the mixtures cf. the pure stuffs, and the role they play in the mixture. Suspensions have a stuff in liquid state, called *continuous medium* or dispersion medium, and a stuff in the solid state, called *dispersed phase*, where their bearers, stuffs, can play each role depending on what is mixed. Take, e.g., the suspension Mud, where liquid water acts as continuous medium and sand as dispersed phase, whereas liquid water is the dispersed phase in Fog in the continuous medium air; hence, they are roles the stuffs play in the mixture, not that the stuffs are continuous medium (resp. dispersed phase).

Formalising this, we start with HeterogeneousMixture that has at least two types of stuff and granules (Eq. 10), inheriting from MixedStuff that it has at least two stuffkinds.

$$\text{HeterogeneousMixture} \sqsubseteq \text{Mixture} \sqcap \ge 2 \text{ hasSubStuff.}(\text{MixedStuff} \sqcup \text{PureStuff}) \sqcap$$
$$\ge 2 \text{ hasGranuleType.}(\text{Molecule} \sqcup \text{MultiMoleculeParticle}) \tag{10}$$

For its two subtypes, we have to take into consideration the state that the stuffs are in, as that is an essential characteristic of the mixture. This is a property of a substance only, not as a reified solid, liquid, or gas (which have their own properties, like crystalline or malleable). A SolidHeterogeneousMixture is composed of stuffs that are in the solid state, and Suspension has the stuff that plays the continuous medium in the liquid state with stuff in the solid state dispersed in it, more than one kind of solid stuff may be suspended in the liquid continuous medium, and we use the common inheresIn relationship (from foundational ontologies) to relate roles with their bearers. Typing hasState with domain Stuff and range StuffState (i.e., $\exists$ hasState.$\top \sqsubseteq$ Stuff and $\top \sqsubseteq \forall$hasStuff.StuffState), we define the two classes as follows:

$$
\text{SolidHeterogeneousMixture} \equiv \text{HeterogeneousMixture} \sqcap
$$
$$
\geq 2 \text{ hasSubStuff.}(\text{Stuff} \sqcap \exists\text{hasState.Solid}) \tag{11}
$$
$$
\text{Suspension} \equiv \text{HeterogeneousMixture} \sqcap \exists\text{hasSubStuff.}(\text{Stuff} \sqcap
$$
$$
\exists\text{hasState.Liquid} \sqcap \exists\text{inheresIn}^-.\text{ContinuousMedium}) \sqcap
$$
$$
\exists\text{hasSubStuff.}(\text{Stuff} \sqcap \exists\text{hasState.Solid} \sqcap \exists\text{inheresIn}^-.\text{DispersedPhase}) \tag{12}
$$

Homogeneous Mixed Stuff. In HomogeneousMixtures, the *mixed stuffs are distributed evenly* across the mixture[1]. There are two categories of stuff that can be created and remain a stable homogeneous mixture: solutions and colloids, where the former exists as one phase and the latter exists as two or more phases (which is sometimes also referred to as a homogeneous heterogeneous stuff); a *phase* is a physically distinct portion of the system, where the stuff occupying that region of space has uniform properties. A true Solution is a combination of at least two stuffs where the mixing occurs at the molecular level where some chemical reaction occurs, and the resultant is one phase. This can occur such that (*i*) one stuff that plays the role of Solute dissolves in the other stuff that plays the Solvent role such that no new compounds are formed, other than ignorable changes—like an -OH group to a -O$^-$ + H$^+$—in the solution, e.g., some dissolved sugar in a cup of tea, or (*ii*) it can be compound-forming in a chemical reaction; e.g., to dissolve gold in aqua regia to obtain a solution with new AuCl$_4^-$ molecules. One can introduce a symmetric solutionFormingRelation, which is a stuff-forming relation between the solute and solvent, but also here one cannot assert that the stuffs that play the solute and solvent role must be distinct, so the solutionFormingRelation is only typed with Solvent as its domain and Solute as its range. Formally, a solution is made of at least two kinds of stuff where one plays the solvent and the other one(s) play(s) the solute role (Eq. 13), and each solvent must have at least one solute (Eq. 14).

$$
\text{Solution} \equiv \text{HomogeneousMixture} \sqcap \exists\text{hasSubStuff.}(\text{Stuff} \sqcap \exists\text{inheresIn}^-.\text{Solute} \sqcap
$$
$$
\text{hasGranuleType.}(\text{Atom} \sqcup \text{Ion} \sqcup \text{Molecule})) \sqcap \exists\text{hasSubStuff.}(\text{Stuff} \sqcap
$$
$$
\text{inheresIn}^-.\text{Solvent} \sqcap \text{hasGranuleType.}(\text{Atom} \sqcup \text{Ion} \sqcup \text{Molecule})) \sqcap
$$
$$
\exists\text{hasNrOfPhase.int}_{=1} \tag{13}
$$
$$
\text{Solvent} \sqsubseteq \exists\text{solutionFormingRelation.Solute} \tag{14}
$$

The other subclass of HomogeneousMixture is Colloid, which is a mixture with intermediate particle size, where one kind of stuff that plays the dispersed phase, is

---

[1] Note that 'homogeneous' can mean sameness of the parts, one phase, and/or macroscopic sameness, depending on the literature consulted [25].

microscopically dispersed *evenly* throughout another stuff, which acts as the continuous (or dispersion) medium; e.g., milk, mayonnaise, agar, and marshmallow. Particle size is the main distinguishing characteristic of colloids compared to solutions; practically, the liquid colloids can be distinguished from liquid solutions using the Tyndall effect[2] and among themselves based on either (*i*) the state of the continuous medium and dispersed phase (dispersion colloids), (*ii*) hydrophobicity (associational colloids), or (*iii*) it has molecules of colloidal dimension, i.e., very large molecules, dispersed in the medium (molecular colloids). For instance, whipped cream is a Foam that has as continuous medium stuff that is in its liquid state and as dispersed phase a stuff that is in its gaseous state; pigmented ink and blood are Sols that have as continuous medium stuff that is liquid and a dispersed phase with solid stuff; and milk and mayonnaise are Emulsions that have a liquid continuous medium and dispersed phase. Soap is a micellar (associational) colloid, with an aqueous liquid containing micelles formed by molecules with a hydrophilic head and hydrophobic tail. Latex and starchy stuffs with large polymers, such as wallpaper glue, are examples of molecular colloids.

These characteristics result in the second distinction with solutions: a colloid has at least two phases whereas solutions have only one. The phases of a dispersion colloid can be distinguished typically only under a microscope, and therefore they are perceived as homogeneous and possibly easily misrepresented as a solution. Third, the colloid has properties of its own, such as its freezing point, that is different from the separate stuffs making up the colloid.

Note that one cannot simply pour whipping cream into a bowl and it will become whipped cream by simple contact with the air, or put together oil and egg yolk arbitrarily and expect to obtain mayonnaise. They have to be mixed in a specific way such that the globules/particles are gradually added to the continuous medium and obtain the required surface tension to remain stable. As such, one can consider a specific *colloid-forming relation* between the distinct stuffs that compose the colloid, of which an instance comes into existence only when the stuff that plays the role of dispersed phase is mixed gradually with the continuous medium in order to become a stable colloid. Thus, the colloidFormingRelation holds between the continuous medium that inheres in some stuff and the dispersed phase that inheres in some stuff, not the stuffs per sé. One can philosophise whether they are roles the stuffs in the colloid play or the component-stuffs are occupiers of three-dimensional spaces that, in turn, fulfill a particular role in the space that the amount of colloid occupies. Here, we take the former, more compact, formalization. Formally, the general characterisation of Colloid is in Eq. 15. The dispersion colloid Gel is included as Eq. 16; the other seven follow the same pattern with the differences in states: Emulsion as a stuff in liquid state dispersed in another stuff that is also in liquid state and has the role of continuous medium; Foam as a gas dispersed in liquid; LiquidAerosol as a liquid dispersed in gas; Sol as a solid dispersed in liquid; SolidAerosol as a solid dispersed in gas; SolidFoam as a gas dispersed in solid; and SolidSol as a solid

---

[2] A beam of light passing through a true (liquid) solution is not visible, but light passing through a colloid will be reflected by the larger particles and therefore the light beam is visible.

dispersed in solid; they are included in the OWL file.

Colloid $\equiv$ HomogeneousMixture $\sqcap$ $\exists$hasNrOfPhase.int$_{\geq 2}$ $\sqcap$

$= 1$hasSubStuff.(Stuff $\sqcap$ $\exists$hasState.StuffState $\sqcap$ $\exists$inheresIn$^-$.ContinuousMedium) $\sqcap$

$= 1$hasSubStuff.(Stuff $\sqcap$ ($\exists$hasState.StuffState) $\sqcap$ ($\exists$inheresIn$^-$.DispersedPhase)) (15)

Gel $\equiv$ DispersionColloid $\sqcap$ $= 1$ hasSubStuff.(Stuff $\sqcap$ $\exists$hasState.Solid $\sqcap$

$\exists$inheresIn$^-$.ContinuousMedium)$\sqcap$ $= 1$ hasSubStuff.(Stuff $\sqcap$ $\exists$hasState.Liquid $\sqcap$

inheresIn$^-$.DispersedPhase) $\sqcap$ $\exists$hasNrOfPhase.int$_{\geq 2}$ (16)

One can elaborate on surfactants, stabilizers, and enhancers; e.g., for whipping cream in homebaking, one can add solid sugar powder and cornstarch to keep the whipped cream stiff for longer, i.e., stabilise the colloid against unfavourable environmental conditions. Also, there are more types of gel, which are useful for a pure chemistry ontology, but have not been included in the stuff ontology due to its highly specialised usage; e.g., a ringing gel is a gel "with energy dissipation in the acoustic frequency range" [1].

This concludes the overview of the 25 categories of stuff, of which 16 are defined (see OWL file for the other definitions).

4   Implementation and Evaluation of the Core Ontology

As mentioned in the introduction, the stuff ontology is aimed at bridging the foundational with the domain ontologies, keeping usability in mind. It meets all of Scherp et al.'s desirable core ontology features [27]—axiomatisation, extensibility, reusability, separation of concerns, and modularity—and we add usability. In the remainder of this section, we describe how these features are met.

4.1   OWL version of the Stuff Ontology

The introduction of Section 3 mentioned concessions were made to represent the knowledge in OWL, notably the design choice to stay within a decidable fragment of first order logic. The Stuff Ontology is highly axiomatised nevertheless, and has 52 classes, 18 object properties, 266 axioms and is in $\mathcal{SHIQ}(D)$ (OWL 2 DL). Because availing of automated classification services can be of use, especially for the colloids and solutions, it is more useful to not use just a generic untyped inheresIn relation, but one where the domain and range are declared in a way relevant for the ontology, being one where the range is Stuff and domain is StuffRole that subsumes ContinuousMedium, DispersedPhase, Solute, and Solvent. Therefore, srInheresIn is introduced as an object subproperty of inheresIn. Then, when an ontologist adds, e.g., Water, Sand, and Mud, with the water as the continuous medium and sand the dispersed in water, the reasoner classifies Mud as a subclass of Suspension, which it would not have done if we had used inheresIn. Also disjointness axioms have been added where relevant, and most entities have annotations with explanations and examples. The ontology and the extended versions (introduced below) are available online at http://www.meteck.org/files/ontologies/.

4.2   Modelling Guidance for the Main Categories of Stuff

Most types of stuff in the Stuff Ontology have a quite elaborate axiomatization, which potentially hampers its usability. Although it is not a highlighted feature of core ontologies, we deem efforts toward *usability* relevant, for it is needed to facilitate reusability in the field. In addition, options such as Ontology Design Patterns [14] and templates [13] can help and serve the modularity feature of core ontologies, and templates have been shown to be particularly useful with core ontologies, for being at the appropriate level of granularity according to the evaluation carried out by [13]. However, this will work for the Stuff Ontology only once one knows which stuffkind it is. To this end, we designed a decision diagram that in an informal way guides the domain ontology modeller to the appropriate type of stuff. This diagram is included in Fig. 2 and is intended as an informal aid and as a general overview of the Stuff Ontology's contents.

Let us step through it for Mayonnaise. It is not made up of only one type of atom, molecule or larger particles of the same type, hence, it is a MixedStuff. The stuffs it is made up of are evenly distributed throughout, hence it is a HomogeneousMixture. Let's say we do not know whether it consists of one phase, so we move to the alternative question asking whether the component stuffs of mayonnaise—egg yolk and oil—keep their phase, which is 'yes', hence, it is a Colloid. It has nothing to do with hydrophobicity or very large molecules, hence it is a Dispersion Colloid. As both the egg yolk and oil are liquids, option a) is chosen, and we arrive at the endpoint where mayonnaise is an Emulsion. A contextual template or stuffkind-dependent ODP can then be generated to facilitate adding the definition of the domain entity. A contextualised table on the left in Fig. 3 would suffice as input to generate the axiom on the right in the figure.

A separate `stuff-example.owl` contains several domain stuff entities to illustrate the automated classification of stuffkinds in the correct category, such as Mayonnaise and Gold. These entities are distinctly domain ontology entities and therefore they are not included in the Stuff Ontology itself; likewise, a line has been drawn not to include the fine-grained chemistry scientific knowledge (such as the aforementioned ringing gel). Thus, the feature of separation of concerns has been adhered to.

4.3   Ontology Interoperability

To evaluate whether the Stuff Ontology can serve as a core ontology that bridges foundational ontologies and domain ontologies, we first link it to DOLCE and BFO, and subsequently turn to domain ontologies.

Linking to a Foundational Ontology. We tested linking the Stuff Ontology to DOLCE-Lite and BFO v1.1.1, which was successful and these combined ontologies are also online. One might argue against aligning it to BFO because it does not have stuff, but the EnvO is being aligned to BFO [7], entailing that stuff has to be handled in some way. The links in brief: Stuff is made equivalent to DOLCE's Amount of matter and a subclass of material_entity in BFO, both

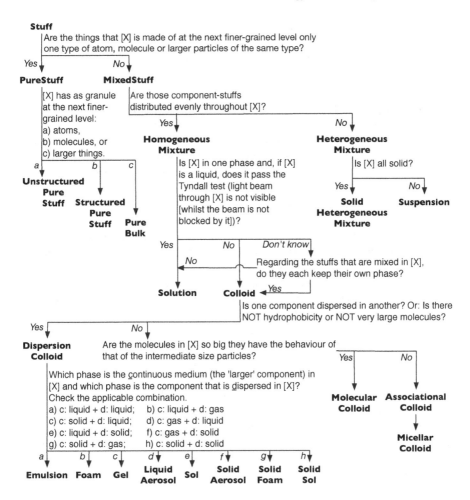

Fig. 2. Decision tree to find the principal kind of stuff of a domain stuff entity

A. Extensible sample template

Feature	Answer
Mayonnaise has as sub-stuff:	Eggyolk
Mayonnaise has as sub-stuff:	Oil
The stuff that is the continuous medium is:	Egg yolk
The stuff that is dispersed in it is:	Oil
Click here to add more sub-stuffs	

B. Definition added to the ontology

Mayonnaise ≡ DispersionColloid ⊓
= 1 hasSubStuff.(Eggyolk ⊓ ∃hasState.Liquid ⊓
∃srInheresIn⁻.ContinuousMedium) ⊓
= 1 hasSubStuff.(Oil ⊓ ∃hasState.Liquid ⊓
srInheresIn⁻.DispersedPhase) ⊓ ∃hasNrOfPhase.int$_{=2}$

Fig. 3. Template to easily ask for the required variables (A), and the definition it will then populate (B), shown for the example where we know Mayonnaise is an Emulsion

also have the 'auxiliary' classes used in the Stuff Ontology, such as PhysicalObject linked to dolce:Physical object and bfo:object, and StuffRole is made a subclass of bfo:role and of dolce:Non-physical endurant. hasPart is made equivalent to dolce:part and inheresIn is made a subrelation of generic-dependent. There are no mappings for the object properties to BFO, because relations are only in the BFO-related Relation Ontology, not in BFO v.1.1.1. The resultant stuff-dolcelite.owl and stuff-bfo11.owl are consistent, and available at the aforementioned URL.

Stuff Ontology for Domain Ontologies: Interoperability. Core ontologies should be useful for domain ontologies, notably to improve the quality, broaden interoperability, and to compute interesting derivations. Due to space limitations, we only provide use cases of ontology interoperability with a few classes (milk, mud, blood, and sugar) and a note on relations, so as to illustrate the underlying modelling issues and solution.

Consider again Milk, which is a colloid *irrespective of one's preferred context*, i.e., the 'nature' of that thing is being a type of stuff. Looking at some of the afore-mentioned ontologies, one notes that Cyc has it as a type of bodily secretion [8] and Galen[3] has it as a NAMEDBodySubstance, which therewith complicate adding soy milk, whereas SNOMED CT [29] has it as a type of Dairy foods and Envo [7] combines the two views by having it as subclass of both 'animal derived beverage' and 'milk product' (both are subclasses of 'food product'), whereas another environment ontology, tailored to microbes (MEO[4]), has it as a portion of secreted substance from the mammary gland, which is an organ, which is an animal-associated habitat for micro-organisms. Linking up the interpretations of milk across the various ontologies and that is least disruptive for the source ontologies, is that in all cases, the milk that is referred to is a stuff and, more precisely an emulsion. The Stuff Ontology can facilitate such interoperability and serve as a 'lingua franca' of the stuffs, either by having links from a stuff ontology extended with domain stuffs, containing, say, a domain-stuff:Milk ⊑ stuff:Emulsion, or where a domain ontology adds a subsumption link to emulsion, e.g., envo:'milk' ⊑ stuff:Emulsion. In a similar way, one can reconcile Mud, which is a stuff:Suspension of itself, whereas in the domain ontologies, it ihas as direct superclass any of the following: it is a meo:rock, sand and soil (which is a meo:geosphere), an envo:'environmental material', cyc:liquid ground, and a cyc:mixture. Likewise, Galen considers Blood as a subclass of Soft tissue, whereas Cyc and SNOMED CT have it as a body fluid (among other things), but, as a stuff, it is in any case a Sol (colloid with liquid continuous medium and solid dispersed phase). Sugar is somewhat trickier: MEO and Envo categorise it as food product (a role it plays), whereas Cyc and SNOMED have it as subclass of Carbohydrate and Organic compound, respectively. However, as a stuff, table sugar/sucrose Sugar is a StructuredPureStuff, and its granule, the molecule $C_{12}H_{22}O_{11}$, is the carbohydrate.

Besides aiding interoperability with respect to classes, it also does so for the relations (OWL object properties). cyc:granuleOfStuff, biotop:'has granular part' and [18]'s ingredients all match the notion of hasGranuleType, so one either can replace those relations or link each to the Stuff Ontology's hasGranuleType. Knowledge about relating component-stuffs is not widely represented in the ontologies, for

---

[3] http://www.co-ode.org/ontologies/galen#Milk; last accessed: 4-7-2014.

[4] http://purl.jp/bio/11/meo/MEO_0000629; last accessed: 4-7-2014.

it requires a careful analysis between portions, parts, and substuffs. hasSubStuff can already aid with some aspects; e.g., adding which beverages hasSubStuff some alcohol can be represented in SUMO, Cyc, or SNOMED CT, knowing that they then have the same representation of that knowledge and are interoperable on that aspect. Generally, though, the issues with portions, sub-quantities, contiguous parts, scattered parts, and summation principles are yet to be resolved fully (see, e.g., [12,16,21] for preliminary results), and we expect that the Stuff Ontology can assist in resolving that, for it already eliminates some philosophical debates on scattered portions (like sending oil molecules to Venus), as individual molecules are not portions of mixtures, and likewise it sets conditions on parts and portions especially regarding colloids and solid heterogeneous mixtures.

5   Conclusions

The gap between foundational and domain ontologies regarding stuff (matter/mass/substance) was filled by applying the idea of a 'bridging' core ontology: the Stuff Ontology. The ontology distinguishes between pure and mixed stuffs, and their sub-categories, such as solutions, colloids, and suspensions, and includes a few core relationships, such as a stuff's granule type and what stuffs a stuff is made of. The Stuff Ontology is highly axiomatised and in OWL DL for practical usability, it was successfully aligned to the DOLCE and BFO foundational ontologies. A decision diagram provides modeling guidelines applicable to the stuffs in domain ontologies, enhancing their quality and interoperability.

Current work concerns the interaction with portions and parts, and future work pertains to a use case on modelling food and bulk goods in food processing.

References

1. Alemán, J., et al.: Definitions of terms relating to the structure and processing of sols, gels, networks, and inorganic-organic hybrid materials. Pure and Applied Chemistry 79(10), 1801–1829 (2007)
2. Barnett, D.: Some stuffs are not sums of stuff. The Philosophical Review 113(1), 89–100 (2004)
3. Beisswanger, E., Schulz, S., Stenzhorn, H., Hahn, U.: BioTop: An upper domain ontology for the life sciences - a description of its current structure, contents, and interfaces to OBO ontologies. Applied Ontology 3(4), 205–212 (2008)
4. BFO: Basic formal ontology, http://www.ifomis.org/bfo (last accessed February 2012)
5. Bittner, T., Donnelly, M.: A temporal mereology for distinguishing between integral objects and portions of stuff. In: Proceedings of AAAI 2007, Vancouver, Canada, pp. 287–292 (2007)
6. van Brakel, J.: The chemistry of substances and the philosophy of mass terms. Synthese 69, 291–324 (1986)
7. Buttigieg, P.L., et al.: The environment ontology: contextualising biological and biomedical entities. Journal of Biomedical Semantics 4, 43 (2013)
8. Cyc: Opencyc, http://www.cyc.com/platform/opencyc (version October 8, 2012) (last accessed: July 2, 2014)

9. Davis, E.: Ontologies and representations of matter. In: Proceedings of AAAI 2010, Atlanta, Georgia, USA, July 11-15. AAAI Press (2010)
10. Degtyarenko, K., et al.: ChEBI: a database and ontology for chemical entities of biological interest. Nucleic Acids Res. 350, D344–D350 (2008)
11. Donnelly, K.A.-M.: A short communication - meta data and semantics the industry interface: What does the food industry think are necessary elements for exchange? In: Sánchez-Alonso, S., Athanasiadis, I.N. (eds.) MTSR 2010. Communications in Computer and Information Science, vol. 108, pp. 131–136. Springer, Heidelberg (2010)
12. Donnelly, M., Bittner, T.: Summation relations and portions of stuff. Philosophical Studies 143, 167–185 (2009)
13. Francescomarino, C.D., Ghidini, C., Khan, M.T.: Grounding conceptual modelling templates on existing ontologies. In: Proceedings of KEOD 2013, Vilamoura, Portugal, September 19-22. INSTICC, pp. 199–206. Scitepress (2013)
14. Gangemi, A., Presutti, V.: Ontology design patterns. In: Staab, S., Studer, R. (eds.) Handbook on Ontologies, pp. 221–243. Springer (2009)
15. Garcia, A., et al.: Developing ontologies within decentralized settings. In: Semantic e-Science. Annals of Information Systems, vol. 11, pp. 99–139. Springer (2010)
16. Guizzardi, G.: On the representation of quantities and their parts in conceptual modeling. In: Proceedings of FOIS 2010. IOS Press, Toronto (2010)
17. Herre, H.: General Formal Ontology (GFO): A foundational ontology for conceptual modelling. In: Theory and Applications of Ontology: Computer Applications, ch. 14. Springer, Heidelberg (2010)
18. Höfling, B., Liebig, T., Rösner, D., Webel, L.: Towards an ontology for substances and related actions. In: Fensel, D., Studer, R. (eds.) EKAW 1999. LNCS (LNAI), vol. 1621, pp. 191–206. Springer, Heidelberg (1999)
19. Jakubke, H.D., Jeschkeit, H.: Concise Encyclopedia Chemistry [translated from the German "ABC Chemie". Walter de Gruyter & Co (1993)
20. Keet, C.M.: A Formal Theory of Granularity. Phd thesis, KRDB Research Centre, Faculty of Computer Science, Free University of Bozen-Bolzano, Italy (April 2008)
21. Keet, C.M., Artale, A.: Representing and reasoning over a taxonomy of part-whole relations. Applied Ontology 3(1-2), 91–110 (2008)
22. Loggerhead Nesting Ontology, http://bioportal.bioontology.org/ontologies/1024 (last accessed: January 27, 2012)
23. Masolo, C., Borgo, S., Gangemi, A., Guarino, N., Oltramari, A.: Ontology library. WonderWeb Deliverable D18 (2003), http://wonderweb.semanticweb.org (ver. 1.0, December 31, 2003)
24. Needham, P.: Compounds and mixtures. In: Handbook of the Philosophy of Science. Philosophy of Chemistry, vol. 6, pp. 271–290. Elsevier (2011)
25. Needham, P.: Macroscopic mixtures. Journal of Philosophy 104, 26–52 (2007)
26. Niles, I., Pease, A.: Towards a standard upper ontology. In: Proceedings of FOIS 2001, Ogunquit, Maine, October 17-19 (2001)
27. Scherp, A., Saathoff, C., Franz, T., Staab, S.: Designing core ontologies. Applied Ontology 6(3), 177–221 (2011)
28. Silberberg, M.S.: Chemistry: the molecular nature of matter and change, 4th edn. McGraw Hill Higher Education (2006)
29. SNOMED CT, http://www.ihtsdo.org/snomed-ct/ (version January 31, 2014) (last accessed: July 3, 2014)
30. SUMO, http://www.ontologyportal.org/ (last accessed: May 2, 2012)
31. Thakur, M., Donnelly, K.A.M.: Modeling traceability information in soybean value chains. Journal of Food Engineering 99, 98–105 (2010)
32. Zimmerman, D.W.: Coincident objects: Could a 'stuff ontology' help? Analysis 57(1), 19–27 (1997)

Feasibility of Automated Foundational Ontology Interchangeability

Zubeida Casmod Khan[1,2] and C. Maria Keet[1]

[1] Department of Computer Science, University of Cape Town, South Africa
mkeet@cs.uct.ac.za
[2] Council for Scientific and Industrial Research, Pretoria, South Africa
zkhan@csir.co.za

Abstract. While a foundational ontology can solve interoperability issues among the domain ontologies aligned to it, multiple foundational ontologies have been developed. Thus, there are still interoperability issues among domain ontologies aligned to different foundational ontologies. Questions arise about the feasibility of linking one's ontology to multiple foundational ontologies to increase its potential for uptake. To answer this, we have developed the tool SUGOI, Software Used to Gain Ontology Interchangeability, which allows a user to interchange automatically a domain ontology among the DOLCE, BFO and GFO foundational ontologies. The success of swapping based on equivalence varies by source ontology, ranging from 2 to 82% and averaging at 36% for the ontologies included in the evaluation. This is due to differences in coverage, notably DOLCE's qualities and BFO and GFO's roles, and amount of mappings. SUGOI therefore also uses subsumption mappings so that every domain ontology can be interchanged, preserves the structure of the ontology, and increases its potential for usability.

1 Introduction

The growth in the amount of Semantic Web applications and ontology-mediated interoperability of complex software applications pushes demands for infrastructure to facilitate with semantic interoperability. Already from the early days of the Semantic Web, foundational ontologies have been proposed as a component to facilitate such interoperability, for they provide common high-level categories so that domain ontologies linked to them are also interoperable [7]. Over the past 15 years, multiple foundational ontologies have been developed, such as DOLCE, BFO [7], GFO [1], SUMO [9], and YAMATO [8]. This introduced the issue of semantic conflicts for domain ontologies that are linked to different foundational ontologies, if those foundational ontologies are indeed really different, and new questions for ontology engineers, chiefly:

1. Which foundational ontology should one choose to link one's domain ontology O_A to?
2. If O_A is linked to foundational ontology O_X, then is it still interoperable with domain ontology O_B that is linked to foundational ontology O_Y?

K. Janowicz et al. (Eds.): EKAW 2014, LNAI 8876, pp. 225–237, 2014.

3. Is it feasible to automatically generate links between O_A and O_Y (which one may not know in sufficient detail), given O_A is linked to O_X?
4. If there are issues with the former, what is causing it? Or: in praxis, which entities of O_X are typically used for mappings with domain ontologies that may not be present, or present in an incompatible way, in O_Y?

The first question has been answered with ONSET [5], which considered the requirements but did not take into account what has been used in praxis. That is, ONSET cannot be used to answer the fourth question, which, may indicate actual modelling motivations and content of O_A to choose O_X over O_Y, assuming O_X has those things being represented in O_A that O_Y does not have. If O_Y has all those things as well, then there must be another reason why O_X was chosen.

The aim of this paper is to answer questions 3 and 4, above. To achieve this, we created SUGOI, a *Software Used to Gain Ontology Interchangeability*, which automatically interchanges the foundational ontology a domain ontology is linked to, as, to the best of our knowledge, no such tool exists yet. The current version can interchange between DOLCE, BFO, and GFO, for their mappings have been studied in detail [3,6], but the system is designed for extensibility so as to handle any 'swap' (only new mapping files have to be provided). SUGOI and its supplementary material are available from the foundational ontology library RO-MULUS at http://www.thezfiles.co.za/ROMULUS/ontologyInterchange.html. We conducted an evaluation with 16 ontologies, using both quantitative and qualitative means. The overall 'raw interchangeability' based solely on the equivalence mappings among the foundational ontologies, is 36.18% on average, ranging from 2.04% to 81.81%, depending mainly on the source ontology. If one permits subsumption mappings for the interchange, then one's foundational ontology can be fully swapped for another. The main reasons for any 'low' interchange is a combination of limited foundational ontology mappings that maintain consistency of the resultant ontology, and coverage of the foundational ontology, in particular when that is used in the domain ontology to foundational ontology alignment.

The remainder of the paper is structured as follows. The design of SUGOI is described in Section 2, which is followed by the experimental evaluation in Section 3. A discussion is presented in Section 4 and conclusions in Section 5.

2 SUGOI Ontology Interchangeability Tool

To answer the questions concerning interchanging domain ontologies among foundational ontologies, we have developed SUGOI, Software Used to Gain Ontology Interchangeability. We describe the input files and algorithm of SUGOI.

2.1 SUGOI's Input Files

SUGOI has been designed to interchange domain ontologies between DOLCE, BFO, and GFO by using OWL mapping files. For the foundational ontology mediation, we will use the results obtained by [3,6]: its equivalence and subsumption mappings between entities in the three ontologies have been investigated in detail, are logically consistent, and are available as machine-processable OWL files from the ontology repository ROMULUS [4]. Because several ontology files are used in the interchangeability, we describe here the terms used for each one:

- The *Source Ontology* ($^s\mathcal{O}$) that the user wants to interchange, which comprises the *Source Domain Ontology* ($^s\mathcal{O}_d$), with the domain knowledge component of the source ontology, the *Source Foundational Ontology* ($^s\mathcal{O}_f$) that is the foundational ontology component of the source ontology that is to be interchanged, and any equivalence or subsumption mappings between entities in $^s\mathcal{O}_d$ and $^s\mathcal{O}_f$.
- The *Target Ontology* ($^t\mathcal{O}$) which has been interchanged, which comprises the *Target Domain Ontology* ($^t\mathcal{O}_d$), with the domain knowledge component of the target ontology, and the *Target Foundational Ontology* ($^t\mathcal{O}_f$) that is the foundational ontology that the user has selected to interchange to, and any equivalence or subsumption mappings between entities in $^t\mathcal{O}_d$ and $^t\mathcal{O}_f$.
- *Mapping ontology:* the mapping ontology between the $^s\mathcal{O}_f$ and the $^t\mathcal{O}_f$.
- *Domain entity:* an entity from $^s\mathcal{O}_d$ or $^t\mathcal{O}_d$.

The algorithm is described in the next subsection.

2.2   Foundational Ontology Interchangeability Algorithm

The general idea of the algorithm behind SUGOI is that it accepts a $^s\mathcal{O}$ consisting of a $^s\mathcal{O}_d$ linked to a $^s\mathcal{O}_f$ (either DOLCE, BFO or GFO) and converts it to a $^t\mathcal{O}$ with a different $^t\mathcal{O}_f$. For this, SUGOI must have access to all the foundational ontologies and the mapping ontologies. The $^s\mathcal{O}$ is provided by the user. It does not matter whether the $^s\mathcal{O}_d$ is linked to a foundational ontology by an import or a merge. SUGOI accesses the remainder of the ontologies either by loading the ontology from the online URI, or by loading it from an offline file, depending on the version in use. Since the algorithm refers to independent ontology files, any changes in the foundational ontologies and mappings will not affect either the algorithm fundamentally or the software. Also, any implementation can be extended easily, as other foundational ontologies and mappings are developed by including the new ontology file paths or URIs.

Twenty mapping files are pre-loaded into SUGOI, allowing the user to interchange between DOLCE, BFO and GFO modules bi-directionally. These mappings do not result in an inconsistency, because any alignment that did that has been removed [3]. After the interchange process, all the domain entities from the $^s\mathcal{O}_d$ are present in the $^t\mathcal{O}_d$. SUGOI links domain entities from the $^s\mathcal{O}_d$ to the $^t\mathcal{O}_f$ as follows. SUGOI maps a domain entity's superentity in the $^s\mathcal{O}_f$ to its corresponding superentity in the $^t\mathcal{O}_f$ using the mapping ontology. This is illustrated in Fig. 1 for the entity dmop:DataType from the DMOP ontology [2], changing the link from DOLCE to one in GFO, and this resulting axiom is called a *GT, good target linking axiom*. If the domain entity's superentity does not have a corresponding mapping entity, SUGOI then treats that superentity as a domain entity and looks for a corresponding mapping entity at a higher level up in the taxonomy. Thus, eventually, the domain entity from the $^s\mathcal{O}_d$ is mapped with on-the-fly subsumption. This is displayed for interchanging the entity dmop:Strategy in Fig. 1, and this resulting axiom is called a *BT, bad target linking axiom*.

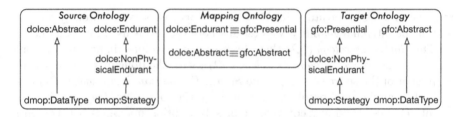

Fig. 1. Examples of interchanging domain entities dmop:DataType and dmop:Strategy from $^s\mathcal{O}_f$ DOLCE to $^t\mathcal{O}_f$ GFO with SUGOI, using equivalence and subsumption mappings, respectively

The main steps of the algorithm are thus as follows:
1. Create a $^t\mathcal{O}$.
2. Copy axioms from the $^t\mathcal{O}_f$ to the $^t\mathcal{O}$.
3. Copy the $^s\mathcal{O}_d$ (domain axioms) to the $^t\mathcal{O}$.
4. Map the $^s\mathcal{O}_d$ domain entities to the $^t\mathcal{O}_f$ using the mapping ontology.
5. Perform on-the-fly subsumption if a domain entity from previous step is not linked to a $^t\mathcal{O}_f$.
6. Delete $^s\mathcal{O}_f$ entities that are not referenced by the domain entities in the $^t\mathcal{O}$.

The full algorithm can be accessed at the ROMULUS repository at the aforementioned URL, and it is illustrated in the next example.

Example 1. The BFO-aligned Subcellular Anatomy Ontology (SAO) is linked to DOLCE by SUGOI as follows.
1. Create a new ontology file, a $^t\mathcal{O}$: `sao-dolce.owl`.
2. Copy the entire $^t\mathcal{O}_f$ to the $^t\mathcal{O}$: copy the OWLized DOLCE ontology into `sao-dolce.owl`.
3. Copy the axioms from the $^s\mathcal{O}_d$ to the $^t\mathcal{O}$: e.g., the axiom sao:Membrane Surface $\sqsubseteq$ bfo:Object_boundary exists in the $^s\mathcal{O}$ SAO, which is added to the `sao-dolce.owl` $^t\mathcal{O}$ and is referred to as a 'new' axiom.
4. Change the 'new' axioms to reference $^t\mathcal{O}_f$ entities, if mappings exist: for the example in the previous step, no mapping exists for bfo:Object_boundary between BFO and DOLCE, so it proceeds to the next step.
5. If a mapping does not exist, perform on-the-fly subsumption: continuing with the example, bfo:Object_boundary has a superclass bfo:Independent_Continuant and the mapping ontology has bfo:Independent_Continuant $\equiv$ dolce:endurant, so bfo:Object_boundary $\sqsubseteq$ dolce:endurant is added to `sao-dolce.owl`.
6. Delete entities that exist in the $^t\mathcal{O}$ that are from the $^s\mathcal{O}_f$ but do not appear in an axiom with entities from the $^t\mathcal{O}_d$, resulting in the final $^t\mathcal{O}$, `sao-dolce.owl`.

3   Experimental Evaluation

The first purpose of the quantitative evaluation is to assess whether SUGOI successfully interchanges a $^s\mathcal{O}$ to a $^t\mathcal{O}$ and to determine the amount of the ontology that will be effectively interchanged, which refers to those entities within the $^t\mathcal{O}$ that have been mapped with equivalence relations, thereby not required to use parts of the $^s\mathcal{O}_f$ in the $^t\mathcal{O}$. Second, to carry out a qualitative assessment of the entities and axioms to uncover what contributes to (un)successful interchangeability. Finally, we consider two domain ontologies linked to foundational ontologies to cross-check whether there are any major differences between the manual and automated mappings.

3.1 Materials and Methods

Materials. The SUGOI desktop application online version was used for the automated interchangeability, Protégé v4.3 for data on ontology changes, the foundational ontologies in OWL, the mapping ontologies available in ROMULUS, and a set of real ontologies to evaluate. Based on the $^s\mathcal{O}_f$ of the ontologies, SUGOI loads five mapping files, for interchanging between DOLCE↔BFO, BFO↔GFO, GFO↔DOLCE, DOLCE↔GFOBasic, and GFOBasic↔BFO. The sample size was 16 source ontologies covering various subject domains, such as data mining, animals, dermatology, and spatial scenes, of which 5 have DOLCE as $^s\mathcal{O}_f$, 6 with BFO, and 3 with GFO, and 2 ontologies for the comparison between manual alignments to BFO and DOLCE and the automated alignments. All test files can be downloaded from the SUGOI page on ROMULUS.

Methodology. The procedure for the experiment is as follows. *Preprocess domain ontologies* to checking whether each $^s\mathcal{O}$ uses the latest version of its respective $^s\mathcal{O}_f$ (DOLCE-Lite v397, BFO v1.1, and GFO v1.0) and whether the ontology import URIs are correct, and fix where necessary. *Perform interchangeability* by running SUGOI twice for each $^s\mathcal{O}$ to acquire its respective target ontologies; e.g., if the $^s\mathcal{O}_f$ is GFO, we generate two versions for the $^t\mathcal{O}$, one with DOLCE and another with BFO. *Evaluate interchangeability* as follows:

1. Compare the metrics of the domain entities of the target ontologies to those of the $^s\mathcal{O}$.
2. Compare the $^t\mathcal{O}$ to the $^s\mathcal{O}$ using the compare feature in Protégé. Protégé generates a list of entities that have been added, deleted and modified. Its 'modified entities' refers to the axioms that are used to define the entities, and whether they have been changed. In each $^t\mathcal{O}$, the entities that are modified are those that reference the mappable classes from their respective foundational ontologies.
3. Running the reasoner for the $^t\mathcal{O}$ to detect if there are unsatisfiable entities.
4. Analyse the metrics of the $^s\mathcal{O}_f$ entities that exist in the target ontologies.
5. Analyse the *raw interchangeability* of each $^t\mathcal{O}$, i.e., the amount of the $^t\mathcal{O}$ that has been correctly interchanged using equivalence mappings thereby not referring to the $^s\mathcal{O}_f$ entities. This is calculated from the $^t\mathcal{O}$ as follows: Let *GT, good target linking axioms*, represent the sum of axioms that link domain ontology entities and $^t\mathcal{O}_f$ entities in the $^t\mathcal{O}$. Let *BT, bad target linking*

axioms, represent the sum of axioms that link domain ontology entities and $^s\mathcal{O}_f$ entities in the $^t\mathcal{O}$; the raw interchangeability is calculated as follows:

$$Raw\ interchangeability = \frac{|GT|}{|GT + BT|} \times 100 \tag{1}$$

For instance, recall Fig. 1: the subsumption with dolce:NonPhysicalEndurant in the $^t\mathcal{O}$ counts toward the bad target linking axioms, whereas dmop:DataType ⊑ gfo:abstract counts as a good target linking axiom. SUGOI generates the raw interchangeability and ontology metrics in its log file for each $^t\mathcal{O}$.

6. Analyse and compare the DOLCE- and BFO-linked BioTop and Stuff ontologies with SUGOI's interchangeability. We interchange in both directions and compare the output with the original ontologies.

Because there are not many domain ontologies linked to a foundational ontology, there will be insufficient data to conduct a full statistical analysis to compare the results for different interchanges.

3.2   Results and Discussion

We describe the analysis of the interchanged ontologies, a more detailed entity-level analysis, and then the comparison with the manual mappings.

Analysis of the Interchanged Ontologies. After minor preprocessing of DMOP and SAO, all ontologies were successfully interchanged. Table 1 displays the domain entities in the $^s\mathcal{O}_d$ of the $^s\mathcal{O}$ and the domain entities of the $^t\mathcal{O}_d$-component of the $^t\mathcal{O}$ for the source ontologies. The 'modified entities' are those where a subsumption changed in the process; e.g., in the original DOLCE version of the DMOP ontology, the dmop:DecisionBoundary class is a subclass of dolce:abstract, which is modified in the GFO version, where dmop:DecisionBoundary is a subclass of gfo:Abstract. Such changes were collected from Protégé, which is illustrated for the example in Fig. 2.

Comparing the metrics of the domain entities of the $^s\mathcal{O}_d$ and $^t\mathcal{O}_d$ shows there are one or more extra domain entities in the $^t\mathcal{O}_d$, indicating the amount of $^s\mathcal{O}_f$ entities that have been added to the $^t\mathcal{O}_d$ (recall Example 1 and Fig. 1). The number of domain ontology entities increases from $^s\mathcal{O}_d$ to $^t\mathcal{O}_d$: e.g., $\delta = (749 - 739) = 7$ when interchanging DMOP to a GFO-aligned version (see Table 1), which is due to some absent mappings between the $^s\mathcal{O}_f$ and $^t\mathcal{O}_f$.

The same occurs with the set of BFO-aligned and GFO-aligned $^s\mathcal{O}$, and they differ for each case. Among others, bfo:Object_boundary is added to the $^t\mathcal{O}$ when the SAO ontology is interchanged from BFO to DOLCE, because there is no mapping from bfo:Object_boundary to a DOLCE entity, whereas in the interchange to GFO, bfo:object_boundary maps to gfo:Material_boundary, so sao:Membrane Surface becomes a subclass of gfo:Material_boundary.

Table 1. Comparison of the ^sO_d entities to the ^tO_d entities and raw interchangeability; interchang. = raw interchangeability and avg = average.

Source and Target ontology	^sO_d to ^sO_f links	Domain Classes	Domain OP	Domain Entities	Modified entities	Raw interchangeability
Source domain ontologies linked to DOLCE with target domain ontologies						
dmop	409	739	140	1350		
dmop-bfo		749	154	1377	43	4.88%
dmop-gfo		745	154	1373	54	11.65%
naive_animal	41	416	15	438		
naive_animal-bfo		422	24	453	20	21.95%
naive_animal-gfo		421	24	452	22	25.58%
ontoderm	14	239	28	301		
ontoderm-bfo		244	30	308	47	28.57%
ontoderm-gfo		243	30	307	49	42.85%
scene	18	172	74	246		
scene-bfo		175	78	253	3	50.00%
scene-gfo		174	78	252	4	50.00%
sego	43	75	43	139		
sego-bfo		89	55	165	32	29.54%
sego-gfo		88	53	162	32	36.36%
Correlation ^sO_d-^sO_f links and interchang.:	-0.79			*Avg for DOLCE:*		*30.02%*
Source domain ontologies linked to BFO with target domain ontologies						
bco	26	63	62	146		
bco-dolce		67	62	150	19	65.39%
bco-gfo		66	62	149	20	67.86%
epidemiology	15	169	4	173		
epidemiology-dolce		174	4	178	13	60.00%
epidemiology-gfo		173	4	177	15	68.75%
ero	97	3910	123	4114		
ero-dolce		3918	123	4122	13	32.99%
ero-gfo		3917	123	4121	51	52.85%
ido	77	150	0	150		
ido-dolce		151	0	151	64	81.81%
ido-gfo		151	0	151	65	81.81%
proper_name	13	30	34	64		
proper_name-dolce		33	34	67	31	61.53%
proper_name-gfo		32	34	66	26	76.92%
sao	54	728	36	809		
sao-dolce		732	36	813	29	50.00%
sao-gfo		731	36	812	29	55.17%
Correlation ^sO_d-^sO_f links and interchang.:	-0.33			*Avg for BFO:*		*62.90%*
Source domain ontologies linked to GFO with target domain ontologies						
pid	98	135	2	137		
pid-dolce		138	9	147	22	14.29%
pid-bfo		139	9	148	4	2.04%
gfo-bio	70	90	6	96		
gfo-bio-dolce		103	12	115	19	20.27%
gfo-bio-bfo		103	13	116	19	17.56%
gfo-bio-meta	14	127	6	139		
gfo-bio-meta-dolce		142	13	161	6	20%
gfo-bio-meta-bfo		142	13	161	8	19.69%
Correlation ^sO_d-^sO_f links and interchang.:	-0.66			*Avg for GFO:*		*15.64%*
Correlation all ^sO_d-^sO_f links and interchang.: -0.44				*Avg for all:*		*36.18%*

Modified DecisionBoundary	Description Superclass changed	Baseline Axiom DecisionBoundary SubClassOf abstract	New Axiom DecisionBoundary SubClassOf Abstract

Fig. 2. A change for the dmop:DecisionBoundary class when interchanged to a GFO ^tO

The number of entities in each $^t\mathcal{O}$ that are from the $^s\mathcal{O}_f$ follows from the extra domain entities in Table 1. In terms of these metrics, ontologies with a small difference in $^s\mathcal{O}_d$ and $^t\mathcal{O}_d$ numbers, i.e., having a low number of $^s\mathcal{O}_f$ entities, perform best because they only contain few entities that cannot be mapped with equivalence, while ontologies with a high number of $^s\mathcal{O}_f$ entities perform worst because they contain many domain entities that cannot be mapped with equivalence. The IDO ontology has the least number of $^s\mathcal{O}_f$ entities in its $^t\mathcal{O}_d$ (only 1), thus it performs the best, whereas the gfo-bio-meta performs the worst with 15 $^s\mathcal{O}_f$ entities in its $^t\mathcal{O}_d$. The extra domain entities in a $^t\mathcal{O}$ ontology cause an increase in the number of *BT, bad target linking axioms*, which causes a lower raw interchangeability. The raw interchangeability values for the $^t\mathcal{O}$ files are shown in the last column of Table 1.

The interchanged ontologies are consistent, except for `ido-dolce.owl` and `ido-gfo.owl`, but `ido.owl` $^s\mathcal{O}$ was already unsatisfiable due to conflicting disjointness and subclass axioms among some domain entities.

After reasoning the ontologies, we manually compared the inferences of the domain entities of the $^s\mathcal{O}$ ontologies to the $^t\mathcal{O}$ ontologies to investigate whether different foundational ontologies influence these domain-specific inferences. For this set of domain ontologies, there was no change in the inferences.

Entity-Level Analysis. Let us now consider those extra domain entities, which are those that are commonly used in domain ontologies, but do not have corresponding equivalence mappings among the foundational ontologies; or: the main 'culprits' for a low interchangeability. Table 2 displays these results. For DOLCE-aligned $^s\mathcal{O}$ ontologies, the object property dolce:has-quality has been referenced the most at 308 times, followed by dolce:has-quale 180 times, which are used for relating an endurant (e.g., apple) to a property (e.g., colour) and a value (e.g., red). Hence, domain ontologies linked to DOLCE heavily use DOLCE's features for representing properties and values. While there is some support for representing properties and values in BFO and GFO, they are not represented in the same way. BFO does not have any object properties, so while properties are supported using bfo:quality, there is no object property to link together an entity and its property. GFO does have a gfo:has_value and a gfo:value_of that correspond to those DOLCE entities 'in spirit', but this is not asserted in the corresponding mapping file due to conflicting domain and range axioms that would result in an unsatisfiable ontology. Other DOLCE entities that have been referenced many times include dolce:inherent-in, and dolce:abstract-region. For BFO-interchanged ontologies, the bfo:Role entity has been used the most, at 72 times; perhaps the results could be improved if we consider interchanging these ontologies using the Functional-Participation module of DOLCE that covers roles. Other frequently used BFO entities include bfo:Continuant, and bfo:Site. It might appear that bfo:Continuant could be mapped to the dolce:Endurant and gfo:Presential. This is not the case: bfo:Continuant subsumes bfo:quality, and dolce:quality is disjoint from dolce:Endurant so it would result in an inconsistency in the $^t\mathcal{O}$ if we did. It causes other inconsistencies when bfo:Continuant is mapped to gfo:Presential.

Table 2. The number of times (N) a source foundational ontology entity is referenced in target ontologies for the total set of interchanged ontologies

DOLCE entity	N	BFO entity	N	GFO entity	N
has-quality	308	Role	72	plays_role	80
has-quale	180	Continuant	36	part_of	52
inherent-in	88	Site	30	has-participant	47
abstract-region	60	Function	19	has_part	34
non-physical-endurant	28	ProcessualEntity	18	has_property	34
particular	26	ObjectAggregate	17	on_level	32
non-physical-object	20	FiatObjectPart	8	played_by	30
mediated-relation	18	RealizableEntity	6	Biological_level	28
mediated-relation-i	14	GenericallyDependent Continuant	6	has_role	20
part	14	Disposition	4	instance_of	20
other DOLCE entities (aggregated)	170	other BFO entities (aggregated)	13	other GFO entities (aggregated)	124

Recall that the raw interchangeability measures the amount of the domain entities that have been interchanged using equivalence mappings (see Table 1). Given the set of satisfiable equivalence mappings—7 for DOLCE to BFO, 10 for BFO to GFO, and 15 for GFO to DOLCE [3]—it is no surprise that the average raw interchangeability for the source ontologies is only 36.18%. The set of BFO ontologies had the highest raw interchangeability (62.90%), followed by DOLCE (30.02%) and lastly GFO (15.64%). BFO has the highest raw interchangeability probably because it is a bare taxonomy with no entity axioms (other than disjointness axioms) and no object properties. The entities of DOLCE and GFO have many axioms that cause dependencies between entities, therefore if a domain entity is related to a foundational ontology entity, other foundational ontology entities are also affected.

In general, the raw interchangeability differs greatly for the target ontologies which is due to two counterweighting factors. First, the number of links between the $^s\mathcal{O}_d$ and $^s\mathcal{O}_f$ has a moderate negative correlation with the raw interchangeability for DOLCE and GFO; see Table 1. Thus, a larger number of links between $^s\mathcal{O}_d$ and $^s\mathcal{O}_f$ entities for DOLCE and GFO ontologies can cause a *lower* raw interchangeability values (for the set of BFO $^s\mathcal{O}_f$, the correlation is much weaker). Second, the raw interchangeability is slightly *higher* when there are more mappings between source and target foundational ontologies among the interchanged ones: there are more DOLCE to GFO mappings (15) than DOLCE to BFO mappings (7), and the average interchangeability for the test ontologies are 33.29% and 26.99%, respectively. The same pattern exists for BFO to DOLCE vs BFO to GFO (58.62% vs 67.23%) and for GFO to BFO vs GFO to DOLCE (13.10% vs 18.19%). This does not hold for their aggregates, though, where the effect is dampened due to the large variation in raw interchangeability. The 'low' raw interchangeability values reveals that foundational ontology coverage and entity representation differs considerably. In some cases, there is no corresponding entity to interchange to while at other times there are seemingly similar entities to map to (recall property and value treatment in the ontologies), but the entity definition differs such that they cannot be mapped.

Table 3. The BioTop and Stuff $^{t}\mathcal{O}$ ontology metrics regarding interchangeability and change in cross comparison

Target ontology ($^{t}\mathcal{O}$), with the last component of the name the $^{t}\mathcal{O}_f$	Raw interchangeability	New entities	Modified entities	Additional mappings
biotop-bfo-ro-dolce.owl	41.18%	25	60	4
biotop-dolce-ro-bfo.owl	27.59%	67	54	6
stuff-bfo-dolce.owl	80.00%	12	17	1
stuff-dolcelite-bfo.owl	45.45%	8	14	3

Computing a 'transitive interchangeability' is a moot point, as the raw interchangeability is already substantially less than 100%. Besides the extra domain entities from the base cases, this is exacerbated when the $^{s}\mathcal{O}$ does not import the entire $^{s}\mathcal{O}_f$. For instance, DMOP has only a subset of DOLCE, so interchanging to BFO, resulting in `dmop-bfo.owl`, and then back, resulting in `dmop-bfo-dolce.owl`, SUGOI includes the entire DOLCE foundational ontology in the second interchange, causing it to have more axioms than the original DMOP $^{s}\mathcal{O}$.

Comparing SUGOI to Manual Mappings. Lastly, we evaluate SUGOI's interchangeability with the BFO and DOLCE versions of BioTop and Stuff to compare the existing manual mappings with the automatically generated ones.

The ontologies were interchanged in both directions (the BFO versions to DOLCE and vv.), and the raw interchangeability measure, and other metrics for the $^{t}\mathcal{O}$ ontologies are displayed in Table 3, which are in the same range as with the other ontologies (cf. Table 1). The interchangeability measure for the BioTop ontologies stems from the different coverage in the two foundational ontologies. For instance, in the original DOLCE-aligned version, biotop:physical boundary $\sqsubseteq$ dolce:feature, while in the original BFO-aligned version, it is not directly subsumed by a BFO entity. This also means that the manual versions of BioTop will differ from the interchanged versions. Comparing the interchanged versions of BioTop (e.g., `biotop-bfo-ro-dolce.owl`) to the original manual versions (e.g., `biotop-dolce.owl`), we note that there are some new and modified entities, and additional $^{t}\mathcal{O}_d$ to $^{t}\mathcal{O}_f$ subsumption axioms identified by SUGOI. One of the additional links in `biotop-dolce-ro-bfo.owl` is, biotop:ImmaterialObject $\sqsubseteq$ bfo:MaterialEntity, which is a consequence of biotop:ImmaterialObject $\sqsubseteq$ dolce-physical-endurant in the original `biotop-dolce-ro.owl`, and there is a new subsumption biotop:ValueRegion $\sqsubseteq$ dolce:endurant in `biotop-bfo-ro-dolce.owl`, which is also due to the $^{s}\mathcal{O}$, for biotop:ValueRegion $\sqsubseteq$ bfo:IndependentContinuant was asserted in the original `biotop-bfo-ro.owl`.

For the cross comparison of the Stuff ontologies, there are new and modified entities, and additional mapping axioms in the Stuff $^{t}\mathcal{O}$ ontologies. One of the additional links in `stuff-dolcelite-bfo.owl` is, stuff:Endurant $\equiv$ bfo:IndependentContinuant, while in `stuff-bfo-dolce.owl`, there is, stuff:Perdurant $\equiv$ dolce:process (a consequence of stuff:perdurant $\equiv$ bfo:process in the `stuff-bfo.owl`).

Overall, the Stuff ontology performed better in terms of raw interchangeability than BioTop, and compares well to the manual effort. However, the importance of using SUGOI for interchangeability in both ontologies is demonstrated by the fact that there were some missing mappings from the manual ontologies. Thus, it is best to use SUGOI in conjunction with manual interchange to ensure that all the relevant mappings have been implemented.

4 Discussion

Considering the results together, the average raw interchangeability for all the target ontologies is 36.18% (ranging between 2.04% to 81.81%), which means there are typically more links thanks to subsumption rather than equivalence. This is due to the fact that the set of equivalence mappings among the foundational ontologies is limited, and in some cases, those non-mapped entities from the ${}^s\mathcal{O}_f$ are heavily used in the alignment of the ${}^s\mathcal{O}_d$ to the ${}^t\mathcal{O}_f$, as seen by dolce:has-quality (Table 2). Foundational ontology developers may wish to add those entities to broaden the foundational ontology's coverage and therewith increase its interoperability. For the time being, it means that domain ontology developers should choose a foundational ontology carefully.

Interchangeability surely can be performed, and the subsumption mappings added by SUGOI improve the quality of the ${}^t\mathcal{O}$ in that extra domain entities are subsumed by the relevant ${}^t\mathcal{O}_f$ entities, resulting in a 'clean' taxonomy, i.e., entities that cannot be mapped via equivalence are not by default mapped as subclasses of owl:Thing or topObjectProperty outside the scope of the ${}^t\mathcal{O}_f$.

The interchanged ontologies are usable and SUGOI can be used as an initial tool used to achieve semantic interoperability with regards to foundational ontologies. The best results (higher raw interchangeability) were obtained for DOLCE ontologies when interchanging to GFO, for BFO ontologies when interchanging to GFO, and for GFO ontologies when interchanging to DOLCE.

We now return to the questions posed in the introduction. Regarding question 3: it is indeed feasible to automatically generate links between a domain ontology and a different foundational ontology, although the results based on equivalence-only mappings depend on the source ontology and its amount of links to its ${}^s\mathcal{O}_f$. Permitting subsumption, then the whole ontology can be interchanged to another foundational ontology. Regarding question 4: the issues observed are due to a combination of varying foundational ontology coverage (notably quality properties and roles), the amount of mappings between foundational ontologies, and the amount of links between the domain and foundational ontology components of the source ontology. The former problem could be solved with foundational ontology developers extending the coverage of their ontologies. The latter is more complex and requires a deep semantic change and unification about entity representation among ontology developers.

5 Conclusion

We presented the SUGOI tool, which automatically changes a source ontology's foundational ontology to another, maintaining alignments between the domain ontology component and the chosen foundational ontology (either DOLCE, BFO, or GFO). This automation enabled an investigation into the feasibility of aligning automatically one's ontology to another foundational ontology. The success of such a 'swap' based only on equivalence among entities in foundational ontologies differs by source ontology, ranging from 2 to 82% success, and averaging at 36% for the 16 ontologies included in the evaluation. Comparing SUGOI to manual dual mappings, it did outperform manual efforts, in the sense of having found additional alignments, but also missed a few, thus a final manual check is advisable. The large differences in interchangeability success are due mainly to differences in coverage of the foundational ontology (notably: qualities and roles), the number of alignment axioms between the source domain and foundational ontology, and to a lesser extent also the amount of mappings between each pair of foundational ontologies. SUGOI also uses subsumption mappings so that every domain ontology can be interchanged, preserving the structure of the ontology.

For future work, we consider creating mappings between other foundational ontologies and the existing ontologies in SUGOI. The community could also assist with this by submitting mappings in ROMULUS's community page. Given the insights on usage of a foundational ontology's content coverage and domain to foundational ontology mappings, we also plan to extend ONSET [5] with such fine-grained aspects.

References

1. Herre, H.: General Formal Ontology (GFO): A foundational ontology for conceptual modelling. In: Theory and Applications of Ontology: Computer Applications, ch. 14, pp. 297–345. Springer, Heidelberg (2010)
2. Keet, C.M., Lawrynowicz, A., d'Amato, C., Hilario, M.: Modeling Issues, Choices in the Data Mining Optimization Ontology. In: Proceedings of the 10th International Workshop on OWL: Experiences and Directions (OWLED 2013), Montpellier, France, May 26-27. CEUR Workshop Proceedings, vol. 1080, CEUR-WS.org (2013)
3. Khan, Z., Keet, C.M.: Addressing issues in foundational ontology mediation. In: 5th International Conference on Knowledge Engineering and Ontology Development (KEOD 2013), Vilamoura, Portugal, September 19-22, pp. 5–16. Scitepress – Science and Technology Publications (2013)
4. Khan, Z.C., Keet, C.M.: The foundational ontology library ROMULUS. In: Cuzzocrea, A., Maabout, S. (eds.) MEDI 2013. LNCS, vol. 8216, pp. 200–211. Springer, Heidelberg (2013)
5. Khan, Z., Keet, C.M.: ONSET: Automated foundational ontology selection and explanation. In: ten Teije, A., Völker, J., Handschuh, S., Stuckenschmidt, H., d'Acquin, M., Nikolov, A., Aussenac-Gilles, N., Hernandez, N. (eds.) EKAW 2012. LNCS, vol. 7603, pp. 237–251. Springer, Heidelberg (2012)
6. Khan, Z., Keet, C.M.: Toward semantic interoperability with aligned foundational ontologies in ROMULUS. In: Seventh International Conference on Knowledge Capture (K-CAP 2013). ACM proceedings, Banff, Canada, June 23-26, pp. 23–26 (2013) (poster/demo)
7. Masolo, C., Borgo, S., Gangemi, A., Guarino, N., Oltramari, A.: Ontology library. WonderWeb Deliverable D18 (2003), http://wonderweb.semanticweb.org (ver. 1.0, December 31, 2003)

8. Mizoguchi, R.: YAMATO: Yet Another More Advanced Top-level Ontology. In: Proceedings of the Sixth Australasian Ontology Workshop. Conferences in Research and Practice in Information, pp. 1–16. ACS, Sydney (2010)
9. Niles, I., Pease, A.: Towards a standard upper ontology. In: Welty, C., Smith, B. (eds.) Proceedings of the 2nd International Conference on Formal Ontology in Information Systems (FOIS-2001), Ogunquit, Maine, October 17-19 (2001)

Automating Cross-Disciplinary Defect Detection in Multi-disciplinary Engineering Environments

Olga Kovalenko[1], Estefanía Serral[2], Marta Sabou[1],
Fajar J. Ekaputra[1], Dietmar Winkler[1], and Stefan Biffl[1]

[1] Christian Doppler Laboratory for Software Engineering
Integration for Flexible Automation Systems,
Vienna University of Technology,
Favoritenstrasse 9-11/E188, A-1040 Vienna
{firstname.lastname}@tuwien.ac.at
[2] Department of Decision Sciences and Information Management, KU Leuven
Naamsestraat 69, B-3000 Leuven, Belgium
estefania.serralasensio@kuleuven.be

Abstract. Multi-disciplinary engineering (ME) projects are conducted in complex heterogeneous environments, where participants, originating from different disciplines, e.g., mechanical, electrical, and software engineering, collaborate to satisfy project and product quality as well as time constraints. Detecting defects across discipline boundaries early and efficiently in the engineering process is a challenging task due to heterogeneous data sources. In this paper we explore how Semantic Web technologies can address this challenge and present the Ontology-based Cross-Disciplinary Defect Detection (OCDD) approach that supports automated cross-disciplinary defect detection in ME environments, while allowing engineers to keep their well-known tools, data models, and their customary engineering workflows. We evaluate the approach in a case study at an industry partner, a large-scale industrial automation software provider, and report on our experiences and lessons learned. Major result was that the OCDD approach was found useful in the evaluation context and more efficient than manual defect detection, if cross-disciplinary defects had to be handled.

1   Introduction

Multi-disciplinary engineering (ME) projects represent complex environments, where different disciplines (e.g., mechanical, electrical and software engineering), have to collaborate efficiently in order to deliver high-quality end products and to satisfy tight timeframes [12]. An example ME project is designing a power plant and corresponding control system. In ME projects, engineering data is spread over numerous heterogeneous data sources derived from various discipline-specific tools and corresponding data models and data formats. Typically the tools are loosely coupled with limited capabilities for cross-disciplinary data exchange or/and data analysis. As a consequence, risks of deviations and defects in project data increase.

Errors made during the early development stages are especially critical, as they can potentially affect the artifacts of all latter phases. Staying undetected, such defects can

K. Janowicz et al. (Eds.): EKAW 2014, LNAI 8876, pp. 238–249, 2014.
© Springer International Publishing Switzerland 2014

lead to costly corrections during the commission phase or even to failures during the operation phase. Hence, ensuring consistency of project data and detecting emerging deviations and defects early are crucial requirements [6]. To this end, handling cross-disciplinary defects raises additional challenges. A cross-disciplinary defect is a defect that can only be identified by analyzing the data from several disciplines. For instance, the sensor type specified in the physical topology (mechanical engineering) of the automation system has to match the information in the corresponding electrical plan (electrical engineering) and the value range for control variables (software engineering) to describe a correct system. It is important to mention that interrelations between data of different disciplines are often not explicitly documented, but instead are only implicitly available as internal knowledge of the engineers. As the cross-disciplinary relations are not represented in a machine-understandable way, they cannot be automatically checked. Therefore, cross-disciplinary defect detection typically requires manual checking by the engineers, which is time consuming and error-prone. Thus, there is a need for effective and efficient defect detection methods, including cross-disciplinary defect detection, in ME projects.

In this paper we present an ontology-based approach for automated defect detection across discipline boundaries. Ontologies allow representing the data models of different engineering disciplines and/or tools and cross-disciplinary interrelations between the heterogeneous project data in a machine-understandable form, thus, enabling automated processing and analysis across disciplines. Comprehensive queries can be defined and executed in order to (a) check whether or not project data satisfies specified cross-disciplinary dependencies; and (b) to detect deviations and candidate defects in the ME project data. As an advantage the Ontology-based Cross-Disciplinary Defect Detection (OCDD) approach does not require the project participants to change their well-known tools and workflows.

The remainder of the paper is structure as follows. Section 2 presents related work; Section 3 describes the engineering practice in ME projects; Section 4 introduces the OCDD approach in the context of an industrial case study; Section 5 reports on preliminary evaluation within the case study at the industry partner; Section 6 discusses the implementation strategy of the proposed approach in ME settings; and Section 7 concludes the paper and depicts future work.

2   Related Work

This section summarizes related work on defect detection in multi-disciplinary engineering (ME) projects and the use of semantic web approaches in industrial contexts.

Defect Detection in ME Environments. Engineers of individual disciplines typically apply isolated and discipline-specific tools and data models while designing their artifacts. Within each discipline, well-defined approaches are used for quality assurance (QA) and engineering data analysis according to domain specific industry standards and best practices, e.g., simulation of electrical circuits and systems [16]; or static analysis methods (e.g., inspections or code analysis techniques [8]) and testing of software components [13]. However, in ME environments these isolated disciplines have to collaborate and exchange data – a major challenge for defect detection and QA. Defects and inconsistencies have to be detected as early as possible to minimize risks, solve conflicts, and improve product quality.

In [2] an openness metric for a systematic assessment of interoperability capabilities in ME projects has been applied to a set of selected tools. The main outcome was that isolated tools can support data exchange standards, e.g., XML or AutomationML[1] to enable collaboration between disciplines. However, loosely coupled tools do not support cross-disciplinary QA. Tool suites, e.g., Comos[2], typically cover a range of disciplines and provide functionality also for cross-disciplinary collaboration. These tools suites include a common data model that could enable basic QA tasks, e.g., defect detection. As for the drawbacks there may be some reduction of feature sets compared to isolated and highly specific solutions. In addition, project participants have to switch from their well-known tools to the all-in-one solution which might represent a barrier regarding acceptance, time and cost. Therefore, there is a need for approaches and tool-support for the engineers in ME projects to: (a) explicitly specify the cross-disciplinary interrelations between the heterogeneous engineering artifacts; (b) perform data analysis and detect defects across disciplines: and c) keep their customary engineering workflows and tools.

Semantic Web-Based Approaches. Semantic based solutions have been developed for various industries such as the aeronautical industry [1], the automotive industry [5], chemical engineering [11], heavy industries [15], factory automation [9] or, more broadly, manufacturing in general [10,14]. As opposed to these efforts, which typically focus on a single domain (with the notable exception of [4, 5]), we aim to support mechatronic systems, which, by definition combine the work of multiple engineering disciplines such as mechanical, electrical and software engineering. This combination of disciplines is a key differentiating feature of our efforts with respect to the predominantly mono-domain approaches reported so far in the literature.

The major goal of the various ontology based solutions reported so far is the integration and consolidation of engineering data [15, 19]. Such integration is a prerequisite to enable a range of intelligent applications such as decision support [1], automatic cost estimation [10], semantic-aware multiagent systems for manufacturing [11] or enterprise specific tasks such as bid analysis, market analysis and continuous process improvement by analyzing and integrating employee feedback [18]. The identification of errors, faults and defects across engineering models from different disciplines is an important but less frequent application and has only been reported by [4]. A mono-disciplinary defect detection system for identifying faults of electronic control units in cars has been achieved using ontologies and rules at AUDI[3].

---

[1] AutomatonML: https://www.automationml.org
[2] COMOS:
http://www.automation.siemens.com/mcms/plant-engineering-software
[3] http://www.w3.org/2001/sw/sweo/public/UseCases/Audi/

3   The Engineering Process in Multi-Disciplinary Environments

Multi-disciplinary engineering (ME) projects, e.g., in the automation systems engineering (ASE) domain, typically require concurrent engineering [7]. Due to tight project delivery times and project constrains engineering teams work in parallel rather than sequentially, often in a geographically distributed setting. This requires adjusting the engineering process and including a set of synchronizations at each project stage to (a) propagate changes across disciplines and (b) identify early defects and inconsistencies across disciplines from concurrent changes in heterogeneous project data. Figure 1 shows the data synchronization process with defect detections mechanisms.

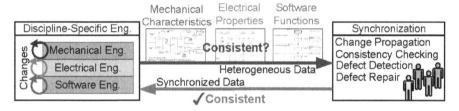

Fig. 1. Synchronization Process in Multi-Disciplinary Engineering Projects

The main aim of synchronization is addressing different types of heterogeneities that exist in ASE projects: technical heterogeneity (various engineering tools and technologies applied), semantic heterogeneity (dissimilar data models and formats), and process heterogeneity (tailored development processes). To manage these heterogeneities engineers from different disciplines work together during the synchronization on a) propagating changes that were made to data of a discipline since the last synchronization; and b) checking the consistency of engineering data across disciplines. If inconsistencies have been detected, a next step is to define actions and responsible roles for getting to a consistent state by defect repair or conflict resolution. Such checking is performed iteratively, until the data is proved to be consistent.

Two important types of defects affect engineering processes (a) *intra-disciplinary defects* (affect data within one discipline) and (b) *cross-disciplinary defects* (affect data in more than one discipline), e.g., changing a sensor (mechanical engineering) might have an effect on the related software component (software engineering) and might lead to defects if not addressed properly. While intra-disciplinary defects are usually discoverable by discipline-specific tools, cross-disciplinary defects are detected and fixed mainly during the synchronization phase. Because of the lack of tool support, cross-disciplinary data analysis is usually performed manually by project engineers, which is time consuming and error-prone.

Based on the described above, it is necessary in ME projects to provide efficient and effective mechanisms for defect detection. These mechanisms should be aware of the following requirements: (a) different disciplines involved; (b) large number of heterogeneous engineering artifacts; (c) cross-disciplinary dependencies in the project data; and d) concurrent engineering.

4   Automating Cross-Disciplinary Defect Detection: A Power Plant Automation System Case Study

This section presents the ontology-based cross-disciplinary defect detection (OCDD) approach for ME projects and introduces it within a case study at an industry partner. Figure 2 gives an overview on the approach and contrasts it with a traditional manual defect detection.

In traditional settings (lower part of Figure 2) the data and data models of the involved disciplines (e.g., mechanical, electrical and software engineering) are completely isolated and locked in discipline-specific tools using heterogeneous data models and data formats. Therefore all cross-disciplinary data exchange and analysis activities (including defect detection) rely on the knowledge of domain experts and require manual processes.

With the OCDD approach (upper part of Figure 2) an ontology layer is created for (1) capturing explicitly the discipline specific data models and knowledge in corresponding ontologies and (2) defining mappings between these ontologies corresponding to cross-disciplinary dependencies. This knowledge layer enables the automation of the defect detection process as follows. Firstly, domain experts formulate consistency checks focusing on the engineering objects that are important in more than one discipline. Secondly, a knowledge engineer translates the checks defined by the domain experts into corresponding SPARQL queries to be executed over the created ontological system, thus performing the cross-disciplinary data analysis and defect detection in an automated way.

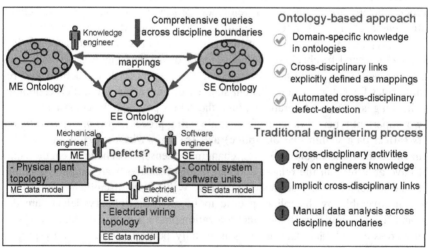

Fig. 2. Ontology-based Cross-Disciplinary Defect Detection (OCDD) vs. a traditional manual approach in ASE (ME – mechanical engineering; EE – electrical eng.; SE – software eng.).

We continue with an overview of a case study in a ME project at an industry partner, a large-scale industrial automation software provider (Sections 4.1- 4.3).

4.1   Case Study Overview

The case study was performed in the ME project concerning the development of a power plant and the corresponding control system. Engineering data from three domains were considered: (a) hardware configuration (HC) domain (sub-part of mechanical engineering), responsible for designing the physical plant topology; (b) control system (CS) domain (a sub-part of software engineering), responsible for developing PLC code for the corresponding control system; and (c) project configuration (PC) domain, responsible for managing the projects' data, people involved in the development and history of changes in the engineering data of these projects.

The following links, implicitly known by the project engineers, exist between these domains: (a) *variables* link CS and HC domains, i.e. for each device a set of global variables from the PLC code, are defined for its inputs and outputs; and (b) *artifacts* link the PC domain with HC and CS domains, i.e. an artifact can represent either a code unit or a software variable on a CS side; or a certain hardware device on a HC side.

4.2   Case Study: Knowledge Representation

We hereby describe the knowledge representation for the Hardware Configuration (HC), Control System (CS) and Project Configuration (PC) domains. All presented ontologies are OWL ontologies.

Hardware Configuration Ontology

The HC domain operates with data about devices, their inputs and outputs and variables that get and set values on certain inputs/outputs. Corresponding ontology was populated by transformation from the XML files obtained from the industry partner.

Figure 3 presents the part of the ontology relevant within the case study. Arrows denote the object properties. An important concept in the ontology is *Device*, which represents a specific device within a power plant (e.g., a temperature sensor). Specifying device information is stored via concept *DeviceDef*. Another important concept is *Variable*, which represents variables defined on devices' inputs and outputs. E.g., value measured by a specific temperature sensor will be set as a value of the corresponding variable. *VariableDef* comprises additional variable information, such as its size, type, and extra flags. Variables are grouped via *VarGroup*, which is assigned to a certain device. A specific device can have many variable groups assigned to it.

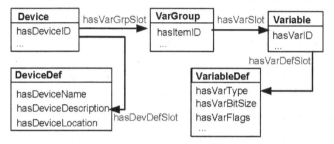

Fig. 3. Part of the Hardware Configuration Ontology relevant within the case study

Control System Ontology

The CS domain manages the control system software. Corresponding ontology (depicted in Figure 4) was obtained by transformation from the XML files. The data is compliant with the IEC61131-3 standard for representing programmable logic controllers.

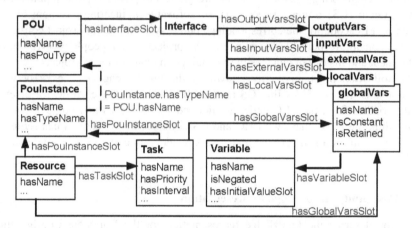

Fig. 4. Part of the Control System Ontology relevant within the case study

An important concept within this ontology is *POU* (program organization unit), which can represent a function, a function block (containing a set of functions) or a program (containing a set of functions and functions blocks). Every POU has an *Interface*, where the variables are declared. The *Variable* concept generalizes five different variable types: *global variable* (visible within all POUs), *local variable* (visible within one POU); *external variable* (referencing a global variable); *input variable* (transferred to a specific POU as an input parameter before execution); and *output variable* (takes a value after the POU execution). The concepts *globalVars*, *localVars*, *externalVars*, *inputVars* and *outputVars* comprise a set of variables of a corresponding type, which can be then assigned to a specific *Interface* (for local, external, input and output variables) or to a specific *Resource* or *Task* (for global variables).

Resource represents a device controller. For each resource a set of tasks are defined. *Task* combines a set of POUs with the execution configuration. To be executed in run-time *POU* must be assigned to a resource and/or task. This is done via concept *PouInstance* (similar to classes and their instances in Object Oriented Programming). POU instances exist only in run-time and refer to a name of a corresponding POU (a dashed arrow in Figure 4 depicts this connection that should have been represented via object property, but due to peculiarities of data representation in initial XML files, must be checked additionally, by comparing the string values of the properties *POU.hasName* and *PouInstance.hasTypeName*.

Project Configuration Ontology

The PC domain comprises more general project related information such as: engineering projects under development; project members and their responsibilities; and the history of changes in the engineering data of these projects. Figure 5 presents the ontology part relevant within the case study.

The *Project* concept represents an engineering project and comprises such details as its id, name, start and end dates and current stage. Engineers working in a project are represented via the concept *ProjectMember*. Every project member has a set of assigned responsibilities. *Responsibility* is a tuple relating a specific project with a specific project role. The following project roles are defined in the ontology: "RequirementsEngineer", "Modeler", "Developer", "Tester", "Validator" and "ProjectLeader". Thus, a project member can be a tester in one project and developer in another. *Artifact* represents various artifacts that are managed during the development (e.g. a specific variable or a piece of code). *Activity* represents a single change in the project engineering data and is used to store a history of changes. Following information is defined for each activity: who performed it? (refers to a *ProjectMember*); which artifact was influenced? (refers to an *Artifact*); what kind of activity it was? (refers to *ActivityType*, which can be "Create", "Delete", "Modify" or "Validate").

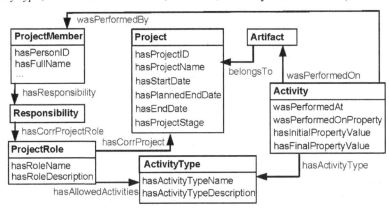

Fig. 5. Part of the Project Configuration Ontology relevant within the case study

4.3   Case Study: Cross-Disciplinary Defect Detection

In the case study we focus on checking the variable data across the HC, CS and PC domains. Variables are important engineering objects in ASE and often link several domains/disciplines. In particular, variables are defined on the devices inputs and outputs (HC domain); then the same variable data are included into the PLC code (CS domain); and finally there are changes made on variable data (PC domain). According to the industry partner up to 40,000 variables can be managed in a specific project [12], which is a hard task, if doing this with the traditional manual approach.

To make the relations between the variables in HC, CS and PC domains explicit, the following mappings have been defined: a) *CS:Variable* and *HC:Variable* are specified as subclasses of *PC:Artifact*; and b) *CS:Variable* is specified to be equivalent to *HC:Variable*. Although few and straightforward, these mappings already enable executing comprehensive checks on variable data across domain boundaries, which was not possible to perform automatically before. Below two sample cross-disciplinary checks are explained in details (SPARQL implementation can be found online[4]).

Q1: Which global variables on CS side are not declared on HC side? Each global variable declared in the control system software (CS ontology) should be declared on a specific device input or output in the hardware system topology (HC ontology). If a corresponding declaration is missing on the HC side, this might indicate two possible problems: a) either there is a redundant global variable (CS side); b) or a variable declaration is missing in the physical system topology (HC side).

Q2: Which changes on global variables declared at a certain device were not allowed by a project role of the project member that performed them? Each project member has a project role (or a set of them) that specifies which activities (s)he can perform in this project (e.g., a developer can create, modify and delete artifacts, while a validator can only validate). If there are doubts on the consistency of global variables in a project, one way to find the cause could be checking whether someone has performed an activity not allowed by his role. If such changes are found, corresponding global variables are the first candidates to be tested for consistency.

Of course, the range of possible checks over HC, SC and PC domains is not limited to variable data only. For instance, there is an implicit connection between the *CS:Resource* and *HC:Device* (both represent specific aspects of a hardware device) and at the same time they both can be seen as an *PC:Artifact*. After defining explicit mappings, it becomes possible to perform various checks concerning hardware devices across the domains (similar to those described above concerning variables).

5   Evaluation of the Case Study Results

In this section we discuss the results of prototypic implementation of OCDD approach obtained within the case study in the ME project at the industry partner.

We performed several interviews with the domain experts at the industry partner to ask for their feedback and opinion on the OCDD approach comparing with a traditional manual defect detection approach, with a particular focus on the foreseen benefits and limitations of applying the OCDD in practice. The interviews were semi-structured (acc. to [3]) and were performed in two stages: 1) requirements capture: the desired consistency checks for the case study were identified and formulated; and 2) approach validation: to validate that the captured requirements were efficiently addressed by the OCDD approach.

In the interviews, the industry experts were concerned about the additional modeling complexity introduced: it is necessary to specify an ontology for each discipline and the mappings between the ontologies. Since the domain experts at the industry partner do not possess such skills in their current setup, this also implies the need for a Knowledge Engineer to manage semantic technologies.

In spite of these concerns, the industry experts do believe that the approach provides valuable improvements: 1) the cross-disciplinary relations between the

---

[4] SPARQL implementation of the queries in this paper: 128.130.204.52/ekaw14-queries.html

engineering artifacts are explicitly specified and presented in machine-understandable form; 2) having the connections defined in a machine understandable format makes possible to identify the exact relevant data set (in the engineering data of other disciplines) that must be checked to solve a defect; 3) knowing the defect's origin, it is possible to identify how this defect was produced, and therefore, take measures to avoid it in the future; 4) defects across the disciplines can be detected automatically, leading to significant time savings and higher recall compared to the traditional manual defect detection approach. Experts at the industry partner also estimated the overall effectiveness of the OCDD approach as being higher due to the fact that the process relies on formally defined parameters (data models and relations between them) and not on subjective human-based estimation.

6   Discussion

This section discusses in details specific aspects of the implementation strategy of the proposed OCDD approach.

Domain Knowledge Modeling. Ontology enables gathering knowledge from the heterogeneous data sources and tools within the domain (e.g. CAE tools that correspond to the mechanical engineering) and making it explicit. However, this means extra time and complexity for modeling the domain knowledge in terms of classes, relations and axioms. This step requires close collaboration of the engineers of the ME project and knowledge engineer(s), as the domain experts typically have no expertise in the semantic web technologies. From the positive side, knowledge captured by the ontology is reusable, flexible and customizable and, therefore, can be easily used to implement the cross-disciplinary defect detection in next projects.

Data Import. Most of the engineering tools allow their data to be exported in one of the widely used formats, e.g. XML or spreadsheet data. In this case, there are tools already available that support automated data transformation from these formats into ontology (for an instance, XMLTab[5] and MappingMaster[6]). In the worst case, if the data can be only obtained in a proprietary tool format, one converter has to be implemented for each engineering tool. Although this requires extra effort from the project engineers, once the converters have been implemented they can be reused for the next projects, as the tool data model typically is stable and do not change with time.

Comprehensive Querying. Semantic technologies provide high expressiveness and enable (in contrary to UML diagrams and SQL queries) the possibility to create mappings between different models and to query the different models (corresponding to disciplines) at the same time. For the time being, cross-disciplinary data analysis and defect detection are mainly performed manually in industrial ME practice. For instance, several engineers from different disciplines (e.g. mechanical engineering and software engineering) typically spend several days to complete one or at most several specific consistency checks for their engineering artifacts. Having in mind that a number of checks are needed during the synchronization and at least several syn-

---

[5] http://protegewiki.stanford.edu/wiki/XML_Tab
[6] http://protege.cim3.net/cgi-bin/wiki.pl?MappingMaster

chronizations are needed during the ME project development, the ability to automatically execute checks (encoded in SPARQL queries) will significantly reduce the time and efforts to perform the cross-disciplinary data analysis in a ME project.

Limited Scalability of Ontologies. Semantic web technologies provide an expressive and explicit way to define domain knowledge, mappings, and queries. However, the performance of the data storage and the memory usage become challenging when managing larger datasets (e.g., millions of instances) [17]. Especially high computational load is to be expected when it comes to reasoning and querying for large instance data sets [19]. Therefore, the difficulty of using semantic technologies is the need for very powerful computer hardware to perform within reasonable time. In future work, we would like to analyze how a selection of specific mapping and querying techniques and/or technologies can help mitigating these problems.

Domain-Expert Support. In the current approach, a knowledge engineer is needed to work with semantic web technologies since domain experts do not typically have the appropriate skills. This could be mitigated by creating a GUI that hides the technological details and allows the domain experts performing the needed activities to manage the project data (e.g., data import, creation of mappings, and querying). This will also encourage the usage of the system from non-experts in semantic web.

7   Conclusion and Future Work

In the multi-disciplinary engineering projects (ME) participants from different engineering disciplines collaborate to deliver a high-quality end product. Typically, the disciplines are rather isolated and use heterogeneous data models to represent common concepts in the project team. Therefore, it is difficult to efficiently analyze data and perform defect detection activities across the disciplines. In this paper we introduced the ontology-based cross-disciplinary defect detection (OCDD) approach that supports automated cross-disciplinary defect detection. We presented the preliminary evaluation based on prototypical implementation of the OCDD approach in a case study ME project at an industry partner, an industrial automation software provider. Major result was that the OCDD approach was found useful in the evaluation context and more efficient than traditional manual defect detection if heterogeneous data originating from different engineering disciplines have to be handled.

As future work we plan a) to align our domain ontologies to existing domain-agnostic, core engineering ontologies that model concepts and patterns suitable for representing any type of engineering knowledge (e.g. MASON [10] and OntoCAPE [11]); and to existing ontologies partially covering one of the domains of interest (e.g., the W3C Organization ontology[7] partially covers Project Configuration domain); b) to investigate how the selection of a certain mapping and querying mechanism influences the efficiency of the approach; and c) to provide a user-friendly interface for data querying to hide the complexity of SW technologies from domain experts.

---

[7] http://www.w3.org/TR/vocab-org/

References

1. Adams, T., Dullea, J., Clark, P., Sripada, S., Barrett, T.: Semantic integration of heterogeneous information sources using a knowledge-based system. In: Proceedings of 5th International Conference on Computer Science and Informatics (CS&I 2000), Citeseer (2000)
2. Fay, A., Biffl, S., Winkler, D., Drath, R., Barth, M.: A method to evaluate the openness of automation tools for increased interoperability. In: Proceedings of 39th Annual Conference of the IEEE Industrial Electronics Society, IECON 2013, pp. 6844–6849. IEEE (2013)
3. Gray, D.E.: Doing research in the real world. Sage (2009)
4. Hästbacka, D., Kuikka, S.: Semantics enhanced engineering and model reasoning for control application development. Multimedia Tools and Applications 65(1), 47–62 (2013)
5. Hefke, M., Szulman, P., Trifu, A.: An ontology-based reference model for semantic data integration in digital production engineering. In: Proceedings of the 15th eChallenges Conference. Citeseer (2005)
6. Kovalenko, O., Winkler, D., Kalinowski, M., Serral, E., Biffl, S.: Engineering process improvement in heterogeneous multi-disciplinary environments with the defect causal analysis. In: Proceedings of the 21st EuroSPI Conference (2014)
7. Kusiak, A.: Concurrent engineering: automation, tools, and techniques. John Wiley & Sons (1993)
8. Laitenberger, O., DeBaud, J.M.: An encompassing life cycle centric survey of software inspection. Journal of Systems and Software 50(1), 5–31 (2000)
9. Lastra, J.L.M., Delamer, I.M.: Ontologies for production automation. In: Advances in Web Semantics I, pp. 276–289. Springer (2009)
10. Lemaignan, S., Siadat, A., Dantan, J.Y., Semenenko, A.: MASON: A proposal for an ontology of manufacturing domain. In: IEEE Workshop on Distributed Intelligent Systems: Collective Intelligence and Its Applications, DIS 2006, pp. 195–200. IEEE (2006)
11. Morbach, J., Wiesner, A., Marquardt, W.: OntoCAPE - a (re) usable ontology for computer-aided process engineering. Computers & Chemical Engineering 33(10), 1546–1556 (2009)
12. Mordinyi, R., Winkler, D., Moser, T., Biffl, S., Sunindyo, W.D.: Engineering object change management process observation in distributed automation systems projects. In: Proceedings of the 18th EuroSPI Conference, Roskilde, Denmark (2011)
13. Naik, S., Tripathy, P.: Software testing and quality assurance: theory and practice. John Wiley & Sons (2011)
14. Obitko, M., Marik, V.: Ontologies for multi-agent systems in manufacturing domain. In: Proceedings of the 13th International Workshop on Database and Expert Systems Applications, pp. 597–602. IEEE (2002)
15. Peltomaa, I., Helaakoski, H., Tuikkanen, J.: Semantic interoperability-information integration by using ontology mapping in industrial environment. In: Proceedings of the 10th International Conference on Enterprise Information Systems – ICEIS 2008, pp. 465–468 (2008)
16. Sage, A.P., Rouse, W.B.: Handbook of systems engineering and management. John Wiley & Sons (2011)
17. Serral, E., Mordinyi, R., Kovalenko, O., Winkler, D., Biffl, S.: Evaluation of semantic data storages for integrating heterogeneous disciplines in automation systems engineering. In: 39th Annual Conference of the IEEE Industrial Electronics Society, pp. 6858–6865 (2013)
18. Uschold, M., King, M., Moralee, S., Zorgios, Y.: The enterprise ontology. The Knowledge Engineering Review 13(01), 31–89 (1998)
19. Wiesner, A., Morbach, J., Marquardt, W.: Information integration in chemical process engineering based on semantic technologies. Comp. & Chem. Eng. 35(4), 692–708 (2011)

Querying the Global Cube: Integration of Multidimensional Datasets from the Web

Benedikt Kämpgen, Steffen Stadtmüller, and Andreas Harth

Institute AIFB, Karlsruhe Institute of Technology, Karlsruhe, Germany
{benedikt.kaempgen,steffen.stadtmueller,harth}@kit.edu

Abstract. National statistical indicators such as the Gross Domestic Product per Capita are published on the Web by various organisations such as Eurostat, the World Bank and the International Monetary Fund. Uniform access to such statistics will allow for elaborate analysis and visualisations. Though many datasets are also available as Linked Data, heterogeneities remain since publishers use several identifiers for common dimensions and differing levels of detail, units, and formulas. For queries over the Global Cube, i.e., the integration of available datasets modelled in the RDF Data Cube Vocabulary, we extend the well-known Drill-Across operation over data cubes to consider implicit overlaps between datasets in Linked Data. To evaluate more complex mappings we define the Convert-Cube operation over values from a single dataset. We generalise the two operations for arbitrary combinations of multiple datasets with the Merge-Cubes operation and show the feasibility of the analytical operations for integrating government statistics.

1 Introduction

Given the Open Data policy of governments and intergovernmental organisations, citizens can access many statistical datasets online. For example, one can find the Gross Domestic Product of countries per year from Eurostat, the World Bank and the International Monetary Fund. Integrating such multidimensional datasets will allow for more complete answers and detailed comparisons of indicators. For example, the GDP of a country from one and the population from another dataset allow analysts to compute the GDP per Capita and to cross-check these derived values with values from other publishers.

Towards providing uniform access, many datasets are also made available – directly or by third-parties – as Linked Data reusing the RDF Data Cube Vocabulary (QB), the quasi-standard for publishing multidimensional datasets. Although analytical operations over QB datasets have been defined [5] and indicators from two datasets can be compared in visualisations [3] integration is still difficult [13] if datasets:

- contextualise their indicators with different dimensions, e.g., "geo-location", "time" or "gender",
- use different names for the same dimensions, e.g., "geo" and "location" or dimension values, e.g., "DE" and "Germany",

K. Janowicz et al. (Eds.): EKAW 2014, LNAI 8876, pp. 250–265, 2014.

- provide different levels of detail, e.g., regional or national level,
- use different units of measurement, e.g., "Million Euro" and "Euro",
- and publish datasets derived from other datasets, e.g., "GDP per Capita" computed via "Nominal GDP" divided by "Population".

Defining a global schema over heterogeneous datasets published as Linked Data is challenging since related work has so far concentrated on relational settings [2] with few sources that are centrally integrated. Relationships between different datasets are often buried in informal descriptions, and the routines to resolve semantic conflicts are provided in code or external background information [10]. After introducing preliminaries and a motivating scenario in Section 2 and before describing related work in Section 6, and concluding with Section 7, we provide the following contributions:

- We define the Global Cube using the Drill-Across operation [6] over datasets published as Linked Data. We describe how to derive previously unknown values in the Global Cube using OWL axioms as well as conversion [10] and merging correspondences [2] (Section 3).
- We analyse the complexity of generating the Global Cube (Section 4) and show the feasibility of our approach for government statistics (Section 5).

2   Preliminaries and Government Statistics Scenario

We use the common Multidimensional Data Model (MDM) of Data Cubes as a conceptualisation of QB datasets since we then can apply analytical operations such as Slice and Dice [5,7]: An MDM consists of data cubes (instances of qb:DataSet) with facts (instances of qb:Observation). Every data cube defines measures (instances of qb:MeasureProperty) and dimensions (qb:Dimension-Property). Every fact in the data cube has a value for each of the measures and dimensions. The values of the measures are functionally dependent on the values of the dimensions, i.e., for every possible combination of dimension values, only one fact can be contained in the data cube. Members are the possible dimension values and may be grouped into levels along hierarchies (e.g., instances of qb:CodeList).

For instance, see Table 1 for an overview of data cubes from existing datasets to which an integration system should provide access. The table shows in the rows all data cubes and in the columns all their dimensions. The cells give example members for a dimension, "-" if the dimension is not and "..." if the dimension may be used.

For readability reasons, we describe URIs with namespaces[1], slightly abusing the W3C CURIE syntax for expressing compact URIs. Relative URIs such as :DE are defined by the data source in the respective context.

Since most publishers – also of our scenario data cubes – follow the practice of using an unspecific measure sdmx-measure:obsValue and a dimension indicating the measured variable, e.g., estatwrap:indic_na and gesis:variable,

---

[1] Use http://prefix.cc/ to look up prefix definition.

Table 1. Overview of data cubes in rows with their dimensions in columns and dimension members available in the scenario in cells

Cube \Dimension	estatwrap:geo	estatwrap:unit	dcterms:date	gesis:geo	gesis:variable	estatwrap:indic_na	estatwrap:sex	estatwrap:age
eurostat:id/ tec00115#ds (GDP Growth)	:DE...	:PCH_PRE.	2001...	-	-	-	-	-
allbus: ZA4570v590.rdf#ds (Unemploy. Fear)	-	-	2004...	:00...	:v590_1...	-	-	-
eurostat:id/ tsdcc310#ds... (EU 2020 Indicator)	:DE...	...	2001...	-	-	...	...	...
eurostat:id/ nama_aux_gph#ds (GDP Per Capita)	:DE...	:EUR_HAB.	2001...	-	-	:NGDPH...	-	-
eurostat:id/ nama_gdp_c#ds (GDP Components)	:DE...	:MIO_EUR.	2001...	-	-	:B1G, :D21_M-_D31	-	-
eurostat:id/ demo_pjan#ds (Population)	:DE...	-	2001...	-	-	-	:F...	:Y18...

and since cubes with multiple measures can be transformed to this form by introducing a new measure dimension, for the remainder of this paper we assume data cubes to have only one general measure, sdmx-measure:obsValue.

Every multidimensional element is published by a data source identified by the namespace. The eurostat namespace[2] makes available thousands of data cubes with indicators about European countries from Eurostat. For instance, the *GDP Growth* with the growth rate of the gross domestic product of all European countries per year, with the unit "percentage change on previous period" (:PCH_PRE) and for the geo dimension denoting Germany as :DE. Also, Eurostat provides citizens with EU 2020 Indicators, e.g., the energy dependence, productivity, and intensity as well as the greenhouse gas emission. Table 1 gives an example of one of those datasets; every *EU 2020 Indicator* cube exhibits the geo and time dimension and can contain other dimensions from the same data source. *GDP Components* provides granular values from which other indicators can be computed. For instance, the Nominal GDP (GDP at market prices) can be computed from adding the "Total gross value added" (estatwrap:indic_na of :B1G) and "Taxes less subsidies on products" (:D21_M_D31); similarly, the Nominal GDP divided by the *Population* should result in the *GDP Per Capita*.

The allbus namespace[3] provides information about "attitudes, behaviour and social structure in Germany" from the Cumulated German General Social Survey (ALLBUS). Among others, we can retrieve a survey where German employees were asked about their fear of becoming unemployed (*Unemploy. Fear*). The measure describes the number of answers for a given question. The allbus:variable dimension denotes the type of answers given "No fear",

---

[2] http://estatwrap.ontologycentral.com/
[3] http://lod.gesis.org/lodpilot/ALLBUS/

"Yes, of becoming unemployed", "Yes, of having to change employer"[4]. The :geo dimension describes the participants' country, e.g., Germany is denoted via :00.

An analytical query over a data cube can be described as a nested set of OLAP operations and executed using SPARQL over QB datasets [6,5,7]: Projection selects measures from a data cube; Dice filters for facts with certain members as dimension values; Slice sets dimensions to an implicit *ALL* member so that they can be aggregated over and removed; and Roll-Up aggregates dimension members to a higher level of the dimension hierarchy. Measures are aggregated using an aggregation function, e.g., described by the measure or by the user in the query [5]. We now describe three example queries that citizens may want to pose over the available datasets.

Unemployment Fear and GDP Growth (UNEMPLOY): Citizens want to compare the indicator about unemployment fear with the "GDP Growth" over time for Germany to get insights about the relation between GDP and employees' perceived situation.

Comparing EU 2020 - Indicators (EU2020): Here, citizens want to aggregate and compare important metrics about European countries by average for all countries and to show the aggregated numbers per year, so that trends of important indicators for European countries become visible.

GDP per Capita from Different Sources (GDP_CAP): Here, citizens may want to confirm that the GDP per Capita per country and year provided by different institutions and derived from different datasets is equal to increase their trust in Open Data.

3   Building the Global Cube

In this section, we introduce an integrated view over data cubes, the Global Cube, and show how to increase its size using mappings between data cubes.

We describe the data of a cube ds $\in$ DataCube as a relation ds(D1, D2, ..., Dn, M) with dimension(ds) the set of dimensions used by a cube and M the unspecific measure sdmx-measure:obsValue. The relation contains all possible dimension-member combinations on a specific level of detail, possibly with M = null. We use functional datalog for describing rules about relations.

Definition 1 defines Drill-Across, the basic operation for integrating cubes.

Definition 1 (Drill-Across). *Given two data cubes ds1(D11, D12, ..., D1n, M1) and ds2(D21, D22, ..., D2n, M2), we define Drill-Across: DataCube × DataCube → DataCube [6] and Drill-Across(ds1, ds2) = ds3 as follows: If Dimensions(ds1) != Dimensions(ds2) then ds3(D31, ..., D3n, M3), with Dimensions(ds3) = Dimensions(ds1) ∪ Dimensions(ds1) empty, i.e., its relation contains no tuples; else then D1i = D2i, 1 <= i <= n and the following rule holds: ds3(D1, ..., Dn, M) :- ds1(D1, ..., Dn, M1), ds2(D1, ..., Dn, M2), M = f(M1, M2), with f(M1, M2) defined as follows: If (M1 != null AND M2 == null) then M1; else if (M1 == null AND M2 !=*

---

[4] allbus:variable.rdf#v590_1 to allbus:variable.rdf#v590_3

null) then M2; else if (M1 == M2) then M1; else "Integrity Constraint Violation".

As stated in other work [9,1], Drill-Across requires as input two data cubes with the same dimensions and for the resulting cube computes an *Outer Join* of facts on the dimensions. Different from existing work, we consider the more general case where the same measure may be used by the input data cubes; in case two facts from the two cubes have identical dimension-member combinations and different values for the measures, the resulting cube violates the constraint to not have different measure values for the same dimension-member combination (IC-12 in QB specification; can also be denoted by ``integrity constraint violation'' :- ds(D1, ..., Dn, M1), ds(D1, ..., Dn, M2), M1 != M2). Use-case-specific conflict resolution is then possible.

Based on Drill-Across, Definition 2 defines the Global Cube.

Definition 2 (Global Cube). *Given a set of available cubes {ds1, ..., dsn} with dimension the set of all dimensions of these available data cubes, we define the Global Cube globalcube(D1, ..., Dn, M) with dimension(globalcube) = dimension. The Global Cube is defined in terms of the available cubes; given cube dsi(Di1, ..., Dik, Mi), the following rule holds: globalcube(all, ..., Di1, ..., Dik, all ..., Mi) :- dsi(Di1, ..., Dik, Mi). We denote with all the ALL member [8] aggregating over all possible values in the dimension. Thus, dimensions not used in available cubes are regarded as sliced with respect to the Global Cube. An OLAP query Q over the Global Cube with S sliced dimensions then can be answered by:*

$Q(globalcube) = Drill-Across_{ds\in DataCube, dimension \backslash S \subseteq dimension(ds)} Q(ds).$

Since Drill-Across is commutative, the Global Cubes does not depend on the order of Drill-Across operations.

For instance, we can define a Global Cube by the data cubes Unemploy. Fear and GDP Growth for our UNEMPLOY query. We use a function-like syntax to describe that cubes are modified along OLAP operations parametrised with elements from the MDM to eventually result in a cube to be displayed to the user, e.g., in a pivot table: Slice(Dice(Projection(-GlobalCube, {sdmx-measure:obsValue qb4o:avg}), (estatwrap:geo = eurostat-geo:DE)), {estatwrap:unit, gesis:variable}). Here, the unit and variable dimensions are sliced and the average of measures over all years for Germany requested. We can use a nested set of analytical operations as in Listing 1.1 to describe the query in terms of the two available cubes.

Listing 1.1. Nested set of analytical operations for UNEMPLOY query

```
1  Drill-Across(
2  Slice(Dice(Projection(Base-Cube(eurostat:id/tec00115#ds),
3                        {sdmx-measure:obsValue qb4o:avg}),
4            (estatwrap:geo = eurostat-geo:DE)),
5        {estatwrap:unit, gesis:variable}),
6  Slice(Dice(Projection(Base-Cube(allbus:ZA4570v590.rdf#ds),
7                        {sdmx-measure:obsValue qb4o:avg}),
```

```
8        (estatwrap:geo = eurostat-geo:DE)),
9      {estatwrap:unit, gesis:variable})
10 )
```

However, this query only returns results if Unemploy. Fear and GDP Growth – despite their heterogeneous structures according to Table 1 – exhibit a dimension `estatwrap:geo` and a member `eurostat-geo:DE`. Therefore, in the following, we present two possibilities to reduce heterogeneities between data cubes to increase the number of answers returned for queries over the Global Cube: 1) Slicing of dimensions and mappings between shared dimensions and members, and 2) converting and merging of data cubes.

3.1   Drill-Across with Shared Dimension Mappings in Linked Data

To execute the analytical query given in Listing 1.1, we need to evaluate the query plan of a nested set of OLAP operations over QB datasets.

Every sub-query-plan of OLAP operations not including the Drill-Across operation we can evaluate using the *OLAP-to-SPARQL algorithm* [8] where every analytical operation is evaluated using parts of a SPARQL query. Similarly, given the RDF describing two input cubes re-using QB and sharing all their dimensions, we can evaluate the Drill-Across operation using SPARQL. See Listing 1.2 for an example SPARQL query for our previous OLAP query (Listing 1.1).

Listing 1.2. SPARQL for UNEMPLOY Drill-Across query

```
1  select ?geo0 ?date0 f(avg(?obsValue1), avg(?obsValue2))
2  where {
3  OPTIONAL { ?obs1 qb:dataSet eurostat:id/tec00115#ds;
4      estatwrap:geo ?geo0;
5      dcterms:date ?date0;
6      sdmx-measure:obsValue ?obsValue1 .
7  FILTER (?geo0 = eurostat-geo:DE) }
8  OPTIONAL { ?obs2 qb:dataSet allbus:ZA4570v590.rdf#ds;
9      estatwrap:geo ?geo0;
10     dcterms:date ?date0;
11     sdmx-measure:obsValue ?obsValue2 .
12 FILTER (?geo0 = eurostat-geo:DE)
13 }} group by ?geo0 ?date0
```

Here, for each of the two input cubes, we query for observations linked via `qb:dataSet` to the respective QB dataset URI (line 3 and 8); the observations from both datasets we join on the values of their dimension properties (4,5 and 9,10) and bind the values of their measures to separate variables (6,11) and combine them with f(M1, M2) with f resolving possible integrity constraint violations (1)[5]. Various optimisations such as materialisation [9] are possible but not the topic of this paper. The integration of more than two data cubes is possible by chaining Drill-Across operations.

---

[5] In this example, no conflict resolution would be done but the values of the two cubes displayed to the user, e.g., using the concat function.

Drill-Across requires data cubes to use the same dimensions and members. Dimensions and members are shared if the same URIs or literal values are used; for instance, `:dim` is shared by `:ds1` and `:ds2` if the following patterns bind:

```
1  :ds1 qb:structure/qb:component/qb:dimension :dim.
2  :ds2 qb:structure/qb:component/qb:dimension :dim.
```

For instance, since GDP Growth and Unemploy. Fear both use `dcterms:date` and literal values for years such as 2006, drill-across over the time dimension can directly be done. However, different RDF terms may be used and only implicitly represent shared dimensions and members. For instance, the GDP Growth and Unemployment Fear cubes use different geo dimensions, `estatwrap:geo` and `gesis:geo`, as well as different members representing Germany, `:DE` and `:00`.

To allow the implicit definition of shared dimensions and members, we assume that the standard OWL semantics hold. OWL axioms can either be loaded from existing Linked Data or manually added to the system. There are different ways to indicate shared dimensions and members in Linked Data, e.g., `owl:sameAs`, `owl:equivalentProperty`, and `rdfs:subPropertyOf`.

For instance, GDP Growth and Unemploy. Fear share `estatwrap:geo` and `gesis:geo` if the dimensions are linked via `owl:equivalentProperty`; after also stating `eurostat-geo:DE owl:sameAs gesis-geo:00`, the query from Listing 1.1 will bring together GDP Growth and Unemploy. Fear for Germany.

3.2   Conversion and Merging Correspondences Between Data Cubes

We now define more complex mappings between data cubes. A Conversion Correspondence according to Definition 3 describes relationships between two cubes in terms of their dimension-member combinations (`inputmember`, `outputmember` $\in 2^{Dimension \times Member}$), i.e., how facts with certain members on dimensions in an `inputcube` can be converted to facts with other members on such dimensions in an `outputcube`. The actual conversion is described using a conversion function `f` $\in$ `Function` that describes how the value of the measure of the `outputcube` can be computed by the value of the measure of the `inputcube` and that may be implemented in any programming language [10].

Definition 3 (Conversion Correspondence). *We define a Conversion Correspondence adapted from correspondences over relational data [2] and conversion functions [10] as follows: ConversionCorrespondence = { (inputmembers, outputmembers, f) $\in 2^{Dimension \times Member} \times 2^{Dimension \times Member} \times$ Function } with Function: String $\rightarrow$ String. Given two data cubes ds1(D11, ..., D1n, M1) and ds2(D21, ..., D2n, M2) with D1i = D2i, 1 <= i <= n. A conversion correspondence cc between the cubes, cc(ds1) = ds2, holds if the following rule holds: ds2(D21, ..., D2n, M2) :- ds1(D11, ..., D1n, M1), inputmember $\in$ inputmembers hold for ds1, outputmember $\in$ outputmembers hold for ds2, D1i $\in$ dimension(ds1) \ inputmembers : D1i = D2i, f(M1) = M2.*

We define a Convert-Cube operation with `Convert-Cube: DataCube × ConversionCorrespondence → DataCube` to denote the application of a conversion correspondence to an input data cube to result in a new derived cube with the same structure as the input cube: `Convert-Cube(ds1, cc) = ds2 <=> cc(ds1) = ds2`.

For instance, the relationship between the member "Million Euro" and "Euro" in Eurostat can be described with the following correspondence: `MIO2EUR =` $(\{(\text{estatwrap:unit, eurostat-unit:MIO\_EUR})\}, \{(\text{estatwrap:unit, eurostat-unit:EUR})\}, f(x) = 1,000,000 \cdot x)$ The application of `MIO2EUR` over the GDP Components data cube is denoted by `Convert-Cube(estatwrap:id/nama_gdp_c#ds, MIO2EUR)` and returns a new data cube containing values with unit "Euro". To allow the consecutive application of conversion correspondences to a data cube in a nested set of Convert-Cube operations, each Convert-Cube operation we evaluate using a SPARQL 1.1 CONSTRUCT query generating the RDF of the derived cube to which in turn another Convert-Cube operation can be applied. Listing 1.3 shows the SPARQL query for our example.

Listing 1.3. Evaluation of `MIO2EUR` over GDP Components data cube.

```
1   CONSTRUCT {
2   ds12c44:ds qb:structure ?dsd .
3   _:outputobs qb:dataSet ds12c44:ds;
4       estatwrap:unit eurostat-geo:EUR;
5       gesis:geo ?gesisgeo;
6       estatwrap:geo ?estatwrapgeo;
7       estatwrap:indic_na ?estatwrapindicna;
8       dcterms:date ?dctermsdate;
9       sdmx-measure:obsValue ?outputvalue1 .
10  } where { {
11  select ?dsd ((1000000 * ?inputvalue1) as ?outputvalue1)
             ?estatwrapgeo ?dsd1 ?dctermsdate ?estatwrapindicna
             ?estatwrapgeo   ?inputvalue1
12  where {
13  estatwrap:id/nama_gdp_c#ds qb:structure ?dsd .
14  ?inputobs qb:dataSet estatwrap:id/nama_gdp_c#ds;
15      estatwrap:unit eurostat-unit:MIO_EUR;
16      gesis:geo ?gesisgeo;
17      estatwrap:geo ?estatwrapgeo;
18      estatwrap:indic_na ?estatwrapindicna;
19      dcterms:date ?dctermsdate;
20      sdmx-measure:obsValue ?inputvalue1 .
21  } } }
```

The SPARQL CONSTRUCT query can be divided by triple patterns in the body (line 13 to 20 in Listing 1.3) that provide bindings for triple patterns in the head (line 2 to 9) that in turn define the constructed triples. Since in our implementation no functions are possible in triple patterns (see `1000000 * ?inputvalue1`), we surround body triple patterns with a SPARQL SELECT query. The query generates for every fact in the input cube with unit eurostat-unit:MIO_EUR a new fact with unit eurostat-unit:EUR in an output cube with the same structure (dimensions and measures); the value of the (generic) measure is $1,000,000$ times the value of the input cube's measure. Along this example, we explain how a cube and a conversion correspondence as input to a Convert-Cube operation can be translated to the respective SPARQL CONSTRUCT query. The body triple patterns are created in the following steps:

1. **Dataset Triples:** We bind the data structure definition and observations from the dataset URI of the input cube (line 13 and 14).
2. **Inputmembers Triples:** For each dimension-member combination in inputmembers, we add a respective triple pattern (15).
3. **Dimensions Triples:** For each dimension from the input cube which is not contained in inputmembers, we bind from the observation the value for the dimension URI to a variable derived from the dimension URI to refer back to it in the head triple patterns later (16 to 19). Since the data cubes share their geo dimensions, there are triple patterns for gesis:geo and estatwrap:geo.
4. **Measures Triples:** For each measure in inputcube, we bind from the observation the value to a variable that is unique per measure for referral in other parts of the rule (20).
5. **Function Triples:** For each measure in inputcube, we bind a variable for the derived dataset's measure with an expression for function f with the input variable of f replaced by the respective measure variable (11).

Similarly, we create the triple patterns in the head:

1. **Dataset Triples:** We introduce a URI for the derived output dataset (e.g., by a combination of unique IDs for the original dataset and the conversion correspondence); we add the data structure definition of the input dataset to the output dataset (line 1); we add new observations to the output dataset using a blank node (line 2)
2. **Outputmembers Triples:** For each dimension-member combination in outputmembers, we add a respective triple pattern (line 4).
3. **Dimension Triples:** For each dimension from the input cube which is not contained in outputmembers, we add to the new observation the dimension values of the observation in the body (line 5 to 8).
4. **Measure Triples:** For each measure in inputcube, we assign to the respective measure in the derived observation the variable describing the converted value from the body (9)

The Dimension Triples make sure that the derived data cube has the same dimensions as the input cube and copy all dimension values not touched by the conversion correspondence. For that, contrary to the Open-World assumption in Linked Data, we have to assume all dimensions stated by the data structure definition of the input dataset to be known.

The SPARQL query is evaluated over the RDF representing the data cube to generate the derived cube. To answer a query over the Global Cube, we need to take into account all derived data cubes, including those derived by nested Convert-Cube operations. Given an OLAP query with nested Convert-Cube operations, any Convert-Cube operation is evaluated using one evaluation of the respective SPARQL CONSTRUCT query over the input data cube's RDF. Iteratively, the RDF of the input data cube may first need to be derived by the evaluation of another Convert-Cube operation. In the next section, we will describe an analysis of the number of derived data cubes in the Global Cube.

Conversion correspondences we can extend to merging correspondences to combine values from two cubes. A merging correspondence according to Definition 4 describes how facts with certain members on dimensions in two data cubes can be merged to facts in a third data cube with members on such dimensions and with the same structure as the first input cube.

Definition 4 (Merging Correspondence). *We define* `MergingCorrespondence` *=* `{ (inputmembers1, inputmembers2, outputmembers, f)` $\in$ $2^{Dimension \times Member}$ $\times$ $2^{Dimension \times Member}$ $\times$ $2^{Dimension \times Member} \times$ `Function` `}` *with* `Function: String` $\times$ `String` $\to$ `String`. *Given three data cubes* `ds1(D11,D12 ..., D1n, M1)`, `ds2(D21, ..., D2n, M2)`, *and* `ds3(D31, ..., D3n, M3)` *with* `D1i = D3i`, `1 <= i <= n`. *A merging correspondence* `mc` *between the three cubes,* `mc(ds1, ds2) = ds3` *holds if the following rule holds:* `ds3(D31, ..., D3n, M3) :- ds1(D11, ..., D1n, M1)`, `ds2(D21, ..., D2n, M2)`, `inputmember1` $\in$ `inputmembers1` *hold for* `ds1`, `inputmember2` $\in$ `inputmembers2` *hold for* `ds2`, `outputmember` $\in$ `outputmembers` *hold for* `ds3`, `D1i` $\in$ `dimension(ds1) \ inputmembers1 : D1i = D3i`, `f(M1, M2) = M3`.

We define a Merge-Cubes operation with `Merge-Cubes: DataCube` $\times$ `DataCube` $\times$ `MergingCorrespondence` $\to$ `DataCube` to denote the application of a merging correspondence to two input data cubes to result in a derived cube.

The following example computes the Nominal Gross Domestic Product (NGDP) from the sum of two GDP component indicators: `COMPUTE_GDP` = `({(estatwrap:indic_na, eurostat-indic_na:B1G)}, {(estatwrap:indic_na, eurostat-indic_na:D21_M_D31)}, {(estatwrap:indic_na, eurostat-indic_na:NGDP)}`, $f(x_1, x_2) = x_1 + x_2$). And the following example computes the GDP per Capita in Euro per Inhabitant from the Nominal GDP and the Population: `COMP_GDP_CAP` = `({(estatwrap:indic_na, eurostat-indic_na:NGDP), (estatwrap:unit, eurostat-unit:EUR)}, {(estatwrap:sex, eurostat-sex:T), (estatwrap:age, estatwrap-age:TOTAL)}, {(eurostat:indic_na, eurostat-indic_na:NGDPH), (eurostat:unit, eurostat-unit:EUR_HAB)}`, $f(x_1, x_2) = x_1/x_2$). Here, from the second input cube only facts are selected that contain measures for all genders and age groups, assuming they describe the population. The algorithm to evaluate Convert-Cube using a SPARQL CONSTRUCT query can be extended to the Merge-Cubes operation.

4   Analysis of the Global Cube

Given a set of data cubes and conversion and merging correspondences, an algorithm to generate all derived data cubes to answer a query over the Global Cube may not terminate since correspondences can be infinitely nested.

If we require that the same correspondence is not applied repeatedly we can give an upper bound estimation of the number of (derived) cubes based on ds datasets and mc merging and conversion correspondences: $noderivedds(ds, mc)$.

For that, we define a recursive function $noc(dp, ds, mc)$ that distinguishes the depth dp of a nested set of correspondence applications with $noc(0, ds, mc) = ds$, $noc(dp, ds, mc) = mc * (noc(dp - 1, ds, mc - 1) + 2 * \sum_{0<=i<=dp-1} noc(dp - 1, ds, mc - 1) * noc(i, ds, mc - 1))$. In the recursion, we need to consider the ordering of inputs to the merging, i.e., the consecutive application of merging correspondences in the left, right and both inputs. Then, $noderivedds(ds, mc) = noc(0, ds, mc) + noc(1, ds, mc) + \ldots + noc(mc, ds, mc)$.

As an example, for our GDP_CAP query we assume the GDP Per Capita, the GDP Components, and the Population as data cubes, MIO2EUR as conversion, and COMP_GDP and COMP_GDP_CAP as merging correspondences. The maximum number of (derived) datasets is given by: $noderivedds(3, 3) = noc(0, 3, 3) + noc(1, 3, 3) + noc(2, 3, 3) + noc(3, 3, 3) = 3 + 27 + 1,296 + 252,720 = 254,046$.

However, most derived data cubes are empty, e.g., MIO2EUR(GDP Per Capita) since GDP Per Capita does not contain values with unit "Million Euro". Therefore, if we require in a nested application of correspondences that outputmembers of the first correspondence fit inputmembers of the second correspondence, the number of derived datasets in many cases will be reduced.

To generate all possible derived data cubes in our GDP_CAP query, we use a functional Datalog program, where we define the datasets using relation dataset(Ds), dimensions using dimension(Ds, Dim) and dimension-member combinations using dimensionmember(Ds, Dim, Mem); also, we define every conversion and merging correspondence using four rules for 1) generating the dataset, 2) copying over the dimensions, 3) copying over the dimension-members, and 4) setting the new dimension member. For instance, rule 1) for MIO2EUR is as follows: dataset(mio2eur(X)) :- dataset(X), dimension(X,unit), (\+ dimensionmember(X,unit,Z); dimensionmember(X,unit,mioeur)).

Running the program in XSB Prolog, we now only get 54 derived datasets – including a computation of the GDP per Capita via comp_gdp_per_cap(comp_gdp-(mio2eur(gdpcomponents),mio2eur(gdpcomponents)),population), to evaluate using SPARQL. The computation would take milliseconds on commodity hardware, since the program would only contain 14 atoms and 12 rules; the facts do not need to be represented in the program since we find matches between datasets to convert or merge only by looking at the definition of correspondences, i.e., output- and inputmembers.

We may want to allow cycles in the definition of input-/outputmembers, e.g., conversion correspondences MIO2EUR and EUR2MIO. In this case we can design an algorithm that terminates with the application of conversion and merging correspondences when no new facts can be added to the Global Cube:

Sketch of Proof. According to Definition 1 of Drill-Across and Definition 2 of the Global Cube, an "Integrity Constraint Violation" is returned for a measure if two input cubes during the computation of the Global Cube contain different measure values for identical dimension-member combinations.

Only different dimension-member combinations can provide new facts, all other data cubes either provide facts with the same measure value or an "Integrity Constraint Violation". If dimension-member combinations are limited, so are derived datasets that provide new facts to the Global Cube.

The number of dimension-member combinations is limited: Considering ds datasets as special combinations and the order of combining combinations, cc conversion and mc merging correspondences provide at max $(ds + cc + mc)!$ combinations of dimension-member combinations.   □

In our example, this would result in $(3 + 1 + 2)! = 720$ possible combinations.

5   Evaluation: Integrating Government Statistics

Figure 1 illustrates how a client issues the *GDP_CAP* query (using the query language MDX) to the designed integration system over a Global Cube defined by data cubes GDP Per Capita, GDP Components and Population. The integration engine 1) loads and validates available data cubes defined by QB datasets (Base-Cube), 2) translates the query over the Global Cube to a logical operator query plan over the available as well as all derived data cubes, 3) transforms the logical to a physical operator query plan with iterators that 4) are then executed. Here, MIO2EUR converts "Million Euro" to "Euro", COMP_GDP computes the Nominal GDP, and COMP_GDP_CAP computes the GDP Per Capita which in the Global Cube is brought together with values from the GDP Per Capita data cube.

We implemented all operations, including the Drill-Across, Convert-Cube, and Merge-Cubes operations, in *OLAP4LD*, an Open-Source Java engine for

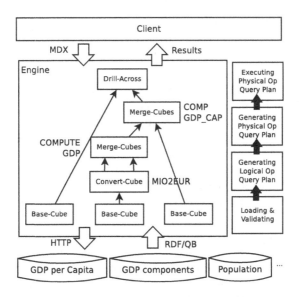

Fig. 1. Overview of integration system

analytical queries over multidimensional datasets published as Linked Data[6]. OLAP4LD uses a directed crawling strategy to load and validate all data cubes into a Sesame Repository (v2.7.10) as embedded triple store. Due to lack of space, in the further descriptions we assume all available data cubes loaded[7].

Given a query and a set of available datasets, the logical query plan is automatically generated per Definition 2 of the Global Cube, and by automatically applying mappings between shared dimensions and members as well as convert and merging correspondences.

Drill-Across is implemented as a nested loop join directly over the results of the *OLAP-to-SPARQL algorithm* [8]. OWL semantics we evaluate using a duplication strategy by repeatedly executing SPARQL INSERT queries implementing entailment rules of equality[8].

Every SPARQL query defined by a Convert-Cube and Merge-Cubes operation is evaluated once and the result is loaded in the triple store for usage by consecutive operations.

Setup: For the *UNEMPLOY* query, we created `owl:sameAs` mappings between the `:geo` dimensions and the identifier for Germany `:DE` and `:00` from Eurostat and Gesis. For *EU2020*, we selected four and eight EU 2020 Indicator datasets that surely overlap, e.g., the energy dependence, productivity, and intensity. For *GDP_CAP*, we created a ConversionCorrespondence for *MIO2EUR* and MergingCorrespondences for *COMPUTE_GDP*, and *COMP_GDP_CAP*.

Every query motivated in our scenario we executed five times on an Ubuntu 12.04 workstation with Intel(R) Core(TM) i5 CPU, M520, 2.40GHz, 8 GB RAM, 64-bit on a JVM (v6) with 512M initial and 1524M maximum memory allocation.

Results from Evaluating Drill-Across: Table 2 gives an overview of experiment results. We compare query results from previous experiments executing Drill-Across with the OLAP engine Mondrian over MySQL for query processing (UNEMPLOY_1, EU2020_1a, EU2020_1b) [7] and from executing our Drill-Across implementation (UNEMPLOY_2, EU2020_2a, EU2020_2b). The experiments are comparable since we used the same machine.

We successfully integrated the GDP Growth from Eurostat[9] and the Unemployment Fear from ALLBUS and found overlaps for Germany in 2004 and 2006. Mappings between implicitly shared dimensions and members were considered. Also, for the EU2020 query, we successfully integrated four and eight datasets.

Loading and validating datasets takes much less time than with our previous implementation which results from the directed crawling strategy and from a switch from *qcrumb.com* to Sesame as a SPARQL query engine. L&V also includes the time for reasoning. Most time is spent in executing several queries for multidimensional elements (MD) and in generating the logical and physical

---

[6] https://code.google.com/p/olap4ld/

[7] Additional information can be found on the evaluation website of the paper:
http://linked-data-cubes.org/index.php/Global_Cube_Evaluation_EKAW14

[8] http://semanticweb.org/OWLLD/#Rules

[9] Apparently, dataset http://estatwrap.ontologycentral.com/id/tsieb020#ds in Eurostat was replaced by dataset tec00115 after conducting these experiments.

Table 2. For every experiment, number of integrated datasets #DS, triples #T, observations #O, look-ups #LU, and average elapsed query times in sec for loading and validating datasets (L&V), executing (MD) a certain number of metadata queries (#MD), generating the logical query plan (LQP), generating the physical query plan (PQP), executing the physical query plan (EQP), and total elapsed query time (T).

Experiment	#DS	#T	#O	#LU	L&V	MD	#MD	LQP	PQP	EQP	T
UNEMPLOY_1	2	20,268	350	22	283	-	-	-	-	0.073	273
UNEMPLOY_2	2	3,897	362	12	11	5	41	3	3	0.036	22
EU2020_1a	4	24,636	1,247	26	654	-	-	-	-	0.161	654
EU2020_2a	4	19,714	2,212	12	18	15	67	3	3	0.094	39
EU2020_1b	8	35,482	2,682	34	1,638	-	-	-	-	0.473	1,638
EU2020_2b	8	38,069	3,992	20	47	40	103	6	10	0.151	103

query plans (LQP+PQP). Our experiments with 2, 4, and 8 datasets indicate that MD, LQP, PQP and EQP increase linearly. LQP includes the time for interpreting the query language (MDX) and building a nested set of OLAP operations. PQP includes the time to run the *OLAP-to-SPARQL algorithm* [8]. Executing the SPARQL queries and Drill-Across operations (EQP) only takes a fraction and is similar to processing time in the OLAP engine [7].

Results from Evaluating Convert-Cube and Merge-Cubes: To show the feasibility of conversion and merging correspondences, we manually built the logical query plan as illustrated in Figure 1 for comparing GDP per Capita from different datasets. Consequently, no time is spent for metadata queries and generating the logical query plan. For an efficient materialisation of all derived data cubes, a more scalable RDF engine would be needed.

We successfully executed the GDP_CAP query, the resulting cube allows us to compare computed and the given GDP per Capita as stored in Eurostat. By the small divergence between the computed and the given values, we presume that the computations are correct; for instance, for UK in 2010, the Nominal GDP is directly given as $27,800$ and computed as $27,704$ Euro per Inhabitant.

On average, the query takes 246sec. We load 1,015,044 triples. Note, these do not only come from 16 lookups to the three integrated datasets, but also from loading derived datasets to the embedded triple store. Similarly, in total, the engine loads or creates 126,351 observations. The long time of 119sec for the 10 look-ups, loading, and validating results from the fact that integrated datasets per se are larger than the datasets we have loaded in previous experiments, e.g., the Population data cube is described by more than 22MB of RDF/XML.

Generating the physical operator query plan with on average 16sec is fast, but executing the query plan with an average of 111sec takes as long as loading and validating. This is because different from the pipelining strategy of the Drill-Across iterator to directly process the results of a previous iterator, for Convert-Cube and Merge-Cubes the physical query plan involves materialising data cubes as derived cubes and storing them in the embedded triple store for the next iterator. From 111sec needed for processing the physical query plan, on average 91sec (82%) was spent on generating and storing the derived datasets.

6   Related Work

Some authors [1,6] allow drill-across over cubes with not fully shared dimensions, e.g., dimensions with different granularity such as monthly and yearly, and for which one dimension can be defined as the association of several ones for which a mapping is needed, e.g., latitude/longitude versus point geometry.

Tseng and Chen [13] define several semantic conflicts, e.g., implicitly shared dimensions and inconsistent measures, that are manually solved using XML transformations. Different from these approaches to overcome heterogeneities, we keep a strict Drill-Across definition and allow solving of semantic conflicts with abstract conversion and merging relationships.

For finding relationships between multidimensional datasets common ontology matching approaches are less suitable [15]. Torlone [12] automatically match heterogeneous dimensions by checking requirements of shared dimensions such as coherence and soundness; similar to our work, they use joins and materialisation approaches. We focus on more complex mappings explicitly given by experts.

Wilkinson and Simitsis [14] propose flows of hypercube operators as a conceptual model from which ETL processes can be generated. The Linked-Data-Fu language [11] uses N3 rules for describing complex data processing interactions on the Web. A rule engine could possibly improve our query processing approach, e.g., by bulk-loading, crawling and query processing in parallel threads and if backtracking from a query is supported. However, N3 does not support functions such as needed in our conversion and merging correspondences. Also, we provide an abstraction layer specific to multidimensional datasets published as Linked Data. Etcheverry and Vaisman [5] map analytical operations to SPARQL over RDF but do not define multi-cube operations and mappings.

Siegel et al. [10] introduce the notion of semantic values – numeric values accompanied by metadata for interpreting the value, e.g., the unit – and propose conversion functions to facilitate the exchange of distributed datasets by heterogeneous information systems. Calvanese et al. [2] describe a rule-based approach to automatically find the matching between two relational schemas. We extend their approaches to data cubes published as Linked Data.

Diamantini et al. [4] suggest to uniquely define indicators (measures) as formulas, aggregation functions, semantics (mathematical meaning) of the formula, and recursive references to other indicators. They use mathematical standards for describing the semantics of operations (MathML, OpenMath) and use Prolog to reason about indicators, e.g., for equality or consistency of indicators. In contrast, we focus on heterogeneities occurring in terms of dimensions and members, and allow conversions and combinations.

7   Conclusions

As the number of statistical datasets published as Linked Data is growing, citizens and analysts can benefit from methods to integrate national indicators, despite heterogeneities of data sources. In this paper, we have defined the Global Cube based on the Drill-Across operation over cubes published as QB datasets.

The number of answers of queries over the Global Cube can be increased via OWL mappings as well as more complex conversion and merging relationships between datasets. Results from a scenario integrating government statistics indicate that – if a more scalable RDF engine is used – the operations can provide the foundations for an automatic integration of datasets.

Acknowledgements. This work was partially supported by the German Research Foundation (I01, SFB/TRR 125 "Cognition-Guided Surgery"), the German Federal Ministry of Education and Research (Software Campus, 01IS12051), and the EU's 7th Framework Programme (PlanetData, Grant 257641).

References

1. Abelló, A., Samos, J., Saltor, F.: Implementing Operations to Navigate Semantic Star Schemas. In: Proceedings of DOLAP. ACM Press (2003)
2. Calvanese, D., De Giacomo, G., Lenzerini, M., Nardi, D., Rosati, R.: Data Integration in Data Warehousing. International Journal of Cooperative Information Systems 10, 237–271 (2001)
3. Capadisli, S., Auer, S., Riedl, R.: Linked Statistical Data Analysis. Semantic Web Challenge 2013 (2013)
4. Diamantini, C., Potena, D., Storti, E.: A Logic-Based Formalization of KPIs for Virtual Enterprises. Advanced Information Systems, 274–285 (2013)
5. Etcheverry, L., Vaisman, A.A.: Enhancing OLAP Analysis with Web Cubes. In: Simperl, E., Cimiano, P., Polleres, A., Corcho, O., Presutti, V. (eds.) ESWC 2012. LNCS, vol. 7295, pp. 469–483. Springer, Heidelberg (2012)
6. Gómez, L.I., Gómez, S.A., Vaisman, A.A.: A Generic Data Model and Query Language for Spatiotemporal OLAP Cube Analysis Categories and Subject Descriptors. In: Proceedings of EDBT (2012)
7. Kämpgen, B., Harth, A.: Transforming Statistical Linked Data for Use in OLAP Systems. In: Proceedings of the 7th I-Semantics (2011)
8. Kämpgen, B., Harth, A.: No size fits all – running the star schema benchmark with SPARQL and RDF aggregate views. In: Cimiano, P., Corcho, O., Presutti, V., Hollink, L., Rudolph, S. (eds.) ESWC 2013. LNCS, vol. 7882, pp. 290–304. Springer, Heidelberg (2013)
9. Shukla, A., Deshpande, P.M., Naughton, J.F.: Materialized View Selection for Multi-cube Data Models. In: Proceedings of EDBT, pp. 269–284 (2000)
10. Siegel, M., Sciore, E., Rosenthal, A.: Using semantic values to facilitate interoperability among heterogeneous information systems. Transactions on Database Systems (1994)
11. Stadtmüller, S., Harth, A.: Data-Fu: A Language and an Interpreter for Interaction with Read / Write Linked Data. In: Proceedings of WWW (2013)
12. Torlone, R.: Two approaches to the integration of heterogeneous data warehouses. Distributed and Parallel Databases 23(1), 69–97 (2007)
13. Tseng, F., Chen, C.: Integrating heterogeneous data warehouses using XML technologies. Journal of Information Science 31 (2005)
14. Wilkinson, K., Simitsis, A.: Designing Integration Flows Using Hypercubes. In: Proceedings of EDBT/ICDT (2011)
15. Zapilko, B., Mathiak, B.: Object property matching utilizing the overlap between imported ontologies. In: Presutti, V., d'Amato, C., Gandon, F., d'Aquin, M., Staab, S., Tordai, A. (eds.) ESWC 2014. LNCS, vol. 8465, pp. 737–751. Springer, Heidelberg (2014)

VOWL 2: User-Oriented Visualization of Ontologies

Steffen Lohmann[1], Stefan Negru[2], Florian Haag[1], and Thomas Ertl[1]

[1] Institute for Visualization and Interactive Systems (VIS),
University of Stuttgart, Universitätsstr. 38, 70569 Stuttgart, Germany
{steffen.lohmann,florian.haag,thomas.ertl}@vis.uni-stuttgart.de
[2] Faculty of Computer Science, Alexandru Ioan Cuza University,
Strada General Henri Mathias Berthelot 16, 700483 Iasi, Romania*
stefan.negru@info.uaic.ro

Abstract. Ontologies become increasingly important as a means to structure and organize information. This requires methods and tools that enable not only ontology experts but also other user groups to work with ontologies and related data. We have developed VOWL, a comprehensive and well-specified visual language for the user-oriented representation of ontologies, and conducted a comparative study on an initial version of VOWL. Based upon results from that study, as well as an extensive review of other ontology visualizations, we have reworked many parts of VOWL. In this paper, we present the new version VOWL 2 and describe how the initial definitions were used to systematically redefine the visual notation. Besides the novelties of the visual language, which is based on a well-defined set of graphical primitives and an abstract color scheme, we briefly describe two implementations of VOWL 2. To gather some insight into the user experience with the new version of VOWL, we have conducted a qualitative user study. We report on the study and its results, which confirmed that not only the general ideas of VOWL but also most of our enhancements for VOWL 2 can be well understood by casual ontology users.

Keywords: Ontology, visualization, owl, vowl, visual language, semantic web, protégé, prefuse, d3, svg, user study.

1 Introduction

Ontologies describe the concepts and relationships in an area of knowledge using a logic-based language that enables automated reasoning. They are no longer exclusively used by ontology experts but also by non-expert users in various domains. However, especially these casual users often have difficulties to understand ontologies.

Ontology visualizations can help in this regard by assisting in the exploration, verification, and sensemaking of ontologies [15,26]. They can be particularly useful for casual users, but may also give expert users a new perspective on ontologies. While several ontology visualizations have been developed in the last couple of years, they either focus on specific aspects of ontologies or are hard to read for casual users. Furthermore, many visualizations are tailored for a specific task or use special types of diagrams that must first be learned to understand the visualization.

---

* Stefan Negru is now with MSD IT Global Innovation Center.

K. Janowicz et al. (Eds.): EKAW 2014, LNAI 8876, pp. 266–281, 2014.
© Springer International Publishing Switzerland 2014

In order to fill this gap and provide a more intuitive and user-oriented visualization for ontologies, we developed the Visual Notation for OWL Ontologies (VOWL). An early version of VOWL [34] has been compared to the UML-based visualization of ontologies [33]. Based on insights from the comparison, we have completely reworked the VOWL notation and developed version 2 with significant improvements and more precise mappings to OWL. One of the main goals of VOWL 2 is to define a visual language that can also be understood by casual users with only little training. In this paper, we present the considerations and concepts of VOWL 2 in detail. Two implementations of VOWL 2 demonstrate its applicability and usability. In addition, we report on a user study that compares VOWL 2 to the two related ontology visualizations GrOWL [24] and SOVA [25].

2 Related Work

Quite a number of visualizations for ontologies have been presented in the last couple of years [10,15,23]. While some of them are implemented as standalone applications, most are provided as plugins for ontology editors like Protégé [3].

2.1 Graph Visualizations of Ontologies

Many approaches visualize ontologies as graphs, which is a natural way to depict the structure of the concepts and relationships in a domain of knowledge. The graphs are often rendered in force-directed or hierarchical layouts, resulting in appealing visualizations. However, only few visualizations show complete ontologies, but most focus on certain aspects. For instance, OWLViz [21], OntoTrack [27], and KC-Viz [31] depict only the class hierarchy of ontologies. OWLPropViz [37], OntoGraf [11], and FlexViz [12] represent different types of property relations, but do not show datatype properties and property characteristics required to fully understand ontologies.

A smaller number of approaches provide more comprehensive graph visualizations that represent all key elements of ontologies. Unfortunately, the different ontology elements are often hard to distinguish in the visualizations. For instance, TGViz [5] and NavigOWL [22] use very simple graph visualizations where all nodes and links look the same except for their color. This is different in GrOWL [24] and SOVA [25], which define more elaborated notations using different symbols, colors, and node shapes. However, as the notations of both GrOWL and SOVA rely symbols from description logic [6] and abbreviations, they are not perfectly suited for casual users. Furthermore, the visualizations created with GrOWL and SOVA are characterized by a large number of crossing edges which has a negative impact on the readability.

Other graph visualizations focus on specific tasks. The RelFinder [17], for instance, visualizes relationships between individuals described by ontologies and makes these relationships interactively explorable. GLOW uses a radial tree layout and hierarchical edge bundles [19] to depict relationships within ontologies [20]. Both approaches provide some insight into links between certain classes and individuals, but they do not give an overview of the complete ontology.

2.2   Ontology Visualizations Based on Specific Diagram Types

There are also a number of works that use other types of diagrams than graph visualizations to represent ontologies. For instance, Jambalaya [36] and OWL-VisMod [14] use treemaps to depict the class hierarchy of ontologies. Jambalaya additionally provides a nested graph visualization called SHriMP that allows to split up the class hierarchy into different views [36]. CropCircles is a related visualization technique that visualizes the class hierarchy of ontologies with the goal to support the identification of "undermodeled" ontology parts [38]. All these approaches visualize once again mainly the class hierarchy, without considering other property relations.

Cluster Maps use a visualization technique that is based on nested circles and has also been successfully applied to ontologies [13]. Instead of showing the class hierarchy, Cluster Maps visualize individuals grouped by the classes they are instances of. Similar techniques are used in VisCover [28] and OOBIAN Insight [2] that additionally provide a number of interactive filtering capabilities. Another related approach is gFacet [18], where individuals are grouped by their classes and can be filtered by selecting linked individuals or data values. While using appealing visualizations, these tools show only a selection of classes along with their instances but do not provide complete visualizations of ontologies.

A powerful type of diagram related to OWL and often reused to visualize ontologies is the class diagram of the Unified Modeling Language (UML) [4]. Precise mappings between OWL and UML class diagrams are specified in the Ontology Definition Metamodel (ODM) [1], among others. A major drawback of such attempts is that they require some knowledge about UML class diagrams. Although many people with an IT background are familiar with these types of diagrams, people from other domains have difficulties interpreting them correctly, as we also found in the aforementioned comparative study [33].

2.3   Discussion of Related Work

Looking at the related work, some common characteristics stand out: Most visualizations utilize a well-known type of diagram for ontology visualization (graph visualization, treemap, UML) and focus on specific aspects of ontologies. Only few attempts aim for a comprehensive ontology visualization. Even less approaches provide an explicit description of the visual notation, i.e. a specification that precisely defines the semantics and mappings of the graphical elements. Often, there is no clear visual distinction between different property types or between classes, properties, and individuals.

Furthermore, many works implement a stepwise approach of ontology exploration, where only a root class is shown at the beginning and the user has to navigate through the visualization. With VOWL, we rather aim for an approach that provides users with an overview of the complete ontology and let them subsequently explore parts of it in depth, following the popular Visual Information Seeking Mantra of "overview first, zoom and filter, then details-on-demand" [35]. We chose this approach as we consider it important to give users a visual impression of the size and topology of the ontology before they start to explore it any further.

Most importantly, we aim for an intuitive visualization that is also comprehensible to users less familiar with ontologies, while most of the related work has rather been designed for ontology experts.

3   VOWL 2: Visual Notation for OWL Ontologies

Based upon our review of related work and the comparative evaluation [33], we decided to retain numerous traits of the initial VOWL version (VOWL 1). As already mentioned, graphs seem to be a natural and intuitive way to represent the structure of ontologies, which is confirmed by many of the related work reported above. VOWL is based on a mapping of OWL elements to graphical depictions that are combined into a graph representing the ontology. For VOWL 2, we have reworked these mappings and taken into account the exact semantics of all definitions from OWL that were considered. In particular, we have broken down the components of VOWL to a set of basic building blocks consisting of shapes and colors that express specific aspects of the OWL elements (datatype or object properties, different class and property characteristics, etc.), also considering possible combinations thereof.

VOWL 1 included an integrated view that would display the TBox of an ontology along with information from the ABox. Comments from the initial user study on VOWL 1, however, led us to conclude that concerns about the scalability of the integrated view were justified. Even with few instances per class, additional information, such as property values of instances, would be difficult to show without creating lots of clutter. Therefore, VOWL 2 focuses on displaying primarily the TBox and only optionally integrates some ABox information in the visualization itself, but rather recommends to display this information in another part of the user interface.

3.1   Basic Building Blocks of VOWL

The basic building blocks of VOWL 2 are a clearly defined set of graphical primitives and a color scheme. In addition, VOWL 2 uses a force-directed graph layout along with splitting rules that specify which elements are multiplied in the visualization.

Graphical Primitives. VOWL 1 defined graphical representations for a number of OWL concepts. For VOWL 2, we took into account those definitions, but based the visualization upon a more abstract and systematic approach. The alphabet of the visual language is now formed by only a handful of graphical primitives and features. Table 1(a) lists these primitives and the ontology elements they are applied to.

As the visualization of individual instances was not considered crucial for most contexts, classes are simply depicted as a circle in VOWL 2, without any additional elements to accommodate instance information. Where available and desired, the number of instances may still be implied by modifying the radius of the circle compared to the default radius. VOWL 2 does not specify a particular scaling method for the circle sizes, but good results may be achieved with a logarithmic or square-root scaling in most cases. The class representation of owl:Thing has a fixed size, as it usually does not carry any particular domain information and as all individuals in an ontology are instances of owl:Thing according to the OWL specification.

Like in VOWL 1, property relations are expressed by labeled arrows. The labels do not have individual arrowheads any more, as the user study revealed that their intended direction was often ambiguous, particularly for vertical edges. Other edges, like those for subproperty relations, are completely left out and replaced by additional texts in the labels or interactive features to reduce the number of edge crossings and to facilitate the implementation of VOWL.

As the use of description logic and other symbols to express concepts such as the union or the intersection of classes can be unnecessarily confusing to lay users, VOWL 2 avoids such symbols or combines them with graphical representations reminiscent of Venn diagrams to more clearly communicate the underlying set operations.

Table 1. Graphical primitives and color scheme forming the basic building blocks of VOWL

(a) Graphical primitives

Primitive	Application
◯	classes
◠	properties
▷ ▶	property directions
▭	datatypes, property labels
▪▪▪▪ ▪▪▪▪▪▪	special classes and properties
text number symbol	labels, cardinalities

(b) Excerpt of the VOWL color scheme

Name	Color	Application
General		classes, object properties, disjoints
Rdf		elements of RDF and RDF Schema
External		external classes and properties
Deprecated		deprecated classes and properties
Datatype		datatypes, literals
Datatype property		datatype properties
Highlighting		highlighted elements

Color Scheme. Since the results of the user study on VOWL 1 showed that colors are very helpful in identifying the different elements, a stronger focus was placed on creating systematic coloring rules for VOWL 2. We therefore created a color scheme that clearly defines foreground and background colors for all elements based on a number of attributes. While colors in the VOWL 1 specification were statically linked to the visual elements, VOWL 2 defines colors by their function, for example, to mark deprecated or external elements. Where several of the color mappings may apply, priority rules are specified. For instance, the deprecated color has priority over the external color according to the VOWL 2 specification.

VOWL 1 and most related approaches rely either on a concrete set of colors or do not specify colors at all. We acknowledged that a specific color scheme may not always be adequate and therefore defined the VOWL 2 color scheme in a more flexible way by using abstract color names, such as the ones listed in Table 1(b). Although the VOWL 2 specification recommends a particular color mapping, it is meant merely as a default suggestion and any references to colors in the specification can be treated as variables. In addition, the color scheme comes with guidelines on how the colors should relate to each other in order to encode the VOWL semantics.

3.2   Visual Elements and Graph Visualization

The VOWL 2 specification includes graphical representations for the most common OWL elements based on the aforementioned primitives and colors. A selection thereof is shown in Figure 1.[1] In several cases, information is redundantly encoded. For example, equivalent classes both carry a double border as well as several class names in their label, and external classes both adhere to the external color as defined in the color scheme and sport the hint "external" beneath their name. While the colors improve the overview in most situations, the additional texts ensure that even in the absence of colors, the important aspects of the ontology are still intelligible. Moreover, we wanted to make the visualization more self-explanatory with the text representations.

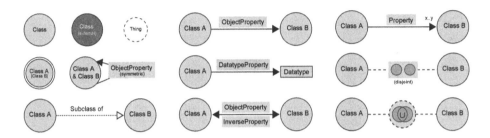

Fig. 1. A selection of visual elements from the VOWL 2 specification

As participants of the VOWL 1 user study stated the desire for an interactive highlighting of certain information and relationships, some of the visual element definitions in VOWL 2 include guidelines on how to design interactive implementations. For example, while the aforementioned subproperty relation is no longer expressed by an arrow in VOWL 2, hovering over a subproperty is defined to automatically highlight its parent property and vice-versa in interactive contexts.

The visual elements are combined to a graph representing the entire ontology. By default, VOWL graphs are visualized using a force-directed layout. In order to relax the energy of that layout and to reduce the visual importance of certain frequently referred to but generic ontology elements, some elements can be multiplied to appear more than once in a VOWL graph. While this was already the case for owl:Thing in VOWL 1, we have systematically defined generic splitting rules in VOWL 2. These rules determine that there may be no multiplication for elements, multiplication across the entire graph, or multiplication for each connected class. The VOWL 2 specification relies on such rules to define the splitting of owl:Thing into several representations, as well as that of certain other elements, such as datatypes or literals.

---

[1] The graphical representations of further OWL elements are defined in the VOWL 2 specification that is publicly available on the web at the persistent URL http://purl.org/vowl. Most of the remaining representations are variations of the ones presented in Figure 1 and visualize specific property characteristics (e.g. functional, transitive) or other set operators (e.g. intersection, complement), among others.

Figure 2 shows two visualizations of the main component of the Friend of a Friend (FOAF) vocabulary, one created with VOWL 1 and the other with VOWL 2 [34]. The visualizations contain several of the visual elements described above and exemplify some of the differences between VOWL 1 and VOWL 2. Another important difference of the two visualizations is that the VOWL 1 visualization has been manually created with a vector graphics editor (cf. [34]), while the VOWL 2 visualization has been automatically generated and only slightly adapted using the WebVOWL implementation that is presented in the next section.

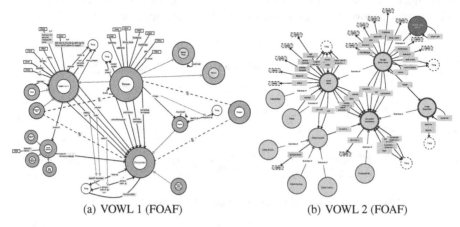

(a) VOWL 1 (FOAF)   (b) VOWL 2 (FOAF)

Fig. 2. Friend of a Friend (FOAF) vocabulary visualized with (a) VOWL 1 and (b) VOWL 2

3.3   Implementations of VOWL 2

We have implemented VOWL 2 in two different tools that demonstrate its applicability and usability: ProtégéVOWL and WebVOWL. ProtégéVOWL is a Java-based plugin for the aforementioned ontology editor Protégé and makes use of the visualization toolkit Prefuse [16].[2] It implements the VOWL 2 specification to a large extent and uses the data model supplied by the underlying Protégé API.

WebVOWL is a standalone application based on web technologies and the visualization library D3 [7]. Figure 3 shows a screenshot of WebVOWL where it is used to visualize the Personas Ontology [32]. Instead of implementing an OWL parser itself, it defines a JSON structure that the ontology needs to be converted into. This makes WebVOWL independent from a particular OWL parser and broadly applicable. WebVOWL additionally allows to export the entire ontology visualization or any portion of it as SVG image that can be opened in other programs, edited, shared, and printed.

Both implementations use physics simulations provided by the visualization toolkits to generate the force-directed graph layouts. The forces are iteratively applied in these simulations, resulting in an animation that dynamically positions the nodes. The users

---

[2] A demo of ProtégéVOWL has been presented at ESWC 2014 [30].

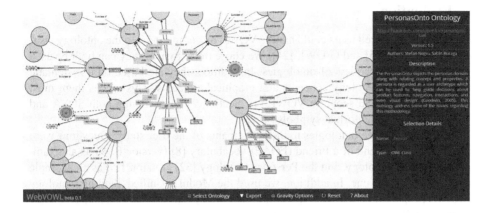

Fig. 3. Screenshot of WebVOWL with a visualization of the Personas Ontology

can smoothly zoom in to explore certain ontology parts in detail or zoom out to analyze the global structure of the ontology. They can pan the background and move elements around, which results in a repositioning of the nodes by animated transitions, triggered by the force-directed layout. Both implementations support interactive highlighting and display additional information on the selected elements on demand (in Figure 3, the class "Person" is selected). Moreover, the force-directed layout can be adapted, as the attraction forces between nodes can be modified and the automatic layout can be suspended in favor of a manual repositioning of nodes. Since datatypes have a separate attraction force, they can be placed in close proximity to the classes they are connected with, to emphasize their radial arrangement and increase readability.

The user interfaces of both tools consist of three parts (see Figure 3): A *viewer* displaying the VOWL visualization, a *sidebar* listing details about the element that is selected, and the *controls* allowing to adapt the force-directed graph layout and providing further options, such as a function to export the VOWL visualization as SVG image. We developed the tools, in particular WebVOWL, so that they can be used in different interaction contexts, including settings with touch interaction. For instance, zooming can not only be performed with the mouse wheel but also with a double click/touch or two fingers zooming gestures on the canvas. As some interactive features, such as mouseover effects, may not be available in all interaction contexts (e.g. when using touch interfaces), we took care that they are not crucial for the interaction or for understanding the ontology.[3]

To the best of our knowledge, WebVOWL is the first tool for comprehensive ontology visualization that is completely based on open web standards. Related tools running in web browsers, such as FlexViz [12] or OOBIAN Insight [2], are implemented with technologies like Adobe Flex or Microsoft Silverlight that require proprietary browser plugins. The tool LodLive [9] is technically more related to WebVOWL but focuses on the visual exploration of Linked Data and does not visualize ontologies.

---

[3] Both tools are released under the MIT license and are publicly available at http://vowl.visualdataweb.org

4   Evaluation

We evaluated how well users could handle VOWL by comparing it to the ontology visualizations SOVA [25] and GrOWL [24]. We chose those two, as they can both be used to gain a general overview of ontologies. In addition, they are based on a systematic mapping between ontology concepts and graphical elements. This makes them most related in purpose and scope to VOWL (cf. Section 2), even though both SOVA and GrOWL include some formal symbols.

We presented three ontologies to the participants of the user study: Questions were asked about the Friend of a Friend (FOAF) vocabulary [8] (version 0.99) as an example of a smaller ontology, and the Personas Ontology [32] (version 1.5) as an example of a more extensive one. In addition, we used the Modular Unified Tagging Ontology (MUTO) [29] (version 1.0) as a small training ontology, to give participants an opportunity to familiarize themselves with each visualization approach and the user interface of the respective implementation.

The FOAF vocabulary visualized with SOVA and GrOWL is shown in Figure 4, the VOWL representation of FOAF was already depicted in Figure 2(b). While both WebVOWL and ProtégéVOWL are, in principle, conformant with the VOWL 2 specification, the implementation of WebVOWL had progressed further at the time of the study, which is why the VOWL visualizations were shown in WebVOWL. The SOVA visualizations were generated with the respective plugin for Protégé [25], while for the GrOWL visualizations, we used the Java tool presented in [24]. The Java tool supports either the creation of a new ontology or the visualization of an existing one in a force-directed layout, which was what we used. Note that the force-directed layouts arrange the graphs differently each time the ontologies are loaded into the tools, as these layouts are inherently non-deterministic.

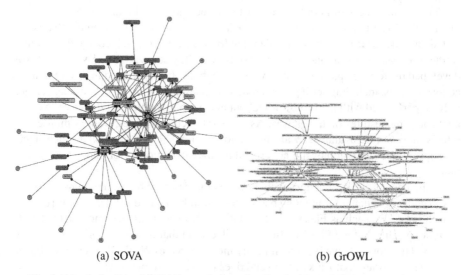

(a) SOVA   (b) GrOWL

Fig. 4. Friend of a Friend (FOAF) vocabulary visualized with (a) SOVA and (b) GrOWL

4.1 Tasks

We prepared 18 comprehension tasks, six per visualization, and among those, three for each of the two ontologies (FOAF and Personas Ontology). The tasks reflected questions that users working with ontologies would have to pose in order to identify, use, or edit parts of the ontologies. Some of the tasks featured the same or similar questions, referring to different ontologies. A full list of the tasks is provided in Table 2.

Table 2. Tasks of the user study (translated from German to English). Groups of six tasks were applied to the three visualizations (column *V*), which were presented in a balanced order (i.e. *V* = 1 was either GrOWL, SOVA, or VOWL). In each of these groups, there were three tasks per ontology (column *O*), FOAF (*F*) and PersonasOnto (*P*).

V	O	Question
1	F	Which classes appear to be crucial for the ontology?
		Which data properties does the class *Person* have?
		Is the class *Spatial Thing* equivalent to any other class? If so, to which?
	P	How many *different* (i.e. not equivalent) classes are approximately visible in total?
		Which classes are subclasses of the class *Resource*?
		Do the classes *Place* and *Organization* have any properties in common? If so, which ones?
2	F	Which classes have been imported (from other ontologies)?
		Which data properties does the class *Document* have?
		Is the class *Document* equivalent to any other class? If so, to which?
	P	Which classes appear to be crucial for the ontology
		Which classes are subclasses of the class *Persona*?
		The property *isPartOfTest* refers to the class *UsabilityTest*. For which classes is this property defined?
3	F	How many *different* (i.e. not equivalent) classes are approximately visible in total?
		Which data properties does the class *Image* have?
		Is the class *PersonalProfile* equivalent to any other class? If so, to which?
	P	Can you recognize any classes that serve as a generalization of many subclasses?
		Which classes are subclasses of the class *Scenario*?
		Do the classes *Participant* and *Goals* have any properties in common? If so, which ones?

The tasks also forced study subjects to analyze the visualizations and recognize relationships between ontology elements, just like actual users of ontologies would have to. While we did check the correctness of the answers, we were primarily interested in the comments made by the participants during task completion. Therefore, we asked participants to adhere to the "think-aloud" method and state everything they were thinking, feeling, considering, or doing with respect to the visualizations.

4.2 Other Material

We also prepared a brief printed introduction to the topic of ontologies. It included a quick overview of the concepts relevant to the study, comprising classes, properties, subclassing, equivalent classes, set operators, and imported ontology elements. Moreover, we printed a table for each of the evaluated visualizations, showing how the concepts are depicted in the given notations and how a very small exemplary ontology that combines some of the elements could look like. Finally, a questionnaire about the experienced ease-of-use was prepared for each visualization, and an additional questionnaire asked for the prior knowledge of the participants.

Implementations of the three visualizations—the SOVA plugin (version 0.8.1) for Protégé, the GrOWL Java application (version 0.02), and WebVOWL (version 0.1) in a Mozilla Firefox browser—were installed and running on the test computer. In the case of SOVA, the plugin version 0.8.1 was the latest available version at the time of conducting the user study. Unfortunately, that version did not support the display of datatype properties, which is why tasks related to datatype properties had to be skipped in SOVA. The three ontologies (MUTO, FOAF, and Personas) were loaded in each of the visualization applications and displayed on a 24" TFT monitor at a resolution of 1920×1200 pixels.

4.3 Participants

We chose to conduct the study with participants who may have to work with ontologies at some point, though not necessarily with formal ontology languages like OWL— in short, casual ontology users. We recruited six researchers from various fields of information technology (*not* including Semantic Web technologies) between 29 and 57 years of age. All participants were roughly familiar with the idea of ontologies and/or had some knowledge in related topics, such as object-oriented class structures, UML class diagrams or ER diagrams for database modeling. Two of them had worked with ontologies in the past, but only to a limited extent and without making use of formal representations.

The tested ontologies were unknown to the study participants. While two participants had already heard about the FOAF project, they had never seen the FOAF ontology before. Another two of the participants had some passing knowledge about the topic of ontology visualization, but none of them had ever used any of the three visualizations evaluated in the study.

4.4 Design and Procedure

The study had a mixed design, so that participants could compare the different visualizations. The presentation of the three visualizations was counterbalanced to avoid order effects. The order of the tasks remained fixed, as some of them would require incremental knowledge. In combination with the counterbalancing of the visualizations, this resulted in a setting where each task had to be solved for each of the visualizations by some of the participants. Likewise, the FOAF ontology was always shown before the Personas Ontology, as the latter has a larger size and is more difficult to grasp.

Participants first had to complete the questionnaire about their prior knowledge before being shown the introduction to ontologies. Meanwhile, it was announced that in the case of any doubt, questions for clarification could be asked at any point before or during the study. After briefly familiarizing themselves with the relevant concepts, participants had to use the three visualizations, one at a time.

For each visualization, participants were first provided with the printed table explaining the notation and had an opportunity to explore the MUTO ontology on screen. When they felt sufficiently familiar with the visualization, they had to perform the three tasks for each of the two ontologies, i.e. for FOAF and the Personas Ontology. The study supervisor would note down any of the participants' statements as well as the solutions they arrived at.

After completing the tasks for all three visualizations, participants received the questionnaire on which they had to rate each visualization by the criteria of clarity, learnability, ease of finding elements, mappings between visual and conceptual elements, use of colors, and use of shapes. Each criterion was accompanied by a short explanation, as given in Figure 5.

4.5   Results

In general, participants could solve most of the tasks correctly (84%). Two participants gave up solving some of the tasks in GrOWL, as the implementation lacked a feature to search for specific elements and the participants could not find these elements by visually scanning the graph. Figure 5 illustrates how participants rated the three visualizations based on the criteria of the questionnaire.

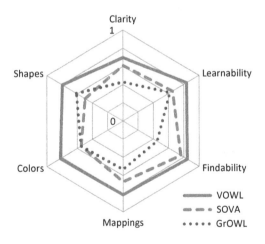

Clarity:
Perceived clarity of the visualization.

Learnability:
Perceived ease of learning how to use the visualization.

Findability:
Convenience of finding specific elements.

Mappings:
Perceived comprehensibility of the mapping between elements of the ontology and visualization.

Colors:
Helpfulness of colors for comprehension of the visualization.

Shapes:
Helpfulness of shapes for comprehension of the visualization.

Fig. 5. User ratings of the visualizations based on different criteria

Comments were generally favorable toward VOWL ("properties and classes can be distinguished very well", "not so much tangle and less edges [compared to the other visualizations]"), which was especially praised for the clear visual distinction of classes, properties, and other ontology elements. Several participants pointed out that classes could easily be recognized due to their different shape and size compared to other visual elements. The text labels indicating the meaning of various VOWL elements were mostly thought of as beneficial; one participant even stated that there was no need to use the printed table as the VOWL visualization was very self-explanatory. On the other hand, one participant with UML knowledge found some of the labels to be unnecessarily cluttering the visualization, such as the *subclass* text on the UML-inspired class inheritance arrows. Participants considered the animated force-directed layout in all three visualizations to be beneficial, as nodes would to some extent arrange themselves. One participant remarked that circles are a good choice for representing classes in VOWL, as arrow heads of edges pointing to a class would align nicely around its circle with minimal overlapping.

Overall, VOWL 2 was assessed to be well readable and the participants emphasized the comparably low number of edges and, in particular, edge crossings. This effect was achieved both by avoiding several edges present in other visualizations, such as between equivalent classes, and by applying splitting rules for node multiplication, as described in Section 3.2. All but one of the participants understood the way equivalent classes are displayed. Two more participants asked for a clarification, as they wondered whether there would be multiple copies of the double-ringed equivalent class circles, one for each equivalent class, or only one in all.

As opposed to that, the general base class owl:Thing was indeed displayed several times according to the splitting rules of VOWL 2 (cf. Section 3.2). Interestingly, this was instantly understood and pointed out whenever participants encountered owl:Thing in one of the tasks solved in VOWL. While multiple copies of owl:Thing at first create slightly more nodes, the edges linking to those owl:Thing nodes are overall shorter and with less edge crossings, again contributing to the aforementioned impression that VOWL does not feature a 'maze of edges'.

Many of the other comments dealt with implementation-specific issues. The most important features asked for (when they were missing) or praised (when they were present) were a continuous zooming feature—for which most participants preferred the mousewheel, as offered in VOWL and SOVA—and a search facility to quickly find particular classes (or other elements) by name, which was present in SOVA, and in a limited fashion also available in WebVOWL due to the built-in browser text search. Furthermore, a highlighting feature that changes the color of all directly connected nodes upon hovering the mouse cursor over one node, like the one available in SOVA, was stated to be useful. It was, however, noted, that such a highlighting should not completely replace the original node colors.

5   Conclusions and Future Work

In an earlier effort to create a uniform visual notation for OWL ontologies, we developed a first version of VOWL [34]. Based upon that work, related endeavors, as well as findings from a user study [33], we have redesigned large parts of the notation to create VOWL 2, a visual language that can also be understood by casual ontology users. We have described the key considerations, features, and capabilities of VOWL 2 and have presented two implementations of the visualization, a plugin for the widely used ontology editor Protégé and a responsive web application. Moreover, we have reported on a qualitative user study that compared VOWL 2 to two related ontology visualizations to get a better understanding of its readability and usability. We found that users were able to solve a majority of the tasks correctly and received overall favorable comments concerning VOWL 2.

5.1   Summary of Study Results

The qualitative user study provided us with some insights into how users perceive various features of VOWL 2:

– Structurally, the design of the graph visualization that allows moving nodes with the pointing device was welcomed, and the force-directed layout would cause highly connected nodes to be easily recognizable. Study participants would frequently use the opportunity to reposition single nodes in the graph manually in order to get a clearer understanding of the connections present.
– Due to the force-directed layout, disjoint subgraphs can get pushed out of sight. Hence, the question of adding some invisible link to create a slight attraction to the main part of the graph still needs to be tackled.
– The user study revealed that the idea of multiplying general nodes (e.g. owl:Thing or rdfs:Literal) so they do not appear overly important can be understood by users.
– The unification of equivalent nodes causes a cleaner apperance for the graph visualization. However, although the equivalence relationship was correctly recognized in the user study, several users were unsure whether equivalent classes are displayed as several nodes, each referring to the other nodes, or as only one node.
– The fact that many elements are explicitly labeled evoked mostly positive feedback among the study participants. One of the study participants stated that VOWL 2 is so self-explanatory that no notation reference was needed at all, while others commented that some of the labels could be removed from the visualization without loss of clarity. Thus, it seems to be advisable to give users a choice whether such labels are displayed.

5.2   Open Issues

The ontologies used in the study, which were of a relatively moderate size (comprising 7, 22, and 53 classes), could still be handled in VOWL 2. However, there is no upper limit for the size of ontologies, both because a vast number of topics can be covered in one ontology, and because an ontology can be modeled down to an arbitrary level of detail. Graph visualizations are, on the other hand, viable only up to a certain graph size, at which point the overview is lost and the graph is not easily usable any more. VOWL 2 mitigates this only slightly based on its splitting rules and the unification of equivalent classes. Ongoing research on VOWL will have to look into means of dealing with this problem, at latest when VOWL is used to analyze the connections and alignments across several ontologies. Solutions will incorporate both considerations on the automatic and manual detection of ontology parts that carry context-specific importance, so parts of the ontology can be temporarily hidden or bundled, as well as general strategies for handling large graphs used in the field of graph visualization.

A related issue exists due to the fact that ontology elements have no inherent relative location information. Therefore, all elements are initially placed in a random manner in the force-directed layout. While this does not influence a single session of work with the VOWL depiction of an ontology, it prevents the users to create a "mental map" of the visualization that is valid for several sessions, as the elements are at different locations every time the VOWL graph is rendered. Future work will have to develop reasonable guidelines on how to best place ontology elements so their positioning follows a reproducible pattern.

References

1. Ontology Definition Metamodel, http://www.omg.org/spec/ODM/
2. OOBIAN Insight, http://dbpedia.oobian.com
3. Protégé Wiki, http://protegewiki.stanford.edu/wiki/Visualization
4. Unified Modeling Language, http://www.uml.org
5. Alani, H.: TGVizTab: An ontology visualisation extension for protégé. In: 2nd Workshop on Visualizing Information in Knowledge Engineering, VIKE 2004 (2003)
6. Baader, F., Calvanese, D., McGuinness, D.L., Nardi, D., Patel-Schneider, P.F.: The Description Logic Handbook: Theory, Implementation, and Applications. Cambridge University Press (2003)
7. Bostock, M., Ogievetsky, V., Heer, J.: D3 data-driven documents. IEEE Transactions on Visualization and Computer Graphics 17(12), 2301–2309 (2011)
8. Brickley, D., Miller, L.: FOAF Vocabulary Specification 0.99 (2014), http://xmlns.com/foaf/spec/
9. Camarda, D.V., Mazzini, S., Antonuccio, A.: Lodlive, exploring the web of data. In: Proceedings of the 8th International Conference on Semantic Systems, I-SEMANTICS 2012. ACM (2012)
10. Dadzie, A., Rowe, M.: Approaches to visualizing linked data: A survey. Semantic Web 2(2), 89–124 (2011)
11. Falconer, S.: OntoGraf (2010), http://protegewiki.stanford.edu/wiki/OntoGraf
12. Falconer, S.M., Callendar, C., Storey, M.-A.: A visualization service for the semantic web. In: Cimiano, P., Pinto, H.S. (eds.) EKAW 2010. LNCS, vol. 6317, pp. 554–564. Springer, Heidelberg (2010)
13. Fluit, C., Sabou, M., van Harmelen, F.: Ontology-based information visualization: Toward semantic web applications. In: Visualizing the Semantic Web, pp. 36–48. Springer (2002)
14. García-Peñalvo, F.J., Colomo-Palacios, R., García, J., Therón, R.: Towards an ontology modeling tool. a validation in software engineering scenarios. Expert Systems with Applications 39(13), 11468–11478 (2012)
15. Geroimenko, V., Chen, C.: Visualizing the Semantic Web: XML-Based Internet and Information Visualization, 2nd edn. Springer (2006)
16. Heer, J., Card, S.K., Landay, J.A.: Prefuse: A toolkit for interactive information visualization. In: Proceedings of the SIGCHI Conference on Human Factors in Computing Systems, CHI 2005, pp. 421–430. ACM (2005)
17. Heim, P., Lohmann, S., Stegemann, T.: Interactive relationship discovery via the semantic web. In: Aroyo, L., Antoniou, G., Hyvönen, E., ten Teije, A., Stuckenschmidt, H., Cabral, L., Tudorache, T. (eds.) ESWC 2010, Part I. LNCS, vol. 6088, pp. 303–317. Springer, Heidelberg (2010)
18. Heim, P., Ziegler, J., Lohmann, S.: gFacet: A browser for the web of data. In: Proceedings of the International Workshop on Interacting with Multimedia Content in the Social Semantic Web, IMC-SSW 2008, vol. 417, pp. 49–58. CEUR-WS.org (2008)

19. Holten, D.: Hierarchical edge bundles: Visualization of adjacency relations in hierarchical data. IEEE Transactions on Visualization and Computer Graphics 12(5), 741–748 (2006)

20. Hop, W., de Ridder, S., Frasincar, F., Hogenboom, F.: Using hierarchical edge bundles to visualize complex ontologies in glow. In: Proceedings of the 27th Annual ACM Symposium on Applied Computing, SAC 2012, pp. 304–311. ACM (2012)

21. Horridge, M.: OWLViz (2010), http://protegewiki.stanford.edu/wiki/OWLViz

22. Hussain, A., Latif, K., Rextin, A., Hayat, A., Alam, M.: Scalable visualization of semantic nets using power-law graphs. Applied Mathematics & Information Sciences 8(1), 355–367 (2014)

23. Katifori, A., Halatsis, C., Lepouras, G., Vassilakis, C., Giannopoulou, E.: Ontology visualization methods – a survey. ACM Computer Surveys 39(4) (November 2007)

24. Krivov, S., Williams, R., Villa, F.: GrOWL: A tool for visualization and editing of owl ontologies. Web Semantics: Science, Services and Agents on the World Wide Web 5(2), 54–57 (2007)

25. Kunowski, P., Boiński, T.: SOVA – Simple Ontology Visualization API (2012), http://protegewiki.stanford.edu/wiki/SOVA

26. Lanzenberger, M., Sampson, J., Rester, M.: Visualization in ontology tools. In: Proceedings of the International Conference on Complex, Intelligent and Software Intensive Systems, CISIS 2009, pp. 705–711 (2009)

27. Liebig, T., Noppens, O.: OntoTrack: A semantic approach for ontology authoring. Web Semantics: Science, Services and Agents on the World Wide Web 3(2-3), 116–131 (2005)

28. Liebig, T., Noppens, O., von Henke, F.W.: Viscover: Visualizing, exploring, and analysing structured data. In: Proceedings of the IEEE Symposium on Visual Analytics Science and Technology, VAST 2009, pp. 259–260. IEEE (2009)

29. Lohmann, S.: Modular unified tagging ontology, MUTO (2011), http://purl.org/muto/core#

30. Lohmann, S., Negru, S., Bold, D.: The ProtégéVOWL plugin: Ontology visualization for everyone. In: Proceedings of ESWC 2014 Satellite Events. Springer (to appear, 2014)

31. Motta, E., Mulholland, P., Peroni, S., d'Aquin, M., Gomez-Perez, J.M., Mendez, V., Zablith, F.: A novel approach to visualizing and navigating ontologies. In: Aroyo, L., Welty, C., Alani, H., Taylor, J., Bernstein, A., Kagal, L., Noy, N., Blomqvist, E. (eds.) ISWC 2011, Part I. LNCS, vol. 7031, pp. 470–486. Springer, Heidelberg (2011)

32. Negru, S.: PersonasOnto (2014), http://blankdots.com/open/personasonto.html

33. Negru, S., Haag, F., Lohmann, S.: Towards a unified visual notation for owl ontologies: Insights from a comparative user study. In: Proceedings of the 9th International Conference on Semantic Systems, I-SEMANTICS 2013, pp. 73–80. ACM (2013)

34. Negru, S., Lohmann, S.: A visual notation for the integrated representation of OWL ontologies. In: Proceedings of the 9th International Conference on Web Information Systems and Technologies, WEBIST 2013, pp. 308–315. SciTePress (2013)

35. Shneiderman, B.: The eyes have it: A task by data type taxonomy for information visualizations. In: Proceedings of the 1996 IEEE Symposium on Visual Languages, VL 1996, pp. 336–343. IEEE (1996)

36. Storey, M.-A., Noy, N.F., Musen, M., Best, C., Fergerson, R., Ernst, N.: Jambalaya: An interactive environment for exploring ontologies. In: Proceedings of the 7th International Conference on Intelligent User Interfaces, IUI 2002, pp. 239–239. ACM (2002)

37. Wachsmann, L.: OWLPropViz (2008), http://protegewiki.stanford.edu/wiki/OWLPropViz

38. Wang, T.D., Parsia, B.: CropCircles: Topology sensitive visualization of OWL class hierarchies. In: Cruz, I., Decker, S., Allemang, D., Preist, C., Schwabe, D., Mika, P., Uschold, M., Aroyo, L.M. (eds.) ISWC 2006. LNCS, vol. 4273, pp. 695–708. Springer, Heidelberg (2006)

What Is Linked Historical Data?

Albert Meroño-Peñuela[1,2] and Rinke Hoekstra[1,3]

[1] Department of Computer Science, VU University Amsterdam, NL
{albert.merono,rinke.hoekstra}@vu.nl
[2] Data Archiving and Networked Services, KNAW, NL
[3] Faculty of Law, University of Amsterdam, NL

Abstract. Datasets that represent historical sources are relative new-comers in the Linked Open Data (LOD) cloud. Following the standard LOD practices for publishing historical sources raises several questions: how can we distinguish between RDF graphs of primary and secondary sources? Should we treat archived and online RDF graphs differently in historical research? How do we deal with change and immutability of a triplified History? To answer these fundamental questions, we model *historical primary and secondary sources* using the OntoClean metaprop-erties and the theories of perdurance and endurance. We then use this model to give a definition of Linked Historical Data. We advocate a set of publishing practices for Linked Historical Data that preserve the on-tological properties of historical sources.

Keywords: Semantic Web, Linked Data, Historical Data.

1 Historical Sources as RDF Graphs

Historical sources have traditionally been encoded in different formats: from papyrus to digital images, through books, tapes, photographs and newspapers. It is not difficult to see the benefits of publishing historical sources as Linked Open Data [7]. However, it is unclear whether standard Linked Data modeling and publication pipelines are suitable for historical sources. If the Semantic Web is to serve as both paradigm and infrastructure for conducting historical research on the Web, it is fundamental to address the representation of historical sources and to understand their essential ontological properties. In this paper we are interested in modeling the essential ontological properties of historical sources in order to make explicit to what extent current methodologies are adequate.

Independence and *reliability* of sources are fundamental issues historians take into account in scholarly writing [5]. To address these, historians distinguish be-tween *primary* and *secondary* sources. Primary sources are "original materials created at the time under study that have not been altered or distorted in any way" [2,1]; e.g. the diary of Anne Frank (1947) or the Dutch historical censuses (1795–1971)[1]. Secondary sources are "documents that relate or discuss infor-mation originally presented elsewhere, written after the fact with the benefit of

---

[1] See http://www.volkstellingen.nl/

K. Janowicz et al. (Eds.): EKAW 2014, LNAI 8876, pp. 282–287, 2014.

hindsight" [1]; e.g. socio-historical analysis on the content of the Dutch historical censuses [8]. A fundamental difference between the two is that primary sources must be *immutable*: they cannot be altered once they are created. Traditionally, immutability of sources is achieved through *archiving* them, either as books (in a library or book archive), as physical objects (in a museum archive), or more recently as digital objects and preserved Linked Data (in a digital archive). The archive is the authority that protects the primary source from change, providing *independence* and *reliability*. As a consequence, primary sources are always inevitably detached to some extent from their original context. Secondary sources are attempts from historians to recreate this context.

A strict requirement then is that RDF graphs of primary sources need to be immutable as well. But how does RDF deal with change over time [9]?

> Intuitively speaking, changes in the universe of discourse can be reflected in the following ways:
> 1. An IRI, once minted, should never change its intended referent.
> 2. Literals, by design, are constants and never change their value.
> 3. A relationship that holds between two resources at one time may not hold at another time.
> 4. RDF sources may change their state over time. That is, they may provide different RDF graphs at different times.
> 5. Some RDF sources may, however, be immutable snapshots of another RDF source, archiving its state at some point in time.

Statement 1 is problematic: a primary source that changes keeps its IRI although its identity is changed (see Section 2). In addition, statements 4 and 5 have important consequences for historical sources. First, it follows the *alive-dead* Linked Data dichotomy: on the one hand, there is a *living* LOD cloud that is constantly updated and changed; on the other hand, a *dead* and archived LOD cloud exists as old snapshots of what once was alive. This situation corresponds to the life cycle of primary and secondary sources. All sources are first ordinary living LOD data, but the fact that they are *archived to preserve their immutability* turns them into primary sources. The metaphor of the *alive-dead* LOD serves well the purpose of primary and secondary sources as RDF graphs. For a primary source to be represented as an RDF graph, it is necessary (and sufficient) to be archived and preserved from change. This implies that primary source RDF graphs are always detached to some extent from their original context, as any other primary source. Consequently, (a) outgoing links of the dataset to other resources; and (b) schemas, vocabularies or ontologies used to model the datset might be partially lost or unavailable. RDF graphs of secondary sources, on the other hand, live in the LOD cloud similar to other datasets.

2   An Ontological Framework for Historical Sources

What are the basic ontological properties that characterize historical sources? In order to come with appropriate proposals on how to publish historical primary and secondary sources as LOD, we first need to understand their fundamental characteristics. We apply the philosophical stances of *perdurance* and *endurance* and the OntoClean methodology of [4] to study ontological properties that apply to historical sources; we model these sources according to their properties.

Perdurantism holds that ordinary things like animals, boats and planets have temporal parts (things persist by *perduring* through time). *Endurantism* is the stance that ordinary things do not have temporal parts; instead, things are wholly present whenever they exist (things persist by *enduring*) [6]. The DOLCE ontology [3] translates these stances to two types of entities: *endurants* and *perdurants*, which can be characterized by whether or not they can exhibit change in time. Endurants "can "genuinely" change in time, in the sense that the very same endurant as a whole can have incompatible properties at different times; perdurants cannot change in this sense, since none of their parts maintain identity in time." Secondary sources, such as comments, notes, articles, annotations, are *endurants*; at any point in time they can be appreciated as a whole, while they still may undergo changes (e.g. working papers). Primary sources, on the other hand, have the same enduring properties, but *cannot* change: if any of their properties change, they lose identity. The accumulation over time of secondary sources that share a dependency on a primary source form our "body of knowledge" about the historical entity represented by the primary source. This body of knowledge is an **endurant** (similar to item 4 in Section 1). On the other hand, the "state of our knowledge" at any point in time is a *slice* of that body of knowledge: a set of snapshots of these endurants we call **strong endurants**.

Distinguishing between perdurants and endurants is closely related to the question of identity: if sources can change over time, how can we guarantee that they are the same entity? To help answering this question, we use the OntoClean methodology [4]. Following OntoClean, some properties are essential to *all* their instances; we call these properties **rigid** (**+R**). For instance, an entity having the property of *being a person* is guaranteed to preserve its identity even if other of his properties change, because *being a person* is rigid. Properties that are not essential for *some* of their instances are called **non-rigid** (**-R**); of these, properties that are not essential to *all* of their instances (i.e. required to change) are called **anti-rigid** ($\sim$**R**). According to this, the property of a source being primary is +R, because being primary is essential to all sources (i.e. if it stops being a primary source, it no longer exists); the property of being secondary is $\sim$**R**, since secondary sources may become primary sources through archiving.

Another way of looking at identity of historical sources consists of considering them as *sortals*. A **sortal** (**+I**) is a class all of whose instances are identified in the same way. The class of secondary sources does not carry any identity criteria (i.e. a secondary source cannot be identified by any predefined set of characteristics). On the other hand, a primary source is always **+I**: its identity criteria cover all of its properties (in order for something to be a primary source, none of its properties is allowed to change).

Unity (**+U**) is the metaproperty of classes all of whose individuals are *wholes* under the same relation. A *whole* is an instance that, in opposition of *mere sums*,

Table 1. Ontological metaproperties of historical sources

Secondary sources	Primary sources
Endurant	(Strong) Endurant
Alive datasets	Dead datasets
Non-timestamped resources	Timestamped resources
Dereferenceable IRIs	Archive-only-dereferenceable IRIs
Anti-rigid $\sim$**R**	Rigid +**R**
Dependent (on the primary Source) +**D**	Independent -**D**
Not a sortal -**I**	A sortal +**I**
Unity +**U**	Anti-unity $\sim$**U**

does not create new instances of the same class it belongs to when an arbitrary subsection of such instance is considered. For instance, splitting a piece of *clay* in two, constitutes two pieces of *clay* (it is a *mere sum*), while this does not typically happen with e.g. instances of the class *person* (a *whole*). Primary sources are **anti-unity** ($\sim$**U**), since any part in which a primary source may decompose creates a new primary source. Think of historical objects for which only certain parts could be preserved; these parts constitute the genuine primary source. In case new parts of the object were found, these would constitute different independent primary sources. Secondary sources are +**U** because specific relations between their parts preserve their integrity as wholes, and arbitrary parts of them do not constitute secondary sources anymore.

Finally, a property is **dependent** (+**D**) if each instance of it implies the existence of another entity [4]. Primary sources are **independent** (-**D**), given that they can exist independently of other entities. However, secondary sources are +**D**: every secondary source is always *about* some existing primary source.

Table 1 shows the correspondence between the properties of primary and secondary sources. We model historical sources using the study of this Section and the considerations made in Section 1.

3   Linked Historical Data: From Modeling to Publishing

The model proposed in Section 2 conflicts with some of the basic LOD publishing principles, more concretely with the openness of the Web. The AAA rule (Anyone can say Anything about Any topic) is one of the essential principles of the Web, which also holds for RDF data. The IRI of a primary source can be used by anyone as a subject of an RDF statement; this changes the graph of the primary source, and breaks the basic principle of immutability of primary sources (see Section 1). In this Section we investigate mechanisms to publish Linked Historical Data as LOD according with the model of Section 2.

To solve this conflict, we propose *dereferenceability* as a mechanism to preserve the fundamental properties of primary sources and their interplay with secondary sources. Concretely, we propose a dereferencing service for authoritative digital archives hosting RDF graphs with two essential characteristics: *reliability* and *independence* (the overlap with the requirements for historical sources in

Section 1 is no coincidence). First, dereferenceability is the *only* mechanism by which users may know that they are talking about a primary source. Hence, it is necessary that, when asked, the authoritative archive provides information on whether it *knows* something about such primary source or not (e.g. via SPARQL ASK queries). This way we achieve *reliability*: the only reliable primary source triples are those for which the archive returns some description. This will not happen with triples about the primary source issued by anybody else.

Second, when users dereference triples of a primary source, they get back *copies* of it, where all IRIs are replaced by new ones, but refer back to the original primary source IRI (or IRIs inside the primary source graph) through `prov:wasDerivedFrom` relations. This way we achieve *independence*: new statements (i.e. secondary sources) refer to this qualified copy independently on the original contents of the in-archive primary source graph, preserving its independence and immutability. Alternatively, the resolution creates a new FRBR (Functional Requirements for Bibliographic Records[2]) expression of the same FRBR work, but then the primary source is also an expression (the first).[3] URN resolution mechanisms (cf. DOIs) could also be used, such that users have to use a trusted dereferencing service at the archive location to obtain the primary source data (e.g. crossref dereferences DOIs at `http://dx.doi.org/` to the document's publisher landing page, or to an RDF representation of the source).

With our proposed model and publishing study, we can now answer the question: what is Linked Historical Data? Historical data is the union of *primary sources P* and *secondary sources S*: (a) a *primary source P* is an accumulation of strong-endurant, dead, timestamped, only-archive-dereferenceable, rigid, independent, sortal, and anti-unity resources; (b) a *secondary source S* is an accumulation of endurant, alive, non-timestamped, dereferenceable-by-anyone, anti-rigid, dependent, non-sortal, and unity resources; (c) statements in S contain links to statements in P; and (d) for any time t in which a statement of P is made, and for any time t' in which a statement of S is made, $t' > t$.

In this paper we argue for an ontological model and a consequent adequate publication of historical sources as RDF graphs in the LOD cloud. We advocate the use of the OntoClean methodology and DOLCE to give characterizations of *primary* and *secondary sources*. We propose the implementation of specific IRI dereferencing services in digital archives to preserve these fundamental properties of historical sources in the form of *independence* and *reliability*.

Acknowledgements. This work was supported by the Computational Humanities Programme of the KNAW (see `http://ehumanities.nl`) and the Dutch national program COMMIT. We acknowledge suggestions contributed by colleagues, especially Christophe Guéret.

---

[2] See `http://www.loc.gov/cds/downloads/FRBR.PDF`

[3] An *expression* is "the specific intellectual or artistic form that a work takes each time it is 'realized.'" For instance, an expression of Beethoven's 9th Symphony might be each draft of the musical score he writes down – not the paper itself, but the music thereby expressed.

References

1. Australia, J.C.U.: Primary, secondary and tertiary sources.
   http://libguides.jcu.edu.au/primary
2. Benjamin, J.R.: A Student's Guide to History. Bedfors/St. Martin's, Boston (2004)
3. Gangemi, A., Guarino, N., Masolo, C., Oltramari, A., Schneider, L.: Sweetening ontologies with DOLCE. In: Gómez-Pérez, A., Benjamins, V.R. (eds.) EKAW 2002. LNCS (LNAI), vol. 2473, pp. 166–181. Springer, Heidelberg (2002)
4. Guarino, N., Welty, C.A.: A Formal Ontology of Properties. In: Dieng, R., Corby, O. (eds.) EKAW 2000. LNCS (LNAI), vol. 1937, pp. 97–112. Springer, Heidelberg (2000), http://dx.doi.org/10.1007/3-540-39967-4_8
5. Helge S. Kragh: An Introduction to the Historiography of Science. Cambridge University Press (1989)
6. Katherine Hawley: "Temporal Parts". The Stanford Encyclopedia of Philosophy (Winter edn.) (2010),
   http://plato.stanford.edu/archives/win2010/entries/temporal-parts/
7. Meroño-Peñuela, A., Ashkpour, A., van Erp, M., Mandemakers, K., Breure, L., Scharnhorst, A., Schlobach, S., van Harmelen, F.: Semantic Technologies for Historical Research: A Survey. Semantic Web Journal (2012)
8. Boonstra, O.W.A., Doorn, P.K., van Horik, M.P.M., van Maarseveen, J.G.S.J., Oudhof, J.: Twee eeuwen Nederland geteld. Onderzoek met de digitale Volks-, Beroeps- en Woningtellingen 1795–2001. DANS en CBS (2007)
9. World Wide Web Consortium: RDF 1.1 Concepts and Abstract Syntax., http://www.w3.org/TR/rdf11-concepts/

A Quality Assurance Workflow for Ontologies Based on Semantic Regularities

Eleni Mikroyannidi[1], Manuel Quesada-Martínez[2], Dmitry Tsarkov[1],
Jesualdo Tomás Fernández Breis[2], Robert Stevens[1], and Ignazio Palmisano[1]

[1] University of Manchester, Oxford Road, Manchester M13 9PL
{mikroyannidi,tsarkov,stevens,palmisano}@cs.manchester.ac.uk
[2] Universidad de Murcia, IMIB-Arrixaca, CP 30100 Murcia
{manuel.quesada,jfernand}@um.es

Abstract. *Syntactic regularities* or *syntactic patterns* are sets of axioms in an OWL ontology with a regular structure. Detecting these patterns and reporting them in human readable form should help the understanding the authoring style of an ontology and is therefore useful in itself. However, pattern detection is sensitive to syntactic variations in the assertions; axioms that are semantically equivalent but syntactically different can reduce the effectiveness of the technique. Semantic regularity analysis focuses on the knowledge encoded in the ontology, rather than how it is spelled out, which is the focus of syntactic regularity analysis. Cluster analysis of the information provided by an OWL DL reasoner mitigates this sensitivity, providing measurable benefits over purely syntactic patterns - an example being patterns that are instantiated only in the entailments of an ontology. In this paper, we demonstrate, using SNOMED-CT, how the detection of semantic regularities in entailed axioms can be used in ontology quality assurance, in combination with lexical techniques. We also show how the detection of *irregularities*, i.e., deviations from a pattern, are useful for the same purpose. We evaluate and discuss the results of performing a semantic pattern inspection and we compare them against existing work on *syntactic regularity* detection. Systematic extraction of *lexical*, *syntactic* and *semantic patterns* is used and a quality assurance workflow that combines these patterns is presented.

1 Introduction

In ontology engineering (in this paper, ontology stands for Web Ontology Language ontology, or OWL ontology), the use and recognition of patterns is important during authoring as it facilitates ontology understanding, verification of compliance with coding guidelines, best practices and mandated axiom patterns [1]. A regular ontology, i.e., an ontology with regular structure, shows coherent organisation of the knowledge. For example, biomedical ontologies like SNOMED-CT[1] [19] or FMA[2] [16,17] mandate regular design for similar concepts such as symmetrical parts of the body or description of diseases. A regular

---

[1] http://goo.gl/aOSJm
[2] http://goo.gl/mbvama

K. Janowicz et al. (Eds.): EKAW 2014, LNAI 8876, pp. 288–303, 2014.
© Springer International Publishing Switzerland 2014

design should ease the maintenance and extension of the ontology and is thus a desirable quality of an ontology.

We call a set of axioms with reoccurring (regular) syntactic structure a *syntactic regularity* or *syntactic pattern* [9]. The terms regularity and pattern will be used interchangeably in the remainder of this paper.

A regularity can be expressed with a *generalisation*, or *generalised axiom*. A *generalisation* is an axiom in which some of the entities are replaced with variables. An *instantiation* is an axiom, occurring in an ontology, where all variables are bound to actual entities or expressions.

An example generalisation and one of its *instantiations*, found in SNOMED-CT, are shown in Figure 1. In Figure 1 the link between generalisation and instantiation is in the variable bindings (e.g. ?C is bound to 'Chronic kidney disease stage 3 (disorder)'. The RoleGroup property is used syntactically to group together closely related characteristics like morphologies, disorders etc [18]. Clustering based methods for detecting such syntactic regularities using the Regularity Inspector for Ontologies (RIO) framework and their use for quality assurance are described in [9,10].

Regularity:

?C ⊑ ?D ⊓ ∃RoleGroup.(∃'Clinical course (attribute)'.'Chronic (qualifier value)')

Bindings:

?C = 'Chronic kidney disease stage 3 (disorder)',

?D = 'Chronic renal impairment (disorder)'

Example Instantiation:

'Chronic kidney disease stage 3 (disorder)' ⊑ 'Chronic renal impairment (disorder)'

⊓ (∃RoleGroup(∃'Clinical course (attribute)'.'Chronic (qualifier value)'))

Fig. 1. Example regularity and axiom instantiation found in SNOMED-CT

SNOMED-CT is the official clinical terminology in many countries, and is internationally considered to be key for the achievement of semantic interoperability in healthcare [4,24]. Previous work on quality assurance for SNOMED-CT, with respect to its patterns, has been done with manual inspection of its asserted axioms and the formulation of queries to detect irregularities, such as missing restrictions [15,14].

Such quality assurance is usually guided through *lexical patterns* in the labels of an ontology's components. We call a *lexical pattern* a set of classes whose labels share a common group of consecutive words [12].

For example, the documentation for SNOMED-CT states that terms having the keyword "Chronic" in their label should instantiate the following documented pattern:

?Chronic_class ⊑ ?Findings ⊓ ∃RoleGroup.'Chronic (qualifier value)'

In this documented pattern, the variable ?Chronic_class holds all entities from the ontology that have the keyword "chronic" in their label while the variable ?Finding holds entities which are defined as 'findings' in the ontology, related with the chronic entity. The syntactic regularity in Figure 1, detected by RIO, conforms to this pattern.

It has been observed in [10] that intended design patterns, like "Chronic", are not fully revealed by syntactic analysis, as they can be only partially instantiated in the asserted axioms, while portions of them only appear in the ontology entailments [10]. As a result, these regularities revealed by inference are invisible to analysis of syntatic patterns. The inclusion of entailments in the detection is therefore required to gain a better overview of the ontology structure in terms of its regularities or irregularities.

Moreover, syntactic variations without semantic consequences can influence the detection of syntactic regularities, while the ontology entailments are not affected by such changes. This syntactic sensitivity is likely to cause ontology engineers to spend more effort to understand the underlying patterns.

Similar to a syntactic regularity, a *semantic regularity* abstracts over a set of entailments with the same repetitive structure. The concepts of generalisation and instantiation are extended to cover semantic regularities as well as syntactic regularities.

The contribution of this paper is as follows: (1) We present an extension to RIO for dealing with entailments and use it detect semantic regularities. We present the Knowledge Explorer Graph (KE), which is a tool for entailment extraction. (2) We describe a new Ontology Quality Assurance Workflow (QAW) by combining the existing approach in RIO with the detection of semantic regularities, guided by lexical pattern analysis. (3) We extend the analysis in [10] to other parts of SNOMED-CT and highlight benefits in terms of isolating irregularities by using semantic patterns.

We show that , by detecting patterns that escape syntactic analysis, semantic pattern analysis gives a better overview of the structure of an ontology than the syntactic patterns alone; this is demonstrated by presenting cases in which entities share semantic patterns but not syntactic ones.

1.1   Related Work

Related work on the detection of patterns in ontologies has mainly focused on the supervised detection of regularities. The method for matching axioms with ontology design patterns described in [8] cannot detect knowledge patterns [2] and only detects patterns included in the Ontology Design Pattern catalogue. TEIRESIAS [3] supports the exploration of structural patterns, but the process is guided by the user. In the same context, supervised methods for mining patterns from ontologies with DL-safe rules [7] and through SPARQL queries [20] have been proposed. The methods presented in this paper are unsupervised and are not limited to identifying the patterns existing in a catalogue. In terms of lexical pattern detection, the authors in [22] formalized the concept of simple and complex labels, and use them to define and detect "defining axioms".

2   Pattern-Based Ontology Quality Assurance Workflow

Figure 2 shows our Quality Assurance Workflow (QAW), which couples lexical pattern detection with semantic and syntactic pattern detection. This QAW

(Figure 2) is based on the notion of *"lexically suggest and logically define"* [14]. This means that terms that appear to have regularities in their names should instantiate a corresponding pattern in their axioms (e.g. terms with the "Chronic" keyword in their label should instantiate a pattern with the 'Chronic (qualifier value)').

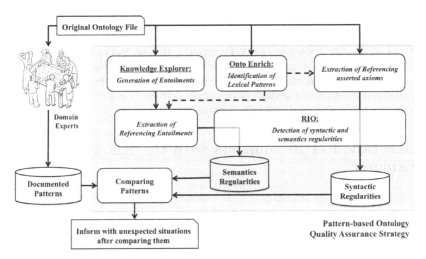

Fig. 2. The pattern-based Quality Assurance Workflow (QAW) for an ontology

First, we use the OntoEnrich tool [12] for detecting entities in the ontology matching a particular lexical pattern.

Second, we extract asserted axioms (for detecting syntactic regularities) and entailed axioms (for detecting semantic regularities) that reference these entities.

Third, we apply RIO on the extracted axioms to compute syntactic [9] and semantic regularities respectively. For the computation of semantic regularities, we first perform clustering on the signature of the extracted entailments to find groups of similar entities with respect to their usage in the entailments. After, we rewrite the semantic regularities as generalisations.

Lastly, we evaluate the patterns obtained, inspecting and comparing the syntactic and semantic regularities. We also evaluate these regularities with respect to an expected group of patterns, which are documented or suggested by the ontology developers. This can help isolate irregularities; for example, spotting entities that have a common lexical pattern but are missing a corresponding axiomatic pattern.

3   Detection of Lexical Patterns in an Ontology

The details for the automatic extraction of lexical patterns are described in [13]. Our method initially processes the ontology with $\mathcal{O}$ and extracts the labels, which are split into tokens using any white space character as a delimiter. Then, we create a graph using the label tokens. Each token is represented as a node in a graph, and two tokens that appear consecutively and in consistent order in a label are linked through an edge in the graph. Finding a lexical pattern of length N tokens requires navigation through N edges starting from an initial node. We can obtain the whole set of lexical patterns within an ontology by repeating the process in all the nodes of the graph.

A coverage threshold is used by our method to guide the lexical pattern detection, enabling filtering out of less frequent lexical patterns. For example, lexical patterns that appear in two labels might be considered insignificant. In SNOMED-CT, the most frequent lexical patterns are *disorder* (22.3%) and *procedure* (17.09%), but they are also very general. In this work, an initial analysis of SNOMED-CT will be performed at different coverage thresholds to select the lexical patterns that will form the input to the next steps of the workflow. Examples of a multi-word lexical pattern are *benign neoplasm of* or *biopsy of*, which are found in 632 and 988 labels respectively.

4   Generation of Entailments with the Knowledge Explorer

The axioms entailed by an ontology are extracted with the *Knowledge Explorer* (KE); an API for providing a graph of the TBox entailments, based on the completion graph generated by the FaCT++ tableaux reasoner [23]. For the entailment generation, we use KE with the whole ontology as input and then we extract the entailments referencing entities within a lexical pattern.

KE is an extension of the OWLAPI OWLReasoner: it is a Java interface that allows client code to explore the completion tree built by a tableaux reasoner. The interface and documentation of KE are available on the OWLAPI web site[3]. The KE provides convenient methods for the computation of entailments occurring between complex classes. The entailments obtained through KE have the same characteristics of soundness and completeness of the implementing reasoner; the advantage over using a plain reasoner is that KE allows faster access to the completion graph, not available through OWLReasoner.

Conceptually, KE represents a graph based on the exploration of a single model that a reasoner builds while it checks the TBox consistency. More formally,

Definition 1 (Completion graph). *The* completion graph *is a directed graph* $G = \langle V, E, \mathcal{L} \rangle$, *where* V *is a nonempty set of* nodes, $E \subseteq V \times V$ *is a set of* edges, *and* $\mathcal{L}$ *maps every* $v \in V$ *to a set of classes, and every* $e \in E$ *to a set of properties.*

Such a completion graph is produced by a tableaux-based reasoner during satisfiability check. A completion graph corresponding to a satisfiability check for a class A w.r.t. ontology $\mathcal{O}$ (whether or not $\mathcal{O} \models A \sqsubseteq \bot$) has the features [6]:

1. There is a root node $r \in V$ such that $A \in \mathcal{L}(r)$
2. For every class $B \in \mathcal{L}(r)$, $O \models A \sqsubseteq B$, where A and B are classes.
3. Every edge in the graph corresponds to a $\exists R.C$ or $\geq nR.C$ class in a label[4] of its starting nodes.

---

[3] http://goo.gl/VqEaU2
[4] The label here is different from the label of Section 3.

4. For every node x and class C, the reasons for $C \in \mathcal{L}(x)$ include:
   - There is a class B: $B \in \mathcal{L}(x)$ and $\mathcal{O} \models B \sqsubseteq C$;
   - There is a node y: $(y, x) \in E$ and $R \in \mathcal{L}(y, x)$ and either $\exists R.C \in \mathcal{L}(y)$ or $\forall R.C \in \mathcal{L}(y)$

Entailments Considered: The entailments that are extracted from KE are of the form $A \sqsubseteq B$ and $A \equiv B$, where A is always an atomic class and B can be an atomic or complex class. Both trivial (i.e., asserted) entailments and non-trivial entailments are included in the set of extracted entailments.

The grammar for B is:

$$B \rightarrow \top | A | B \sqcap B | \exists R.B$$

This grammar leads to infinite instantiations, which is due to the possibility of an infinite number of non-trivial entailments. For example, we can have entailments of the form $A \sqsubseteq \exists R.A$, $A \sqsubseteq \exists R.R.A$ and so on. In order to extract a finite set of entailments and to ensure the termination of exploration in KE, we rely on the reasoner. The models of a concept expression must be tree-like. They might have infinite branches, which can be unrolled cycles or infinitely long branches. In such cases, the reasoner uses blocking techniques to ensure termination [5]. Thus, the KE provides only the part of a branch up to its first repetition. This cover both infinitely long branches and unrolled cycles.

There are also implementation restrictions: at the time of writing, the following cannot be directly extracted from the KE: (1) expressions containing non-simple properties, e.g. $\mathcal{O} \models A \sqsubseteq \exists R.C$, where R is a non-simple property[5]. These expressions are not explored further and they are skipped. (2) in Definition 1, for $\exists R.C \in \mathcal{L}(y)$ or $\forall R.C \in \mathcal{L}(y)$, R is always an object property. These limitations are dependent on the current FaCT++ implementation, not on the KE interface itself.

Computation of Entailments: Algorithm 1 computes a set of entailments S from the KE. To achieve this, it uses the recursive Algorithm 2 (GETFILLERS(R)) to explore all descendant nodes to the ROOTNODE. Algorithm 1 in step 10 calls the function CHECKENTAILMENTS (Algorithm 3) to check if the created axioms α, β are entailed by the ontology $\mathcal{O}$. This guarantees that extracted entailments from the KE are always valid. In addition, KE provides several methods to access the graph, namely: (1) GETROOTNODE(A) returns the root node of a graph for a class A; (2) GETLABEL(x) returns a set $\{B : B \in \mathcal{L}(x)\}$ (3) GETPROPERTIES(x) returns $\{R : \exists y, (x, y) \in E, R \in \mathcal{L}(x, y)\}$; (4) GETNEIGHBOURS($x, R$) returns $\{y : (x, y) \in E, R \in \mathcal{L}(x, y)\}$;

Algorithm 1 can be used with any consistent OWL-DL ontology as it does not add any constraints on the reasoning process.

5   Semantic Pattern Detection

We use a pattern detection process similar to the knowledge discovery process [21]. The main steps for the computation of semantic regularities are: (1) extraction of a set of entailments n from the KE; (2) computation of pairwise

---

[5] Non-simple property is defined in [11].

Algorithm 1. ComputeKnowledgeExplorationAxioms($\mathcal{O}$)

Input: $\mathcal{O}$ an ontology
Output: A set of entailments S, such that $\mathcal{O} \models S$;
1: $S \leftarrow \emptyset$
2: **for all** $A \in Sig(\mathcal{O})$ that $\mathcal{O} \not\models A \sqsubseteq \bot$ **do**
3:     $R \leftarrow \text{GETROOTNODE}(A)$
4:     **for all** $p \in \text{GETPROPERTIES}(R)$ **do**
5:         $F \leftarrow \emptyset$ ▷ p-fillers
6:         **for all** $N \in \text{GETNEIGHBOURS}(R, p)$ **do**
7:             $F \leftarrow F \cup \text{GETFILLERS}(N)$
8:         **end for**
9:     **end for**
10:     $S \leftarrow S \cup \text{CHECKENTAILMENTS}(A, p, F)$
11: **end for**
12: **return** S

Algorithm 2. getFillers (R)

Input: A node R
Output: A set of complex classes Fillers;
1: Fillers $\leftarrow \text{GETLABEL}(R) \cup \{\top\}$
2: **for all** $p \in \text{GETPROPERTIES}(R)$ **do**
3:     **for all** $N \in \text{GETNEIGHBOURS}(R, p)$ **do**
4:         **for all** $C \in \text{GETFILLERS}(N)$ **do**
5:             Fillers $\leftarrow$ Fillers $\cup \{\exists p.C\}$
6:         **end for**
7:     **end for**
8: **end for**
9: **return** Fillers

---

similarity distances for all the entities in the $Sig(n)$; (3) computation of clusters of similar entities in the $Sig(n)$; (4) formulation of generalisations that describe clusters of similar entities. Steps (2)-(4) are similar to the detection of syntactic regularities described in [9], thus we do not show details on these steps but just an outline. The main difference is that the detection of syntactic regularities is done on the basis of asserted axioms while the detection of semantic regularities is done on the basis of entailments.

To demonstrate the main points for the semantic pattern computation we will use a simplified example from SNOMED-CT with three classes, e1 =Chronic kidney disease stage 3 (disorder), e2 =Chronic lung disease (disorder), e3 =Chronic eczema (disorder). A subset of their extracted entailments based on KE is shown in Table 1.

Entity Pairwise Similarity Distance. In order to decide the variable in our patterns (e.g. ?chronic_class variable that holds all chronic entities or entities with similar content) we perform clustering in the signature of the entailments. The clusters of similar entities are represented with variables in the generalisations.

In clustering, the distance measure defines the shape of clusters. In RIO, the distance between two entities is defined with respect to their usage in the entailments. For its computation we use a replacement function for abstracting the entailments. That is:

Replacement Function ϕ. Given an ontology $\mathcal{O}$, and a set of entailments S for $\mathcal{O}$, we define $\Phi = \{$?class, ?objectProperty, ?dataProperty, ?star $\}$ a set of four symbols that do not appear in the $Sig(\mathcal{O})$. A placeholder replacement is a function $\phi : Sig(\mathcal{O}) \rightarrow Sig(\mathcal{O}) \cup \Phi$ which, when applied to an entity $e \in Sig(S)$, returns: (1) one of e, ?star or ?class if e is a class name; (2) one of e, ?star or

---

Algorithm 3. checkEntailments (A, p, Fillers)

Input: a class A, objectProperty p, a set of classes Fillers;
Output: A set of entailments S, such that $\mathcal{O} \models S$

1: $S \leftarrow \emptyset$
2: **for all** $C \in$ Fillers **do**
3:     Axiom $\alpha \leftarrow$ A $\sqsubseteq \exists$p.C $\sqcup$A $\equiv \exists$p.C
4:     **if** $\mathcal{O} \models \alpha$ **then** $S \leftarrow S \cup \{\alpha\}$
5:     **end if**
6:     Axiom $\beta \leftarrow$ A $\sqsubseteq \forall$p.C $\sqcup$A $\equiv \forall$p.C
7:     **if** $\mathcal{O} \models \beta$ **then** $S \leftarrow S \cup \{\beta\}$
8:     **end if**
9: **end for**
10: **return** S

?objectProperty if e is an object property name; (3) one of e, ?star or ?dataProperty if e is a data property name; (4) one of e, ?star or ?individual if e is an individual name. Thus, the ϕ decides whether or not to replace an entity e with a symbol based on some decision criteria. Since the set of entailments S we extract contains only class names and object property names, only cases (1) and (2) are relevant in this work. Then, the pairwise distance between two entities is defined as:

Definition 2 (Distance). *Let $\mathcal{O}$ be an ontology, S a set of entailments for $\mathcal{O}$, σ_i and σ_j two entities from $Sig(S)$, Σ and ϕ a placeholder replacement function. We denote A_i the set $\{\phi(Ax(\alpha)), \alpha \in S, \sigma_i \in Sig(\alpha)\}$, i.e: the set of placeholder replacements for the entailments in S that reference σ_i. We define the distance between the two entities, $(\sigma_i, \sigma_j) \in \Sigma x \Sigma$ as:*

$$d(\sigma_i, \sigma_j) \leftarrow \frac{|A_i \cup A_j| - |A_i \cap A_j|}{|A_i \cup A_j|}$$

The distance between two entities e_1, e_2 is computed as an overlap between their referencing entailments that have been transformed into more abstract forms by the placeholder function ϕ. The defined distance is always in the interval $[0,1]$, where 0 means that the two entities are identical and 1 that they have no similarity.

ϕ is used to enable comparison between the referencing entailments of e_1 and e_2. Different decision criteria can be used for ϕ; Here we use a *popularity based replacement function*, which has been used previously in [9] and determines our distance as follows: When computing $d(e_1, e_2)$, for each entailment a where either occurs, the function replaces e_1 or e_2 with ?star and decides whether to replace the other entities with a placeholder depending on their popularity across all the entailments that have the same *structure* as a

The application of ϕ in the entailments of e1, e2, e3[6] when computing the pairwise distances will result in the abstracted entailments of Table 2. Thus, the distances are computed as an overlap of the entailments from Table 2 and are $d(e1, e2)=0.5$, $d(e1, e3)=0$, $d(e2, e3)=0.5$.

Clustering and Generalised Entailments. We use *agglomerative hierarchical clustering (AHC)*; it is a common solution to unsupervised detection of

---

[6] For simplicity, we consider only the entailments of Table 1 as referencing entailments of e1, e2, e3.

Table 1. Example entailments of three SNOMED-CT 'Chronic' classes

a1 = 'Chronic kidney disease stage 3' ⊑ 'Disease'
a2 = 'Chronic kidney disease stage 3' ⊑ 'Chronic renal impairment'
a3 = 'Chronic kidney disease stage 3' ⊑ ∃RoleGroup.(∃'Clinical course'. ('SNOMED CT Concept' ⊓ 'Descriptor' ⊓ 'Time patterns' ⊓ 'Special atomic mapping values' ⊓ 'Courses' ⊓ 'Special disorder atoms' ⊓ 'Qualifier value' ⊓ Chronic)
b1 = 'Chronic lung disease' ⊑ Disease
b2 = 'Chronic lung disease' ⊑ Disorder of body system
b3 = 'Chronic lung disease' ⊑ ∃RoleGroup.(∃'Clinical course'. ('SNOMED CT Concept' ⊓ 'Descriptor' ⊓ 'Time patterns' ⊓ 'Special atomic mapping values' ⊓ 'Courses' ⊓ 'Special disorder atoms' ⊓ 'Qualifier value' ⊓ Chronic)
c1 = 'Chronic eczema' ⊑ Disease
c2 = 'Chronic eczema' ⊑ Disorder of integument
c3 = 'Chronic eczema' ⊑ ∃RoleGroup.(∃'Clinical course'. ('SNOMED CT Concept' ⊓ 'Descriptor' ⊓ 'Time patterns' ⊓ 'Special atomic mapping values' ⊓ 'Courses' ⊓ 'Special disorder atoms' ⊓ 'Qualifier value' ⊓ Chronic)

clusters, and we use it in favor of other algorithms like k-means as we do not have a predetermined number of clusters.

An AHC algorithm takes as input a *proximity matrix* that holds all pairwise distances for the entities in the $Sig(S)$, where S is the set of entailments in which we are interested in finding patterns. AHC initialises every cluster with a single entity and merges clusters as long as all pairwise distances between the two clusters are less than 1 (maximal distance). In every agglomeration step the proximity matrix is updated according to the Lance-Williams formula [21].

After the computation of clusters, the generalisations (semantic patterns) are formed with respect to these clusters. In particular, the entailments that reference entities in a cluster are rewritten by replacing such entities with its corresponding cluster variable. In our example, the entities e1, e2, e3 end up in the same cluster (cluster_1), while 'Disease' ends up in cluster_18 along with another 15 classes. Thus, the generalisation ?c_1 ⊑ ?c_18 has a1 from Table 1 as instantiation. The final generalisation should not be confused with the intermediate abstractions of Table 2 used for computing the pairwise distances.

Variable Naming: Having an informative name for a variable of a cluster should facilitate the inspection of the generalisations by ontology engineers. The name of a variable is selected to be the name of the least common subsumer of the entities in the corresponding cluster. If the least common subsumer is the ⊤ (owl:Thing) entity, then a generic name is selected as the name of the cluster variable (e.g. c_i, where i denotes the sequence of the cluster like ?c_15 to denote cluster number 15). With this approach we try, when possible, to give variables a name that indicates the type of entities it holds.

Table 2. Abstracted entailments of e1, e2, e3 for the computation of their pairwise distances

Entailments of e1 for computing distances $d(e1, e2)$ and $d(e1, e3)$
$\phi(a1) =$?star $\sqsubseteq$ 'Disease'
$\phi(a2) =$?star $\sqsubseteq$?class
$\phi(a3) =$?star $\sqsubseteq$ ∃RoleGroup.(∃?objectProperty.
('SNOMED CT Concept' ⊓ 'Descriptor' ⊓ 'Time patterns'
⊓ ?class ⊓ 'Courses' ⊓ ?class ⊓ 'Qualifier value' ⊓ Chronic)

Entailments of e2 for computing distances $d(e2, e1)$ and $d(e2, e3)$
$\phi(b1) =$?star $\sqsubseteq$ 'Disease'
$\phi(b2) =$?star $\sqsubseteq$ Disorder of body system
$\phi(b3) =$?star $\sqsubseteq$ ∃RoleGroup.(∃?objectProperty.
('SNOMED CT Concept' ⊓ 'Descriptor' ⊓ 'Time patterns'
⊓ ?class ⊓ 'Courses' ⊓ ?class ⊓ 'Qualifier value' ⊓ Chronic)

Entailments of e3 for computing distances $d(e3, e1)$ and $d(e3, e2)$
$\phi(c1) =$?star $\sqsubseteq$ Disease
$\phi(c2) =$?star $\sqsubseteq$?class
$\phi(c3) =$?star $\sqsubseteq$ ∃RoleGroup.(∃?objectProperty.
('SNOMED CT Concept' ⊓ 'Descriptor' ⊓ 'Time patterns'
⊓ ?class ⊓ 'Courses' ⊓ ?class ⊓ 'Qualifier value' ⊓ Chronic)

Measuring Regularity: For checking the impact of regularities we define the following metric: Given a set of G generalisations (patterns), instantiated by A entailments, then the *mean instantiations per generalisations (MIPG)* is $MIPG = \frac{|A|}{|G|}$. Other metrics for assessing the patterns is the combination of number of clusters with the number of generalisations and mean instantiations per generalisation. For example, having many clusters, shows that RIO detected more deviations from a regularity. This can be verified by the number of generalisations which is high and the MIPG value which in that case is low. That means, that the user has to inspect many more regularities in order to get an intuition about the construction of the corresponding clustered entities.

6   Application of the QAW in SNOMED-CT

Our analysis consists of the following main steps: (1) Detection of entities with a particular lexical pattern. (2) Extraction of referencing asserted axioms (for detecting syntactic regularities) or entailments (for detecting semantic regularities) of these entities. (3) Application of RIO to the extracted axioms or entailments for the computation of syntactic and semantic regularities respectively. (4) Comparison of the syntactic and semantic regularities. (5) Verification of dominant regularities with expected patterns. (6) Isolation of irregularities. The irregularities we are dealing with are *(a) missing descriptions* with respect to a documented pattern, *(b) lexical irregularities.*

The analysis is divided into two parts: *(a) a qualitative analysis* performed with six sets of entities extracted from SNOMED-CT for which we can check

patterns with SNOMED-CT's documentation and with prior work on quality
assurance for SNOMED-CT; and *(b) a quantitative analysis* performed with a
larger set of 308 lexical patterns and extracted entities for which we describe
syntactic and semantic regularities and show how the workflow we suggest for
quality assurance can be generalised for different sets of entities that instantiate
a lexical pattern.

For the analysis we used the January 2013 release of SNOMED-CT. This
version consists of 296 529 axioms and is in the $\mathcal{EL}$ profile. The statistical analysis
along with the files containing the regularities can be found online[7].

6.1   Qualitative Analysis

An analysis similar to the one performed in [14,10] is done on six cases whose
label should comply with their axiomatic description. These six patterns refer
to (1) classes whose name includes the word "chronic" in the beginning or in
the middle of their label and are expected to be subclasses of ∃RoleGroup.Chronic
(qualifier value); (2) classes whose name includes the word "acute" in the beginning or in the middle of their label and are expected to be subclasses of
∃RoleGroup. Sudden onset AND/OR short duration (qualifier value), (3) classes whose
name includes the word "present" and are expected to be subclasses of the
∃RoleGroup.Present (qualifier value), (4) classes whose name includes the word "absent" and are expected to be subclasses of the ∃RoleGroup.Absent (qualifier value),
(5) classes that have the keywords "right" or (6) "left" in their names and
are expected to be subclasses of ∃Laterality (attribute).Right (qualifier value) and
∃Laterality (attribute).Left (qualifier value) respectively. We will call these sets of
entities *target entities*. In [10] pattern inspection was carried out on syntactic
patterns only.

Table 3 shows the analysis of semantic patterns for the target entities. Figure 3
shows the semantic patterns expected to be found for chronic and acute entities
along with one example instantiation. For the remaining cases, the results are
similar.

Comparison of Syntactic and Semantic Regularities: As shown in Table 3, there is a difference between syntactic and semantic regularities. Semantic
regularities are more uniform; that is because the entities with lexical patterns
are distributed in fewer clusters and the expected patterns are better formed
in most cases; we have fewer variations in the generalisations that refer to an
expected pattern. Also, because we consider the entailments, we do not miss any
information on the instantiation of the expected pattern. Therefore, semantic
regularities do not suffer from syntactic variations.

Semantic Irregularities: We compare the results with existing work on
quality assurance for "chronic", "acute" in [14]. Although this analysis uses
on an older version of SNOMED-CT (May 2010), the discrepancies still exist.
Our analysis also highlighted additional discrepancies. In particular, 14% of the
chronic classes do not instantiate the documented pattern, i.e., do not conform
to it; this includes the irregular classes reported in [14]. Only 2% of the chronic
classes conform to the pattern in the asserted axioms. This percentage increases
to 86% when considering the otnology entailments. Similarly for the other sets of

---

[7] http://goo.gl/RvvNL

Table 3. Regularity analysis, for the six sets of terms

Lexical pattern	Chronic		Acute		Present		Absent		Left		Right	
	Synt.	Sem.	Synt.	Sem.	Synt.	Sem.	Synt.	Sem.	Synt.	Sem.	Synt.	Sem.
# entities with a lexical regularity	1219		1611		747		443		2377		2105	
# referencing axioms/entailments of target entities	1593	25160	1774	31247	1956	12021	940	7844	2767	64251	2455	58848
# clusters	373	598	397	685	371	334	201	299	591	750	489	760
# of clusters that include the target entities	196	3	240	5	142	3	78	3	382	7	310	4
# of generalisations describing the target entities	1018	1844	1137	1880	914	1393	232	1050	1715	2112	1527	2032
# of instantiations referring to the target entities	1474	25160	1670	31247	1881	12021	891	7844	2580	64251	2244	58848
# of target entities that were excluded from clusters	573	0	723	0	143	0	83	0	941	0	889	0
# of generalisations whose instantiations refer to the documented pattern	2	3	6	1	10	2	7	2	3	1	4	2
# of instantiations referring to the documented pattern	26	1053	61	717	349	1041	108	330	52	589	51	586

classes—5% (61) of the "acute" classes is conform to the pattern in the asserted axioms, raising to 45% in the entailments. "Left" and "right" are more irregular as we have 75% of the "Left" classes and 72% of the "right" nonconformant classes.

Lexical Irregularities: The analysis of semantic regularities revealed entities whose referencing entailments were instantiating one of the expected patterns, but this was not followed by the label of their name. Such discrepancies were highlighted in the classes with the "present" lexical pattern. In particular, 294 were entailed to instantiate the documented pattern, without having the word "present" in their label. An example is the entity 'History of - diphtheria (situation)'; although its name is missing the keyword "Present", it is inferred to have a relationship with the Known present (qualifier value). This might be an intended deviation by the developers or a mistake in the labeling of these entities. Such irregularities can be isolated and reported to domain experts by our method; this is not possible with syntactic pattern analysis, as shown above; standard reasoning is not useful in this respect either, since the classes are not unsatisfiable. Semantic pattern analysis brings therefore a measurable improvement to the techniques available in this area.

6.2   Quantitative Analysis

The outline of this analysis is similar to the qualitative but it is missing the verification of false positives and false negatives. Here, based on the lexical pattern analysis we highlight 308 cases from SNOMED-CT and we show how our method can work for other sets of entities.

Detection of Lexical Patterns: To narrow down the scope of our analysis we pick lexical patterns that have the same coverage in the ontology as the ones

Generalisation:

?c_1 ⊑ ∃RoleGroup(∃Clinical course (attribute)(?c_1 ⊓ ?c_103 ⊓ ?c_143 ⊓ ?c_18))

Total Instantiations: 607

Example Bindings:

?c_103:CLASS = [Time patterns (qualifier value), Special disorder atoms (qualifier value),
    Courses (qualifier value), Special atomic mapping values (qualifier value),
    Qualifier value (qualifier value)]

?c_18:CLASS = [SNOMED CT Concept (SNOMED RT+CTV3)],

?c_143:CLASS = [Descriptor (qualifier value)],

?c_1:CLASS = [Chronic (qualifier value), Chronic renal failure syndrome (disorder)]

Example Instantiation:

'Chronic renal failure syndrome (disorder)' ⊑ ∃RoleGroup.
    (∃Clinical course (attribute).(SNOMED CT Concept (SNOMED RT+CTV3)
        ⊓ Descriptor (qualifier value) ⊓ Time patterns (qualifier value)
        ⊓ Special atomic mapping values (qualifier value) ⊓ Courses (qualifier value)
        ⊓ Special disorder atoms (qualifier value) ⊓ Qualifier value (qualifier value)
        ⊓ Chronic (qualifier value)))

(a) A semantic regularity describing the chronic pattern

Generalisation:

?c_1 ⊑ ∃RoleGroup.(∃Clinical course (attribute).(?c_157 ⊓ ?c_3 ⊓ ?c_35))

Total Instantiations: 736

Example Bindings

?c_35:CLASS = [Time patterns (qualifier value), Special disorder atoms (qualifier value),
    Courses (qualifier value), Sudden onset AND/OR short duration (qualifier value),
    Special atomic mapping values (qualifier value), Descriptor (qualifier value)]

?c_3:CLASS = [SNOMED CT Concept (SNOMED RT+CTV3)],

?c_157:CLASS = [Qualifier value (qualifier value)],

?c_1:CLASS = [Acute bacterial endocarditis (disorder)]

Example Instantiation:

Acute bacterial endocarditis (disorder) ⊑ ∃RoleGroup.(∃Clinical course (attribute)
    (SNOMED CT Concept (SNOMED RT+CTV3) ⊓ Descriptor (qualifier value)
        ⊓ Time patterns (qualifier value) ⊓ Special atomic mapping values (qualifier value)
        ⊓ Courses (qualifier value) ⊓ Special disorder atoms (qualifier value)
        ⊓ Qualifier value (qualifier value) ⊓ Sudden onset AND/OR short duration (qualifier value)))

(b) A semantic regularity describing the acute pattern

Fig. 3. Semantic regularities in SNOMED-CT describing (a) the "chronic" pattern and
(b) the "acute" documented pattern respectively

we picked for the qualitative analysis. The extraction of lexical patterns is based on the methods presented in [13] and we used the OntoEnrich tool [12]. The six lexical patterns of the qualitative analysis had a coverage between 0.1%–0.4% in the entities of the ontology. Thus, in the quantitative analysis we extract all classes that appear to have a lexical pattern in 0.1%–0.4% of the entities of the ontology. The intuition behind this is that this interval has more chances to contain labels that are relatively more meaningful with respect to the content of the ontology.

Table 4 is similar to Table 3 and it shows the total mean values for the syntactic and semantic regularities we generated for the 308 lexical patterns we processed according to the workflow of Figure 2.

Table 4. Average values of syntactic and semantic regularities for the 308 cases(extracted based on lexical patterns)

	Syntactic	Semantic
# entities with a lexical regularity (target entities)	521.2	
# referencing axioms/entailments of target entities	1086.57	10792.96
# clusters	218.79	203.82
# clusters that included the target entities	98.06	2.64
# generalisations describing the target entities	714.11	602.37
mean instantiations per generalisation	1.52	17.052
# of target entities that were excluded from clusters	291.42	0

The results in Table 4 show that the semantic regularities for classes with a lexical pattern are more uniform than syntactic regularities;the target entities are distributed in fewer clusters than in the syntactic regularities. Also although for the computation of the semantic regularities, both trivial and non-trivial entailments are considered, these are described with fewer generalisations. On the contrary, on the computation of the syntactic regularities, RIO produces more generalisations due to syntactic variations. The syntactic variations of the asserted axioms, also explain the fact that in the syntactic regularities many of the target entities are excluded from clusters and they do not have a detectable regularity. These results are comparable to the findings we get for the known cases presented in Table 3.

7 Conclusions

We have presented a novel approach to unsupervised detection of semantic patterns in an ontology based on cluster analysis of entities with similar usage in entailments. We introduced the Knowledge Explorer (KE) and presented the methods for extracting a finite set of entailments with a specific grammar from KE, that are used as an input to our algorithms for detecting semantic patterns. Future work will involve the inclusion of other types of entailments, such as class and property assertions and the comparison of alternative grammars.

We also presented a pattern based approach for quality assurance of large and complex ontologies, like SNOMED-CT. The quality assurance method we demonstrate checks the conformance with the pattern based construction of an ontology. In particular, the methods we suggest are based on the detection of lexical patterns in the terms of an ontology and then the detection of corresponding semantic regularities to verify conformance to an expected pattern. The work-flow is based on the intuition that terms with similar lexical description should also have a common logical description.

We tested and evaluated this hypothesis with six cases from SNOMED-CT. The results show the ability to gain meaningful patterns from the inferences of an ontology that can facilitate detection of quality assurance issues.

Our method highlighted entities that did not explicitly instantiate a pattern in their asserted axioms, but were found to instantiate it in the entailments of the ontology; lexical irregularities in the entities were also revealed – such cases could not be discovered by syntactic tools and could be only discovered by an ontology engineer after querying the ontology in question. The quantitative analysis performed with 308 similar cases in SNOMED-CT showed that the combination of lexical patterns with the patterns that RIO can reveal can be useful to inspect the construction of portions of the ontology, with strong implications for quality assurance in ontologies. The qualitative analysis showed that semantic patterns provide an improved picture of an intended pattern and the deviations from that pattern.

Acknowledgments. Manuel Quesada-Martínez is funded by the Spanish Ministry of Science and Innovation through TIN2010-21388-C02-02 and fellowship BES-2011-046192.

References

1. Blomqvist, E., Sandkuhl, K.: Patterns in ontology engineering: Classification of ontology patterns. In: ICEIS (3), pp. 413–416 (2005)
2. Clark, P.: Knowledge patterns. Knowledge Engineering: Practice and Patterns, pp. 1–3 (2008)
3. Davis, R.: Interactive transfer of expertise: Acquisition of new inference rules. Artificial Intelligence 12(2), 121–157 (1979)
4. European Commission. Semantic interoperability for better health and safer healthcare. deployment and research roadmap for Europe (2009) ISBN-13: 978-92-79-11139-6
5. Glimm, B., Horrocks, I., Motik, B.: Optimized Description Logic Reasoning via Core Blocking. In: Giesl, J., Hähnle, R. (eds.) IJCAR 2010. LNCS, vol. 6173, pp. 457–471. Springer, Heidelberg (2010)
6. Horrocks, I., Kutz, O., Sattler, U.: The even more irresistible SROIQ. In: Principles of Knowledge Representation and Reasoning, pp. 57–67 (2006)
7. Józefowska, J., Lawrynowicz, A., Lukaszewski, T.: Towards discovery of frequent patterns in description logics with rules. Rules and Rule Markup Languages for the Semantic Web, 84–97 (2005)
8. Khan, M.T., Blomqvist, E.: Ontology design pattern detection-initial method and usage scenarios. In: SEMAPRO 2010, The Fourth International Conference on Advances in Semantic Processing, pp. 19–24 (2010)
9. Mikroyannidi, E., Iannone, L., Stevens, R., Rector, A.: Inspecting regularities in ontology design using clustering. In: Aroyo, L., Welty, C., Alani, H., Taylor, J., Bernstein, A., Kagal, L., Noy, N., Blomqvist, E. (eds.) ISWC 2011, Part I. LNCS, vol. 7031, pp. 438–453. Springer, Heidelberg (2011)
10. Mikroyannidi, E., Stevens, R., Iannone, L., Rector, A.: Analysing Syntactic Regularities and Irregularities in SNOMED-CT. Journal of biomedical semantics 3(1), 8 (2012)

11. Motik, B., Patel-Schneider, P., Parsia, B., Bock, C., Fokoue, A., Haase, P., Hoek-stra, R., Horrocks, I., Ruttenberg, A., Sattler, U., et al.: OWL 2 Web Ontology Language: Structural Specification and Functional-Style Syntax. In: W3C Recommendation, 2nd edn., vol. 11 (2012)

12. Quesada-Martínez, M., Fernández-Breis, J.T., Stevens, R.: Enrichment of OWL ontologies: a method for defining axioms from labels. In: Moss, L., Sleeman, D. (eds.) Proceedings of the International Workshop on Capturing and Refining Knowledge in the Medical Domain (KMED 2012), Galway, Ireland, pp. 5–10 (2012)

13. Quesada-Martínez, M., Fernández-Breis, J.T., Stevens, R.: Lexical characterization and analysis of the bioPortal ontologies. In: Peek, N., Marín Morales, R., Peleg, M. (eds.) AIME 2013. LNCS, vol. 7885, pp. 206–215. Springer, Heidelberg (2013)

14. Rector, A., Iannone, L.: Lexically suggest, logically define: Quality assurance of the use of qualifiers and expected results of post-coordination in SNOMED CT. Journal of Biomedical Informatics 45(2), 199 (2012)

15. Rector, A.L., Brandt, S., Schneider, T.: Getting the foot out of the pelvis: modeling problems affecting use of SNOMED CT hierarchies in practical applications. Journal of the American Medical Informatics Association 18(4), 432–440 (2011)

16. Rosse, C., Mejino, J., et al.: A reference ontology for biomedical informatics: the Foundational Model of Anatomy. Journal of biomedical informatics 36(6), 478–500 (2003)

17. Rosse, C., Mejino Jr., J.L.: The foundational model of anatomy ontology. In: Anatomy Ontologies for Bioinformatics, pp. 59–117. Springer (2008)

18. Spackman, K., Dionne, R., Mays, E., Weis, J.: Role grouping as an extension to the description logic of ontylog, motivated by concept modeling in snomed. In: Proceedings of the AMIA Symposium, p. 712. American Medical Informatics Association (2002)

19. Spackman, K.A., Campbell, K.E., Côté, R.A.: SNOMED RT: a reference terminology for health care. In: Proceedings of the AMIA Annual Fall Symposium, p. 640. American Medical Informatics Association (1997)

20. Šváb-Zamazal, O., Scharffe, F., Svátek, V.: Preliminary results of logical ontology pattern detection using sparql and lexical heuristics. In: Proceedings of the Workshop on Ontology Patterns (WOP-2009) (2009)

21. Tan, P.-N., Steinbach, M., Kumar, V.: Introduction to Data Mining. Addison-Wesley (2005)

22. Third, A.: Hidden semantics: what can we learn from the names in an ontology? In: Proceedings of the Seventh International Natural Language Generation Conference, Utica, IL, USA (May 2012)

23. Tsarkov, D., Horrocks, I.: faCT++ description logic reasoner: System description. In: Furbach, U., Shankar, N. (eds.) IJCAR 2006. LNCS (LNAI), vol. 4130, pp. 292–297. Springer, Heidelberg (2006)

24. Wang, Y., Halper, M., Min, H., Perl, Y., Chen, Y., Spackman, K.: Structural methodologies for auditing snomed. Journal of Biomedical Informatics 40(5), 561–581 (2007)

Adaptive Knowledge Propagation in Web Ontologies

Pasquale Minervini, Claudia d'Amato, Nicola Fanizzi, and Floriana Esposito

Department of Computer Science - University of Bari, Italy
{firstname.lastname}@uniba.it

Abstract. The increasing availability of structured machine-processable knowledge in the WEB OF DATA calls for machine learning methods to support standard reasoning based services (such as query-answering and logic inference). Statistical regularities can be efficiently exploited to overcome the limitations of the inherently incomplete knowledge bases distributed across the Web. This paper focuses on the problem of predicting missing class-memberships and property values of individual resources in Web ontologies. We propose a transductive inference method for inferring missing properties about individuals: given a class-membership/property value learning problem, we address the task of identifying relations which are likely to link similar individuals, and efficiently propagating knowledge across such (possibly diverse) relations. Our experimental evaluation demonstrates the effectiveness of the proposed method.

1 Introduction

Standard query answering and reasoning services for the Semantic Web [2] (SW) largely rely on deductive inference. However, purely deductive reasoning with SW representations suffers from several limitations: inference tasks can be computationally complex, and distributed knowledge bases (KBs) are often characterized by incomplete and conflicting knowledge. In this context, many complex tasks (such as query answering, clustering or ranking) are ultimately based on assessing the truth value of ground facts. Deciding on the truth of specific facts (assertions) in SW knowledge bases requires to take into account the *open-world* form of reasoning adopted in this context: a failure on ascertaining the truth of a given fact does not imply that such fact is false, but rather that its truth value cannot be deductively inferred from the KB (e.g. because of a temporary lack of knowledge). This differs from the *Negation As Failure*, commonly used with databases and logic programs. Other issues are related to the distributed nature of the data across the Web. Cases of contradictory answers or flawed inferences may be caused by distributed pieces of knowledge that may be mutually conflicting.

The prediction of the truth value of an assertion can be cast as a *classification* problem to be solved through *statistical learning*: individual resources in an ontology can be regarded as statistical units, and their properties can be statistically inferred even when they cannot be deduced from the KB. Several approaches have been proposed in the SW literature (see [15] for a recent survey). A major issue with the methods proposed so far is that the induced statistical models (as those produced by kernel methods, tensor factorization, etc.) are either difficult to interpret by experts and to integrate in logic-based SW infrastructures, or computationally impractical.

K. Janowicz et al. (Eds.): EKAW 2014, LNAI 8876, pp. 304–319, 2014.

Related Work. A variety of methods have been proposed for predicting the truth value of assertions in Web ontologies: those include generative models [16], kernel methods [12], upgrading of propositional algorithms [11], matrix and tensor factorization methods [14, 19]. An issue with existing methods is that they either rely on a possibly expensive search process, or induce statistical models that are often not easy to interpret by human experts. Kernel methods induce models (such as separating hyperplanes) in a high-dimensional feature space implicitly defined by a kernel function. The underlying kernel function itself usually relies on purely syntactic features of the neighborhood graphs of two individual resources (such as their common subtrees [12] or isomorphic subgraphs [21]). In both cases, there is not necessarily a direct translation in terms of domain knowledge. Latent variable and matrix or tensor factorization methods such as [14, 16, 19] try to explain the observations in terms of latent classes or attributes, which also may be non-trivial to describe using the domain's vocabulary. The approach in [11] tries to overcome this limitation by making use of complex features defined using the ontology's terminology; however, this method involves a search process in a possibly very large feature space, which might not be feasible in practice.

Contribution. We propose a transductive inference method for predicting the truth value of assertions, which is based on the following intuition: individuals that are *similar* in some aspects tend to be linked by specific relations. Yet it may be not straightforward to determine such relations for a given learning task. Our approach aims at identifying such relations, and permits the efficient propagation of information through chains of related individuals. It turns out to be especially useful with real-world *shallow* ontologies, i.e. those with a relatively simple, fixed terminology and populated by very large amounts of instance data such as citation or social networks, in which related entities tend to influence each other. These are particularly frequent in the context of the *Linked Open Data* [7] (LOD).

Unlike other approaches, the proposed method can be used to identify which relations are likely to link examples with similar characteristics. Similarly to graph-based semi-supervised learning (SSL) methods [5], we rely on a similarity graph linking pairs of similar examples, for propagating knowledge among them. SSL methods are often designed for propositional representations, while the proposed method addresses the problem of learning from real ontologies, where examples (represented by individuals in the KB) can be interlinked by diverse relations. In particular, this article makes the following contributions:

- A method for efficiently *propagating* knowledge among similar examples: it leverages a similarity graph, which plays a critical role in the propagation process.
- An approach to *learning* an optimal similarity graph for a given prediction task, by leveraging a set of semantically diverse relations among examples in the ontology.

To the best of our knowledge, our approach is the first to explicitly identify relations that semantically encode similarities among examples w.r.t. a given learning task. The method proposed in this article is a significant advance w.r.t. our previous work in [13], in which we adopt kernel-defined weights to construct the similarity graph. However, such weights were lacking a meaningful interpretation.

The remainder of the paper is organized as follows. In Sect. 2, we review the basics of semantic knowledge representation and reasoning tasks, and we introduce the concept of *transductive learning* in the context of semantic KBs. In Sect. 3, we illustrate the proposed method, which is based on the efficient propagation of information among related examples, and address the problem of identifying which relations are likely to link similar examples. In Sect. 4, we provide empirical evidence for the effectiveness of the proposed method. In Sect. 5, we summarize the proposed approach, outline its limitations and discuss possible future research directions.

2 Transductive Learning with Web Ontologies

We assume the knowledge base (KB) is encoded in a syntactic variant of some *Description Logic* [1] (DL), and describes a set of objects, their attributes and relations. Basics elements are *atomic concepts* $N_C = \{C, D, \ldots\}$ interpreted as subsets of a domain of objects (e.g. Person or Article), and *atomic roles* $N_R = \{R, S, \ldots\}$ interpreted as binary relations on such a domain (e.g. friendOf or authorOf). Domain objects are represented by *individuals* $N_I = \{a, b, \ldots\}$, each associated to a domain entity (such as a person in a social network, or an article in a citation network).

Specifically, we consider KBs in the OWL 2 language [1], which has its theoretical foundations in DLs: concepts and roles are referred to as *classes* and *properties*, respectively. Classes, properties and individuals are represented in the ontology by their URIs. Each DL provides a set of constructors that can be used to build complex concept descriptions using atomic concepts and roles.

A DL KB $\mathcal{K} = \langle \mathcal{T}, \mathcal{A} \rangle$ is composed by two main components: a *TBox* $\mathcal{T}$, which contains terminological axioms, and an *ABox* $\mathcal{A}$, which contains ground axioms (called *assertions*) about individuals. In the following, we will denote as $\mathsf{Ind}(\mathcal{A})$ the set of individuals occurring in $\mathcal{A}$.

As inference procedure, *Instance Checking* consists in deciding whether $\mathcal{K} \models Q(a)$ (where Q is a query concept and a is an individual) holds. Because of the *Open-World Assumption*, instance checking may provide three possible outcomes, i.e. i) $\mathcal{K} \models Q(a)$, ii) $\mathcal{K} \models \neg Q(a)$ and iii) $\mathcal{K} \not\models Q(a) \wedge \mathcal{K} \not\models \neg Q(a)$. This means that failing to deductively infer the membership of an individual a to a concept Q does not imply that a is a member of its complement $\neg Q$.

It is also possible to express more complex queries: given a (infinite) set of variables N_V, a *Conjunctive Query* q is a conjunction of concept or role atoms ($C(v)$ or $R(v, v')$, with $v, v' \in N_V \cup N_I$) built on the signature of $\mathcal{K}$. The set of its variables $\mathrm{VAR}(q)$ is composed by *answer variables* and (existentially) *quantified variables*. Informally, a binding of the variables w.r.t. some model of $\mathcal{K}$ determines the satisfiability of a query and a result via the answer variables values. $\mathcal{K} \models q$ denotes the satisfiability of q w.r.t. all models of $\mathcal{K}$.

In this work, we focus on *transductive learning* [20] rather than *inductive learning*. Inductive learning focuses on the creation of general rules, which are then applied to test cases, while transductive learning focuses on generalizing directly from observed training cases to specific test cases.

---

[1] OWL 2 W3C Recommendation: http://www.w3.org/TR/owl-overview/

The main motivation behind the choice of transductive learning is described by the *main principle* in [20]: "If you possess a restricted amount of information for solving some problem, try to solve the problem directly and never solve a more general problem as an intermediate step. It is possible that the available information is sufficient for a direct solution but is insufficient for solving a more general intermediate problem".

On the ground of the available information, the method proposed in this work aims at learning a *labeling function* for a given target class that can be used for predicting whether examples, represented by individuals in the knowledge base, are members of a target class C (positive class) or to its complement $\neg C$ (negative class), when this cannot be deductively inferred. This setting is closely related to the *transductive classification* setting in e.g. [22].

Formally, the problem can be defined as follows:

Definition 2.1 (Transductive Class-Membership Learning).
Given:

- *a target* class C *in a KB* $\mathcal{K}$;
- *a set of examples* $X \subseteq \mathsf{Ind}(\mathcal{A})$ *partitioned into:*
  - *a set of* positive examples: $X_+ \triangleq \{a \in X \mid \mathcal{K} \models C(a)\}$;
  - *a set of* negative examples: $X_- \triangleq \{a \in X \mid \mathcal{K} \models \neg C(a)\}$;
  - *a set of* neutral *(unlabeled) examples:* $X_0 \triangleq \{a \in X \mid a \notin X_+ \wedge a \notin X_-\}$;
- *a set of* labeling functions $\mathcal{F}$ *with domain* X *and range* $\{-1, +1\}$, *i.e.*

$$\mathcal{F} \triangleq \{\mathbf{f} \mid \mathbf{f} : X \to \{+1, -1\}\};$$

- *a* cost function $\mathrm{cost}(\cdot) : \mathcal{F} \mapsto \mathbb{R}$ *defined over labeling functions in* $\mathcal{F}$;

Find $\mathbf{f}^* \in \mathcal{F}$ *minimizing* $\mathrm{cost}(\cdot)$ *w.r.t.* X:

$$\mathbf{f}^* \leftarrow \arg\min_{\mathbf{f} \in \mathcal{F}} \mathrm{cost}(\mathbf{f}).$$

The transductive learning task is cast as the problem of finding a *labeling function* $\mathbf{f}^*$ for a target class C, defined over a finite set of *labeled* (if positive or negative) and *unlabeled* (if their membership to the target class cannot be determined) examples X, which minimizes an arbitrary cost criterion. The set of examples X is a subset of the individuals occurring in the KB.

Example 2.1 (Transductive Class-Membership Learning). Consider an ontology modeling an academic domain. The problem of learning whether a set of researchers is affiliated to a given research group or not, provided a set of positive and negative examples of affiliates, can be cast as a *transductive class-membership learning* problem: examples (consisting in a subset of the individuals in the ontology, each corresponding to a researcher), represented by the set X, can be either *positive, negative* or *neutral* depending on their membership to a target class `ResearchGroupAffiliate`. The transductive learning problem reduces to finding the best labeling function $\mathbf{f}$ (according to a given criterion, represented by the cost function), providing a membership value for each example in X.

In this work, we leverage the diverse relations holding among examples in the ontology to *propagate* knowledge, in the form of label information, among similar examples.

The method proposed in this article is related to *graph-based semi-supervised learning* [5] (SSL) methods. In particular, it is based on the *cluster assumption*: if two examples are in the same cluster, then their class memberships should be similar. Similarly to graph-based SSL methods, we define a similarity graph over examples, and look for a labeling function **f** that *varies smoothly* across similar examples (i.e. those linked together in the similarity graph).

3   Knowledge Propagation

In this section we present a new method, named *Adaptive Knowledge Propagation* (AKP), for solving the learning problem in Def. 2.1 in the context of Web ontologies. In Sect. 3.1 we show how a (weighted) similarity graph defined over examples can be efficiently used to propagate label information among similar examples. The effectiveness of this approach strongly depends on the choice of the similarity graph (represented in the following by its adjacency matrix **W**). In Sect. 3.2, we show how the matrix **W** can be learned from examples, by leveraging their relationships within the ontology.

3.1   Transductive Inference as an Optimization Problem

We now propose a solution to the transductive learning problem in Def. 2.1. As discussed in the end of Sect. 2, we look for a labeling function $\mathbf{f}^*$ defined over examples X, which is both consistent with labeled examples, and *varies smoothly* across examples in the same cluster (according to the cluster assumption). In the following, we assume that a (weighted) similarity graph over examples in X is already provided. Such a graph is represented by its adjacency matrix $\mathbf{W}$, such that $\mathbf{W}_{ij} = \mathbf{W}_{ji} \geq 0$ if $x_i, x_j \in X$ are *similar*, and 0 otherwise. As in [5, ch. 11], we assume that $\mathbf{W}_{ii} = 0$. A solution to the problem of learning $\mathbf{W}$ from examples is proposed in Sect. 3.2.

Formally, each labeling function **f** can be represented by a finite-size vector, where $\mathbf{f}_i \in \{-1, +1\}$ is the label for the i-th element in the set of examples X. According to [22], labels can be enforced to vary smoothly among similar examples by considering a cost function with the following form:

$$E(\mathbf{f}) \triangleq \frac{1}{2} \sum_{i=1}^{|X|} \sum_{j=1}^{|X|} \mathbf{W}_{ij} (\mathbf{f}_i - \mathbf{f}_j)^2 + \epsilon \sum_{i=1}^{|X|} \mathbf{f}_i^2, \tag{1}$$

where the first term enforces the labeling function to vary smoothly among similar examples (i.e. those connected by an edge in the similarity graph), and the second term is a L_2 regularizer (a penalty on the *complexity* of the labeling function) with weight $\epsilon > 0$ over **f**. A labeling for unlabeled examples in X_0 is obtained by minimizing the function $E(\cdot)$ in Eq. 1, constraining the value of $\mathbf{f}_i$ to 1 (resp. -1) for all positive examples $x_i \in X_+$ (resp. negative examples $x_i \in X_-$).

Let $L \triangleq X_+ \cup X_-$ and $U \triangleq X_0$ represent labeled and unlabeled examples, and $\mathbf{f}_L$, $\mathbf{f}_U$ their labels respectively. Constraining the labeling function $\mathbf{f}_U$ to take only discrete values on unlabeled examples (i.e. $\mathbf{f}_i \in \{-1, +1\}, \forall x_i \in X_0$) has two main drawbacks:

- The labeling function $\mathbf{f}$ can only provide a *hard* classification (i.e. $\mathbf{f}_U \in \{-1, +1\}^{|U|}$), without any measure of confidence;
- The function $E(\cdot)$ defines the energy function of a discrete Markov Random Field, and calculating the marginal distribution over labels $\mathbf{f}_U$ is inherently difficult [10].

To overcome these problems, in [22] authors propose a continuous relaxation of $\mathbf{f}_U$, where labels for unlabeled examples are represented by real values (i.e. $\mathbf{f}_U \in \mathbb{R}^{|U|}$). This allows for a simple, closed-form solution to the problem of minimizing the function $E(\cdot)$ for a given value of $\mathbf{f}_L$, where $\mathbf{f}_L$ represents the labels for labeled examples.

Application to Class-Membership Learning. We can solve the learning problem in Def. 2.1 by minimizing the cost function $E(\cdot)$ in Eq. 1, for a given labeling for labeled examples $\mathbf{f}_L$. Eq. 1 can be rewritten as [22]:

$$E(\mathbf{f}) = \mathbf{f}^T(\mathbf{D} - \mathbf{W})\mathbf{f} + \epsilon \mathbf{f}^T = \mathbf{f}^T(\mathbf{L} + \epsilon\mathbf{I})\mathbf{f}, \tag{2}$$

where $\mathbf{D}$ is a diagonal matrix such that $\mathbf{D}_{ii} = \sum_{j=1}^{|X|} \mathbf{W}_{ij}$ and $\mathbf{L} \triangleq \mathbf{D} - \mathbf{W}$ is the *graph Laplacian* of $\mathbf{W}$. Reordering the vector $\mathbf{f}$ and matrices $\mathbf{W}$ and $\mathbf{L}$ w.r.t. the membership of examples to L and U, they can be rewritten as:

$$\mathbf{f} = \begin{bmatrix} \mathbf{f}_L \\ \mathbf{f}_U \end{bmatrix}, \quad \mathbf{W} = \begin{bmatrix} \mathbf{W}_{LL} & \mathbf{W}_{LU} \\ \mathbf{W}_{UL} & \mathbf{W}_{UU} \end{bmatrix}, \quad \mathbf{L} = \begin{bmatrix} \mathbf{L}_{LL} & \mathbf{L}_{LU} \\ \mathbf{L}_{UL} & \mathbf{L}_{UU} \end{bmatrix}. \tag{3}$$

The problem of finding a real valued labeling function $\mathbf{f}_U$ which minimizes the cost function $E(\cdot)$ for a given value of $\mathbf{f}_L$ has a closed form solution [22]:

$$\mathbf{f}_U^* = (\mathbf{L}_{UU} + \epsilon\mathbf{I})^{-1}\mathbf{W}_{UL}\mathbf{f}_L. \tag{4}$$

Complexity. A solution for Eq. 4 can be computed efficiently in nearly-linear time w.r.t. $|X|$. Indeed computing $\mathbf{f}_U^*$ can be reduced to solving a linear system in the form $\mathbf{A}\mathbf{x} = \mathbf{b}$, with $\mathbf{A} = (\mathbf{L}_{UU} + \epsilon\mathbf{I})$, $\mathbf{b} = \mathbf{W}_{UL}\mathbf{f}_L$ and $\mathbf{x} = \mathbf{f}_U^*$. A linear system $\mathbf{A}\mathbf{x} = \mathbf{b}$ with $\mathbf{A} \in \mathbb{R}^{n \times n}$ can be solved in nearly linear time w.r.t. n if the coefficient matrix $\mathbf{A}$ is *symmetric diagonally dominant*[2] (SDD). An algorithm for solving SDD linear system is proposed in [9]: its time-complexity is $\approx O(m \log^2 n)$, where m is the number of non-zero entries in $\mathbf{A}$ and n is the number of variables in the system of linear equations. In Eq. 4, the matrix $(\mathbf{L}_{UU} + \epsilon\mathbf{I})$ is SDD, since the graph Laplacian $\mathbf{L}$ is SDD [18].

3.2 Learning to Propagate Knowledge in Web Ontologies

The approach to propagate knowledge across similar examples discussed in Sect. 3.1 relies on a similarity graph, represented by its adjacency matrix $\mathbf{W}$.

The underlying assumption of this work is that some relations among individuals in the KB might encode a similarity relation w.r.t. a specific target property or class: identifying such relations can help to propagate information among similar examples, and provide new knowledge about the domain.

---

[2] A matrix $\mathbf{A}$ is SDD iff $\mathbf{A}$ is symmetric (i.e. $\mathbf{A} = \mathbf{A}^T$) and $\forall i : \mathbf{A}_{ii} \geq \sum_{i \neq j} |\mathbf{A}_{ij}|$.

In literature, this phenomenon is also referred to as *Homophily* [3]: a relation between examples (such as *friendship* in a social network) can be correlated with those individuals being similar w.r.t. a set of properties (such as political views, hobbies, religious beliefs). However, depending on the learning task at hand, not all relations are equally effective at encoding similarities between examples. For example, in a social network, friends may tend to share common interests, while quiet people may tend to prefer talkative friends and vice-versa.

In this work, we represent each distinct relation type by means of an *adjacency matrix* $\tilde{\mathbf{W}}$, such that $\tilde{\mathbf{W}}_{ij} = \tilde{\mathbf{W}}_{ji} = 1$ iff the relation $\mathtt{rel}(x_i, x_j)$ between x_i and x_j holds in the ontology (i.e. $\mathcal{K} \models \mathtt{rel}(x_i, x_j)$). The predicate $\mathtt{rel}$ might represent any generic relation between examples (e.g. friendship or co-authorship). For simplicity, we assume $\tilde{\mathbf{W}}_{ii} = 0, \forall i$.

Given a set of adjacency matrices $\mathcal{W} \triangleq \{\tilde{\mathbf{W}}_1, \ldots, \tilde{\mathbf{W}}_r\}$, according to the assumption that not all relations are equally important in the construction of the similarity graph, we define $\mathbf{W}$ as a linear combination of the matrices in $\mathcal{W}$:

$$\mathbf{W} \triangleq \sum_{i=1}^{r} \mu_i \tilde{\mathbf{W}}_i, \quad \text{with } \mu_i \geq 0, \forall i \tag{5}$$

where each μ_i, is a parameter representing the contribution of the matrix $\tilde{\mathbf{W}}_i$ in the construction of $\mathbf{W}$. Non-negativity in μ enforces that $\mathbf{W}$ has non-negative weights, and therefore that the corresponding graph Laplacian $\mathbf{L}$ is PSD [18]. This ensures that the problem of finding a global minimum for Eq. 2 has a unique solution that can be calculated in closed form. In the following, we propose a solution to the problem of efficiently learning the parameters $\{\mu, \epsilon\}$ from a set of labeled and unlabeled examples.

Parameters Learning. The parametric form of $\mathbf{W}$ is fully specified by the parameters μ in Eq. 5, which reflect the importance of each relation in the construction of the similarity graph. In addition, the approach in Sect. 3.1 depends on the choice of a regularization parameter ϵ. In this work, we propose learning the parameters $\Theta \triangleq \{\mu, \epsilon\}$ by *Leave-One-Out* (LOO) *Error minimization*. Provided that propagation can be performed efficiently, we are able to directly computing the LOO error: it is defined as the summation of reconstruction errors obtained by considering each labeled example, in turn, as unlabeled, and predicting its label.

Let $U_i \triangleq U \cup \{x_i\}$ and $L_i \triangleq L - \{x_i\}$: w.l.o.g. we assume that the label of the left-out example $x_i \in L$ is in the first position of the new real valued labeling vector $\mathbf{f}_{U_i}$. Let $\ell(x, \hat{x})$ be a generic, differentiable loss function (e.g. $\ell(x, \hat{x}) = |x - \hat{x}|$ for the absolute loss, or $\ell(x, \hat{x}) = (x - \hat{x})^2/2$ for the quadratic loss). The LOO Error is formally defined as follows:

$$\mathcal{Q}(\Theta \mid \mathbf{f}_L) \triangleq \sum_{i=1}^{|L|} \ell(\mathbf{f}_i, \hat{\mathbf{f}}_i), \tag{6}$$

where $\mathbf{e}^T \triangleq (1, 0, \ldots, 0) \in \mathbb{R}^{u+1}$ and $\hat{\mathbf{f}}_i \triangleq \mathbf{e}^T (\mathbf{L}_{U_i U_i} + \epsilon \mathbf{I})^{-1} \mathbf{W}_{U_i L_i} \mathbf{f}_{L_i}$ represents the continuous label value assigned to x_i as if such a value was not known in advance.

The vector $\mathbf{e}^T$ is needed to select the predicted label for the left-out example $x_i \in L$. This leads to the definition of the following criterion for learning the parameters $\boldsymbol{\Theta}$:

Definition 3.1 (Minimum LOO Error Parameters). *Given a set of labeled (resp. un-labeled) examples L (resp. U) and a set of adjacency matrices $\mathcal{W}$, each corresponding to a relation type, the* minimum LOO Error Parameters $\boldsymbol{\Theta}^*_{LOO}$ *are defined as follows:*

$$\boldsymbol{\Theta}^*_{LOO} = \arg \min_{\substack{\boldsymbol{\Theta}=\{\boldsymbol{\mu},\epsilon\} \\ \boldsymbol{\mu}\geq 0, \epsilon>0}} \mathcal{Q}(\boldsymbol{\Theta} \mid \mathbf{f}_L) + \lambda\|\boldsymbol{\Theta}\|^2, \tag{7}$$

where the function $\mathcal{Q}$ is defined as in Eq. 6 and $\lambda \geq 0$ weights a L_2 regularization term which controls the complexity of parameters $\boldsymbol{\Theta}$.

The objective function in Def. 3.1 is differentiable and can be efficiently minimized by using gradient-based function minimization approaches such as gradient descent. Let $\mathbf{Z}_i = (\mathbf{L}_{U_i U_i} + \epsilon\mathbf{I})$: the gradient of $\mathcal{Q}$ w.r.t. a parameter $\theta \in \boldsymbol{\Theta}$ is given by:

$$\frac{\partial \mathcal{Q}(\boldsymbol{\Theta} \mid \mathbf{f}_L)}{\partial \theta} = \sum_{i=1}^{|L|} \frac{\partial \ell(\mathbf{f}_i, \hat{\mathbf{f}}_i)}{\partial \hat{\mathbf{f}}_i} \left[\mathbf{e}^T \mathbf{Z}_i^{-1} \left(\frac{\partial \mathbf{W}_{U_i L_i}}{\partial \theta} \mathbf{f}_{L_i} - \frac{\partial \mathbf{Z}_i}{\partial \theta} \mathbf{f}^*_{U_i} \right) \right]. \tag{8}$$

3.3 Identifying Meaningful Relations

In Sect. 3.2, we expressed the adjacency matrix of the similarity graph $\mathbf{W}$ as a linear combination of adjacency matrices $\tilde{\mathbf{W}}_i \in \mathcal{W}$, each corresponding to a distinct relation type among examples within the ontology (such as friendship or co-authorship). We now discuss the problem of efficiently retrieve possibly non-trivial, yet meaningful, relations among examples in X.

Simply retrieving binary relations encoded by atomic roles in the KB might fail to capture a number of meaningful, semantically relevant, relations among examples. For example, in an academic domain, the KB may contain each researcher's group affiliations (e.g. by means of a `affiliatedTo` atomic role), but the relation "sharing the same affiliation" between researchers might not be captured by any atomic role between examples in X. To overcome this issue, we rely on Conjunctive Queries (CQs), described in Sect. 2, to retrieve relations between examples. For example, the relation "sharing the same affiliation" between $a, b \in X$ can be assessed by means of the following CQ:

$$? : \exists z.(\texttt{affiliatedTo}(a, z) \wedge \texttt{affiliatedTo}(b, z)),$$

where $z \in N_V$ is a *non-distinguished* variable.

In this work, we leverage the relations between examples holding in the KB for constructing the similarity graph; in particular, we consider relations that can be expressed using CQs. However, the number of such relations might be very large. To overcome this problem, in empirical evaluations (see Sect. 4), we considered two types of such relations holding between pairs of examples $a, b \in X$:

– *Simple* relations, i.e. those encoded by CQs in the form:

$$? : \mathbf{r}(a, b),$$

where $\mathbf{r} \in N_R$ is an atomic role;

– *Composite* relations, i.e. those corresponding to CQs in the form:

$$? :\exists z.(\mathbf{r}(a,z) \wedge \mathbf{r}(b,z)) \quad \text{or} \quad ? :\exists z.(\mathbf{r}(z,a) \wedge \mathbf{r}(z,b)),$$

where $\mathbf{r} \in N_R$ and $z \in N_V$.

Current technologies allow to efficiently retrieve complex relations holding among examples. CQs can be expressed in the SPARQL-DL [17] query language. SPARQL-DL seems particularly convenient for the task: it is a specialization of SPARQL, sharing its syntax and working under OWL's *Direct Model-Theoretic Semantics*[3]. SPARQL-DL queries generalize CQs as they admit variables standing for property names (allowing to retrieve different types of complex relations among individuals at once) together with *non-distinguished variables,* i.e. those that are bound to entities that need not be interpreted as specific individuals in the queried ontology.

Example 3.1. Given a KB $\mathcal{K}$, suppose that statistical units (i.e. individuals of interest) are all persons, represented by members of the concept foaf : Person. Assume that relations of interest correspond to the result of CQs in the form:

$$? :\exists z.(\texttt{foaf : Person}(a) \wedge \texttt{foaf : Person}(b) \wedge \mathbf{r}(a,z) \wedge \mathbf{r}(b,z)),$$

where $\mathbf{r} \in N_R$, $a,b \in N_I$ and $z \in N_V$. Such relations can be retrieved by a single SPARQL-DL query:

```
SELECT DISTINCT ?p ?q ?r WHERE {
  ?p a foaf:Person .
  ?q a foaf:Person .
  ?p ?r _:o .
  ?q ?r _:o .
  ?r rdf:type owl:ObjectProperty .
}
```

Note that the variable _:o is a *non-distinguished variable* which does not need to be materialized in the KB (i.e. represented by an asserted individual).   ∎

This approach to retrieving complex relations presents multiple advantages: a single SPARQL-DL query can capture a large class of CQs, thanks to the use of variables in place of role names. We will use the following short-hand notations to describe more concisely relations elicited during the empirical evaluation phase:

$$\mathbf{rel}_1 \circ \mathbf{rel}_2^{-1}(a,b) \equiv \exists z.(\mathbf{rel}_1(a,z) \wedge \mathbf{rel}_2(z,b)),$$
$$\mathbf{rel}_1^{-1} \circ \mathbf{rel}_2(a,b) \equiv \exists z.(\mathbf{rel}_1(z,a) \wedge \mathbf{rel}_2(b,z)),$$

where $\mathbf{rel}_1, \mathbf{rel}_2 \in N_R$, $a,b \in X$ and $z \in N_V$.

3.4 Summary of the Proposed Method

The method, which we refer to as *Adaptive Knowledge Propagation* (AKP), can be summarized by the following steps:

---

[3] http://www.w3.org/TR/owl2-direct-semantics

1. Retrieve relations among examples in X using SPARQL-DL queries, and create a set of adjacency matrices $\mathcal{W} = \{\tilde{\mathbf{W}}_1, \ldots, \tilde{\mathbf{W}}_r\}$, one for each relation type.
2. Given a labeling for labeled examples $\mathbf{f}_L$, find the minimum Leave-One-Out Error parameters Θ^*_{LOO} defined in Def. 3.1, by solving the constrained optimization problem in Eq. 7 (e.g. by using a gradient-based optimization method).
3. Use the learned parameters $\Theta^*_{LOO} = \{\mu, \epsilon\}$ to find a labeling for unlabeled examples $\mathbf{f}_U$, by first calculating the adjacency matrix of the similarity graph $\mathbf{W}$ as in Eq. 5, and then propagating knowledge across the graph as in Eq. 4.

4   Empirical Evaluation

The method discussed in Sect. 3 was experimentally evaluated in comparison with other approaches proposed in the literature on a variety of assertion prediction problems. Sources and datasets for reproducing the experiments are available at https://code.google.com/p/akp/. We now describe the setup of experiments and their outcomes.

4.1   Setup

In empirical evaluations, we used an open source DL reasoner [4] for answering the SPARQL-DL queries.

Ontologies. We considered three real world ontologies: the AIFB PORTAL Ontology [5], the DBPEDIA 3.9 Ontology [4] and the BRITISH GEOLOGICAL SURVEY (BGS) Ontology [6]. The characteristics of these ontologies are outlined in Tab. 1.

The AIFB PORTAL Ontology relies on knowledge from the SWRC Ontology and metadata available from the Semantic Portal of the AIFB institute: it models key concepts within a research community, such as persons, articles, technical reports, projects and courses (e.g. ~ 500 individuals belong to the class foaf : Person and ~ 2400 to the class foaf : Document). DBPEDIA [4] makes structured information extracted from Wikipedia available in the LOD cloud, providing unique identifiers for the described entities that can be dereferenced over the Web: DBPEDIA 3.9, released in September 2013, describes 4.0 million entities. The BRITISH GEOLOGICAL SURVEY Ontology is part of an effort by the British Geological Survey, a premier center for earth science, to publish geological data (such as hydro-geological, gravitational and magnetic data). In particular, the ontology models knowledge on 11697 "Named Rock Units".

Experimental Setting. The proposed method, denoted AKP, is summarized in Sect. 3.4. We used *Projected Gradient Descent* to minimize the Leave-One-Out Error in Eq. 6 w.r.t. available labels $\mathbf{f}_L$ (using the absolute loss as loss function), together with an intermediate line search to assess the step size and early stopping. The regularization parameter λ in Eq. 6 was fixed to $\lambda = 10^{-8}$, preventing the parameters to diverge.

---

[4] Pellet v2.3.1 – http://clarkparsia.com/pellet/

[5] http://www.aifb.kit.edu/web/Wissensmanagement/Portal

[6] http://data.bgs.ac.uk/, as of March 2014

Table 1. Ontologies considered in the experiments

Ontology	DL Language	#Axioms	#Individuals	#Properties	#Classes
AIFB PORTAL [12]	$\mathcal{ALEHO(D)}$	268540	44328	285	49
DBPEDIA 3.9 [4] Frag.	$\mathcal{ALCH}$	78795	16606	132	251
BGS [21]	$\mathcal{ALI(D)}$	825133	87555	154	6

Before each experiment, the class-membership relations that were the target of the prediction task were removed from the ontology. Following the related evaluation procedures in [12, 21], members of the target class were considered as *positive examples*, while an equal number of *negative examples* was randomly sampled from unlabeled examples. Remaining instances (i.e. neither positive nor negative) were considered as *neutral* (unlabeled) *examples*. Results are reported in terms of *Area Under the Precision-Recall Curve* (AUC-PR), a measure to evaluate rankings also used in e.g. [14]. In each experiment, we considered the problem of predicting the membership to each of several classes: for each of such classes, we performed a 10-fold cross validation (CV), and report the average AUC-PR obtained using each of the considered methods.

We used the same 10-folds partitioning across experiments related to each of the datasets. For such a reason, we report statistical significance tests using a paired, non-parametric difference test (Wilcoxon T test). We also report diagrams showing how using a smaller random sample of labeled training examples (i.e. 10%, 30%, 50%, . . ., a plausible scenario for a number of real world settings with limited labeled training data), and using the remaining examples for testing, affects the results in terms of AUC-PR.

Setup of the Compared Methods. We compare AKP with state-of-the-art approaches proposed for learning from ontological KBs. Specifically, we considered two kernel methods: Soft-Margin SVM (SM-SVM) and Kernel Logistic Regression (KLR), together with different kernel functions suited for ontological KBs: we used the *Intersection SubTree* [12] (IST) and the *Weisfeiler-Lehman* [21] (WL) kernels for ontological KBs. We also considered the SUNS [19] relational prediction model.

The RDF graph used by kernel functions and SUNS was materialized as follows: all $\langle \text{s}, \text{p}, \text{o} \rangle$ triples were retrieved by means of SPARQL-DL queries (where p was either an object or a data-type property) together with all *direct type* and *direct sub-class* relations. As in [12], IST kernel parameters were selected in $d \in \{1, 2, 3, 4\}$ and $\lambda_{ist} \in \{0.1, 0.3, \ldots, 0.9\}$, and WL kernel parameters in $d, h \in \{1, 2, 3, 4\}$ (where d represents the depth of the considered neighborhood graph). In SM-SVM, in order to obtain a ranking among instances, we applied the logistic function s to the decision boundary f instead of the sign function (which is commonly used in the classification context), thus obtaining $s(f(\cdot)) : \mathcal{X} \rightarrow [0, 1]$. In SM-SVM, the parameter C was selected in $C \in \{0.0, 10^{-6}, 10^{-4}, \ldots, 10^4, 10^6\}$, while in KLR the weight λ_k associated to the L_2 regularizer was selected in $\lambda_k \in \{10^{-4}, 10^{-3}, \ldots, 10^4\}$. In the SUNS relational prediction model, parameters t and λ were selected in $t \in \{2, 4, 6, \ldots, 24\}$ and $\lambda_s \in \{0, 10^{-2}, 10^{-1}, \ldots, 10^6\}$. All parameters were selected by grid optimization, using a 10-fold cross validation (CV) within the training set.

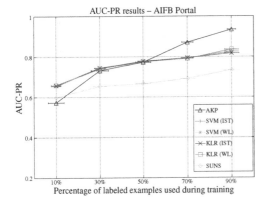

Fig. 1. AIFB PORTAL – Left: AUC-PR results (mean, std.dev.) estimated by 10-fold CV, obtained varying the percentage of labeled examples used for training – Right: AUC-PR results estimated by 10-fold CV: ▼/▽ (resp. ▲/△) indicates that AKP's mean is significantly higher (resp. lower) in a paired Wilcoxon T test with $p < 0.05$ / $p < 0.10$

4.2   Results

Experiments with the AIFB PORTAL Ontology. As in [12,21], the learning task consisted in predicting the affiliations of AIFB staff members to research groups. Specifically, in a set of 316 examples (each representing a researcher in the ontology), the task consisted in predicting missing affiliations to 5 distinct research groups. Empirical results are described in Fig. 1. The table (right) summarizes the overall AUC-PR results on the research group affiliation prediction task, obtained via 10-fold CV (one per research group, in a *one-versus-all* setting). The plot shows average AUC-PR values describes results obtained with a limited number of labeled training examples, and leaving the rest to the test: error bars (pictured horizontally) represent twice the standard deviation.

The proposed method AKP yields significantly higher AUC-PR values in comparison with the other considered methods, where statistical significance was calculated with a Wilcoxon T test with $p < 0.05$. By identifying those relations that are likely to link persons with similar research group affiliations, it shows that AKP can be used to discover new knowledge about the domain of an ontology. Tab. 2 shows a sample of the relations considered for the affiliation prediction task, among a total of 77 retrieved (all *composite*) relations, together with a measure of their relevance (given by their associated weight μ_i, described as either LOWER if $\mu_i \approx 0$, and HIGHER otherwise). As expected, AKP recognizes that authors sharing publications or interests, teaching the same courses or sharing their office are very likely to be affiliated to the same research group (unlike e.g. sharing the same academic title).

In this experiment, each AKP run took an average of ~ 500 seconds on a single core of an Intel®Core™i7 processor, showing that it can be used in practice for learning from real KBs.

Experiments with the DBPEDIA 3.9 Fragment. Similarly to [14], we evaluated the proposed approach on the task of predicting political party affiliations to either the

Table 2. Relations considered in the AIFB PORTAL and the DBPEDIA 3.9 Ontologies

AIFB PORTAL		DBPEDIA 3.9	
HIGHER μ_i	LOWER μ_i	HIGHER μ_i	LOWER μ_i
publications^{-1} o publications	title o title^{-1}	vicePresident	successor
interest o interest^{-1}	mobile o mobile^{-1}	president	predecessor
lecturer^{-1} o lecturer	road o road^{-1}	region o region^{-1}	religion o religion^{-1}
room o room^{-1}	webpage o webpage^{-1}	district o district^{-1}	award o award^{-1}

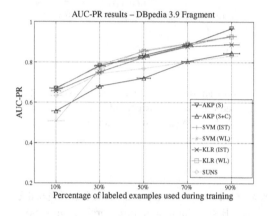

Method	AUC-PR (mean ± var.)	S	S+C
AKP (S)	0.967 ± 0.003		▲
AKP (S+C)	0.845 ± 0.035	▼	
SUNS	0.832 ± 0.019	▼	
SMSVM (IST)	0.930 ± 0.011	▽	
SMSVM (WL)	0.930 ± 0.011	▽	
KLR (IST)	0.888 ± 0.029	▼	
KLR (WL)	0.927 ± 0.012	▽	

Fig. 2. DBPEDIA 3.9 Ontology – Left: AUC-PR results (mean, st.d.) estimated by 10-fold CV, obtained varying the percentage of labeled examples used for training – Right: AUC-PR results estimated by 10-fold CV: ▼/▽ (resp. ▲/△) indicates that AKP's mean is significantly higher (resp. lower) in a paired Wilcoxon T test with $p < 0.05$ / $p < 0.10$

Democratic and the Republican party for 82 US presidents and vice-presidents from DBPEDIA 3.9. The experiment illustrated in [14] uses a small RDF fragment containing the president and vicePresident predicates only.

In this experiment, we used a real-life fragment of DBPEDIA 3.9 obtained by means of a crawling process, containing a number of irrelevant and possibly noisy entities and relations. Following the extraction procedure in [8], the DBPEDIA 3.9 RDF graph was traversed starting from resources representing US presidents and vice-presidents: all immediate neighbors, i.e. those with a recursion depth of 1, were retrieved, together with their related schema information (direct classes and their super-classes, together with their hierarchy). All extracted knowledge was used to create a KB whose characteristics are outlined in Tab. 1. For efficiency reasons, parameters in the WL kernel were fixed to $d = 1$ and $h = 1$.

In this experiment, the total number of retrieved relations (both *simple* and *composite*) was higher than the number of instances itself: 82 US presidents and vice-presidents were interlinked by 25 simple relations and 149 composite relations. This differs from other empirical evaluations discussed in this paper, in which instances are linked by a more limited number of, exclusively composite, relations. For such a reason, we evaluated two variants of the proposed method: AKP (S), which only uses simple relations,

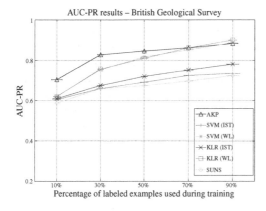

Method	AUC-PR (mean ± var.)	
AKP	0.887 ± 0.014	
SUNS	0.724 ± 0.022	▼
SMSVM (IST)	0.735 ± 0.026	▼
SMSVM (WL)	0.887 ± 0.010	
KLR (IST)	0.781 ± 0.020	▼
KLR (WL)	0.900 ± 0.007	

Fig. 3. BGS Ontology – Left: AUC-PR results (mean, st.d.) estimated by 10-fold CV, obtained varying the percentage of labeled examples used for training – Right: AUC-PR results estimated by 10-fold CV: ▼/▽ (resp. ▲/△) indicates that AKP's mean is significantly higher (resp. lower) in a paired Wilcoxon T test with $p < 0.05$ / $p < 0.10$

and AKP (S+C), which uses both simple and composite relations. Experimental results are summarized in Fig. 2. AUC-PR values obtained with AKP (S) are significantly higher than those provided by the other considered methods ($p < 0.05$, except for three cases in which $p < 0.10$). This was not true for AKP (S+C): relying on both simple and composite relations greatly increased the variance in AUC-PR results. An explanation for this phenomenon is in the *curse of dimensionality* [6]: as the number of considered relations grows, it becomes increasingly difficult to identify those that effectively encode similarities among examples.

AKP was able to identify which relations are likely to link same party affiliates, some of which are summarized in Tab. 2: it was able to find that the vice president is likely to belong to the same party of the president; that representatives covering a role under the same president are likely to belong to the same party; or that representatives elected in the same region are likely to belong to the same party. On the other hand, AKP recognized that sharing the same religion, profession, nationality or awards does not necessarily mean sharing the same party affiliation.

Experiments with the BRITISH GEOLOGICAL SURVEY Ontology. As in [21], we evaluated AKP on the *Lithogenesis* prediction problem in the BRITISH GEOLOGICAL SURVEY Ontology. The problem consisted in predicting the value of the property hasLithogenesis in a set of 159 named rock units labeled with their corresponding lithogenetic type. As in [21], we focus on two learning tasks, consisting in the prediction of two major lithogenetic types: "Alluvial" and "Glacial".

Results are summarized in Fig. 3. AKP provides significantly higher AUC-PR values, in comparison with kernel methods using the IST kernel and SUNS ($p < 0.05$). The difference between results obtained with AKP and by kernel methods using the WL kernel was not statistically significant, confirming the effectiveness of the WL kernel on this specific dataset (see [21]). However, while the statistical models produced with the WL kernel only have non-trivial geometrical interpretations, those learned by AKP explicitly represent the importance of relations in the propagation process.

Also in this case, AKP was able to extract relations between rock units that are likely to link rocks with similar lithogenetic types. For example, among a total of 23 relations (all *composite*) it emerged that rocks with similar geographical distributions, thickness and lithological components were likely to share their lithogenetic type, while their geological theme and oldest geological age were not considered informative.

5 Conclusions and Future Work

In this work, we propose a semi-supervised transductive inference method for statistical learning in the context of the WEB OF DATA. Starting from the assumption that some relations among examples in a Web ontology can encode similarity information w.r.t. a given prediction task (pertaining a particular property of examples, such as a specific class-membership), we propose a method, named *Adaptive Knowledge Propagation*, for i) identifying which relations are likely to link similar examples in the ontology, and ii) efficiently propagating knowledge across related examples, leveraging the diverse nature of such relations.

We empirically show that the proposed method is able to identify which relations are likely to link examples that are similar w.r.t. a given aspect, and that this information can provide new knowledge about the ontology. We also show that AKP provides significantly better or competitive results, in terms of AUC-PR, in comparison with current state-of-the-art methods in the literature. We are currently investigating probabilistic ways of learning how to propagate knowledge among examples; the use of different loss functions, optimization methods and regularization terms; and the automatic identification and selection of more complex relations between examples.

Acknowledgments. This work fulfills the objectives of the PON 02_00563_3489339 project "PUGLIA@SERVICE - Internet-based Service Engineering enabling Smart Territory structural development" funded by the Italian Ministry of University and Research (MIUR).

References

1. Baader, F., Calvanese, D., McGuinness, D.L., Nardi, D., Patel-Schneider, P.F. (eds.): The Description Logic Handbook. Cambridge University Press (2007)
2. Berners-Lee, T., Hendler, J., Lassila, O.: The Semantic Web. Scientific American 284(5), 34–43 (2001)
3. Bhagat, S., Cormode, G., Muthukrishnan, S.: Node classification in social networks. In: Aggarwal, C.C. (ed.) Social Network Data Analytics, pp. 115–148. Springer (2011)
4. Bizer, C., Lehmann, J., Kobilarov, G., Auer, S., Becker, C., Cyganiak, R., Hellmann, S.: DBpedia - a crystallization point for the Web of Data. J. Web Sem. 7(3), 154–165 (2009)
5. Chapelle, O., Schölkopf, B., Zien, A. (eds.): Semi-Supervised Learning. MIT Press (2006)

6. Hastie, T., Tibshirani, R., Friedman, J.: The elements of statistical learning: data mining, inference and prediction, 2nd edn. Springer (2008)
7. Heath, T., Bizer, C.: Linked Data: Evolving the Web into a Global Data Space. Synthesis Lectures on the Semantic Web. Morgan & Claypool Publishers (2011)
8. Hellmann, S., Lehmann, J., Auer, S.: Learning of OWL Class Descriptions on Very Large Knowledge Bases. Int. J. Semantic Web Inf. Syst. 5(2), 25–48 (2009)
9. Kelner, J.A., Orecchia, L., Sidford, A., Zhu, Z.A.: A simple, combinatorial algorithm for solving sdd systems in nearly-linear time. In: Boneh, D., et al. (eds.) Proceedings of STOC 2013, pp. 911–920. ACM (2013)
10. Koller, D., Friedman, N.: Probabilistic Graphical Models: Principles and Techniques. MIT Press (2009)
11. Lin, H.T., Koul, N., Honavar, V.: Learning Relational Bayesian Classifiers from RDF Data. In: Aroyo, L., Welty, C., Alani, H., Taylor, J., Bernstein, A., Kagal, L., Noy, N., Blomqvist, E. (eds.) ISWC 2011, Part I. LNCS, vol. 7031, pp. 389–404. Springer, Heidelberg (2011)
12. Lösch, U., Bloehdorn, S., Rettinger, A.: Graph kernels for RDF data. In: Simperl, E., Cimiano, P., Polleres, A., Corcho, O., Presutti, V. (eds.) ESWC 2012. LNCS, vol. 7295, pp. 134–148. Springer, Heidelberg (2012)
13. Minervini, P., d'Amato, C., Fanizzi, N., Esposito, F.: Transductive inference for class-membership propagation in web ontologies. In: Cimiano, P., Corcho, O., Presutti, V., Hollink, L., Rudolph, S. (eds.) ESWC 2013. LNCS, vol. 7882, pp. 457–471. Springer, Heidelberg (2013)
14. Nickel, M., Tresp, V., Kriegel, H.P.: A Three-Way Model for Collective Learning on Multi-Relational Data. In: Getoor, L., et al. (eds.) Proceedings of ICML 2011, pp. 809–816. Omnipress (2011)
15. Rettinger, A., Lösch, U., Tresp, V., d'Amato, C., Fanizzi, N.: Mining the Semantic Web: Statistical learning for next generation knowledge bases. Data Min. Knowl. Discov. 24(3), 613–662 (2012)
16. Rettinger, A., Nickles, M., Tresp, V.: Statistical Relational Learning with Formal Ontologies. In: Buntine, W., Grobelnik, M., Mladenić, D., Shawe-Taylor, J. (eds.) ECML PKDD 2009, Part II. LNCS, vol. 5782, pp. 286–301. Springer, Heidelberg (2009)
17. Sirin, E., Parsia, B.: SPARQL-DL: SPARQL Query for OWL-DL. In: Golbreich, C., et al. (eds.) OWLED. CEUR Workshop Proceedings, vol. 258. CEUR-WS.org (2007)
18. Spielman, D.A.: Algorithms, Graph Theory, and Linear Equations in Laplacian Matrices. In: Proceedings of ICM 2010, pp. 2698–2722 (2010)
19. Tresp, V., Huang, Y., Bundschus, M., Rettinger, A.: Materializing and querying learned knowledge. In: Proceedings of IRMLeS 2009 (2009)
20. Vapnik, V.N.: Statistical learning theory. Wiley, 1 edn. (September 1998)
21. de Vries, G.K.D.: A Fast Approximation of the Weisfeiler-Lehman Graph Kernel for RDF Data. In: Blockeel, H., Kersting, K., Nijssen, S., Železný, F. (eds.) ECML PKDD 2013, Part I. LNCS, vol. 8188, pp. 606–621. Springer, Heidelberg (2013)
22. Zhu, X., Ghahramani, Z., Lafferty, J.D.: Semi-Supervised Learning Using Gaussian Fields and Harmonic Functions. In: Fawcett, T., et al. (eds.) Proceedings of ICML 2003, pp. 912–919. AAAI Press (2003)

Using Event Spaces, Setting and Theme to Assist the Interpretation and Development of Museum Stories

Paul Mulholland[1], Annika Wolff[1], Eoin Kilfeather[2], and Evin McCarthy[2]

[1] Knowledge Media Institute, The Open University, Walton Hall, Milton Keynes, UK
{p.mulholland,a.l.wolff}@open.ac.uk
[2] Digital Media Centre, Dublin Institute of Technology, Aungier Street, Dublin, Ireland
{eoin.kilfeather,evin.mccarthy}@dit.ie

Abstract. Stories are used to provide a context for museum objects, for example linking those objects to what they depict or the historical context in which they were created. Many explicit and implicit relationships exist between the people, places and things mentioned in a story and the museum objects with which they are associated. We describe an interface for authoring stories about museum objects in which textual stories can be associated with semantic annotations and media elements. A recommender component provides additional context as to how the story annotations are related directly or via other concepts not mentioned in the story.

The approach involves generating a concept space for different types of story annotation such as artists and museum objects. The concept space is predominantly made up of a set of events, forming an event space. The concept spaces of all story annotations can be combined into a single view. Narrative notions of setting and theme are used to reason over the concept space, identifying key concepts and time-location pairs, and their relationship to the rest of the story. Story setting and theme can then be used by the reader or author to assist in interpretation or further evolution of the story.

Keywords: Storytelling, museums, concept space, event space, theme, setting.

1   Introduction

Stories are often used in the presentation of museum objects. The story describes a context of the object, describing for example, how the object was created, or how the artwork can be seen as a response to conditions of the time. A story may relate multiple museum objects, describing how the creation of one was in reaction to, or in some way influenced, by another. Stories therefore provide a valuable mechanism for interpreting museum objects and understanding them within a wider context.

Museum storytelling is not the preserve of the museum professional. Museum organizations understand and expect stories to be told by their visitors. Rowe et al. [1] distinguish between the large, overall story of the exhibition and the small, personal stories associated with it. These small stories may originate from the visitor, triggered by something in the exhibition. For example, the visitor may recall a personal experience related

K. Janowicz et al. (Eds.): EKAW 2014, LNAI 8876, pp. 320–332, 2014.

to a museum object in the exhibition. Museums may also use small stories themselves to help visitors to relate to the overall story, for example, presenting the (possibly fictional) story of a character that lived at a certain time in order to bring it to life. O'Neil [2] describes how Kelvingrove Art Gallery and Museum in Glasgow selected a set of 100 stories through a process of public consultation to assist visitor interpretation of the exhibits. The use of storytelling in museums can be seen as part of a more general trend away from the presentation of museum works according to classification schemes (such as time periods and art schools). For example, Dion suggests that the paintings of Manet are better understood if exhibited with the paintings he was reacting against, rather than other impressionist paintings from 30 years later [3].

Many relationships can exist between the concepts (people, places, museum objects) mentioned in museum stories. Some of these relationships may be articulated in the story, while others may remain implicit. For example, the story may mention two artists but only touch on the connections between them. The story author may assume or be unaware of these connections. The reader may fail to establish these connections for themselves.

As well as implicit or explicit relationships between the concepts of the story, much more could potentially be said about how each story concept connects to further concepts currently lying outside the scope of the story. For example, participants in the story will be involved in many more activities, and mentioned locations will be the site of other events. Art objects mentioned in the story, may feature in many more events concerning, for example, their creation, acquisition and display. Unmentioned national or international events may have influenced what happened in the story. Some of these external links may assist the reader or author. Many more may be a distraction or irrelevance from the perspective of the story. We propose to employ the narrative concepts of setting and theme to provide a focus and abstraction for how the potentially large knowledge space around the story is explored, in which themes are key concepts of the story and settings are times and places at which events in the story occurred. This approach was inspired by our earlier work on the analysis of museum stories, manually annotated according to their constituent events, to understand what the story reader saw as important [4].

Stories are generally understood as comprising events, which are emplotted into structures that express relationships across those events, and are then narrated for an audience [5]. Many semantic and knowledge-based research applications developed for the museum sector adopt an event-based approach. This can be explained in terms of the richness of event-based representations for reasoning and their use in aligning heterogeneous knowledge sources [6] as well as their affordance for story representation. A number of event ontologies have been developed including LODE [7] and SEM [8]. The CIDOC CRM ontology [9] facilities an event-based approach to the representation of heritage and cultural knowledge. Heritage applications that utilize an event-based approach include the work of Hyvönen et al. [10] in the development of an event-based gazetteer of the First World War using Linked Data sources. Similarly, van den Akker et al. [11] utilize an event-based representation of heritage in which events are used as points of connection between historical concepts.

The rest of the paper is structured as follows. Section 2 describes a model of museum story authoring in which a story can be authored and semantically annotated alongside a recommender component that provides additional context. Section 3 shows how an event-based concept space can be generated and aggregated across story annotations. Section 4 describes how themes can be identified from the concept space and made available to the user for navigation. Section 5, describes how settings can be derived from the events of a concept space. Section 6, shows how settings themselves can be used to produce a concept space bringing in national and international perspectives on the events of the story. Section 7 describes a preliminary evaluation of the approach.

2   A Model of Museum Story Authoring

Museum objects are often presented alongside stories that supply a context. For example, the story might recount a mythological tale depicted in the object or describe how the life of the artist influenced the work. The story itself provides a branching-off point to explore other people, places, events as well as other stories and museum objects. In this work, we present a lightweight approach to authoring museum stories. The museum authoring component is paired with a recommender component that provides access to the surrounding context of the story. The link between the two components is the set of annotations associated with the story.

Fig. 1. The authoring environment for writing stories and adding media and annotations

The story authoring environment (see figure 1) and recommender component were implemented as modules in the Drupal Content Management System [12]. The annotations of the story are associated with Freebase topics, using a variant of Freebase Suggest customized for the Drupal environment. The story text can also be associated with media elements (images, videos). The story text and associated media objects are themed for presentation according to a pre-defined template.

The recommender component produces a concept space from the Freebase annotations associated with the story. The recommender component can be used both by the author to assist in story development and by the reader to explore beyond the story.

Annotations are used to generate a concept space comprising associated attributes (e.g. name and description of an artwork) and events (e.g. creation, ownership and exhibition events of an artwork) of the annotation. Narrative notions of setting and theme are then used to extract elements from the concept space of potential greater relevance to the author or reader.

In the narratology literature, themes are defined as the most central concepts of a story. Tomashevsky [13] argues that stories need themes for coherence and give context that can assist interpretation. Themes derived from the concept space suggest new concepts not annotated in the story. These may be used by the author to extend the scope of the story or by the reader to understand more about the story and its context. For example, a theme could relate to a person that is connected to a number of people mentioned in the story, thereby potentially extending the story as well as uncovering connections between annotations already associated with the story.

Settings are the derived from the time and location attributes of events in the concept space. The author or reader can use identified settings (such as London 1900-1905) as a starting point to find out about other events associated with the setting. Settings may also suggest relationships between times and locations mentioned in the story that may not be explicit in the text itself.

The recommender component is implemented as a Drupal module that uses the Freebase API to query and retrieve information and store it locally in the installation. The timeline.js library is used to visualize event spaces. A Drupal background process module is used to retrieve and process information from Freebase asynchronously in order not to disrupt user interaction with the system.

Although the surrounding context is not, and may never be, part of the story itself, narrative principles were adopted to represent and process story context for a number of interrelated reasons. First, events allow translation of knowledge represented using a range of different schemas into a homogenous form. This allows different types of reasoning to be applied across the events (such as theme and setting identification) and the events to be presented in accessible ways to the user, for example, using timelines. Second, theme and setting identification from the concept space allows what may potentially be the most interesting aspects brought to the attention of the reader or author. Third, navigating related sets of events in terms of setting and theme allows the concept space to be traversed using a type of abstraction different from that found in knowledge graph navigation tools (e.g. Sig.ma [14], Sindice [15]), though still maintaining a reasonable degree of domain independence. This abstraction may better fit the tasks of the author (e.g. "I need to say more about the historical context in which this happened") or questions of the reader ("In what other ways are the people in this story connected?"). The following sections describe how the concept space of a story is generated and how theme and setting are calculated and used.

3 Generating the Concept Space of Story Annotations

The concept space of a story is the aggregation of the concept spaces of the story annotations. First, we describe how a concept space is generated for one annotation, then how it is combined to provide a concept space for the story. The concept space of a single annotation is modeled as a mixture of direct attributes and events associated with the annotation. The same knowledge can often be modeled as either events or as direct properties of an entity [16]. For example, the birth and death of an artist can be modeled as a single life event with start and end dates, a pair of birth and death events, or as "date of birth" and "date of death" attributes of the person.

Some things are difficult to model as events such as the art movement associated with an artist. Their membership generally has no time or location data and is often a post-hoc interpretation of the artist's work. This can be contrasted with membership of an educational or learned institution, which is often an objectively recorded event with time and location information. For other types of data there can be significant information loss if an event-based or similar approach is not used. For example, the owners of an artwork and the durations of their ownership are more effectively represented in an event-based form rather than as an "owned by" property of the museum object.

The decision on whether to model knowledge as events or attributes can also be influenced by professional practice and the intended purpose to which the knowledge will be put. Through our own work, we found a preference among museum professionals to model birth and death as attributes, and to use these as part of the identifier for a person. Reasoning over the events of an artist's life (e.g. objects created, education history, membership of professional bodies) could throw up interesting connections to other artists. However, relationships based on birth and death events were not found to be interesting to the user [17]. This aligns with the observation made by Mäkelä et al [18] who found library indexers preferred to model birth and death as direct properties of a person rather than events.

Issues of knowledge representation, museum professional practice and intended uses of the knowledge were therefore used to determine appropriate events and attributes of key types of annotation. For artists, activities such as artwork creation, education, exhibition production, authoring, organization membership, awards and nominations were modeled as events. Associated artistic movements, birth and death were modeled as direct attributes.

The events and attributes of a story annotation are retrieved from Freebase using the topic and MQL APIs. The topic API is used to retrieve the name, description and associated image of the annotation. The topic API is also used to retrieve the notable types of a Freebase topic (e.g. whether a person is primarily known as an artist, author, actor, etc.). The Freebase MQL API is used first to retrieve additional knowledge based on the type of the annotation. For example, if a topic is of type "people/person" then date of birth, date of death and education history can be retrieved. Birth and death are then represented as attributes of the annotation. Education history is represented as events associated with the person. If a topic had the type "/visual_art/art_subject" (i.e. had been a subject of one or more artworks), then the associated artworks are represented as artwork creation events associated with the subject.

All event-based knowledge is stored using both the original Freebase properties as well as a mapping to a simple event schema. The schema, which grew out of our previous work with museum professionals modeling events, closely aligns with the LODE [7] and CIDOC CRM [9] ontologies. The event properties used are agent, location, start_time, end_time, activity and tag, in which the tag property is used to associate any other entities with the event. The agent, location and tag properties are equivalent to respectively the involvedAgent, involvedObject and atPlace properties of the LODE ontology. The CIDOC CRM properties had_participant, took_place_at, starts and finishes are equivalent to the agent, location, start_time and end_time properties. Activity denotes event type such as artwork creation.

A story annotation for the Impressionist painter Claude Monet (see figure 2), has a concept space that first includes the name, associated image, notable type and description field. This is followed by any retrieved direct attributes such as date of birth. Below the derived themes and settings is the associated event space. The direct attributes of the annotation and the attributes of the included events are all shown as navigation links. These links generate a new concept space around that associated concept. The entire event space or events of one activity (e.g. object creation) can be visualized on a timeline (excluding events for which there is no time information) (see figure 3). In a similar way, a concept space is generated for all annotations of a story, in which the events associated with each annotation are aggregated into a singe event space.

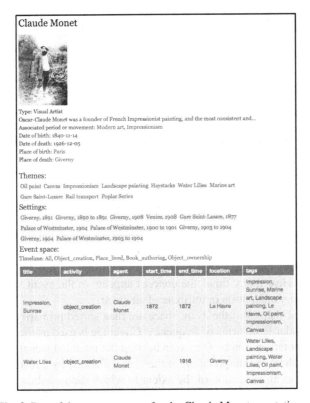

Fig. 2. Part of the concept space for the Claude Monet annotation

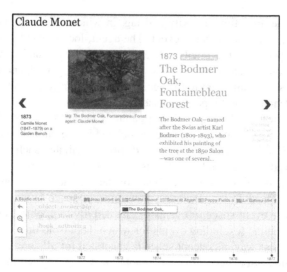

Fig. 3. Timeline of the event space of Claude Monet

4   Identifying Themes from a Concept Space

The event space created by the annotations of a story can be relatively large to navigate, easily containing over 100 events. Themes identified from the event space can assist the author or reader in making sense of the event space and understanding what is potentially of greatest interest from the perspective of the current story. As described earlier, themes are central concepts that bind together the other elements of the story. The story already has a candidate set of themes in the form of its annotations. The additional concepts (people, places, objects, etc.) contained in the concept space of the story are evaluated as candidate themes, in terms of how they bind together the annotations of the story.

Themes can be generated for any single or multi-annotation event space. The concepts contained in the event space are scored in terms of:

Coverage - How many story annotations they are associated with either as direct attributes of the annotation (such as art movement) or through co-occurring in an event with the annotation.

Frequency - How many times the concept appears in the event space as either an attribute of a story annotation or attribute of an event.

The candidate themes of the event space are then sorted primarily in terms of coverage and secondarily in terms of frequency. Coverage is used as the primary measure as the story annotations can be seen as indicating the intended meaning of the story (if added by an author) or interpretation of the story (if added by a reader). The measure of coverage gives an indication of the extent to which each candidate theme from the concept space binds together these annotations of the story. For example, a person that worked with each person annotated in the story could be of potential interest to the author or reader.

Frequency is used as a secondary measure to order themes that are associated with the same number of annotations. Frequency on its own would be a poor indicator of theme for a concept space aggregated across a set of annotations. For example, a person may be frequently associated with one of the annotations but have no connection to the others. This person would though be a potentially strong theme when exploring that single annotation. In this case, as each candidate theme has an association to the sole annotation of interest, only frequency can be used to determine theme. Frequency alone would therefore reveal for example a regular collaborator.

Figure 4 shows the themes associated with a story that has three annotations: the Impressionist painters Camille Pissarro, Claude Monet and Paul Cézanne. The top n themes are shown (n is specified in a configuration parameter). The top themes are those concepts in the concept space that connect to the most annotations, ordered by frequency. As all three participated in events involving the creation of Impressionist artworks, themes concerned with the art materials used, associated art movement and style of artwork predominate in the theme list. The art school Académie Suisse features higher in the theme list than Post-Impressionism even through it has a far lower frequency in the event space. This is because all three artists attended the school but all three are not associated with Post-Impressionism. If we contrast the themes with those associated solely with Claude Monet (figure 2) Académie Suisse does not feature as it has a lower frequency in that single annotation event space than themes such as Water Lillies.

Camille Pissarro, Claude Monet, Paul Cézanne

Tags:

Claude Monet   Paul Cézanne   Camille Pissarro

Themes:

Oil paint   Canvas   Impressionism   Landscape art   Genre art   Portrait   Art exhibition   Académie Suisse

Post-Impressionism   Still life

Fig. 4. Themes of a concept space for Camille Pissarro, Claude Monet and Paul Cézanne

The annotations (termed "Tags" in the interface), shown above the themes, are also ordered using the same thematic principles, primarily by the number of other annotations with which they are associated and secondarily by frequency. This gives an indication of how central each of the annotations are to the story. For example, if the annotations comprised an art teacher or pioneer and a number of other artists with which they worked (who did not necessarily work with each other), then the teacher or pioneer would head the list.

5   Identifying Settings from the Events of a Concept Space

Settings indicate both when and where something happened in a story. Setting is important as it identifies a point in time and space where characters or other objects in the story intersected. The candidate settings of an event space are all the times and locations associated in an event. A setting may include a time point (for events that have only a start or end time) or a time span (for events that have both a start and end time). Candidate settings are ranked using a similar approach to theme ordering. Settings are primarily ordered according to coverage, defined as the number of annotations associated with events featuring that particular setting.

Frequency is again used as the secondary ordering principle. Frequency is defined as the number of times the setting features in the event space. Figure 5 shows the settings derived from the event space of three story annoations: The Bodmer Oak, Fontainebleau Forest (an artwork by Monet), Chicago and 1900. These annotations could be associated with a story about the artwork being owned by Chauncey J. Blair in Chicago 1990. The highest ranked setting of the aggregated event space is Chicago 1990 as there is an event of Blair's ownership of the artwork that contains all three of the annotations. The next setting is New York 1873-1900. This refers to a single event about the artwork whose timespan (1873-1900) covers the annotation 1900, but is located in New York rather than Chicago.

Suggested settings may identify relationships between location and time annotations that are not made explicit in the story itself. For example, the story may mention, at various points, a year and an artist but not make the connection that the artist created an artwork in that particular year.

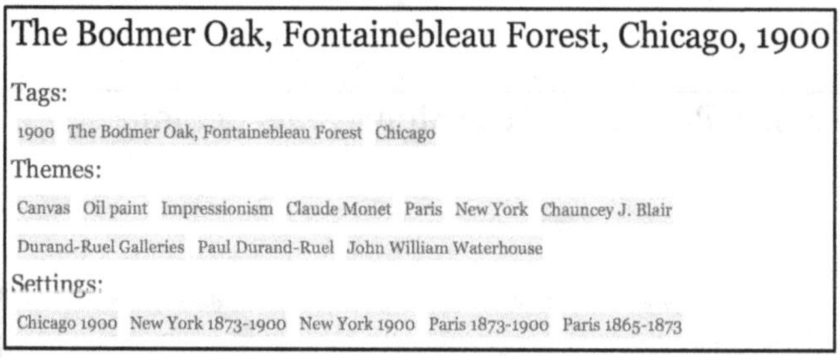

The Bodmer Oak, Fontainebleau Forest, Chicago, 1900

Tags:

1900   The Bodmer Oak, Fontainebleau Forest   Chicago

Themes:

Canvas   Oil paint   Impressionism   Claude Monet   Paris   New York   Chauncey J. Blair

Durand-Ruel Galleries   Paul Durand-Ruel   John William Waterhouse

Settings:

Chicago 1900   New York 1873-1900   New York 1900   Paris 1873-1900   Paris 1865-1873

Fig. 5. Settings derived from the event space of three story annotations

Similarly to themes, settings can be derived from the event space of a single annotation. In this case, as all events will have an association with the annotation, the settings can only ordered by frequency. When calculating the frequency of each setting within the event space only exact matches of time and location are considered. Temporal or spatial containment is not used. For example, an event with a setting of Paris 1880 would not be treated as an additional instance of the setting France 1880-1890. Using location and temporal containment to calculate smaller scale settings as contributing to the larger scale settings would imply some causal or other relationship between their associated events, which might not be the case. Events associated with the setting France 1880-1890 may have had no influence upon the events associated with the setting Paris 1880, and vice versa. Temporal and spatial containment is though used when presenting the event space of a setting to the author or reader. This is covered in the next section.

6   Generating the Event Space and Themes of a Setting

A setting can be used to generate a further space of events related to that setting. Events are retrieved that match as well as contain the setting in terms of location and time. This gives the user a view of larger scale events that may, but not necessarily, have had an influence on the events directly associated with the setting. So for example, if a setting was derived from the creation of an artwork and that setting fell during a national or global conflict then details of that conflict would be included in the event space of the setting. However, it is left to the reader or author to consider whether that could be relevant to the current story.

A set of themes can also be generated for the event space of the setting. However, as a setting rather than an annotation list is used to identify the events, only frequency is used to rank candidate themes. Figure 6 shows some of the events presented for the setting Paris 1865-1873, which was one of the settings suggested for the story in the previous section. In this case the local art events have been supplemented with national and international events such as the Paris Commune, which may help contextualize the local events more closely related to the story.

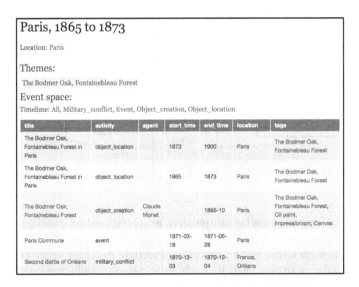

Fig. 6. Themes and events of the setting Paris 1865-1873

7   Navigating between the Story, Concepts and Settings

The story authoring environment and associated recommender component provide a number of ways of navigating the knowledge space surrounding a story. Starting from the story itself, the reader or author can explore either the concept space of an individual story annotation or the aggregated concept space of all annotations. A single or set of annotations can have an associated set of themes. Each theme links to the concept space for that theme concept. The direct attributes of the annotation (such as art movement) or the attributes of the event space (e.g. people, objects) can also be used to navigate to their associated concept space. Single or aggregated concept spaces can also have associated settings that each link to a further event space that can draw in larger scale national and international events that give further context to the setting. The possible pathways are illustrated in figure 7.

8   Preliminary Evaluation

A small observational study was conducted to gain insight into how the recommender component would support searching for different types of information in comparison to other information sources, namely web pages and Freebase. A task was devised around two artists, Dante Gabriel Rossetti and William Holman Hunt, who were both founders of the Pre-Raphaelite Brotherhood. The first question asked 'what artistic movement were they linked to?' in which participants should find that they were both founders of the Pre-Raphaelite Brotherhood. The second required participants to make a value judgement and asked 'what important artworks did they create?' The final question asked 'what relationships can you find between them and other artists?'

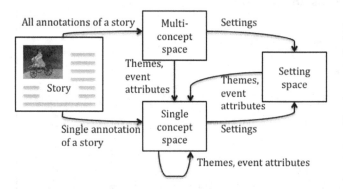

Fig. 7. Navigation paths between the story, its concepts and associated settings

Participants were either given access to i) Freebase pages about the two artists ii) the recommender page generated for each artist, plus the multi-annotation page that merged both artists, or iii) an artist biography for each taken from www.tate.org.uk. There were two participants for each version (six in total).

Preliminary findings suggest that the recommender facilitates finding information that links artists. For example, participants were significantly faster in linking both artists to the Pre-Raphaelite Brotherhood than in the other conditions. For question two, participants relied heavily on written text for making value judgements about important artworks. For the third question, when describing the relationship between artists, without fail the participants used the terms available to describe the nature of the relationship, rather than discovering or choosing their own.

In summary, the recommender appeared to facilitate discovering information that linked more than one artist, whereas a web-type resource made it easier to answer a question which required a value judgement to be made, so that participants could rely on the judgement of others who had written the text (participants did not appear to naturally want to dig further and decide importance for themselves). Similarly when describing relationships, the information available heavily influenced what was selected and the terms used to describe the relationship, even though further searching of the resources could have provided further information that could have been used.

9   Conclusions and Future Work

This paper has described an approach to assisting the authors and readers of museum stories to better understand and explore the surrounding context. The approach draws on the narrative notions of setting and theme to traverse the surrounding knowledge space according to concepts that help to tie together the elements of the story and the times and places associated with the events of the story. In a future evaluation we wish to investigate the types of pathways that users take through the knowledge space when guided by setting and theme, and look at how that is affected by features of the story and user characteristics. In terms of event reasoning, we intend to look at whether graph-based approaches and the weighting of event properties could be used to improve the ranking of settings and themes.

Acknowledgements. This work was partially funded by the DECIPHER (270001) EU 7th Framework Programme project in the area of Digital Libraries and Digital Preservation.

References

1. Rowe, S., Wertsch, J., Tatyana, K.: Linking Little Narratives to Big Ones: Narrative and Public Memory in History Museums. Culture and Psychology 16(2), 96–112 (2002)
2. O'Neill, M.: Essentialism, adaptation and justice: Towards a new epistemology of museums. Museum Management and Curatorship 21(2), 95–116 (2006)
3. Corrin, L.C., Kwon, M., Bryson, N.: Mark Dion. London, Phaidon (1997)
4. Wolff, A., Mulholland, P., Collins, T.: Storyscope: Using Theme and Setting to Guide Story Enrichment from External Data Sources. In: ACM Hypertext (2013)
5. Mulholland, P., Wolff, A., Collins, T.: Curate and storyspace: An ontology and web-based environment for describing curatorial narratives. In: Simperl, E., Cimiano, P., Polleres, A., Corcho, O., Presutti, V. (eds.) ESWC 2012. LNCS, vol. 7295, pp. 748–762. Springer, Heidelberg (2012)
6. Mäkelä, E., Hyvönen, E., Ruotsalo, T.: How to deal with massively heterogeneous cultural heritage data – lessons learned in CultureSampo. Semantic Web 3, 85–109 (2012)
7. Shaw, R., Troncy, R., Hardman, L.: LODE: Linking Open Descriptions of Events. In: Asian Semantic Web Conference, pp. 153–167 (2009)
8. van Hage, W.R., Malaise, V., Segers, R., Hollink, L., Schreiber, G.: Design and use of the Simple Event Model (SEM). Journal of Web Semantics 9(2) (2011)

9. Le Boeuf, P., Doerr, M., Ore, C.E., Stead, S. (eds.): Definition of the CIDOC Conceptual Reference Model (2014), http://www.cidoc-crm.org

10. Hyvönen, E., Lindquist, T., Törnroos, J., Mäkelä, E.: History on the Semantic Web as Linked Data - An Event Gazetteer and Timeline for World War I. In: CIDOC (2012)

11. Van den Akker, C., Legêne, S., Van Erp, M., et al.: Digital hermeneutics: Agora and the online understanding of cultural heritage. In: ACM WebSci Conference (2011)

12. http://www.drupal.org

13. Tomashevsky, B.: Thematics. Russian Formalist Criticism: Four Essays, pp. 62–95. University of Nebraska, Lincoln (1965) Lemon, L.T., Reis, M.J.

14. http://sig.ma

15. http://sindice.com

16. Stasinopoulou, T., Bountouri, L., Kakali, C., et al.: Ontology-Based Metadata Integration in the Cultural Heritage Domain. In: International Conference on Asian Digital Libraries (2007)

17. Wolff, A., Mulholland, P., Cornelli, J.: Prototype for Reasoning Across Narratives. DECIPHER Project Deliverable D3.4.1 (2013)

18. Mäkelä, E., Hypén, K., Hyvönen, E.: BookSampo - Lessons Learned in Creating a Semantic Portal for Fiction Literature. In: International Semantic Web Conference (2011)

Functional-Logic Programming for Web Knowledge Representation, Sharing and Querying

Matthias Nickles

Insight Centre for Data Analytics and Department of Information Technology
National University of Ireland, Galway
`matthias.nickles@deri.org`

Abstract. We propose a unified approach to semantically rich knowledge representation, querying and exchange for the Web, based on functional-logic programming. JavaScript- and JSON-based so-called information scripts serve as a unified knowledge representation and query format, with logical reasoning being a constraint solving or narrowing task. This way, our framework provides a highly versatile, easy to use and radically different alternative compared to conventional forms of knowledge representation and exchange for the Web.

Keywords: Knowledge representation, JSON-LD, JSON, JavaScript, Functional-Logic Programming, Relational Programming, Linked Data, Semantic Web.

1 Introduction and Related Work

With this position paper, we propose a functional-logic (FL) approach to expressive knowledge representation, querying and exchange for the Web which is directly based on a popular Web scripting language (JavaScript/JSON). Doing so, we aim to address serious issues with existing Semantic Web (SW) and Linked Data (LD) technologies: while RDF(S) has a foothold in the area of Linked Open Data (LOD), standard semantic technologies (including RDF and OWL) are arguably lacking acceptance in other large communities of potential SW/LD users, in particular those of Web software developers and many non-institutional knowledge providers. Instead, the use of "non-semantic" data formats like JSON, CSV, XML and relational database formats is prevalent in these areas. Furthermore, RDF is severely restricted in terms of logical expressiveness and reasoning capabilities (in particular in connection with SPARQL).

As a response to these issues, we propose so-called *information scripts* as a knowledge format which is at the same time more versatile and likely much easier to use (for non-logicians) than traditional SW or LD technologies. Information scripts are directly encoded using plain JavaScript and/or JSON (JavaScript Object Notation) - languages which are already familiar to many users. First-order features and querying are both based on existentially quantified (query) variables (related to but going beyond RDF's blank nodes), and deduction as well as query processing can be realized in a unified and expressive way as a straightforward constraint solving task. Main advantage over RDF besides the likely better comprehensibility to many people is the ability to formalize "real" logical formulas (including quantified variables, rules and negation).

K. Janowicz et al. (Eds.): EKAW 2014, LNAI 8876, pp. 333–338, 2014.
© Springer International Publishing Switzerland 2014

One flavor of our approach (Sect. 2.2) can be seen on the syntax level as an extension of JSON-LD [1] and allows for the inclusion of links in the form of URIs, but there is no requirement to make any link to RDF(S).

The closest related older approach is the Relational-Functional Markup Language RFML [3]. However, whereas RFML is a new FL language with XML syntax, we propose the direct use of an existing off-the-shelf language (namely JS/JSON) for representation, logical inference and queries. Other related works include approaches to "semantic programming" [5]. But in contrast to these, we do not aim for an integration of existing SW languages into general purpose programming languages. The idea to use query expressions for logic programming can also be found in [4], and the de facto unification of queries and logical rules can already be found in Datalog [2]. The concept of using boolean functions for logic programming is long known in the area of FL programming (e.g., [6]). MiniKanren [7] shares with us the goal to integrate logic programming directly into a host programming language, and can be implemented using general purpose languages including JS. However, our approach is syntactically even more lightweight and focuses on being a knowledge representation framework, compatible with JSON, while miniKanren focuses on being a programming language.

2 Information Scripts

We propose two concrete flavors of the idea outlined so far: 1) the direct use of a defined subset of JavaScript (JS) as a knowledge representation language, and 2) a variant of 1) which uses JSON (or JSON-LD) as underlying serialization format. Both variants (which can be combined) are called *information scripts*. Variant 1) uses syntactically plain JS scripts which can be embedded in Web pages and transferred in exactly the same way as any other parts of Web pages (e.g., microformats or embedded metadata). Only if we want to process queries over information scripts, we need additional functionality, however, this functionality could be provided as JS code also.

JS programs are ideal for this purpose since they are already meant to be transferred between hosts via the Internet, they can even be serialized to JSON if needed (if functions are encoded as source code), and modern browsers have sophisticated security mechanisms in place to ensure that programs do not harm client systems.

2.1 JavaScript as a Logic Language

The basic idea of FL programming is straightforward: logical rules and facts are represented by functions with a boolean result. Predicates become names of functions from their respective domain to type boolean. Logical connectives (including negation) are represented by boolean operators. Parameters of boolean functions correspond to universally quantified logical variables. *Query expressions* are used to obtain instantiations of existentially quantified logical variables (EQVs) (sometimes called *query variables* or just *logical variables*) for which boolean expressions with these variables evaluate to true. EQVs are represented using ordinary JS variables. Various sound evaluation mechanisms for FL programming languages exist, such as various forms of *narrowing* [6] and constraint solving. A way to approach evaluation technically would be by adding basic constraint solving capabilities in the form of a JS library or some external off-the-shelf constraint solver.

The syntax of information scripts is simple: informally, an *information script* is a non-empty set of JS function definitions of the form function pred(params) {...}, where pred is a predicate name. Each function needs to be referentially transparent, must not have any side effects, and must return a value of type boolean (variants might relax some of these restrictions, e.g., allow arbitrary result types). The list of parameters (which can be of any type) can be empty. We also need two predefined functions which both invoke the constraint solver (or some other kind of reasoner):

solveBind(qe[,v][,domains]) accepts a query expression qe in the form of an anonymous boolean function which in turn accepts a number of query variables (EQVs). solveBind returns an array of JS values which are those instances of the EQVs for which the call of qe returns boolean value true. Optionally, the set of EQVs whose instances shall be returned can be restricted to some subset (parameter v). Large or infinite domains could be handled by variants of solveBind which return their results incrementally in a lazy fashion (e.g., as a data stream). Inference using solveBind(qe) is undecidable, but if decidability is really required, information scripts would have to be restricted to some decidable fragment. Optionally, domains for the EQVs can be provided.

exists(qe[,domains]) is similar to solveBind(qe), but it just returns false or true - the latter if there are any instances of the EQVs for which qe is satisfied.

An information script is therefore encoded using a subset of plain JS (we use the EC-MAScript 6 standard syntax in the examples below, just to be able to encode anonymous functions syntactically nicely as Lambda abstractions). The syntax might look unusual at first for a logic language, but even though this issue could easily be fixed using a simple syntax preprocessor, a feature of this approach is precisely that the functional nature of rules is not concealed - logical rules are actually also (boolean) functions, and their "function nature" should allow programmers who are not familiar with logic programming or SW technologies to understand the meaning of an information script immediately, once the concept of query variables has been introduced. Example:

```
<script type="information">
function person(x) {
    return x == "ann" || x == "bertrand" || x == "charles" ||
           x == "dottie" || x == "evelyn" || x == "fred" ||
           x == "george" || x == "bill"; }
function parent(x,y) {
    return x=="dottie" && y =="george" || x == "evelyn" &&
           y == "george" || x == "bertrand" && y == "dottie" ||
           x == "ann" && y == "dottie" || x == "anne" && y == "bill"
           || x == "charles" && y == "evelyn"; }
function sameGenCousins(x,y) {
    return (x == y && person(x) ||
            exists(($x1, $y1) => (parent(x, $x1) && parent(y, $y1)
                                && sameGenCousins($x1, $y1)) )); }
</script>
```

Functions person(x) and parent(x,y) are rules (in the FL programming sense) although they actually define sets of ground facts such as person("ann"). Note that there is no requirement for the bodies of these functions to use boolean connectives; just as well we could obtain within the bodies of `person(x)` and `parent(x,y)` the person names and parent-relationships from some database or remote server using appropriate JS code. `sameGenCousins` is a recursive rule which states that two persons are same generation cousins whenever they are identical or if they have parents which are in turn same generation cousins. In classical logic, we would write this rule as $\forall x, y : x = y \lor \exists x_1, y_1 : parent(x, x_1) \land parent(y, y_1) \land sameGenCousins(x_1, y_1) \rightarrow sameGenCousins(x, y)$. Function `exists` calls the constraint solver and returns true *iff* for *some* instances of EQV `$x1` and EQV `$y1` condition `parent(x,$x1) && parent(y,$y1) && sameGenCousins($x1,$y1)` is satisfied. As an example for a query using the knowledge encoded in the script above, we call `solveBind(($x, $y) => sameGenCousins($x, $y))`, resulting in an array of tuples of same generation cousins

`[["ann","ann"], ... , ["dottie","evelyn"], ["ann","charles"]]`.

Observe that our approach so far does not enforce the use of any ontology or schema, or a namespace. There are at least two ways to add a schema or ontology if required: 1) switch from JS to a typed functional language (e.g., TypeScript or PureScript, which both compile to plain JS). This allows to attach type information to function parameters and thus simple schema functionality. 2) Model ontological constraints using the information script itself: e.g., `function person(x) {return user(x);}` asserts that every "user" is also a "person" (*is-a* relation of two concepts).

2.2 Non-ground JSON for Knowledge Representation and Queries

With the approach described above, ground knowledge is represented using JS terms such as `parent(dottie,charles)`. While this is compatible with data representation formats using ground terms as in logic programming, a more compact format using JSON as serialization format might be more handy in the context of the Web. In the following, we therefore propose a variant of the above which employs JSON (or a JSON application such as JSON-LD or Apache Avro) as representation format. We still require `solveBind` (Sect. 2.1), but query expressions, non-ground facts and rules (again in the form of boolean functions) can now optionally be embedded directly into a JSON document, which thus might contain logical variables (in the form of EQVs).

Concretely, we lift JSON to the first-order level by allowing certain JavaScript expressions and logic variables as property (key) values. We call such "higher-order JSON documents" *non-ground JSON* (NG-JSON). NG-JSON documents are valid JSON documents. They can contain expressions and logical variables in string form (e.g., `"age": "$age >= 18"`) and their semantics is operationally defined by a grounding process which maps them to their instances, i.e., a (possibly empty) set of ground JSON files where non-ground expressions have been replaced with their respective results (this does not imply that such an extension must be actually performed). The denotation of a NG-JSON document is not ground if values of logical variables are functions themselves (in JS, functions are first-class citizens), but we ignore this possibility here for lack of space. Note that the extensional form does not need to be finite (infinite groundings, if required, could be handled again by using lazy data streams). The NG-JSON document, which might be significantly more compact than its set of groundings, can either be directly transmitted to the client or knowledge consumer, or it could be expanded to ground data on server-side (similarly to *stored procedures* in DBMS). As an example for NG-JSON, consider the following document which specifies properties of persons (some omitted for lack of space):

```
[ {   "name": "John Smith",
      "@id": "http://johnsmith.com",
      "age": 23,
      "parents": [
          { "name": "Alice Springs" },
          { "name": "Tom Smith" } ],
      "adultSiblings": "$x.age > 17 && isSibling(this, $x)"
  },
  {   "name": "Mary Hippler",
      "age": 25,
      "parents": [
          { "name": "Alice Springs" },
          { "name": "Tom Smith" } ]
  },
  {   "name": "William Smith",
      "age": 16,
      "parents": [
          { "name": "Alice Springs" },
          { "name": "Tom Smith" } ]
  } ]
```

Like any NG-JSON, this example is a valid JSON file (with optional JSON-LD elements which are handy in a Web context, like @id for URIs). Only non-ground property is John's property "adultSiblings", which represents all objects (instances of EQV $x) which fulfill constraint isSibling(this, $x). In our example, the only valid instance of $x is the person with name Mary Hippler.

$x.age > 17 && isSibling(this, $x) is just syntactic sugar for

($x) => $x.age > 17 && isSibling(this, $x). this is a JS keyword which here refers to person John (as a JS object). The definition of rule isSibling is omitted (isSibling is a boolean function which simply checks if two persons are different and have the same parents. It could be provided either as a function-type property or in the way described in Sect. 2.1). An even more compact way to write this example could avoid the repetition of the values of parents using a JS expression.

Grounding is a context-sensitive operation - we need to know the domains of EQVs. In the example, the domain of $x is the set of all top-level objects in the NG-JSON document, but this is *not* necessarily so. We could allow for, e.g., numerical ranges or databases as domains, and provide a way to specify a context which is shared among different documents (a solution might involve JSON-LD's @context).

The same NG-JSON document can be seen both as a *data generator* (which "generates" all valid expansions of non-ground slots) and as a query (which instantiates the EQVs with values from the context, e.g., from some given database or objects in the NG-JSON document itself).

To obtain ground document(s), there are two possibilities: we can expand a non-ground expression to an array obtained from a solveBind call (see Sect. 2.1) (the result for the example would look like the NG-JSON document, but with `"adultSiblings": [{"name":"Mary Hippler", "age": 25, ...}]` instead of the current non-ground key/value pair `"adultSiblings": "$x...`).

Alternatively, we can create a set of ground JSON documents where each ground document represents one particular logical variable assignment. E.g., if the non-ground value of John's property "age" would be `"$age >= 21 && $age <= 23"`, grounding this way would generate *three* ground JSON documents with three different persons with name John Smith with three different ages 21, 22 and 23. Properties which trigger the former kind of expansion should be appropriately labeled in the NG-JSON document (this is omitted in the example code above).

Technically, the grounding of a NG-JSON document is a two-step process (details omitted for lack of space): firstly, we parse (de-serialize) the document as normal into an array of objects (here: persons), with the exception that each property value which is a string containing a lambda expression is converted into the respective anonymous function (this can be done by providing JSON.parse() with a suitable key (property) handler). Secondly, the array of objects is traversed and for each property p (here: `adultSiblings`) which contains an anonymous function, the anonymous function is passed as an argument to function `solveBind`. The result of `solveBind` is then used to ground property p. Some care is required to pass on the proper execution object context for keyword `this` with each `solveBind` and `isSibling` call.

3   Conclusions

With this paper, we have proposed a new, script-based approach to formal knowledge representation, querying and sharing. While this work certainly leaves room for refinements (e.g., how to express properties of properties?) and does not strive for coverage of all technical details, it is hoped that it provides a contribution towards semantic technologies which are more suitable for many Web-related tasks and Web-related software development than most existing Semantic Web approaches. Future work includes technical refinements and additions (such as formal specifications of query semantics and contexts), and an experimental evaluation.

References

1. http://www.w3.org/TR/json-ld/
2. Gallaire, H., Minker, J. (eds.): Logic and Data Bases, Symposium on Logic and Data Bases, Centre d'études et de recherches de Toulouse (1977); Advances in Data Base Theory (1978)
3. Boley, H.: Markup Languages for Functional-Logic Programming. Procs. 9th WFLP 2000 (2000)
4. Polleres, A., Wallner, J.: On the Relation Between SPARQL1.1 and Answer Set Programming. Journal of Applied Non-Classical Logics (JANCL) 23(1-2), 159–212 (2013)
5. Oren, E., Heitmann, B., Decker, S.: ActiveRDF: Embedding Semantic Web data into object-oriented languages. In: Web Semantics: Science, Services and Agents on the World Wide Web (2008)
6. Hanus, M., Lucas, S.: An Evaluation Semantics for Narrowing-Based Functional Logic Languages. Journal of Functional and Logic Programming 2001(2) (2001)
7. Byrd, W.: Relational Programming in miniKanren: Techniques, Applications, and Implementations. PhD dissertation (2009)

Inferring Semantic Relations by User Feedback

Francesco Osborne and Enrico Motta

Knowledge Media Institute, The Open University, MK7 6AA, Milton Keynes, UK
{francesco.osborne,e.motta}@open.ac.uk

Abstract. In the last ten years, ontology-based recommender systems have been shown to be effective tools for predicting user preferences and suggesting items. There are however some issues associated with the ontologies adopted by these approaches, such as: 1) their crafting is not a cheap process, being time consuming and calling for specialist expertise; 2) they may not represent accurately the viewpoint of the targeted user community; 3) they tend to provide rather static models, which fail to keep track of evolving user perspectives. To address these issues, we propose Klink UM, an approach for extracting emergent semantics from user feedbacks, with the aim of tailoring the ontology to the users and improving the recommendations accuracy. Klink UM uses statistical and machine learning techniques for finding hierarchical and similarity relationships between keywords associated with rated items and can be used for: 1) building a conceptual taxonomy from scratch, 2) enriching and correcting an existing ontology, 3) providing a numerical estimate of the intensity of semantic relationships according to the users. The evaluation shows that Klink UM performs well with respect to handcrafted ontologies and can significantly increase the accuracy of suggestions in content-based recommender systems.

Keywords: Ontology, User Modelling, Recommender Systems, Ontology-based User Modelling, Data Mining, Ontology Learning, Community-based Ontologies.

1 Introduction

In the last ten years, ontology-based recommender systems have been shown to be effective tools for predicting user preferences and suggesting items. Many of them [1,2,3,4] build user models as overlays of the domain ontology and use variations of the spreading activation technique for propagating the user feedback on certain items to related concepts. This solution allows recommender systems to suggest items that are semantically similar to the ones that the user liked and to compare users according to their preferences on a variety of concepts. In most cases, the ontologies used by these methods are manually crafted in OWL, both to facilitate sharing and because this language enjoys good tool support.

There are however some issues associated with the ontologies adopted by these approaches, such as: 1) their crafting is not a cheap process, being time consuming and calling for specialist expertise; 2) they may not represent accurately the viewpoint of the targeted user community; 3) they tend to provide rather static models, which fail to keep track of evolving user perspectives.

K. Janowicz et al. (Eds.): EKAW 2014, LNAI 8876, pp. 339–355, 2014.

A common way to craft these ontologies is to consult domain experts, who however, may disagree on how to represent the different semantic relationships or may propose solutions that, while describing a correct formalization of the domain, may not be the most adequate for a recommender system. For example, users may take decisions on the basis of features that were instead neglected in the expert crafted ontology. Of course, it is possible to evaluate a first draft of the ontology on a sample of users and then iterate the crafting process; however this is a time consuming and expensive process. Moreover, the final product is a static knowledge base that will eventually need to undergo new modifications, e.g., when adding new categories of items to the recommender system.

For all these reasons, a more appealing perspective is to consider the domain ontology, and in particular the semantic relationships between concepts, as something dynamic, which can be learned, adjusted and adapted according to the emergent semantics that characterize a group of users. The idea of deriving community-based ontologies from social networks or folksonomies has been investigated by a number of authors, yielding promising results [5,6]. A possible drawback of these ontologies is that they usually strongly depend on the community taken into consideration. However, this actually becomes an advantage when the aim is to adapt an ontology to that same community. Adapting ontologies to specific users is also the idea which gave origin to personal ontology views [7] (POVs), which proved to be effective tools in assisting tasks like web navigation and search, allowing the users to classify items according to their own mental categories [8].

We thus propose to combine these two ideas (extracting ontologies from communities and tailoring an ontology to particular users) in the context of recommender systems by exploiting user ratings for eliciting emergent semantics and then adapting the ontology to these users for improving the recommendation accuracy. The flow of information thus becomes bidirectional: the user preferences are used to adapt and enrich the domain ontology and the ontology is exploited to infer additional user preferences.

In particular, we want to be able to select among the possible ontologies describing a certain domain the one which works best in forecasting the preferences of a specific group of users, by exploiting state of the art algorithms for propagating user preferences in ontology-based recommender systems, such as those presented in [1,2,4]. Hence, we do not claim that an ontology crafted or enriched by means of user feedback would necessary be the most complete or formally correct representation of a domain: only that it will work better than the available alternatives for that specific task.

As an example, by analysing user ratings we may detect that users who like the Italian cheese "Gorgonzola" tend to like also "Blue Danish" more often than one might expect on the basis of their actual semantic relationships: in fact in that ontology they may simply be two subclasses of "Cheese", with no property in common. Hence, this situation can be addressed by analysing these two types of products, discovering that they are both blue mould cheeses and then adding either a common superclass, "Blue Mould Cheese", or a related property. Analogously, we may also learn the intensity of the different semantic relationships according to the users. For example, we may discover that the relationship between "Wine" and "White Wine" is stronger than the one between "Juice" and "Orange Juice", even if both relationships are *subClassOf*.

We can then use this knowledge to compute a more accurate semantic distance between concepts and thus foster the recommendation process.

As a contribution to addressing this issue, we propose *Klink UM* (Klink for User Modelling), an algorithm which generates semantic relationships between concepts using as input the user ratings on items associated with keywords. Klink UM is a modified version of *Klink* [9], an algorithm designed by the authors of this paper to mine semantic relationships between research areas. Klink was developed for Rexplore [10], a novel tool that provides a variety of functionalities and visualizations to support users in exploring information about the academic domain. Klink UM uses similar statistical and machine learning techniques for finding hierarchical and similarity relationships between keywords associated with rated items and can be used for: i) building a conceptual taxonomy from scratch, ii) enriching and correcting an existing ontology, iii) providing a numerical estimate of the intensity of the semantic relationships according to a group of users.

The rest of the paper is organized as follows. In section 2, we describe the Klink UM algorithm, focusing in particular on the changes with respect to the original Klink algorithm. In section 3 we evaluate the approach i) by comparing the generated taxonomies with two gold standard human crafted ontologies and ii) by applying Klink UM to a content-based recommender system with the aim of increasing the accuracy of recommendations. Section 4 deals with the related work. In section 5 we summarize the main conclusions and outline future directions of research.

2   The Klink UM Algorithm

2.1   Overview of the Approach

Most ontology-based recommender systems rely mainly on the conceptual taxonomy defined by semantic relationships such as *subClassOf* [1,2,4]. Klink UM can be used to infer both hierarchical and similarity relationships and adopts by default the SKOS model[1], a standard way to represent knowledge organization systems using RDF. In SKOS it is possible to express a taxonomy by stating that a concept is more or less specific than another. Thus, the hierarchical links detected by Klink UM (see section 2.3) are mapped to *skos:broaderGeneric,* a property from the *SKOS 5 model*, which indicates that a concept is broader than another. For example, "Music" is broader than "Rock Music". Similarly, strong similarity links between concepts (see section 2.3) are mapped to the *relatedEquivalent* relationship, which we define as a sub-property of *skos:related*, to indicate that two particular ways of referring to a concept can be treated as equivalent. A trivial case is when there are lexical variations of the same tag, e.g., "rock-music" and "Rock Music".

Klink UM can be used in two modalities: i) to build a conceptual taxonomy and ii) to enrich, correct and/or give suggestions for improving an existing ontology. In the first case the input is a collection of user ratings associated with keywords, tags or

---

[1] http://www.w3.org/2004/02/skos/

categories and the result is an OWL model and a matrix associating each relationship with an intensity score. In the second case, the input includes also the original ontology and the output yields the enriched ontology, the intensity matrix and, when possible, some suggestions for further modifications.

When feeding an ontology to Klink UM, it is also possible to associate a weight to each semantic relationship. The higher the weight, the more resilient to changes will be the relationship. The given ontology is treated as a taxonomy shaped by hierarchical links whose strength is defined by the weights. The links will be included in the set of hierarchical links discovered by Klink UM (section 2.3) and may be deleted if stronger links are found (section 2.5). It is however possible to preserve a relationship despite any counter-evidence by assigning a weight equal to infinity.

The approach herein presented includes several new features with respect to the (original) Klink algorithm. Among them: 1) the possibility of using user ratings as input, 2) the ability to examine and correct an existing ontology and 3) the capacity of suggesting changes to an ontology or signalling discrepancies between the ontology and the user feedback.

Pseudocode 1 – **The KlinkUM Algorithm**

```
function KlinkUM (RATINGS, KEYWORDS, OWL, OWL_weights) returns
(NEW_OWL, NEW_OWL_weights) {
    RATINGS = a set of user ratings on the keywords/tags/categories;
    KEYWORDS = a set of keywords/tags/categories;
    OWL = a initial OWL Ontology, optional;
    OWL_weight = the weights associated with the ontology relationships, optional;
    con_prob = computeConditionalProbabilities(RATINGS); // Step 1
    keywords_to_merge=true;
    while (keywords_to_merge) {
        foreach K in KEYWORDS {
            co_keywords = selectKeywordsWithRatingsInCommon(K);
            foreach K2 in co_keywords { // Step 2
                linkH = computeHL(K, K2, con_prob, RATINGS);
                // hierarchical link
                if (linkH > tₕ) links["H", K, K2]= linkH;
                else if (not the first loop) {
                    linkS = computeSL(K, K2, RATINGS);
                    // strong similarity link
                    if (linkS > tₛₛ) links["S", K, K2]= linkS;
                    // weak similarity link
                    else if (linkS > tᵥₛ) links["WS", K, K2] = linkS;
                }
            }
        }
    links = filterKeywords(KEYWORDS, links); // Step 3
    if (not the first loop) { // Step 4
        if (at least one weak similarity link in links)
```

```
   clusters = clusterSimilarityLinks(links);
  if (at least one strong similarity link in links)
   KEYWORDS = mergeKeywords(links, KEYWORDS);
  else keywords_to_merge = false;
  }
 }
 links = fixLoops(links); // Step 5
 links = enforceStructuralRequirements(links,  OWL_weight);
 OWL_NEW = OWL; // Step 6
 foreach (link or concept discrepancy between OWL and links)
   NEW_OWL = proposeModification(discrepancy);
 foreach (cluster in clusters)
   NEW_OWL = alertForMissingPropertyOrSuperClass(cluster);
 NEW_OWL_weights = normalizeWeights(links);
 return NEW_OWL, NEW_OWL_weights;
}
```

The steps of the algorithm are the followings:

1) The matrix representing user ratings on the keywords is used for computing the conditional probability that a user who has given a positive or negative feedback on keyword x would give the same feedback on keyword y.
2) Each keyword is compared with the other keywords with which it shares at least n ratings in common in order to infer the *hierarchical links*, which shape the conceptual taxonomy, and the *strong/weak similarity links*, which denote the degree of similarity between keywords. The detection of the latter depends on the taxonomy (see section 2.3.2), thus they are computed only after the first loop.
3) The keywords are filtered and tidied up and those that do not relate to other keywords or appear to be outside the target domain are excluded;
4) If this is not the first loop, the keywords that share a strong similarity link are merged, and the keywords that share a weak one are clustered together. Steps 2-4 are repeated with the new keywords obtained by merging the keywords with inferred equivalence relationships, until no new *similarity link* is inferred.
5) The links are tidied up by deleting loops and redundancies; the user's requirements on the structure are enforced;
6) If an initial ontology was given, a series of suggested *modifications* with respect to it and some *alerts* about possibly missing properties or super concepts may be proposed to the user. The algorithm returns an OWL file and a matrix yielding the detected intensity of hierarchical and similarity relationships.

We will now explain more in detail how the individual steps are carried out.

2.2   Step 1 – From Ratings to Conditional Probability

Klink UM relies on variations of the subsumption model [11,12] for detecting hierarchical links. The subsumption model is used for finding hierarchical relationships between terms associated with documents. Term x is said to subsume term y if two conditions holds: $P(x|y) = 1$ and $P(y|x) < 1$, e.g., if y is associated to documents that are a subset of the documents x is associated to. Usually the first condition is relaxed in $P(x|y) > \alpha$, since it is quite improbable to find a perfect relationship, with $0.7 < \alpha < 0.8$.

As discussed in [9], Klink originally computed the conditional probability of keyword x given keyword y by using the ratio of the co-citations to the total citations of y. Since Klink UM considers ratings instead of co-citations, it calculates the conditional probability that a user who has a positive or negative opinion on x will have the same opinion on y. This is computed as the ratio between common positive/negative feedbacks and the total positive/negative feedbacks received by a keyword. A rating from a user above/below her/his average rating by a chosen threshold constitutes a positive/negative feedback on a keyword. Let us consider the case in which a user rates 7 the keyword "Beer", 8 the keyword "Wine" and has an average rating of 6.5. If we choose a threshold for the difference equal to 1, Wine has a positive feedback, but not so Beer. With a threshold equal to 0.5 both receive a positive feedback. We call this a *common positive feedback*, since it relates to the same user. Thus for a common positive feedback the difference between the given rating and the average rating of the user must be positive and higher than a threshold for both keywords. The *common negative feedback* follows the same rule with the difference that in this case the difference must be negative. Even if in many systems a user is not allowed to rate directly the keywords, the rating of a keyword can be estimated by using the average rating of the items associated with it.

For example, if keyword A received 50 feedbacks and 25 of them were in common with keyword B, the conditional probability of the feedbacks $P_f(B|A)$ is equal to 0.5, indicating a very strong relationship between the two keywords. To have a better idea about the direction of the subsumption relationship, we need to compute also $P_f(A|B)$: for example if $P_f(A|B)=0.1$ we have a good evidence that A may be a sub-concept of B, since many people who like A also like B, whereas only a limited number of people who like B are into A. However, if $P_f(A|B)=0.5$ we will still be clueless about the direction of the relationship: A and B might be similar concepts or even synonymous.

2.3   Step 2 – Inferring Hierarchical and Similarity Relationships

In this section we will elaborate on inferring the hierarchical and similarity links between keywords. We will use the first kind of link to build the conceptual taxonomy, and the second one to merge together keywords that point to a single concept and to suggest relationships between concepts that may not be explicit in the initial ontology.

For the following steps we will also need a way to estimate how similar two keywords are according to the users. Collaborative item-based filtering recommenders [13] make the assumption that items similarly rated by a common pool of users will also be similar. Hence, a common way to estimate the similarity of a pair of items is given by the cosine similarity between their vectors of user ratings. Here we adopt the same method to compute the similarity between keywords and we estimate the rating implicitly assigned to a keyword by a user as the average of the ratings given to the pool of items tagged with the keyword.

2.3.1   Inferring Hierarchical Links

A hierarchical link of keyword x with respect to y is inferred when the difference between the conditional probabilities $P_f(y|x)$ and $P_f(x|y)$ is high enough and the two terms are considered fairly similar by the users. More formally, we compute the strength of the hierarchical relationship as:

$$L(x,y) = \left(\frac{P_f\,(y|x)}{ln(D_x+1)} - \frac{P_f\,(x|y)}{ln(D_y+1)} \right) \cdot cos(\hat{x},\hat{y}) \cdot (1 + nameSim(x,y)) \quad (1)$$

where $cos(\hat{x},\hat{y})$ is the cosine similarity between the two rating vectors associated to the keywords; D_i is the number of items associated with keyword i; $nameSim(x,y)$ is the ratio between the longest common substring of x and y and the length of the longer of these two keywords.

The first factor of the formula will give the direction of the relationships, while the other two will estimate its strength. We assume in fact that two classes of items have stronger relationships if they are considered similar by the users and (optionally) share a significant part of their name. The number of items associated with a keyword is needed to balance the cases, not so uncommon during the cold start phase, in which a relatively smaller keyword may have received a higher number of feedbacks than its super-concept. This may bias the sample and reverse the link direction.

A hierarchical link is inferred when $L(x,y) > t_h$ and then x is considered a candidate for becoming a sub-concept of y. The value of $L(x,y)$ will also be used to weight the intensity of a semantic relationship.

2.3.2 Inferring Similarity Links

A naive way to detect similarity links between keywords would be to consider all the couple of keywords with a cosine similarity higher than a certain threshold. However, in a conceptual taxonomy is perfectly normal for related concepts, such as siblings, to be quite similar, especially in the lower levels. For this reason, using directly the cosine similarity would usually yield clusters of concepts under a common branch of the taxonomy. In fact, this same idea was actually used by Chuang and Chien [14] for generating topic hierarchies.

Hence, to infer a similarity link, we should not only check that two keywords are generally similar, but also that they are more similar to each other than they are with their siblings and super-concepts. We are thus looking for a similarity that can not be solely explained by their placement in the conceptual taxonomy.

Hence, we detect the similarity links between two keywords x and y by means of the following formula:

$$S(x,y) = \frac{cos(\hat{x},\hat{y})}{max\left(cos_{sup}(x,y), cos_{sib}(x,y)\right)+1} \quad (2)$$

where $cos_{sup}(x,y)$ and $cos_{sib}(x,y)$ are the average cosine similarities with the common immediate super-concepts and the common sibling concepts. We consider as siblings of x the immediate sub-concepts of the immediate super-concepts of x, according to the detected hierarchical relationships. Root concepts are considered siblings to each other.

Using this formula we infer two kinds of links: the strong similarity link and the weak one. The first correspond to $S(x,y)>t_{ss}$, the second to $S(x,y)>t_{ws}$, where $t_{ss}> t_{ws}$.

The strong similarity link is used for the identification of synonymous or related keywords that point to the same concept. The weak similarity link is utilized for the detection of clusters of similar keywords that may indicate the presence of an implicit super-concept or propriety, not reflected by the current ontology.

2.3.3   Estimating the Threshold Values

Assigning a sound value to t_h, $t_{ss,}$ and t_{ws} is important for generating a conceptual taxonomy that is optimized for inferring user preferences. While it is possible to assign these values empirically and vary them according to the desired sensitivity as we did in [9], in most cases it is better to rely on an automatic method. Hence, we use the Nelder-Mead algorithm [15], which is a derivative-free optimization method, used to solve parameter estimation problems when the function values are uncertain. It considers the parameters to be found as vertices of a simplex, which is a generalization of the notion of a tetrahedron to arbitrary dimensions. Then it performs a sequence of geometrical transformations on it, aimed at minimising an evaluation function.

In this case we need a function that measures the ability of the ontology in yielding sound suggestions to the users. We assume that an ontology will be better at this task if it is able to assist the generation of a list of preferred items with a high correlation to the correct ones. Hence, we adopt as evaluation function the Spearman's rank correlation coefficient ρ computed between the lists of items suggested by using spreading activation [4] on 50% of the rated items and the list produced by ordering the other half according to their ratings. This similar procedure was used in [3,4] for evaluating the accuracy of ontology-based recommender systems and will also be used in section 3.2 for evaluating the performance of Klink UM.

The Spearman's coefficient provides a non-parametric measure of statistical dependence between two ordinal variables and gives an estimate of the relationship between two variables using a monotonic function. It is defined as the Pearson correlation coefficient between ranked variables. Here, we prefer the former rather than the latter, since it is able to handle ties, which can be frequent during the cold-start phase or in the case of data sparsity.

2.4   Step 3 and 4 – Keyword Filtering and Merging

To filter out keywords that are just noise or irrelevant to the domain in hand, Klink UM applies three techniques: 1) it deletes keywords without inferred relationships with any other keyword; 2) it uses the common feedback distributions to detect and delete keywords that are too general; 3) it uses external knowledge from web pages about a domain to check the estimated dimension of the keywords in that same domain and then deletes those under a certain threshold. These methods are also used in Klink, and discussed more thoroughly in [9].

The keywords which share a strong similarity link are considered synonymous, thus they will be merged and at the next iteration of the algorithm they will be considered as a single keyword with a rating vector given by the average of the rating vectors of the merged keywords. The keywords that share a weak link will be clustered together, but they will preserve their individuality. The cluster will be used to generate the alert relative to potential discrepancies between the original ontology and the perspective of the users. In fact the clustered keywords point to a situation that should be recognized also in the ontology, for example by adding a common super-concept or a shared property. Both merging and clusterization are implemented by means of a bottom-up single-linkage hierarchical clustering algorithm which uses the inverse of $S(x,y)$ as the distance between the keywords.

The algorithm will then return to step 2 if new similarity links are inferred in this iteration, otherwise it will proceed to step 5.

2.5   Step 5 – Tidying up the Keywords and Adjusting the Links

The links are reassessed by detecting loops in the model and breaking them up by eliminating the weaker links in terms of $L(x,y)$. Redundant links are also deleted. A redundant link is a link that is unnecessary because implicit in other relationships: for example if A is a sub-concept of B and B a sub-concept of C, we do not need to state explicitly that A is a sub-concept of C.

This phase includes the enforcement of the user requirements on the structure. At the moment Klink UM supports two main structure boundaries, which are the maximum number of super and sub concepts. They are implemented by deleting the links in excess with lower $L(x,y,)$ score. As anticipated in section 2.2, a semantic relationship included in the initial ontology with an assigned weight w can be deleted only for inserting links with $L(x,y)>w$.

2.6   Step 6 – Suggestions and OWL Creation

If the algorithm did not receive an ontology in input, it outputs an OWL model and the matrix containing the detected intensity scores of the semantic relationships (equal to $L(x,y)$). These scores can be used to weigh the links of the conceptual taxonomy and enhance a variety of approaches [1,2,4] that rely on graph-based distance to assess semantic similarity between concepts.

As stated before, Klink UM produces the OWL ontology by mapping the hierarchical links to the *skos:broaderGeneric* semantic relationships and the strong similarity links to the *relatedEquivalent* relationships. However it is up to each individual implementation to decide whether to use the default SKOS-based model or to produce instead an alternative representation of the hierarchical structure.

If an input ontology is given, the algorithm generates a list of suggestions that can be answered with a yes or no by the user. For each detected discrepancy between the given ontology and the generated one, the algorithm suggests a modification to the original ontology, e.g., adding a new *skos:broaderGeneric* relationship between two previously unrelated concepts. At the moment Klink UM can suggest: 1) to add a relationship, 2) to delete a relationship, 3) to add a concept, 4) to delete a concept. After the user validates the suggestions, the algorithm proceed to generate a new OWL model. Of course the user can also decide to trust Klink UM and accept all suggestions by default.

At the end, Klink UM will also yield a warning about potentially neglected properties linking the component of the clusters found via the *weak similarity links*. These clusters in fact suggest the existence of a relationship between their elements, which affect the user ratings, but do not appear in the domain ontology. In this case, Klink UM does not try to implement any automatic modification, and only reports potential problems that an ontology engineer may want to address.

3   Evaluation

In this section we aim to prove that 1) Klink UM can generate conceptual taxonomies similar enough to the ones crafted by human experts and 2) the ontologies generated or enriched by Klink UM are tailored to a particular group of users, and thus particularly useful for recommendation purposes.

Hence, in the first part we will measure the F-measure between conceptual taxonomies generated by Klink and gold standard expert crafted ontologies. In the second part we will compare the accuracy of the suggestions yielded by a content-based recommendation system when using a human crafted ontology, the same ontology enriched by Klink UM, and an automatically generated ontology.

3.1   Ontology Generation

In order to evaluate the ability of Klink UM to generate a conceptual taxonomy from scratch we used two ontologies, designed about two years ago by experts in the gastronomic domain and ontology engineers for an adaptive application called WantEat [16], developed as part of the PIEMONTE Project. WantEat is an application for Android and iPhone that allows a user to explore the "slow food" domain. The users can give a feedback by tagging, voting, visiting and bookmarking both items and categories. In this case, items are gastronomic products, such as a particular Parmesan cheese sold by a certain producer, while categories include general concepts, such as "Parmesan Cheese", "Fat Cheese" and "Cheese".

The two ontologies are 1) *Cold Cuts*, a three level ontology with 19 classes, describing the different cuts of meat and 2) *Drinks*, a three level ontology with 33 classes, describing different kinds of drinks. Our hypothesis is that Klink UM should be able to generate OWL ontologies that are very similar to the human crafted ones by analysing user ratings on the concepts included in the ontology. This approach was tested against the classic subsumption method as in [11] and [12], using the conditional probability that the average user who likes/dislikes keyword x will have the same relationship with keyword y, as described in section 2.2.

We used the dataset collected for [4] which includes user ratings on cuts of meat (in particular cold cuts) and on drinks obtained by means of online questionnaires. The ratings ranged between 0 and 10 and the threshold for the negative/positive feedback described in Section 2.2 was set to 1. The initial sample for the *Cold Cuts* included 1392 ratings given by 87 subjects, 19-45 years old, recruited according to an availability sampling strategy. The sample for the *Drinks* ontology included 7623 ratings given by 231 subjects, in the age range 19-38 years old, similarly recruited.

We ran Klink UM and the baseline method 10 times for each different set of randomized input data and compared the generated ontologies with the two original gold standard ontologies, using the average recall, precision and F-measure (that is their harmonic mean) of the inferred relationships.

Figure 1 shows the F-measure of the two approaches with respect to the *Cold Cuts* and the *Drinks* ontologies. Clearly, in both cases Klink UM performs better than the subsumption method, with the two resulting curves showing a statistically significant difference ($p<10^{-12}$, according to the chi-square test). Klink UM is able to obtain at the largest sample size a Precision of 96% with a Recall of 94% for *Drinks* (N= 7623) and a Precision of 87% with a Recall of 80% for *Cold Cuts* (N=1392).

The performance of Klink UM depends on two factors: 1) the fraction of keywords voted by the average user (μ) and 2) the number of ratings. The first component is important since Klink UM needs to compare the votes of the same user on different keywords in order to infer the hierarchical links: if these data are too sparse, this becomes difficult. The left panel of Figure 2 shows the Klink UM performance on both *Drinks* and *Cold Cuts* as a function of μ. It can be seen that it performs well for both ontologies, with the *Drinks* dataset yielding better results thanks to its higher number of ratings.

The right panel of Figure 2 highlights the trade-off relationship between the number of ratings and the μ value for the *Drinks* dataset. If μ is high enough, Klink UM is able to obtain very good results even with a low number of ratings: with $\mu = 0.8$, Klink UM is able to reach an F-measure of 75% with only 5000 ratings, whereas with $\mu = 0.5$ it needs 7000 ratings to reach the same F-measure.

It is interesting to notice that the curves exhibit a progressively increasing crowding with the increasing value of μ; the gap between the curves corresponding to $\mu = 0.4$ and $\mu = 0.6$ is ten times larger than the gap between $\mu = 0.8$ and $\mu = 1$. The chi-square test confirms this behaviour: the probability that the difference between the $\mu = 0.4$ and $\mu = 0.6$ curves may be ascribed to chance is $p < 10^{-12}$, increasing to $p = 2\times10^{-7}$ for the $\mu = 0.6$ and $\mu = 0.8$ curves, and finally losing statistical significance with $p = 0.93$ for the $\mu = 0.8$ and $\mu = 1$ curves.

Figure 3 shows a portion of the version of the *Drinks* ontology generated by Klink UM, highlighting the intensity of the subsumption relationships according to the users. For example, it appears that "Spumante" (the Italian version of Champagne) is considered a less typical "Wine" than "Red Wine" and "White Wine". Thus if we want the ontology to mirror this perception we should differentiate "Spumante" from its siblings "Red Wine" and "White Wine" by adding a property or by using a different super-concept for "Spumante". Of course a group of users with different background and drinking habits may have a different idea on this subject.

The placement of fruit-flavoured liquor under Wine is formally a mistake since accordingly to the human crafted ontology it should be under Hard Liquor. However by looking at the ratings we can see in this case a stronger correlation with the Wine concept. As the number of ratings increase this may be revealed as a statistical fluctuation or rather it may confirm that our users considered it more similar to the Wine concept. Hence, the ontology used for recommendation purpose may be modified accordingly, e.g., by adding a common property.

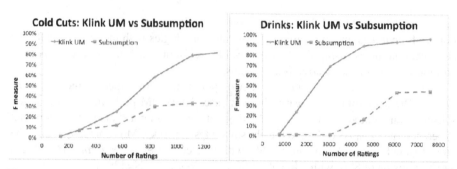

Fig. 1. F-measure of Klink UM and the Subsumption method for the *Cold Cuts* and the *Drinks* datasets

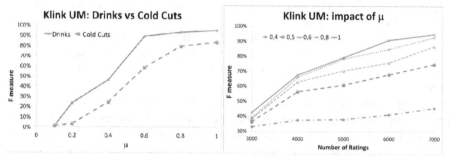

Fig. 2. On the left: the performance of Klink UM in the two tests as a function of μ. On the right: the trade-off between μ and ratings for the *Drinks* dataset.

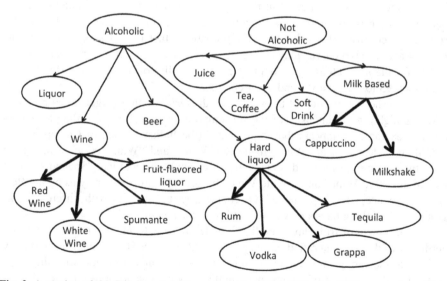

Fig. 3. A portion of the *Drinks* ontology generated by Klink UM with 5000 user ratings. The width of a link is proportional to the detected intensity of the semantic relationship.

3.2   Ontology Enrichment and Generation for Content-Based Recommender Systems

Many state of the art approaches use ontologies or conceptual taxonomies for inferring additional user interests from an initial set of ratings and then suggesting items. A standard technique is to use spreading activation to propagate user interests from a set of initial concepts or items to the semantically related concepts. To measure the ability of Klink UM in assisting the recommendation process we will use the approach described in Cena et al [4], which was shown to outperform other similar techniques, such as [1,2]. The links between concepts were weighted by the intensity detected by Klink UM (see formula 1), when available.

In particular we will compare the accuracy of three approaches, namely:

- Spreading activation on an expert crafted ontology (labelled **S**)
- Spreading activation on an expert crafted ontology, corrected and enriched by accepting by default Klink UM suggestions (labelled **SE**)
- Spreading activation on a conceptual taxonomy generated from scratch by Klink UM (labelled **SG**)

To compute the accuracy we rely on the *Drinks* dataset described in the previous section. The accuracy of a certain approach was measured by giving to it only a certain fraction r of user ratings and then comparing the produced recommendations with the true user preferences. The comparison was done using Spearman's rank correlation coefficient ρ, the well known non-parametric measure of statistical dependence, which we already discussed in Section 2.3.1.

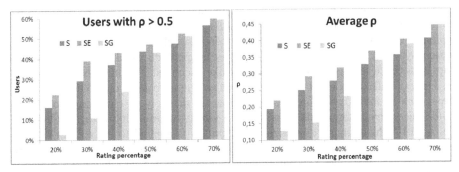

Fig. 4. Average ρ (left panel) and number of users with $\rho > 0.5$ (right panel), when taking as input a certain rating percentage r for the three techniques

Figure 4 shows the performance of the three approaches for different percentages of input ratings. SE always outperforms S, and is significantly different from it for $r \leq 30\%$ ($0,002 \leq p \leq 0.026$, according to the chi-square test). In fact, as highlighted by the right panel of the figure 4, when $r \leq 30\%$, SE obtains on the average 8.1% more user with $\rho > 0.5$ than S, while for $40\% \leq r \leq 70\%$, the difference is reduced to 4.3%. Hence, especially in the cold-start phase or in situations of data sparsity, when the system does not yet know much about user preferences, Klink UM is able to significantly improve the quality of the recommendation by enriching the initial ontology.

The SG algorithms, which tries to learn the conceptual taxonomy from scratch, does not perform as well as S for $r \leq 40\%$. However, for higher values of r SG is not significantly different from S and SE ($0.67 \leq p \leq 0,98$) and for $r \geq 60\%$ the performance of SE and S are almost identical, both of them being superior to S. Hence, while it takes a decent amount of user feedback to learn the conceptual taxonomy from scratch, once this is achieved, the results are indistinguishable from the version that relies on the expert crafted ontology. Hence, SG seems a viable option especially for systems that can rely on a good number of user ratings and for which the manual crafting of the domain ontology is not easy, e.g. very large online stores. In all other cases the best solution appears to start with a human crafted ontology and then to enrich and correct it accordingly to the user needs.

4   Related Work

In the first part of this section, we will describe the state of the art in techniques to infer conceptual taxonomies or semantic relationships. In the second part we will highlight the main works relative to ontology-based recommender systems, which can benefit from Klink UM.

The idea of extracting ontologies from user communities is thoroughly discussed in the work of Mika [5], which extends the traditional bipartite model of ontologies with the social dimension, proposing a tripartite model of actor, concepts and instances. Similarly, Specia et al [6] extract semantics from folksonomies by clustering tag sets and detecting highly related tags corresponding to concepts in ontologies.

The automatic inference of semantic relationships is usually addressed by means of two approaches. The first was developed in the area of computational linguistic and exploits lexico-syntactic patterns [17], the second uses clustering techniques [18]. The Lexico-Syntactic Pattern Extraction (LSPE) is an approach which discovers relationships between terms by exploiting patterns like "such as...", "and other...", and so on. For example, De Cea et al [19] use this technique to infer ontological relationships, such as *subClassOf*. Instead the approaches that rely on clustering techniques build a hierarchy of keywords according to a variety of similarity metrics. For example, in [14] a hierarchical clusterization algorithm is applied to the context of web pages and a top-down partitioning is used to generate a multi-way-tree taxonomy from the binary tree. The *TaxGen* framework [20] uses instead a hierarchical agglomerative clustering algorithm and text mining techniques for building a taxonomy from a set of documents. Also Klink UM uses a hierarchical algorithm and similarity distances between keywords, but only for the inference of the similarity links and for the detection of potentially missing superclasses or properties.

The subsumption approach, exploited also by Klink UM, was introduced in Sanderson and Croft [11]. Also Schmitz et al [12] use a subsumption-based model for inducing a faceted ontology from *Flickr* tags. The metric we propose for finding hierarchical links exploits the same idea, but considers also the reciprocal conditional probability and other factors, such as the cosine similarity between keywords. The subsumption approach inspired also the GrowBag algorithm [21], which uses a biased *PageRank* algorithm to exploit second order co-occurrences.

While Klink UM aims to adapt an ontology to a groups of users, other approaches tailor ontologies to specific users, resulting in personal ontology views [7]. For example, Haase et al [8] proposed a method for assisting users in the management of their personal ontologies with the aim of yielding more accurate recommendations.

Klink UM can be useful especially for ontology-based recommenders [1,2,3,4], since it makes it easier to craft and update an ontology targeted to a group of users. It can currently identify only hierarchical and similarity relationships, however most works in the fields also rely solely on these relationships. For example Middleton et al [1] exploit the user feedback on research papers and use the hierarchical relationships between classes to infer other topics of interest. In Sieg et al [2] the ontology is treated as a semantic network and the interest values are updated by means of spreading activation. Cena et al [4] propose instead a multi-directional anisotropic interest propagation which is able to spread user feedback also to instances.

Many other methods exploit the ontology graph structure to compute the distance between concepts. For example, Resnik et al presented a semantic similarity measure [22] based on information content in a taxonomy that is computed as the negative logarithm of the probability of occurrence of the class in a text *corpus*. Other methods, such as [3], use instead shared and distinctive OWL properties rather than a graph-based distance. Similar approaches are also applied to determine the similarity between Linked Data entities [23]. For example, Freitas et al. [24] introduce a query mechanism for Linked Data based on the combination of entity search, semantic relatedness and spreading activation. We believe that Klink UM can be helpful to all these approaches as a support for computing a fit-for-purpose conceptual similarity between concepts.

5   Conclusions

In this work we presented Klink UM, an extension of the Klink algorithm which is able to detect relationships between keywords and create or enrich an ontology starting from a set of user ratings on the keywords, with the aim of tailoring the ontology to a specific group of users.

We tested the ability of Klink UM to build a conceptual taxonomy from scratch and to assist the recommendation process. In the first task it overperformed the subsumption approach obtaining an F-measure of 95% for the *Drinks* test (N= 7623) and of 83% for the *Cold Cuts* test (N=1392). In the second one, the approach relying on an ontology enriched by Klink UM outperformed the one relying on the human crafted one, especially in conditions of data sparsity ($p \leq 0.03$). Moreover, after a good number of user ratings, the conceptual taxonomy crafted by Klink UM performed as well as the human crafted enriched ontology ($p \geq 0.67$).

Klink UM can also be used for generating suggestions about potential missing properties, that may have been forgotten or considered irrelevant when the ontology was crafted. Hence, it allows ontology engineers and domain experts to gain an interesting user-centred prospective.

The next step will be to have Klink UM recognizing groups of people with different views of the domain in order to build different version of the domain ontology, tailored to them [25]. We also are working on novel heuristics for detecting a higher number of semantic relationships.

References

1. Middleton, S.E., Shadbolt, N.R., De Roure, D.C.: Ontological user profiling in recommender systems. ACM Transactions on Information Systems (2004)
2. Sieg, A., Mobasher, B., Burke, R.: Web search personalization with ontological user profiles. In: Proceeding of the 16th ACM Conference on Information and Knowledge Management, CIKM 2007, pp. 525–534. ACM (2007)
3. Cena, F., Likavec, S., Osborne, F.: Property-based interest propagation in ontology-based user model. In: Masthoff, J., Mobasher, B., Desmarais, M.C., Nkambou, R. (eds.) UMAP 2012. LNCS, vol. 7379, pp. 38–50. Springer, Heidelberg (2012)
4. Cena, F., Likavec, S., Osborne, F.: Anisotropic propagation of user interests in ontology-based user models. Information Sciences (2013)
5. Mika, P.: Ontologies are us: A unified model of social networks and semantics. In: Gil, Y., Motta, E., Benjamins, V.R., Musen, M.A. (eds.) ISWC 2005. LNCS, vol. 3729, pp. 522–536. Springer, Heidelberg (2005)
6. Specia, L., Motta, E.: Integrating folksonomies with the semantic web. In: Franconi, E., Kifer, M., May, W. (eds.) ESWC 2007. LNCS, vol. 4519, pp. 624–639. Springer, Heidelberg (2007)
7. Chaffee, J., Gauch, S.: Personal ontologies for web navigation. In: Proceedings of CIKM 2000 (2000)
8. Haase, P., Hotho, A., Schmidt-Thieme, L., Sure, Y.: Collaborative and Usage-Driven Evolution of Personal Ontologies. In: Gómez-Pérez, A., Euzenat, J. (eds.) ESWC 2005. LNCS, vol. 3532, pp. 486–499. Springer, Heidelberg (2005)
9. Osborne, F., Motta, E.: Mining Semantic Relations between Research Areas. In: Cudré-Mauroux, P., et al. (eds.) ISWC 2012, Part I. LNCS, vol. 7649, pp. 410–426. Springer, Heidelberg (2012)
10. Osborne, F., Motta, E., Mulholland, P.: Exploring Scholarly Data with Rexplore. In: Alani, H., et al. (eds.) ISWC 2013, Part I. LNCS, vol. 8218, pp. 460–477. Springer, Heidelberg (2013)
11. Sanderson, M., Croft, B.: Deriving concept hierarchies from text. In: Proceedings of the SIGIR conference, pp. 206–213 (1999)
12. Schmitz, P.: Inducing Ontology from Flickr Tags. In: Proceedings of the 15th International Conference on World Wide Web (WWW), Edinburgh, UK (2006)
13. Sarwar, B., Karypis, G., Konstan, J., Riedl, J.: Item-based collaborative filtering recommendation algorithms. In: Proceedings of the 10th International Conference on World Wide Web (pp, pp. 285–295. ACM (2001)
14. Chuang, S., Chien, L.: A practical web-based approach to generating topic hierarchy for text segments. In: Proceedings of the 13th ACM Conference on Information and Knowledge Management, Washington, D.C., USA (2004)
15. Olsson, D.M., Nelson, L.S.: The Nelder-Mead simplex procedure for function minimization. Technometrics 17(1), 45–51 (1975)

16. Console, L.: Piemonte Team: WantEat: interacting with social networks of intelligent things and people in the world of enogastronomy. In: Proceedings of the Workshop on Interacting with Smart Objects, pp. 1–6 (2011)

17. Morin, E.: Automatic acquisition of semantic relations between terms from technical corpora. In: Proceedings of the 5th International Congress on Terminology and Knowledge Engineering (1999)

18. Assadi, H.: Construction of a regional ontology from text and its use within a documentary system. In: Guarino, N. (ed.) Formal Ontology in Information Systems, Proceedings of FOIS-98, Trento, Italy, pp. 236–249 (1999)

19. De Cea, G., de Mon, I., Montiel-Ponsoda, E.: From Linguistic Patterns to Ontology Structures. In: Proceding of the 8th Conference on Terminology and Artificial Intelligence (2009)

20. Müller, A., Dorre, J.: The TaxGen Framework: Automating the Generation of a Taxonomy for a Large Document Collection. In: Proceedings of the 32nd Hawaii International Conference on System Sciences, vol. 2, pp. 20–34 (1999)

21. Diederich, J., Balke, W., Thaden, U.: Demonstrating the Semantic GrowBag: Automatically Creating Topic Facets for FacetedDBLP. In: Proceedings of JCDL 2007. ACM, New York (2007)

22. Resnik, P.: Semantic similarity in a taxonomy: An information-based measure and its application to problems of ambiguity in natural language. Journal of Artificial Intelligence Research 11, 95–130 (1999)

23. Di Noia, T., Mirizzi, R., Claudio Ostuni, V., Romito, D., Zanker, M.: Linked Open Data to support Content-based Recommender Systems. In: Proceeding of the International Conference on Semantic Systems, I-Semantics (2012)

24. Freitas, A., Oliveira, J.G., O'Riain, S., Da Silva, J.C., Curry, E.: Querying linked data graphs using semantic relatedness: A vocabulary independent approach. Data & Knowledge Engineering 88, 126–141 (2013)

25. Osborne, F.: A POV-Based User Model: From Learning Preferences to Learning Personal Ontologies. In: Carberry, S., Weibelzahl, S., Micarelli, A., Semeraro, G. (eds.) UMAP 2013. LNCS, vol. 7899, pp. 376–379. Springer, Heidelberg (2013)

A Hybrid Semantic Approach to Building Dynamic Maps of Research Communities

Francesco Osborne, Giuseppe Scavo, and Enrico Motta

Knowledge Media Institute, The Open University, MK7 6AA, Milton Keynes, UK
{francesco.osborne,giuseppe.scavo,e.motta}@open.ac.uk

Abstract. In earlier papers we characterised the notion of *diachronic topic-based communities* –i.e., communities of people who work on semantically related topics at the same time. These communities are important to enable topic-centred analyses of the dynamics of the research world. In this paper we present an innovative algorithm, called Research Communities Map Builder (RCMB), which is able to automatically link diachronic topic-based communities over subsequent time intervals to identify significant events. These include topic shifts within a research community; the appearance and fading of a community; communities splitting, merging, spawning other communities; and others. The output of our algorithm is a map of research communities, annotated with the detected events, which provides a concise visual representation of the dynamics of a research area. In contrast with existing approaches, RCMB enables a much more fine-grained understanding of the evolution of research communities, with respect to both the granularity of the events and the granularity of the topics. This improved understanding can, for example, inform the research strategies of funders and researchers alike. We illustrate our approach with two case studies, highlighting the main communities and events that characterized the World Wide Web and Semantic Web areas in the 2000 – 2010 decade.

Keywords: Semantic Web, Community Detection, Change Detection, Trend Detection, Pattern Recognition, Data Mining, Scholarly Data.

1   Introduction

Understanding the dynamics of research communities is a challenging and important task. As Yan et al [1] point out, there is a need for "better tools for identifying emergent trends and the development of new scholarly communities." In particular, we need to be able i) to capture effectively the relationships between authors and *research topics*, ii) to learn how these evolve over time, and iii) to understand how research communities interact with each other, trading topics and researchers.

Current approaches to these tasks, e.g., [2,3,4,5], suffer from a number of limitations. First, they model research topics simply as keywords, failing to capture the semantic relationships that can exist between topics and thus reducing the opportunities for a sophisticated modelling of topic spaces [6]. They also tend to focus on 'static snapshots' of research communities [2,4,5] and do not take into account the dynamic

K. Janowicz et al. (Eds.): EKAW 2014, LNAI 8876, pp. 356–372, 2014.
© Springer International Publishing Switzerland 2014

aspects associated with the evolution of the *research trajectories* of authors (i.e., which topics they work on over time). As we know, communities are dynamic entities that may merge, split and evolve by incorporating new topics and visions [1,7,8]. By analysing the trajectories of different authors and identifying similarities between them it becomes possible to go beyond such static snapshots, to develop models of the evolution of topic-centred research communities. This approach makes also possible to estimate the effects of specific external events (e.g., grants, new technologies, historical events) on the research dynamics.

In Osborne et al. [9] we took a first step to addressing the aforementioned limitations by presenting Temporal Semantic Topic-Based Clustering (TST), an algorithm which identifies *temporal topic-based communities,* i.e., communities grouping authors who share similar research trajectories[1].

In this paper we present an innovative algorithm, called Research Communities Map Builder (RCMB), which is able to automatically link diachronic topic-based communities over subsequent time intervals to identify significant events. These include topic shifts within a community; the appearance and fading of a community; communities splitting, merging, spawning other communities; etc. The output of RCMB is a map of research communities, annotated with the detected events, which provides a concise visual representation of the dynamics of a research area. RCMB is integrated in Rexplore [10], a system that capitalises on innovative integrated solutions in semantic technologies and data mining to support users in exploring and making sense of scholarly data.

These research maps can be important for a variety of tasks and users. For example, they can help research managers to understand which are the main research communities in a field, in which directions they are evolving, and how they interact, to inform critical decisions on funding and recruitment policies. Editors can use research maps to ensure timely editorial decisions, e.g., by detecting emerging themes for special issues. Researchers can use them for making sense of new trends and identifying appropriate collaborators. Moreover, by analysing the history of research communities it is possible to learn good practices. For example, we can investigate how scientific communities adapt and cooperate to implement visions into concrete technologies (as the Semantic Web community did with Linked Data) and try to replicate successful stories. Finally, discovering how groups of researchers are influenced

---

[1] Some readers have objected to our use of the term "community" to refer to groups of researchers who work on the same topic or follow similar research trajectories. They argue that the term "community" implies interaction between its members –e.g., as it is the case for communities extracted from interactions on social media, while (naturally!) it does not follow that two people working on the same topic have any interaction or are even aware of each other existence. Our view is that this objection is unwarranted, as it is predicated on an unnecessary narrowing of the semantics of the word "community". This is commonly used to refer to groups of people who share common characteristics, as e.g., when we talk about the "international community" or the "academic community", and does not actually require explicit interaction between the members of a particular community, when this is defined on the basis of shared characteristics.

by technological breakthroughs, grants or visions, and how they interact to generate new ideas and technologies, can allow us to predict future research trends.

We will illustrate our approach with two case studies, highlighting the main communities and events that characterized the World Wide Web (WWW) and Semantic Web (SW) areas in the 2000 – 2010 decade.

2   State of the Art

Community detection is a popular topic in computer science and has been addressed using a variety of techniques. Most of this work deals with graphs (e.g., co-authorship networks) and their topological structure rather than exploiting the topic similarity of the members. Current approaches to community detection are usually classified according to the strategy they employ [5], as either heuristic [11] or optimization-based methods [12]. However, from the point of view of capturing coherent topic-centric research communities, both fail to correctly cover all people who work in a research area (lack of recall) and also typically include individuals interested in different topics (lack of precision).

More recently, there has been a growing interest in topic-based communities [1], i.e., communities generated on the basis of topic similarities between individuals, rather than on their connections in a graph. These communities can in fact be used to describe the evolution of topics in a research area [7]. For example, Upham et al. [3] presented an analysis of "knowledge communities", defined as intellectually cohesive, organic inter-organizational forms. Similarly to our approach, they detect communities by using a clustering scheme that produces dynamic clusters over a timeline. However, they focus mainly on the citation graph and on language-level similarities between publications to identify communities. In contrast with this approach, we focus instead on identifying the research trajectories shared by groups of authors. Zhao et al. [5] identify topic-based communities by analyzing co-authorship networks. Their method lacks however the temporal dimension, which is needed for detecting research trends. Other techniques focus on identifying dynamic trends within an individual topic. For example, Racherla and Hu [13] identify topic communities by exploiting a topic similarity matrix and assigning a predefined research topic to each document and author. This approach however fails to take into account the fact that most research communities cannot be described by a single topic, being most often characterized by a distribution of related topics [7].

Topic models, which compute the similarity of entities according to shared keywords, can also be seen as a form of community detection. These methods usually rely on the detection of latent topics for capturing semantic dependencies between keywords and exploit Probabilistic Latent Semantic Indexing (pLSI) [14] or Latent Dirichlet Allocation [15]. For example the Author-Conference-Topic (ACT) model [16] treats authors as probability distributions over topics, conferences and journals extracted by means of an unsupervised learning technique. Our approach is instead based on a semantic characterization of research topics, which are connected by three types of semantic relations. These are generated automatically from a corpus of publications by means of Klink [6], an algorithm that combines machine-learning and statistical methods to populate an OWL ontology with semantic relations between research topics. Another possibility is to exploit human-made ontologies for describing scholarly data [17], which however should be adapted for describing topics relationships and need to be kept constantly up-to-date.

RCMB integrates TST [9], which adopts a Fuzzy C-Means (FCM) [18] clustering algorithm that exploits a novel similarity metric on vectors of *semantic topics* in subsequent years. Similarly, Yan et al. [4] use a K-Means algorithm to examine a paper-to-paper network based on shared word relations, while Van Eck and Waltman [2] exploit modularity-based clustering techniques for detecting research communities. Differently from these approaches, we focus on authors' research trajectories rather than on papers, as our aim is to identify diachronic communities and their dynamics, rather than simply detecting the existence of a community in a certain time interval. Another important feature of RCMB is its ability of linking together communities over time intervals. Similarly, Yan at al. [1] use cosine similarity over the topic distributions and empirically set thresholds to detect links between communities. RCMB however brings this idea further by taking into account also the migrations of authors from one community to another and finding automatically the relevant thresholds by minimizing an evaluation function with the Nelder-Mead algorithm [19]. In addition, RCMB relies on the chi-square test and a sliding window algorithm to detect significant changes in the topic distribution of a community. Similar statistical approaches are applied in the field of prospective disease surveillance [20] and in the field of change detection, such as scene change detection [21].

3   The Research Communities Map Builder

In this section we will describe in detail the Research Communities Map Builder algorithm, which generates a map of the main communities within a given topic.

Most methods for detecting topic-based communities [1,2,4,7] use keywords as proxies for research topics. Hence, pairs of obviously related terms, e.g., "Semantic Web" and "Linked Data", are considered as unrelated entities. We instead rely on the Klink algorithm [6] to address this issue and generate an ontology describing a structured set of semantic topics. Specifically, Klink is able to infer three kinds of semantic relationships between keywords, which are *skos:broaderGeneric* (topic, T_1 is a sub-topic of topic T_2), *relatedEquivalent* (two topics are alternative names for the same research area) and *contributesTo* (research in topic T_1 is an important contribution to research in topic T_2). Hence, the topic vectors representing the publications are modified by labelling with topic T_1 any publication tagged with topic T_2, if T_2 is sub-topic of T_1 or equivalent to T_1.

RCMB takes as input i) a research area (e.g., Semantic Web); ii) a time interval (e.g., 2000-2006); iii) a granularity index (e.g., 3), which will determine the length of the intervals to be processed (e.g., 2000-2002, 2002-2004, 2004-2006); iv) a number of authors *active* in the research area, associated with their publications; and v) a knowledge base, automatically populated by Klink, specifying the semantic topics and their relationships. We define as active in a research area, say R, any author who has at least one publication a year in R, during the time interval considered.

The output is a map of the research communities within the research area in question, describing for each year of the time interval the existing communities, the topic shifts (i.e., changes in some of the major topics which characterize a community); and a number of other significant events that alter the research landscape, such as the splitting of a community. RCMB relies on statistical methods to infer topic shifts and on heuristic rules to detect six kinds of important events. More formally, RCMB is described by the following pseudo code:

```
Function RCMB (main_topic, time_interval, granularity_index, authors,
topic_kb) {
  // Split the time interval in multiple intervals with a length equal to the granularity
  and the last year of an interval being the first year of the next interval
  time_intervals = splitTimeInterval(time_interval, granularity);
  // Extract the semantic topic vectors from the publication (Sec. 3.1)
  stv = semanticTopicExtraction(authors, topic_kb);
  // Weights each topic accordingly to its similarity with main_topic (Sec. 3.1)
  wstv = topicWeighting(stv, main_topic);
     foreach (time_intervals as t) {
     // Clusters authors in fuzzy communities using FCM (Sec. 3.2)
     initial_centroids = substractiveMethod(wstv[t]);
     communities[t] = FCM(wstv[t], initial_centroids);
  }
  // Infer the shifts of interest (Sec. 3.3)
  shifts = inferTopicsShifts(communities);
  // Links communities in different time intervals (Sec. 3.4)
  s_links = estimateStrongLinks(communities, shifts);
  w_links = estimateWeakLinks(communities, shifts);
  // Detect additional shifts of interest (Sec. 3.3)
  shifts = inferTopicsShifts2(shifts, communities, s_links);
  // Detect key events (Sec. 3.5)
  events = inferEvents(communities, s_links, w_links, shifts );
  map = buildMap(communities, s_links, w_links, shifts, events);
  return map; }
```

In the following sections we will discuss in details the steps of the algorithm. The first three steps (described in Section 3.1 and 3.2) are actually a slight modification of the TST algorithm [9], thus they will be explained only briefly here.

3.1   Semantic Topic Integration and Topic Vector Weighing

In this step we extract the semantic topics from the publications to represent each author as a semantic topic distribution over subsequent years. We do so by building a matrix for each author which records the number of publications on each topic in each year. Hence, every row of the matrix associates a year with a topic vector that describes the author's interests at the time. The vector already takes into account the *skos:broaderGeneric* and the *relatedEquivalent* relationships, since the topics tagging each paper were corrected accordingly. Then, for each pair of topics sharing a *contributesTo(T_1, T_2)* relationship in each topic vector, we also increment the score associated with topic T_2 by a fraction $CT(T_1)$ of the score of T_1, computed as:

$$CT(T) = \sum_{i=1}^{n} P\big(T\big|ct(i,T)\big)^{\varphi}$$

where $ct(i,T)$ indicates the set of topics associated with the i-th publication that are in a *contributesTo* relationship with T. $P\big(T\big|ct(i,T)\big)$ is the probability that a paper with such a set of topics is also tagged with area T (or with a topic having a *broaderGeneric* or *relatedEquivalent* relationship with T) at the publication date of the i-th paper. The summation is carried out over the number n of publications that are not already associated with T but have at least one topic in a *contributesTo* relationship with T.

Moreover, to privilege the communities strongly related to the research area given as input to RCMB (the "main topic"), we weigh each topic according to its relationship with the main topic. Given a topic T, the weight $W(T)$ is calculated as follows:

$$W(T) = 1 + k\frac{C(T)}{S(T)}$$

where $C(T)$ is the number of co-occurrences of topic T with the main topic in the selected time interval; $S(T)$ is the number of total occurrences of the topic T in the selected time interval, and k is an arbitrary constant that can be tuned to amplify the effect of the weight on the system.

Hence, the resulting topic vectors take into account all the semantic relationships discussed before and privilege the topics more similar to the given research area.

3.2   Fuzzy Clustering Based on Temporal Topic Similarity

We employ a Fuzzy C-means algorithm (FCM) [18] over the *weighted semantic topic vectors* in the timeframe to compute the clusters. We use a fuzzy clustering technique since researchers are often members of multiple communities.

For clustering authors according to their shared topic trajectory over the years we use a similarity metric called *ATTS (Adjusted Temporal Topic Similarity)*. ATTS is computed by averaging the cosine similarities of the semantic topic vectors over progressively smaller intervals of time. We first define the *TTS (Temporal Topic Similarity)* between author A and author B in the interval t_1-t_2 as:

$$TTS(A,B,t_1,t_2) = \sum_{i=0}^{\lfloor log_2(t_2-t_1)\rfloor} \frac{\left[\left(\sum_{j=0}^{2^i-1} TS\left(A,B,t_1+\left\lceil\frac{j\cdot(t_2-t_1)}{2^i}\right\rceil,t_1+\left\lfloor\frac{(j+1)\cdot(t_2-t_1)}{2^i}\right\rfloor\right)\right)/2^i\right]}{\lfloor log_2(t_2-t_1)\rfloor}$$

where $TS(A,B,t_1,t_2) = \cos(\sum_{i=t_1}^{t_2}\hat{a}_i, \sum_{i=x}^{t_2}\hat{b}_i)$, $\hat{a}_i$ and $\hat{b}_i$ are the topic vectors of the two authors in the i-th year and $cos(s,t)$ is the cosine similarity.

To account for those cases in which an author may not be present in all the years of the timeframe, we define the *adjusted temporal topic similarity* ATTS as:

$$ATTS(A,B,t_1,t_2) = TTS(A,B,t_1,t_2)\cdot\frac{I_s^{\gamma}}{I_s^{\gamma}+I_{ns}^{\gamma}} + P\cdot\frac{I_{ns}^{\gamma}}{I_s^{\gamma}+I_{ns}^{\gamma}},$$

where I_s is the number of years in which both authors were active, I_{ns} is the remaining number of years, P is a constant equal to the average TTS of n random couples of authors in the given timeframe ($n=500$ in the prototype), and $\gamma>1$ a parameter for weighing their relationship ($\gamma=2$ in the prototype).

Since ATTS is a similarity metric, while a FCM needs a distance, we use as norm the inverse of the ATTS minus 1.

In order to choose the candidate centroids for the FCM algorithm we use the subtractive clustering method [22], which estimates the initial centroids by assigning a potential to each individual in the dataset according to its number of neighbours. FCM returns a list of cluster centroids and a partition matrix where each author is associated with its degree of membership to each cluster. The returned centroids are actually the topic vectors of the communities in each year, allowing for an easy detection of shifts and changes throughout the years. By summing the vectors over the years and selecting the topics with the highest values, it is possible to label communities in terms of their most significant topics.

3.3   Detecting Topic Shifts

One of the main advantages of using communities characterized by an evolving distribution of topics is that we can study the dynamic changes in the research interests of the community. In this section we describe an automatic method which detects that a certain community underwent a topic shift and outputs an explanation. (e.g., the topic shift was mainly produced by the growth of the "Mobile Device" topic). As shown in the pseudo code, RCMB infers community topic shifts in two occasions. The first time is before linking the communities (*inferTopicsShift* function), because these initial topic shifts will be used to estimate the threshold value for the linking process (see Section 3.4). The procedure is then run again on the linked communities (*inferTopicsShifts2* function), to allow the detection of topic shifts across the given time intervals.

We define a *topic shift* as a statistically significant change in the topic distribution of a community which occurred in a certain time interval. We compute the null hypothesis p that the difference between two topic distributions of the same community in two subsequent time t_1 and t_2 are due to random fluctuations by using the *chi-square test*; if $p \leq 0.05$, the two distributions are considered different and a topic shift is detected in the time interval $[t_1-t_2]$.

After detecting the topic shift it is also important to detect which topics were the main protagonists of this event. We do so by applying the chi-square test to the topic distributions, excluding each time a different topic, and selecting the topic whose absence yields the bigger increment in the p value. If after excluding this topic we still obtain $p \leq 0.05$, the procedure is repeated to select another topic, until p > 0.05.

In most cases the topic shift does not happen abruptly in one year, but it is a gradual process. Thus we implemented a sliding window algorithm that checks for a topic shift by comparing the initial topic distribution in time t with the topic distributions in time $t+1, t+2... t+n$ (n=10 in the prototype). The same procedure is repeated after incrementing t, until $t = m-1$, where m is the total number of years in the investigated interval.

This algorithm may output different topic shifts that point to the same real life phenomenon (e.g., the growth of topic T in community C at the beginning of 2000), but we want to select only the ones that would be more significant for a human user. We assume that a human would prefer a sharp shift over a slow one and would prefer to recognize it as soon as possible: hence, if two or more topic shifts share part of the same time interval (e.g., 2000-2002 and 2000-2003) we keep only the shortest one, and if they have the same length, we keep the oldest one.

3.4   Linking Communities

We will now discuss the RCMB approach to linking a number of communities on a timeline, and automatically detecting their interactions. The inputs are the temporal topic-based communities detected in different time intervals, with the last year of an interval being the first year of the subsequent interval –e.g., 2000-2002, 2002-2004 and so on. The topic vector of the year in common between two successive intervals is then used to compute the *community similarity* (CS) between each couple of communities. CS, which assesses the possibility that two communities in different time intervals C and D are actually the same one, is computed as:

$$CS(C,D) = \left(cos(\widehat{c_y}, \widehat{d_y}) + aut(C,D)\right)/2$$

where C and D are two communities in subsequent time intervals, y is the year they have in common (e.g., last year of C and first year of D), $cos(\widehat{c_y}, \widehat{d_y})$ is the cosine similarity between the communities topic distribution in year y, and $aut(C,D)$ is the percentage of authors which moved from C to D. $CS(C,D)$ varies between 0 and 1, with a high value pointing to the fact that C and D denote the same community in different intervals.

As in [1], the CS(C,D) measure is used to detect two different links between communities. We define two thresholds, t_s and t_w, with $t_s > t_w$. When $CS(C,D) \geq t_s$ we infer a *strong link*, when instead $t_w \leq CS(C,D) < t_s$ we infer a *weak link*.

The *strong link* is defined as a link that connects the same community in subsequent timeframes –e.g., the link that connects the "Ontology" community of SW in the 2004-2006 interval with the "Ontology" community of SW in 2006-2008.

The *weak link* is defined as the link that connects community C_1 with community C_2 in a subsequent timeframe, if C_1 has an impact over C_2 in terms of migrating authors and/or topics. For example a weak link can be established between the "Intelligent Agent" community and the "Semantic Web Services" community, if a number of authors from the first one flow into the second.

Estimating the correct value for t_s and t_w is vital for generating a legitimate and useful map of research communities. We determine those values by using the Nelder-Mead algorithm [19], which is a derivative-free optimization method. The Nelder-Mead algorithm is used to solve parameter estimation problems where the function values are uncertain or subject to noise. It works by defining a simplex, whose vertices represent the parameters to be found, and then performing a sequence of geometrical transformations on it, aimed at decreasing an evaluation function. Hence, we need an evaluation function that will estimate the quality of the links.

It is possible to use as evaluation function the F-Measure between the links in a generated map and those from a human generated gold standard. However it is not trivial to find the right group of experts and it may be argued that the threshold values obtained within a certain research area may not be feasible to be reused for a different one. We thus propose a different solution, which uses a number of preferable properties that a map should possess to be practical and readable.

The properties on which we focus are:
- Ideally the communities should not appear intermittently, since it would be unrealistic to assume that a community keep disappearing and reappearing.

- Ideally the communities that fade out should contribute to other communities; it would be odd if both the authors and the topics suddenly disappear from a map without any explanation. More formally this means that communities on the verge of disappearing should have at least one exiting weak link.
- Ideally the communities that receive a weak link should observe a topic shift, since they are being modified by the inflow of another community.
- The definition of strong link entails that two strong links should not 1) fork from a community or 2) merge into two different communities.

From these preferable properties we derive the Map Evaluation Function (MEF):

$$MEF = (I \, w_I + D \, w_D + NTS \, w_{NTS} + SLF \, w_{SFL} + SLM \, w_{SFM}) - (WL + SL)$$

where, I is the number of times a community disappeared and then reappeared in a subsequent year, D the number of times a community disappears without any exiting link in the previous time interval, NTS the number of times a weak link does not produce a topic shift, SLF the number of strong links forking, and SLM the number of strong links merging. WL and SL define the ratio between the sum of all weak/strong links and the average number of communities in an interval; the purpose of these components is to avoid that the best solution would yield a low or null number of links. The components of this function are attuned by means of weights (i.e., $w_I, w_{SFL}, w_{SFM}, w_D, w_{NTS}$) that can be set empirically or learnt by maximizing, using the Nelder-Mead algorithm, the F-Measure between the links of the generated community and the links of a human crafted gold standard.

We take the minimum values of t_s and t_w that minimize the MEF. As an initial parameter estimation for the Nelder-Mead algorithm, we use $t_s = 0.5$ and $t_w = 0.25$.

3.5   Detecting Other Key Events

The two kinds of links, which connect the communities in subsequent years, are also exploited for automatically detecting six other kinds of typical dynamics. These events are detected by applying the following heuristic rules:

1. If a community has no strong links with any precedent interval communities, we detect an event of **type 1**, i.e., the **appearance** of a community.
2. If a community has no strong links with any subsequent interval communities, we detect an event of **type 2**, i.e., the **fading** of a community.
3. If two or more communities are linked to one community in the subsequent interval and one of the inlinks is a strong link, we detect an event of **type 3.A**, i.e., the **assimilation** of one or more communities into the community C characterized by the strong link. If the communities fade after the event, they are labelled as **absorbed by C**, else they are labelled as **contributing to C**.
4. If two or more communities are linked to one community in the subsequent interval and none of the inlinks is a strong link, we detect an event of **type 3.B**, i.e., the **merging** of two or more communities in a new community C. If the communities fade after the event, they are labelled as **merged in C**, else they are labelled as **contributing to C**.
5. If a community is linked to more than one community in the subsequent interval and one of the links is a strong one we detect an event of **type 4.A**, i.e., the **forking** of one or more communities out of the community characterized by the strong link.

6. If a community is linked to more than one community in the subsequent interval and none of the links is a strong one we detect an event of **type 4.B**, i.e., the **splitting** of a community into multiple communities.

It should be noted that, from the definition of strong link, it follows that we should never have more than one of them in 3.A and 4.A events. However, the opposite may actually happen in practice and the conflict is then solved by considering as strong link only the one with the highest *CS*.

The final output of RCMB is a data structure that we call 'map of research communities', describing the detected communities within a certain topic, the links, the topic shifts and the other detected events. A map of research communities can be used as a knowledge base and visualized in a variety of ways. For example Rexplore [10] currently implements a view in which communities are represented as nodes in a graph and linked to the related authors, affiliations and countries. In this paper we will instead use a timeline based visualization (see Figures 1 and 2), which is particularly useful for highlighting the evolution and interactions of research communities.

4   Mapping the Dynamics of WWW and SW

In this section we discuss the most interesting events that we detected by applying RCMB to two research areas: World Wide Web (WWW) and Semantic Web (SW). For each of these areas we will highlight the main topic-based communities and how they evolved in the time interval 2000-2010. Since an in-depth analysis of all significant dynamics and patterns discovered in these two areas would take too much space, here we will provide broad overviews of these areas and we will elaborate only on the most interesting automatically detected patterns. We will support our analysis by evidencing the most significant changes in the topic distributions of the communities and the flow of authors between them. We will also show examples of *representative authors*. These are defined as members of a community who fit well the community profile (i.e., they are very similar to the community centroid) and have an H-Index of at least 10. For readability, we will label some communities only with their one or two most significant topics (e.g., "Semantic Web Services" community rather than the "Semantic Web Services, Web Service Composition, Web Service Discovery" community).

Our study was based on a dataset built from data retrieved by means of the API provided by Microsoft Academic Search (http://academic.research.microsoft.com). We first retrieved authors and papers labelled with WWW and SW or with their first 150 co-occurring topics. By running the Klink algorithm over these keywords we detected about 700 semantic relationships between them. We then run RCMB on WWW and SW in the 2000-2010 time interval with a granularity of 3. The average number of authors selected in each year was 932 for WWW and 646 for SW.

4.1   Modelling the Dynamics of the World Wide Web Research Area

WWW is a major area of computer science and contains a variety of communities continuously renewed by the introduction of new technologies and topics. Figure 1 shows the main communities and trends in the WWW area in the timeframe 2000-2010. For year 2000, the RCMB algorithm yielded eight main communities: "Information

Retrieval" (210 authors), "HCI, User Interface" (178), "E-Commerce, User Behaviour" (167), "Intelligent Agents" (150), "Query Languages, Data Structures" (149), "Data Mining" (142), "Internet Services, Mobile Agents, Middleware" (90) and "Semantic Web, Artificial Intelligence" (86).

It should be noted that the number of authors does not represent the total of authors who happen to work in some of these topics, but only those who 1) have at least one publication per year in the WWW area and 2) share a common research trajectory with the other authors of the community, i.e. have a similar topic distribution in the same years[2].

We will now examine more closely some of the trends within the WWW area. As shown in Figure 1, in 2002 some authors from the "Data Mining" community (about 55% of them) merged with the "Query Languages, Data Structures" community, while others (43%) flew into the "Information Retrieval" community. The merging of "Data Mining" and "Query Languages, Data Structures" in 2002 gave birth to a novel community that counted 245 authors with a hybrid topic distribution, since it was composed by authors who appeared to be interested both in "Query Languages" and in "Data Mining".

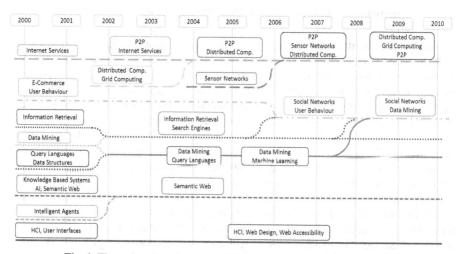

Fig. 1. The main research communities in WWW and their trajectories

Moreover, since 2004, the topic distribution of the "Data Mining" community continued to evolve, being progressively enriched by topics representing "Machine Learning" approaches, such as "Neural Networks" and "Genetic Algorithms". Also the "Internet Services, Mobile Agents, Peer To Peer" community went through some interesting changes. In fact, after 2002, the "Peer to Peer" component became prominent in this community, growing from 11% to almost 50%.

It can be hypothesised that this phenomenon was linked to the emergence in 2001-2002 of influential web applications relevant to the Peer To Peer area, such as BitTorrent,

---

[2] Since RCMB returns fuzzy clusters, for the sake of this analysis we assigned each author to the communities for which she/he had a membership score > 0.4.

Kademlia and Gnutella. Indeed the behaviour of this community appears to be very sensitive to technological shifts: in 2004 it merged with the "Distributed Computing, Grid Computing" community, and in 2006 with "Sensor Networks", finally becoming the "Distributed Computing, Grid Computing, Peer To Peer" community.

The main transformation in the 2000-2010 timeframe for the WWW research area is however the emergence of the "Social Networks" community in 2006, the same year in which Facebook went public outside USA. According to RCMB, the "Social Networks" community drew its authors mainly from the "E-Commerce, User Behaviour" (31%), "Information Retrieval" (27%), "Data Mining" (18%) and "Semantic Web" (18%) communities. The topic distribution of "Social Networks" in 2006 includes: "Social Network" 52%, "User Behaviour" 18%, "Complex Networks" 14%, "E-Commerce" 12% and "Knowledge Based Systems" 10%. It should be noted that, since we are using Klink, the main components tend to be high-level topics, which implicitly include the lower level ones. Thus "Social Networks" actually includes other areas, such as "Social Web", "Social Media", "Collaborative Networks" etc. It is possible to examine each of these components, but here we will instead focus on the big picture. In 2008 there is again a strong flow of authors from the "Data Mining" community to the "Social Networks" community (32%). This migration causes a topic shift in the community, which becomes more focused on "Data Mining", "Information Retrieval" and "Machine Learning" at the expense of "User Behaviour" and "Complex Network". In fact, Social Networks became a major domain for researchers in Data Mining in these years.

4.2   Modelling the Dynamics of the Semantic Web Research Area

The Semantic Web area is a particularly interesting one to be analysed in the timeframe 2000-2010, since it became officially recognised only in 2000. It is thus possible to study how authors from other areas gradually enriched the Semantic Web environment and how the main communities within the Semantic Web area were created. Figure 2 provides an overview of trends in the Semantic Web. At the beginning of 2000, we detect 3 main communities: "Knowledge Based Systems, AI, Ontology" (77 authors), "Intelligent Agents, Software Agents, Multi Agent Systems" (47), "WWW, Data Models, RDF" (61).

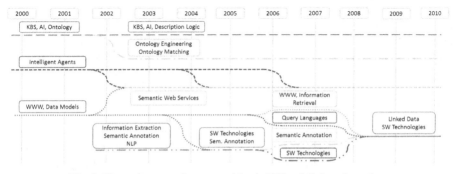

Fig. 2. The main research communities in SW and their trajectories

These communities are composed by the initial authors setting up the Semantic Web area and indeed represent the three main classes of experts needed to generate this novel area according to the vision of Tim Berners Lee et al. [23]. In the following years, these original groups will interact and merge with each other to create new communities.We can see in Table 1 that by 2002-2004 the scenario has changed and we now have four new communities. Specifically, in 2002 the "Knowledge Based Systems" community split into two different branches: about 22% of the authors migrated to "Ontology Engineering, Ontology Matching" (116 authors) and 58% to "Knowledge Based Systems, AI, Description Logic" (212 authors), which in 2004 would create the OWL standard. In the same year, some authors from the "WWW, Data Models" and the "Intelligent Agents" communities came together to build the "Semantic Web Services" community. According to RCMB, the authors from "Intelligent Agents" kept flowing to "Semantic Web Services" in the 2002-2006 interval, and eventually "Intelligent Agents" went under the critical mass to be considered as a main community for the SW. This insight is actually confirmed by a 2007 editorial titled "Where are all the Intelligent Agents?" [24] in which Jim Hendler, one of the founders of the SW area, observed that the role of agent research in SW at that time was not as strong as envisaged in the original 2001 vision.

Table 1. Novel Semantic Web communities in 2002-2004

Topics	Rep. Authors	Topics	Rep. Authors
002-2004: KBS, AI, Description Logic (212)		**2002-2004: Semantic Web Services** (149)	
KBS: 26 % AI: 22 % Des. Logic: 16 % Ontology: 6 % Logic Prog. : 5 %	F. Van Harmelen, P. Patel-Schneider, I. Horrocks, S. Bechhofer, J. Heflin, P. Hayes, D. McGuinness, C. Welty.	SW Services: 30 % WS Composition : 15 % WS Discovery: 9 % WWW: 7 % SW Tech.: 6 %	B. Norton, K. Verma, A. Sheth, N. Srinivasan, S. Kumar Agarwal, U. Keller, J. Miller, C. Patel, S. McIlraith.
2004: O. Alignment., O. Engin. (116 authors)		**2002-2004: Inf. Extraction, Sem. Ann., NLP** (63)	
Ontologies: 21 % KBS: 11 % O. Alignment: 10% O. Engineering: 7% Sem. Matching: 5%	S. Castano, N. Silva, J. Euzenat, A. Ferrara, Y. Kalfoglou, M. Ehrig, S. Montanelli, J. M. Rocha.	Inf. Extraction: 26 % Sem. Annotation: 18 % Natural Language: 18 % KBS: 7 %	Y. Wilks, B. Popov, H. Cunningham, T. Declerck, A. Dingli, M. Vargas-Vera, K. Bontcheva, F. Ciravegna.

The fourth novel community to appear in 2002 is the "Information Extraction, Semantic Annotation, Natural Language Processing" community, which has a hybrid composition, acquiring authors from "Knowledge Based Systems, AI, Description Logic" (18%), "WWW, Data Models" (14%), and "Intelligent Agents" (12%). In 2004 this community is enriched again by authors from the "WWW, Data Models" community and becomes the "Semantic Web Technologies, Semantic Annotation" community. In 2006, this community splits into "Semantic Web Technologies, World Wide Web, Ontologies" (51% of the authors) and in "Semantic Annotation, Knowledge Based Systems, Semantic Wikis" (38% of the authors). The former appears to focus primarily on the design and use of ontologies and SW technologies, while the latter focuses on the task of annotating the World Wide Web. One of their most significant outputs was DBpedia [25], the RDF based version of Wikipedia, which today provides a widely used information source in the Linked Data environment. In the meantime, the original "WWW, Data Models" community followed a parallel track and also split in 2006: 30% of the authors became part of the novel "WWW, Information Retrieval" community while 32% became part of the "Query Languages, Data Models" community. "WWW, Information Retrieval" focused on methods to exploit semantic markups for Information Retrieval on the WWW, whereas "Query Languages, Data Models" gave birth to SPARQL [26], the W3C candidate recommendation query language for RDF.

By 2008 these four communities had crafted a multitude of RDF resources (e.g., DBpedia), a query language (SPARQL) and a variety of approaches for exploiting Semantic Web Technologies. Soon after, they all merged into the "Linked Data, Semantic Web Technologies, Information Retrieval" community, focusing on the key task of building a large-scale Semantic Web. Indeed, about 48% of the authors from the original "WWW, Data Model" community and 52% of the authors from the 2004 "Information Extraction" community eventually flowed into the "Linked Data" community. These trends provide a good example of how a community of researchers started with a vision that was ahead of its time, split into sub-communities, which tackled different elements of the problem, and then merged again years later, once the key components of the vision had become established.

5   Evaluation

In this section we compare the RCMB algorithm with other approaches and show how the different techniques introduced in Section 3 incrementally improve the identification of well-formed research communities.

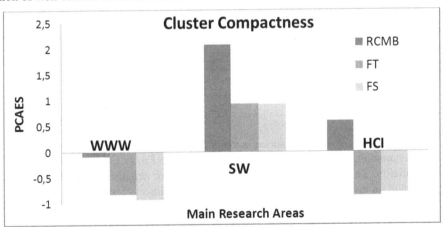

Fig. 3. PCEAS of the cluster sets returned by RCMB, FT and FS

In particular, we tested four different methods: 1) Fuzzy C-Mean (FCM) using cosine similarity on regular keywords, 2) FCM using cosine similarity on semantic topics (**FS**), 3) FCM using TTS on semantic topics (**FT**) and 4) FCM using TTS on weighted semantic topics (**RCMB**). We ran these approaches on WWW, SW and Human Computer Interaction research areas in the timeframe 2000-2010 and compared the detected clusters by using *PCAES* [27], a standard validity index for fuzzy clustering. PCAES varies between $-n$ and n, where n is the number of clusters. A large PCAES value means that each cluster is compact and well separated from the others. As shown by Figure 3 in all cases RCMB performs much better than the other two approaches in term of cluster compactness, yielding a PCAES 129±41% higher than FT and FS. According to the chi-square test, the differences between RCMB and either FT or FS are statistically significant (p=0.03), thus we can say that the semantic techniques discussed in this paper also allow finding more compact clusters.

The left panel of Table 2 describes the communities detected by the different approaches in the WWW area. The clusters in the left column are the communities with more than 50 authors discovered by at least one of the algorithms. The performance of RCMB and FT is close, with FT detecting all communities detected by RCMB but one. FS misses out three communities detected by RCMB, but in contrast with both RCMB and FT highlights the "Data Structures, Data Models" community. Hence, RCMB and FT appear to perform better than FS on the basic community identification task.

Table 2. Left Panel: main communities of WWW in 2000-2010. Right Panel: Topics associated with the main WWW communities in 2000-2010 according to RCMB and FC.

Clusters	RCMB	FT	FS
Inf. Retrieval, Search Eng.	Y	Y	Y
Semantic Web, AI	Y	Y	Y
P2P, Dis. Compu-	Y	Y	Y
Data Mining, Inf. Retrieval	Y	Y	Y
Social Networks	Y	Y	N
E-Commerce	Y	Y	N
HCI, Design	Y	N	N
Data Structures, Data Models	N	N	Y

RCMB	Baseline Fuzzy C-Mean
Information Retrieval, Search Engines, Web Search	Search Engine, Web Search, Digital Libraries, Inf. Retrieval
Semantic Web, AI, KBS, Intelligent Agents	SW, Linked Data, Semantic Web Services
Data Mining, Information Retrieval	Data Mining, Data Streams
Social Networks, Complex Networks, User Behavior	Astrophysics Data System, Xml Document, Query Language
Peer To Peer, Distributed Computing, Sensor Networks	Web Design, Web Engineering, Cosmic Ray, E-Commerce
HCI, Design Process, Learning Process, Web Accessibility	Ubiquitous Computing, Communication Systems
E-Commerce, Information Technology	Web Interface, Eclipsing Binaries, Variable Stars

The right panel of Table 2 shows a comparison between the main topics of the WWW communities according to both RCMB and the Fuzzy C-Mean using the cosine similarity. The absence of semantics has an evident negative impact both on the clusters and on their topic distribution. The first three clusters found by FC may probably be mapped to the "Information Retrieval", "Semantic Web" and "Data Mining" clusters detected by RCMB, but the others appear to be very noisy.

6   Conclusions

In this paper we have presented the Research Communities Map Builder (RCMB), an algorithm which builds maps of research communities, describing for each year in a given interval the main communities within a given topic, the topic shifts and a number of other key events. The resulting map of research communities can be used in a variety of ways to study the evolution of the communities within a given topic, their interactions, and how they are influenced by each other or by external events, such as a technological breakthrough.

For the future, we plan to build on this work and develop methods able to forecast topic shifts and key events, e.g., to estimate the probability that a new topic will emerge in a certain community or that two communities will merge in the coming years. We also intend to develop new knowledge-based techniques, able to provide comprehensive explanations for the identified dynamics.

References

1. Yan, E., Ding, Y., Milojević, S., Sugimoto, C.R.: Topics in dynamic research communities: An exploratory study for the field of information retrieval. Journal of Informetrics 6(1), 140–153 (2012)
2. Van Eck, N.J., Waltman, L.: Software survey: VOSviewer, a computer program for bibliometric mapping. Scientometrics 84(2), 523–538 (2010)
3. Upham, S.P., Rosenkopf, L., Ungar, L.H.: Innovating knowledge communities. Scientometrics 83(2), 525–554 (2010)
4. Yan, E., Ding, Y., Jacob, E.: Overlaying communities and topics. Scientometrics 90(2), 499–513 (2012)
5. Zhao, Z., Feng, S., Wang, Q., Huang, J.Z., Williams, G.J., Fan, J.: Topic oriented community detection through social objects and link analysis in social networks. Knowledge-Based Systems 26, 164–173 (2012)
6. Osborne, F., Motta, E.: Mining Semantic Relations between Research Areas. In: Cudré-Mauroux, P., et al. (eds.) ISWC 2012, Part I. LNCS, vol. 7649, pp. 410–426. Springer, Heidelberg (2012)
7. Ding, Y.: Community detection: topological vs. topical. Journal of Informetrics 5(4), 498–514 (2011)
8. Upham, S.P., Small, H.: Emerging research fronts in science and technology: patterns of new knowledge development. Scientometrics 83(1), 15–38 (2010)
9. Osborne, F., Scavo, G., Motta, E.: Identifying diachronic topic-based research communities by clustering shared research trajectories. In: Presutti, V., d'Amato, C., Gandon, F., d'Aquin, M., Staab, S., Tordai, A. (eds.) ESWC 2014. LNCS, vol. 8465, pp. 114–129. Springer, Heidelberg (2014)
10. Osborne, F., Motta, E., Mulholland, P.: Exploring Scholarly Data with Rexplore. In: Proceedings of the 12th International Semantic Web Conference (2013)
11. Flake, G.W., Lawrence, S., Giles, C.L., Coetzee, F.M.: Self-organization and identification of web communities. Computer 35(3), 66–70 (2002)
12. Smyth Guimera, R., Amaral, L.A.N.: Functional cartography of complex metabolic networks. Nature 433(7028), 895–900 (2005)
13. Racherla, P., Hu, C.: A social network perspective of tourism research collaborations. Annals of Tourism Research 37(4), 1012–1034 (2010)
14. Hofmann, T.: Probabilistic latent semantic indexing. In: The 22nd Conference on Research and Development in Information Retrieval (pp, Berkeley, CA, pp. 50–57 (1999)
15. Blei, D.M., Ng, A.Y., Jordan, M.I.: Latent Dirichlet allocation. Journal of Machine Learning Research 3, 993–1033 (2003)
16. Tang, J., Zhang, J., Yao, L., Li, J., Zhang, L., Su, Z.: ArnetMiner: extraction and mining of academic social networks. In: Proceeding of KDD 2008, pp. 990–998 (2008)

17. Peroni, S., Shotton, D.: FaBiO and CiTO: ontologies for describing bibliographic resources and citations. In: Web Semantics: Science, Services and Agents on the WWW, vol. 17 (2012)

18. Bezdek, J.C., Ehrlich, R., Full, W.: FCM: The fuzzy c-means clustering algorithm. Computers and Geosciences 10(2), 191–203 (1984)

19. Olsson, D.M., Nelson, L.S.: The Nelder-Mead simplex procedure for function minimization. Technometrics 17(1), 45–51 (1975)

20. Neill, D.B., Moore, A.W., Sabhnani, M., Daniel, K.: Detection of emerging space-time clusters. In: Proceedings of the Eleventh ACM SIGKDD International Conference on Knowledge Discovery in Data Mining, pp. 218–227. ACM (2005)

21. Sethi, I.K., Patel, N.V.: Statistical approach to scene change detection. In: Symposium on Electronic Imaging: Science & Technology. SPIE (1995)

22. Chiu, S.L.: Fuzzy model identification based on cluster estimation. Journal of Intelligent and Fuzzy Systems 2(3), 267–278 (1994)

23. Berners-Lee, T., Hendler, J., Lassila, O.: The Semantic Web. Scientific American 284(5), 28–37 (2001)

24. Hendler, J.: Where are all the Intelligent Agents? A Letter from the Editor in Intelligent Systems IEEE (May/June 2007)

25. Auer, S., Bizer, C., Kobilarov, G., Lehmann, J., Cyganiak, R., Ives, Z.G.: DBpedia: A nucleus for a web of open data. In: Aberer, K., et al. (eds.) ASWC 2007 and ISWC 2007. LNCS, vol. 4825, pp. 722–735. Springer, Heidelberg (2007)

26. Pérez, J., Arenas, M., Gutierrez, C.: Semantics and Complexity of SPARQL. In: Cruz, I., Decker, S., Allemang, D., Preist, C., Schwabe, D., Mika, P., Uschold, M., Aroyo, L.M. (eds.) ISWC 2006. LNCS, vol. 4273, pp. 30–43. Springer, Heidelberg (2006)

27. Wu, K.L., Yang, M.S.: A cluster validity index for fuzzy clustering. Pattern Recognition Letters 26(9), 1275–1291 (2005)

Logical Detection of Invalid SameAs Statements in RDF Data

Laura Papaleo[1], Nathalie Pernelle[1], Fatiha Saïs[1], and Cyril Dumont[1]

Université de Paris-Sud, Laboratoire de Recherche en Informatique,
Bâtiment 650, F-91405 Orsay Cedex, France
`firstname.lastname@lri.fr`
`http://www.lri.fr`

Abstract. In the last years, thanks to the standardization of Semantic Web technologies, we are experiencing an unprecedented production of data, published online as *Linked Data*. In this context, when a typed link is instantiated between two different resources referring to the same real world entity, the usage of *owl:sameAs* is generally predominant. However, recent research discussions have shown issues in the use of *owl:sameAs*. Problems arise both in cases in which sameAs is automatically discovered by a data linking tool erroneously, or when users declare it but meaning something less 'strict' than the semantics defined by OWL. In this work, we discuss further this issue and we present a method for logically detect invalid sameAs statements under specific circumstances. We report our experimental results, performed on OAEI datasets, to prove that the approach is promising.

Keywords: RDF identity link, sameAs, Linking quality & validation.

1 Introduction

The Semantic Web is a *'Web of Data'*, where data can be processed by machines, extending the principles of the Web from *documents* to *data* [1]. In this context, resources can be accessed using the conventional Web architecture (URIs) and it is possible to link resources using named relations. Today, we are experiencing an unprecedented production of resources, published as *Linked Open Data* (LOD, for short). This is leading to the creation of a global data space containing billions of assertions [2]. RDF [13] provides formal ways to build these assertions. Working in the LOD is basically about using the Web to create *typed links* (in RDF) between data from different sources. Most of the RDF links connecting resources coming from different data sources are *RDF identity links*, called also *sameAs statements*. They are defined using the *owl:sameAs* property, thus expressing that two URI references actually refer to the same thing. Unfortunately, many existing identity links do not reflect such genuine identity, as argued recently within the research community [5,4]. So, as numerous independently developed data sources have been published over internet as Linked Data, the *problem of identity* is now casting a shadow over the shininess of the Semantic Web [11,5].

K. Janowicz et al. (Eds.): EKAW 2014, LNAI 8876, pp. 373–384, 2014.

It is becoming extremely important to develop means of *data and linking quality assurance*. The study of the quality of data and links in the LOD cloud may be particularly useful in applications that want to consume Linked Data as well as in Semantic Web frameworks dedicated to data linking or data integration.

In this work, we investigate and design a logical method to detect invalid sameAs statements, by looking at the descriptions associated to the instances involved. We suppose that, in case of multiple data sources, mappings between properties are provided. Our approach is local, in the sense that, we build a contextual graph 'around' each one of the two resources involved in the sameAs statement and we study the descriptions provided in these contextual graphs. The construction of the contextual graph is based on properties that have specific characteristics (functional, local completeness). We claim that, when logical conflicts are encountered, the initial RDF identity link is 'inconsistent', meaning that it requires further investigation (supervised or automatic). We tested the approach on sameAs statements provided by linking tools that have been applied on Ontology Alignment Evaluation Initiative (OAEI) datasets, showing that our research direction is promising.

The remainder of this paper is organized as follows. In Section 2 related works are described. In Section 3, we present the conceptual building blocks of our approach, while Sections 4 and 5 are dedicated to the formulation of the problem and the generation of the rules. In Sections 6 and 7 we present the logical method and the experimental results.Finally, in Section 8 some concluding remarks are drawn.

2   Related Works

How to evaluate and assess the quality of data and links in the Linked Data Cloud is a generally novel problem, growing its importance in the last years, as the research community can, now, work with a massive quantity of data coming from multiple data sources.

In [6] the authors present a 'global approach' where they analyzed the structural properties of large graphs of identity links focusing the attention on general network properties such as degree distributions and URI counts, without analyzing the quality. Recently, in [10] the authors describe another global approach in a framework dedicated to the assessment of Linked Data mappings using network metrics. Five different metrics have been performed on a set of known good and bad links concluding that most of these metrics are not meaningful with respect to the evaluation of the quality of an identity link. In [4], the author illustrates how to assess the quality of *owl:sameAs* links, using a constraint-based method. In the work, an interesting formalization of the problem in a graph-based fashion is presented, but the evaluation of the quality of the identity link is, in the end, performed using only one property, namely the name of each entity. The results are interesting, but as claimed but the author himself, it could be important to include advanced similarity measures and the evaluation of more properties. In [5,12] the authors studied the problem of the quality of RDF identity links from a general point of view, making observations about the varying use of *owl:sameAs* in Linked Data. They proposed an ontology called the Similarity Ontology (SO) that aims at better classifying the different level of similarity between items in different data sources. However, the quality evaluation of the *owl:sameAs* links is performed manually, assessing around 250 *owl:sameAs* links in an Amazon Mechanical Turk experiment.

In this paper we propose a method which analyzes more information than simply the resource name, as opposite to [4]. Our approach is 'local', differently from [6,10] as we assess the correctness of a sameAs statement by studying the information described in contextual sub-graphs built according to specific criteria. To the extent of our knowledge, there not exist similar logical methods in the literature.

To complete this Section, we need to recall that there exist a lot of interesting methods related to *owl:sameAs* link discovery (see [7] as recent survey). This is also referred as the 'coreference problem' in Semantic Web. The reader can, for example, see the works in [9,21,18] or, more recently those in [25,23,16]. However, *sameAs statement quality assessment* is, generally, different from the coreference problem. From the 'coreference prospective', the goal is to analyze the knowledge related to two resources in order to decide if one new assertion can be added to the knowledge base. In various domains, there are generally accepted naming schemata [2]. If two resources in the knowledge base both support one or more of these identification schema, the implicit relationship between entities can be made explicit as identity link, automatically. This can be true, for example, in case of a unique code such as the italian 'Codice Fiscale' that can be derived through a deterministic algorithm from a person's name and his/her date and place of birth, or the International Standard Book Number (ISBN) which is a unique numeric commercial book identifier. When no shared naming schema exist, RDF identity links are usually generated by evaluating the similarity of entities using more or less complex similarity functions. These functions generally take into account sub-parts of resource description that is known to be discriminative enough as, for example, inverse functional properties or composite keys. Few linking tools are interested in generating *owl:differentFrom* links, as for example [20]. This idea of partitioning the resources into groups of 'different resources' is used also in blocking methods as [22]. Then, data linking tools will search for sameAs links only within a group. However, in such approaches, only direct data-type properties are taken into account. Instead, once a sameAs statement exists in the knowledge base, it could be interesting to analyze different properties (not only inverse functional). To clarify this point, let us consider a very simple example: we have two resources (books) b_1 and b_2 both described using two data-type properties *isbn* and *pages*. We assume, for example, that the property *isbn* is inverse functional and *pages* is only functional. In order to infer $sameAs(b_1, b_2)$, it is sufficient to check if the values of *isbn* are equal. Using the semantics of *owl:sameAs* it is possible to infer that the values of the property pages are equivalent. If they are not, one can detect a conflicting case contingent on the semantics of $sameAs(b_1, b_2)$. In conclusion, it is sure that the two problems are entailed and, as immediate future activities, we are planning to deepen the analysis of their interconnection, especially in the case of complex and hybrid linking methods that are recently emerging.

3   Preliminaries

In this Section we present the theoretical framework in order to define the building blocks for the logical invalidation approach.

Definition 1. *RDF Graph.* [17]
An RDF graph is a set of RDF triples. The set of nodes of an RDF graph is the set of subjects and objects of triples in the graph.

Given an infinite set U of URIs, an infinite set B of blank nodes and an infinite set L of literals, a RDF triple is a triple $\langle s, p, o \rangle$ where the subject $s \in (U \cup B)$, the predicate $p \in U$ and the object $o \in (U \cup B \cup L)$. A *RDF triple* represents an assertion: if the triple $\langle s, p, o \rangle$ exists, the logical assertion $p(s, o)$ holds. An RDF graph G is simply a collection of RDF triples and it can be seen as a set of statements describing partially (or completely) a certain knowledge.

Definition 2. *SameAs Statement.* [6]
A SameAs statement sameAs(s, o) is an RDF triple $\langle s, owl : sameAs, o \rangle$ in an RDF graph G which connects two RDF resources s and o by means of the owl:sameAs predicate.

Such an *owl:sameAs* statement indicates that two URI references refer to the same *thing* : the individuals have the same 'identity' [15]. Given an RDF graph G as defined above, the OWL2 RL rules define the owl:sameAs as being reflexive, symmetric, and transitive, and they axiomatize the standard replacement properties.

Definition 3. *Property-based walk of length* n $w_{\{n,s,P\}}$.
Given an RDF graph G, a node s in G, given a set P of properties defined for G, a Property-based walk of length n $w_{\{n,s,P\}}$ is an alternating sequence of nodes and predicates $\{v_0 \equiv s, p_0, v_1, p_1, v_2, \ldots, v_{n-1}, p_{n-1}, v_n\}$, such that

- *$v_0, \ldots, v_{n-1}$ are resources in G, $\forall i = 0, \ldots, n-1$ $v_i \in U$,*
- *v_n is a literal in G, $v_n \in L$*
- *each triple $\{v_i, p_i, v_{i+1}\}$ in the sequence is an RDF triple in G such as $p_i \in P$*
- *all the resources in the walk are distinct from one another. Thus, for each pair of resource $\{v_i, v_j\}$, v_i and v_j are not the same resource, with $\{i, j\} \in [0, \ldots, n-1]$ (they have different URIs).*

In the definition we suppose that each predicate in G has an associated weight 1 that expresses its existence (its length). $w_{\{n,s,P\}}$ is basically a path in the RDF graph without cycle and of length n, involving $n + 1$ node, n resources defined by URIs and 1 node as a literal. It can be seen also as a collection of assertions selected according to specific conditions (the starting resource s and the set of properties P). In other words, with a walk $w_{\{n,s,P\}}$ in the graph G, we select a sequence of assertions in some way related to the resource s. This means also that, for every RDF triple $\langle v_i, p_i, v_{i+1}\rangle$ in $w_{\{n,s,P\}}$ the fact $p_i(v_i, v_{i+1})$ holds.

Definition 4. *m-degree Contextual Graph* $G_{\{m,s,P\}}$
Given and RDF graph G and a node $s \in G, s \in U$, an integer number m and a set P of properties defined for G, a m-degree Contextual Graph $G_{\{m,s,P\}}$ for s is a sub-graph of G such that every node $v_i \in G_{\{m,s,P\}}$ belongs to a property-based walk of length n, with $n \leq m$.

A m-degree contextual graph for a resource s can be seen as a subset of knowledge pertinent to s, bounded by the set of predicates P. Given an RDF graph G, in which circles identify resources with URI and rectangles represent literals, Figure 1-(left) shows a walk $w_{\{2,s,P=\{P_0,P_1\}\}}$ for the resource s. The walk has length 2 and involves the properties P_0 and P_1. Figure 1-(right) shows a 2-degree contextual graph $G_{\{2,s,P=\{P_0,...,P_4\}\}}$ for the same resource s. It involves the properties P_0, P_1, P_2, P_3 and P_4.

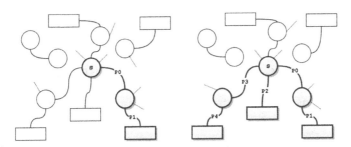

Fig. 1. (left) a walk of degree 2 for the resource s, $w_{\{2,s,P=\{P_0,P_1\}\}}$. (right) The contextual graph $G_{\{2,s,P=\{P_0,...,P_4\}\}}$ of degree 2 for the same resource s.

4   Problem Statement

The problem we are addressing is to check if a sameAs statement can be invalidated and eventually explain this deduction. We need to check for inconsistencies in the assertion $sameAs(x, y)$ according to the knowledge provided in the RDF graph G.

Our approach relies on building two contextual graphs (see Section 3), for x and y respectively and on reasoning on the assertions contained in these two graphs. The building blocks of the problem are the following:

- An RDF graph G
- two resources x and y, such that x, y are resources in G
- the triple $\langle x, owl : sameAs, y\rangle$ (or $sameAs(x, y)$) belonging to G
- a set of properties P in G

- a value n representing the depth of the contextual graphs
- the contextual graphs $G_{\{n,x,P\}}$ and $G'_{\{n,y,P\}}$ for x and y

The problem becomes the evaluation of the following rule:

$$G_{\{n,x,P\}} \wedge G'_{\{n,y,P\}} \wedge sameAs(x,y) \Rightarrow \bot$$

The construction of the contextual graphs depends on the predicates (properties) we select and the value n. Indeed, in complex RDF graph, which can combine data coming from multiple data sources, limiting the depth of a contextual graph could be wise. The main reason is that long property-based walks can lead to not relevant piece of information which can eventually confuse the validation process. In Figure 2 we show an example of what we want to build. In this case, the statement $sameAs(x,y)$ must be validated, and a value $n = 2$ has been selected. The set of properties P has been defined as $\{P_0, \ldots, P_4\}$. The image shows the two contextual graphs extracted for x and y. In the following Section we explain how we want to choose the predicates.

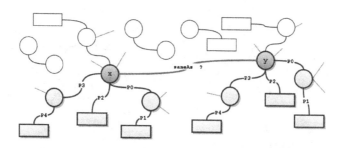

Fig. 2. The statement $sameAs(x,y)$ must be validated. The two 2-degree contextual graphs extracted for x and y are highlighted.

5   Properties Selection and Rules Generation

In this work, we chose to use (inverse) functional properties and those properties declared as local complete. Here, we explain and motivate this choice, describing the logical rules we add in the resolution system.

5.1   Functional and Inverse Functional Properties

Let us suppose that p_1 is a functional property. It can be expressed logically as follows [15]:

$$p_1(r,v) \wedge p_1(r,v') \Rightarrow v \equiv v'$$

If we want to validate $sameAs(x,y)$ and we have a mapped functional property p_1, with $p_1(x,w)$ and $p_1(y,w_1)$, and we can assert in some way that $w \not\equiv w_1$ then:

$$sameAs(s,o) \wedge p_1(s,w) \wedge p_1(o,w_1) \wedge w \not\equiv w_1 \Rightarrow \bot$$

We have an inconsistency. A similar reasoning can be done for inverse functional properties. In these situations, if we assume that the assertions already in the RDF graph are true and we have 'doubts' only on the sameAs statement, we can conclude that this latter has problems. In our approach, taking into consideration functional properties, we basically add the following rules for every property p_i, p_j, p_k in the contextual graphs we are considering.

- $R_{1_{FDP}} : sameAs(x,y) \wedge p_i(x,w_1) \wedge p_i(y,w_2) \rightarrow synVals(w_1,w_2)$
- $R_{2_{FOP}} : sameAs(x,y) \wedge p_j(x,w_1) \wedge p_j(y,w_2) \rightarrow sameAs(w_1,w_2)$
- $R_{3_{IFP}} : sameAs(x,y) \wedge p_k(w_1,x) \wedge p_k(w_2,y) \rightarrow sameAs(w_1,w_2)$

Note that $R_{1_{FDP}}$ is for data-type properties and $R_{2_{FOP}}$ and $R_{3_{IFP}}$ are for object-type properties. $synVals$ and $\neg synVals$ are further described in Section 6. Given a property p in the graph G, the knowledge of p being a functional property can be already present among the assertions in G or derived after, collecting knowledge from experts or gathering it externally (existing ontologies, additional assertions on the Web and so on.)

5.2 Local Completeness

The closed-world assumption is in general inappropriate for the Semantic Web due to its size and rate of change [14]. But in some domains and specific contexts, local-completeness for RDF predicates (properties) could be assured. A good example for a multi-valued local complete property could be one representing the authors of a publication. When a predicate is like that, it should be declared *closed* in the specific knowledge base, making a local completeness assumption. A Local Completeness (LC) rule specifies that the resource is complete for a subset(s) of information (on a particular ontology): the information contained in the resource is all the information for the subset (specified by the rule) of the domain. In an RDF graph G, we declare the following OWL2 RL rule for each property that fulfills LC:

- $R_{4_{LC}} : sameAs(x,y) \wedge p(x,w_1) \rightarrow p(y,w_1)$

where p is a predicate defined in the RDF graph G, x and y are object-type resources in G ($x, y \in U$) and w_1 is a literal ($w_1 \in L$). This rule will be used to discover inconsistencies since negative facts can be inferred because of the local completeness, as explained in the next Section. Given a property p, the knowledge of 'local completeness' for p can be asserted by an expert or discovered using semi-automatic approaches.

6   The Invalidation Approach

In this Section we present our invalidation approach, on the basis of all the definitions and reasoning made so far. Given G the initial RDF graph with U the set of resources in G with URIs. Given $sameAs(x,y)$ the input sameAs statement to validate, where $x, y \in U$. Let F be a set of facts, initially empty, and L the set of literals for G.

1. Build a set F_1 of $\neg synVals(w_1, w_2)$, for each pair of semantically different w_1 and w_2, with $w_1, w_2 \in L$.
2. Choose a value n indicating the depth of the contextual graphs
3. Build the contextual graphs for x and y considering (inverse) functional properties and local complete properties
   - For all the (inverse) functional properties $p_{i_{FP}}$ add the relative set of RDF facts to F, considering the rules $R_{1_{FDP}}, R_{2_{FOP}}, R_{3_{IFP}}$ in Section 5.
   - For each $p_{i_{LC}}$ that falls in the contextual graphs and fulfills the local completeness (i.e. $R_{4_{LC}}$ is declared), add to F a set of facts in the form $\neg p_{i_{LC}}(s, w)$ if w is different to all the w' s.t. $p_{i_{LC}}(s, w')$ belongs to F, using F_1. Note that $w, w' \in L$.
4. Apply iteratively unit resolution until saturation [19] using
   $$F \cup CNF^1\{R_{1_{FDP}}, R_{2_{FOP}}, R_{3_{IFP}}, R_{4_{LC}}\}.$$

Note also that disjointness of classes can be provided as input and considered in the resolution.

The set of $\neg synVals(w_1, w_2)$ with $w_1, w_2 \in L$ can be obtained using different strategies. It is possible, for example, to perform a pre-processing step in which we build a clustering of the values according to specific criteria. To clarify, consider a simple example of names of cities in a specific domain: it is possible to pre-process all the possible values and assert that $synVals('Paris', 'ParisCity')$ and that $\neg synVals('Paris', 'Milan')$ and so on. Thus, the evaluation is based on determining if two values w_1, w_2 belong to the same cluster. Another situation arises when the values are 'well defined' as in the case of enumeration, dates, years, geographical data or some types of measures. In these cases, the evaluation is again a simple syntactic comparison of the values. If they are the same, they are equivalent, otherwise they are not equivalent.

7   Experimental Results and Discussion

A prototype of our validation framework has been implemented in Java using the AIMA library for the resolution. In this Section we present the results of the experiments we performed for assessing the quality of the set of sameAs statements computed by different linking methods, respectively presented in [20], [24] and [26].

In [20] the sameAs statements are computed according to similarity measures over specific property descriptions, as in [26] where similarity between entities is iteratively calculated by analyzing specific features. In [24], instead sameAs statements are computed on the basis of a novel algorithm for key discovery. All the above methods have produced results on the Person-Restaurants (PR) data test available for the instance matching contest OAEI 2010 (IM@OAEI2010) [3]. For the key discovery method, we started from the links obtained by the method considering only the *name* of the restaurant as a key. According to the knowledge

---

[1] CNF: Conjunctive Normal Form.

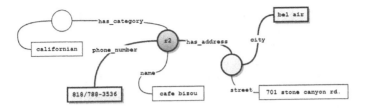

Fig. 3. An instance of restaurant in the dataset 'restaurant1' Given the functional properties *phone_number*, *has_address* and *city*, a contextual graph of degree 2 is depicted

base, we considered as 'meaningfully' functional the properties *phone_number* and *has_address* that describe a restaurant and *city* that describes an address[2]. Thus, given a sameAs statement in the form *sameAs(x, y)* we computed the contextual graph of degree 2 considering the three functional properties listed before. Figure 3 shows an example of the contextual graph computed for a restaurant in the first dataset 'restaurant1' (already mapped). To build the $\neg synVals$ (set F_1) for the values of the properties selected, we did a normalization of the values. For *phone_number*, we removed all the additional characters (e.g. '/', '-', and so on), leaving only the numbers. We note that the same number of digits are given for all the phone numbers. For *city*, we removed words which can be not meaningful such as 'city', the character '(' and so on. A $\neg synVals$ is declared for each pair of syntactically different pairs of values. To explain the results obtained, let us consider the answers collected by applying our invalidation approach on the sameAs statements computed by [24]. Note that, in this case, the analysis is performed using properties completely different from those used in the computation of the identity links. Over the 90 sameAs statements computed, 4 were wrong with respect to the gold standard. We are able to detect 3 of these 4 erroneous links. The only one we cannot detect is the one linking restaurant 91 defined in dataset 1 to restaurant 711 defined in dataset 2. By looking at the properties, the two restaurants share the same phone number and the same city. They even share the same street name. So an inconsistency cannot be detected. Most probably, they represent the same commercial site providing different services (they have different categories). In addition we classify as 'wrong sameAs' 5 statements which, with respect to the gold standard, are in fact good sameAs statements. The reason is that, in every statement *sameAs(x, y)*, the restaurants x and y have different phone number or different city (or both). This type of result can be seen dually. On the one hand this could mean, for example, that a restaurant can have two phone numbers, so maybe the property *phone_number* is not functional. On the other hand, there can be errors in the data (for example 'los angeles' and 'los feliz') and the computation of the $\neg synVals$ has been imprecise. In any case, the good idea is to highlight the inconsistency to the

---

[2] Note that both the previous methods aligned the two initial datasets in order to compute the sameAs statements. We considered the same alignment in the explanation of the results.

user (expert) and ask for confirmation or correction. Table 1 shows a tabular summary of our tests, including accuracy, recall and precision of the method. The table indicates as: *(i)* **TC**: total cases to be considered, namely the number of *sameAs* found by the linking algorithm. *(ii)* **RG**: the number of the sameAs statements really wrong, wrt the gold standard. *(iii)* **TN**: (true negative), the number of statements which we detected 'good' and were actually correct (wrt the gold standard). *(iv)* **TP**: (true positive), the number of statements which we detected 'wrong' and were actually wrong (wrt the gold standard). *(v)* **FP** (false positive), the number of statements which we detected 'wrong' but were actually correct. *(vi)* **FN**: (false negative), the number of real wrong statements which we could not detect. Additionally, by definition, $accuracy = (TP + TN)/TC$, $recall = TP/(TP + TN)$ and $precision = TP/(TP + FP)$.

Table 1. Results of our approach on the sameAs links provided by the linking methods. We report the accuracy, recall and precision for the invalidation approach (IA) and the overall precision (LM+IA) in the last column.

Linking Method	LM precision	TC	RG	TN	TP	FN	FP	accuracy	recall	IA precision	LM+IA precision
[24]	95.55%	90	4	81	3	1	5	93,34%	75%	37%	98.85%
[20]	69.71%	142	43	94	38	5	5	92.9%	88.4%	88.4%	95.19%
[26]	90.17%	112	11	86	11	0	16	86.60%	100%	42.30%	100%

In conclusion, our results showed that, when our validation tool is applied after one of the linking tool, the precision of each tool can be improved, namely for [24] we pass from a precision of 95.55% to 98.85%, for [20] from a precision of 69.71% to 95.19% and finally for [26] from a precision of 90.17% to 100%.

8   Concluding Remarks

In the last years, the amount of data published on online as Linked Data is growing significantly. In this context, the usage of *owl:sameAs* is generally predominant when linking resources from different data sources. Recent research discussions within the Linked Data community have shown that the use of *owl:sameAs* may be incorrect. Hence, the needs of methods to assure and validate the quality of links in RDF stores.

In this paper we argued on the problem of evaluating sameAs statements.We designed a logical evaluation method which relies on the descriptions associated to the resources involved in the sameAs statement.Our method analyzes the functional properties and the properties defined as local complete. It builds a contextual graph for each resource and assesses the equality of each description involved. We formulated the necessary concepts and formally presented the approach, indicating the set of rules we use. We experimented the method with 3 datasets of sameAs statements produced by 3 different linking tools. The analysis of the results proved that, by applying our method after the linking, the precision is improved. We are working on completing the comparison with other methods, e.g.[8,16].

In the future, we are planning to explore different research directions. First, we are going to run experiments on more complex datasets. Second, we are working in the formalization of a set of rules for the re-qualification of a 'wrong' sameAs statement, in cases in which two resources represent the same conceptual element but at *different levels of details*. We want extend our approach using similarity measures on property values, allowing us to work with data with typos errors. As ultimate goal, we are aiming at designing an integration framework where knowledge base can be assessed, enhanced and visualized, using inferences on data and links, including data fusion, links corrections, and organization of the knowledge and the data at different levels of abstraction.

Acknowledgment. Work supported by the French National Research Agency: Quality and Interopera bility of Large Catalogues of Document project (QUALINCA-ANR-2012-CORD-012-02), by the Digiteo research cluster (digiteo.fr) within the framework of its OMTE programme and by the software group of the LRI lab.

References

1. Berners-Lee, T., Hendler, J., Lassila, O.: The semantic web. Scientific American 284(5), 34–43 (2001)
2. Bizer, C., Heath, T., Berners-Lee, T.: Linked data - the story so far. International Journal Semantic Web Information Systems 5(3), 1–22 (2009)
3. OEAI Campaign. Im@oaei2010 - persons-restaurants (pr) dataset (April 2014)
4. de Melo, G.: Not quite the same: Identity constraints for the Web of Linked Data. In: Proc. of the 27th Conference on Artificial Intelligence. AAAI Press (2013)
5. Ding, L., Shinavier, J., Finin, T., McGuinness, D.L.: owl:sameAs and Linked Data: An Empirical Study. In: International Web Science Conference (2010)
6. Ding, L., Shinavier, J., Shangguan, Z., McGuinness, D.L.: SameAs networks and beyond: Analyzing deployment status and implications of owl:sameAs in linked data. In: Patel-Schneider, P.F., Pan, Y., Hitzler, P., Mika, P., Zhang, L., Pan, J.Z., Horrocks, I., Glimm, B. (eds.) ISWC 2010, Part I. LNCS, vol. 6496, pp. 145–160. Springer, Heidelberg (2010)
7. Ferrara, A., Nikolov, A., Scharffe, F.: Data linking. J. Web Semantics 23(1) (2013)
8. Ghazvinian, A., Noy, N.F., Jonquet, C., Shah, N., Musen, M.A.: What four million mappings can tell you about two hundred ontologies. In: Bernstein, A., Karger, D.R., Heath, T., Feigenbaum, L., Maynard, D., Motta, E., Thirunarayan, K. (eds.) ISWC 2009. LNCS, vol. 5823, pp. 229–242. Springer, Heidelberg (2009)
9. Glaser, H., Jaffri, A., Millard, I.: Managing co-reference on the semantic web. In: WWW 2009 Workshop: Linked Data on the Web, LDOW 2009 (April 2009)
10. Guéret, C., Groth, P., Stadler, C., Lehmann, J.: Assessing linked data mappings using network measures. In: Simperl, E., Cimiano, P., Polleres, A., Corcho, O., Presutti, V. (eds.) ESWC 2012. LNCS, vol. 7295, pp. 87–102. Springer, Heidelberg (2012)
11. Halpin, H., Hayes, P.J.: When owl: sameas isn't the same: An analysis of identity links on the semantic web. In: Proc. of the WWW 2010 Workshop on Linked Data on the Web. CEUR-WS.org Proceedings, vol. 628 (2010)

12. Halpin, H., Hayes, P.J., Thompson, H.S.: When owl: sameas isn't the same redux: A preliminary theory of identity and inference on the semantic web. In: Workshop on Discov. Meaning OntheGo in Large Heter. Data, pp. 25–30 (2011)
13. Heath, T., Bizer, C.: Linked Data: Evolving the Web into a Global Data Space, 1st edn. Morgan & Claypool (2011)
14. Heflin, J., Muñoz-Avila, H.: LCW-based agent planning for the semantic web. In: Ontologies and the Semantic Web Workshop, pp. 63–70. AAAI Press (2002)
15. Hitzler, P., Krötzsch, M., Parsia, B., Patel-Schneider, P.F., Rudolph, S. (eds.): OWL 2 Web Ontology Language: Primer. W3C Recommendation (2009), http://www.w3.org/TR/owl2-primer/
16. Hogan, A., Zimmermann, A., Umbrich, J., Polleres, A., Decker, S.: Scalable and distributed methods for entity matching, consolidation and disambiguation over linked data corpora. J. Web Sem. 10, 76–110 (2012)
17. Lassila, O., Swick, R.R.,. WWW Consortium.: Resource description framework (RDF) model and syntax specification (2004)
18. Pernelle, N., Saïs, F., Safar, B., Koutraki, M., Ghosh, T.: N2R-Part: Identity Link Discovery using Partially Aligned Ontologies. In: International Workshop on Open Data, Paris, France (June 2013)
19. Robinson, G., Wos, L.: Paramodulation and theorem-proving in first-order theories with equality. In: Automation of Reasoning 2: Classical Papers on Computational Logic, pp. 298–313. Springer (1969)
20. Saïs, F., Niraula, N.B., Pernelle, N., Rousset, M.C.: LN2R a knowledge based reference reconciliation system: OAEI2010 results. In: International Workshop on Ontology Matching OM2010, vol. 689. CEUR-WS.org Proceedings (2010)
21. Saïs, F., Pernelle, N., Rousset, M.-C.: Combining a logical and a numerical method for data reconciliation. In: Spaccapietra, S. (ed.) Journal on Data Semantics XII. LNCS, vol. 5480, pp. 66–94. Springer, Heidelberg (2009)
22. Song, D., Heflin, J.: Automatically generating data linkages using a domain-independent candidate selection approach. In: Aroyo, L., Welty, C., Alani, H., Taylor, J., Bernstein, A., Kagal, L., Noy, N., Blomqvist, E. (eds.) ISWC 2011, Part I. LNCS, vol. 7031, pp. 649–664. Springer, Heidelberg (2011)
23. Song, D., Heflin, J.: Domain-independent entity coreference for linking ontology instances. J. Data and Information Quality 4(2), 7:1–7:29 (2013)
24. Symeonidou, D., Armant, V., Pernelle, N., Saïs, F.: SAKey: Scalable Almost Key Discovery in RDF Data. In: Janowicz, K., et al. (eds.) ISWC 2014. LNCS, vol. 8796, pp. 33–49. Springer, Heidelberg (2014)
25. Taheri, A., Shamsfard, M.: Instance coreference resolution in multi-ontology linked data resources. In: Takeda, H., Qu, Y., Mizoguchi, R., Kitamura, Y. (eds.) JIST 2012. LNCS, vol. 7774, pp. 129–145. Springer, Heidelberg (2013)
26. Yves, J.R., Shironoshita, E.P., Kabuka, M.R.: Ontology matching with semantic verification. Web Semantics 7(3), 235–251 (2009)

Integrating Know-How
into the Linked Data Cloud

Paolo Pareti[1,2], Benoit Testu[1], Ryutaro Ichise[1],
Ewan Klein[2], and Adam Barker[3]

[1] National Institute of Informatics, Tokyo, Japan
p.pareti@sms.ed.ac.uk, benoit.testu@u-psud.fr, ichise@nii.ac.jp
[2] University of Edinburgh, Edinburgh, United Kingdom
ewan@inf.ed.ac.uk
[3] University of St Andrews, St Andrews, United Kingdom
adam.barker@st-andrews.ac.uk

Abstract. This paper presents the first framework for integrating procedural knowledge, or "know-how", into the Linked Data Cloud. Know-how available on the Web, such as step-by-step instructions, is largely unstructured and isolated from other sources of online knowledge. To overcome these limitations, we propose extending to procedural knowledge the benefits that Linked Data has already brought to representing, retrieving and reusing declarative knowledge. We describe a framework for representing generic know-how as Linked Data and for automatically acquiring this representation from existing resources on the Web. This system also allows the automatic generation of links between different know-how resources, and between those resources and other online knowledge bases, such as DBpedia. We discuss the results of applying this framework to a real-world scenario and we show how it outperforms existing manual community-driven integration efforts.

1 Introduction

The Web contains a large amount of procedural knowledge, or *know-how*, in many domains of human interests, ranging from cooking recipes to software tutorials and social skills. As such, it has become one of the major sources of knowledge for anybody who is interested in performing a task. Online knowledge also has the potential for helping machines to understand and reason over common-sense human activities [9]. However, the potential for applying this knowledge is severely restricted due to its lack of structure, the diversity of representation formats and its isolation from other knowledge sources. In this context, we argue that Linked Data is an ideal representation for overcoming these restrictions on using know-how at web-scale. The main contributions of this paper are:

- The description of the first framework that can automate the creation and the integration of know-how into the Linked Data Cloud.
- The validation of this framework with a concrete implementation which outperforms existing know-how integration efforts.

K. Janowicz et al. (Eds.): EKAW 2014, LNAI 8876, pp. 385–396, 2014.

The main benefit of a formal representation of human know-how is to allow machines to better understand human processes, making them reusable in different applications. We adopt a generic definition of the term process which includes any entity which has the potential for being performed, such as step-by-step instructions.

We present a framework that overcomes the limitations of the existing know-how and enables it to be integrated into the Linked Data Cloud. This framework can be divided in two components:

- Knowledge Extraction and Representation. This framework allows the automatic formalization of existing know-how based on a generic and lightweight Linked Data vocabulary. This component addresses the limitation of the lack of explicit structure and shared semantics.
- Linked Data Integration. This framework can automatically discover links between processes and other existing Linked Data. This component addresses the problem of the isolation of individual processes from related knowledge.

This framework has been implemented and validated in a real-world scenario. We have applied it to two different large-scale know-how repositories and created a Linked Data representation of over 200,000 processes. These processes have been integrated both with each other and with DBpedia [2]. We have compared the quality of the results with existing user-generated links and we have tested them in a practical application.

2   Problem Formulation

The problem addressed by this paper is the *effective* integration of a particular kind of procedural knowledge, that we call *human know-how*, into the Linked Data Cloud. The integration will be considered effective if the quality of the generated links can be shown superior to a real-world benchmark. We define human know-how as the procedural knowledge that involves humans as the main actors. Other well-known types of procedural knowledge, such as programming languages or business workflows, are excluded by this definition as they are meant to be executed by artificial agents such as computers. The formal representation of human know-how presents some unique challenges:

- Knowledge can be vague, erroneous or missing. For example, the details on how to perform a step might not be specified.
- Knowledge is distributed across different repositories on the Web.
- Knowledge is in constant evolution. New processes can be defined and existing processes can be modified.

Considering these challenges, we propose two requirements that are necessary to make human know-how machine understandable. The first requirement is that the knowledge representation language needs to be generic and lightweight. A generic representation is required because human know-how covers many different domains. This representation also needs to be lightweight in order to avoid inconsistencies or wrong inferences when integrating conflicting or erroneous information from distributed sources. This does not exclude the possibility of adopting other logic-heavy representations if required for specific applications.

The second requirement is that it should be possible to automatically generate structured knowledge about a process from the unstructured user-generated representation. A manual approach is impractical for two reasons: first, because of the large number of existing know-how resources and second, because of their evolution over time, which would require constant revisions.

3   Related Work

3.1   Procedural Knowledge Representation

There is a rich body of research into methods of representing and reasoning with procedural knowledge, for example in the Automated Planning and Problem Solving Methods fields. These systems, however, are not sufficiently lightweight and generic to conveniently represent human know-how. Logic-heavy representations, such as OWL-S [8] and the Process Specification Language (PSL) [4], require the information about a process to be complete and correct. Their application in the human know-how domain is therefore inconvenient, as it would constantly face the problem of inconsistencies and wrong inferences.

Another limitation of existing languages is domain specificity. OWL-S, for example, defines a process as a "specification of the ways a client may interact with a service" [8]. This definition is not compatible with a more general interpretation of a process which might not involve neither clients nor services. Lastly, languages might not be sufficiently expressive. For example, the vocabulary defined by Schema.org[1] currently lacks relations to define the decomposition of a process into steps. The arguments that we have made to show the limitations of OWL-S, PSL and Schema.org can also be applied to other existing languages.

3.2   Human Know-How Extraction

Several research projects have already attempted to extract human know-how from manually generated instructions. One of the most frequent approaches, based on Natural Language Processing (NLP), has been used to extract knowledge from domain-independent know-how repositories, such as wikiHow[2] [1], [6] as well as domain-specific ones, like the medical domain [12]. An approach based on statistical analysis has also been used to extract procedural knowledge from a more diverse set of Web documents not necessarily focused on know-how [3].

These approaches were used to obtain a deep logical understanding of the processes which resulted in a loss of accuracy, as most user-generated instructions are inherently vague and cannot be analyzed reliably. Our system, instead, does not require a particular level of detail in the formalization. For this reason, the

---

[1] http://schema.org/
[2] http://www.wikihow.com/

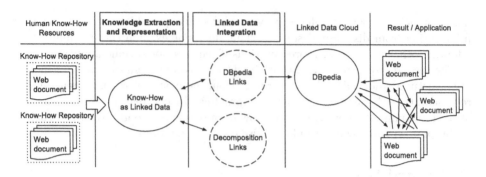

Fig. 1. Diagram of the human know-how integration framework

structure of a process is extracted only when this can be done with confidence. This situation occurs when such structure already exists, for example when the steps of a process have been clearly divided into an ordered list.

3.3 Applications of Human Know-How

A machine understandable representation of human know-how can be applied in a wide variety of areas ranging from Information Retrieval to Service Recommendation [9]. Two notable applications will be discussed here, namely Activity Recognition and process automation. The goal of Activity Recognition is to identify a top level activity (or intention) from a set of observations [7]. The intention of preparing tea, for example, could be inferred after observing an agent boiling water and placing a tea bag in a cup. A challenge faced by Activity Recognition systems is the acquisition of a model of the activities to be recognized. This model can be extracted from human know-how on the Web and used to recognize common human activities [11].

Another notable application of formalized human know-how involves the automation of activities. One experiment that attempted this kind of automation employed a robotic agent [13]. This agent attempted to perform the activity of preparing a pancake by following user-generated instructions retrieved from a wikiHow website. This experiment explored the potential of human know-how for process automation and highlighted the importance of integrating individual processes with external sources of knowledge. Artificial agents, in fact, require more information about a process than what can typically be extracted from a single set of instructions, as they lack human common sense. Knowledge about an ingredient, for example, allowed the agent to learn what it looked like and whether, by virtue of being perishable, it might be found in the refrigerator.

4   Methodology

The integration of human know-how into the Linked Data Cloud requires solving a number of different problems. The most important of those are the representation

Table 1. The vocabulary to represent processes

Prefix	Namespace
prohow:	`http://vocab.inf.ed.ac.uk/prohow#`

Term	Definition when X is the subject and Y is the object
`prohow:has_step`	Y can help accomplishing/obtaining X
`prohow:has_method`	Y can be accomplished/obtained instead of X
`prohow:requires`	Y should be accomplished/obtained before doing X

of know-how as Linked Data and the generation of links to external sources of information. Our framework addresses each of those issues with a different component. Figure 1 schematizes the general workflow of our system. The input of the system is a set of human know-how resources. These resources are analyzed by the first component of our framework, namely **Knowledge Extraction and Representation**, and converted into Linked Data. This Linked Data representation is integrated with the Linked Data Cloud by the second component of our framework: **Linked Data Integration**. This last component generates two kinds of links, namely links to DBpedia (DBpedia links) and links between processes (decomposition links). More details about these two components will be provided in the next subsections.

4.1 Knowledge Extraction and Representation

In section 3.1 we discussed several issues in reusing existing knowledge representation languages in the human know-how domain. This lead us to the development of a Linked Data vocabulary which is both lightweight and generic [10]. This vocabulary is sufficient to represent the two main concepts that can be reliably extracted from semi-structured human know-how. These concepts, namely dependencies and process decompositions, play a key role in most procedural knowledge representation formalisms. This vocabulary is based on just three properties, as shown in Table 1.

`prohow:has_step` This property can be used to decompose a complex process into its various sub-processes. For example, this property could connect the process "make a pancake" with its step "mix the ingredients".

`prohow:has_method` This property can connect a process with an alternative way of achieving it. For example, this property could connect the process "make a pancake" with the more specific process "make a lemon pancake".

`prohow:requires` This property defines a dependency between two entities. The process "put the mix on a pan", for example, depends on the process "mix the ingredients", which should be done in advance.

These relations can also be used to connect processes with objects. In our example, the process "put the mix on a pan" could specify the object "pancake mix" as a requirement using the `prohow:requires` relation. In the human know-how domain, the distinction between processes and objects is often vague.

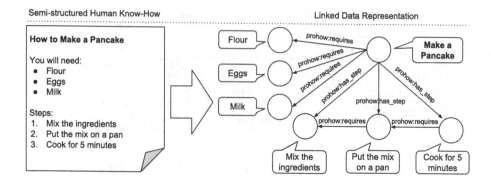

Fig. 2. Extraction of the Linked Data representation of human know-how

Knowledge Extraction from Know-How Repositories. Our approach to knowledge extraction is focused on semi-structured resources. Examples of those resources can be found in the wikiHow and Snapguide[3] websites. The structure of those resources typically contains: (1) a title denoting the main task that the process achieves, (2) the category of the process, (3) a list of the distinct requirements of the process, (4) a hierarchical structure of the steps of the process and (5) the order in which the various steps should be performed. Our approach extracts this structure to reliably decompose a process into a number of entities and relations. A simplified example of such extraction is depicted in Figure 2. Each extracted entity is given a unique URI and it is linked with the other entities of the same process. Finally, each entity is connected with its human-understandable representation using the Open Annotation Data Model.[4]

The main advantages of our approach are two. First, our extraction is accurate because it is only based on the existing structure of the processes. Second, our approach is applicable to processes described in different formats, like pictures and videos, as it does not rely on format-specific techniques like NLP. The main disadvantage of our approach is that it is only applicable to semi-structured resources. We argue that this is not a severe limitation because a large amount of know-how on the Web has some degree of structure. This structure is spontaneously created by Web users as it leads to less ambiguous instructions which are more human understandable. Like the DBpedia project [2], our system exploits the existing structure of a particular kind of Web repositories to create a large and generic nucleus of Linked Data.

4.2 Linked Data Integration

The representation of human know-how as Linked Data is an important step in making such processes machine understandable. The benefits of this representation, however, are limited by the amount of knowledge contained in a single

---

[3] http://snapguide.com/

[4] http://www.openannotation.org/

set of instructions. Instructions on "how to apply for a job", for example, might mention the step "submit a resume" without explaining what a "resume" is, and how it can be produced. This is a limitation for human users, which might need to search for additional knowledge in order to understand the instructions. This limitation is even more critical for machines, which cannot compensate for the missing knowledge with common sense.

Linked Data integration can overcome this limitation by allowing artificial agents to complement the information contained in a single set of instructions with existing related knowledge. Linked Data is the ideal infrastructure for this type of integration, as it allows the creation of links between distributed knowledge sources on the Web. Our framework allows the discovery of two of the most common kinds of links for human know-how. The first kind follows the concepts of inputs and outputs by linking the objects involved in a process with the corresponding DBpedia entities of the same type. The second kind links the steps of a process with other related processes. It should be noted that our Linked Data Integration component creates new links which did not exist before. Unlike our Knowledge Extraction and Representation component, it is not only based on user-generated structure but it utilizes also other techniques, like NLP and Machine Learning, which result in a margin of error.

DBpedia Links. Integrating human know-how with DBpedia involves finding links between procedural and declarative knowledge. Two of the most common relations at the intersection of these types of knowledge are the concepts of inputs and outputs. The process "make a pancake", for example, can be seen as a process which outputs an object of type "pancake" and requires, among others, the ingredient "milk" as an input. Our system attempts to identify the DBpedia type of inputs and outputs by analyzing their textual label. The label of each entity is processed by the DBpedia Lookup service[5] to identify related DBpedia entities. Among those entities, our system chooses the one which has the highest textual similarity with the original label.

Input entities are selected among the requirements of a process. Output entities, instead, are selected among the labels of the top-level processes which contain a *creation verb*. A creation verb is verb which semantically implies the creation of its object, such as the verbs "create", "produce" and "build". The object of the creation verb is considered as a candidate output. For example, for the top-level process "make a pancake", the word "pancake" would be considered as a possible output because the verb "make" is a creation verb.

The discovery of both input and output types allows the discovery of input/output (I/O) links between processes. An I/O link indirectly connects a process that outputs an entity of a given type with another process that requires an entity of the same type. For example, the same DBpedia entity might be linked to (1) the input "cover letter" of the process on "how to apply for a job" and (2) the output of the process "how to write a cover letter". The combination of these two links forms an I/O link between the two processes.

---

[5] http://wiki.dbpedia.org/lookup/

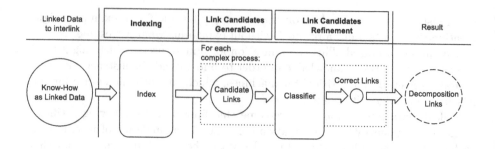

Fig. 3. Diagram of the generation of the decomposition links between processes

Decomposition Links. Step decomposition links are used to connect abstract processes with their steps, steps with their sub-steps and so forth. Within a finite set of instructions, the steps at the bottom of this decomposition hierarchy can be considered *primitive* processes. A primitive process is a process that cannot be decomposed further into sub-processes. Instructions on "how to apply for a job", for example, might mention the step "prepare a resume" without explaining how this can be achieved. Processes which are not primitive are called *complex*.

The execution of a primitive process assumes that the agent following the instructions is able to perform it without requiring any further information. This assumption might be incorrect both for human and artificial agents, thus creating the need to retrieve additional information. In order to exploit related knowledge, our system generates decomposition links between primitive processes and related complex processes. For example, the primitive step "prepare a resume" could be linked to a set of detailed instructions on "how to prepare a resume".

Our system for generating decomposition links is divided into the three main phases schematized in Figure 3. The first phase involves indexing the textual descriptions of all the processes using an efficient text search engine. This phase addresses the scalability issue caused by the large number of links to consider.

During the second phase, the index is queried to retrieve a small subset of candidate primitive entities to link. These are chosen on the basis of their textual similarity with the the complex process considered. When analysing the complex process with label "how to prepare a resume", for example, we might search the index for primitive entities containing the words "prepare" and "resume".

The third and last phase is meant to refine the set of candidate entities by removing those which are not related with the complex process considered despite having a high text similarity. To do this, a number of features are extracted from each candidate entity with the respect to the complex process considered. These features are then processed by a classifier to decide whether an entity should be linked or not. Examples of the features that can be computed between two entities are the Inverse Document Frequency of the words in common, the number of shared categories, and the number of words in common between the contexts. The context of an entity can be obtained by considering the description of the other entities belonging to the same set of instructions. The keywords "apply"

Table 2. Statistics of the knowledge extraction (May 23rd 2014)

	wikiHow	Snapguide	Total
Number of main processes	167,232	44,464	211,696
Total number of entities	1,871,468	737,768	2,609,236

Table 3. Results of the DBpedia integration experiment

	Inputs	Outputs	Total
Number of linked entities	255,101	4,467	259,568
Number of different DBpedia types linked	8,453	3,439	10,166
Precision	96% (P_I)	98.3% (P_O)	96% (P_{I+O})

and "job", for example, could be included in the context of the step "prepare a resume" if this step is related to the task "how to apply for a job".

5 Implementation

To evaluate our framework we have applied it in a large-scale real-world scenario. Our knowledge extraction system analyzed the web pages of the wikiHow and Snapguide websites, two of the largest sources of semi-structured human know-how on the Web. Each web page containing instructions was analyzed and its structure was converted into Linked Data. In total, over 200,000 processes were extracted. More details about this extraction are listed in in Table 2.

After extracting the Linked Data representation of a large number of processes, we applied our Linked Data integration system. Our system followed the method described in section 4.2 to discover the links between DBpedia entities and the inputs and the outputs of the processes. The results of this experiment can be found in Table 3. The precision was manually evaluated separately for the inputs (P_I) and the outputs (P_O) on 300 randomly selected links for each type. A link was considered wrong (1) if it linked an entity which was not an input or an output of the process or (2) if the type of the input or output did not correspond to the linked DBpedia type.

Lastly, our Linked Data integration system generated decomposition links between different processes. Following the method described in section 4.2, all the entities extracted from human know-how were indexed using the text search engine Apache Lucene.[6] For each complex and primitive process pair, 34 features were computed and classified by the WEKA [5] implementation of a Random Forest classifier. The process pairs classified as correct were linked and added to the set of the discovered decomposition links. The classifier was trained using a manually classified set of 1000 randomly-generated links.

The results of our knowledge extraction and integration experiment are available online through the HowLinks[7] Web application. This application demonstrates

---

[6] http://lucene.apache.org/core/
[7] http://w3id.org/prohow/main/

how Linked Data can be used to have an integrated visualization of both procedural and declarative knowledge retrieved from different sources.

6   Evaluation

To understand the significance of the results of our integration experiment, we need to compare them with a relevant benchmark. Since our system is the first to integrate human know-how, we cannot compare our results with a previous experiment. We can however compare them with an existing manual integration effort that is being performed by the wikiHow community. The members of this community, in fact, are not only active in the creation and the refinement of individual sets of instructions, but are also actively creating links between different processes. This community effort can be seen as evidence of the human benefits of know-how integration.

To evaluate the results of this community effort we have extracted all the user-generated links found in the description of each wikiHow process. These links have been split into two groups. The first group consists of the links found in the requirements of a process. These links typically connect a required object to a process that can produce such object. As such, they have the same functional role of the I/O links found by our system. The second group is made of the links found in the steps of the process. These links connect a step with another process which provides additional information about that step. As such, they have the same functional role of the decomposition links found by our system.

Having identified a comparable set of links, we proceeded to compute three quality metrics on both results set. These quality metrics are the following:

- Precision of the links. Correct links should provide relevant information on how to perform or obtain the linked entity. For example, our system correctly linked the step "Avoid smoking cigarettes, cigars or pipes around the baby" with the relevant process "How to Avoid Smoking". The wikiHow community integration, instead, linked this step with the irrelevant processes "How to Smoke a Cigar" and "How to Prevent Frozen Water Pipes".
- Number of links found.
- Coverage of the links. This metric evaluates the number of processes which contain at least one link to another process. A better integration is achieved when the links are evenly spread between the various entities.

The result of this comparison can be seen in Table 4. For each of the two types of links generated by the wikiHow community (**WH-C**), the precision has been evaluated manually on 200 randomly selected links. The precision of the I/O links generated by our system (**WH+S**) is defined as the probability that both the input and the output links involved are correct: $P_{I/O} = P_I * P_O$. As such, it can be derived from the precision values shown in Table 3. The precision of the decomposition links generated by our system (**WH+S**) is determined by the precision of the classifier used to select them. This precision was evaluated using 10-fold cross validation.

Table 4. Comparison of the wikiHow community integration (**WH-C**) with the results of our integration of wikiHow (**WH**) and of both wikiHow and Snapguide (**WH+S**)

	WH-C	WH	WH+S
Precision of I/O links	65%	94.3%	94.1%
Number of I/O links	4,560	93,883	183,094
Coverage of I/O links	3,342 (1.9%)	35,169 (21%)	58,029 (27.4%)
Precision of decomposition links	71%	82.1%	82.4%
Number of decomposition links	101,496	127,468	193,701
Coverage of decomposition links	45,250 (27.1%)	69,859 (41.8%)	90,217 (42.6%)
Total precision of the links	70.7%	87.3%	88.1%
Total number of links	106,056	221,351	376,795
Total coverage of the links	45,999 (27.5%)	84,350 (50.4%)	114,166 (53.9%)

It should be noted that the links generated by the wikiHow community only interlink wikiHow resources. On the contrary, our system integrates procedural knowledge both from the wikiHow and the Snapguide repositories. To make a fair comparison, Table 4 also shows the evaluation of the links generated by our system which only connect wikiHow resources (**WH**).

The result of our evaluation shows how our automatic approach to human know-how integration significantly outperforms manual community-based integration efforts. This is shown for all the metrics considered and for both types of links. This result demonstrates how our framework can be used to significantly increase the value of human know-how by automatic means. We take this result as strong evidence for the effectiveness of our integration framework.

7   Conclusion

This paper has described the first framework for the integration of human know-how into the Linked Data Cloud. Human know-how is an important source of knowledge on the Web, but its potential applications are limited by a general lack of structure and isolation from other knowledge. We have surveyed attempts to overcome these limitations both by user communities, trying to manually add structure and links to human know-how, and by existing research projects, trying to exploit this knowledge to develop intelligent systems. None of these approaches, however, automated the integration of this type of knowledge.

We proposed a Linked Data framework to automate both the extraction of human know-how, and its integration with related knowledge. We chose Linked Data as the ideal format to represent distributed knowledge on the Web. To validate this framework, we have applied it in a real-world scenario. First, this framework generated the Linked Data representation of over 200,000 processes by extracting human know-how from the wikiHow and Snapguide websites. Lastly, we have used our framework to link these processes both with each other and with DBpedia entities. We have evaluated the quality of these links and showed how they significantly outperform existing community-based integration efforts.

This result demonstrates how the integration of human know-how as Linked Data can immediately benefit Web users by allowing them to access the vast amount of know-how on the Web more efficiently. The application of this knowledge to develop intelligent systems has not been investigated and remains a promising direction for future work.

References

1. Addis, A., Borrajo, D.: From Unstructured Web Knowledge to Plan Descriptions. In: Soro, A., Vargiu, E., Armano, G., Paddeu, G. (eds.) Information Retrieval and Mining in Distributed Environments. Studies in Computational Intelligence, vol. 324, pp. 41–59. Springer, Heidelberg (2010)
2. Auer, S., Bizer, C., Kobilarov, G., Lehmann, J., Cyganiak, R., Ives, Z.G.: DBpedia: A Nucleus for a Web of Open Data. In: Aberer, K., Choi, K.-S., Noy, N., Allemang, D., Lee, K.-I., Nixon, L.J.B., Golbeck, J., Mika, P., Maynard, D., Mizoguchi, R., Schreiber, G., Cudré-Mauroux, P. (eds.) ASWC 2007 and ISWC 2007. LNCS, vol. 4825, pp. 722–735. Springer, Heidelberg (2007)
3. Fukazawa, Y., Ota, J.: Automatic Modeling of User's Real World Activities from the Web for Semantic IR. In: Proceedings of the 3rd International Semantic Search Workshop, pp. 5:1–5:9 (2010)
4. Grüninger, M., Menzel, C.: The Process Specification Language (PSL) Theory and Applications. AI Magazine 24(3), 63–74 (2003)
5. Hall, M., Frank, E., Holmes, G., Pfahringer, B., Reutemann, P., Witten, I.H.: The WEKA Data Mining Software: An Update. SIGKDD Explorer Newsletter 11(1), 10–18 (2009)
6. Jung, Y., Ryu, J., Kim, K.-M., Myaeng, S.-H.: Automatic Construction of a Large-Scale Situation Ontology by Mining How-To Instructions from the Web. Web Semantics: Science, Services and Agents on the World Wide Web 8(2-3), 110–124 (2010)
7. Kim, E., Helal, S., Cook, D.: Human Activity Recognition and Pattern Discovery. IEEE Pervasive Computing 9(1), 48–53 (2010)
8. Martin, D., Burstein, M., Hobbs, J., Lassila, O., McDermott, D., McIlraith, S., Narayanan, S., Paolucci, M., Parsia, B., Payne, T., et al.: OWL-S: Semantic markup for web services. W3C member submission (2004)
9. Myaeng, S.-H., Jeong, Y., Jung, Y.: Experiential Knowledge Mining. Foundations and Trends in Web Science 4(1), 71–82 (2013)
10. Pareti, P., Klein, E., Barker, A.: A Semantic Web of Know-how: Linked Data for Community-centric Tasks. In: Proceedings of the 23rd International Conference on World Wide Web Companion, pp. 1011–1016 (2014)
11. Perkowitz, M., Philipose, M., Fishkin, K., Patterson, D.J.: Mining Models of Human Activities from the Web. In: Proceedings of the 13th International Conference on World Wide Web, pp. 573–582 (2004)
12. Song, S.-k., Oh, H.-s., Myaeng, S.H., Choi, S.-p., Chun, H.-w., Choi, Y.-s., Jeong, C.-h.: Procedural Knowledge Extraction on MEDLINE Abstracts. In: Zhong, N., Callaghan, V., Ghorbani, A.A., Hu, B. (eds.) AMT 2011. LNCS, vol. 6890, pp. 345–354. Springer, Heidelberg (2011)
13. Tenorth, M., Klank, U., Pangercic, D., Beetz, M.: Web-Enabled Robots. IEEE Robotics Automation Magazine 18(2), 58–68 (2011)

A Dialectical Approach to Selectively Reusing Ontological Correspondences

Terry R. Payne and Valentina Tamma

Department of Computer Science, University of Liverpool,
Liverpool L69 3BX, United Kingdom
{T.R.Payne,V.Tamma}@liverpool.ac.uk

Abstract. Effective communication between autonomous knowledge systems is dependent on the correct interpretation of exchanged messages, based on the entities (or vocabulary) within the messages, and their ontological definitions. However, as such systems cannot be assumed to share the same ontologies, a mechanism for autonomously determining a mutually acceptable alignment between the ontologies is required. Furthermore, the ontologies themselves may be confidential or commercially sensitive, and thus neither systems may be willing to expose their full ontologies to other parties (this may be pertinent as the transaction may only relate to part, and not all of the ontology). In this paper, we present a novel inquiry dialogue that allows such autonomous systems, or *agents* to assert, counter, accept and reject correspondences. It assumes that agents have acquired a variety of correspondences from past encounters, or from publicly available alignment systems, and that such knowledge is *asymmetric* and *incomplete* (i.e. not all agents may be aware of some correspondences, and their associated utility can vary greatly). By strategically selecting the order in which correspondences are disclosed, the two agents can jointly construct a bespoke alignment whilst minimising the disclosure of private knowledge. We show how partial alignments, garnered from different alignment systems, can be reused and aggregated through our dialectical approach, and illustrate how solutions to the *Stable Marriage* problem can be used to eliminate ambiguities (i.e. when an entity in one ontology is mapped to several other entities in another ontology). We empirically evaluate the performance of the resulting alignment compared to the use of randomly selected alignment systems, and show how by adopting a sceptical mentalistic attitude, an agent can further reduce the necessary disclosure of ontological knowledge.

1 Introduction

The volume and diversity of data, devices and services across the internet is rapidly increasing, with low-cost sensors and personal devices (such as smartphones) being the drivers of some of the fastest growing sources and consumers of data. With the huge diversity and volume of data expected to further increase in the near future, collaboration and coordination between different systems is essential [3]. Intelligent applications (e.g. *agents*) need flexible and scalable mechanisms to facilitate and comprehend data and thus exploit this wealth of knowledge, based on the underlying semantics of the entities within the data. Although such entities are typically defined within an *ontology*, the agents may differ in the vocabulary (and ontologies) they assume, thus compromising seamless *semantic interoperability* between dynamic and evolving systems.

K. Janowicz et al. (Eds.): EKAW 2014, LNAI 8876, pp. 397–412, 2014.

Knowledge integration has traditionally depended on the creation of *alignments* [11] between pairs of ontologies, where an alignment consists of a set of *correspondences* between related entities. The ontology alignment community has proposed many diverse approaches that *align* pairs of ontologies to find these sets of correspondences; however, most rely on the ontologies to be fully shared [9], and no single approach can provide a panacea for all ontology pairs. This raises the question *"what alignments or alignment mechanisms should be used/reused by two agents to align their ontologies?"*

The question is further exacerbated in those cases when neither agent may be prepared to disclose some (or all) of its ontology. The notion of privacy preserving information sharing has been advocated by a number of previous efforts [1,4,5,12,18,19,24]. Various use-cases for which it is necessary to introduce some form of privacy preservation in the schema, in the data or both have been identified [1,4], including monitoring healthcare crisis, facilitating e-commerce, outsourcing, and end-to-end integration. More recently, the notion of preserving privacy when matching schemas and ontologies was proposed as a way of allowing different parties to interoperate whilst limiting the sharing of information concerning the ontologies used to model the different applications [18,5]. Likewise, from a game-theoretic perspective, an agent may want to keep part (or all) of its ontological knowledge private, and consequently may not want to share or disclose it to other agents, as the disclosed ontological axioms could be exploited by other, self-interested agents (and thus have intrinsic value to the owner if kept private), were agents to compete over multiple transactions.

The existence of alternate, pre-computed alignments has been exploited by several alignment negotiation approaches, which aggregate the constituent correspondences [8,15,17,22]. However, certain correspondences may be found frequently by different alignment approaches, whereas others could be spurious or erroneous, and only appear rarely. Thus, different correspondences may have different levels of *utility* representing the likelihood that they will be successfully utilised in future scenarios. Furthermore, different alignment systems may map entities from one ontology to alternate entities in the other ontology, leading to *ambiguity*. Naively combining these can result in undesirable behaviour, such as incoherence and inconsistency within the ontologies, rendering the resulting alignment unusable. If we assume that agents can acquire such alignments through past experience, it follows that different agents will typically be only aware of a subset of the possible correspondences between two ontologies, and thus the knowledge of one agent can be very different to that of another. Hence, they need to agree on what correspondences they believe to be the most relevant to a given context or task to resolve ambiguous combinations, whilst behaving rationally; i.e. only disclosing and proposing *viable* correspondences that are relevant to the communication task.

An *Inquiry Dialogue* is a dialogue between two parties that strives to establish knowledge in order to achieve some goal (such as answering a question or solving a problem) [23]. Typically, such a dialogue starts from an open problem, whereby neither party has the full solution, but both actively engage with each other to arrive at a consensual solution. In this paper, we present our novel inquiry dialogue (called the *Correspondence Inclusion Dialogue - CID*) that allows two agents to take turns in asserting, countering, accepting and rejecting the correspondences that each is aware of, in order to establish a mutually acceptable alignment between their respective ontologies. It assumes that:

i) the agents have acquired correspondences from past encounters, or from publicly available alignment systems; ii) each agent associates a *utility* to each correspondence it knows of (representing a weight the agents ascribe to that correspondence based on past experience, or some other knowledge); and iii) agents do not automatically expose their full knowledge bases to other agents, but rather selectively disclose only that knowledge deemed relevant to the negotiation. As this knowledge is *asymmetric* and *incomplete* (i.e. neither agent involved in the dialogue will be aware of all of the possible correspondences, and the utility of each correspondence can differ greatly between agents), the agents use the inquiry dialogue to: 1) ascertain the joint acceptability of each correspondence; and to 2) select an unambiguous set of correspondences which reduces the possibility of the resulting alignment being incoherent. We present the dialogue, and illustrate through examples how this dialectical approach can identify mutually acceptable correspondences, even when knowledge of different correspondences is asymmetric. We show how the *Stable Marriage* algorithm [10,13,14,16] can be adapted to resolve ambiguities emerging from the aggregation of correspondences or entailed by an agent's individual ontology. Finally, we demonstrate how the number of correspondences that need to be shared can be greatly reduced, by selectively disclosing them based on their perceived utility.

The remainder of this paper is organised as follows: the *Correspondence Inclusion Dialogue* is presented in Section 2, and is then evaluated in Section 3. Related work is presented in Section 4, before concluding in Section 5.

2 The Correspondence Inquiry Dialogue

The *Correspondence Inclusion Dialogue* enables two agents to exchange knowledge about ontological correspondences through a dialogical game that satisfies the following: 1) each agent is aware of a set of correspondences, each with an associated *utility*; 2) there should be no *ambiguity* with respect to either the source entities in the resulting alignment, or the target entities; 3) if alternative choices of correspondences exist, the selection should be based on the *joint utility* of both agents; 4) no correspondences should be selected where their joint utility is less than some defined *admissibility threshold*; and 5) the alignment should be generated by disclosing as few beliefs as possible.

2.1 The Inquiry Dialogue Moves

The dialogue consists of a sequence of communicative acts, or *moves*[1], whereby agents take turns to assert the viability of some correspondence c for inclusion in a mutually acceptable final alignment, AL, and respond to such assertions by: i) confirming the acceptability of c; ii) rejecting the acceptability of c; or iii) proposing alternate correspondences in the case of ambiguity. Each agent discloses its private *utility* over the inclusion of c in the alignment AL, and the agents' goal is to rationally identify an unambiguous set of correspondences deemed viable by both agents, given an *admissibility threshold* ϵ. The dialogue assumes there are always exactly two agents (referred to here

---

[1] The moves of the *Correspondence Inclusion Dialogue* are formally presented in [20].

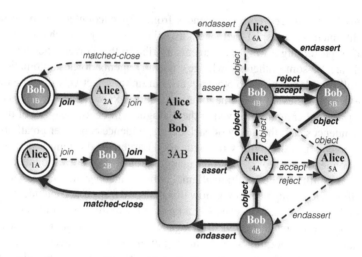

Fig. 1. The dialogue as a state diagram. Nodes indicate the agent whose turn it to utter a move. Moves uttered by Alice are labelled with a light font / dashed edge, whereas those uttered by Bob are labelled with a heavy font / solid edge.

as *Alice* and *Bob*) who participate in the dialogue, and that each agent plays a role in each dialogue move; i.e. an agent is either a *sender* x or *recipient* $\hat{x}$.

The *moves* of the dialogue are summarised in Table 1, and the corresponding state diagram is given in Figure 1. The syntax of each move at time s is of the form $m_s = \langle x, \tau, \phi, \phi^{att} \rangle$, where x represents the identity of the agent making the move; τ represents the move type; ϕ is a tuple that represents a belief that agent x has for a correspondence and the utility it associates to that correspondence; whereas ϕ^{att} represents a belief for some correspondence that the agent is countering or objecting to. For some moves, it may not be necessary to specify one or either beliefs; in which case they will be empty or unspecified (represented as *nil*).

Agents take turns to utter *assert* moves (i.e. to transition from state 3AB in Figure 1). A sender x can also make multiple moves in certain circumstances, such as an *accept* or *reject* move (see states labelled 4A for *Alice* and 4B for *Bob* in Figure 1). This enables an agent to accept or reject a disclosed correspondence before making some other move (such as raising a *object* move), or signalling its intention to end a negotiation round (through an *endassert* move).

2.2 Ontologies, Correspondences and Beliefs

The agents negotiate over the viability of different correspondences that could be used to align the two agents' ontologies. The dialogue therefore assumes that each agent maintains an ontological model $\mathcal{O}$, which represents the agent's knowledge about the environment, and its background knowledge (domain knowledge, beliefs, tasks, etc.). $\mathcal{O}$ is modelled as a set of axioms describing classes and their relations.[2]

---

[2] Here we restrict the ontology definition to classes and roles.

Table 1. The set $\mathcal{M}$ of legal moves permitted by the Correspondence Inquiry Dialogue

Syntax	Description
$\langle x, join, \text{nil}, \text{nil} \rangle$	Agents assert the *join* move to participate within the dialogue.
$\langle x, assert, \phi, \text{nil} \rangle$	The agent x will *assert* the belief ϕ for a correspondence c that is believed to be viable for inclusion into the final alignment AL, and is the undisclosed belief with highest personal utility.
$\langle x, object, \phi, \phi^{att} \rangle$	An agent can *object* to some correspondence c^{att} if it knows of another correspondence c that shares one of the two entities in c^{att}, i.e. ambiguous(ϕ, ϕ^{att}), and $\kappa_c^{est} \geq \kappa_{c^{att}}^{joint}$. The agent utters the *object* move to: 1) inform the recipient of the senders personal utility of the disclosed correspondence c^{att} through the belief ϕ^{att}; and 2) propose an alternative correspondence c by asserting the belief ϕ.
$\langle x, accept, \phi, \text{nil} \rangle$	If the agent received a belief ψ for c in the previous move, and $\kappa_c^{joint} \geq \epsilon$, then the agent can confirm this by accepting the correspondence and sharing its own personal utility in ϕ, where ϕ and ψ represent the different beliefs about the same correspondence.
$\langle x, reject, \psi, \text{nil} \rangle$	If the agent received a belief ψ for c in the previous move, but was not viable (i.e. $\kappa_c^{joint} < \epsilon$), then the agent can reject this simply by returning the original belief ψ.
$\langle x, endassert, \text{nil}, \text{nil} \rangle$	If an agent has no more objections to make about the correspondences negotiated since the previous assert, it can then indicate this by uttering an *endassert* move. Once both agents have uttered this move sequentially, a new *assert* move can be uttered, or the dialogue can close.
$\langle x, close, \text{nil}, \text{nil} \rangle$	If an agent has no more correspondences that could be viable, but that have not been disclosed, then it can utter a *close* move. However, the dialogue does not terminate until both agents utter a sequence of *close* moves (known as a *matched-close*).

During any given encounter, the sender and the recipient use only part of their ontological model (i.e. they use their "working" ontology $\mathcal{W}$) to communicate. This could be based on an ontology module relevant to the task [6,8], or the agent's ontological knowledge may comprise several different ontologies (as illustrated in Figure 2). To avoid confusion, the sender's ontology is denoted $\mathcal{W}^x$, whereas the recipient's ontology is $\mathcal{W}^{\hat{x}}$, and $\widetilde{\mathcal{W}}$ denotes the *ontology signature*; i.e. the set of class and property names used in $\mathcal{W}$. Both $\mathcal{W}^x$ and $\mathcal{W}^{\hat{x}}$ are fragments[3] of the sender and recipient ontologies (respectively) that denote each agent's private subset of the ontology used to model the corresponding entities used in the transaction. We also assume that agents do not disclose their "working" ontologies, and hence the participants involved in the encounter have no knowledge about whether these ontologies overlap completely, partially, or in the worst case not at all (which would imply that no interaction would be possible [8]).

For agents to interoperate in an encounter, they need to determine an *alignment* AL between the two working ontology fragments $\mathcal{W}^x$ and $\mathcal{W}^{\hat{x}}$ for that encounter. An alignment [9] consists of a set of *correspondences* that establish a logical

---

[3] We do not prescribe the logical properties exhibited by the fragment, but refer to the work on ontology modularisation, e.g. [6].

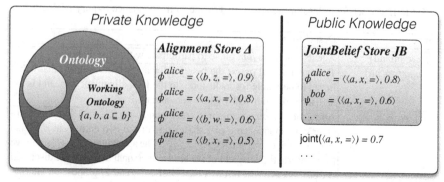

Fig. 2. The knowledge model assumed by each agent. Only alignments grounded in the Working Ontology $\mathcal{W}$ are listed in *Alice's* Alignment Store Δ. As the correspondence $\langle a, x, = \rangle$ has been *asserted* and *accepted* by the agents, they appear in *Alice's* Joint Belief Store JB. As Alice knows both her, and *Bob's* belief for this correspondence, she can calculate the joint belief.

relationship[4] between the entities (classes, properties or roles, and instances) belonging to each of the two ontologies. The universe of all possible correspondences is therefore denoted $\mathcal{C}$.

Definition 1. *A **correspondence** is a triple denoted $c = \langle e, e', r \rangle$ such that $e \in \widetilde{\mathcal{W}^x}$, $e' \in \widetilde{\mathcal{W}^{\hat{x}}}$, $r \in \{=\}$.*

Agents associate a private, static *utility* κ_c to a correspondence, which represents the *admissibility* of c in the alignment AL. The tuple $\langle c, \kappa_c \rangle$, where $0 \le \kappa_c \le 1$, is a *belief* an agent holds on a correspondence c. We refer to beliefs sent by x as ϕ, the beliefs sent by $\hat{x}$ (to x) as ψ, and the set of all beliefs is denoted $\mathcal{B}$. The function corr : $\mathcal{B} \mapsto \mathcal{C}$ returns the correspondence c for some belief. The aim of the dialogue is to select an *unambiguous* (i.e. where no entity appears more than once) set of viable correspondences, $AL \subseteq \mathcal{C}$, which maps between the entities in $\mathcal{W}^x$ and $\mathcal{W}^{\hat{x}}$, and whose joint utility is at least as great as the admissibility threshold ϵ. The function ent(c) returns a set containing the two entities e and e' for the correspondence c.

Each agent manages a private knowledge base, known as the *Alignment Store* (Δ), which holds the beliefs an agent has over its correspondences, and a public knowledge base, or *Joint Belief Store* (JB), which contains correspondences that have been shared (see Figure 2). We distinguish between the sender's stores, Δ^x and JB^x, and the recipient's stores, $\Delta^{\hat{x}}$ and $JB^{\hat{x}}$, respectively. The sender's joint belief store JB^x ($JB^{\hat{x}}$ for the receiver) contains beliefs that are exchanged as part of the dialogue and hence contains beliefs sent and received by x (conversely $\hat{x}$). Throughout the dialogue, both agents will be aware of all of the beliefs shared[5]; i.e. $JB^x = JB^{\hat{x}}$.

---

[4] We only consider *logical equivalence* (as opposed to *subsumption* ($\sqsubseteq$) and *disjointness* ($\perp$)), as it has the property that correspondences are symmetric; i.e. $\langle e, e', = \rangle$ is logically equivalent to $\langle e', e, = \rangle$, and thus can be easily used by either agent. Furthermore, the majority of alignment generation systems only computes equivalence correspondences.

[5] We will not distinguish between the two stores JB^x and $JB^{\hat{x}}$ in the remainder of this paper.

2.3 Aggregating Beliefs and the Upper Bound

Within the dialogue, the agents try to ascertain the unambiguous, mutually acceptable correspondences to include in the final alignment AL by selectively sharing those correspondences that are believed to have the highest utility. Once each agent knows of the other agent's utility for a given correspondence c, it can calculate c's *joint utility*, and check if it is greater than or equal to the *admissibility threshold*, ϵ. This threshold is used to filter out correspondences with a low utility (i.e. when $\kappa_c < \epsilon$), whilst minimising the number of beliefs disclosed. The function joint : $C \mapsto [0, 1]$ returns the *joint utility* for some correspondence $c \in C$. This results in either: 1) κ_c^{joint} calculated based on the utilities for both agents (if both utilities have been disclosed); or 2) κ_c^{est} for a conservative upper estimate, if only one of the two utilities is known.

When deciding which correspondences are viable for inclusion in the final alignment AL the agents might chose between two opposite mentalistic attitudes for the admission of disclosed correspondences: *sceptical* and *credulous* acceptability. These attitudes reflect whether or not an agent is prepared to accept the viability of new, hitherto unknown correspondences from its peers. A *sceptical* attitude is one where the agent may have reservations or doubts about the acceptability of new correspondences; thus a correspondence is only considered within the dialogue if it is known by all agents involved; i.e. c is potentially acceptable *iff* $c \in \Delta^x \cap \Delta^{\hat{x}}$. This attitude will eliminate the possibility of further correspondences being proposed if one agent has considered all of its correspondences (this can happen in highly asymmetric cases, where an agent may have acquired a large number of possibility conflicting correspondences). However, there may be contexts whereby an agent may be *knowledge poor* (i.e. it possess little knowledge), and thus needs to acquire new correspondences from other agents. Therefore, an agent may choose to adopt a *credulous* attitude, whereby it will accept the potential viability of any correspondence that is suggested by its peers. This gullibility may initially be necessary to allow an agent to acquire knowledge of some correspondences, but could result in a larger number and diversity of correspondences being considered. Thus a correspondence will be considered within the dialogue if it is known by at least one agent involved; i.e. c is potentially acceptable *iff* $\exists \Delta \in \{\Delta^x \Delta^{\hat{x}}\}, c \in \Delta$.

These two attitudes will affect the way in which the joint utility is calculated (Definition 2, below), and whether or not a correspondence is considered in the dialogue. When the sender x receives a belief ψ from $\hat{x}$ ($\psi \in JB^x$) on a correspondence c, it can assess the joint utility for c as the average between its own utility and the one by $\hat{x}$, assuming that x holds a belief on c, i.e. $\phi \in \Delta^x$ (**Case 1**). If, however, x has no prior knowledge of c (i.e. $\phi \notin \Delta^x$), then the acceptability of the correspondence, and its joint utility will depend on the mentalistic attitude of the agent. If the agent adopts a *sceptical* attitude, then the correspondence will be rejected, and the joint utility for c will be zero (**Case 2a**). However, if the agent adopts a *credulous* attitude, then the joint utility will depends only on $\kappa_c^{\hat{x}}$ (**Case 2b**). Finally, if x holds a belief on c that has not yet been disclosed to $\hat{x}$ ($\phi \in \Delta^x; \phi \notin JB^x$) and if ψ has not been disclosed by $\hat{x}$ ($\psi \notin JB^x$), then $\kappa_c^{\hat{x}}$ can only be estimated (**Case 3**). The *upper bound*, κ_{upper}^x is explained below.

Table 2. The individual and joint utilities for the correspondences in the examples

Correspondence c	κ_c^{Alice}	κ_c^{Bob}	Credulous joint(c)	Sceptical joint(c)
$\langle$publication, paper, $=\rangle$	0.8	0.6	**0.7**	**0.7**
$\langle$article, paper, $=\rangle$	0.5	0.8	**0.65**	**0.65**
$\langle$article, submittedPaper, $=\rangle$	0.6	0.4	**0.5**	**0.5**
$\langle$article, reviewedPaper, $=\rangle$	0.9	—	**0.45**	**0**
$\langle$author, publisher, $=\rangle$	—	0.2	**0.1**	**0**
$\langle$publication, reviewedPaper, $=\rangle$	0.1	—	**0.05**	**0**
$\langle$editor, editor-in-chief, $=\rangle$	0.3	0.3	**0.3**	**0.3**

Alice	Bob
ID: Entity $e \in \mathcal{W}^{Alice}$	**ID:** Entity $e' \in \mathcal{W}^{Bob}$
a: publication	**w:** submittedPaper
b: article	**x:** paper
c: author	**y:** publisher
d: editor	**z:** reviewedPaper
	v: editor-in-chief

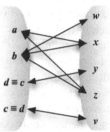

Fig. 3. The entities in the two working ontologies with identifiers used in Figure 2 and Table 3, and the bipartite graph that represents correspondences between the ontological entities

Definition 2. *The function* joint : $\mathcal{C} \mapsto [0,1]$ *returns the* joint utility *for some* $c \in \mathcal{C}$, *where* $c = \text{corr}(\phi) = \text{corr}(\psi)$:

$$
\text{joint}(c) = \begin{cases} \text{avg}(\kappa_c^x, \kappa_c^{\hat{x}}) & \textbf{Case 1: } \psi \in JB^x; \phi \in \Delta^x \\ 0 & \textbf{Case 2a: (sceptical) } \psi \in JB^x; \phi \notin \Delta^x \land \phi \notin JB^x \\ \kappa_c^{\hat{x}} & \textbf{Case 2b: (credulous) } \psi \in JB^x; \phi \notin \Delta^x \land \phi \notin JB^x \\ \text{avg}(\kappa_c^x, \kappa_{upper}^x) & \textbf{Case 3: } \phi \in \Delta^x; \phi, \psi \notin JB^x \end{cases}
$$

Example 1: Bob *makes the move* $\langle bob, assert, \langle \langle$publication, paper, $=\rangle, 0.6\rangle, nil\rangle$. *Alice adds the belief* $\psi^{bob} = \langle \langle$publication, paper, $=\rangle, 0.6\rangle$ *into her Joint Belief store, JB (Figure 2). She then responds with the move* $\langle alice, accept, \langle \langle$publication, paper, $=\rangle, 0.8\rangle, nil\rangle$, *which is also stored in JB. Now both beliefs have been disclosed, the joint belief* joint($\langle$publication, paper, $=\rangle$) *can be calculated; i.e.* avg(0.8, 0.6) = 0.7.

Each agent takes turns to propose a belief regarding some correspondence, and the other participant confirms if the actual joint utility $\kappa_c^{joint} \geq \epsilon$. Proposals are made by identifying an undisclosed correspondence with the highest degree of belief κ_c^x. As the dialogue proceeds, each subsequent correspondence asserted will have an equivalent or lower degree of belief than that previously asserted by the same agent.

Example 2: *It is Bob's turn to assert a new correspondence. If he were starting a new dialogue, he would assert the correspondence* $\langle \langle$article, paper, $=\rangle, 0.8\rangle$, *as this would be the one with the highest utility* κ_c^{Bob}. *But in a separate dialogue, the correspondences* $\langle \langle$article, paper, $=\rangle, 0.8\rangle$ *and* $\langle \langle$publication, paper, $=\rangle, 0.6\rangle$ *have already been disclosed. So the next one to assert is* $\langle \langle$article, submittedPaper, $=\rangle, 0.4\rangle$, *as this is the undisclosed correspondence with the highest utility. However, he first has to determine if the estimated joint utility is* $\geq \epsilon$.

Whenever a correspondence is asserted, or included in an objection, the agent should check that its estimated joint utility is not less than the *admissibility threshold*, ϵ. Because the estimate is an upper estimate, the actual joint utility could be lower, and the correspondence still rejected. Agents determine this upper estimate by exploiting the fact that assertions are always made on the undisclosed correspondence with the highest utility. Thus, if one agent asserts some correspondence, the other agent's utility for that asserted correspondence will never be greater than their own previous assertion. Therefore, each agent maintains an *upper bound*, κ_{upper}^x, corresponding to the other agents assertions (prior to the dialogue, $\kappa_{upper}^x = 1.0$).

Example 3: In example 2, Bob *wanted to assert* $\langle\langle\text{article}, \text{submittedPaper}, =\rangle, 0.4\rangle$, *but needed to determine if the estimated joint utility* $\geq \epsilon$. Alice's *previous assertion was for the correspondence* $\langle\langle\text{publication}, \text{paper}, =\rangle, 0.8\rangle$, *and therefore* $\kappa_{upper}^x = 0.8$. *If we assume that* $\epsilon = 0.5$, Bob *can determine that the estimated* $joint(\langle\text{article}, \text{submittedPaper}, =\rangle) = avg(0.4, 0.8) = 0.6 \geq \epsilon$, *and thus makes the assertion.*

2.4 Ambiguity and Stable Marriage

Ambiguities occur when more than one correspondence maps several entities in the source ontology to a single entity in the target ontology (or vice versa). This can prevent semantic interoperability and possibly result in logical incoherence. Objections can be made to an ambiguous belief, once it has been asserted. An ambiguity can be determined if there is some entity that exists in the correspondences of two beliefs or if there is a logical equivalence between the source or the target entities that exist in the correspondences of two beliefs.

Definition 3. Ambiguity *(*ambiguous(ϕ, ϕ')*) occurs given beliefs* ϕ, ϕ', $\phi \neq \phi'$ *iff*

1. $\text{ent}(\text{corr}(\phi)) \cap \text{ent}(\text{corr}(\phi')) \neq \varnothing$ *if there are no equivalence relations – either asserted or inferred – between the entities in* $\widetilde{\mathcal{W}}^x$; *or*
2. $\mathcal{W}^x \models \text{ent}(\text{corr}(\phi)) \equiv \text{ent}(\text{corr}(\phi')) : \text{ent}(\text{corr}(\phi)), \text{ent}(\text{corr}(\phi')) \in \widetilde{\mathcal{W}}^x$.

The notion of ambiguity includes the cases where correspondences become ambiguous as a consequence of an equivalence relation existing between some of their entities (due to an agent's ontology). Whilst these equivalence relations are not frequent, they can still occur and these cases need to be handled appropriately, especially when the equivalence relations occur in one agent's ontology, and are not reflected in the other's.

A belief ϕ can *object* to another belief ϕ' if they result in an *ambiguity*, and the joint utility for ϕ is greater than or equal to that of ϕ', and above the admissibility threshold, ϵ. This objection can also be referred to as an *attack*.

Definition 4. *Given two beliefs* $\phi, \phi', \phi \neq \phi'$, attacks$(\phi, \phi')$ *is true iff* ambiguous$(\phi, \phi') \wedge$ joint$(\text{corr}(\phi)) \geq$ joint$(\text{corr}(\phi')) \geq \epsilon$.

Attacks are represented in the dialogue as *object* moves. There are two scenarios where an agent responds with *object*:

1. when a new correspondence has appeared in a previous *assert* or *object* move. In this case, the sender needs to respond with its own belief of the correspondence, but may also want to raise its own objection.

2. when there is an undisclosed correspondence that could be used to attack a previously disclosed correspondence. This is where agents can identify other attacks on ambiguous correspondences.

Example 4: Alice *asserts the correspondence* $\langle\langle\text{article}, \text{submittedPaper}, =\rangle, 0.6\rangle$. Bob *realises that he has an alternate correspondence,* $\langle\langle\text{article}, \text{paper}, =\rangle, 0.8\rangle$, *which shares the entity "article". He estimates the joint utility for this alternate correspondence as* $joint(\langle\text{article}, \text{paper}, =\rangle) = avg(0.8, \kappa^x_{upper}) = 0.7$ *(here,* $\kappa^x_{upper} = 0.6$*), which is* $\geq joint(\langle\text{article}, \text{submittedPaper}, =\rangle) = 0.5$, *i.e. the joint utility for Alice's asserted correspondence. Therefore* Bob *makes the move*[6] $\langle bob, object, \langle\langle\text{article}, \text{paper}, =\rangle, 0.8\rangle, \langle\langle\text{article}, \text{submittedPaper}, =\rangle, 0.6\rangle\rangle$.

Thus, the dialogue generates a set of possibly ambiguous joint-beliefs, $Ag = \{b \mid b = \langle c, \kappa^{joint}_c\rangle\}$, that should be included in the final alignment AL, where each b represents the belief regarding the inclusion of some correspondence c, and joint(c) represents the joint degree of belief for that correspondence.

As the correspondences represent a mapping between two sets of entities in the two ontologies, the set Ag can be transformed into a bipartite graph $G = (U, V, E)$, where U and V are sets of vertices corresponding to the entities in the two working ontologies; i.e. $U \subseteq \mathcal{W}^x$ and $V \subseteq \mathcal{W}^{\hat{x}}$, and E is a set of edges corresponding to the mappings between the entities (an example appears in Figure 3). However, an undesirable property of this graph is that it now includes nodes with a degree greater than one due to objections within the dialogue that can lead to alternate correspondences for a given entity.

Algorithm 1. Generate preferences for entities in beliefs

Input: Set of sorted beliefs $Ag = \{b = \langle\langle e_s, e_t, =\rangle, \kappa_c\rangle$ in descending order of utility
U : list of individual source entities or set of equivalent entities $e \in Ag$, $Pref^U = \varnothing$
V : list of individual source entities or set of equivalent entities $e' \subset Ag$, $Pref^V = \varnothing$
Output. A match specifying the ordering of preferences $Pref^U$ for the entities in U, and
$\quad\quad Pref^V$ for the entities in V

sk
for *every* $e \in U$ **do**
$\quad$ **for** *every* $b \in Ag$ **do**
$\quad\quad$ **if** *(*$e == e_s$*)* **then**
$\quad\quad\quad$ append e_s to $Pref^U(e)$;

for *every* $e' \in V$ **do**
$\quad$ **for** *every* $b \in Ag$ **do**
$\quad\quad$ **if** *(*$e' == e_t$*)* **then**
$\quad\quad\quad$ append e_t to $Pref^V(e')$;

In order to ensure that each entity is mapped to no more than one entity by the correspondences in the alignment (also known as one-to-one correspondences) we propose

---

[6] Note that *Bob* responds by providing his belief over *Alice's* asserted correspondence, and also provides his belief for the attacking correspondence.

an approach to resolve ambiguities based on the *Stable Marriage* problem [10], using a variant of the recursive algorithm originally proposed by McVittie and Wilson [16] for problems with unequal sets, that allows an exhaustive search of all possible solutions, rather than returning just one of the two extreme solutions, i.e. those known in the literature as *male-optimal solution* and *female-optimal solution*. The Stable Marriage problem is a well-known problem of finding a *matching* between two sets, whereby a *matching* M in the bipartite graph G is a subset of the edges E such that each vertex appears at most once in M. It acquired its name due to the original problem being presented as that of finding the stable marriages between a set of n men and n women, whereby for each man and woman, a strict ordering of their preferences for members of the opposite gender is given. If a solution resulted in there being no two people of the opposite gender who would rather be married to each other than their current partners, then it was said to be *stable*. In [10], Gale and Shapley proved that it was possible to find a solution (known as *male-optimal* as it was optimal for the men, but pessimal for women) in polynomial time. Other variants of the problem have looked at finding the optimal solution for both sets (based on the joint rank order) using an $O(n^4)$-time algorithm [13], or finding solutions with ties (a good survey of the problem and its variants can be found at [14]).

The recursive form of McVittie and Wilson's algorithm [16] assumes two sets of vertices, whereby the set that proposes (i.e. the male set) should be the larger of the two sets. The male-optimal solution is initially found; the marriage of man i in a stable marriage S is then broken, forcing him to take a poorer choice in his list. Correspondingly, this means that the woman who was previously married to i now has the opportunity of getting a better choice in her list. The algorithm continues for all men i until no more solutions are found.

To use this solution to find a match in the set Ag of (possibly ambiguous) correspondences, the two sets of entities were required, together with a strict-order preference for each entity. The set U (and conversely V) of entities was constructed such that $\forall b \in Ag: b = \langle\langle e, e', =\rangle, \kappa_c\rangle, e \in U, e' \in V$. A strict descending ordering of the beliefs over κ_c was then generated, and used to compute the preferences, as shown in Algorithm 1. When the ambiguities arise because of equivalence relations in one of the two working ontologies (case 2 in Definition 3), then both entities are included in the set U (and conversely V), they are assigned to the same vertex with two edges each with its preference determined by the beliefs over the correspondences involving equivalent entities. The algorithm iterates through the sorted beliefs in Ag, and generates an ordered list of preferences of the target entities for each source entity, and vice versa. In case of equivalent entities the Stable Marriage algorithm determines the stable match by adding one additional correspondence to the final match, $c = \langle e, e', =\rangle$ where $e \equiv \bar{e}$. The list of preferences resulting from the correspondences listed in Table 2 are given in Table 3 for both the sceptical and credulous attitude.

3 Empirical Evaluation

In this section, we empirically determine how effective our dialectical approach is in finding mutually acceptable alignments by investigating the alignment solutions found,

Table 3. The preference orders for the bipartite graph of possible correspondences illustrated in Figure 3 for the two mentalistic attitudes given the joint beliefs presented in Table 2

Credulous		Sceptical	
Preferences for entities $e \in U$	Preferences for entities $e' \in V$	Preferences for entities $e \in U$	Preferences for entities $e' \in V$
a: $x, z;$	**v:** $\langle cd \rangle;$	**a:** $x;$	**w:** $b;$
b: $x, w, z;$	**w:** $b;$	**b:** $x, w;$	**x:** $a, b;$
$\langle cd \rangle$: $v, y;$	**x:** $a, b;$	$\langle cd \rangle$: $v;$	**v:** $\langle cd \rangle;$
	y: $\langle cd \rangle;$		
	z: $b, a;$		

and the cost (in terms of messages exchanged). We show how the number of correspondences shared can be minimised (depending on the mentalistic attitude of the agent; i.e. whether it is *sceptical* or *credulous*) whilst still performing as well as, or better than some alignment approach selected at random, and show how the admissibility-threshold ϵ can affect the resulting alignments, by eliminating possibly spurious or erroneous correspondences (i.e. those will little evidence to support their validity).

The following three hypotheses have been tested using OAEI[7] 2013 data sets:

1. The alignments constructed using the dialectical approach presented here are at least comparable (if not better) than those generated by current alignment methods, when measured using the *precision, recall* and *f-measure* metrics;
2. By carefully selecting the admissibility threshold, the number of correspondences disclosed can be significantly reduced without sacrificing the quality of the resulting alignment (depending on the mentalistic attitude assumed).

The Ontology Evaluation Alignment Initiative (OEAI) 2013 Conference Track maintains various ontologies describing the same conceptual domain (conference organisation) and alignments between pairs of ontologies, generated by 24 different ontology alignment approaches. Seven ontologies were selected as these were accompanied by *reference alignments* (defined by a domain expert), resulting in 24 different alignments for each pair of ontologies, and $\frac{7!}{(7-2)!2!} = 21$ pairwise ontology combinations.

The empirical evaluations were conducted over each of the 21 ontology pairs (i.e. for each experiment, an agent would be assigned an ontology, but would have no knowledge of the ontology of its interlocutor). As the dataset included 24 alignments from a variety of different Alignment Approaches for each ontology pair [11]; each experiment consisted of randomly selecting and reusing 20 of the 24 alignments, and then dividing them equally between the two agents (such that each agent has prior knowledge of only 10 alignments, and no alignment was shared by both agents).

As each of the alignments was generated independently, a number of correspondences were found in more than one alignment. Thus, each agent calculated the utility for each correspondence κ_c for each c by determining the probability of finding it in its own alignments. Experiments were repeated for different admissibility thresholds; as 20 alignments were divided between the two agents, the threshold was varied in twentieths; e.g. $\epsilon = \frac{2}{20}$ required there to be at least two instances of a correspondence c to be found (i.e. joint$(c) \geq \frac{2}{20}$) before c was considered. Each experiment was repeated 500 times. The resulting alignments were evaluated using the *precision, recall* and

---

[7] http://oaei.ontologymatching.org

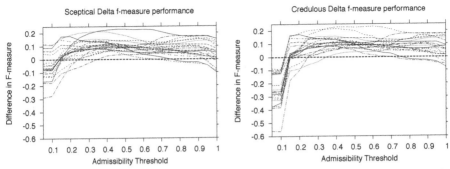

Fig. 4. The performance (in terms of $\Delta f_{\mathcal{D}}$) for all 21 ontology pairs with the *sceptical* (left) and *credulous* (right) mentalistic attitudes. Values above $y = 0$ indicate alignments that scored higher in terms of f-measure than that achieved on average when selecting an existing alignment at random.

f-measure metrics, where: **precision** (p) is the proportion of correspondences found by the dialogue that are correct (i.e. in the *reference alignment*); **recall** (r) is the proportion of correct correspondences with respect to the number of correspondences in the *reference alignment*; and the **f-measure** (f) represents the harmonic mean of p and r.

Hypothesis 1 (Generating Alignments through Dialogue): A baseline was generated by assuming that a naive approach for finding an alignment would consist of an agent randomly picking and using one of the pre-defined alignments. Thus, we compute the average performance of the 24 alignment methods for each ontology pair. The comparative performance of the alignments generated by the dialogue is reported by calculating the average difference in precision ($\overline{p_{\mathcal{D}}}$) and recall ($\overline{r_{\mathcal{D}}}$) for each ontology pair with respect to the baseline alignments. Figure 4 illustrates how, in most cases, the f-measure performance of the dialogue is significantly higher than that achieved by selecting an alignment at random (i.e. in the range $0.25 \leq \epsilon < 0.9$ for both mentalistic attitudes). The graph plots the difference in f-measure (denoted $\Delta f_{\mathcal{D}}$) between that achieved using the average alignments ($\overline{f_{\mathcal{A}}}$), and that achieved by the dialogue for all 21 ontology pairs (i.e. values above zero indicate a better f, whereas those below are worse). In general, as the admissibility threshold increased, the precision of the resulting alignment increased, whereas recall decreased. At $\epsilon > 0.45$, recall fell below that obtained when selecting an alignment at random, whereas precision was higher; ranging from $\overline{p_{\mathcal{D}}} = 0.01$ at $\epsilon = 0.25$ to $\overline{p_{\mathcal{D}}} = 0.28$ at $\epsilon = 1$. The maximum p occurs at $\epsilon = 1$ for *cmt-ekaw* (resulting in a 75% increase).

The dialogue performance degrades for low and high thresholds. When $\epsilon = 0.05$ (i.e. no filtering), a large number of correspondences appear in the alignment, yielding a high r but very low p, suggesting that although the correct correspondences were found, a high number of incorrect ones were also included. Whilst this could be a property of the dataset used (several alignments include a number of rare, but erroneous correspondences), it demonstrates the value of eliminating low utility correspondences (e.g. in this case, those that were found in the source alignments with low frequency). When $\epsilon > 0.9$, a high number of correspondences are eliminated (an average of 6.4% of each agent's correspondences appear in the final alignment), resulting in a slight drop in $\Delta f_{\mathcal{D}}$. This support hypotheses 1 & 2 when the admissibility threshold is used.

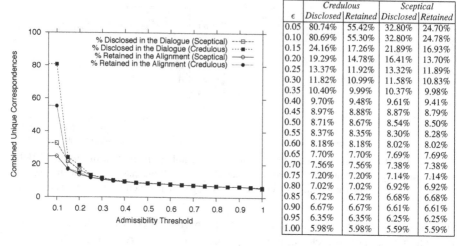

	Credulous		Sceptical	
ϵ	Disclosed	Retained	Disclosed	Retained
0.05	80.74%	55.42%	32.80%	24.70%
0.10	80.69%	55.30%	32.80%	24.78%
0.15	24.16%	17.26%	21.89%	16.93%
0.20	19.29%	14.78%	16.41%	13.70%
0.25	13.37%	11.92%	13.32%	11.89%
0.30	11.82%	10.99%	11.58%	10.83%
0.35	10.40%	9.99%	10.37%	9.98%
0.40	9.70%	9.48%	9.61%	9.41%
0.45	8.97%	8.88%	8.87%	8.79%
0.50	8.71%	8.67%	8.54%	8.50%
0.55	8.37%	8.35%	8.30%	8.28%
0.60	8.18%	8.18%	8.02%	8.02%
0.65	7.70%	7.70%	7.69%	7.69%
0.70	7.56%	7.56%	7.38%	7.38%
0.75	7.20%	7.20%	7.14%	7.14%
0.80	7.02%	7.02%	6.92%	6.92%
0.85	6.72%	6.72%	6.68%	6.68%
0.90	6.67%	6.67%	6.61%	6.61%
0.95	6.35%	6.35%	6.25%	6.25%
1.00	5.98%	5.98%	5.59%	5.59%

Fig. 5. Average Percentage of Messages disclosed in the dialogue, and included in AL

Hypothesis 2 (Communication Costs): To establish the percentage of correspondences shared, and of that selected in the final alignment, the total number of correspondences known by the two agents was calculated for each experiment, and used to determine: 1) the percentage of correspondences that were then disclosed as part of the negotiation; and 2) the percentage of correspondences that were subsequently found in the final alignment AL. A further analysis was conducted to compare the effect of the two mentalistic attitudes on the number of correspondences shared. The results are plotted in Figure 5 against different admissibility thresholds.

The difference between the *credulous* and *sceptical* attitudes is clear when $\epsilon \le 0.25$. As suggested for the previous hypothesis, each agent may posses a number of low utility correspondences that are not shared. If the agents adopt a *sceptical* attitude, then these correspondences known only by the agent will be rejected by its interlocutor, and thus typically will not appear in the dialogue. This is supported by the results in the table in Figure 5, whereby at $\epsilon = 0.05$ (i.e. no filtering), only 32.8% of correspondences are disclosed. However, if an agent adopts a *credulous* attitude, then such correspondences will be considered, despite being known by only one agent (80.74% of correspondences are disclosed). In both cases, at low admissibility thresholds, there is a difference in the percentage of correspondences disclosed and those in the final alignment (at $\epsilon = 0.1$, there is a difference of 25.39% (credulous) and 8.02% (sceptical)), suggesting that many correspondences are eliminated as a result of ambiguity. However, the number of ambiguous cases drops to zero for $\epsilon > 0.55$, as the number of correspondences disclosed and appearing in the final alignment converge. This result supports our second hypothesis.

4   Related Work

A number of different approaches have addressed the reconciliation of heterogeneous ontologies by using some form of rational reasoning. In [2] an ontology negotiation protocol was discussed to enable agents to exchange parts of their ontology by a process of successive interpretations, whereas [7] presented an approach whereby agents shared an explicit goal to collaboratively evolve a common ontology. Whilst these approaches resolve semantic interoperability through negation to achieve semantic *homogeneity*, other approaches attempt to align the heterogeneous ontologies through negotiation; typically through the use of *argumentation* [15,22]. Argumentation has been used as a rational means for agents to select ontology correspondences based on the notion of partial-order preferences over their different properties (e.g. structural vs terminological) [15]. A variant was also proposed [22] which represented ontology mappings as disjunctive queries in Description Logics. Typically, these approaches have used a course-grained decision metric based on the *type* of correspondence, rather than whether or not each correspondence was *acceptable* to each agent (given other mutually accepted correspondences), and do not consider the notion of private, or asymmetric knowledge (the correspondences are assumed to be publicly accessible). A Max-Sum algorithm was used in [21] for synthesising ontology alignment methods whilst maximising social welfare in a group of interacting agents. Although similar to the aims of our study, [21] assumes that all agents have knowledge of the ontologies to align, and each agent is associated with an alignment method with its own preferences on the assessed relation, and quantified by a degree of confidence.

5 Conclusions

We have formally presented and empirically evaluated an inquiry dialogue that facilitates negotiation over asymmetric and incomplete knowledge of ontological correspondences. Our dialogue enables two agents to selectively disclose private beliefs regarding the *utility* of ontological correspondences. Ambiguities (i.e. when the combination of several correspondences erroneously map different entities in one ontology to a single entity in another) are resolved using a *Stable Marriage* algorithm, that identifies one-to-one mappings between entities. Furthermore, the notion of credulous and sceptical mental attitudes was described, which determines how agents respond to unknown correspondences. The dialogue was implemented and empirically evaluated using correspondences found in alignments sourced from 24 different approaches over 21 ontology pairs (from OAEI 2013), and using a set of reference alignments. The results supported the hypotheses that, by filtering low probability correspondences, alignments generated by our dialogue performed as well as selecting an existing alignment approach at random, whilst significantly reducing the number of correspondences disclosed.

References

1. Agrawal, R., Evfimievski, A., Srikant, R.: Information sharing across private databases. In: Proceedings of the 2003 ACM SIGMOD International Conference on Management of Data, pp. 86–97. ACM (2003)
2. Bailin, S., Truszkowski, W.: Ontology negotiation: How agents can really get to know each other. In: Truszkowski, W., Hinchey, M., Rouff, C.A. (eds.) WRAC 2002. LNCS, vol. 2564, pp. 320–334. Springer, Heidelberg (2003)

3. Barnaghi, P., Sheth, A., Henson, C.: From data to actionable knowledge: Big data challenges in the web of things [guest editors' introduction]. IEEE Intelligent Systems 28(6), 6–11 (2013)
4. Clifton, C.: Kantarcio lu, M., Doan, A., Schadow, G., Vaidya, J., Elmagarmid, A., Suciu, D.: Privacy-preserving data integration and sharing. In: Proceedings of the 9th ACM SIGMOD Workshop on Research Issues in Data Mining and Knowledge Discovery, pp. 19–26. ACM (2004)
5. Cruz, I.F., Tamassia, R., Yao, D.: Privacy-preserving schema matching using mutual information. In: Barker, S., Ahn, G.-J. (eds.) Data and Applications Security 2007. LNCS, vol. 4602, pp. 93–94. Springer, Heidelberg (2007)
6. Cuenca Grau, B., Horrocks, I., Kazakov, Y., Sattler, U.: Modular reuse of ontologies: Theory and practice. J. of Artificial Intelligence Research (JAIR) 31, 273–318 (2008)
7. van Diggelen, J., Beun, R.J., Dignum, F., van Eijk, R.M., Meyer, J.J.C.: Anemone: an effective minimal ontology negotiation environment. In: Proceedings of AAMAS 2006, pp. 899–906 (2006)
8. Doran, P., Tamma, V., Payne, T.R., Palmisano, I.: Dynamic selection of ontological alignments: a space reduction mechanism. In: Proceedings of IJCAI 2009, pp. 2028–2033 (2009)
9. Euzenat, J., Shvaiko, P.: Ontology Matching. Springer (2007)
10. Gale, D., Shapley, L.S.: College admissions and the stability of marriage. The American Mathematical Monthly 69(1), 9–15 (1962)
11. Grau, B.C., Dragisic, Z., Eckert, K., Euzenat, J., et al.: Results of the ontology alignment evaluation initiative 2013. In: Proc. 8th ISWC workshop on ontology matching (OM), pp. 61–100 (2013)
12. Inan, A., Kantarcioglu, M., Ghinita, G., Bertino, E.: Private record matching using differential privacy. In: Proceedings of the 13th International Conference on Extending Database Technology, pp. 123–134. ACM (2010)
13. Irving, R.W., Leather, P., Gusfield, D.: An efficient algorithm for the 'optimal' stable marriage. J. ACM 34(3), 532–543 (1987)
14. Iwama, K., Miyazaki, S.: A survey of the stable marriage problem and its variants. In: Proceedings of the International Conference on Informatics Education and Research for Knowledge-Circulating Society, ICKS 2008, pp. 131–136. IEEE Computer Society, Washington, DC (2008)
15. Lacra, L., Blacoe, I., Tamma, V., Payne, T., Euzenat, J., Bench-Capon, T.: Argumentation over ontology correspondences in MAS. In: Proceedings of AAMAS, pp. 1285–1292 (2007)
16. McVitie, D., Wilson, L.: Stable marriage assignment for unequal sets. BIT Numerical Mathematics 10(3), 295–309 (1970)
17. Meilicke, C.: Alignment Incoherence in Ontology Matching. Ph.D. thesis, Dissertation, Universität Mannheim, Mannheim (2011)
18. Mitra, P., Liu, P., Pan, C.C.: Privacy-preserving ontology matching. In: AAAI Workshop on Context and Ontologies (2005)
19. Mitra, P., Pan, C.C., Liu, P., Atluri, V.: Privacy-preserving semantic interoperation and access control of heterogeneous databases. In: Proceedings of the 2006 ACM Symposium on Information, Computer and Communications Security, pp. 66–77. ACM (2006)
20. Payne, T.R., Tamma, V.: Negotiating over ontological correspondences with asymmetric and incomplete knowledge. In: Proceedings of AAMAS 2014, pp. 517–524 (2014)
21. Spiliopoulos, V., Vouros, G.A.: Synthesizing ontology alignment methods using the max-sum algorithm. IEEE TKDE 24(5), 940–951 (2012)
22. Trojahn dos Santos, C., Quaresma, P., Vieira, R.: Conjunctive queries for ontology based agent communication in MAS. In: Proceedings of AAMAS 2008, pp. 829–836 (2008)
23. Walton, D., Krabbe, E.: Commitment in Dialogue: Basic Concepts of Interpersonal Reasoning. SUNY series in Logic and Language, State University of New York Press (1995)
24. Zhang, N., Zhao, W.: Distributed privacy preserving information sharing. In: Proceedings of the 31st International Conference on VLDB, pp. 889–900. VLDB Endowment (2005)

Uncovering the Semantics of Wikipedia Pagelinks

Valentina Presutti[1], Sergio Consoli[1], Andrea Giovanni Nuzzolese[1],
Diego Reforgiato Recupero[1], Aldo Gangemi[1,2],
Ines Bannour[2], and Haïfa Zargayouna[2]

[1] STLab-ISTC Consiglio Nazionale delle Ricerche, Rome, Italy
[2] Université Paris 13 - Sorbonne Paris Cité - CNRS, France

Abstract. Wikipedia pagelinks, i.e. links between Wikipages, carry an intended semantics: they indicate the existence of a factual relation between the DBpedia entity referenced by the source Wikipage, and the DBpedia entity referenced by the target Wikipage of the link. These relations are represented in DBpedia as occurrences of the generic "wikiPageWikilink" property. We designed and implemented a novel method to uncover the intended semantics of pagelinks, and to represent them as semantic relations. In this paper, we test our method on a subset of Wikipedia, showing its potential impact for DBPedia enrichment.

1 Introduction

Wikipedia proved to be an extremely valuable resource for the Semantic Web. In fact, DBpedia (its RDF version) is the most important hub of Linked Open Data [1] and one of the resources most used as training/background knowledge for Semantic Web methods.

However, DBpedia mostly includes structured knowledge from Wikipedia infoboxes, and categories. There is a huge amount of knowledge in Wikipedia that is only expressed as natural language content, which is the case also for the Web in general, and that is worth to annotate with structured data, e.g. by means of RDFa, and to be transformed to Linked Data for fostering the development of the Semantic Web.

Current knowledge extraction (KE) systems address very well the task of linking pieces of text to Semantic Web entities (e.g. `owl:sameAs`) by means of named entity recognition (NER) methods, e.g. NERD[1] [7], FOX[2], conTEXT[3] [9], DBpedia Spotlight[4], Stanbol[5]. Some of them also perform sense tagging, adding knowledge about entity types (`rdf:type`). However, Wikipedia (and DBpedia) can be enriched also with semantic relations different from `owl:sameAs` and `rdf:type`, i.e. factual relations between entities.

---

[1] http://nerd.eurecom.fr
[2] http://aksw.org/Projects/FOX.html
[3] http://context.aksw.org/app/
[4] http://dbpedia-spotlight.github.com/demo
[5] http://stanbol.apache.org

K. Janowicz et al. (Eds.): EKAW 2014, LNAI 8876, pp. 413–428, 2014.

A *pragmatic trace* of a semantic relation between two entities in Wikipedia is the presence of pagelinks, i.e. links between wikipages. In fact, when we include a pagelink in a wikipage, we usually assume that a semantic relation exists between the entity referenced by the page, i.e. the triple subject, and the entity referenced by the target page, i.e. the triple object. For example, a link to "Usenet" in the Wikipedia page of "John McCarthy"[6] suggests a semantic relation between those two entities.

This hypothesis is also supported by a previous study [12], in which we have extracted encyclopedic knowledge patterns for DBpedia types, based on Wikipedia pagelinks. In [12], a user study showed that Wikipedia pagelinks determine relevant descriptive contexts for DBpedia entities at the type level, which suggests that pagelinks mirror relevant semantic relations between DBpedia entities.

Revealing the semantics of pagelinks has a high potential impact for the amount of Wikipedia knowledge that can be published in machine readable form, while keeping an anchoring to corresponding natural language expressions (the textual context of pagelinks). Notably, Wikipedia includes ~136.6M[7] pagelinks. These pagelinks are represented as triples from a generic RDF property "dbpo:wikiPageWikiLink"[8]. Although some of them overlap with infobox data (~ 4%), most of them are not semantically characterized.

Our aim is to type pagelinks with the semantic relations that they implicitly convey, by making them explicit. How to do this automatically? We want to use the text surrounding pagelinks. This, in addition to the pragmatic trace, i.e. the pagelink itself, provides us with a *linguistic trace* of such semantic relations. In fact, the text within which we include a pagelink usually expresses directly or indirectly its intended semantics. For example, the sentence:

"McCarthy often commented on world affairs on the Usenet forums"

explains the semantics of the relation between the entity "John McCarthy" and "Usenet". Currently, DBpedia represents such link as follows:

dbpedia:John_McCarthy[9] dbpo:wikipagewikilink dbpedia:Usenet

Our aim is to automatically annotate these links with semantic relations based on the sentences expressing their meaning. As for this example, we want to produce something like:

dbpedia:John_McCarthy myont:commentsOnForum dbpedia:Usenet

and when possible, to align the produced property to an existing semantic Web property.

In this paper, we describe a novel approach, named *Legalo*[10], for automatically typing pagelinks, and we evaluate its performance on a subset of Wikipedia.

---

[6] Cf. http://en.wikipedia.org/wiki/John_McCarthy_
   (computer_scientist)

[7] M stands for millions.

[8] Prefix dbpo: stands for http://dbpedia.org/ontology/

[10] A demo of Legalo specialized on Wikipedia pagelinks is available at
   http://wit.istc.cnr.it/stlab-tools/legalo/wikipedia

Legalo is based on a pipeline of components, which has at its core a machine reader, i.e. FRED[11] [14]. FRED transforms natural language text to a formal RDF/OWL graph representation. Legalo implements a set of graph pattern-based rules for extracting, from FRED graphs, formal binary relations that capture the semantics of specific links.

This approach can be generalized and applied to any web page and its links; the reader is invited to visit an online demo of a generalized version of Legalo, which demonstrates the generality of the method[12].

The contribution of this paper can be summarized as follows:

- a novel method for automatic labeling of Wikipedia pagelinks, which performs property label generation, and graph-based relation extraction;
- an online tool named *Legalo*, which implements and demonstrates such method;
- a user-based evaluation of Legalo on a subset of Wikipedia.

The paper is structured as follows. In Section 2 we discuss related work. Section 3 illustrates the data sources that we have used in our study, while Section 4 describes our approach for automatic labeling of pagelinks. Section 5 presents our results and the evaluation of our approach. Finally, Section 6 discusses results and future developments.

2   Related Work

The closer domain to our research is relation extraction. There are a number of valuable contributions in this field. Notably, Open Information Extraction (OIE)[13] is a project whose aim is to parse the Web and build a knowledge base of triplets extracted from recognized facts. One of the main tools developed in this project is Ollie [10]. Typical results of relation extraction tools such as OIE are not represented as RDF properties, making them hardly reusable for e.g. annotating links with RDFa tags. A possible reuse of OIE in the context of Legalo is to exploit its knowledge base as a lexical resource providing labels for designing more accurate naming strategies for semantic relations, at least for direct connections among entities.

NELL[14] [3] is a learning tool that since 2010 processes the web for building an evolving knowledge base of facts, categories and relations. We used NELL in our work in an attempt to align the semantic relations resulting from Legalo to NELL ontology.

The main difference between approaches such as OIE and NELL (and in general relation extraction tools), and Legalo is that the formers focus on extracting mainly direct relations between entities, while Legalo focuses on revealing the semantics of relations between entities that are suggested by the presence of links

---

[11] http://wit.istc.cnr.it/stlab-tools/fred/
[12] http://wit.istc.cnr.it/stlab-tools/legalo
[13] http://openie.cs.washington.edu/
[14] http://rtw.ml.cmu.edu/rtw/

in Web pages, and that can be also indirect i.e., expressed by longer paths or n-ary relations. Legalo novelty also resides in performing property label generation, and graph-based relation extraction.

FRED[15] [14] is a tool that transforms natural language text in RDF/OWL graphs with an event-based representation approach. Both NELL and FRED are *machine readers* although they use different approaches. FRED is based on Discourse Representation Theory (DRT) and Frames [2], and builds its knowledge bases by formalizing natural language text. FRED graphs captures very well the semantics of natural language sentences by performing a deep text analysis. As discussed in Section 4, Legalo builds on top of FRED for synthesizing binary relations representing the semantics of pagelinks, hence responding to a requirements of better cognitive ergonomics than n-ary relations, which are the typical representation patterns in FRED graphs.

Legalo includes a matching approach for identifying existing Semantic Web properties that can be aligned to its produced binary relations, for disambiguation purposes. In this research work, we focused more on the property name design strategies for producing binary relations than on the alignment procedure, although our results are reasonably satisfying also in this respect (cf. Section 5). Most ontology alignment methods [5] (cf. see the Ontology Alignment Evaluation Initiative[16]) work on comparing and aligning collection of ontologies (typically addressing the same knowledge domain). Our task instead is closer to string matching as our input values are two properties accompanied with, in the best case, a `rdfs:comment` describing their intended semantics, and sometimes having defined domain and range. In future work, we intend to investigate how to exploit existing ontology matching methods as well as entity linking tools such as SILK [8] in attempt to improve alignment results.

3   Data Sources

In the context of this work we have used a number of data sources.

Wikipedia and Wikipedia Pagelinks. Wikipedia is a collaboratively built encyclopedia on the Web. Currently, English Wikipedia contains ~4.5M articles[17]. Each Wikipedia page refers to one entity: these entities are represented in DBpedia, the RDF version of Wikipedia. The Wikipedia Pagelinks dataset[18] represents internal links between DBpedia instances as they occur in their corresponding Wikipedia pages. This dataset counts ~136.6M `dbpo:wikiPageWikiLink` triples (as of version 3.9). We use a subset of Wikipedia pages and their pagelinks as testing sample for evaluating our approach.

---

[15] http://wit.istc.cnr.it/stlab-tools/fred/
[16] http://oaei.ontologymatching.org/
[17] Source: http://en.wikipedia.org/wiki/Wikipedia:Size_of_Wikipedia, July 2014.
[18] http://wiki.dbpedia.org/Downloads39

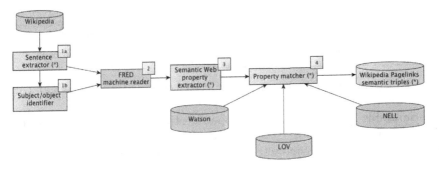

Fig. 1. Pipeline implemented by Legalo for automatic typing Wikipedia pagelinks based on their linguistic trace, i.e. natural language sentence including links. Numbers indicate the order of execution of a component in the pipeline. The output of a component i is passed as input to the next $i+1$ component. (*) denotes tools developed in this work, which are part of our contribution.

Given a sentence including a link, our method creates a RDF property synthesizing the link's semantics. When possible, it aligns this property to existing Semantic Web properties retrieved from three different sources:

- **Watson**[19] [4] is a service that provides access to Semantic Web knowledge, in particular ontologies;
- **Linked Open Vocabularies (LOV)**[20] is an aggregator of Linked Open vocabularies (including DBpedia), and provides services for accessing their data;
- **Never-Ending Language Learning (NELL)**[21] [3] is a machine learning system that extracts structured data from unstructured Web pages and stores it in a knowledge base. It runs continuously since 2010. From the learnt facts, NELL team has derived an ontology of categories and properties: it includes 548 properties at the moment[22].

4   Legalo: A Method and Tool for Typing Pagelinks

Legalo[23] is based on a pipeline of components and data sources, executed in the sequence illustrated in Figure 1. In [6], we experimented the same pipeline for automatic typing DBpedia entities, and applied it on the whole Wikipedia producing an ontology of Wikipedia entity types, derived from their natural language definitions [13]. Such result supports our hypothesis that the same approach can show promising results for automatic labeling of pagelinks.

---

[19] http://watson.kmi.open.ac.uk/WatsonWUI/
[20] http://lov.okfn.org/dataset/lov/
[21] http://rtw.ml.cmu.edu/rtw/
[22] http://nell-ld.telecom-st-etienne.fr/
[23] A demo of Legalo is available at http://wit.istc.cnr.it/
      stlab-tools/legalo/wikipedia

In 1972, Cobb moved to Sydney, Australia, where his work appeared in alternative magazines such as The Digger. Independent publishers Wild & Woolley published a "best of" collection of the earlier cartoon books, *The Cobb Book* in 1975. A follow-up volume, *Cobb Again*, appeared in 1978.

Fig. 2. A fragment of the wikipage wp:Ron_Cobb including two sentences with links

1a. Sentence Extractor. Given a DBpedia entity $subj_e$ (and its corresponding Wikipedia page $page(subj_e)$), this component collects its pagelinks triples (from the Wikipedia Pagelinks dataset, cf. Section 3). For each triple:

$$subj_e \; \texttt{dbpo:wikiPageWikiLink} \; obj_e$$

it extracts the natural language sentences in $page(subj_e)$ including links to $page(obj_e)$, by performing the following actions.

First, it performs a cleaning procedure on $page(subj_e)$: removing special characters, infoboxes, tables, lists, external references, pictures, and captions. Then, for each pagelink, it extracts the text starting after a dot, and ending with a dot, which includes a link to $page(obj_e)$. Sentences are stored in a RDF graph by associating them to the pair $(subj_e, obj_e)$. All red links and disambiguation pages are discarded; redirect pages are handled by substituting their URIs with the redirected objects. For example, given the fragment of the page wp:Ron_Cobb[24] depicted in Figure 2[25] the sentence extractor will store the data shown in Table 1.

Table 1. Data extracted by the sentence extractor from the wikipage fragment shown in Figure 2

link ID	$subj_e$	obj_e	sentence
L1	dbpedia:Ron_Cobb	dbpedia:Sydney	In 1972, Cobb moved to Sydney, Australia, where his work appeared in alternative magazines such as The Digger.
L2	dbpedia:Ron_Cobb	dbpedia:Australia	In 1972, Cobb moved to Sydney, Australia, where his work appeared in alternative magazines such as The Digger.
L3	dbpedia:Ron_Cobb	dbpedia:The_Digger_(alternative_magazine)	In 1972, Cobb moved to Sydney, Australia, where his work appeared in alternative magazines such as The Digger.

1b. Subject/Object Identifier. This component has the role of identifying subject and object of a semantic relation suggested by a pagelink, and their lexicalizations in the associated sentence.

In Wikipedia (and Wikis in general) each $page(subj_e)$ is a representative for one entity, i.e. $subj_e$, hence it is reasonable to assume that all its links suggest semantic relations having $subj_e$ as subject and the links' targets as objects. In this case, we know a priori the DBpedia entities playing the roles of subject and object, respectively: they are given by the sentence extractor as shown above.

---

[24] Prefix wp: stands for http://en.wikipedia.org/wiki/
[25] Links are shown as underlined text.

Although this assumption is reasonable, there are pagelink sentences that refer to entities other than $subj_e$, but still they are associated with pagelinks of $subj_e$. We identify and keep only those sentences (and their associated pagelinks) that include an explicit lexical reference $lex(subj)$ to $subj_e$. To this aim we use the DBpedia Lexicalizations Dataset[26]. For example, the wikipage wp:Ron_Cobb includes a link to wp:Sydney in the sentence:

"In 1972, Cobb moved to Sydney, Australia, where his work appeared in alternative magazines such as The Digger."

This sentence will be kept and stored in our dataset as it contains the term "Cobb", which is a lexicalization of dbpedia:Ron_Cobb. The same wikipage includes a link to wp:Los_Angeles_Free_Press in the sentence:

"Edited and published by Art Kunkin, the Los Angeles Free Press was one of the first of the underground newspapers of the 1960s, noted for its radical politics."

This sentence will be discarded as it does not include any lexicalization of dbpedia:Ron_Cobb. The RDF dataset shown in Table 1 will be updated by this component with the following data:

Table 2. Data extracted by the sentence extractor from the wikipage fragment shown in Figure 2

link ID	$lex(subj)$	$lex(obj)$
L1	Cobb	Sydney
L2	Cobb	Australia
L3	Cobb	The Digger
L4	Cobb	Wild & Woolley

2. Machine Reading (FRED). Each stored sentence is parsed by FRED[27] [14], which produces its RDF/OWL graph representation. The resulting graph is stored as a named graph and associated with its corresponding pair (pagelink, sentence). FRED implements an event-based representation of natural language text. Hence, relations between entities are mainly represented as n-ary relations. For example, the FRED graph for the sentence:

"In 1972, Cobb moved to Sydney, Australia, where his work appeared in alternative magazines such as The Digger."

is depicted in Figure 3. Let us consider the pagelink connecting "Cobb" and "Sydney". The resulting graph correctly represents an event occurrence fred:move_1[28] of type fred:Move (i.e. n-ary relation), having fred:Cobb and

---

[26] http://wiki.dbpedia.org/Datasets/NLP?v=yqj

[27] FRED is available online at http://wit.istc.cnr.it/stlab-tools/ fred

[28] Prefix fred: stands for http://www.ontologydesignpatterns.org/ fred/domain.owl - this is the namespace of ontology entities extracted by FRED, and can be customized by users.

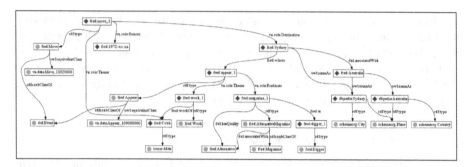

Fig. 3. FRED graph for the sentence: *"In 1972, Cobb moved to Sydney, Australia, where his work appeared in alternative magazines such as The Digger"*

fred:Sydney as arguments. If we consider the pagelink connecting "Cobb" and "The Digger" we can find a semantic connection between them within the FRED graph involving an event occurrence of type fred:Appear having two arguments (representing Cobb's work and alternative magazines) that are respectively connected to fred:Cobb and fred:Digger.

On one hand, this event-based representation of a sentence is excellent if we give priority to completeness and richness aspects. On the other hand, from a cognitive ergonomics perspective, it is desirable (when possible) to represent such connections as binary relations. Binary relations provide a semantic "cognitive shortcut" addressing many Linked Data applications; additionally, they can be used for annotating pagelinks by means of RDFa. The aim of Legalo is to synthesize such connections as binary relations.

3. Semantic Web Property Extractor. This component is in charge of extracting from FRED graphs, the subgraphs connecting $subj_e$ and obj_e, and generating a binary relation expressing the semantics of their connection. One of the main novel aspects of Legalo resides in this component, which performs property label generation and graph-based relation extraction.

Elements' IDs in FRED graphs reflect the terms used in the text, *modulo* a normalization performed by means of a stemming process. FRED graphs also include a set of metadata triples[29] that associate each graph entity to its corresponding text spans. For example, the term "Australia", starting from the text span "31" and ending at text span "40" in the sentence *"In 1972, Cobb moved to Sydney, Australia, where his work appeared in alternative magazines such as The Digger."* denotes the entity fred:Australia in the graph depicted in Figure 3. The following triples provide this information[30].

---

[29] These triples are not returned in the graph-view result of FRED at http://wit.istc.cnr.it/stlab-tools/fred/, they are returned with all other serialization output options.

[30] Prefix pos: stands for http://www.essepuntato.it/2008/12/ earmark#, semio: stands for http://ontologydesignpatterns. cp/owl/semiotics.owl#, and xmls: stands for http://www.w3.org/2001/XMLSchema#

```
fred:offset_31_40_Australia
        a  pos:PointerRange ;
            rdfs:label "Australia"^^xmls:string ;
            semio:denotes fred:Australia ;
            pos:begins "31"^^xmls:nonNegativeInteger ;
            pos:ends "40"^^xmls:nonNegativeInteger ;
```

The Semantic Web property extractor component, for each pair *(pagelink, sentence)* takes as input the lexicalizations of subject and object, and the associated named graph. With respect to the above example, the extractor will receive the data shown in Table 3.

Table 3. Example of input data to the Semantic Web property extractor for the pagelink (`dbpedia:Ron_Cobb`, `dbpedia:Australia`) associated with the linguistic trace "In 1972, Cobb moved to Sydney, Australia, where his work appeared in alternative magazines such as The Digger"

link ID	sentence	*lex(subj)*	*lex(obj)*	**NG ID**
L2	In 1972, Cobb moved to Sydney, Australia, where his work appeared in alternative magazines such as The Digger.	Cobb	Australia	NG1201[31]

The component performs the following actions: (i) it identifies the nodes denoted by *lex(subj)* and *lex(obj)* in the FRED graph, using the text span metadata; (ii) it extracts all subgraphs connecting the two identified nodes; (iii) it produces a Semantic Web property.

To design the strategies implemented by this component for step (iii), we used a combined top-down and bottom-up approach. The top down approach consists in concatenating all labels of graph entities in the extracted subgraphs belonging to the `fred:` namespace, including the more general types of intermediate nodes. With this strategy, each link was associated to a number of properties resulting from different possible paths, each having different length. The bottom-up approach consisted in evaluating a sample of ~200 cases, which showed that the minimum path lengths produced the best names for properties. Also, by means of this empirical observation, we noticed that when subjects and objects are connected through an event node, the best strategy is to exclude all labels of arcs and types that connect the subject to the event node[32].

Additionally, we associate some of the thematic roles of events arguments to specific labels. For example, in the above example, the entity `fred:Australia` plays the role `vn.role:Destination`[33], which is associated to the term "to". The association between thematic roles and labels is shown in Table 4.

---

[32] A detailed description of the algorithm can be temporarily found at `http://stlab.istc.cnr.it/stlab/Legalo`, which would be included in a future extended article.

[33] Prefix `vn.role:` stands for `http://www.ontologydesignpatterns.org/ont/vn/abox/role/`

Table 4. Labels associated with thematic roles used for producing binary relation names

Thematic role	label	Thematic role	label
vnrole:Actor1	with	vnrole:Actor2	with
vnrole:Agent	by	vnrole:Beneficiary	for
vnrole:Destination	to	vnrole:Instrument	with
vnrole:Topic	about		

As a result, referring to the example above, the produced triple is:

`dbpedia:Ron_Cobb fred:moveTo dbepdia:Australia`

4. Property Matcher. The aim of this component is to align the produced properties to existing properties defined in Semantic Web ontologies and vocabularies. As described in Section 3, we used three main sources for retrieving semantic property candidates. For assessing their similarity with the property produced by the Semantic Web property extractor component, we implemented a string matching algorithm, which computes a Levenshtein distance metrics [11] between the two property IDs.

4.1 Discussion

The current implementation of Legalo has some limitations that are worth discussing, and that are subject of ongoing research.

- there is not yet a strategy to ignore pagelinks that most probably correspond to loose or non-sensical relations;
- subject and object identification are based on design assumptions that are hardly portable to contexts different from wikis.

The version of Legalo presented in this paper is specialized on revealing the semantics of Wikipedia pagelinks, which are represented as RDF triples in the DBpedia Pagelinks dataset. Wikipedia pagelinks translate to triples having DBpedia entities as subjects and objects, which are identified based on the wiki design principle that a wikipage represents only one entity.

Legalo works under the hypothesis that a pagelink provides a pragmatic trace of a semantic relation between such two DBpedia entities. With respect to the aissues listed, it relies on the "one-subject-only" wiki design principle as far as subject and object identification are concerned, and assumes that all pagelinks indicate potential relevant relations between the two given entities.

These assumptions are not always robust and certainly they may loose their validity if Legalo is applied to types of Web content other than wikis. We are currently investigating how to identify subject and object of a relation suggested by a link, and how to classify links in order to discard those who probably translate to loose or non-sensical relations. Since we are now focusing on a generalized version of Legalo approach, results of this ongoing study could be also applied to improve the Wikipedia specialized version.

5   Results and Evaluation

In this section, we report the results of our work and evaluate them in terms of precision and recall.

Legalo[34] implements the approach described in Section 4. The goal of this study is to evaluate its potential, and identify weaknesses that to be patched, towards the large scale application on the whole Wikipedia.

To this aim, we have performed an experiment on a subset of Wikipedia pages and their corresponding pagelinks, taken from the Wikipedia Pagelinks dataset[35]. The experiment results are published as RDF data and accessible through a SPARQL enpoint[36], and have been evaluated by means of a user study described in the remaining of this section.

Building the Evaluation Sample. To build our experimental setting we have randomly selected 1,000 distinct DBpedia entities, and their corresponding Wikipedia pages, having at least 10 Wikipedia pagelinks[37]. The random selection has been run for each top-level type of the DBpedia ontology (version 3.9) by considering the frequency of instances *per* each of these types on the overall DBpedia.

We have extracted from the collected Wikipedia pages all sentences embedding the selected Wikipedia pagelinks, and stored them together with their corresponding pairs ($subj_e$, obj_e) in a RDF triplestore[38].

During this process, some pagelinks have been discarded because we could not find a sentence embedding the link. For example, this happens when a link is found in a table, list, or infobox. From the resulting data, we only kept entries including a sentence with an explicit lexicalization of $subj_e$.

The result of this process led us to collect 1,192 pairs (pagelink, sentence), corresponding to 442 distinct subject entities, i.e. $subj_e$. It has to be noted that discarded sentences sometimes express a relation between $subj_e$ and obj_e. However, they include an indirect reference to $subj_e$, for example by means of anaphoras.

Of these 1,192 sentences we kept only those that are parsable by FRED, i.e. those for which FRED returned a non-empty graph[39], and having at least a sub-graph connecting $subj_e$ and obj_e either through a direct path of any length, or through an event occurrence.

The final sample set consists of 629 pairs *(pagelink, sentence)*, each associated with a FRED graph.

---

[34] http://wit.istc.cnr.it/stlab-tools/legalo/wikipedia
[35] http://wiki.dbpedia.org/Downloads39
[36] http://isotta.cs.unibo.it:9191/sparql
[37] We empirically noticed in [12] that this guarantees enough text in the page.
[38] Virtuoso, http://virtuoso.openlinksw.com/
[39] Empty graph output from FRED is mainly caused by the presence of ill formatted characters.

Binary Relations for Pagelinks. We ran Legalo on the corpus described above, and this process produced 629 new binary relations (referred to as p_{new} from now on), which are retrievable through a SPARQL endpoint[40].

The matching process performed against LOV[41], NELL[42] [3], and Watson[43] [4] returned a number of proposed alignment properties (referred to as p_{sw} from now on) for 250 distinct p_{new}, with a threshold on the editing distance value (Levenshtein distance), normalized as *difference percentage*[44], set to 0.7.

The user-based evaluation involved three raters, who are computer science researchers familiar with linked data, but not familiar with Legalo. Independently, they have judged the results of Legalo based on two separate tasks, using a Likert scale of five values.

User-Based Evaluation of p_{new}. The first task consisted in judging a new produced property p_{new} based on a pagelink and its associated sentences. For each p_{new} raters have been provided with:

- $lex(subj)$
- $lex(obj)$
- sentence
- p_{new}

Table 5. An example of evaluation entry for p_{new}

$lex(subj)$	$lex(obj)$	sentence	p_{new}
Cobb	Spain	While Cobb was in Spain working on Conan the Barbarian, Spielberg supervised the rewrite into the more personal E.T. and ended up directing it himself.	fred:locatedIn

Table 5 shows an example of evaluation entry for p_{new}. The following evaluation guidelines have been provided to the raters:

> Express your judgment on the following statement, by assigning one of the values shown in Table 6 to each row.
> *"Property p_{new} captures the essential semantics of the relation between subject and object as it is expressed by the sentence."*

The results of the user-based evaluation of p_{new} are reported in Table 7. The three raters have independently judged the produced properties p_{new} very well designed and accurate (F-measure 0.83) in capturing the semantics of their associated pagelinks and linguistic trace, with a high inter-rater agreement (Kendall's

---

[40] http://isotta.cs.unibo.it:9191/sparql
[41] http://lov.okfn.org/dataset/lov/
[42] http://rtw.ml.cmu.edu/rtw/
[43] http://watson.kmi.open.ac.uk/WatsonWUI/
[44] bit.ly/1qd45AQ

Table 6. Likert scale values and associated criteria for evaluating p_{new}

Likert value	Judgement criteria
Strongly agree	The property is very well defined.
Agree	The property captures the relation semantics but the name can be improved.
Neutral	The property captures only partly the relation semantics but can be used.
Disagree	The property does not really capture the semantics of the relation.
Strongly Disagree	The property expresses something completely different from the relation semantics.

W 0.73). This result suggests that Legalo approach for automatically designing Semantic Web properties satisfies the cognitive-based requirements of this task, i.e. to generate a property name acceptable to a human for expressing a given intensional semantics.

Table 7. Evaluation results on the accuracy of p_{new}

Number of p_{new}	Precision	Recall	F-measure	Kendall's W[45]
629	0.72	0.97	0.83	0.73

User-Based Evaluation of Alignments *(p_{new}, p_{sw}).* The second evaluation task consisted in judging the proposed alignments to existing Semantic Web properties p_{sw} based on the information provided by their metadata i.e., comments and labels, and their domain and range (when available).

For each pair (p_{new}, p_{sw}) raters have been provided with the data of the previous evaluation entries extended with:

- p_{sw}
- rdfs:comment of p_{sw}
- rdfs:label of p_{sw}
- rdfs:domain of p_{sw}
- rdfs:range of p_{sw}

Table 8. An example of evaluation entry for the alignment between p_{new} and p_{sw}

p_{new}	p_{sw}	rdfs:comment	rdfs:label	rdfs:domain	rdfs:range
fred:locatedIn	geo:locatedIn[46]	Indicates that the subject resource is located in the object feature			geo:Feature

An example of evaluation entry for the alignment between p_{new} and p_{sw} is shown in Table 8.

The following evaluation guidelines have been provided to the raters:

Express your judgment on the following statement, by assigning one of the values shown in Table 9 to each row.
"Properties p_{new} and p_{sw} are interchangeable"

The results of the user-based evaluation of the alignments between p_{new} and p_{sw} are reported in Table 10. The three raters have independently judged the

---

[45] Kendall's W measures the inter-rater agreement. Values ranges from 0 (complete disagreement) to 1 (complete agreement).
[46] Prefix geo: stands for http://www.geonames.org/ontology#

Table 9. Likert scale values and associated criteria for evaluating alignments between p_{new} and p_{sw}

Likert value	Judgement criteria
Strongly agree	The two properties have exactly the same sense or p_{sw} is more general than p_{new}.
Agree	The two properties have a similar sense, enough to be either used for representing the same relation between subject and object.
Neutral	I am not sure if the two properties have the same sense.
Disagree	The properties have slightly different senses
Strongly Disagree	The properties have completely different senses.

Table 10. Evaluation results on the accuracy of the alignment between p_{new} and p_{sw}

# p_{new} with at least one p_{sw}	Total # of (p_{new}, p_{sw})	Levenshtein threshold	Precision	Kendall's W
250	693	0.7	0.84	0.76

proposed alignment very accurate (Precision 0.84) with a high inter-rater agreement (Kendall's W 0.76).

6   Discussion and Conclusion

The results of our experiment are very promising, although they also show that there is room for improvement.

Non-sense or Loose Relations. As for the production of p_{new}, the data collected by means of the user-based evaluation is a good source for observing possible emerging patterns indicating when a sentence does not express a strong relation between subject and object of a link. In fact, it can be the case sometimes that a link is put in a sentence just because it is a good practice do to so. Although we have noticed that such cases are not many, detecting them can allow us to improve the precision of our results by removing some of the p_{new} that represent "non-sense" relations.

Better Naming. Other emerging patterns can be observed from recurrent subgraph forms connecting subjects and objects, for which we can design more accurate naming strategies for p_{new}, hence improving their cognitive adequacy and alignment results. Additionally, we have analysed only a subset of thematic roles relations that are used by FRED for characterizing the participation of entities in event occurrences. In fact, thematic roles provide useful means for defining labels that can further improve p_{new} naming design strategies.

Alignment to Existing Semantic Web Properties. As for the alignment procedure, there is also space for improvement, since we addressed this task by computing a simple Levenshtein distance. More sophisticated alignment methods such as those resulting from the Ontology Alignment Initiative[45] or other approaches for entity linking such as SILK[46] [8] can be investigated for enhancing the alignment results. An interesting result is that our alignment results are

---

[45] http://oaei.ontologymatching.org/
[46] http://wifo5-03.informatik.uni-mannheim.de/bizer/silk/

good in terms of precision, although all properties that have been matched with a distance score > 0.70 came only from Watson[47] [4] and LOV[48]. We observed that properties retrieved from NELL[49] [3] all had an editing distance < 0.70 and almost none of them were judged appropriate. This suggests, in our opinion, that our naming design strategies are closer to the one used by humans, i.e. property names are cognitively well designed. In fact, Watson and LOV are repositories of Semantic Web authored ontologies and vocabularies, while NELL properties result from and artificial concatenation of categories learnt automatically.

As for the alignment recall, we could not compute a standard recall metrics because it is impossible to compute False Negative results i.e., all existing Semantic Web properties that would match p_{new} but that we did not retrieve. The relatively high number of missing properties suggests on one hand that a more sophisticated alignment method is needed. On the other hand, if we combine this result with the high value of accuracy of p_{new} and the proposed alignments between p_{new} and p_{sw}, it is reasonable to hypothesize that many cases reveal a lack of intensional coverage in Semantic Web vocabularies, and that our method can help filling this gap.

Conclusion. We have presented a novel approach, named *Legalo*, for uncovering the semantics of hyperlinks based on formal representation of natural language text, and heuristics associated with subgraph-patterns. The main novel aspects of Legalo approach are: property label generation, automatic link tagging, graph-based relation extraction.

Our hypothesis is that pagelinks provide a pragmatic trace of semantic relations between two entities, and that such semantic relations, their subjects and objects, can be revealed by processing their linguistic traces, i.e. sentences embedding pagelinks. Our experiment shows promising results: we produce accurate binary properties (F-measure 0.83) and provide alignments with a precision value of 0.84. A demo of Legalo Web service is available online[50], and the binary properties produced in this study can be accessed by means of a sparql endpoint[51].

Ongoing Work and Future Work. Currently, we are developing a generalized version of Legalo, able to work on any webpage and its hyperlinks. Referring to Figure 1, we focus on generalizing component 1*a* and 1*b*, as the *Semantic Web Property Extractor* and the rest of the pipeline are not Wikipedia-specific, although they can be further improved. The challenge is to design strategies for identifying subject and object of a semantic relation denoted by a hyperlink: a task *per-se* on the general Web. A preliminary demo of a generalized approach is available online[52]: it uses NER and disambiguation on DBpedia for addressing subject/object

---

[47] http://watson.kmi.open.ac.uk/WatsonWUI/
[48] http://lov.okfn.org/dataset/lov/
[49] http://rtw.ml.cmu.edu/rtw/
[50] http://wit.istc.cnr.it/legalo/wikipedia
[51] http://isotta.cs.unibo.it:9191/sparql
[52] http://wit.istc.cnr.it/stlab-tools/legalo/

identification. As future work, we intend to perform a large scale processing of hyperlinks for revealing their semantics. Additionally, we want to combine crowdsourcing annotation of results with a learning procedure that would allow Legalo to improve its design strategies, based on emerging recurrent subgraph patterns.

Acknowledgments. This work has been partly funded by the LabEx Empirical Foundations of Linguistics[53].

References

1. Bizer, C., Heath, T., Berners-Lee, T.: Linked data - the story so far. Int. J. Semantic Web Inf. Syst. 5(3), 1–22 (2009)
2. Bos, J., Nissim, M.: Combining discourse representation theory with framenet. In: Frames, Corpora, and Knowledge Representation, pp. 169–183. R. Rossini Favretti and Bononia University Press (2008)
3. Carlson, A., Betteridge, J., Kisiel, B., Settles, B., Hruschka Jr, E.R., Mitchell, T.M.: Toward an architecture for never-ending language learning. In: Proceedings of the Twenty-Fourth Conference on Artificial Intelligence, AAAI 2010 (2010)
4. d'Aquin, M., Motta, E., Sabou, M., Angeletou, S., Grindinoc, L., Lopez, V., Guidi, D.: Towards a new generation of semantic web applications. IEEE Intelligent Systems 23(3), 80–83 (2008)
5. Euzenat, J., Shvaiko, P.: Ontology Matching, 2nd edn., pp. 1–511. Springer (2013)
6. Gangemi, A., Nuzzolese, A.G., Presutti, V., Draicchio, F., Musetti, A., Ciancarini, P.: Automatic typing of dbpedia entities. In: International Semantic Web Conference (1), pp. 65–81 (2012)
7. Rizzo, G., Troncy, R., Hellmann, S., Bruemmer, M.: NERD meets NIF: Lifting NLP extraction results to the linked data cloud. In: LDOW, 5th Wks. on Linked Data on the Web, Lyon, France (April 2012)
8. Isele, R., Bizer, C.: Active learning of expressive linkage rules using genetic programming. J. Web Sem. 23, 2–15 (2013)
9. Khalili, A., Auer, S., Ngonga Ngomo, A.-C.: ConTEXT – lightweight text analytics using linked data. In: Presutti, V., d'Amato, C., Gandon, F., d'Aquin, M., Staab, S., Tordai, A. (eds.) ESWC 2014. LNCS, vol. 8465, pp. 628–643. Springer, Heidelberg (2014)
10. Mausam, Schmitz, M., Bart, R., Soderland, S., Etzioni, O.: Open language learning for information extraction. In: Proceedings of Conference on Empirical Methods in Natural Language Processing and Computational Natural Language Learning, EMNLP-CONLL (2012)
11. Navarro, G.: A guided tour to approximate string matching. ACM Comput. Surv. 33(1), 31–88 (2001)
12. Nuzzolese, A.G., Gangemi, A., Presutti, V., Ciancarini, P.: Encyclopedic Knowledge Patterns from Wikipedia Links. In: Aroyo, L., Welty, C., Alani, H., Taylor, J., Bernstein, A., Kagal, L., Noy, N., Blomqvist, E. (eds.) ISWC 2011, Part I. LNCS, vol. 7031, pp. 520–536. Springer, Heidelberg (2011)
13. Nuzzolese, A.G., Presutti, V., Gangemi, A., Musetti, A., Ciancarini, P.: Aemoo: exploring knowledge on the web. In: WebSci, pp. 272–275 (2013)
14. Presutti, V., Draicchio, F., Gangemi, A.: Knowledge extraction based on discourse representation theory and linguistic frames. In: ten Teije, A., Völker, J., Handschuh, S., Stuckenschmidt, H., d'Acquin, M., Nikolov, A., Aussenac-Gilles, N., Hernandez, N. (eds.) EKAW 2012. LNCS, vol. 7603, pp. 114–129. Springer, Heidelberg (2012)

---

[53] http://www.labex-efl.org

Closed-World Concept Induction for Learning in OWL Knowledge Bases

David Ratcliffe[1,2] and Kerry Taylor[2,1]

[1] College of Engineering and Computer Science
Australian National University, Canberra ACT 2601, Australia
[2] CSIRO Digital Productivity
CS & IT Building 108, North Road, Australian National University
GPO Box 664, Canberra, ACT 2601, Australia
{david.ratcliffe,kerry.taylor}@csiro.au

Abstract. We present a general-purpose method for inducing OWL class descriptions over data and knowledge captured with RDF and OWL in a closed-world way. We combine our approach with a top-down refinement-based search with Description Logic (DL) expressions which incorporates OWL background knowledge. Our methods are designed for speed and scalability to support analysis tasks like data mining over large knowledge-rich data sets. We compare our methods to a state-of-the-art DL learning tool with respect to a large benchmark problem to demonstrate the speed and effectiveness of our approach.

Keywords: concept induction, data mining, machine learning, DL, RDF, OWL.

1 Introduction

1.1 Motivation

Semantic Web technologies such as the Resource Description Framework (RDF) data model and the Web Ontology Language (OWL) have experienced wide uptake in recent years, particularly within the life sciences. Of particular interest to us are domains which seek to collect and organise large amounts of data and knowledge using RDF and OWL to aid experts in exploring their data. For example, the Crystallisation Data Exchange (XDX) Consortium in the field of protein crystallisation in structural biology aims to collect and integrate experimental data and knowledge with an OWL ontology to help domain experts construct hypotheses about experimental conditions which might be efficient crystallisation catalysts [1]. Similarly, the Kidney and Urinary Pathway Database (KUPKB) collects and organises data and knowledge with an OWL ontology relating to experiments in renal biology to help domain experts construct hypotheses about the causes of renal complications [2]. In domains such as these, automating hypothesis generation in light of data and formal background knowledge captured with OWL is possible with data mining and machine learning methods which have the potential to aid in the search for new scientific knowledge.

K. Janowicz et al. (Eds.): EKAW 2014, LNAI 8876, pp. 429–440, 2014.

Methods and systems have emerged in recent years for automatically inducing OWL concept expressions from RDF instance data. The goal of such methods so far has been to produce OWL concept descriptions which perfectly characterise a class for integration into an ontology, or which induce concepts to capture a classification rule or an interesting cluster in RDF data. These methods have the benefit of utilising expressive background ontologies to structure the search space and to provide an expressive yet comprehensible domain-specific vocabulary with which to pose hypotheses. Many of these such methods bring to bear theoretical results from concept learning in Inductive Logic Programming to Description Logics which underpin the formal semantics of OWL. Most notably, top-down refinement-based search methods have been explored with the DL-LEARNER [3], YINYANG [4], DL-FOIL [5] and FR-ONT [6] systems. Besides DL-LEARNER, these systems use hypothesis languages with limited expressivity and base their learning methods on instance checking under the open-world assumption which can be computationally expensive.

In our work, we aim to improve upon the expressivity, speed and scalability of these methods so as to make them viable for data mining large RDF/OWL knowledge-bases. To achieve this, we have focussed on constraining the search space of OWL expressions under a *closed-world assumption* (CWA), which is commonly employed in machine learning and data mining, yet is uncommon for use with OWL. In this paper, we formally characterise a closed-world interpretation for concept induction in the expressive concept language known as $\mathcal{ALCOQ}$ and describe how it can be used to limit the search space to improve speed and scalability of the search for concept expressions. We also describe how induction with a closed-world assumption can lead to concepts which are unsatisfiable under an open-world assumption with respect to a background ontology.

2 Concept Learning in Description Logics

The setting in which we are considering concept induction involves an OWL background ontology with a set of RDF data which are assertions of instances of various concepts and roles in the ontology. Amongst these is a set of classes $\mathbf{P} = \{P_1, \ldots, P_n\}$ for $n \geq 1$ which are called *label classes* which capture disjoint sets of named instances (RDF resources) which are *examples* for a learning problem. In the *supervised machine learning classification* $(n > 1)$ setting, we usually aim to induce concept expressions which describe examples from one label class and none other. *Unsupervised learning* $(n = 1)$ aims to induce a hypothesis which captures a significant proportion of a set of examples (e.g. a *cluster*).

The remainder of this section is organised as follows. §2.1 formally introduces Description Logics (DLs); §2.2 describes a closed-world interpretation for use in learning expressive DL expressions; §2.3 introduces a refinement-based search method for concept induction, and §2.4 concludes with some considerations for closed-world concept induction against open-world background knowledge.

2.1   Description Logics

Description Logics (DL) are a family of knowledge representation languages based on decidable fragments of first-order logic [7]. The formal semantics of OWL is underpinned by various DLs, such as $\mathcal{SROIQ}$ which provides semantics for the OWL2-DL profile[1]. OWL classes and properties are described as concepts and roles (respectively) in DL terminology, which we will now use interchangeably throughout this paper. A DL *knowledge base* is a pair $\mathcal{K} = (\mathcal{T}, \mathcal{A})$, where $\mathcal{A}$ is called the *assertional box* (ABox) which contains a set of *assertions* declaring named individuals to be known as *instances* of *concepts* such as $Car(c_0)$, $Engine(e_0)$ and to associate individuals with roles, such as $hasEngine(c_0, e_0)$. $\mathcal{T}$ is called the *terminological box* (TBox) containing a set of *inclusion axioms* which assert implications between instances belonging to one concept (role) as also belonging to another concept (role) in the form $C \sqsubseteq D$, denoting that all instances (tuples) of concept (role) C imply membership in concept (role) D, for example $Car \sqsubseteq Vehicle$ ($hasEngine \sqsubseteq hasPart$). An *interpretation* is a pair $(\Delta^{\mathcal{I}}, \cdot^{\mathcal{I}})$ where $\Delta^{\mathcal{I}}$ represents the set of all domain individuals and $\cdot^{\mathcal{I}}$ is a mapping from any concept C to a subset of the domain $C^{\mathcal{I}} \subseteq \Delta^{\mathcal{I}}$, any role R to $R^{\mathcal{I}} \subseteq \Delta^{\mathcal{I}} \times \Delta^{\mathcal{I}}$ and individuals i to an element $i^{\mathcal{I}} \in \Delta^{\mathcal{I}}$. For example, the instances $c_0^{\mathcal{I}}, e_0^{\mathcal{I}} \in \Delta^{\mathcal{I}}$, $c_0^{\mathcal{I}} \in Car^{\mathcal{I}}$, $e_0^{\mathcal{I}} \in Engine^{\mathcal{I}}$ and the tuple $\langle c_0^{\mathcal{I}}, e_0^{\mathcal{I}} \rangle \in hasEngine^{\mathcal{I}}$. We say that an interpretation $\mathcal{I}$ is a *model* of (or, *satisfies*) $\mathcal{T}$ if, for all axioms $C \sqsubseteq D$ in $\mathcal{T}$, we have $C^{\mathcal{I}} \subseteq D^{\mathcal{I}}$. A knowledge base $\mathcal{K}$ is said to *entail* some assertion $C(i)$ as $\mathcal{K} \models C(i)$ if, for all interpretations $\mathcal{I}$, $i \in C^{\mathcal{I}}$ (also, $\mathcal{I} \models C(i)$).

2.2   Closed-World DL Interpretation

An *open-world assumption* (OWA) is typically made of the DLs which underpin OWL knowledge-bases, in that if $\mathcal{K} \not\models \psi$, then it does not follow that $\mathcal{K} \models \neg\psi$ which would otherwise follow under a *closed-world assumption* (CWA). For example, if it cannot be shown that $x^{\mathcal{I}} \in C^{\mathcal{I}}$, then we do not assume that $x^{\mathcal{I}} \in (\neg C)^{\mathcal{I}}$, yet under a closed-world assumption the latter would be implied.

An appropriate closed-world interpretation which is applicable to the expressive DL known as $\mathcal{SROIQ}$ (corresponding to OWL2-DL) knowledge bases has been described by Tao et. al. [8] as the *IC-interpretation* for handling integrity constraints in OWL. This interpretation is defined as the pair $(\mathcal{I}, \mathcal{U})$ where $\mathcal{I}$ is a $\mathcal{SROIQ}$ interpretation defined over the domain $\Delta^{\mathcal{I}}$ and $\mathcal{U}$ is the set of all first-order models of a $\mathcal{SROIQ}$ knowledge base. The interpretation function $\cdot^{\mathcal{I},\mathcal{U}}$ maps concepts and roles to sets as follows, where the set N_I contains the named individuals of $\mathcal{K}$:

$$C^{\mathcal{I},\mathcal{U}} = \{x^{\mathcal{I}} : x \in N_I \text{ s.t. } \forall \mathcal{J} \in \mathcal{U}, x^{\mathcal{J}} \in C^{\mathcal{J}}\}$$
$$R^{\mathcal{I},\mathcal{U}} = \{\langle x^{\mathcal{I}}, y^{\mathcal{I}} \rangle : x, y \in N_I \text{ s.t. } \forall \mathcal{J} \in \mathcal{U}, \langle x^{\mathcal{J}}, y^{\mathcal{J}} \rangle \in R^{\mathcal{J}}\}$$

The interpretations $C^{\mathcal{I},\mathcal{U}}$ and $R^{\mathcal{I},\mathcal{U}}$ contain only what is *known* in $\mathcal{K}$, and all other known individuals (or tuples thereof) are assumed to lie in the negation $(\neg C)^{\mathcal{I},\mathcal{U}}$

---

[1] See http://www.w3.org/TR/owl2-direct-semantics/ for more details.

and $(\neg R)^{\mathcal{I},\mathcal{U}}$ respectively. The interpretation extends to arbitrary concept expressions in $\mathcal{ALCOQ}$ inductively as follows, where $\sharp$ denotes set cardinality:

$$\top^{\mathcal{I},\mathcal{U}} = \Delta^{\mathcal{I},\mathcal{U}}$$
$$\bot^{\mathcal{I},\mathcal{U}} = \emptyset$$
$$(\neg A)^{\mathcal{I},\mathcal{U}} = \Delta^{\mathcal{I},\mathcal{U}} \setminus A^{\mathcal{I},\mathcal{U}}$$
$$(C \sqcap D)^{\mathcal{I},\mathcal{U}} = C^{\mathcal{I},\mathcal{U}} \cap D^{\mathcal{I},\mathcal{U}}$$
$$(C \sqcup D)^{\mathcal{I},\mathcal{U}} = C^{\mathcal{I},\mathcal{U}} \cup D^{\mathcal{I},\mathcal{U}}$$
$$\{x\}^{\mathcal{I},\mathcal{U}} = \{x : x \in \Delta^{\mathcal{I},\mathcal{U}}\}$$
$$(\exists R.C)^{\mathcal{I},\mathcal{U}} = \{x : x \in \Delta^{\mathcal{I},\mathcal{U}} \text{ s.t. } \exists y.\langle x,y \rangle \in R^{\mathcal{I},\mathcal{U}} \wedge y \in C^{\mathcal{I},\mathcal{U}}\}$$
$$(\forall R.C)^{\mathcal{I},\mathcal{U}} = \{x : x \in \Delta^{\mathcal{I},\mathcal{U}} \text{ s.t. } \forall y.\langle x,y \rangle \in R^{\mathcal{I},\mathcal{U}} \rightarrow y \in C^{\mathcal{I},\mathcal{U}}\}$$
$$(\geqslant n R.C)^{\mathcal{I},\mathcal{U}} = \{x : x \in \Delta^{\mathcal{I},\mathcal{U}} \text{ s.t. } \sharp\{y.\langle x,y \rangle \in R^{\mathcal{I},\mathcal{U}} \wedge y \in C^{\mathcal{I},\mathcal{U}}\} \geqslant n\}$$
$$(\leqslant n R.C)^{\mathcal{I},\mathcal{U}} = \{x : x \in \Delta^{\mathcal{I},\mathcal{U}} \text{ s.t. } \sharp\{y.\langle x,y \rangle \in R^{\mathcal{I},\mathcal{U}} \wedge y \in C^{\mathcal{I},\mathcal{U}}\} \leqslant n\}$$

This interpretation has several properties which make it suitable for efficient concept induction for data mining and machine learning in DL knowledge-bases. Firstly, the closed-world assumption is often used in data mining and machine learning, as we commonly assume that knowledge of our example instance data is complete. Secondly, concept learning algorithms which generate hypotheses typically evaluate them in terms of their *coverage* over the example data. In a DL setting, hypotheses as concept expressions are checked for their example coverage by *instance checking*. With an open-world assumption, instance checking is performed by entailment which can be computationally expensive for knowledge-bases with expressive background ontologies, such as N2ExpTime-complete for OWL2-DL based on $\mathcal{SROIQ}$ [9]. Learning algorithms which induce and test very many concept expressions rely on performing coverage testing quickly, so the high complexity of instance checking by entailment over expressive DLs is an impediment to learning, as we cannot afford to re-classify the knowledge-base each time a new candidate expression is generated to determine its cover. Furthermore, coverage checking by entailment in an open-world will fail to indicate instance membership in concepts such as $\forall r.C$, $\leqslant^n r.C$ or $\neg C$ unless explicitly asserted against equivalent expressions in the ABox. However, inducing concepts with these constructs may be helpful and effective in characterising hypotheses.

One approach to address the complexity of coverage checking for concept learning is taken by the DL-LEARNER system which pre-classifies the knowledge-base (wrt. $\mathcal{I}$) with a reasoner. This computes the set of all named individuals in the interpretation of each concept and role in $\mathcal{K}$. While initially complex, the resulting completed ABox then contains all possible *known* assertions about atomic concepts and roles in the TBox, which reflects their $(\mathcal{I},\mathcal{U})$ interpretation. The interpretation of any arbitrary $\mathcal{ALCOQ}$ concept C can then be computed directly with respect to the definition of $(\mathcal{I},\mathcal{U})$, which admits an exponential-time algorithm in the size of the expression and the size of the completed ABox. While not yet formally described, this technique has been referred to as Fast Instance Checks (FIC) in the DL-LEARNER system [10]. Basically, a check proceeds by testing if some named instance $a^{\mathcal{I},\mathcal{U}} \in C^{\mathcal{I},\mathcal{U}}$ by querying the ABox for named instances of sub-expressions of C in a top-down, depth-first backtracking manner until an interpretation is found which satisfies C. When incorporated into a learning algorithm which generates concepts as candidates in a search, this method is known as *learning by interpretation*: we test if the known instances in the ABox are a model of C under $(\mathcal{I}, \mathcal{U})$. We will later show that this method of instance checking can be very fast in practice as it relies on a static database of instances for which re-classification of the knowledge-base is not required.

2.3   Inducing Concepts with Refinement Operators

To induce concept expressions in a knowledge-base, so-called *refinement operators* can be used to traverse the space of concepts which are ordered by the subsumption relation $\sqsubseteq$ (a partial order over concept expressions). Formally, if $(S, \sqsubseteq)$ is the ordered space of concepts, a downward (upward) refinement operator ρ is a mapping from S to 2^S such that for any $C \in S$ we have $C' \in \rho(C)$ implies $C' \sqsubseteq C$ ($C \sqsubseteq C'$). C' is called a *specialisation* (*generalisation*) of C. For example, concept C may be specialised with a refinement step which produces the expression $C \sqcap D$. Clearly, as $C \sqcap D \sqsubseteq C$, this is a downward refinement step. Other steps which provide downward (upward) refinements can be defined over the other elements of the hypothesis language. Detailed treatments of various refinement operators for expressive and inexpressive DLs and their properties have recently been explored by Lehmann and Hitzler [11].

The space of concept expressions induced by $\sqsubseteq_{(\mathcal{I}, \mathcal{U})}$ may be more constrained than the space induced by $\sqsubseteq_{\mathcal{I}}$. For example, consider the axiom $C \sqsubseteq_{\mathcal{I}} D \in \mathcal{T}$, where $C \equiv_{(\mathcal{I}, \mathcal{U})} D$. In this case, we can discard the concept C and prefer the more general D for the purposes of concept induction in a closed-world. Also, consider the case where $\mathcal{I} \not\models C \sqcap D \sqsubseteq \bot$ (i.e. C and D are not disjoint in the original knowledge-base). Despite this, the absence of any named individual as an instance of both C and D mean that they are disjoint under $(\mathcal{I}, \mathcal{U})$, and their conjunction $C \sqcap D$ should never be attempted by the refinement operator.

Prior to executing a learning algorithm, the subsumption relationships between atomic names in N_A and N_R entailed by $(\mathcal{I}, \mathcal{U})$ can be pre-computed to construct a constrained space in which to search for concepts using a refinement operator. For example, in any knowledge-base, there is a finite set M of expressions of the form $(A_0 \sqcap \ldots \sqcap A_i)$ where $i \geqslant 0$, A are atomic concept names or single instance nominals $\{a\}$, and which is *minimal* where no two operands can be related by $\sqsubseteq_{(\mathcal{I}, \mathcal{U})}$. The set M captures concepts comprised of atomic terms which describe a subset of N_I. The set M of such concepts can also be limited to *localised sub-domains* as follows. The set of named example instances for the concept induction problem lie in the top-level *sub-domain* $\Delta_\top^{\mathcal{I}, \mathcal{U}} \subseteq \Delta^{\mathcal{I}, \mathcal{U}}$. A sub-domain Δ_θ captures the set of individuals from N_I in a locally confined context relative to some concept expression θ. For example, consider the expression $A \sqcap \exists r.(\top)$. The sub-domain $\Delta_{\exists r^-.(A)}^{\mathcal{I}, \mathcal{U}} \subseteq \top^{\mathcal{I}, \mathcal{U}}$ captures the set of individuals of $\top$ which are r-successors of those in A. Localised sub-domains can be computed for any such expression relative to the closed-world interpretation and can be used as the basis for defining a *localised* set M_θ which captures only those atomic concept names which are pairwise non-redundant in conjunction to describe instances in the context of θ. This is useful to a refinement operator, for example, in application to the sub-expression $\top$ in this example as $M_{r^-.(A)}$ which captures the non-redundant set of concept expressions which can be used to specialise the expression.

For example, we may compute the set of localised sub-domains for every nested role path which is accessible from the example instances, such as $L = \{\Delta_\top, \Delta_{\exists r^-.\top}, \ldots, \Delta_{\exists s^-.(\exists t^-.(\ldots \top))}\}$. We can then compute the sets M_θ for every $\Delta_\theta \in L$, and use these when refining atomic concepts for each sub-expression in nested role expressions. Note that negated atomic concepts $(\neg A)^{\mathcal{I},\mathcal{U}}$ for any $A \in M_\theta$ can also be defined locally as $\Delta_\theta^{\mathcal{I},\mathcal{U}} \setminus A^{\mathcal{I},\mathcal{U}}$, which can also be compared to other terms in M_θ with respect to $\sqsubseteq_{(\mathcal{I},\mathcal{U})}$.

The concept expressions in M_θ, which we denote C^+, are all the positively-defined minimal expressions capturing instances in the sub-domain of Δ_θ. The subsumption relation $\sqsubseteq_{(\mathcal{I},\mathcal{U})}$ imposes a lattice structure relating the concepts $C^+ \in M_\theta$, and can be used to determine which atomic concepts in M_θ are subsumed, or overlap, any other concept C^+. These atomic concepts can be combined with those concepts which they are subsumed by, or overlap with, as $C^+ \sqcap \neg A$. We define concepts of this kind as C^-, and describe them as being *maximal* if they are of the form $C^+ \sqcap (\sqcap \neg A_i)$ where no term $\neg A_i$ is redundant, and all possible such terms are included for each $C^+ \in M_\theta$. We denote the set of all maximal concepts C^- for some local sub-domain Δ_θ as M_θ^-, which is used when performing generalisation steps in the refinement search by excluding a single $\neg A$ subexpression from the conjunction. Following is an example of a downward (upward) refinement operator $\rho_\theta^\downarrow$ ($\rho_\theta^\uparrow$) which utilises this information for the concept language $\mathcal{ALCOQ}$:

$$\rho_\theta^\downarrow(\bot) \quad = \emptyset \tag{1}$$

$$\rho_\theta^\downarrow(\top) \quad = \{C_1^+ \sqcup \ldots \sqcup C_m^+ \mid C_i^+ \in M_\theta, 1 \leqslant m \leqslant max_\sqcup\} \tag{2}$$

$$\rho_\theta^\downarrow(\phi) \quad = \{\phi \sqcap \neg A \mid A \in M_\theta\} \cup$$
$$\{\phi \sqcap \geqslant^n r.(C_i^+) \mid C_i^+ \in M_{\exists r^-.\theta}, 1 \leqslant n \leqslant max_{\theta,r}\} \cup$$
$$\{\phi \sqcap \leqslant^n r.(C_i^-) \mid C_i^- \in M_{\exists r^-.\theta}^-, 0 \leqslant n \leqslant max_{\theta,r} - 1\} \cup$$
$$\{\phi \sqcap \forall r.(C_i^+) \mid C_i^+ \in M_{\exists r^-.\theta}\} \tag{3}$$

$$\rho_\theta^\downarrow(\bigsqcup \Phi) \quad = \{\bigsqcup \Psi \mid \Psi = \Phi \setminus \{\phi_i\} \cup \rho_\theta^\downarrow(\phi_i), \phi_i \in \Phi\} \tag{4}$$

$$\rho_\theta^\downarrow(\forall r.(\phi)) \quad = \{\forall r.(\psi) \mid \psi \in \rho_{\exists r^-.\theta}^\downarrow(\phi)\} \tag{5}$$

$$\rho_\theta^\downarrow(\geqslant^n r.(\phi)) = \{\geqslant^n r.(\psi) \mid \psi \in \rho_{\exists r^-.\theta}^\downarrow(\phi)\} \tag{6}$$

$$\rho_\theta^\downarrow(\leqslant^n r.(\phi)) = \{\leqslant^n r.(\psi) \mid \psi \in \rho_{\exists r^-.\theta}^\downarrow(\phi)\} \tag{7}$$

$$\rho_\theta^\uparrow(\bot) \quad = \{C_i^- \mid C_i^- \in M_\theta^-\} \tag{8}$$

$$\rho_\theta^\uparrow(\sqcap \Phi) \quad = \{\sqcap \Psi \mid \Psi = \Phi \setminus \{\neg A\}, \neg A \in \Phi\} \tag{9}$$

$$\rho_\theta^\uparrow(\phi) \quad = \{\phi \sqcup \bot\} \tag{10}$$

where $max_\sqcup$ is a pre-set maximum number of disjunct operands, $max_{\theta,r}$ is the maximum number of any r-successors in context θ, and $\sqcap \Phi$ ($\bigsqcup \Phi$) refers to the conjunction (disjunction) of the set of expressions $\Phi = \{\phi_1, \ldots, \phi_n\}$. Note that ρ generates expressions in *negation normal form* (nnf) where $\neg$ only appears in front of atomic concept names A as opposed to negations of arbitrary concepts ($\neg C$ which can always be transformed into equivalent nnf concepts). This refinement operator is *incomplete* in that certain $\mathcal{ALCOQ}$ concept expressions cannot be reached. This is because we do not define role expressions nested within maximum quantified role expressions, as we do not prescribe an *upward* refinement method for such expressions, and the fact that expressions are globally bounded to a pre-set maximum number of disjuncts. The operator ρ also has the properties of *local finiteness* (all refinements of any concept are a finite set of new concepts); *improperness* in that refinements of any concept C may result in a semantically equivalent concept D where $C^{\mathcal{I},\mathcal{U}} = D^{\mathcal{I},\mathcal{U}}$, and *redundancy* in that multiple refinement chains of a single concept C may lead to semantically equivalent concepts. Of these properties, *properness* and *redundancy* most influence the efficiency of the operator to search the space of concepts. However, the refinement steps are largely confined to options which are non-redundant under $(\mathcal{I},\mathcal{U})$, thus reducing the amount of redundancy in the search.

2.4 Considerations for Concept Induction with $(\mathcal{I},\mathcal{U})$

Under the closed-world interpretation $(\mathcal{I},\mathcal{U})$, it is possible to induce a concept expression H which has a non-empty interpretation $H^{\mathcal{I},\mathcal{U}} \neq \emptyset$ but is actually unsatisfiable with respect to a knowledge-base in an open world ($H^{\mathcal{I}} = \emptyset$). For example, consider a knowledge base $\mathcal{K} = (\mathcal{T},\mathcal{A})$ where $\mathcal{A} = \{A(i), p(i,j), C(j)\}$ and $\mathcal{T} = \{A \sqsubseteq {}^{\geqslant 2}p.C\}$. Recall that an interpretation $(\mathcal{I},\mathcal{U})$ is a *model* of $\mathcal{T}$ if, for all axioms $C \sqsubseteq D \in \mathcal{T}$ we have $C^{\mathcal{I},\mathcal{U}} \subseteq D^{\mathcal{I},\mathcal{U}}$. In this example, $A^{\mathcal{I},\mathcal{U}} = \{i\}$ and $({}^{\geqslant 2}p.C)^{\mathcal{I},\mathcal{U}} = \emptyset$ and therefore $(\mathcal{I},\mathcal{U})$ does not satisfy $\mathcal{T}$. The underlying problem here is that the derivation of the interpretation $({}^{\geqslant 2}p.C)^{\mathcal{I},\mathcal{U}}$ relied exclusively on *known* information in $\mathcal{K}$. If information is *missing* from $\mathcal{A}$ with respect to $\mathcal{T}$, it may lead a learning algorithm relying on $(\mathcal{I},\mathcal{U})$ for computing hypothesis coverage to produce an expression which is unsatisfiable with respect to $\mathcal{T}$. In this case, one such expression is $(A \sqcap {}^{\leqslant 1}p.C)$ where $(A \sqcap {}^{\leqslant 1}p.C)^{\mathcal{I},\mathcal{U}} = \{i\}$, but clearly this expression is unsatisfiable with respect to $\mathcal{T}$ as $(A \sqcap {}^{\leqslant 1}p.C)^{\mathcal{I}} = \emptyset$.

A related problem occurs, for example, when the knowledge base $\mathcal{K} = (\mathcal{T},\mathcal{A})$ where $\mathcal{A} = \{P_1(i), P_2(j), p(i,k)\}$ and $\mathcal{T} = \{P_1 \sqsubseteq C, P_2 \sqsubseteq C, C \sqsubseteq \exists p.\top\}$ for the label classes P_1 and P_2. In this case, we find that $(\exists p.\top)^{\mathcal{I}} = \{i^{\mathcal{I}}, j^{\mathcal{I}}, \ldots\}$, however $(\exists p.\top)^{\mathcal{I},\mathcal{U}} = \{i\}$ as no p-successor of j is known in $\mathcal{A}$. From the perspective of a machine learner performing binary classification, the cover of hypothesis $\exists p.\top$ computed by $(\mathcal{I},\mathcal{U})$ appears to correctly describe all instances of partition P_1 and no instances of P_2, and is thus considered a perfect characterisation of P_1. Clearly however, with respect to $\mathcal{T}$, such a characterisation is incorrect.

The situation of inducing an unsatisfiable hypothesis with respect to $\mathcal{T}$ or mischaracterising its performance stems from data which is *missing in $\mathcal{A}$ with respect to $\mathcal{T}$*. In general, a hypothesis H (or a sub-expression thereof) which effectively discriminates examples (or parts thereof) with label P_0 from others in P_1 may only have been induced because data was present in the cover of H for examples in P_0 and was otherwise missing on all those in P_1. It is the *distribution* of missing data which influences an induction method to generate H. However, it is difficult to generally characterise *which* missing data will influence a concept learner to generate problematic concepts, as this depends on the distribution of missing data and the learning strategy. Nevertheless, a method exists for

Algorithm 1. Beam Search for Top-k Concepts

```
 1: F := {⊤}
 2: S := ∅
 3: while ♯F > 0 and ♯S < S_MAX do
 4:     h_max ∈ arg max_{h∈F} util(h)              ▷ Arbitrary equal best hypothesis
 5:     F := F \ {h_max}                           ▷ Remove the chosen best from the frontier
 6:     for all h' ∈ ρ_θ^↓(h_max) do               ▷ For each single-step refinement of h_max
 7:         u_{h'} := util(h')                      ▷ Determine performance based on the cover
 8:         if not insuff(u_{h'}) and ∀s ∈ S, h' ⊑_{I,U} s → u_{h'} > util(s) then
 9:             if suff(u_{h'}) then
10:                 S := S ∪ {h'}
11:             else
12:                 F := F ∪ {h'}
13:                 if ♯F > F_MAX then             ▷ Beam width exceeded
14:                     h_min ∈ arg min_{h∈F} util(h)   ▷ Arbitrary equal worst hypothesis
15:                     F := F \ {h_min}
16:                 end if
17:             end if
18:         end if
19:         S_sub := {s : s ∈ S, s ⊑_{I,U} h' ∧ util(s) ⩽ u_{h'}}
20:         S := (S ∪ {h'}) \ S_sub
21:     end for
22: end while
```

recognising that data is missing in $\mathcal{K}$, which is to perform *integrity checking* of assertions in $\mathcal{A}$ against axioms in $\mathcal{T}$ [8]. This involves testing that, for each axiom $C \sqsubseteq D$ in $\mathcal{T}$, the condition $C^{\mathcal{I},\mathcal{U}} \subseteq D^{\mathcal{I},\mathcal{U}}$ holds[2]. If it does not, instances in $C^{\mathcal{I},\mathcal{U}}$ which are not in $D^{\mathcal{I},\mathcal{U}}$ have missing data. Data missing from D could be handled by excluding any examples incorporating this data from the learning problem, or by entirely pruning sub-parts from all examples where data is missing so the expressions which may otherwise capture them are not relied upon in the learning problem. Alternatively, asserting new data which is detected to be missing may be possible [12].

We believe that the benefits of using $(\mathcal{I},\mathcal{U})$ for efficient coverage testing far outweigh the drawbacks which include the possibility of generating expressions which violate axioms in $\mathcal{T}$. This is particularly the case when we aim to use concept induction to perform analyses over the data such as data mining for patterns, where concepts are induced to be human readable descriptions of interesting patterns in the database, and are not intended to be re-incorporated into the TBox.

2.5   Learning Procedure

Algorithm 1 is a general-purpose beam search for finding the top-k OWL class hypothesis expressions ranked by a utility function, *util*. Hypotheses are refined by $\rho_\theta^\downarrow$ and, if suitable, are stored in a frontier set F in descending order by utility,

---

[2] Possibly subject to expressivity restrictions on the background knowledge [8].

up to some maximum cardinality F_{MAX} (the beam width). The boolean functions *suff* (*insuff*) capture the conditions under which hypotheses can (never) be considered solutions. The definition of *util*, and thus which hypotheses are extracted first from F for refinement at any point in the algorithm, depends on the learning problem. For example, *util* may rank hypotheses based a function of their length (the number of symbols in the expression) together with some *quality* function, $qual(H)$. For example, in an unsupervised learning setting ($\mathbf{P} = \{P_1\}$), *relative frequency* (support) defined as $qual(H) = \frac{\sharp H^{\mathcal{I},\mathcal{U}}}{\sharp P_1}$ can be thresholded as $suff(H) = qual(H) \geqslant 0.75$ (hypotheses covering at least 75% of all examples) and where $insuff(H) = qual(H) < 0.75$. Care must be taken such that *insuff* does not force the rejection of hypotheses which may *increase* their value of $qual$ with further refinements[3]. An example of such a quality function is *accuracy* and is often used in the setting of classification (e.g., $\mathbf{P} = \{P_1, P_2\}$ to describe P_1) as $acc(H) = \frac{|H^{\mathcal{I},\mathcal{U}} \cap P_1| + |P_2 \setminus H^{\mathcal{I},\mathcal{U}}|}{|P_1| + |P_2|}$. Here, we can set $suff(H) = acc(H) \geqslant 0.75$ (solutions have $\geqslant 75\%$ accuracy) and $insuff(H) = |H^{\mathcal{I},\mathcal{U}} \cap P_1| + |P_2| - 0.75(|P_1| + |P_2|) < |H^{\mathcal{I},\mathcal{U}} \cap P_2|$ (capturing the fact that no hypothesis covering less than a certain number of examples from P_1 can ever have an accuracy $\geqslant 75\%$). Line 8 of Algorithm 1 ensures that weak hypotheses which cover subsets of examples of relatively stronger and more general solutions are not considered. Similarly, on line 19, S_{sub} is computed to contain the set of solutions which are subsumed by a hypothesis with a utility at least as strong. Elements of S_{sub} are rejected from the solution set in light of the new hypothesis in this case. The algorithm terminates when at least S_{MAX} solutions are found or the frontier becomes empty, but could be terminated after a fixed time to inspect any current best solutions in S.

3   Implementation and Evaluation

We have tested Algorithm 1 with a Java application written using the OWL-API [13] and the Pellet OWL reasoner [14]. In our implementation, named individuals in local sub-domains are mapped to integers in the range $[0, |\Delta_\theta|]$ to permit efficient set operations when computing the $(\mathcal{I}, \mathcal{U})$ interpretation of concepts. Additionally, our implementation computes all entailments of the form $A_0 \sqsubseteq_{(\mathcal{I},\mathcal{U})} A_1$ between atoms described in §2.3 to infer equivalence, subsumption and disjointness in each local sub-domain prior to executing the algorithm.

   To measure the performance of our learning algorithm and refinement operator, we profiled our software using the carcinogenesis data set[4] for the problem of binary classification. This data set consists of an OWL ontology with 145 classes, 19 properties, and around 22,000 individuals amounting to around 98,000 RDF triples. We tested our software on a 2.8GHz Intel-i7 machine with 8Gb RAM. Loading and classifying the knowledge base using Pellet took 20 seconds and a

---

[3] In machine learning, such functions (including accuracy) are known as not having the property of *anti-monotonicity*.

[4] Available from http://dl-learner.org/wiki/Carcinogenesis

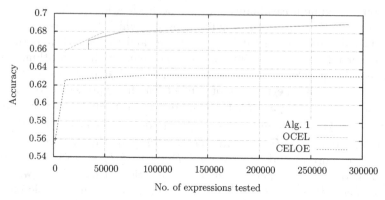

Fig. 1. Plot of the number of hypotheses generated and tested against the best accuracy for the carcinogenesis problem[4]. Each point is labelled with the time in seconds when the new best concept was found. Note that Alg 1., CELOE and OCEL were terminated after 44 seconds, 600 seconds and 2000 seconds, respectively; see Figure 2 for details.

further 20 seconds to compute $(\mathcal{I}, \mathcal{U})$ entailments revealing the relationship of atoms under $(\mathcal{I}, \mathcal{U})$ in each local sub-domain (see §2.3 for more detail).

Alg. 1			OCEL			CELOE		
Accuracy	Searched	Time (s)	Accuracy	Searched	Time (s)	Accuracy	Searched	Time (s)
0.66	33,799	5.2	0.659	10,820	11.1	0.555	987	4.3
0.67	33,725	6.8	0.671	32,829	741	0.626	10,953	11.5
0.68	66,940	9.9	0.6766	42,939	1506	0.632	91,104	98.7
0.69	286,003	44.52	0.6795	48,689	2000	0.632	855,197	600

Fig. 2. Data for Figure 1 showing the time taken to arrive at concepts with particular accuracy after searching and testing a number of concept expressions

We observed that with our implementation, high-accuracy concepts of lengths between 10 and 15 were generated in less than one minute, the best concept being produced after 44.5 seconds with 69.9% accuracy with a fixed maximum false discovery rate of 0.32. We then executed the experiment with DL-LEARNER using each of the main class learning algorithms it implements, OCEL and CELOE, which generate concept expressions in the same DL language $\mathcal{ALCOQ}$. Our goal was to test the speed and efficiency of our method and implementation in finding high-accuracy concepts against these algorithms.

Our first test was with the OCEL algorithm which tested a total of 48,689 expressions in 2000 seconds, locating a concept with a highest accuracy of 67.95%. Secondly, we tried the CELOE algorithm which we let test 855,197 expressions in 600 seconds, locating a concept with a best accuracy of 63.2%. A (truncated) plot of the results are shown in Figure 1. These results show that, for this problem, our implementation significantly outperforms both OCEL and CELOE by locating high-accuracy concepts in much less time, as summarised in Figure 2. Each implementation utilised a single thread to search and test expressions for which coverage was computed using the FIC method (§2.2). We believe that our implementation gained significant advantage from using the constraints implied by the $(\mathcal{I}, \mathcal{U})$ interpretation to speed up both the search for concepts but also their testing, as the interpretation permitted us to store the database in memory at runtime and not require any complex reasoner instance checks. We note that the under-performance of the CELOE algorithm in this test may be explained by the fact that it is geared towards searching for short concepts, whereas high-accuracy concepts for this problem appear to be long.

Note that, in our implementation, the quality function used by the main search algorithm was chosen to align with those used by OCEL and CELOE, which was to use accuracy, accuracy gain and a concept length penalty as $util(H) = acc(H) + 0.5(acc(H) - acc(H')) - 0.2 \cdot length(H)$, where $acc(H)$ is the accuracy of H over the full example data set (see §2.5) and H' is a (parent) concept which was refined in one step to reach H.

4   Conclusion and Future Work

We have presented a closed-world interpretation suitable for concept induction by refinement-based search methods in OWL knowledge bases which may be underpinned by highly expressive description logics. We have also described a refinement operator for the concept language $\mathcal{ALCOQ}$ which leverages the constraints imposed upon the space of concept expressions structured by $\sqsubseteq$ under the closed-world interpretation. We have also presented a general-purpose algorithm for concept induction suitable for a variety of data mining and machine learning tasks involving this refinement operator. Our test over a large dataset representing a benchmark classification problem (carcinogenesis) reveals that our methods and implementation are efficient and outperforms the DL-LEARNER system using either the OCEL or the CELOE class expression algorithms.

Current work includes developing our implementation specifically for performing redundancy-aware top-k pattern mining in parallel, for which the optimisations we have presented in this paper are especially desirable when analysing large knowledge bases using highly expressive DL hypothesis languages. We are also extending the refinement operator to efficiently handle concrete domains to account for OWL datatype expressions, primarily numerical range restrictions. We are aiming to release an implementation of our methods as a branch of the DL-LEARNER implementation which is open-source[5]. Finally, we are currently applying our methods to a large-scale problem in the field of structural biology called protein crystallisation [15,1] for which they were primarily designed.

References

1. Newman, J., Bolton, E.E., Müller-Dieckmann, J., Fazio, V.J., Gallagher, D.T., Lovell, D., Luft, J.R., Peat, T.S., Ratcliffe, D., Sayle, R.A., Snell, E.H., Taylor, K., Vallotton, P., Velanker, S., von Delft, F.: On the need for an international effort to capture, share and use crystallization screening data. Acta Crystallographica Section F Structural Biology and Crystallization Communications 68(3), 253–258 (2012)

---

[5] DL-LEARNER project page: `http://aksw.org/Projects/DLLearner.html`

2. Klein, J., Jupp, S., Moulos, P., Fernandez, M., Buffin-Meyer, B., Casemayou, A., Chaaya, R., Charonis, A., Bascands, J.L., Stevens, R., Schanstra, J.P.: The KUPKB: a novel web application to access multiomics data on kidney disease. FASEB Journal: official publication of the Federation of American Societies for Experimental Biology 26(5), 2145–2153 (2012) PMID: 22345404

3. Lehmann, J.: DL-learner: Learning concepts in description logics. Journal of Machine Learning Research 10, 2639–2642 (2009)

4. Iannone, L., Palmisano, I., Fanizzi, N.: An algorithm based on counterfactuals for concept learning in the semantic web. Applied Intelligence 26(2), 139–159 (2007)

5. Fanizzi, N., d'Amato, C., Esposito, F.: DL-FOIL concept learning in description logics. In: Železný, F., Lavrač, N. (eds.) ILP 2008. LNCS (LNAI), vol. 5194, pp. 107–121. Springer, Heidelberg (2008)

6. Ławrynowicz, A., Potoniec, J.: Fr-ONT: An algorithm for frequent concept mining with formal ontologies. In: Kryszkiewicz, M., Rybinski, H., Skowron, A., Raś, Z.W. (eds.) ISMIS 2011. LNCS, vol. 6804, pp. 428–437. Springer, Heidelberg (2011)

7. Baader, F., Calvanese, D., McGuinness, D.L., Nardi, D., Patel-Schneider, P.F. (eds.): The description logic handbook: theory, implementation, and applications. Cambridge University Press, New York (2003)

8. Tao, J., Sirin, E., Bao, J., McGuinness, D.L.: Integrity constraints in owl. In: AAAI2010: Proceedings of the AAAI Conference on Artificial Intelligence (2010)

9. Kazakov, Y.: RIQ and SROIQ are harder than SHOIQ. In: Proc. KR 2008 (2008)

10. Lehmann, J., Auer, S., Bühmann, L., Tramp, S.: Class expression learning for ontology engineering. Semantics: Science, Services and Agents on the World Wide Web 9(1), 71–81 (2011)

11. Lehmann, J., Hitzler, P.: Concept learning in description logics using refinement operators. Machine Learning 78, 203–250 (2010)

12. Tao, J.: Integrity Constraints for the Semantic Web: An OWL2-DL Extension. PhD thesis, Rensselaer Polytechnic Institute, Troy, NY, USA, AAI3530046 (2012)

13. Horridge, M., Bechhofer, S.: The OWL API: a java API for OWL ontologies. Semantic Web 2(1), 11–21 (2011)

14. Sirin, E., Parsia, D., Grau, B.C., Kalyanpur, A., Katz, Y.: Pellet: A practical OWL-DL reasoner. Web Semantics: Science, Services and Agents on the World Wide Web 5(2), 51–53 (2007)

15. Ratcliffe, D., Taylor, K., Newman, J.: Ontology-based machine learning for protein crystallisation. In: Australasian Ontology Workshop (AOW 2011), Perth, Australia, vol. 132, CRPIT (2011)

YASGUI: Feeling the Pulse of Linked Data*

Laurens Rietveld[1] and Rinke Hoekstra[1,2]

[1] Dept. of Computer Science, VU University Amsterdam, NL
{laurens.rietveld,rinke.hoekstra}@vu.nl
[2] Faculty of Law, University of Amsterdam, NL
hoekstra@uva.nl

Abstract. Existing studies of Linked Data focus on the availability of data rather than its use in practice. The number of query logs available is very much restricted to a small number of datasets. This paper proposes to track Linked Data usage at the *client* side. We use YASGUI, a feature rich web-based query editor, as a measuring device for interactions with the Linked Data Cloud. It enables us to determine what part of the Linked Data Cloud is actually used, what part is open or closed, the efficiency and complexity of queries, and how these results relate to commonly used dataset statistics.

Keywords: SPARQL, Observatory, Linked Data, Semantic Web, Usage analysis.

1 Introduction

As the Linked Data cloud grows both in size and complexity, it becomes increasingly interesting to study how, and what parts are being used for which purpose. There are currently two approaches: the study of query logs, such as provided by the USEWOD series [2], and of gathering dataset statistics [3,7]. Both only partially fulfill their intended purpose because 1) they are restricted to a small number of datasets and 2) the information is collected at the publisher rather than the user-end of the development pipeline. What is missing for analytics over the Linked Data cloud is a dataset independent data collection point, which can act as a kind of observational lens.

Take as analogy the query logs collected by search engines, such as Google or Yahoo. These have become the primary proxies for studying information need on the World Wide Web. This has to do with the unique position those engines have as *the* central filters through which users access the otherwise distributed information. Indeed, the business model of web search giants is founded on their ability to adequately target advertisements to users, based on their search behavior. For the Web of Data, not a single such entry point currently exists. This paper uses statistics generated by YASGUI, a SPARQL client launched in early 2013, which has the potential for becoming such an observational lens for the Linked Data cloud.

---

* This work was supported by the Dutch national program COMMIT.

K. Janowicz et al. (Eds.): EKAW 2014, LNAI 8876, pp. 441–452, 2014.

YASGUI[1], first introduced in the SALAD Workshop [15], is a web-based query editor for the Web of Data that uses the latest web technologies. It is packed with usability features such as auto-completion, syntax highlighting, dataset endpoint search, and sharing functionalities for SPARQL. When given permission to do so, it acts as a measuring device for Linked Data, by tracking the actions of users. This provides insight in how we interact with Linked Data. As YASGUI works for every SPARQL endpoint, it can collect information on more than the Linked Data cloud we were previously aware of, including endpoints inaccessible from the internet. In section 3.1 we show how the information collected through this SPARQL interface increases our knowledge of Linked Data, such as which part of the Linked Data cloud is actually used, what part is open and accessible, the complexity of man-made queries, and the most commonly used namespaces. Our goal is to build a query collection that gives us insight in the of *tasks* performed and *methods* used by Linked Data users.

The matter of uptake is the critical factor as to whether or not YASGUI will eventually collect sufficient, valid, and unbiased data, and can become a proper observational lens. In Section 3 we argue that there are sufficient incentives for users to use it as their point of entry for the Linked Data cloud as it is the most user friendly, intuitive and interactive interface to date.

This paper is structured as follows. In Section 2 we discuss related approaches to the study of the Linked Data cloud, and we review other SPARQL user interfaces. Section 3 outlines our methodology, and summarizes the features of YASGUI. Section 4 discusses how the use of YASGUI allows us to analyze the Linked Data cloud, and what we can observe from the data we gathered since its launch. We conclude in section 5.

2   Related Work

Where Is the Linked Data. The most well known depiction of Linked Data is a "cloud" of 311 connected ("linked") datasets [3]. The size of circles depends on the size of the datasets, and links represent the reuse of identifiers between datasets. Not only is the latest version outdated (November 2011), it is also rather limited in that it is based on metadata that were manually registered in the Datahub CKAN catalog[2] and which have an open license. This makes the analysis quite unreliable and static: there is no check as to whether the size and number of links registered correspond to reality, and there is no indication of whether the data is actually being used.

LODStats [7] assesses the availability of the information in the Datahub. It attempts to access or download registered datasets, and extracts structure and schema characteristics. Results show that for various reasons, only a fraction of the registered data is accessible in practice. Similar to Ding et al. [8], LODStats provides statistics of the popularity of *namespaces* (and thus vocabularies) across a large body of RDF. However, counting namespace occurrence does not give

---

[1] See http://yasgui.org (6 May 2014).

[2] See http://datahub.io (20 Feb. 2014).

insight in the *spread* of a namespace: is it popular within an isolated *cluster* of interlinked datasets, or is its use evenly spread out?

Hogan et al. [11] performed an in depth analysis of the quality of Linked Data that was crawled from the Web as part of the Billion Triple Challenge in 2011[3], focusing in particular on the adherence of the datasets to Linked Data principles such as dereferenceability of URIs. These efforts show that accessibility is hampered by the reliability of services hosting the data. Also, the quality and standards-compliance of Linked Data published is relatively low, given the number of tools that support Linked Data manipulation [1]. SPARQLES [5] continuously tracks the uptime of SPARQL endpoints, which features they support, and which endpoints publish dataset statistics. This is useful for observing the current state of accessible SPARQL endpoints, though again, the set of endpoints is limited to those published on CKAN. Sindice [17] collects data from the Web of Data by crawling web pages for RDFa and Microformat markup. It also collects data from endpoints through a manual procedure (only 8 out of 311 CKAN datasets are indexed). Sindice provides an extensive amount of information about the Web of Data, taking a broader perspective than focusing on SPARQL endpoints alone. In short, we have an incomplete knowledge of what Linked Data is, and how much resides where.

Interfaces to Linked Data. Many SPARQL clients exist, but they lack the feature richness needed to study SPARQL usage across datasets, and to attract sufficient numbers of users. Table 1 lists fourteen currently existing SPARQL clients – that range from very basic to elaborate – and depicts what features they implement. We briefly discuss them below.[4] The YASGUI client is presented separately in Section 3.

SPARQL is a complex language and queries can become quite large. Syntax highlighting and checking can help significantly to improve readability of queries, but the Flint SPARQL Editor is the only client that currently supports it[5]. TopBraid Composer[6] and Flint (and indirectly, the SparQLed editor [6] based on the former) support auto-completion for suggesting classes and properties. This increases transparency, as the auto-completion may suggest information that a user was not aware of.

There are only four clients that fully support access to multiple endpoints. This is because many clients are part of the web front-end of triple stores. Examples are 4Store [10], OpenLink Virtuoso[7], OpenRDF Sesame Workbench [4] and SPARQLer[8]. More generic clients are the Sesame2 Windows Client [4], Glint[9],

---

[3] See http://km.aifb.kit.edu/projects/btc-2011/

[4] Other clients exist, such as NITELIGHT, SPARQLinG, ViziQuer and SPARQLViz, but these were no longer available, or do not work. Contact with the authors behind these tools was either not possible, or did not result in a working tool.

[5] See http://openuplabs.tso.co.uk/demos/sparqleditor (21 Feb. 2014).

[6] See http://www.topquadrant.com/ (21 Feb. 2014).

[7] See http://www.openlinksw.com/

[8] See http://www.sparql.org/ (21 Feb. 2014).

[9] See https://github.com/MikeJ1971/Glint (21 Feb. 2014).

Table 1. SPARQL client feature matrix

Feature	iSPARQL	4Store	OpenLink Virtuoso	SNORQL	SPARQLer	Sesame Workbench	Sesame2 Windows Client	TopBraid Composer	LODatio	Glint	Twinkle	SparqlGUI	SparQLed	Flint SPARQL Editor	YASGUI
Auto-completion	+	-	-	-	-	-	-	-	-	-	-	-	+[a]	+[a]	+[b]
Syntax Highlighting	N/A	-	-	-	-	-	-	+	-	+	-	-	+	+	+
Syntax Checking	N/A	-	-	-	-	-	-	+	-	-	-	-	+	+	+
Multiple Endpoints	-	-	-	-	-	-	±	-	+	+	+	±[c]	-	±[c]	+
Platform independent	+	+	+	+	+	+	-	+	+	-	+	-	+	+	+
Full SPARQL 1.1 syntax	-	+	+	+	+	+	+	+	+	+	+	+	+	+	+
Query retention	-	-	-	-	-	-	+	+	-	+	-	+	-	-	+
File upload	-	-	-	-	-	+	±[d]	+	-	-	+	+	-	-	-[e]
Results rendering	+	-	±[f]	+	±[f]	+	±[f]	+	+	±[f]	±[f]	±[f]	+	+	+
Results download	-	+	+	+	+	+	+	+	-	+	+	+	-	-	+
Visual query interface	+	-	-	-	-	-	-	-	-	-	-	-	-	-	-

[a] Auto-completion of properties and classes available in the triple store

[b] Autocompletion of prefixes/namespaces/properties/classes

[c] Can deal with a limited number of endpoints, e.g. only CORS enabled ones.

[d] File upload requires a local triple store that implements the OpenRDF SAIL API, e.g. OpenRDF Sesame or OpenLink Virtuoso.

[e] File upload is a planned feature, using cloud triple-store services (e.g. dydra.com)

[f] The rendering does not use hyperlinks for URI resources.

Twinkle[10] and SparqlGUI[11]. Other applications fall somewhere in between. The FLINT SPARQL Editor only connects to endpoints which support cross-domain JavaScript (i.e. CORS enabled). This is a problem because not all endpoints are CORS enabled, such as FactForge, CKAN, Mondeca or data.gov. Other editors support only XML or JSON as query results, such as SNORQL[12], which only supports query results in SPARQL-JSON format. TopBraid composer supports querying multiple endpoints only via the the SPARQL SERVICE federated query functionality of SPARQL 1.1. Finally, LODatio indexes the schema from multiple datasets, but not all of them, and not all information is indexed from those that are.

The clients shipped with Virtuoso and 4Store and the Flint SPARQL Editor are Web-based and thus platform independent. Twinkle is a Java application, making it runnable on almost any operating system. Examples of single-platform applications are Sesame2 Windows Client and SparqlGUI: they require

---

[10] See http://www.ldodds.com/projects/twinkle/ (21 Feb. 2014).

[11] See http://www.dotnetrdf.org/content.asp?pageID=SparqlGUI (21 Feb. 2014).

[12] See https://github.com/kurtjx/SNORQL/ (21 Feb. 2014).

Windows. All text-oriented clients provide complete SPARQL syntax support. This is harder to accomplish for clients with a visual query interface, such as iSPARQL.

Query retention allows for easy re-use of important or often used queries. This allows the user to close the application, and resume working on the query later. An example is the 'Query Book' functionality of the Sesame Windows Client. Exploring small RDF graphs should not necessitate the hassle of installing a local triple-store. Several applications such as Twinkle and The Sesame Windows Client support uploading of files.

The raw results to SPARQL queries are very hard to read. All applications except 4Store render the results of SELECT queries as a table. Results typically contain URIs, that invite navigation of the RDF graph. However, not all clients support it (Virtuoso, Twinkle or SparqlGUI). SNORQL allows users to navigate to the Web address of the URI, or the user can click on a link to browse the current endpoint for resources relevant to that URI. Finally, it can be useful to be able to download the results to SPARQL queries, e.g. the results of CON- STRUCT queries are often used in other applications. The only applications that do not support the downloading of results are the FLINT SPARQL editor and SparQLed.

Usage of Linked Data. To better understand the usage of Linked Data, the USEWOD [2] workshop series initiated a challenge to analyze server logs from six well known SPARQL query endpoints (datasets): DBpedia, Semantic Web Dog Food, BioPortal, Bio2RDF, Open-BioMed, and Linked Geo Data.[13] Clearly this only covers a small portion of the number of datasets registered in the Datahub, making it difficult to extrapolate to the full size of the Web of Data. Also, the query logs make no distinction between 'machine queries' – queries executed by applications – and manual interaction with Linked Data [13]. In previous work [16], we quantified exactly this difference, by comparing the YASGUI set of man-made queries with queries taken from server logs (containing mostly machine queries). We showed that queries from each sets differ greatly in size, the range of SPARQL features they use, and complexity.

3   Methodology

The discussion of related work shows that we can only sketch a reliable picture of the Linked Data cloud that includes both the presence and use of datasets if we tap into where interaction with the Linked Data cloud occurs: on the client side. Our method follows two steps, we 1) developed a SPARQL client (YASGUI) that can attract users and allows access to all SPARQL endpoints (Section 3), we then 2) ask permission to log user queries, and analyze these queries along various dimensions such as type, namespaces, endpoints, complexity, etc. (Section 3.1). The results of this analysis are discussed in section 4

---

[13] See http://dbpedial.org, http://data.semanticweb.org, http://bioportal.bioontology.org/, http://www.open-biomed.org.uk/, and http://linkedgeodata.org, respectively.

The Features of YASGUI. YASGUI is a knife that cuts on both sides: it is a tool that makes it easier to interact with Linked Data, and it allows us to gather an unprecedented wealth of usage data if users opt-in. We argue that it is the most complete SPARQL client available, containing unique additional features for auto-completion and collaborative editing, which have not been available in SPARQL interfaces before. We introduced this tool in [15], but will briefly discuss its features here.

YASGUI supports syntax highlighting and checking (like FLINT) but it provides extensive auto-completion features as well: auto-completion of properties and classes are supported, and full namespace URIs of prefixes are added as you type. It supports access to any SPARQL endpoint, and provides auto-completion and searching for endpoints using the CKAN SPARQL endpoint[14]. To access endpoint without Cross-Origin Resource Sharing (CORS) support[15], YASGUI implements a proxy that allows access to all CORS disabled endpoints. Furthermore, YASGUI supports the specification of an arbitrary number of request parameters that are sent along the HTTP request (e.g. the 'soft-limit' parameter of 4Store). YASGUI allows query results to be downloaded as CSV or 'as is' (for raw query results). It provides a tabular view of query results that allows users to browse the Web of Data through clicking on resource URIs.

The YASGUI application state is persistent across sessions: a returning user will see the screen as it was when she last closed the YASGUI browser page. Queries can be bookmarked, and connected to an OpenID account. This way users are able to re-use queries between user sessions, browsers, and computers. Furthermore, YASGUI can generate a permalink for each query. Opening the link in a browser opens YASGUI with the specified query, endpoint and request arguments filled in. We believe this is a welcome feature for people working together with a need to share queries. Finally, YASGUI can be used offline, as a regular desktop application, by means of the HTML5 offline manifest functionality.

Finally, to enable re-use of YASGUI by developers, we publish two separate JavaScript modules: YASQE[16] (a JS SPARQL text area) and YASR[17] (a JS SPARQL result visualizer). Both contain most of the features above, and enable easy integration of the YASGUI tool-set into other Linked Data projects.

3.1 Analysis

This section elaborates on the data we can gather from YASGUI users, the types of analysis we run on the data, and some observations that can be made (section 4). We use Google Analytics[18] to log the actions of users that explicitly allow us to do so: every user is presented with an opt-out form in which users may choose

---

[14] See http://datahub.io (6 May 2014).

[15] See http://www.w3.org/TR/cors/ (21 Feb. 2014).

[16] See http://yasqe.yasgui.org

[17] See http://yasr.yasgui.org

[18] See http://www.google.com/analytics/ (6 May 2014).

Table 2. Statistics on the use of Linked Data as measured from the YASGUI logs

Queries		Complexity		Accessible endpoints	#	%
Total Queries	45.323	≥ 1 joins	54.35%	CKAN endpoints	84	73.45%
Valid Queries	30.482	≥1 VCCpattern	58.37%	Not in CKAN	124	7.61%
Unique Queries	18.162	≥1 VCVpattern	53.68%			
		≥1 CCVpattern	11.92%	**Inaccessible endpoints**	#	%
SELECT	94.52%	≥1 CVVpattern	10.44%	Probably incorrect	447	1.22%
DESCRIBE	0.74%	≥1 VVCpattern	9.87%	Private (local) endpoint	105	11.02%
ASK	1.59%	≥1 VVVpattern	7.76%	Only contains public data	171	6.70%
CONSTRUCT	3.15%	≥1 CCCpattern	0.96%			
INSERT	0.00%	≥1 CVCpattern	0.30%			

to disable logging completely, or to disable logging of endpoints and queries only. User actions include the queries a user executes, the endpoint they use, the time it takes to get the query response[19], the use of the URL shortener service, and more general information such as (an estimate of) the user's location and the local time.

Given these logs we can study the following:

1. How do the SPARQL endpoints registered in CKAN relate to the endpoints used in YASGUI? How big is the overlap?
2. Looking at the datasets hosted by these endpoints, what part of the dataset is actually needed to answer the queries posed against it?
3. What namespaces are most commonly used in the the queries?
4. How complex are the queries, how many are there, what tasks are they used for?

At a more *fine-grained* level, we analyze the complexity of the query sets, using the methods described in [9,14]. We look at two aspects: the triple pattern structure and the number of joins. The number of triple patterns used in queries, as well as the structure of these triple patterns is a good indication of the complexity of queries. We use the method described in [9] to determine types of joins, and the number of joins per query. Each element in a triple can be a variable (V), or a constant (C). For instance, [] `rdf:type ?object` can be classified as V C V. When two triple patterns have one variable in common, the query engine would need to join both. Given the features of YASGUI compared to other clients, we expected that our queries have a higher complexity than SPARQL queries obtained from server-side logs.

---

[19] Logging the execution time of queries is added recently. Therefore, these results are not included in this paper.

4   Results

Since the public launch of YASGUI 1 year ago, it has attracted 2.947 unique visitors from over 74 countries.[20] Until now, 1.709 users (58%) of our users allow full logging, 6% disabled logging of endpoints and queries only, where the remaining 36% disabled logging altogether. Of the 58% who allowed logging, we tracked 45.323 queries, executed against 793 SPARQL endpoints. This means that in total, an estimated additional 25.000 queries were executed through YASGUI without our knowledge. To give some context to the number of visitors: the Semantic Web Dog Food project lists 10.982 unique persons.[21]

Endpoint Usage. We divide the endpoints into five categories (See Table 2). To filter typographic errors, we reduce the list of 931 endpoints to a list of endpoints which only contain those on which more than 1 query was executed. This results in a list of 537 endpoints, for each of which, we check whether this endpoint is accessible and whether it occurs in the Datahub catalog. Inaccessible datasets do not only contain private or closed data: users might store a copy of a CKAN dataset locally for analysis. Therefore, we analyze the namespaces in the corresponding queries of these endpoints: whenever a namespace does not occur in the prefix.cc[22] collection, we assume this endpoint contains private data. This gives us 105 endpoints, from which we can derive that 11.02% of all queries are executed on an endpoint containing private data. In other words, from the YASGUI usage perspective, 89% of the Linked Data Cloud is open, where the other 11% is closed.

Dataset Usage. We can determine what part of each data set is touched by queries, by rewriting all SPARQL SELECT queries to CONSTRUCT queries. This gives us, for each pair of query and endpoint, the triples needed to answer the original SELECT query. We performed this analysis for the 10 most often used datasets that were accessible at the time of the experiment (see Figure 1). This shows that for most endpoints, less than 0.4% of the dataset is actually needed to answer our queries. DBpedia (the most popular endpoint) requires only 0.38% of its size, to answer 8179 queries.

Namespace Usage. The query logs allow us to see what type of information from the Web of Data is used. Namespaces are good candidates to look at, as they reflect the use of often domain specific vocabularies. Table 3 shows the 8 most common namespaces used between all the queries. The RDF type and RDF schema namespaces are the most popular ones. Table 4 compares the pre-LOD statistics of [8] with that of users on Prefix.cc and YASGUI (Prefix.cc provides no numbers, only a ranking). Six out of eight original namespaces are still high

---

[20] Statistics are from May 2014.
[21] Number taken from http://data.semanticweb.org/ (July 2014).
[22] See http://prefix.cc (6 May 2014).

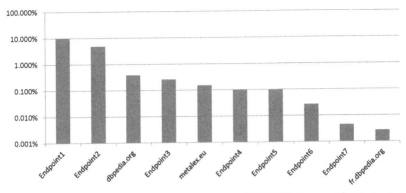

Fig. 1. Query coverage of top 10 used datasets in YASGUI (log scale). Endpoints not available through the Datahub are anonymized.

Table 3. YASGUI: Top 10 namespaces occurring in queries

Namespace	%	#
http://www.w3.org/2000/01/rdf-schema#	16.5%	10.350
http://www.w3.org/1999/02/22-rdf-syntax-ns#	15.9%	9.962
http://dbpedia.org/property/	11.4%	7.142
http://dbpedia.org/resource/	11.0%	6.922
http://dbpedia.org/ontology/	10.9%	6.869
http://xmlns.com/foaf/0.1/	6.2%	3.882
http://dbpedia.org/	3.1%	1.968
http://www.w3.org/2001/XMLSchema#	2.6%	1.642
http://www.w3.org/2002/07/owl#	2.3%	1.437
http://www.w3.org/2004/02/skos/core#	1.6%	1.017

ranked in the Linked Data age. The highly ranked RSS namespace in Prefix.cc can be explained by (non-semantic) web developers. Comparing namespace use between YASGUI and LODStats (Table 5), we can see that DBpedia-based namespaces are more frequently used in queries than that they are reused across datasets. The higher ranked RDF Schema and OWL namespace (9th) in the YASGUI ranking indicates that users do rely on schema information. Using the pairing of namespaces and datasets, we can create a map of the commonalities between datasets.

Query Analysis. Table 2 shows a number of statistics based on a total of 45.323 queries collected via YASGUI. After filtering invalid queries using the Jena[23] query parser, this number drops to 30.482 queries. This large number of invalid queries is partly due to the strict parsing of Jena. Some queries may not conform to the SPARQL standard, but return valid SPARQL results for certain endpoints regardless. For example, a query containing a 'bif:' URI, supported

---

[23] See http://jena.apache.org/ (6 May 2014).

Table 4. Top 8 namespace rankings, comparing Ding et al. [8], Prefix.cc and YASGUI

Namespace	Ding et al.	prefix.cc	YASGUI
http://www.w3.org/1999/02/22-rdf-syntax-ns#	1	2	2
http://www.foaf-project.org/ (or http://xmlns.com/foaf/0.1/)	2	3	6
http://purl.org/dc/elements/1.1/	3	5	10
http://www.w3.org/2000/01/rdf-schema#	4	6	1
http://webns.net/mvcb/	5	39	*none*
http://purl.org/rss/1.0/	6	9	251
http://www.w3.org/2001/vcard-rdf/3.0# (or http://www.w3.org/2006/vcard/ns#)	7	32	20
http://purl.org/vocab/bio/0.1/	8	52	*none*

Table 5. LODStats: Top 10 namespaces based on occurrences in triples

Namespace	LODStats	YASGUI
http://www.w3.org/1999/02/22-rdf-syntax-ns	23.7%	15.9%
http://www.w3.org/2000/01/rdf-schema	15.9%	16.5%
http://purl.org/dc/terms/	10.9%	1.5%
http://www.systemone.at/2006/03/wikipedia	6.0%	*none*
http://d-nb.info/standards/elementset/gnd	5.3%	*none*
http://www.w3.org/2004/02/skos/core	2.8%	1.6%
http://iflastandards.info/ns/isbd/elements	4.7%	0.00%
http://fao.270a.info/property/	2.1%	*none*
http://www.aktors.org/ontology/portal	2.1%	0.00%
http://schema.org	2.1%	0.3%

by Virtuoso endpoints, is marked as invalid. When we remove duplicate queries from the query set, 18.162 queries remain.

We observe that the majority of queries executed via YASGUI are SELECT queries. Both ASK and DESCRIBE queries, amount to a fraction of the YASGUI query logs (1.59% and 0.74% respectively). We believe this shows that users prefer the more common SELECT keyword instead. Rather than the boolean value returned by an ASK query, the user may evaluate the query results from the SELECT query as-is. We expect this is due to the familiarity users have with SELECT queries; only a few of them will opt for an ASK or DESCRIBE query. Interestingly, the number of executed CONSTRUCT queries amounts to only 3.15%, which might indicate that data re-use via SPARQL queries is uncommon. The YASGUI logs show that roughly 7 percentage points out of the SELECT queries is accounted for by SNORQL-style queries.

Another observation concerns the complexity of SPARQL queries. Table 2 shows that 54.35% of the queries contain one or more joins, and the most common triple patterns consists of VCC and VCV triple patterns. Such statistics can be used for optimizing man-made queries, and tell us more about how people query Linked Data. When we take a closer look at the individual queries contained in the logs, we see that we can glean information about more than the queries only. First, following [12], we observe that 72.66% of executed queries are inefficient due to an incorrect or unnecessary use of OPTIONAL: we compared query results *with* and *without* the OPTIONAL to detect these. This high percentage may be partly explained if we consider that SPARQL clients are often used for exploratory tasks. Finding task-trails in query logs [18] will allow us to better detect this behavior.

5   Conclusion

This paper uses YASGUI as a means to analyze the use of Linked Data. Given the richness of features compared to other SPARQL clients, YASGUI is rapidly becoming a popular interface to the Web of Data, positioning itself as a dataset independent data collection point which can act as an of observational lens. We are aware the results presented in this paper are not (yet) fully representative and unbiased. However, alternative dataset statistics suffer from the same problem: these are either based on (outdated) dataset catalogs, or on an opt-in basis, making these statistics incomplete.

Only 1 year after the release of YASGUI, we are already able to analyze a large number of queries. This gives unprecedented insight into how we actually use the Linked Data cloud, and what part of the Linked Data cloud we use. Using the collected data, we were able to analyze the efficiency of queries, what part of the used Linked Data cloud is open or closed, what part of these datasets we use, the complexity of queries, and the shared use of namespaces over all the endpoints.

With an increase in uptake of YASGUI, we will be able to make these claims even stronger, and we will be able to understand the use of Linked Data even better. More data allows us to recognize more fine-grained patterns, e.g. to identify a relation between the structure of a dataset and its queries, which categories of queries exist, and how these query categories relate to typical tasks. This paper shows first steps in this direction. To conclude, this paper introduces a tool, dataset and methodology that increase our knowledge of the use of Linked Data. It allows for analyzing the Linked Data cloud in the broadest sense: what datasets exist, how are they used, and for what purpose? The amount of data we gathered in this short period of time, and the increasing uptake of YASGUI, promises an even clearer picture of Linked Data in the future.

References

1. Beek, W., Rietveld, L., Bazoobandi, H.R., Wielemaker, J., Schlobach, S.: LOD laundromat: A uniform way of publishing other people's dirty data. In: Janowicz, K., et al. (eds.) ISWC 2014. LNCS, vol. 8796, pp. 213–228. Springer, Heidelberg (2014)

2. Berendt, B., Hollink, L., Luczak-Rösch, M., Möller, K., Vallet, D.: Proceedings of USEWOD2013 - 3rd international workshop on usage analysis and the web of data. In: 10th ESWC - Semantics and Big Data, Montpellier, France (2013)
3. Bizer, C., Jentzsch, A., Cyganiak, R.: State of the lod cloud. Version 0.3, 1803 (September 2011)
4. Broekstra, J., Kampman, A., van Harmelen, F.: Sesame: An architecture for storing and querying RDF data and schema information (2001)
5. Buil-Aranda, C., Hogan, A., Umbrich, J., Vandenbussche, P.-Y.: SPARQL web-querying infrastructure: Ready for action? In: Alani, H., et al. (eds.) ISWC 2013, Part II. LNCS, vol. 8219, pp. 277–293. Springer, Heidelberg (2013)
6. Campinas, S., et al.: Introducing rdf graph summary with application to assisted sparql formulation. In: Database and Expert Systems Applications, pp. 261–266. IEEE (2012)
7. Auer, S., Demter, J., Martin, M., Lehmann, J.: LODStats – an extensible framework for high-performance dataset analytics. In: ten Teije, A., Völker, J., Handschuh, S., Stuckenschmidt, H., d'Acquin, M., Nikolov, A., Aussenac-Gilles, N., Hernandez, N. (eds.) EKAW 2012. LNCS, vol. 7603, pp. 353–362. Springer, Heidelberg (2012)
8. Ding, L., Zhou, L., Finin, T., Joshi, A.: How the semantic web is being used: An analysis of foaf documents. In: Proceedings of the 38th Annual Hawaii International Conference on System Sciences (HICSS 2005), pp. 113.3. IEEE Computer Society, Washington, DC (2005)
9. Gallego, M.A., Fernández, J.D., Martínez-Prieto, M.A., de la Fuente, P.: An empirical study of real-world sparql queries. In: 1st International Workshop on Usage Analysis and the Web of Data (USEWOD 2011) at the 20th International World Wide Web Conference (WWW 2011), Hydebarabad, India (2011)
10. Harris, S., Lamb, N., Shadbolt, N.: 4store: The design and implementation of a clustered RDF store. In: 5th International Workshop on Scalable Semantic Web Knowledge Base Systems (SSWS 2009), pp. 94–109 (2009)
11. Hogan, A., Umbrich, J., Harth, A., Cyganiak, R., Polleres, A., Decker, S.: An empirical survey of linked data conformance. J. Web Sem. 14, 14–44 (2012)
12. Loizou, A., Groth, P.T.: On the formulation of performant sparql queries. CoRR abs/1304.0567 (2013)
13. Möller, K., Hausenblas, M., Cyganiak, R., Handschuh, S.: Learning from linked open data usage: Patterns & metrics. In: WebSci10: Extending the Frontiers of Society On-Line, pp. 1–9 (2010)
14. Picalausa, F., Vansummeren, S.: What are real sparql queries like? In: Proceedings of the International Workshop on Semantic Web Information Management, p. 7. ACM (2011)
15. Rietveld, L., Hoekstra, R.: Yasgui: Not just another sparql gui. In: Proceedings of the Workshop on Services and Applications over Linked APIs and Data (SALAD 2013) (2013)
16. Rietveld, L., Hoekstra, R.: Man vs. Machine: Differences in SPARQL Queries. In: ESWC 2014, 4th USEWOD Workshop on Usage Analysis and the Web of Data (2014)
17. Tummarello, G., Delbru, R., Oren, E.: Sindice.com: Weaving the open linked data. In: Aberer, K., et al. (eds.) ASWC 2007 and ISWC 2007. LNCS, vol. 4825, pp. 552–565. Springer, Heidelberg (2007)
18. Weber, I., Jaimes, A.: Who uses web search for what? and how? In: Proceedings of the Fourth ACM International Conference on Web Search and Data Mining, WSDM 2011, pp. 15–24. ACM, New York (2011), http://doi.acm.org/10.1145/1935826.1935839

Tackling the Class-Imbalance Learning Problem in Semantic Web Knowledge Bases

Giuseppe Rizzo, Claudia d'Amato, Nicola Fanizzi, and Floriana Esposito

LACAM – Dipartimento di Informatica
Università degli Studi di Bari "Aldo Moro"
Via E.Orabona 4, 70125 Bari, Italy
firstname.lastname@uniba.it

Abstract. In the Semantic Web context, procedures for deciding the class-membership of an individual to a target concept in a knowledge base are generally based on automated reasoning. However, frequent cases of incompleteness/inconsistency due to distributed, heterogeneous nature and the Web-scale dimension of the knowledge bases. It has been shown that resorting to models induced from the data may offer comparably effective and efficient solutions for these cases, although skewness in the instance distribution may affect the quality of such models. This is known as *class-imbalance* problem. We propose a machine learning approach, based on the induction of *Terminological Random Forests*, that is an extension of the notion of *Random Forest* to cope with this problem in case of knowledge bases expressed through the standard Web ontology languages. Experimentally we show the feasibility of our approach and its effectiveness w.r.t. related methods, especially with imbalanced datasets.

1 Introduction

In the perspective of the Semantic Web (SW) as a global space of data [1], many complex tasks (e.g. query answering, clustering, ranking, etc.) boil down to solving classification problems. In general, such tasks ultimately require the assessment of the truth of ground facts (assertions). Solutions to this kind of problems calls for approaches that may involve pattern matching up to more complex forms of automated reasoning.

In this paper we will consider specifically class-membership prediction problems (as even link-prediction problems can be often reduced to such simpler cases). Deciding on the membership of a given individual to some target concept is not always feasible in a purely deductive approach. This is caused by the inherent uncertainty originated from the heterogeneous and distributed nature of the knowledge bases:

- cases of incomplete information (related to the open-world reasoning);
- cases of conflicting information owing to the decentralized multiplicity and diverse quality of the ontologies that may be involved (in terms of both terminology and assertions).

K. Janowicz et al. (Eds.): EKAW 2014, LNAI 8876, pp. 453–468, 2014.

For these reasons, alternative inductive approaches have been proposed [2]. Particularly, machine learning methods (e.g. see [3]) have been devised to build classification models that exploit the statistical regularities in the data.

However, also data-driven classification based on induced models may be affected by problems originated from heterogeneity and diversity. Indeed the availability of examples and the composition of the training set is crucial for machine learning methods. A relevant *skewness* in the data distribution w.r.t. the classes to be predicted may likely lead to poorly predictive statistical models. Specifically, it has been observed that, depending on the definitions of the concepts and their related assertions, it is very frequent to find more uncertain-membership examples than individuals that belong to the target concept (or to its complement). This has been recognized as an additional problem for inductive methods (a related discussion can be found in [2]) and few supervised algorithms have been developed to tackle it, such as transductive/semi-supervised methods that have been recently proposed [4,5].

Datasets that are characterized by a strong skewness of the example distribution, known as *imbalanced datasets*, require suitable techniques to be adopted for learning in this particular situation [6]. Specifically, in order to infer a general rule for recognizing unseen positive instances, *class-imbalance learning* techniques have been developed [7] for specific domains as the *fraud detection*, where the goal is to recognize most of the examples belonging to the minority class.

An approach that can be employed to deal with this problem is *Ensemble Learning* in which a number of *weak* learners are trained and then a meta-learner is built to combine their answers to improve the performance w.r.t. the single learners. While some ensemble methods aim to reduce the bias of the model (e.g. ADABOOST [8]), other approaches pursue the reduction of the variance. The latter is the case of *bagging*, where each learner is trained on a subset of training instances obtained by a *sampling with replacement* procedure. In this way, ensemble learning techniques can be employed to produce more predictive inductive classifiers than those produced by a single learner. Moving from this idea, we aim to investigate the effectiveness of ensemble learning in order to improve the query answering task in the context of SW knowledge bases. To this purpose, an approach that combines ensemble learning and sampling strategies is proposed.

Specifically, the main contribution of the paper concerns the definition of a framework for the induction of *Terminological Random Forests* for knowledge bases expressed as Web ontologies. This is an ensemble learning approach where the role of the weak classifiers is played by *terminological decision trees* [9] that are induced on re-balanced subsets built from an imbalanced training set. A preliminary empirical evaluation shows a more conservative behavior of the ensemble model compared with an approach based on single-learner.

The remainder of the paper is organized as follows: the next section recalls the basics of learning in the context of SW knowledge bases and with reference to the class-imbalance problems; Sect. 3 presents the novel learning framework for terminological random forests, while in Sect. 4 a preliminary empirical evaluation with its setup and results is described. Finally, Sect. 5 illustrates some conclusions and perspectives for further developments.

2   Class-Imbalance Learning in Description Logics

2.1   Learning Individual Classifiers

We will consider knowledge bases expressed in Description Logics [10] (DLs) as such languages encompass most of the standard SW representations.

A DL *knowledge base* $\mathcal{K} = \langle \mathcal{T}, \mathcal{A} \rangle$ typically contains a terminological part, the set of axioms $\mathcal{T}$, known as the *TBox*, and an assertional part, the set of assertions $\mathcal{A}$, the *ABox*. The set of individuals occurring in $\mathcal{A}$ is denoted by $\mathsf{Ind}(\mathcal{A})$.

The concept learning task in the context of a knowledge base can be formalized as follows:

Definition 1 (learning problem)

Given

- *the knowledge base* $\mathcal{K} = \langle \mathcal{T}, \mathcal{A} \rangle$,
- *a target concept* C,
- *a set of* training examples $\mathsf{Tr} \subseteq \mathsf{Ind}(\mathcal{A})$,
  i.e. individuals for which the intended membership w.r.t. C is known, namely:
    - $\mathsf{Ps} = \{a \in \mathsf{Tr} \mid \mathcal{K} \models C(a)\}$ *(positive examples)*
    - $\mathsf{Ns} = \{b \in \mathsf{Tr} \mid \mathcal{K} \models \neg C(b)\}$ *(negative examples)*
  Tr *may contain also individuals whose membership is not determined:*
    - $\mathsf{Us} = \mathsf{Tr} \setminus (\mathsf{Ps} \cup \mathsf{Ns})$

Find *a concept description D for C (i.e. an axiom $C \equiv D$), such that:*
- $\forall a \in \mathsf{Ps}: \ \mathcal{K} \models D(a)$
- $\forall b \in \mathsf{Ns}: \ \mathcal{K} \models \neg D(b)$

Individuals with an unknown membership w.r.t. the target concept are typical in semi-supervised learning frameworks (such as *transductive learning* [5]). Their occurrence may concern the definition of negative examples. Indeed, in some frameworks it is assumed as a negative example an individual $b \in \mathsf{Ind}(\mathcal{A})$ for which $\mathcal{K} \not\models D(b)$; however, in open-world reasoning, this does not imply that $\mathcal{K} \models \neg D(b)$.

In the following we will use the labels $\mathcal{L} = \{+1, -1, 0\}$ to denote, respectively, the cases of definite membership with respect to C, to $\neg C$, and uncertain membership. Instead of finding a concept description D for C, some algorithms aim at inducing from the training set a *hypothesis* function $h_C : \mathsf{Ind}(\mathcal{A}) \to \mathcal{L}$ such that:

- $\forall a \in \mathsf{Ps}: \ h_C(a) = +1$
- $\forall b \in \mathsf{Ns}: \ h_C(b) = -1$

This function can then be used to predict the label for unseen individuals.

2.2 Sampling Methods for Imbalance Learning

The *class-imbalance* problem [7] concerns the data distribution with respect to classes to be predicted by the classification model. In a binary setting, the problem occurs when training instances belonging to the *majority class* outnumber those belonging to the other (*minority class*). This extends to the settings where models for multiple classes (≥ 3) have to be produced.

In order to tackle this problem, various strategies have been proposed. We will consider those based on sampling. Sampling methods can be employed to rebalance imbalanced datasets so that a classifier can be trained through standard learning algorithms that apply when the distribution of the examples w.r.t. the classes is more uniform.

Sundry sampling strategies have been proposed. A straightforward strategy is based on a random selection of the instances, usually performed by either *over-* or *undersampling* instances. In brief, considering a binary problem setting, in the former case, a selection of the instances of the minority class is replicated until a (more) balanced distribution is reached whereas, in the latter case, instances of the majority class are discarded from the training set.

While oversampling may lead to overfitting the data because of the replicated examples, by adopting an undersampling strategy very informative training examples might be discarded thus compromising the quality of the resulting model. This is why a careful combination with a learning approach should be devised.

3 Learning Terminological Random Forests

The random forest learning approach is now briefly recalled together with the specialization of the *First Order Logic Decision Trees* (FOLDTs) [11] to the target representation.

3.1 Terminological Decision Trees

It has been shown that the concept learning task can be tackled by inducing *Terminological Decision Trees* (TDTs) [9], which represents an extension of the FOLDTs. TDTs are defined as follows:

Definition 2 (terminological decision tree). *Given the knowledge base $\mathcal{K}$, a Terminological Decision Tree is a binary tree where:*

- *each node contains a conjunctive concept description D;*
- *the left and right branches correspond, respectively, to the result of a test (instance checking): $D(a)$?*
- *if a node containing D is the parent of a node containing D' then it must hold that $D' \sqsubseteq D$.*

In the latter case, D' is a specialization of D that can be obtained by applying a *downward refinement operator* ρ w.r.t. the ordering induced by concept subsumption.

We will consider the operator ρ as a mapping with three forms:

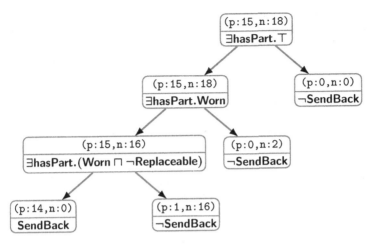

Fig. 1. A simple example of TDT (figure adapted from [9]) with nodes decorated with the number of positive (**p**) and negative (**n**) examples that reached each node in the training phase

ρ_1: adds as a conjunct a concept atom (or its complement), or
ρ_2: refines a sub-description in the scope of an existential restriction, or
ρ_3: refines a sub-description in the scope of an universal restriction.

Note that forms ρ_2 and ρ_3 may be regarded as recursive cases.

Practically, to grow a given node, a set of candidate concept descriptions is generated by means of the refinement operator. Then the best description is selected as the one that maximizes an increment of a *purity* measure w.r.t. the previous level [9]. The underlying idea is to select those descriptions that can better separate positive from negative instances. The purity measure is then the entropy of the positive, negative and uncertain instances.

Fig. 1 proposes an example of TDT. Following Def. 2, its nodes contain DL concept descriptions, which can build upon the signature[1] of the knowledge base $\mathcal{K}$. The intended use of this TDT is predicting whether a car is to be sent back to the factory (SendBack) or can be repaired. We do not show the knowledge base but the counts of training instances that have determined the tree structure. Considering the nodes of the TDT, we can observe that the root concept ∃hasPart.⊤ is progressively specialized. The first immediate refinement is ∃hasPart.Worn, which is installed in the left-child node. This description has been further refined by ρ, and concept ∃hasPart.(Worn ⊓ ¬Replaceable) has been selected, in turn, for its left-child node. In this case the complement of a concept name, ¬Replaceable, is added by the refinement operator in the scope of the existential restriction according to ρ_2. As previously mentioned, each edge

---

[1] For the sake of generality we are not targeting a specific DL: the constructors of $\mathcal{ALC}$ are applied to atoms. Concepts and role names may be defined in terms of a more expressive language adopted for $\mathcal{K}$.

corresponds to the outcome of a test (instance checking). Let a a generic ABox individual, $a \in \mathsf{Ind}(\mathcal{A})$, the edges departing from $\exists\mathsf{hasPart}.\top$ are associated to the test $\exists\mathsf{hasPart}.\top(a)?$. The left branch is associated to the positive while the right one corresponds to the negative case.

3.2   Random Forests

Random Forest (RF) learning [12] is an ensemble learning approach based on a bagging strategy which can be combined with sampling strategies in order to overcome both the overfitting due to the oversampling approach and the loss of information related to the undersampling approach, as described in Sec. 2.

In a generic multi-class learning problem where $\mathcal{L} = \{c_1, c_2, \dots, c_m\}$ is the label set, let F be the set of features that characterize the examples. Growing a random forest amounts to inducing a collection of n decision trees by considering n subsets of the the training set, $D_i \subset \mathsf{Tr}$, $1 \le i \le n$, which are generated by means of sampling with replacement procedure. For each decision tree, only a restricted random subset $A \subseteq F$ of features is considered at each node, where $|A| = f(|F|)$.

After growing the trees using a suitable method, the classification of a new instance a amounts to applying a majority vote rule to the classes predicted by the decision trees $C_i(a) = c_j$, with $j \in \{1, \dots, m\}$:

$$C^\star(a) = \arg\max_{c_j} \sum_{i=1}^{n} I(C_i(a) = c_j)$$

where I is an indicator function[2].

As previously mentioned, RFs can be combined with a sampling strategy. A version of the RF learning algorithm that can cope with the class-imbalance problem is known as *Balanced RF* [13]. The method draws a bootstrap sample from the minority class and randomly selects the same number of instances, with replacement, from the majority class.

3.3   Terminological Random Forests

The notion of *terminological random forest* (TRF) specializes *First Order Logic Random Forests* [14] to cope with the standard representation for SW knowledge bases based on DLs. A TRF is essentially an ensemble of TDTs (see Def. 2). We will now focus on the procedures for growing a TRF and for predicting class-membership of input individuals exploiting a TRF.

Growing TRFs. Alg. 1 describes the procedure for producing a TRF. In order to do this, the target concept C, a training set $\mathsf{Tr} \subseteq \mathsf{Ind}(\mathcal{A})$ and the desired number of trees n are required. As mentioned in Sect. 2, Tr may contain not only

---

[2] $I(x) = 1$ if x is true and $I(x) = 0$ otherwise.

Algorithm 1. The routines for inducing a TRF

---

1   **const:** θ: threshold
2
3   **function** INDUCETRF(Tr : training set; C : concept; $n \in \mathbb{N}$): TRF
4   **begin**
5     $\hat{Pr} \leftarrow$ ESTIMATEPRIORS(Tr, C): {C prior membership probabability estimates}
6     $F \leftarrow \emptyset$
7   **for** $i \leftarrow 1$ **to** n
8       $D_i \leftarrow$ BALANCEDBOOTSTRAPSAMPLE(Tr) {perform undersampling}
9   let $D_i = \langle Ps, Ns, Us \rangle$
10      $T_i \leftarrow$ INDUCETDT($D_i, \top, C, \hat{Pr}$);
11      $F \leftarrow F \cup \{T_i\}$
12   **end**
13
14 **function** INDUCETDT(D : training set; D : concept description; C : target concept; $\hat{Pr}$: priors): TDT
15 **begin**
16   let $D = \langle Ps, Ns, Us \rangle$ {individuals with positive, negative, uncertain membership w.r.t. C}
17    $T \leftarrow$ **new** TDT
18   **if** $|Ps| = 0$ **and** $|Ns| = 0$ **then**
19   **if** $Pr(+1) \geq Pr(-1)$
20   **then** $T.root \leftarrow C$ **else** $T.root \leftarrow \neg C$;
21   **return** T
22   **if** $|Ns| \simeq 0$ **and** $|Ps|/(|Ps| + |Ns| + |Us|) > \theta$ **then**
23      $T.root \leftarrow C$
24   **return** T
25   **if** $|Ps| \simeq 0$ **and** $|Ns|/(|Ps| + |Ns| + |Us|) > \theta$ **then**
26      $T.root \leftarrow \neg C$
27   **return** T
28
29   {random selection of candidate refinements}
30    $S \leftarrow$ RANDOMSELECTION($\rho(D)$)
31
32   {select a subset of features according to $|S|$}
33    $E^* \leftarrow$ SELECTBESTCONCEPT($S, \langle Ps, Ns, Us \rangle$)
34    $\langle \langle P^l, N^l, U^l \rangle, \langle P^r, N^r, U^r \rangle \rangle \leftarrow$ SPLIT($E^*, \langle Ps, Ns, Us \rangle$)
35
36    $T.root \leftarrow E^*$
37    $T.left \leftarrow$ INDUCETDT($\langle P^l, N^l, U^l \rangle, E^*, \hat{Pr}$)
38    $T.right \leftarrow$ INDUCETDT($\langle P^r, N^r, U^r \rangle, E^*, \hat{Pr}$)
39   **return** T
40 **end**

---

positive and negative examples but also of instances with uncertain membership w.r.t. C. The training individuals are sampled with replacement in order to obtain n subsets $D_i \subseteq Tr$, with $i = 1, \ldots, n$.

The sole sampling may fall short to deal with imbalanced datasets, as discussed above. To better tackle this problem, a two-step procedure is required for each D_i. The procedure resorts to *stratified sampling* w.r.t. the class distribution in order to represent instances of the minority class. In the second phase, oversampling or undersampling [7] can be performed on the training set in order to obtain (quasi-)balanced D_i sets (i.e. with a class imbalance that will not affect much the training process). This phase considers the initial data distribution. This means that if an undersampling approach is employed (see the experiments in Sect. 4) and the majority class is the negative one, the exceeding part of the counterexamples is randomly discarded. In the dual case, positive instances are removed. In addition, the sampling procedure removes also all the uncertain instances. In Alg. 1, the procedure that returns the sets D_i implementing this strategy is BALANCEDBOOTSTRAPSAMPLE.

For each D_i, a TDT T_i is built by means of a recursive strategy, which is implemented by the procedure INDUCETDT (adapted from [9]). It distinguishes various cases. The first one uses the prior probability (estimate) to cope with the lack of examples ($|Ps| = 0$ and $|Ns| = 0$) while the second one sets the class label for a leaf node if no positive (resp. negative) example is found while most examples are negative (resp. positive) (i.e. $|Ns| \simeq 0 \wedge |Ps|/(|Ps| + |Ns| + |Us|) > \theta$ or $|Ps| \simeq 0 \wedge |Ns|/(|Ps| + |Ns| + |Us|) > \theta$); the third (recursive) case concerns the availability of both negative and positive examples.

In this case, the current concept description D has to be specialized by means of operator exploring the search space of downward refinements of D. A set of candidate refinements (specializations) $\rho(D)$ is obtained. A subset S of specializations is then selected from S through random sampling (with a call to RANDOMSELECTION). This set is made up of $f(|\rho(D)|)$ concept descriptions. Similarly to the case of propositional RF and following the approach proposed in [14], the number of candidates is set according to the value returned by a function f applied to the cardinality of the set of candidates returned by the refinement operator (e.g. $\sqrt{|\rho(D)|}$). Then, the best description $E^* \in S$ is determined by the SELECTBESTCONCEPT procedure according to the same purity measure employed in [9] and finally it is installed in the current node.

After the assessment of the best concept E^*, the individuals are partitioned by SPLIT for the left or right branch according to the result of the instance-check w.r.t. E^*, maintaining the same group ($P^{l/r}$, $N^{l/r}$, or $U^{l/r}$). Note that a training example a is replicated in both children in case both $\mathcal{K} \not\models E^*(a)$ and $\mathcal{K} \not\models \neg E^*(a)$. The divide-and-conquer strategy is applied recursively until the instances routed to a node satisfy one of the stopping conditions discussed above.

Prediction. After a TRF is produced, predictions can be made relying on the resulting classification model. The related procedure, sketched in Alg. 2, works as follows. Given the individual to be classified, for each tree T_i of the forest, the procedure CLASSIFY returns a class label according to the leaf reached from the root in a path down the tree.

Specifically, the algorithm traverses recursively the TDT performing an instance check w.r.t. the concept contained in each node that is reached: let $a \in \mathsf{Ind}(\mathcal{A})$ and D the concept installed in the current node, if $\mathcal{K} \models D(a)$ (resp. $\mathcal{K} \models \neg D(a)$) the left (resp. right) branch is followed. If neither branch can be followed then the function cannot determine a definite classification[3], therefore it will return the label 0. The service routines ROOT, LEAF and INODE are employed, respectively to get the root node of a given TDT, to test whether a node is a leaf for a tree, and to select the node content.

---

[3] In a new alternative version for this case, the function may follow both branches in parallel and decide on the final classification on the ground of the labels collected at the leaves that are reached.

Algorithm 2. Class-membership prediction

---

 1 **function** CLASSIFYBYTRF(a : individual; F : TRF; C : target concept) : $\mathcal{L}$
 2 **begin**
 3   $count[\ ] \leftarrow$ **new** array {counters of the votes collected from the trees}
 4   **for each** $T \in F$
 5    $l \leftarrow$ CLASSIFY(a, T, C)
 6    $count[l] \leftarrow count[l] + 1$;
 7   **return** $\arg\max_{l \in \mathcal{L}} count[l]$
 8 **end**
 9
10 **function** CLASSIFY(a : individual; T : TDT; C : target concept) : $\mathcal{L}$
11 **begin**
12   $N \leftarrow$ ROOT(T);
13   **while** $\neg$LEAF(N, T) **do**
14    $\langle D, T.\text{left}, T.\text{right} \rangle \leftarrow$ INODE(N)
15   **if** $\mathcal{K} \models D(a)$ **then**
16     $N \leftarrow$ ROOT($T.\text{left}$)
17   **else if** $\mathcal{K} \models \neg D(a)$ **then**
18     $N \leftarrow$ ROOT($T.\text{right}$)
19   **else**
20   **return** 0
21   {leaf case}
22   $\langle D, \text{null}, \text{null} \rangle \leftarrow$ INODE(N)
23   {label assignement}
24   **if** $(D = C)$ **then**
25   **return** $+1$
26   **else** {if $(D = \neg C)$ then}
27   **return** -1
28 **end**

After polling all trees, a majority vote rule is employed to finally assign the class label to the test individual a. Function CLASSIFYBYTRF takes an individual a and a forest F and initializes counters for positive and negative labels, respectively. Then, the algorithm iterates on the forest trees collecting the votes via function CLASSIFY and incrementing the related counter.

4 Preliminary Experiments

The experimental evaluation aims at evaluating the effectiveness of the classification based on the TRF model and the improvement in terms of prediction w.r.t. TDTs. We provide the details of the experimental setup and present and discuss the outcomes.

4.1 Setup

Various Web ontologies have been considered in the experiments (see Tab. 1). They are available on TONES repository[4].

---

[4] http://www.inf.unibz.it/tones/index.php

Table 1. Ontologies employed in the experiments

Ontology	DL Lang.	#Concepts	#Roles	#Disj.Axms	#Individuals
BCO	$\mathcal{ALCHOF}(\mathcal{D})$	196	22	279	112
BioPax	$\mathcal{ALCIF}(\mathcal{D})$	74	70	85	323
NTN	$\mathcal{SHIF}(\mathcal{D})$	47	27	5	676
HD	$\mathcal{ALCIF}(\mathcal{D})$	1498	10	0	639

The parameters of the experiments are the following:

- the number and the kind of query concepts;
- the sampling strategy and the subsequent stratified sampling rate;
- the number of trees per forest;
- the number of randomly selected candidates returned by ρ.

For each ontology, 15 query concepts have been randomly generated by combining (using the conjunction and disjunction operators or universal and existential restriction) 2 through 8 (primitive or defined) concepts of the ontology. The results will be averaged over all concepts per ontology.

Due to the limited population in the considered ontologies, all the individuals occurring in each ontology were employed as (training or test) examples. A 10-fold cross validation design of the experiments was adopted so that the final results are averaged for each of the considered indices (see below).

Concerning the sampling strategy, the TRF learning method was run in two modes:

1. keeping the original class imbalance;
2. using a balanced set of training examples obtained by completely discarding of the uncertain-membership instances and removing the exceeding part of majority class instances

As regards the stratified sampling related to the D_i, three different rates were chosen for the experiments, namely 50%, 70% and 80%.

Finally, forests with an increasing number of trees were considered, namely: 10, 20 and 30. For each tree in a forest, the number of randomly selected candidates was determined as the square root of candidate refinements: $\sqrt{|\rho(\cdot)|}$.

As in previous works [9], to compare the predictions made using RFs against the ground truth assessed by a reasoner[5], the following indices were computed:

- *match* rate (M%): test individuals for which the inductive model and a reasoner agree on the membership (i.e. both +1, −1, or 0);
- *commission* rate (C%): test cases where the determined memberships are opposite (i.e. +1 vs. −1 or viceversa);
- *omission* rate (O%): test cases for which the inductive method cannot determine a definite membership while the reasoner can (0 vs. +1 or −1);

---

[5] The PELLET reasoner was used: http://clarkparsia.com/pellet/

Table 2. Results of experiments on the ontologies in Tab. 1 with no sampling

Ontology	Index	TDT	No Sampling		
			10 trees	20 trees	30 trees
BCO	M%	80.44±11.01	87.99±07.85	87.82±13.86	79.33±22.41
	C%	07.56±08.08	04.32±04.68	02.77±04.77	01.64±02.36
	O%	05.04±04.28	00.09±00.27	00.02±00.04	10.38±19.28
	I%	06.96±05.97	07.61±06.82	09.40±13.93	08.65±14.03
BIOPAX	M%	66.63±14.60	75.93±17.05	75.49±17.05	75.30±16.23
	C%	31.03±12.95	22.11±16.54	18.54±17.80	18.74±17.80
	O%	00.39±00.61	00.00±00.00	00.00±00.00	00.00±00.00
	I%	01.95±07.13	01.97±07.16	01.97±07.16	01.97±07.16
NTN	M%	68.85±13.23	83.42±07.85	83.42±07.85	83.42±07.85
	C%	00.37±00.30	00.02±00.04	00.02±00.04	00.02±00.04
	O%	09.51±07.06	13.40±10.17	13.40±10.17	13.40±10.17
	I%	21.27±08.73	03.16±04.65	03.16±04.65	03.16±04.65
HD	M%	58.31±14.06	67.95±16.99	67.95±16.99	67.95±16.99
	C%	00.44±00.47	00.02±00.05	00.02±00.05	00.02±00.05
	O%	05.51±01.81	06.38±02.03	06.38±02.03	06.38±02.03
	I%	35.74±15.90	25.61±18.98	25.61±18.98	25.61±18.98

- *induction* rate (I%): test cases where the inductive method can predict a definite membership while the reasoner cannot assess it (+1 or −1 vs. 0).

The experiment was carried out on a 2.5 Ghz PC with core i5 processor and 4GB RAM.

4.2 Results

Preliminarily, considering the distribution of the instances w.r.t. the target concepts, we observed that negative instances outnumber the positive ones in BCO and HUMAN DISEASE (HD). In the case of BCO this occurred for all concepts but one with a ratio between positive and negative instances of 1 : 20. In the case of HD this kind of imbalance occurred for all the queries. Moreover, in the case of HD the number of instances with an uncertain-membership is very large (about 90%). On the other hand, in the case of NTN, we noted the predominance of positive instances: for most concepts the ratio between positive and negative instances was 12 : 1 and a lot of uncertain-membership instances were found (again, over 90%). A weaker imbalance could be noted with BIOPAX. For most query concepts the ratio between positive and negative instances was 1 : 5. The class distribution was balanced for three concepts only.

Tables 2-5 present the results of the experiments. We report the values of the various indices, and related standard deviation, averaged over the 10 folds and the 15 target concepts (per ontology).

The experiment outcomes showed how predictions made with TRFs are accurate enough: the overall match rate was high for BCO ontology and for NTN while it was lower for BIOPAX and HD. However, in the latter case, a large induction rate was observed as a consequence of a large number of uncertain-membership instances in the test sets. Conversely, the lack of instances with uncertain-membership in BIOPAX lead to the increase the commission cases.

Table 3. Results of experiments with a sampling rate set to 50%

Ontology	Index	50%		
		10 trees	20 trees	30 trees
BCO	M%	86.27±15.79	86.24±15.94	86.26±15.84
	C%	02.47±03.70	02.43±03.70	02.84±03.70
	O%	01.90±07.30	01.97±07.55	01.92±07.37
	I%	09.36±13.96	09.36±13.96	09.36±13.96
BioPax	M%	75.30±16.23	75.30±16.23	75.30±16.23
	C%	18.74±17.80	18.74±17.80	18.74±17.80
	O%	00.00±00.00	00.00±00.00	00.00±00.00
	I%	01.97±07.16	01.97±07.16	01.97±07.16
NTN	M%	83.41±07.85	83.42±07.85	83.42±07.85
	C%	00.02±00.04	00.02±00.04	00.02±00.04
	O%	13.40±10.17	13.40±10.17	13.40±10.17
	I%	03.17±04.65	03.16±04.65	03.16±04.65
HD	M%	68.00±16.98	68.00±16.99	67.98±16.99
	C%	00.02±00.05	00.02±00.05	00.02±00.05
	O%	06.38±02.03	06.38±02.03	06.38±02.03
	I%	25.59±18.98	25.59±18.98	25.62±18.98

Table 4. Results of the experiments with a sampling rate of 70%

Ontology	Index	70%		
		10 trees	20 trees	30 trees
BCO	M%	84.12±18.27	85.70±16.98	85.52±17.09
	C%	02.16±03.09	02.32±03.39	02.30±03.38
	O%	04.50±12.59	02.65±09.93	02.86±10.04
	I%	09.23±13.98	09.33±13.97	09.31±13.91
BioPax	M%	75.30±16.23	75.30±16.23	75.30±16.23
	C%	18.74±17.80	18.74±17.80	18.74±17.80
	O%	00.00±00.00	00.00±00.00	00.00±00.00
	I%	01.97±07.16	01.97±07.16	01.97±07.16
NTN	M%	83.42±07.85	83.42±07.85	83.42±07.85
	C%	00.02±00.04	00.02±00.04	00.02±00.04
	O%	13.40+10.17	13.40±10.17	13.40±10.17
	I%	03.16±04.65	03.16±04.65	03.16±04.65
HD	M%	68.00±16.99	68.00±16.99	68.00±16.99
	C%	00.02±00.05	00.02±00.05	00.02±00.05
	O%	06.38±02.03	06.38±02.03	06.38±02.03
	I%	25.59±18.98	25.59±18.98	25.59±18.98

The experiments basically showed an improvement of performance in terms of match rate of the TRFs over the TDTs: it was generally higher when TRFs were employed. This improvement was around 7% for BCO, while it was around 9% both for BioPax and HD. The improvement is more noteworthy for NTN, where it was around 15%. The match rate is mainly due to a strong agreement of the weak learners on the label to be predicted. Indeed, we noted that, in the case of BCO ontology, all trees returned the same answer in favor of the correct label. Conversely, commission cases were related to those situations in which votes are distributed evenly w.r.t. the admissible labels.

A further consideration concerns the kind of models produced from the induction of TDTs and TRFs. The effectiveness of this kind of methods is also determined by the quality of the refinements used to produce trees. Indeed, in

Table 5. Results of the experiments with a sampling rate of 80%

Ontology	Index	80%		
		10 trees	*20 trees*	*30 trees*
BCO	M%	76.57±24.28	81.27±19.27	79.33±22.41
	C%	01.45±01.77	01.89±02.65	01.64±02.36
	O%	13.51±22.19	08.05±15.04	10.38±19.28
	I%	08.47±14.03	08.79±13.98	08.65±14.23
BioPax	M%	75.30±16.23	75.30±16.23	75.30±16.23
	C%	18.74±17.80	18.74±17.80	18.74±17.80
	O%	00.00±00.00	00.00±00.00	00.00±00.00
	I%	01.97±07.16	01.97±07.16	01.97±07.16
NTN	M%	83.41±07.85	83.42±07.85	83.42±07.85
	C%	00.02±00.04	00.02±00.04	00.02±00.04
	O%	13.40±10.17	13.40±10.17	13.40±10.17
	I%	03.17±04.65	03.16±04.65	03.16±04.65
HD	M%	68.00±16.99	68.00±16.99	68.00±16.99
	C%	00.02±00.05	00.02±00.05	00.02±00.05
	O%	06.38±02.03	06.38±02.03	06.38±02.03
	I%	25.59±18.98	25.59±18.98	25.59±18.98

some cases, poorly discriminative refinements were found during the training phase. As consequence, the resulting model tended to become more complex with some branches created to accommodate only a few training examples. Due to this situation, known as *small disjuncts problem*, in some cases the TDTs overfitted the training data (turning out to be more error-prone). However, this problem could be mitigated in TRFs that consider the other TDTs in the ensemble.

Concerning the effect of the two-step sampling, the match rate for BCO is higher when no sampling is applied and 10-trees forests were employed. Increasing the number of trees, we can observe a decrease of the match rate and a further increase of the induction cases. On the other hand, the commission rate decreases and a large number of omission cases can be observed in presence of larger forests made up of 30 trees. The omission cases occurred when neither of the TDTs of the forest could assess the membership. This may be due to a strong similarity between the TDTs of the forest, which could be related to the overlap that characterizes the training subsets required to grow each TDT. By setting the sampling rate to 50%, a smaller number of instances was required to train the forest. Likely, the intermediate tests of each TDT were able to better discriminate the instances belonging to the test concept. With a larger number of trees, the behavior did not change significantly. Again, this could be related to the overlap and the subsequent diversification. Due to the increase of the rate for stratified sampling, noisy instances could be added in the learning process, which made the purity measure poorer than the previous cases and hence the refinements became less discriminative.

As regards the results of the experiments with HD, similar considerations with those made for BCO are valid also for this ontology. However, the results of our experiments show that the various forests had approximately the same accuracy. This occurred not only for a specific sampling rate, but also increasing both number of trees and the sampling rate. Although a large stratified sampling allowed to consider more instances than a lower sampling rate, the undersampling of majority class instances probably removed a lot of redundant examples [7], without adding further information for the improvement of the quality of the produced model. This might have occurred also because of the previously mentioned problem of the small disjuncts. In the case of the TDTs and of the TRFs, it means that, while during the training phase, the concepts installed as current node were the same both with and without the application of the sampling strategy. In both cases, the split procedure according to the instance check test sent all the examples along only one branch while the other had no instances for the recursive call (see Fig. 1). Consequently, the difference that could exist between the employment of sampling and not is simply related to the number of instances that were propagated. In this case, only a part of the majority class examples could be considered as useful for learning.

For NTN quite a high omission rate was observed. Again, the performance of TRF models did not change much over all the experiments considering different sampling rates and numbers of TDTs. Again, this is related to the presence of redundant examples. Moreover, some trees turned out to be very poor predictors, unlike those built in the experiments with other ontologies. In this case, the most of the training examples had the same membership w.r.t. the target concepts and hence further refinement steps were not required.

As previously mentioned, the datasets generated for the experiments with BioPax suffered less from the class-imbalance problem compared to those generated for the experiments with the other ontologies. In this case, the different performance w.r.t. the experiments proposed in [9] could be due to the number of generated trees when no sampling is employed. Moreover, the application of stratified sampling and the lack of uncertain-membership instances has led to situations in which each tree is trained on a smaller set of instances.

The execution time for the experiments spanned from few minutes (less than a quarter of hour) for BCO to almost 10 hours for HD for inducing the forests w.r.t. all the 15 target concepts. This difference seems to be directly related to the number of instances as well as non-informative splits that did not allow to produce early leaves for the TDTs in the various forests.

Lessons Learnt and Current Limitations. From the discussion reported above, it can be noted that the proposed method shows various interesting aspects as well as some limitations.

The smallest changes in terms of match rate relating to the number of trees as well as the stratified sampling rate seem to suggest that there is no need to set high values for these parameters. For instance, given a TRF composed by 10 TDTs, with a stratified sampling rate of 50%, we observed competitive results although this combination of parameters values is non-optimal. Therefore it is possible to speed up the training phase and reduce the exploiting of the instance-check service required for the splitting phase in order to potentially improve the scalability of the method.

Finally, the non-informative splittings obtaining according to the description that are returned by the refinement operator may represent a potential bottleneck for the training phase. Particularly, this seems to hold for large ontologies. However, it should be noted that our implementation[6] is not currently optimized and the limitation may be overcome through the parallelization of learning process or by means a Map/Reduce approach [15].

5   Conclusion and Extensions

In this work, we intended to tackle the class-imbalance problem when learning predictive classification models for SW knowledge bases. To address this, we devised an extension of the model based on terminological decision trees. The proposed method combines sampling methods with ensemble learning techniques in order to mitigate some problems deriving from the employment of sampling. As a result, the terminological random forest model has been introduced and a preliminary empirical evaluation with publicly available ontologies has been performed. The experiments have shown how the predictiveness of the new classification model can be sufficiently tolerant to variation of the number of trees and the sampling rate.

In the future, we plan to extend the method along various directions. One direction regards the choice of refinement operator that may be applied in order to generate more discriminative intermediate test. Further ensemble techniques and novel rules for combining the answers of the weak learners could be employed. The experimental evaluation shall be extended in order to provide further evidences in favor of the method by considering larger datasets extracted from the Linked Data cloud [1]. In this perspective, the method could be parallelized in order to employ it as a non-standard way to reason over such datasets. Further investigation may be concerns the application of strategies aiming either to optimize the ensemble or to improve the diversification of the single classifier models in the ensemble, that is an important characteristic of ensemble learning methods [16,17].

Acknowledgments. This work fulfills the research objectives of the PON 02_00563_3470993 project "Vincente - A Virtual collective INtelligenCe ENvironment to develop sustainable Technology Entrepreneurship ecosystems" funded by the Italian Ministry of University and Research (MIUR).

References

1. Heath, T., Bizer, C.: Linked Data: Evolving the Web into a Global Data Space. Synthesis Lectures on the Semantic Web. Morgan & Claypool Publishers (2011)

---

[6] The implementation of the TRF learning algorithm is available at:
https://github.com/Giuseppe-Rizzo/SWMLAlgorithms

2. d'Amato, C., Fanizzi, N., Esposito, F.: Inductive learning for the Semantic Web: What does it buy? Semant. Web 1, 53–59 (2010)
3. Rettinger, A., Lösch, U., Tresp, V., d'Amato, C., Fanizzi, N.: Mining the Semantic Web - Statistical learning for next generation knowledge bases. Data Min. Knowl. Discov. 24, 613–662 (2012)
4. Rettinger, A., Nickles, M., Tresp, V.: Statistical relational learning with formal ontologies. In: Buntine, W., Grobelnik, M., Mladenić, D., Shawe-Taylor, J. (eds.) ECML PKDD 2009, Part II. LNCS, vol. 5782, pp. 286–301. Springer, Heidelberg (2009)
5. Minervini, P., d'Amato, C., Fanizzi, N., Esposito, F.: Transductive inference for class-membership propagation in web ontologies. In: Cimiano, P., Corcho, O., Presutti, V., Hollink, L., Rudolph, S. (eds.) ESWC 2013. LNCS, vol. 7882, pp. 457–471. Springer, Heidelberg (2013)
6. He, H., Garcia, E.A.: Learning from imbalanced data. IEEE Trans. on Knowl. and Data Eng. 21, 1263–1284 (2009)
7. He, H., Ma, Y.: Imbalanced Learning: Foundations, Algorithms, and Applications, 1st edn. Wiley-IEEE Press (2013)
8. Freund, Y., Schapire, R.E.: Experiments with a new boosting algorithm. In: Saitta, L. (ed.) ICML, pp. 148–156. Morgan Kaufmann (1996)
9. Fanizzi, N., d'Amato, C., Esposito, F.: Induction of concepts in web ontologies through terminological decision trees. In: Balcázar, J.L., Bonchi, F., Gionis, A., Sebag, M. (eds.) ECML PKDD 2010, Part I. LNCS, vol. 6321, pp. 442–457. Springer, Heidelberg (2010)
10. Baader, F., Calvanese, D., McGuinness, D., Nardi, D., Patel-Schneider, P. (eds.): The Description Logic Handbook. 2nd edn. Cambridge University Press (2007)
11. Blockeel, H., De Raedt, L.: Top-down induction of first-order logical decision trees. Artif. Intell. 101(1-2), 285–297 (1998)
12. Breiman, L.: Random forests. Machine Learning 45, 5–32 (2001)
13. Chen, C., Liaw, A., Breiman, L.: Using random forest to learn imbalanced data. Technical report, Department of Statistics, University of Berkeley (2004)
14. Assche, A.V., Vens, C., Blockeel, H., Dzeroski, S.: First order random forests: Learning relational classifiers with complex aggregates. Machine Learning 64, 149–182 (2006)
15. Li, B., Chen, X., Li, M.J., Huang, J.Z., Feng, S.: Scalable random forests for massive data. In: Tan, P.-N., Chawla, S., Ho, C.K., Bailey, J. (eds.) PAKDD 2012, Part I. LNCS, vol. 7301, pp. 135–146. Springer, Heidelberg (2012)
16. Fu, B., Wang, Z., Pan, R., Xu, G., Dolog, P.: An integrated pruning criterion for ensemble learning based on classification accuracy and diversity. In: Uden, L., Herrera, F., Bajo, J., Corchado, J.M. (eds.) 7th International Conference on KMO. AISC, vol. 172, pp. 47–58. Springer, Heidelberg (2013), http://dx.doi.org/10.1007/978-3-642-30867-3_5
17. Yin, X.C., Yang, C., Hao, H.W.: Learning to diversify via weighted kernels for classifier ensemble. CoRR abs/1406.1167 (2014)

On the Collaborative Development of Application Ontologies: A Practical Case Study with a SME

Marco Rospocher[1], Elena Cardillo[2], Ivan Donadello[1,3], and Luciano Serafini[1]

[1] Fondazione Bruno Kessler—IRST,
Via Sommarive 18, Trento, I-38123, Italy
{rospocher,donadello,serafini}@fbk.eu
[2] Institute for Informatics and Telematics—IIT-CNR,
Via P. Bucci 17B, Rende, I-87036, Italy
{elena.cardillo@iit.cnr.it}
[3] Department of Information and Communication Technology, University of Trento,
Via Sommarive 9, Trento, I-38123, Italy

Abstract. With semantic technologies coming of age, ontology-based applications are becoming more prevalent. These applications exploit the content encoded in ontologies to perform different tasks and operations. The development of ontologies to be used by a specific application presents some peculiarities compared to the modelling process of other types of ontologies. These peculiarities are related to the choice of the ontology metamodel which should be optimised for the application, and the possibility of an indirect evaluation of the ontology by running the application. In this paper we report the experience of collaboratively building an ontology for an application that supports the development of Individual Educational Plans (IEPs) for pupils with special needs. This application is a commercial product of a Small-Medium Enterprise (SME). The ontology is the result of a one-year long modelling experience that involved more than a dozen users having different expertise and competences, such as educationalists, psychologists, teachers, knowledge engineers, and application engineers. Beside describing the modelling process and tool, we report the lessons learned in collaboratively modelling an application ontology in a very concrete case. We believe our experience is worth reporting as our findings and lessons learned may be beneficial for similar modelling initiatives regarding the development of application ontologies.

1 Introduction

The last couple of decades have seen the growing popularity of ontology-based applications, i.e., applications that exploit the knowledge formalized in ontologies to perform given tasks and operations, like data integration, content classification and recommendation, and knowledge inferencing.[1] While in some cases these

---

[1] For an overview of ontology-based applications, we point the reader to Part IV of [1].

K. Janowicz et al. (Eds.): EKAW 2014, LNAI 8876, pp. 469–484, 2014.
© Springer International Publishing Switzerland 2014

applications exploit available ontologies, there are situations where the ontology is built specifically for the given application (see e.g., [2,3,4,5]). These ontologies, aka *application ontologies* [6], typically formalize various types of content, spanning from domain knowledge on the application context, to content that is application-specific (e.g., content shown in the application interface to support interaction with the user). Furthermore, the formalization of the content in these ontologies may actually depend on the specific way the application exploits the ontology for performing the given tasks and operations.

In this paper, we describe the construction of the *IEP ontology*, an application ontology specifically built to support the development of Individual Education Plans (IEPs) for pupils with special needs (i.e., disabilities). The ontology is at the core of *ePlanning* , a commercial product developed by an Italian Small-Medium Enterprise (SME)[2] that helps teachers in defining educational goals for pupils having an impairment of some functional abilities, proposing them also activities to achieve these goals, and materials that may help performing these activities. The ontology modelling process involved more than a dozen of users with different competences and modelling skills: *domain experts*, like educationalists, psychologists, and teachers, who contributed with their deep knowledge of the pedagogical domain, including functional abilities, goals, activities, and materials; *knowledge engineers*, who contributed with their modelling skills; and, *application engineers*, i.e., developers of ePlanning, who provided the application perspective, especially in terms of ontology requirements and evaluation. With the exception of knowledge engineers, all users involved in the modelling process were employees or collaborators of the SME. To support the modelling activities, and in particular the active contribution of domain experts in the construction of the ontology, we developed a customized version of MoKi [7], a collaborative wiki-based ontology modelling tool in which users provide ontological content via forms. The tool has been used by 13 users, mainly people from the SME, which performed over 6500 editing activities in a one-year period.

The contribution of this paper is two-fold: on the one hand, we present the modelling process and the customization of MoKi adopted to build the IEP Ontology; on the other hand, we report the lessons learned in collaboratively modelling an application ontology in a very concrete case, i.e., the development of an ontology-based commercial application of a SME. We believe our experience is worth reporting as our findings and lessons learned may be beneficial for similar modelling initiatives regarding the development of application ontologies.

The paper is organized as follows. Section 2 introduces the modelling scenario, contextualizing the role of the IEP Ontology in ePlanning. Section 3 presents the modelling process that we followed to build the ontology, while Section 4 describes the customization of MoKi that we used, as well as some statistics on its usage during the modelling activities. Section 5 provides an overview of the current version of the IEP ontology. We discuss the lessons learned from the modelling experience in Section 6, while we conclude in Section 7 with some final remarks.

---

[2] Edizioni Erickson – http://www.erickson.it/

2   Modelling Context

Italian government regulates inclusive education of people with special needs and disabilities [8], defining an IEP as "a document that describes integrated and balanced interventions, prepared for students with disabilities in a given period of time, for the purpose of executing the right to education and training". An IEP has to be built by teachers for each pupil with disabilities and it has to be conceived as integral part of the class teaching programming. Moreover, it could be integrated by contributions of other actors, such as local health operators, psychologists, and family.

In addition to information regarding the pupil's profile (e.g., master data, class characteristics - human resources in support, aids for learning and autonomy, etc.), an IEP is constituted by four main components, which correspond to four phases of planning and work [9]. The *first component* is the Functional Diagnosis (FD), that according to [8] falls to the local health authority or affiliated organizations. The FD describes the functional impairment of the psycho-physical state of the pupil: it is expressed in a profile, in which abilities, capabilities and growth difficulties of the pupil are described. It is drawn up according to the criteria of the bio-psycho-social model that is the basis of the International Classification of Functioning, Disability and Health (ICF).[3] This means that the FD has to be described by relating information on: physical conditions, body functions, body structures, personal activities, social activities, and contextual factors. The *second component* is the Dynamic Funtional Profile (DFP). It follows the FD, carrying out two important functions: *(i)* discussing the clinical components of the FD with additional information derived from school and family; *(ii)* defining the educational goals to be reached at the end of the school year for improving pupil's capabilities and inclusion. According to the timing of implementation, educational goals are distinguished in: (i) final goals (or long-term goals); (ii) intermediate general goals (or medium term goals); and, (iii) immediate directional goals (or short term goals). *Third* and *fourth components* are respectively related to: activities, methodologies, techniques and materials to facilitate the achievement of the set goals; and finally midterm monitoring and checks in case of changing of FD or DFP.

The adoption of ICF as bio-psycho-social classification model useful for the integration between pupil's functional abilities and his social, cultural and personal context, is regulated by the guidelines for inclusive education of disabled pupils, issued by the Italian Ministry of Education University and Research (MEUR) on August 2009. Nonetheless the use of ICF for the implementation of the FD in an IEP is still considered a difficult task by teachers. Two critical aspects of ICF are the amount of codes (1661 for ICF-CY), that makes it difficult to assimilate by domain experts and teachers, and the complexity of its conceptual schema [10]. The complexity of ICF structure was criticized in the literaure by [11], where an ontological analysis of the domain of processes and functioning in ICF is presented.

---

[3] http://www.who.int/classifications/icf/en/

This and other issues motivated: (i) the necessity for a simpler model for representing the domain, mainly focused on the abilities and activities of the pupil in the personal, social and school contexts; and, (ii) the construction of an intelligent system that, based on this simplified model, supports and guides teachers in the definition of an IEP for any pupil.

We thus proposed the design of an ontology, namely the IEP ontology, that serves two purposes: on the one hand, it represents a classification of functional and cognitive abilities (à la ICF); and, on the other hand, it describes a complete model of abilities, educational goals, activities, and educational materials, that could be exploited by an intelligent system (the ePlanning application) to support the automatic creation of an IEP. Note that, as for the creation of IEPs, the involvement of different actors was needed also for building such ontology. Besides domain experts (such as educationalists, psychologists, teachers), who defined domain knowledge on functional abilities, goals, activities, and materials, and knowledge engineers, who guided the modelling activities and supported the formalization, we also involved application engineers, who provided application specific requirements on the ontology content.

In the literature, very few experiences are reported concerning the formalization of knowledge in similar contexts. One example is described in [12], which proposes an ontological formalization of ICF. Authors discussed a preliminary qualitative and quantitative analysis of the relationships used in the "Activities and Participation" component of ICF, trying to identify potential logical problems by defining mapping to SUMO (Suggested Upper Merged Ontology) concepts.

Our work comes alongside the reporting of concrete modelling experiences and lessons learned in collaborative settings, such as the collaborative ontological formalization of ICD-11 presented in [13]. Differently from other works in the literature, our contribution presents the experience of collaboratively modelling an application ontology, i.e., an ontology which is built targeting also the needs and requirements of the specific application it is meant for. Furthermore, the ontology is built in a very concrete case: the development of a commercial ontology-based application in a SME.

3   Modelling Process

The development process of the IEP ontology consisted of four main phases.

Phase 1: Ontology Requirements Specification. At the beginning of the modelling activities, in collaboration with the domain experts and application engineers, we specified the requirements of the IEP ontology by following the Ontology Requirements Specification guidelines described in [14]. The output of this activity was the IEP Ontology Requirements Specification Document (ORSD), a template-based report containing information about the:

- PURPOSE. (i) To provide a classification of functional and cognitive abilities of children and youth persons according to a given conceptual schema defined by expert educationalists and psychologists in the field; (ii) to support the compilation via an intelligent system of Individual Education Plans for pupils having some of their functional abilities compromised.

- SCOPE. The ontology should describe (i) functional and cognitive abilities; (ii) proposals of educational goals to be set in view of some compromised abilities; (iii) examples of activities to be performed to reach the proposed goals; (iv) educational materials that may be used to perform an activity; (v) related information such as sex, age, educational level and school grades, useful to define the pupil's profile.
- IMPLEMENTATION LANGUAGE. OWL.
- INTENDED USERS. Different typologies of users may have to interact with the content stored in the ontology: teachers, clinicians, neuropsychiatrists, educationalists, parents. However, all these users will access the ontology content via the ePlanning application, the main "user" of the ontology.
- INTENDED USES. The ePlanning application interacts with the IEP ontology mainly by querying it, exploiting reasoning, to retrieve content that may help a user in building an IEP.
- NON-FUNCTIONAL REQUIREMENTS. (i) Any annotation (e.g., label, comment) of ontology entities should be provided in Italian; (ii) the ontology should be richly annotated with natural language text, in different forms and using different terminologies (e.g., definitions, explanatory questions), to favour the comprehension and exploitation of its content by a broad spectrum of users (see intended users); (iii) the ontology should contain mappings to relevant classes defined in international health classifications like ICD-10 and ICF-CY; (iv) to keep the ontology simple and to favour its usability in the application, multi-inheritance is not allowed (i.e., a class can be subclass of at most one class);
- FUNCTIONAL REQUIREMENTS. To define the functional requirements of the ontology, we relied on *competency questions* [15], that is questions that an (instantiated) ontology should be able to answer, and that therefore are useful to guide the formalization process. Some of the competency questions that we considered are reported in Table 1.
- PRE-GLOSSARY OF TERMS (excerpt). Functional ability, ICD-10 code, ICF-CY code, activity, short/medium/long term goal, educational material, educational level, school grade, light/medium/severe impairment, sex.

Phase 2: Definition of the Ontology "Metamodel". The second modelling phase was the development of the IEP ontology "metamodel" (aka, "content model"), i.e., the upper ontology which provides the basic structures, definitions, and properties to be used in the ontology: indeed, the actual IEP ontology imports this metamodel, specifying the classes of the latter according to the actual abilities, goals, activities, and materials to be defined. Therefore, in the IEP ontology metamodel we defined general classes like "Ability", "Goal", "Activity", and "Material", as well as properties like those that enable (i) mapping an ability to classes in standard international classifications (e.g. ICF-CY, ICD-10), (ii) asserting that to work on a pupil ability some goals can be set and some activities

Table 1. Excerpt of the IEP ontology competency questions

CQ1. Given the impairment of a functional ability of a pupil, what are the (short
/medium/long term) goals to be set so that the pupil may overcome it?

CQ2. Given the impairment of a functional ability of a pupil, are there other abilities
to be considered that are more specific than it?

CQ3. Given the impairment of a functional ability of a pupil, are there other abilities
to be considered that are more general than it?

CQ4. Given the impairment of a functional ability of a pupil, are there other abilities
that are introductory to it (i.e., to be considered before)?

CQ5. Given the impairment of a functional ability of a pupil, are there other abilities
to be considered that are complementary to it?

CQ6. Given the impairment of a functional ability of a pupil, what are the ICF-CY
and ICD-10 codes associated to it?

CQ7. Given the impairment of a functional ability of a pupil, and a goal set for it,
what activities can be performed if the pupil suffers of severe visual problems?

CQ8. Given an activity, which educational materials can be used to support the
performing of the activity by the pupil?

CQ9. Is this functional ability appropriate according to the sex of the pupil?

---

performed (with the help of some materials), and (iii) expressing that before
working on a pupil ability, other abilities should be considered as well. Other
notions formalized in the IEP ontology metamodel are "Sex", "Level of impairment of an ability", "Timing of implementation", and so on. Another decision
that we took in the metamodel, to cope with the dual purpose of the ontology,
is to require that each ability is expressed both with a class and an individual.[4]
The former is used to favour the construction of the ontology of functional abilities as typically done in standard classifications, i.e., as a taxonomy of classes,
while the latter is used to favour the representation and exploitation of all the
properties and attributes related to an ability (e.g., the fact that a certain ability
is investigated only with pupils of the primary school) in the application. Note
that, as discussed in Phase 3, this modelling choice was completely transparent
to the modellers building the actual IEP ontology.

Phase 3: Formalization of Abilities, Goals, Activities, and Materials. The third
phase of the modelling process consisted in the formal definition of the actual
abilities, goals, activities, and materials in the IEP ontology. Based on the output
of the previous two phases, domain experts were asked to define a taxonomy of
functional abilities, rooted in the metamodel class "Ability", and to provide for
each actual ability the information needed to characterize it according to the
metamodel defined in Phase 2.

As different competencies and expertise (e.g., people having medical background, educationalists, neuropsychiatrists, teachers) were needed to produce
the required quality content, a truly collaborative effort was envisaged: therefore,
to support the team of domain experts in modelling this wealth of content, we

---

[4] *à la* OWL Punning: http://www.w3.org/2007/OWL/wiki/Punning

provided a customized version of MoKi (the Modelling Wiki) [7], a collaborative wiki-based ontology modelling tool. As described in Section 4, the customization mainly consisted in defining ad-hoc forms (based on the ontology metamodel defined in Phase 2) to guide the domain experts in filling in the required content, as well as in providing customized functionalities to browse the content of the ontology under development. Note that, by means of such form based interface, the domain experts were abstracted from the actual formal encoding in the ontology of the content they provided.

Given the availability in a bunch of spreadsheets of some draft version of the taxonomy of abilities (i.e., mainly the name of the abilities and the ability/sub-ability relation between some of them), we automatically preloaded in MoKi the content of these spreadsheets. This preliminary content was then revised and substantially enriched in MoKi by the domain experts.

Phase 4: Ontology Evaluation. Besides checking the IEP ontology against the competency questions defined in Phase 1, by translating them into SPARQL queries that we ran against its evolving versions, we also set up an indirect domain experts and application engineers evaluation by periodically deploying the working-copy of the ontology (thus, potentially incomplete and inaccurate) into the ePlanning application prototype under development. While on the one side this application-focused evaluation favoured the development of the prototype itself, on the other side it sets up the conditions such that domain experts and application engineers were able to spot anomalies, modelling mistakes, or shortcomings of the ontology, by actually "using" the ontology within the prototype. This application-focused evaluation strategy allowed us to detect some modelling issues related either to inaccurate content provided in Phase 3, or even to the IEP ontology metamodel defined in Phase 2, due to wrong or missing modelling assumptions/competency questions (some examples are commented in Section 6). Fixing these later issues actually required to revise some of the competency questions defined in Phase 1 (or the introduction of new competency questions), which in turn triggered a revision of the IEP ontology metamodel and of the MoKi forms.

4   A MoKi for ePlanning

As described in Section 3, domain experts collaboratively and actively participated in the modelling activities by using a customized version of MoKi.[5]

In MoKi, each ontology entity is associated to a wiki page, where users fill in content according to forms that guide them in contributing to the development of the ontology. Figure 1 shows the typical page (and corresponding form) associated to an ontology entity (in this case, the ability "Feeding through baby bottle, shake, with the help of another person"). The top menu allows, among other

---

[5] A description of the general MoKi framework can be found in [7]. In this paper, we highlight the specific features and functionalities customized for the development of the IEP ontology.

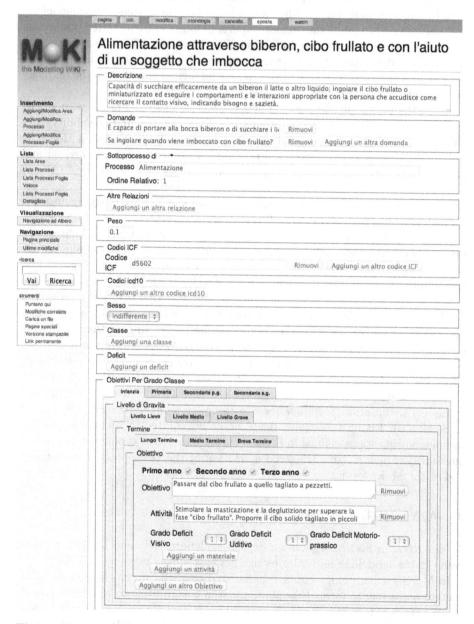

Fig. 1. The form used by the modelling team to edit the IEP ontology with MoKi (Italian labels are explained in Section 4)

things, editing (*modifica*), deleting (*cancella*), and renaming (*sposta*) the ontology entity, as well as checking the history of changes performed on it (*cronologia*). Instead, the left sidebar allows to access functionalities like the adding of a new ontology entity (*Inserimento* group), the listing of ontology entities by type (*Lista* group), and the tree-like browsing of the taxonomical relations in the ontology (*Navigazione ad albero* entry). Furthermore, to support user awareness of the modelling activities on the ontology, users can easily inspect the latest changes performed (*Ultime modifiche* entry).

The form in Figure 1 is designed according to the IEP ontology metamodel, to guide the formalization of the content by domain experts: this way, it provides a standard web-based editing interface, something with which users are familiar, hiding the actual underlying OWL formalization from them. Modellers can insert several annotations, like a description (*Descrizione* box) of the functional ability under definition as well as questions (*Domande* box) that may help end users, typically not very familiar with the domain and the terminology used, to better understand if that ability is something to work on with the pupil. Besides having the possibility of expressing if an ability is more specific than another one (*Sottoprocesso di* box),[6] users can also state that an ability is complementary/preparatory/correlated to another ability (*Altre Relazioni di* box). The *Peso* box is used to represent an application specific attribute that, in combination with some aspects of the pupil's profile, is used to discard abilities in the development of an IEP if they fall below a certain threshold value. Linking to ICF-CY and ICD-10 classifications is enabled via the *Codici ICF* and *Codici ICD10* boxes.[7] The *Sesso, Classe, Deficit* boxes allow to express (i) that the ability applies to males and/or females (e.g., abilities related to female period), (ii) that the ability applies only to pupils of certain school grades and age (e.g., ability to drive vehicles), and (iii) that the ability should always be analysed in pupils with some common impairment (visual/hearing/mobility).

The multi-tab lower part of the form (*Obiettivo Per Grado Classe* box) enables to specify proposals of educational goals (*Obiettivo* field), activities (*Attività* field), and materials (*Aggiungi un materiale* button) based on the educational level (four outermost tabs: *Infanzia, Primaria, Secondaria p.g., Secondaria s.g.* corresponding to pre-primary, primary, lower secondary, and upper secondary school), the severity of impairment of the ability (the three tabs: *Livello Lieve, Livello Medio, Livello Grave*), and the length of the term (i.e., timing of implementation) on which to work with the pupil on that goal (the three tabs: *Lungo Termine, Medio Termine, Breve Termine*). The user can also express that a certain goal applies only to specific school grades of a given educational level (e.g., the three tick boxes: *Primo Anno, Secondo Anno, Terzo Anno*), or that a specific activity can be performed or not depending on the visual/hearing/mobility

---

[6] The "Ordine Relativo" entry is used to keep track of the order in which the subclasses of an ability have to be presented to the user through the ePlanning user interface. See also Section 6.

[7] User can lookup the appropriate ICF-CY and ICD-10 codes directly from the MoKi interface.

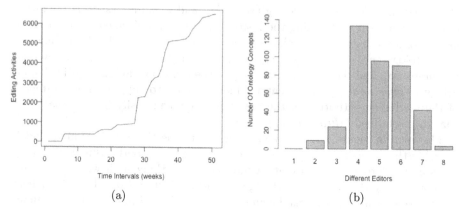

Fig. 2. (a) The cumulative number of editing activities in MoKi (from July 2013 to June 2014); (b) Number of ontology concepts (y axis) edited by distinct users (x axis)

impairments of the pupils (e.g., to avoid proposing activities which require movement to a pupil with some mobility impairment).

MoKi provides fine-grained access control at the level of each single box of the form: that is, based on the group they belong, users can edit or not any specific element of the form. Furthermore, MoKi tracks in detailed logs all the editing activities performed by users as well as all the functionalities they have used while working on the ontology.

4.1   Usage of MoKi

Phase 3 of the modelling process (the one in which MoKi was used to formalize abilities, goals, activities, and materials) has spanned over almost one year (starting date: July 2013).[8] Before starting this modelling phase, we ran a tutorial (with presentations and hands-on sessions) with the modellers explaining them how to use MoKi and all its functionalities in order to participate to the modelling activities.

During the modelling period, 13 users participated to the editing activities in MoKi: seven domain experts (educationalists and psychologists), four teachers, one application engineer, and one knowledge engineer. They produced 6538 editing contributions.[9] Figure 2a shows the cumulative number of editing activities between July 2013 and June 2014. After a slow start, a noticeable burst of editing activities can be seen around week 27, which corresponds to the actual starting of the development of the first prototype of the ePlanning application.

The average number of editing activities per user on the ontologies is 594 (max: 2782, median: 327). On average, each class has been edited approximatively 16

---

[8] At the time of writing this paper, some minor editing activities are still going on.

[9] Note that by "editing contribution/activity" we mean the saving of the MoKi page corresponding to an ontology entity. This can actually correspond to changes on multiple boxes of the form of the page.

Table 2. Metrics about the metamodel and the IEP ontology

	metamodel	IEP Ontology
DL Expressivity	$\mathcal{SROIF(D)}$	$\mathcal{SROIF(D)}$
Classes	20	419
Object Properties	44	44
Datatype Properties	3	3
Individuals	40	20339
Class Axioms	31	1066
Object Properties Axioms	155	155
Datatype Property Axioms	9	9
Individual Axioms	74	198095
Annotations	75	21571

times (with a maximum of 87 editing activities on a single class, and a minimum of 4). Every ontology class was edited by at least 2 distinct users (see Figure 2b), and approximatively 92% of them have been edited by at least four distinct users (35% of the classes have been actually edited even by six to eight distinct users), remarking the truly collaborative nature of this modelling phase.

Concerning the usage of functionalities, the logs show that users tended to monitor the evolution of the ontology (626 times the change history on an ontology entity and the latest changes on the ontology were invoked), and they equally used the list-based (397 times) and tree-based (394 times) views to browse the ontology.

5   The IEP Ontology

Table 2 reports some quantitative metrics of the current version of the IEP ontology.[10] The IEP ontology consists of the metamodel ontology (defined in Phase 2 of the modelling process), and of the content provided by domain experts in MoKi (Phase 3). The first column of the table highlights the contribution of the metamodel ontology, while the values of the second column refer to the complete IEP ontology.

As shown in the table, there is a huge difference in size between the metamodel and the complete ontology (e.g., see the metrics about the number of individuals, class axioms, individual axioms, and annotations). This remarks the quantity of content filled by domain experts in MoKi.[11] A closer look to the IEP ontology content reveals that domain experts defined 399 functional abilities, which are formalized both as classes (see the difference between the two columns for the

---

[10] As the ontology is the core element of the ePlanning application, a commercial product of the SME, we are not allowed to distribute it.

[11] To be precise, domain experts filled in MoKi content that, once exported from MoKi to OWL, produced an ontology with the quantitative specifications reported in Table 2 (i.e., a single entry in a MoKi form may lead to the instantiation of several individuals and individual axioms in the resulting OWL ontology).

entry "Classes" of the table) as well as individuals: 6 of these functional abilities are top-level classes in the hierarchy (aka, *areas*), while 275 of them are leaf classes in the taxonomy (aka, *leaf functional abilities*), i.e., they do not have more specific functional abilities. The taxonomy of classes has a maximum depth of 5. Domain experts, beside adding a description for each functional ability, provided 489 explanatory questions (on average, 1.2 questions per functional ability), that by using a less-formal example-oriented language formulation, aim to help to better understand and discriminate what a given functional ability is about. Concerning the mappings to WHO international classifications, 150 functional abilities are mapped to 262 ICF-CY codes via 305 mapping, while 56 functional abilities are mapped to 63 ICD-10 codes via 101 mappings.

The modelling team also defined 9278 proposals of educational goals, defined for all the 275 leaf functional abilities (on average, 33.7 goals per functional ability), 9171 activities (on average, almost one activity per goal), and 962 educational materials.

6   Discussion and Lesson Learned

The one-year long experience of collaboratively developing an application ontology to be used in a commercial product of a SME let emerge several interesting modelling-related aspects that it is worth sharing.

Importance of Having a "Flexible" Modelling Tool. The customization of MoKi used to develop the IEP ontology has noticeably changed since its first release at the beginning of the modelling phase. On the one hand, several changes were performed on the MoKi forms further to adaptation of the ontology metamodel due to refinements of the ontology requirements. Thanks to the flexibility of the form definition (basically an XML file), we were able to promptly adapt the MoKi editing interface (e.g., addition of new boxes) without requiring any modellers intervention on the content previously introduced (this situation occurred five times during the modelling phase). On the other hand, to better support the modeller activities, we exploited the modularity of the MoKi framework to seamlessly plug-in "on request" functionalities in the tool. For instance, to have a better overview of the whole model, modellers asked for a list-based view of the functional abilities defined in the model, highlighting whether goals are provided for them (and for which educational level/school grade). The addition of functionalities like this one did not affect the modelling activities, both in terms of tool down-time (functionalities can be plugged in "live" in the running web-application) and content (no changes are required on the ontology under construction). The benefit of having a flexible modelling tool was also previously observed in [13], where a different modelling tool was used (iCat).

Benefits in Adopting an Ad-hoc, On-Line, and Collaborative Modelling Tool. At the beginning of the modelling activities, the modelling team was moderately reluctant to adopt MoKi: they were familiar with spreadsheets,[12] and keen to use them also for developing the ontology. Indeed, due to the availability of some preliminary content in spreadsheet form, some initial activities were performed by domain experts in this direction. Several issues rapidly emerged, such as the proliferation of "latest" versions of the document and the considerable human effort required to merge and reconcile contributions from different users in the up-to-date version of the document. While some of these aspects could have been mitigate with the use of some on-line spreadsheet application, the infeasibility of the approach became evident also to modellers as soon as it got clear the wealth and complexity of the content to be represented.

Despite the initial doubts and disinclination, users ended up using extensively the tool, as shown by the 6538 editing activities (we traced more than 22,000 activities in the logs, mainly page accesses/inspections). Users actually exploited in full the on-line "edit wherever you are" capability of the tool, as we traced editing activities from 64 different network domains (compare with the 13 users). As remarked in Section 4.1, users also amply used the functionalities for collaboration awareness and model overview, including those provided ah-hoc for this customization of MoKi.

Early Deployment of an Application Ontology in Its Corresponding System to Improve Ontology Quality. Since the early stages of the ontology construction, we periodically "released" to the application developers the up-to-date version of the ontology, even if incomplete and potentially inaccurate, to bootstrap the development of the application prototype. As a side-effect, this strategy turned out as particularly successful to improve the quality of the ontology itself, as by seeing the ontology in use in the system, domain experts and application engineers were able to better understand the role of the ontology in the system. This helped to detect a number of (application-related) issues that triggered a revision of the ontology (and its metamodel) already during the modelling phase:

Revision or Extension of the Competency Questions. Some competency questions were revised or even added, thus triggering a revision of the ontology metamodel. As an example of the first situation, the detail of the level of impairment (see the drop-down boxes *Grado Deficit Visivo*, *Grado Deficit Uditivo*, *Grado Deficit Motorio-prassico* at the bottom of the form in Figure 1), initially envisaged as relative to goals, was moved to activities, so to discriminate activities (and not goals) that could be performed (or not) based on the profile of the pupil. As an example of the latter, to avoid presenting in ePlanning too many abilities to be investigated by a user when compiling an IEP, an additional box was introduced in MoKi to model a value (*Peso* box in Figure 1, a real number between 0 and 1 representing a sort of likelihood that a functional ability has to be investigated) that, in combination with some aspects of the pupil's profile, enables to filter some abilities to be shown to the user if their value falls below a certain threshold.

---

[12] A quite popular situation, as noted also in [16,13].

This triggered the addition of a further competency question involving the retrieval of this value from the ontology.

Mismatch of Implicit Assumptions. When modelling the subclasses of a given class, domain experts were defining them in a precise order (i.e., class X is the first subclass of Y, Z is the second subclass of Y, and so on), according to some educational best-practices. However, as this requirement was not explicitly made during the ontology specification phase, they discovered when using the ontology in the ePlanning application prototype that this ordering was not preserved, as ordering has to be explicitly modelled in OWL (see e.g., [17]). This triggered a revision of the ontology metamodel, which was adapted to enable the storing of the ordering information (see also the *Ordine Relativo* entry in the *Sottoprocesso Di* box in Figure 1).

Extension of Ontology Non-functional Requirements. In using the ontology within the application prototype, domain experts and application engineers noticed that situations where a class has several direct subclasses (i.e., ≥ 10) were not optimal to favour the development of an IEP with the application (too much content to be shown to the users in a single interaction step). Therefore, domain experts decided to revise the ontology introducing in these situations additional intermediate subclasses (at least 2) between the class and its direct subclasses, so that the former children of the class became direct children of one of these intermediate classes (with each intermediate class having roughly the same number of children). Note that this change affected the ontology, but not its metamodel, and thus did not require any modification of MoKi or its forms.

All these "debugging" situations let us suggest to include the early deployment of application ontologies in their corresponding system (even if under development) as integral part of the modelling activities of this kind of ontologies, to favour the improvement of the quality of the ontology under construction.

On Adopting an Hybrid Ontological Representation for a Multipurpose Ontology. As previously mentioned, one of the requirements of the IEP OWL ontology was its capability to be used both as (i) a traditional *classification* ontology,[13] i.e., where the core elements (i.e., functional abilities in IEP ontology context) are usually modelled as classes, as well as (ii) the main data component of an application system, in which a class-oriented encoding of the core elements to be represented may not be optimal, especially if application-specific content has to be directly asserted on these elements (something typically problematic to formalize on classes in OWL). Arguably, situations like this are indeed not so uncommon in practice.

Instead of over-complicating the formalization of the content in the ontology, introducing ad-hoc representation patterns, we decided to adopt an approach *à la* OWL punning, where each core element has a dual representation as a class and as an individual, the former to be compliant with traditional classification ontologies, while the latter to favour the assertion of application-specific content

---

[13] Like typically done in ontologies in the medical domain (see e.g., [18,19,20]).

on the core elements of the application domain. Note that, thanks to the usage of MoKi for modelling the ontology, this dual-representation approach was completely transparent to the modellers, as the content they provided in MoKi was automatically encoded in the appropriate format when exporting the MoKi content to OWL.

7   Conclusions

In this paper we reported the experience of collaborative modelling an application ontology in the concrete case of the development of a commercial ontology-based application of a SME. The construction of the ontology involved a number of users with different competencies and skills: domain experts and application developers from the SME, as well as external knowledge engineers supporting the formalization. Beside describing the modelling process that was followed and the tool that was used, we reported several lessons learned in collaboratively modelling an ontology specifically built for a given application: among them, we remark the importance of early deploying the application ontology in the system it is meant for (even if under development) already during the modelling activities, to favour the improvement of the ontology quality and the early detection of modelling mistakes and assumptions. Given the very concrete nature of the reported experience (the application will be commercialized from September 2014, having as target users teachers and schools of all levels of the Italian education system), we believe our findings and lessons learned may be beneficial for similar modelling initiatives regarding the development of application ontologies.

Acknowledgements. This work is supported by "ePlanning - Sistema esperto per la creazione di progetti educativo-didattici per alunni con Bisogni Educativi Speciali", funded by the Operational Programme "Fondo Europeo di Sviluppo Regionale (FESR) 2007-2013" of the Province of Trento, Italy.

References

1. Staab, S., Studer, R.: Handbook on Ontologies, 2nd edn. Springer Publishing Company, Incorporated (2009)
2. Zheng, J., Manduchi, E., Stoeckert Jr, C.J.: In: Dumontier, M., Hoehndorf, R., Baker, C.J.O. (eds.) ICBO. CEUR Workshop Proceedings, pp. 62–67. CEUR-WS.org Zheng, J., Manduchi, E., Stoeckert Jr, C.J.: Development of an Application Ontology for Beta Cell Genomics Based On the Ontology for Biomedical Investigations. In: Dumontier, M., Hoehndorf, R., Baker, C.J.O. (eds.) ICBO. CEUR Workshop Proceedings, pp. 62–67. CEUR-WS.org
3. Harrison, R., Chan, C.: Implementation of an application ontology. In: Li, D., Wang, B. (eds.) Artificial Intelligence Applications and Innovations. IFIP, vol. 187, pp. 131–143. Springer, Heidelberg (2005)
4. Antezana, E., Egaña, M., Blondé, W., Illarramendi, A., Bilbao, I., Baets, B.D., Stevens, R., Mironov, V., Kuiper, M.: The cell cycle ontology: an application ontology for the representation and integrated analysis of the cell cycle process. Genome Biol. 10(5), R58 (2009)

5. Mejino, J.L.V., Rubin, D.L., Brinkley, J.F.: Fma-radlex: An application ontology of radiological anatomy derived from the foundational model of anatomy reference ontology. In: AMIA Annu. Symp. Proc., pp. 465–469 (2008)

6. Guarino, N.: Formal Ontology in Information Systems: Proceedings of the 1st International Conference, 1st edn., Trento, Italy, June 6-8. IOS Press, Amsterdam (1998)

7. Ghidini, C., Rospocher, M., Serafini, L.: Modeling in a wiki with moki: Reference architecture, implementation, and usages. International Journal On Advances in Life Sciences 4(4), 111–124 (2012)

8. Presidenza della Repubblica Italiana: Legge-quadro n. 104 per l'assistenza, l'integrazione sociale e i diritti delle persone handicappate (February 5, 1992)

9. Ianes, D., Cramenotti, S.: Il Piano educativo individualizzato - Progetto di vita: Raccolta di buone prassi di PEI compilati e commentati. vol. 3. Edizioni Erickson (2009)

10. Grasso, F.: L'ICF a scuola. L'applicazione agli adempimenti della legge 104/1992: Diagnosi Funzionale, PDF e PEI. Giunti O.S. Organizzazioni Speciali, Firenze (2011)

11. Kumar, A., Smith, B.: The ontology of processes and functions: A study of the international classification of functioning, disability and health. In: Proceedings of the AIME 2005 Workshop on Biomedical Ontology Engineering, Aberdeen, Scotland (2005)

12. Della Mea, V., Simoncello, A.: An ontology-based exploration of the concepts and relationships in the activities and participation component of the International Classification of Functioning, Disability and health. Journal of Biomedical Semantics 3(1), 1–9 (2012)

13. Tudorache, T., Nyulas, C.I., Noy, N.F., Musen, M.A.: Using semantic web in ICD-11: Three years down the road. In: Alani, H., Kagal, L., Fokoue, A., Groth, P., Biemann, C., Parreira, J.X., Aroyo, L., Noy, N., Welty, C., Janowicz, K. (eds.) ISWC 2013, Part II. LNCS, vol. 8219, pp. 195–211. Springer, Heidelberg (2013)

14. Suárez-Figueroa, M.C., Gómez-Pérez, A., Villazón-Terrazas, B.: How to write and use the ontology requirements specification document. In: Meersman, R., Dillon, T., Herrero, P. (eds.) OTM 2009, Part II. LNCS, vol. 5871, pp. 966–982. Springer, Heidelberg (2009)

15. Grüninger, M., Fox, M.S.: Methodology for the Design and Evaluation of Ontologies. In: IJCAI 1995 Workshop on Basic Ontological Issues in Knowledge Sharing (1995)

16. Wolstencroft, K., Owen, S., Krebs, O., Mueller, W., Nguyen, Q., Snoep, J.L., Goble, C.: Semantic data and models sharing in systems biology: The just enough results model and the SEEK platform. In: Alani, H., et al. (eds.) ISWC 2013, Part II. LNCS, vol. 8219, pp. 212–227. Springer, Heidelberg (2013)

17. Drummond, N., Rector, A., Stevens, R., Moulton, G., Horridge, M., Wang, H., Sedenberg, J.: Putting owl in order: Patterns for sequences in owl. In: OWL Experiences and Directions (OWLEd 2006), Athens Georgia (2006)

18. Hèja, G., Surjàn, G., Lukácsy, G., Pallinger, P., Gergely, M.: Galen based formal representation of icd10. I. J. Medical Informatics 76(2-3), 118–123 (2007)

19. Rector, A., Rogers, J.: Patterns, properties and minimizing commitment: Reconstruction of the galen upper ontology in owl. In: Gangemi, A., Borgo, S. (eds.) Proceedings of the EKAW*04 Workshop on Core Ontologies in Ontology Engineering, CEUR (2004)

20. The International Health Terminology Standards Development Organisation.: Snomed clinical terms(snomed ct) - international release. technical reference guide (July 2011)

Relationship-Based Top-K Concept Retrieval for Ontology Search

Anila Sahar Butt[1,2], Armin Haller[1,2], and Lexing Xie[2]

[1] CSIRO, Canberra, Australia
[2] Australian National University
firstname.lastname@anu.edu.au

Abstract. With the recent growth of Linked Data on the Web there is an increased need for knowledge engineers to find ontologies to describe their data. Only limited work exists that addresses the problem of searching and ranking ontologies based on a given query term. In this paper we introduce DWRank, a two-staged bi-directional graph walk ranking algorithm for concepts in ontologies. We apply this algorithm on the task of searching and ranking concepts in ontologies and compare it with state-of-the-art ontology ranking models and traditional information retrieval algorithms such as PageRank and tf-idf. Our evaluation shows that DWRank significantly outperforms the best ranking models on a benchmark ontology collection for the majority of the sample queries defined in the benchmark.

1 Introduction

The growth in Linked Data coupled with the widespread use of ontologies in vertical domains (e.g. bioinformatics, e-commerce, internet-of-things etc.) highlights an increasing need to discover existing ontologies and the concepts and relations within. The benchmark ontology collection that we use in the evaluation of this paper, for example, includes 1022 ontologies that were retrieved through a Web crawl [2]. However, the potential to "reuse" these and other ontologies is hampered by the fact that it is hard to find the right ontology for a given use case. There are several established ontology libraries in vertical domains such as the Open Biological and Biomedical Ontologies library[1] or the BioPortal [14], where keyword queries are still the preferred method to find concepts and relations in the registered ontologies. However, since there may exist many ontologies that contain concepts and relations with their label matching the keyword query, the matches need to be usefully ranked. There has been some previous work, for example [7,1,14,13], to tackle the problem of finding and ranking ontologies. More recently, also dedicated ontology search engines have emerged [21], but the ranking algorithms they use are based only on document-ranking algorithms. Moreover, most of the ranking techniques in these ontology libraries and search engines only consider the popularity of terms in the ontology corpus, often using

---

[1] http://www.obofoundry.org/

K. Janowicz et al. (Eds.): EKAW 2014, LNAI 8876, pp. 485–502, 2014.

the PageRank algorithm, which although effective in some cases [2] hinders the visibility of newly emerged well defined ontologies.

In this paper we propose a new ontology concept retrieval framework that uses a number of techniques to rate and rank each concept in an ontology based on how well it represents a given search term. The ranking in the framework is conducted in two phases. First, our offline ranking algorithm, DWRank, computes the centrality of a concept within an ontology based on its connectivity to other concepts within the ontology itself. Then, the authority of a concept is computed which depends on the number of relationships between ontologies and the weight of these relationships based on the authority of the source ontology. The assumption behind this is that ontologies that reuse and are reused by other ontologies are more authoritative than others. In a second, online query processing phase a candidate set for a *top-k* concept is selected from the offline ranked list of ontologies and then filtered based on two strategies, the diverse results semantics and the intended type semantics. The resulting list of *top-k* ranked concepts is then evaluated against a ground truth derived through a human evaluation published previously [2]. Our evaluation shows that DWRank significantly outperforms the state-of-the-art ranking models on the task of ranking concepts in ontologies for all ten benchmark queries in the ontology collection.

The remainder of the paper is structured as follows. In Section 2 we describe the overall framework and briefly define some of the terms used throughout the paper. Section 3 describes the offline ranking phase of our framework, in particular the DWRank algorithm. Section 4 then describes the online query processing and filtering phase that is independent of the offline ranking model. We evaluate the DWRank algorithm with and without the additional filters in Section 5. We position our work in relation to state-of-the-art in Section 6 before we conclude in Section 7.

2   Relationship-Based Top-k Concept Retrieval

In the following we first define the terms used throughout the paper. We then give a brief overview of the mechanics of the ranking framework.

2.1   Preliminaries

An ontology in this paper refers to a graph based formalisation $O = (V, E, L)$ of a domain knowledge. V is a finite set of nodes where $v \in V$ denotes a domain concept in O, E is the edge set where $(v, v') \in E$ denotes an explicit or implicit relationship between v and v'. L is a labelling function which assigns a label $L(v)$ (resp. $L(e)$ or $L(O)$) to node v (resp. an edge $e \in E$ or the ontology O). In practice the labelling function L may specify (1) the node labels to relate the node to the referent concept, e.g. person, place and role; and (2) the edge labels as explicit relationships between concepts e.g., friendship, work and participation or implicit relationships e.g., sub-concept and super-concept, and (3) the ontology label to relate the ontology to the domain or some identity.

Intra-Ontology Relationships. An intra-ontology relationship $I_a = ((v, v'),$ $O)$ is a directed edge (v, v'), where $(v, v') \in E(O)$ for $v \in V(O)$ and $v' \in V(O)$.

Inter-Ontology Relationships. An inter-ontology relationship $I_e = ((v, v'),$ $O, O')$ is a directed edge (O, O'), where $(v, v') \in E(O)$, $L(v) = L(O)$, $L(v') = L(O')$ and $L(v,v') = owl{:}imports^2$.

Forward Link Concepts. Forward link concepts $C_{FLinks}(v, O)$ is a set of concepts V' in an ontology O, where $V' \subset V(O)$ and $\forall\ v_i \in V'$, $\exists\ (v, v_i) \in E(O)$.

Back Link Concepts. Back link concepts $C_{BLinks}(v, O)$ is a set of concepts V'' in an ontology O, where $V'' \subset V(O)$ and $\forall\ v_j \in V''$, $\exists\ (v_j, v) \in E(O)$.

2.2 Overview of the Framework

The framework is composed of two phases as shown in Fig. 1. The first phase is an offline phase where two indices, i.e. *ConHubIdx* and *OntAuthIdx*, are constructed for the whole ontology corpus. The second phase is an online query processing phase where a query is evaluated and the *top-k* concepts are returned to the user.

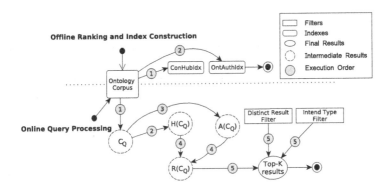

Fig. 1. Relationship-based top-k concept retrieval framework

Offline Ranking and Index Construction: The framework first constructs a *ConHubIdx* on all concepts and *OntAuthIdx* on all ontologies in the ontology corpus O. The *ConHubIdx* maps each concept of an ontology to its corresponding *hub score*. Similarly, the *OntAuthIdx* maps each ontology to its precomputed *authority score*. The *hub score* and *authority score* are defined in Sec. 3.1

---

^{2} http://www.w3.org/2002/07/owl#imports

Online Query Processing: Upon receiving a query Q, the framework extracts the *candidate result set* $C_Q = \{(v_1, O_1), ..., (v_i, O_j)\}$ including all matches that are semantically similar to Q by querying the ontology repository. The *hub score* and *authority score* for all $(v, O) \in C_Q$ are extracted from the corresponding indices as $H(C_Q)$ and $A(C_Q)$ lists. A ranked list $R(C_Q)$ of a candidate result set is computed from $H(C_Q)$ and $A(C_Q)$ along with the text relevancy measure. $R(C_Q)$ is further filtered to satisfy two result set properties, i.e. the *Diverse Result Semantics* and the *Intended Type Semantics*, as introduced in Sec. 4.3.

3   Offline Ranking and Index Construction

In this section the offline ranking phase of the *relationship-based top-k concept retrieval* framework is described (cf. Fig. 2). First, we introduce the ranking model in Section 3.1 and then we introduce the index construction based on the ranking model in Section 3.2.

3.1   DWRank: A *D*ual *W*alk Based *Rank*ing Model

Our ranking model characterises two features of a concept to determine its rank in a corpus:

1. A concept is more important, if it is a *central concept* to the ontology within which it is defined.
2. A concept is more important, if it is defined in an *authoritative* ontology.

More precisely, first, the offline ranking module generates for each concept in the corpus a *hub score*, a measure of the *centrality of a concept*, i.e. the extent that the concept is `related` to the domain for which the ontology is formalised. Second, the *authority score* is generated as a measure of the `authoritativeness` of the ontology. A link analysis algorithm, i.e. PageRank, is performed that leverages the ontological structure and semantics to compute these scores. However, the difference between our model and a traditional PageRank-like algorithms is two-fold. Firstly, we perform the link analysis independently on each ontology to find a *hub score* and then only on the whole ontology corpus considering an ontology as a node and inter-ontology relationships as links. Secondly, we differentiate the type of relationship (i.e. inter-ontology and intra-ontology) and the direction of the walk varies on the basis of the type of the relationship. Our Model *DualWalkRank* is named after its characteristic of a dual directional walk to compute the ranks of concepts.

HubScore: The Centrality of a Concept within an Ontology. The *hub score* is a measure of the centrality of a concept within an ontology. We define a *hub function* h(v,O) that calculates the *hub score*. The *hub function* is characterised by two features:

– **Connectivity:** A concept is more central to an ontology, if there are more *intra-ontology relationships* starting from the concept.

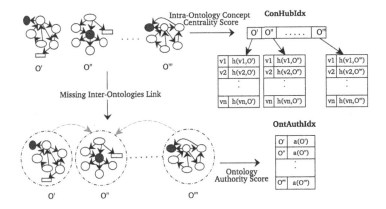

Fig. 2. Offline Ranking and Index Construction Phase

- **Neighbourhood:** A concept is more central to an ontology, if there is an *intra-ontology relationship* starting from the concept to another central concept.

According to these features, a concept accepts the centrality of another concept based on its forward link concepts (like a **hub**). The *hub function* is therefore a complete reverse of the PageRank algorithm [15] where a node accepts scores from its referent nodes i.e. back link concepts. We adopt a Reverse-PageRank [9] as the *hub function* to find the centrality of a concept within the ontology. The hub function is an iterative function and at any iteration k, the *hub function* is featured as Eq.1.

$$h_k(v,O) = \sum_{v_i \in C_{FLinks}(v,O)} \frac{h_{k-1}(v_i,O)}{|C_{BLinks}(v_i,O)|} \tag{1}$$

Within the original PageRank framework there are two types of links in a graph, strong and weak links. The links that actually exist in the graph are *strong links*. *Weak links* are artificially created links by a damping factor α, and they connect all nodes to all other nodes. Since *data-type relationships* of a concept do not connect it to other concepts in an ontology, most PageRank-like algorithms adopted for ontology ranking consider only *object type relationships* of a concept while ignoring others. We adopt the notion of weak links in our *hub function* to be able to also consider *data-type relationships* along with *object-type relationships* for the ontology ranking. We generate a set of artificial concepts $V(O)$ in the ontology that act as a sink for every *data-type relationship* and label these concepts with the data type relationship label. i.e. $\forall v_j \in V'$, $L(v_j') = L(v_i,v_j')$. After incorporating *weak links* and *weak nodes* notions, Eq. 2 reflects the complete feature of our *hub function*.

$$h_k(v,O) = \frac{1-\alpha}{|V|} + \alpha \sum_{v_i \in C_{SFLinks}(v,O) \cup C_{WFLinks}(v,O)} \frac{h_{k-1}(v_i,O)}{|C_{BLinks}(v_i,O)|} \quad (2)$$

In Eq. 2, $C_{SFLinks}(v,O)$ is a set of *strong forward link concepts* and $C_{WFLinks}(v,O)$ is a set of *weak forward link concepts*. Our *hub function* is similar to [22], but varies from it as we consider *weak nodes* and we are not considering relationships weights. The results presented in [22] also justify our choice of ReversePageRank over other algorithms to measure the centrality. We normalise the hub scores of each concept v within an ontology O through the z-score of the concept's hub score after the last iteration of the *hub function* as follows:

$$h_n(v,O) = \frac{h(v,O) - \mu_h(O)}{\sigma_h(O)} \quad (3)$$

In Eq 3, $h_n(v,O)$ is a normalised hub score of v, $\mu_h(O)$ is an average of hub scores of all concepts in the ontology and $\sigma_h(O)$ is the standard deviation of hub scores of the concepts in the ontology.

AuthorityScore: The Authoritativeness of a Concept. The *authority score* is the measure of the authoritativeness of a concept within an ontology. As mentioned earlier, the *authoritativeness of a concept* depends upon the *authoritativeness of the ontology* within which it is defined. Therefore, we define the *authority function* a(O) to measure the *authority score* of an ontology. Our *authority function* is characterised by the following two features:

- **Reuse:** An ontology is more authoritative, if there are more *inter-ontology relationships* ending at the ontology.
- **Neighbourhood:** An ontology is more authoritative, if there is an *inter-ontology relationship* starting from an authoritative ontology to the ontology.

Based on these two features, an *inter-ontology relationship* $I_e((v,v'),O,O')$ is considered as a "positive vote" for the authoritativeness of ontology O' from O. The PageRank is adopted as the *authority function*, whereby each ontology is considered a node and *inter-ontology relationships* are considered links among nodes. Eq. 4 formalise the *authority function* which computes the authoritativeness of O at the kth iteration.

$$a_k(O) = \frac{1-\alpha}{|O|} + \alpha \sum_{O_i \in O_{BLinks}(O)} \frac{a_{k-1}(O_i)}{|O_{FLinks}(O_i)|} \quad (4)$$

In Eq. 4, $O_{BLinks}(O)$ is a set of *back link ontologies* and $O_{FLinks}(O)$ is a set of *forward link ontologies*. The definition of $O_{FLinks}(O)$ (resp. $O_{BLinks}(O)$)

is similar to $C_{FLinks}(v, O)$ (resp. $C_{BLinks}(v, O)$), however, the links are inter-ontology relationships.

Similar to the *hub score*, we also compute the z-score of each ontology after the last iteration of *authority function* as follows:

$$a_n(O) = \frac{a(O) - \mu_a(0)}{\sigma_a(0)} \qquad (5)$$

In Eq. 5, $a_n(O)$ is the normalised authority score of v, $\mu_a(0)$ is an average of the authority scores of all ontologies in the corpus and $\sigma_a(0)$ is the standard deviation of the authority scores of ontologies in 0.

DWRank Score. Finally, we define the *DWRank* $R_{(v,O)}$, as a function of the *text relevancy*, the *normalised hub score* and the *normalised authority score*. The function is described as a quantitative metric for the overall relevance between the query Q and the concept v; and the concept *hub and authority* score as follows:

$$R_{(v,O)} = F_V(v, Q) * [w_1 h(v, O) + w_2 a(O)]$$
$$F_V(v, Q) = \sum_{q \in Q} f_{ss}(q, \phi(q_v)) \qquad (6)$$

In Eq. 6, w_1 and w_2 are the weights for the *hub function* and the *authority function*. $F_V(v, Q)$ aggregates the contribution of all matched words of a node v, in an ontology O, to the query keywords $q \in Q$. f_{ss} returns a binary value : it returns 1 if q has a match $\phi(q_v)$ in v, and 0 otherwise. The metric favours the nodes v that are semantically matched to more keywords of the query Q.

3.2   Index Construction: An Execution of DWRank

In this section, we explain the execution of the *DWRank* model and the construction of the indices.

ConHubIdx. A bi-level index where each entry in the index maps a concept of an ontology to its *normalised hub score* $h_n(v, O)$ as shown in Fig. 2 (top left). To construct the *ConHubIdx* for all ontologies in 0, (1) the *hub function* is executed in an iterative way to get the *hub score* of all the concepts in ontology O, and (2) after the last iteration, we compute the normalised hub scores and (3) insert the concepts along with their normalised hub scores in an ontology to the index.

OntAuthIdx. An index where each entry in the index maps an ontology to its *normalised authority score* $a_n(O)$ as shown in Fig. 2 (bottom left). To construct the *OntAuthIdx* on the corpus 0, (1) the *authority function* is executed to get an *auth score* of all the ontologies in 0, (2) after the last iteration, the normalised authority scores are computed, and (3) the ontology along with its normalised authority scores is inserted as an entry to the index.

Inter-Ontology Relationships Extraction. As we mentioned earlier, the *authority function* leverages the *inter-ontology relationships* that are directed links among ontologies. If ontology *OntA* reuses the resources in ontology *OntB*, ontology *OntA* declares the reuse of resources through an OWL import property i.e. `owl:imports`. Since some ontology practitioners fail to explicitly declare the reuse of ontologies, the `owl:imports` relationships in an ontology are often inaccurate representations of the inter-ontology relationships. We therefore identify the implicit *inter-ontology relationships* by considering the reused resources in the corpus. Finding the implicit inter-ontology relationships involves the following steps:

1. **Missing Relationships Detection:** To find all missing inter-ontology relationships we identify the resources that appear in multiple ontologies. If a resource (referred to as *"reused resource"*) is used in multiple ontologies (referred to as *"hosting ontologies"*) then there must be some inter-ontology relationships. If these relationships are not explicitly defined then there are missing relationships among the ontologies.

2. **Relationship Direction Identification:** Since inter-ontology relationships are directed links between ontologies, another challenge is to find the direction of the missing relationships. A part of the ontology corpus in Fig. 2 (top right), contains a *reused resource* (i.e. filled node) that appears in three different ontologies O', O'' and O'''. In the absence of explicit relationships, some implicit relationships exist and to create these relationships we need to identify the direction of the relationships i.e. from O' to O'' and from O''' to O''. To identify the direction, the *namespace* of the *reused resource* are used. If the namespace of the *reused resource* matches to the *namespace* of a *hosting ontology* (e.g. O''), then the ontology is selected as the *"home ontology"* of the *reused resource* and the inter-ontology relationships are directed from the *hosting ontologies*(i.e. O', O''') to the *home ontology* i.e. O''.

3. **Explicit Relationships Creation:** Once the missing relationships and their directions are identified, we create explicit inter-ontology relationships using `owl:imports` properties.

An important point to consider is that although an ontology *OntA* may reuse more than one resource from another ontology *OntB* there will only be one inter-ontology relationship from *OntA* to *OntB* according to the semantics of the *owl:imports* property. Therefore, independently of the number of resources that are reused in *OntA* from *OntB*, we create a single inter-ontology relationship from *OntA* to *OntB*.

Table 1 and Table 2 show the top five ontologies in the benchmark ontology collection [2] and the corresponding number of inter-ontology relationships that are directed to these ontologies (i.e. *reuse count*) counted through *explicit* and *implicit* relationships, respectively.

Table 1. Top five reused ontologies based on explicit inter-ontology relationships

URI	Count
http://def.seegrid.csiro.au/isotc211/iso19150/-2/2012/basic	36
http://purl.org/dc/elements/1.1/	25
http://www.ifomis.org/bfo/1.1	16
http://www.w3.org/2006/time	16
http://www.ontologydesignpatterns.org/schemas/cpannotationschema.owl	15

Table 2. Top five reused ontologies based on implicit inter-ontology relationships

URI	Count
http://www.w3.org/2002/07/owl#	881
http://www.w3.org/2000/01/rdf-schema	361
http://www.w3.org/1999/02/22-rdf-syntax-ns	298
http://xmlns.com/foaf/0.1/	228
http://www.w3.org/2004/02/skos/core	140

4   Online Query Processing

In this section, we first describe the concept retrieval task and then we outline the online query processing technique that finds the top-k ranked concepts for Q in O with the highest semantic relevance.

4.1   Concept Retrieval Task.

Given a query string $Q = \{q_1, q_2, \ldots, q_k\}$, an Ontology corpus $O = \{O_1, O_2, \ldots, O_n\}$ and a word sense similarity threshold θ, the concept retrieval task is to find the $C_Q = \{(v_1, O_1), \ldots, (v_i, O_j)\}$ from O, such that there is a *surjective function* f_{sj} from Q to C_Q where (a) v has a partial or an exact matched word $\phi(q_v)$ for q $\in$ Q (b) for a partially matched word, $SenSim(q, \phi(q_v)) \geq \theta$. We refer to C_Q as a candidate set of Q introduced by the mapping f_{sj}.

$SenSim(q, \phi(q_v))$ is a word similarity measure of a query keyword and a partially matched word in $L(v)$.

4.2   Query Evaluation

In the online query evaluation (c.f Fig. 3), first a candidate set for a *top-k* concept is selected from the ontology data store i.e. *OntDataStore*, and then the relevance of each concept is calculated based on the formulae defined in Eq. 6.

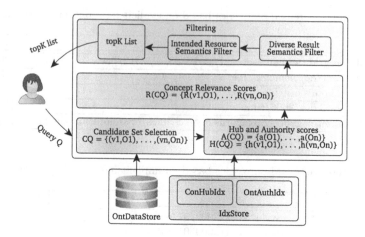

Fig. 3. Online Query Processing

Candidate Result Set Selection. A keyword query evaluation starts with the selection of a candidate set C_Q for Q. A candidate result set C_Q is characterised by two features:

1. To be part of the candidate set a candidate concept v must have at least one exact or partial match $\phi(q_v)$ for any query keyword $q \in Q$ as part of the value of (a) rdfs:label (b) rdfs:comment (c) rdfs:description property; or $\exists$ $q \in Q \mid \phi(q_v)$ is part of $L(v)$.
2. The word sense similarity of q and $\phi(q_v)$ i.e. senSim(q,$\phi(q_v)$) should be greater than the sense similarity threshold θ.

In our current implementation, we check the word sense similarity using WordNet and set a word sense similarity threshold $\theta = 0.85$. Each entry in a candidate list denotes a candidate concept 'v' and is a pair (v, O) (shown in Fig. 3) of v and O where $v \in V(O)$. Since for the *reused resources* there are multiple *hosting ontologies*, therefore 'v' may have multiple entries in a candidate set if it is a *reused resource*.

Concept Relevance. For each entry in the candidate list, two scores are retrieved from the stored indices built during the *offline ranking and index construction phase*. The entry (v, O) is used to retrieve the *hub score* of concept v in ontology O from the *ConHubIdx*, and the *authority score* of ontology O from the *OntAuthIdx*. The two scores are combined according to the formulae of Eq. 6, that provides the final *concept relevance* of each v to the Query Q.

4.3   Filtering Top-k Results

In this section, we discuss the filtering strategies of our framework to enhance the semantic similarity of the results to the keyword query. We introduce two properties for the *top-k* results:

Diverse Results Semantic. Considering the semantics of a query allows us to remove repetitive results from the top-k results to increase the diversity in the result set. As mentioned earlier, if a candidate concept v is reused/extended in 'n' hosted ontologies i.e. $\{O_1, O_2, ..., O_n\}$ then it may appear multiple times in a *candidate result set* (i.e. $C_Q = \{(v, O_1), (v, O_2), ..., (v, O_n)\}$). In this case we remove the duplicates from the candidate result set.

Intended Type Semantic. The semantic differentiates the *intended type* from the *context resource* of a concept. The label of a concept v may have multiple keywords as a description of the concept e.g., the label of a concept in the GND ontology has the keywords "Name of the Person"[3]. Here "Name" is the intended type, whereas "Person" is the context resource. According to the *intended type semantic property* a concept should appear in the *top-k* if and only if its *intended type* matches to at-least one of the query keywords $q \in Q$.

Algorithm 1: TOP-K FILTER

Input: Concept Relevance Map $R(C_Q) = \{[(v_1, O_1), r_1], .. , [(v_n, O_n), r_n]\}$
Output: top-k results $L(C_Q) = \{[(v_1, O_1), r_1], .. , [(v_k, O_k), r_k]\}$

1 $R_s(C_Q)$ /* A map to store intermediate results */
2 **for** $i \in [1, n]$ **do**
3    $e \leftarrow R(C_Q).get(i)$;
4   **if** $R(C_Q).contains(e') \bigcap v(e) = v(e') \cap O(e) \neq O(e')$ **then**
5      $R_s(C_Q).put([(v, O_h), r_h])$;
6   **for** e'' *where* $v(e'') = v$ and $O(e'') \neq O_h$ **do**
7        $R_s(C_Q).put([(v, O''), (r'' - r_h)])$;
8      $R(C_Q).removeAll(e$ where concept is $v)$;
9   **else**
10      $R_s(C_Q).put(e)$;

11 $R_s(C_Q) \leftarrow$ sortByValue($R_s(C_Q)$);
12 **while** $(L(C_Q).size() \leq k) \bigcap (i \in [1, n])$ **do**
13    $e \leftarrow R(C_Q).get(i)$;
14   **if** $\phi (q_v(e))$ *is a multi-keyword match* **then**
15   **if** $I_t(\phi (q_v(e))) = q$ **then**
16        $L(C_Q).put(e)$;
17   **else**
18      $L(C_Q).put(e)$;

19 **return** $L(C_Q)$

Algorithm 1 explains the *top-k results filtering* process. It takes as input a *Concept Relevance Map* $R(C_Q)$ and returns the *top-k* results. First, the *diverse results semantics* are preserved (line 2-10) for $R(C_Q)$, and then the check for

---

[3] http://d-nb.info/standards/elementset/gnd#NameOfThePerson

the *intended type semantics* is applied (line 11-18) until the *top-k* results are retrieved.

A map $R_s(C_Q)$ is initialised to store the intermediate results that preserve the *diverse results semantics*. All candidate concepts in $R(C_Q)$ that appear only once in $R(C_Q)$ preserve the *diverse results semantics*, therefore they become part of $R_s(C_Q)$ (line 10). For all *reused concepts*, first the *home ontology* $O_h(v)$ of the concept v is identified. The entry e= $[(v,O),r] \in R(C_Q)$ for which the ontology of the concept v is its home ontology (i.e. $O=O_h(v)$) becomes part of the $R_s(C_Q)$ (line 5). For all other entries e'' for v a new entry is created by subtracting the relevance score of e i.e. r_h from the r'' and add it to the $R_s(C_Q)$ (line 6-7). The process decreases the relevance score of duplicate entries by a factor of r_h. Then all such e'' from $R(C_Q)$ are removed since they have already been dealt with through candidate concepts of v.

The next step is to check the *intended type semantic*. For brevity, a detailed discussion of the intended type checking is exempted from Algorithm 1. The *ontology structure* and the *Information Retrieval method* are used to identify the *intended type*. For a concept v, its sub-classes, super-classes and inter-ontology relationships are extracted as the context of v. The WS4J[4] API is used to calculate the similarity of different words in the concept v with its context. The word that has a higher similarity score in regards to the context is considered as the intended type of the concept. However, to reduce the cost of ensuring the *intended type semantic* for *top-k* results, the filter is only applied until we retrieved the *top-k* results in the final results L. For this, first the $R_s(C_Q)$ is sorted in a decreasing order based on its relevance score r, so the more relevant results for query Q are at the top of the $R_s(C_Q)$ (line 11). Then the intended type of the candidate concept is checked only until 'k' concepts are selected from $R_s(C_Q)$ or there are no more results in $R(C_Q)$ (line 12). If the concept v has a single exact or partial matched word ϕ $q_v(e)$ then by default it preserves the semantics and becomes part of $L(C_Q)$ (line 18), otherwise we check its *intended type*. If its intended type is equal to the query keyword $q \in Q$, the concept is included in $L(C_Q)$ otherwise, it is ignored.

5 Experimental Evaluation

In the following we present an experimental evaluation of our *relationship based top-k concept retrieval framework* on a benchmark suite CBRBench - Canberra Ontology Ranking Benchmark [2]. We conducted two sets of experiments to evaluate: (1) the effectiveness of the *DWRank ranking model* presented in Sec. 3 and (2) the effectiveness of the additional filtering phase presented in Sec. 4.

5.1 Experimental Settings

To evaluate our approach we use a benchmark suite CBRBench [2], that includes a collection of ontologies, a set of benchmark queries and a ground truth established by human experts. This collection is composed of 1022 ontologies and

---

[4] https://code.google.com/p/ws4j/

ten keyword queries: Person, Name, Event, Title, Location, Address, Music, Organization, Author and Time. The benchmark evaluates eight state-of-the-art ranking algorithms: *Tf-Idf*[17], *BM25*[16], *Vector Space Model* (VSM)[18], *Class Match Measure* (CMM) [1], *PageRank* (PR)[15], *Density Measure* (DEM)[1], *Semantic Similarity Measure* (SSM)[1] and *Betweenness Measure* (BM)[1] on the task of ranking ontologies. We use the performance of these ranking models as the baseline to evaluate our approach. For a fair analysis, we implemented two versions of our approach: (1) DWRank: the DWRank model with the *diverse root semantics* (2) DWRank+Filter: the DWRank model with both the *diverse root semantics* and the *intended type semantics*. The reasoning for two different implementations of top-k concept retrieval framework is, we want to compare the effectiveness of DWRank model with the baseline ranking models and since CBRBench provides distinct top-k results of the baseline algorithms - which means *diverse root semantics* is considered while evaluating the baseline ranking models - therefore the DWRank model along with *diverse root semantics* is implemented in DWRank version. Secondly, the *intended type semantics* can be applied to any of the baseline ranking models to improve its performance, thus, in the DWRank+Filter version we only evaluate the effectiveness of the *intended type semantics filter*. The effectiveness of the framework is measured in terms of its *Precision* (P), *Mean Average Precision* (MAP), *Discounted Cumulative Gain* (DCG) and *Normalised Discounted Cumulative Gain* (NDCG).

5.2 Experimental Results

We next present our findings.

Effectiveness of DWRank. In the first set of experiments, we evaluated the effectiveness of DWRank in comparison with the eight baseline ranking models. We ran the ten sample queries on the ontology collection and retrieved the *top-k* results according to the proposed ranking model. We recorded the P@10, the MAP@10, the DCG@10 and the NDCG@10. The effectiveness measure results of the DWRank are shown in Table 3, where column header corresponds to benchmark query terms and row header corresponds to evaluation metrics.

Table 3. DWRank Effectiveness

	Person	Name	Event	Title	Loc.	Addr.	Music	Org.	Author	Time
P@10	0.9	0.7	1	0.7	0.7	0.8	0.7	0.9	0.8	0.8
MAP@10	0.98	0.82	1	0.88	0.86	0.94	0.80	0.85	0.78	0.74
DCG@10	37.58	19.11	35.12	12.45	24.88	23.53	14.82	33.70	18.24	22.53
NDCG@10	0.51	0.41	0.51	0.26	0.60	0.59	0.4	0.53	0.48	0.49

Next, we compared our results with the baseline for the same dataset with the sample queries. The results are shown in Fig. 4. Each graph here presents an effectiveness measure of a ranking model for all ten queries, where the x-axis

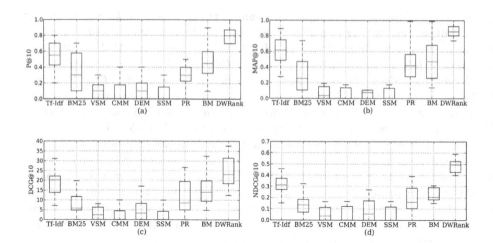

Fig. 4. Effectiveness of Ranking Model

is the *ranking model* and the y-axis is the *unit of measure*. Each box on a graph presents the range of effectiveness measure for 10 sample queries according to the gold standard. Fig. 4 shows the maximum, minimum and average performance of DWRank in comparison to the performance of the baseline ranking models for each of the ten queries. The graph shows that DWRank performs better than the best performing ranking algorithm for most queries. For the *address* query, the P@10 and MAP@10 for DWRank is lower than the other best performing ranking model. However, the maximum average MAP@10 for DWRank on ten queries is 0.84 that is greater than the average of Tf-Idf, the best baseline ranking models, (i.e., 0.55). The box plot also shows that P@10 and MAP@10 of DWRank ranges from 0.7 ~1.0 that means the performance of DWRank is more stable on the ontology collection for the sample queries than the baseline ranking models.

Similarly, the DCG@10 values in Fig. 4(c) and NDCG@10 values in Fig. 4(d) for the ranking models show that DWRank is more effective than the baseline models. The maximum and minimum measures are closer to the *Betweenness Measure (BM)* and the *Tf-Idf* model, however, the average performance of DWRank is much higher than the average performance of the BM and Tf-Idf models.

Fig. 5 compares the MAP@10 (resp. NDCG@10) for DWRank on all ten queries with the maximum MAP@10 (resp. NDCG@10) achieved with any of the baseline ranking model on the sample queries. The result shows that DWRank performs best for MAP@10 (resp. NDCG@10) for all but one query. The experiment confirms our claim about the stable performance of the DWRank algorithm.

Effectiveness of DWRank+Filter. For the evaluation of the filter performance, we ran the ten sample queries of the benchmark collection with the DWRank model extended with the filter proposed earlier, i.e. *intended type semantics*. Fig. 6 shows the effectiveness of DWRank compared to DWRank+Filter.

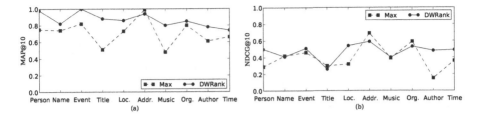

Fig. 5. *MAP@10* and *nDCG@10* for DWRank in comparison with the best value for any ranking model on sample queries

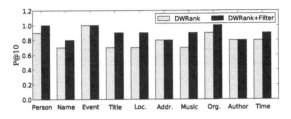

Fig. 6. Filter Effectiveness

The average P@10 increased from 0.8 to 0.9, i.e. a 12 % increase in the effectiveness of the results.

From the evaluation it is obvious that the *filter* improves the overall performance of our framework. A detailed analysis on the precision and recall of the *intended type semantics filter* is omitted from this paper for brevity. However, some *True positive* (TP), *False positive*(FP), *True negative* (TN) and *False negative* (FN) examples regarding our current implementation of the intended type semantic filter are shown in Table 4. We analyse the top-10 results of DWRank without *intended type semantic filter* and then with the filter. For each query if there are TN, FN, FP examples we selected them or otherwise a random TP example.

6   Related Work

The Linked Open Vocabularies (LOV) search engine[5], initiated in March 2011, is to the best of our knowledge, the only purpose-built ontology search engine available on the Web. It uses a ranking algorithm based on the term popularity in Linked Open Data (LOD) and in the LOV ecosystem [21].

There are also some ontology libraries available that facilitate the locating and retrieving of potentially relevant ontology resources [13]. Some of these libraries are domain-specific such as the Open Biological and Biomedical Ontologies library[6] or the BioPortal [14], whereas others are more general such as

---

[5] http://lov.okfn.org
[6] http://www.obofoundry.org/

Table 4. Intended Type Semantic Filter Performance in Relationship-based top-k Concept Retrieval Framework

Query term	Label of concept	Human Judgement	Intended Type Filter Judgement
person	personal communication model	✗	✗
name	gene name	✗	✗
event	academic event	✓	✓
title	spectrum title	✗	✗
location	hematopoiesis location trait	✗	✗
address	E45_address	✓	✗
music	sound and music computing	✗	✗
organization	3D structural organization datrum	✗	✗
author	author list	✓	✗
time	time series observation	✗	✓

OntoSearch [19] or the TONES Ontology Repository[7]. However, as discussed by Noy & d'Aquin [13] only few libraries support a keyword search, only one (Cupboard [4]) supports a ranking of ontologies based on a keyword query using an information retrieval algorithm (i.e. tf-idf), and none support the ranking of resources within these ontologies.

Semantic Search engines such as Swoogle [6] (which was initially developed to rank ontologies only), Sindice.com [20], Watson [5], or Yars2 [10] do allow a search of ontology resources through a keyword query. The ranking in these search engines follows traditional link-based ranking methods [12], in particular adapted versions of the PageRank algorithm [15], where links from one source of information to another are regarded as a 'positive vote' from the former to the latter. Often, these ranking schemes also take the provenance graph of the data into account [11]. AKTiveRank [1], ranks ontologies based on how well they cover specified search terms. Falcon [3] is a popularity-based scheme to rank concepts and ontologies. Other strategies, mainly based on methods proposed in the information retrieval community, are employed in Semantic Search [8], but what all these methods have in common is that they are targeted to rank instances, but do not work well for ranking concepts and properties in ontologies [7,1]. Another related approach is presented in [22] that identifies the most important concepts and relationships from a given ontology. However, the approach does not support ranking concept that belong to multiple ontologies.

7   Conclusion and Future Work

In this paper we have presented a relationship-based *top-k* concept retrieval and ranking framework for ontology search. The ranking model is comprised of two phases, an offline ranking and index construction phase and an online query and

---

[7] http://owl.cs.manchester.ac.uk/repository/

evaluation phase. In the offline ranking phase our DWRank algorithm computes a rank for a concept based on two features, the centrality of the concept in the ontology, and the authority of the ontology that defines the concept. The online ranking phase filters the top-k ranked list of concepts by removing redundant results and by determining the intended type of the query term and removing concept types that are not closely related to the intended query type. We evaluated our DWRank algorithm without the online query processing filters against state-of-the-art ranking models on a benchmark ontology collection and also evaluated the added performance of the proposed filters. The evaluation shows that DWRank outperforms the best performing ranking algorithm for most queries while exhibiting a more stable performance (i.e. MAP@10 of 0.84) than the average of the best performing ranking models of the benchmark (i.e. MAP@10 of 0.55). The filters proposed in the online ranking phase further increased the average P@10 by 12%. Although our algorithm shows significantly improved performance compared to the state-of-the-art in ontology ranking models, we believe further improvements are possible through learning the weights in computing the authority and the hub score using linear classification model. Also, in the online query processing phase we could pre-compute indices for the diverse result semantics and intended type semantics to increase the performance of the online query.

References

1. Alani, H., Brewster, C., Shadbolt, N.: Ranking Ontologies with AKTiveRank. In: Proceedings of the International Semantic Web Conference (ISWC), pp. 5–9 (2006)
2. Butt, A.S., Haller, A., Xie, L.: Ontology search: An empirical evaluation. In: Proceedings of the International Semantic Web Conference, Riva del Gara, Italy, pp. 130–147 (2014)
3. Cheng, G., Ge, W., Qu, Y.: Falcons: searching and browsing entities on the semantic web. In: Proceedings of the 17th International Conference on World Wide Web, pp. 1101–1102. ACM (2008)
4. d'Aquin, M., Lewen, H.: Cupboard — A Place to Expose Your Ontologies to Applications and the Community. In: Proceedings of the 6th European Semantic Web Conference, Berlin, Heidelberg, pp. 913–918 (2009)
5. d'Aquin, M., Motta, E.: Watson, More Than a Semantic Web Search Engine. Semantic Web 2(1), 55–63 (2011)
6. Ding, L., Finin, T., Joshi, A., Pan, R., Cost, R.S., Peng, Y., Reddivari, P., Doshi, V., Sachs, J.: Swoogle: A Search and Metadata Engine for the Semantic Web. In: Proceedings of the 13th ACM International Conference on Information and Knowledge Management, pp. 652–659. ACM, New York (2004)
7. Ding, L., Pan, R., Finin, T.W., Joshi, A., Peng, Y., Kolari, P.: Finding and ranking knowledge on the semantic web. In: Gil, Y., Motta, E., Benjamins, V.R., Musen, M.A. (eds.) ISWC 2005. LNCS, vol. 3729, pp. 156–170. Springer, Heidelberg (2005)
8. Fernandez, M., Lopez, V., Sabou, M., Uren, V., Vallet, D., Motta, E., Castells, P.: Semantic Search Meets the Web. In: Proceedings of the 2008 IEEE International Conference on Semantic Computing, Washington, DC, USA, pp. 253–260 (2008)
9. Fogaras, D.: Where to start browsing the web? In: Innovative Internet Community Systems, pp. 65–79 (2003)

10. Harth, A., Umbrich, J., Hogan, A., Decker, S.: YARS2: A Federated Repository for Querying Graph Structured Data from the Web. In: Aberer, K., et al. (eds.) ASWC 2007 and ISWC 2007. LNCS, vol. 4825, pp. 211–224. Springer, Heidelberg (2007)

11. Hogan, A., Harth, A., Decker, S.: Reconrank: A scalable ranking method for semantic web data with context. In: Proceedings of the 2nd Workshop on Scalable Semantic Web Knowledge Base Systems (2006)

12. Hogan, A., Harth, A., Umbrich, J., Kinsella, S., Polleres, A., Decker, S.: Searching and browsing Linked Data with SWSE: The Semantic Web Search Engine. Web Semantics: Science, Services and Agents on the World Wide Web 9(4), 365–401 (2011)

13. Noy, N.F., d'Aquin, M.: Where to Publish and Find Ontologies? A Survey of Ontology Libraries. Web Semantics: Science, Services and Agents on the World Wide Web 11(0) (2012)

14. Noy, N.F., Shah, N.H., Whetzel, P.L., Dai, B., Dorf, M., Griffith, N., Jonquet, C., Rubin, D.L., Storey, M.-A., Chute, C.G., Musen, M.A.: BioPortal: ontologies and integrated data resources at the click of a mouse. Nucleic Acids Research (2009)

15. Page, L., Brin, S., Motwani, R., Winograd, T.: The PageRank citation ranking: Bringing order to the Web. In: Proceedings of the 7th International World Wide Web Conference, Brisbane, Australia, pp. 161–172 (1998)

16. Robertson, S.E., Walker, S., Jones, S., Hancock-Beaulieu, M.M., Gatford, M.: Okapi at trec-3. NIST SPECIAL PUBLICATION SP, 109–109 (1995)

17. Salton, G., Buckley, C.: Term-weighting approaches in automatic text retrieval. Information Processing & Management 24(5), 513–523 (1988)

18. Salton, G., Wong, A., Yang, C.-S.: A vector space model for automatic indexing. Communications of the ACM 18(11), 613–620 (1975)

19. Thomas, E., Pan, J.Z., Sleeman, D.: Ontosearch2: Searching ontologies semantically. In: Proceedings of the OWLED 2007 Workshop on OWL: Experiences and Directions. CEUR Workshop Proceedings, vol. 258 (2007)

20. Tummarello, G., Delbru, R., Oren, E.: Sindice.com: Weaving the Open Linked Data. In: Aberer, K., et al. (eds.) ASWC 2007 and ISWC 2007. LNCS, vol. 4825, pp. 552–565. Springer, Heidelberg (2007)

21. Vandenbussche, P.-Y., Vatant, B.: Linked Open Vocabularies. ERCIM News 96, 21–22 (2014)

22. Wu, G., Li, J., Feng, L., Wang, K.-H.: Identifying potentially important concepts and relations in an ontology. In: Sheth, A.P., Staab, S., Dean, M., Paolucci, M., Maynard, D., Finin, T., Thirunarayan, K. (eds.) ISWC 2008. LNCS, vol. 5318, pp. 33–49. Springer, Heidelberg (2008)

A Knowledge Driven Approach towards the Validation of Externally Acquired Traceability Datasets in Supply Chain Business Processes

Monika Solanki and Christopher Brewster

Aston Business School
Aston University, UK
{m.solanki,c.a.brewster}@aston.ac.uk

Abstract. The sharing of near real-time traceability knowledge in supply chains plays a central role in coordinating business operations and is a key driver for their success. However before traceability datasets received from external partners can be integrated with datasets generated internally within an organisation, they need to be validated against information recorded for the physical goods received as well as against bespoke rules defined to ensure uniformity, consistency and completeness within the supply chain. In this paper, we present a knowledge driven framework for the runtime validation of critical constraints on incoming traceability datasets encapuslated as EPCIS event-based linked pedigrees. Our constraints are defined using SPARQL queries and SPIN rules. We present a novel validation architecture based on the integration of Apache Storm framework for real time, distributed computation with popular Semantic Web/Linked data libraries and exemplify our methodology on an abstraction of the pharmaceutical supply chain.

1 Introduction and Motivation

Incorporating novel techniques in their processes that contribute towards eliminating disruptions within global supply chains has been a long standing objective for business organisations and companies. Supply chain visibility (SCV) can be summarised as "Visibility is the ability to know exactly where things are at any point in time, or where they have been, and why"[1]. The goal of SCV is to improve and strengthen the supply chain by making near real-time supply chain knowledge readily available to all stakeholders, including the customer.

However, as useful as this knowledge may be, supply chain data is inherently very sensitive to adhoc integration with third party datasets. For a specific stakeholder, effectiveness of the business workflows and decision support systems utilised within its supply chain operations, that ultimately govern the timely fulfillment of its contractual obligations, is directly dependent on the quality and authenticity of the data received from other partners. Before traceability datasets received from external sources and partners can be incorporated and integrated

---

[1] http://www.gs1.org/docs/GS1_SupplyChainVisibility_WhitePaper.pdf

K. Janowicz et al. (Eds.): EKAW 2014, LNAI 8876, pp. 503–518, 2014.

with the supply chain datasets generated internally within an organisation, to be further shared downstream, they need to be validated against information recorded for the physical goods received as well as against bespoke rules, defined to ensure the quality, uniformity, consistency and completeness of datasets exchanged within the supply chain.

In this paper we present a methodology powered by Semantic Web standards and Linked data principles for validating the traceability data sent from one stakeholder to another in the supply chain. Our approach is motivated by four main requirements: (1) The validation should be supply chain domain agnostic, i.e, the constraints must be reusable independently of the goods being tracked. (2) The representation and sharing of traceability data must conform to standards most commonly deployed in supply chains (3) The architecture must be scalable to handle large volumes of streaming traceability data and (4) The constraints must be formalised using widely used Semantic Web standards that are fit-for-purpose. While constraints can be represented using expressive formalisms such as temporal logics, adopting a unified mechanism for representing domain knowledge and constraints eliminates impedance mismatch between the representations, avoids the need for an intermediate mapping language, makes the addition of new constraints easier and simplifies implementation requirements.

Traceability data in supply chains is generated when barcode and RFID readers record traces of products tagged with an EPC (Electronic Product Code), monitoring their movement across the supply chain as specific occurrences of "events". In the proposed framework, description of events is facilitated using EPCIS[2](Electronic Product Code Information Services), a standardised event oriented specifications prescribed by GS1[3] for enabling traceability [4] in supply chains. We exploit two information models: The *EPCIS Event Model* (EEM)[4] based on the EPCIS specification, that enables the sharing and semantic interpretation of event data and *CBVVocab*[5] a companion ontology to EEM for annotating the business context associated with events. In previous work [9] we have shown how EPCIS events can be exploited for the generation of traceability/visibility information that can be shared among supply chain partners as "linked pedigrees". In this paper we show how linked pedigrees received from external partners can be validated against constraints defined using SPARQL queries and SPIN[6] rules. To the best of our knowledge, validating constraints on (real time) supply chain knowledge has so far not been explored both within the Semantic Web and supply chain communities.

The paper is structured as follows: Section 2 presents our motivating scenario from the pharmaceutical supply chain. Section 3 discusses related work. Section 4 highlights the contextual background for the proposed methodology.

---

[2] http://www.gs1.org/gsmp/kc/epcglobal/epcis
[3] http://www.gs1.org/
[4] http://purl.org/eem#
[5] http://purl.org/cbv#
[6] http://www.w3.org/Submission/spin-overview/

Section 5 presents the requirements analysis for constraints. Section 6 formalises the constraints using SPARQL and SPIN rules. Section 7 illustrates our execution environment and highlights implementation details. Section 8 discusses the results of our evaluation. Section 9 presents conclusions.

2   Motivating Scenario

We outline the scenario of a pharmaceutical supply chain, where trading partners exchange product track and trace data using linked pedigrees. Figure 1 illustrates the flow of data for four of the key partners in the chain.

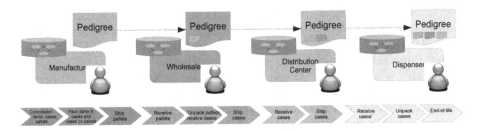

Fig. 1. Trading partners in a pharmaceutical supply chain and the flow of information

The *Manufacturer* commissions[7], i.e., assigns an EPC (Electronic Product Code) to the items, cases and pallets. The items are packed in cases, cases are loaded onto pallets and pallets are shipped. At the Warehouse for the *Wholesaler*, the pallets are received and the cases are unloaded. The cases are then shipped to the various *Distribution centers*. From the Distribution centers the cases are sent to retail *Dispenser* outlets, where they are received and unpacked. Finally, the items are stacked on shelves for dispensing, thereby reaching their end-of-life in the product lifecycle.

EPCIS events are internally recorded for various business steps at each of the trading partner's premises and used for the generation of linked pedigrees. When the pallets with the cases are shipped from the manufacturer's premises to the warehouse, pedigrees encapsulating the set of EPCIS events encoding traceability data are published at an IRI based on a predefined IRI scheme. At the warehouse, when the shipment is received, internal EPCIS events corresponding to the receipt of the shipment are recorded. The IRI of the pedigree sent by the manufacturer is dereferenced to retrieve the pedigree. IRIs of the events corresponding to the transaction (shipping) and consignment (goods) information encapsulated in the pedigree are also dereferenced to retrieve the event specific information for the corresponding business steps. When the warehouse ships the cases to the distribution center, it incorporates the IRI of the manufacturer's pedigree

---

[7] Associates the serial number with the physical product.

in its own pedigree definition. As the product moves, pedigrees are generated with receiving pedigrees being dereferenced and incorporated, till the product reaches its end-of-life stage. Note that pedigrees sent by a distributor may include references to the pedigrees sent by more than one warehouse.

3 Related Work

The need for standards/frameworks that enable the representation of rules and constraints on the Semantic Web, while complementing the existing ontology representation formalisms such as RDF and OWL has received considerable attention [3] in recent years. Several languages, frameworks and models have been proposed, which mostly have their roots in first order logic (Horn rules), Logic programming, action rules (production rule systems such as Jess, Drools) and Deductive databases. A comprehensive tutorial[8] highlights the state of the art in the fundamentals, applications and standards available for Semantic Web rules. OWL 2 Rules have been explicitly addressed in another tutorial[9].

RuleML[10] is a family of rule languages serialised in XML. RuleML [2] covers a wide spectrum of rules from deliberation, derivation, transformation and reaction rules. It serves as a mechanism to interoperate between certain dialects of other rule specifications such as RIF (Rule Interchange Format), Prolog and N3. SWRL[11] is an expressive rule language that can be used to increase the amount of knowledge encoded in OWL ontologies. SWRL extends the set of OWL axioms to include Horn-like rules. It combines OWL DL with the Unary/Binary Datalog RuleML sublanguages of the RuleML. RIF[12] is a W3C standard designed for interchanging rules between different rule systems. Syntactic mappings that are semantics-preserving can be defined by rule systems from their native languages to RIF dialects and back. The standard RIF dialects are Core, BLD and PRD. OWL-RL[13] is a syntactic subset of OWL 2 which is amenable to implementation using rule-based technologies. OWL 2 RL is ideal for enriching RDF data, especially when the data must be massaged by additional rules.

Provision for the specification of rules have also been made in dedicated Semantic Web frameworks, platforms and triple stores such as Jena[14], OWLIM[15] and Apache stanbol[16]

The use of SPARQL as a constraint/rule language based on its CONSTRUCT keyword has long been advocated [7]. SPARQL CONSTRUCT is a SPARQL query that

---

[8] http://silk.semwebcentral.org/iswc2012-rules-tutorial/talk-iswc2012-rules-tutorial.pdf

[9] http://semantic-web-book.org/page/KI_2009_Tutorial

[10] http://www.ruleml.org/

[11] http://www.w3.org/Submission/SWRL/

[12] http://www.w3.org/TR/rif-overview/

[13] http://www.w3.org/TR/owl2-profiles/#OWL_2_RL

[14] http://jena.sourceforge.net/inference/#rules

[15] https://confluence.ontotext.com/display/OWLIMv43/OWLIM-SE+Reasoner#OWLIM-SEReasoner-RuleBasedInference

[16] http://stanbol.apache.org/docs/trunk/components/rules/

returns a graph (set of triples) that is the result of applying the `CONSTRUCT` graph pattern to each match in the `WHERE` clause. Specialised extensions of SPARQL for the rule based processing of events such as EP-SPARQL [1] have also been proposed.

SPIN(SPARQL Inferencing notation) is a SPARQL-based rule and constraint language for the Semantic Web. SPIN links class definitions with SPARQL queries using the SPIN Modeling Vocabulary, to capture constraints and rules. SPIN provides mechanisms to capture reusable SPARQL queries using SPIN templates, which are defined as SPARQL queries parameterized with pre-bound variables. SPIN also makes it possible to define custom SPARQL functions.

The use of SPARQL and SPIN to identify data quality problems on the Semantic Web has been proposed in [5]. The authors use SPIN query templates to parameterise the queries with variables. The data quality problems addressed here include missing values, syntax violations and the like. SPIN has also been used for formalising accounting regulations on the Web [6].

Although we explored the various frameworks briefly reviewed above for specifying the type of supply chain constraints we wanted to express, our choice of SPARQL and SPIN was strongly motivated by the fact that a supply chain may have several partners who may well use systems implemented by different vendors. Achieving interoperability between these systems would be crucial in ensuring that the constraints are validated by every partner without which the entire supply chain would be affected. SPARQL is an existing W3C standard with well-formed query semantics across RDF data, has existing widespread use amongst most RDF query engines and graph stores, and provides sufficient expressivity. SPIN allows one to check the validity of an RDF model by using SPARQL and covers a much larger range of potential constraint specifications than other Semantic rules languages. Further, SPIN rules and constraints can be easily shared on the web together with the class definitions they are associated with.

4   Preliminaries

4.1   EPCIS

An Electronic Product Code (EPC)[17] is a universal identifier that gives a unique, serialised identity to a physical object. EPCIS is a ratified EPCglobal[18] standard that provides a set of specifications for the syntactic capture and informal semantic interpretation of EPC based product information. As the EPC tagged object moves through the supply chain, RFID readers record and transmit the tagged data as "events". Given the scenario in Section 2, we are concerned with three types of EPCIS[19] events: *ObjectEvent* represents an event that occurred

---

[17] http://www.gs1.org/gsmp/kc/epcglobal/tds/tds_1_6-RatifiedStd-20110922.pdf

[18] http://www.gs1.org/epcglobal

[19] Please refer the specification for details.

as a result of some action on one or more entities denoted by EPCs, i.e., commissioning of an object *AggregationEvent* represents an event that happened to one or more EPC-denoted entities that are physically aggregated (constrained to be in the same place at the same time, as when cases are aggregated to a pallet) *TransactionEvent* represents an event in which one or more entities denoted by EPCs become associated or disassociated with one or more identified business transactions, i.e., the shipping of a pallet of goods in accordance to the fulfillment of an order.

4.2   The EEM Ontology

EEM is an OWL 2 DL ontology for modelling EPCIS events. EEM conceptualises various primitives of an EPCIS event that need to be asserted for the purposes of traceability in supply chains. A companion standard to EPCIS is the Core Business Vocabulary(CBV) standard. The CBV standard supplements the EPCIS framework by defining vocabularies and identifiers that may populate the EPCIS data model. *CBVVocab* is an OWL ontology that defines entities corresponding to the identifiers in CBV. Development of both the ontologies was informed by a thorough review of the EPCIS and the CBV specifications and extensive discussions with trading partners implementing the specification. The modelling decisions [10] behind the conceptual entities in EEM highlight the EPCIS abstractions included in the ontology. It is worth noting that in previous work [12] we have already defined a mapping between EEM and PROV-O[20], the vocabulary for representing provenance of Web resources. This implies that when a constraint violation is detected, the events in the history can be interrogated using PROV-O for recovering provenance information associated with the events.

The EEM ontology structure and its alignment with various external ontologies is illustrated in Figure 2. The ontology is composed of modules that define various perspectives on EPCIS. The *Temporal* module captures timing properties associated with an EPCIS event. It is aligned with temporal properties in DOLCE+DnS Ultralite (DUL)[21]. Entities defining the EPC, aggregation of EPCs and quantity lists for transformation events are part of the *Product* module. The GoodRelations[22] ontology is exploited here for capturing concepts such as an Individual Product or a lot (collection) of items, SomeItems of a single type. Information about the business context associated with an EPCIS event is encoded using the entities and relationships defined in the *Business* module. RFID readers and sensors are defined in the *Sensor* module. The definitions here are aligned with the SSN[23] ontology. The *EPCISException* module incorporates the hierarchy of the most commonly observed exceptions [13] occurring in EPCIS governing supply chains.

---

[20] http://www.w3.org/ns/prov-o
[21] http://ontologydesignpatterns.org/ont/dul/DUL.owl
[22] http://purl.org/goodrelations/v1
[23] http://purl.oclc.org/NET/ssnx/ssn

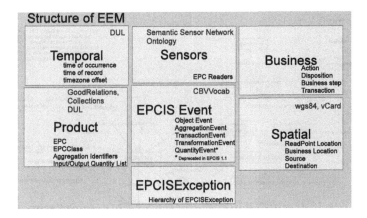

Fig. 2. Structure of EEM and its alignment with external ontologies (noted in blue coloured text)

For further details on EEM and its applications in real world scenarios, the interested reader is referred to [9–12].

4.3 Linked Pedigrees

A Pedigree is an (electronic) audit trail that records the chain of custody and ownership of a drug as it moves through the supply chain. Each stakeholder involved in the manufacture or distribution of the drug adds visibility based data about the product at their end, to the pedigree. Recently the concept of "Event-based Pedigree" [24] has been proposed that utilises the EPCIS specification for capturing events in the supply chain and generating pedigrees based on a relevant subset of the captured events. In previous work [9] we introduced the concept of linked pedigrees in the form of a content ontology design pattern, "OntoPedigree". We proposed a decentralised architecture and presented a communication protocol for the exchange of linked pedigrees among supply chain partners. In [11], we extended OntoPedigree to include provenance metadata as illustrated in Figure 3 and proposed an algorithm for the automated generation of linked pedigrees. For the purpose of completeness, we briefly recall the axiomatisation of a linked pedigree in Figure 4.

The definition highlights the mandatory and optional restrictions on the relationships and attributes for every pedigree that is exchanged between stakeholders. Based on these, we define the requirements on the constraints to be validated for the pedigrees.

---

[24] http://www.gs1.org/docs/healthcare/Healthcare_Traceability_Pedigree_Background.pdf

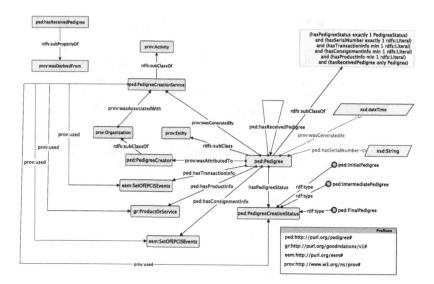

Fig. 3. Graphical Representation of Provenance based OntoPedigree

5   Requirements Analysis for Pedigree Validation

In this section we highlight some of the typical validation requirements on the pedigrees as well as on the traceability data encapsulated in the pedigrees received from upstream partners.

- **Incomplete Pedigree:** When a pedigree is received from an intermediate upstream partner it must include deferenceable URIs to the shipping events and the aggregation events in order to verify the upstream CoC/CoO. If the pedigree is received from the initial partner, it must also include dereferenceable URIs to the commissioning events. The Manchester syntax definition of the pedigree illustrated in Figure 4 highlights the entities that are mandatory and must be validated for any pedigree dereferenced by a supply chain partner.
- **Pedigree Data Has Broken Chain:** A pedigree received from an intermediate upstream partner must include dereferenceable URIs to other pedigrees from any previous partners who may have been in the line of CoO/CoC for the goods. Validation of included pedigrees must be carried out recursively for the upstream partners until pedigrees from the initial partner in the chain have been validated.
- **Pedigree Based, Receiving and Shipping Event Correlation:** When a consignment of physical goods is received, the receiving events and the EPCs recorded as part of the receiving events must correlate with the shipping events in the pedigree and the EPCs included in the shipping events.
- **Temporal Validity of Shipping and Receiving Events:** For a specific consignment, the shipping events must always precede the corresponding

```
Prefix ped: <http://purl.org/pedigree#>
Prefix prov: <http://www.w3.org/ns/prov-o>

Class: ped:Pedigree
       SubClassOf:
        (hasPedigreeStatus exactly 1 ped:PedigreeStatus)
        and (hasSerialNumber exactly 1 rdfs:Literal)
        and (pedigreeCreationTime exactly 1 xsd:DateTime)
        and (prov:wasAttributedTo exactly 1 ped:PedigreeCreator)
        and (ped:hasConsignmentInfo someValuesFrom eem:SetOfEPCISEvents)
        and (ped:hasTransactionInfo exactly 1 eem:SetOfEPCISEvents)
        and (ped:hasProductInfo min 1),
        (prov:wasGeneratedBy only ped:PedigreeCreationService),
        (ped:hasReceivedPedigree only eem:Pedigree),
        prov:Entity
```

Fig. 4. Manchester syntax serialisation of OntoPedigree

receiving events. Further, this delay needs to be corroborated with the actual time taken for the shipment to be transported from the source to the destination.

- **Missing Parent-Child Aggregation:** In a multi-party supply chain, aggregation and disaggregation of goods may happen at several points. Each of these activities have to be recorded and incorporated within the pedigree. Further goods with EPCs that are part of commissioning events and consequently aggregation events have to be accounted for in every phase of aggregation and disaggregation.

6   Formalising the Pedigree Validation Rules

In this section we formalise three of the pedigree validation rules identified in Section 5 using a combination of SPARQL queries and SPIN constraints .

6.1   Constraint1: Incomplete Pedigree (SPIN Constraint)

As per the axiomatisation of a pedigree illustrated in Figure 4, certain attributes and relationships are mandatory. If a pedigree is found to be incomplete, a `PedigreeIncompleteException` needs to be constructed. `PedigreeIncompleteException` is a subclass of `EPCISException` which itself subclasses from `spin:ConstraintViolation`. The textual SPARQL query for validating this constraint can be defined as:

```
#checks for incomplete pedigree
PREFIX ped: <http://purl.org/pedigree#>
PREFIX eem: <http://purl.org/eem#>
PREFIX spin: <http://spinrdf.org/spin#>
```

```
CONSTRUCT
{
  _:b0 a eem:PedigreeIncompleteException;
        spin:violationRoot ?this;
        eem:eventOccurredAt "timeLiteral"xsd:datetime;
        eem:associatedBusinessStep cbv:receiving;
        ....other triples about the exception
        rdfs:label ``Incomplete pedigree exception''.
}
WHERE
{
    ?this a ped:Pediigree;
          ped:hasPedigreeStatus ?PedigreeStatus;
          ped:hasSerialNumber ?serialNumber;
          ped:pedigreeCreationTime ?pedTime;
          prov:wasAttributedTo  ?pedigreeCreator;
          ped:hasConsignmentInfo ?setOfConsEvents;
          ped:hasTransactionInfo SetOfShipEvents;
          ped:hasProductInfo productInfo;
          prov:wasGeneratedBy ?pedigreeGenerationService;
          ped:hasReceivedPedigree ?pedigree.
    FILTER NOT EXISTS{ ped:hasPedigreeStatus ?PedigreeStatus;
                ped:hasSerialNumber ?serialNumber;
                ped:pedigreeCreationTime ?pedTime;
                prov:wasAttributedTo  ?pedigreeCreator;
                ped:hasConsignmentInfo ?setOfConsEvents;
                ped:hasTransactionInfo SetOfShipEvents;
                ped:hasProductInfo productInfo.}
}
```

The FILTER NOT EXISTS clause checks for the mandatory properties, in the absence of which the exception is generated and forwarded to the exception and notification handling modules. A detailed mechanism for representing the triples for the exception itself can be found in [13].

Using the SPIN spin:constraint we link[25] the definition of Pedigree to the constraint.

```
ped:Pedigree spin:constraint
     [ a sp:Construct;
       sp:templates ([..SPIN generated triples
                      for the construct query...])
     ]
```

---

[25] Due to space restrictions we do not reproduce the complete definition here.

6.2   Constraint2: Pedigree Data Has Broken Chain (SPARQL 1.1 Property Path)

The property `hasReceivedPedigree` relates a pedigree received by an *intermediate* partner to the pedigree it has received from upstream/downstream partners. We use SPARQL 1.1 property paths to validate the chain of received pedigrees.

```
CONSTRUCT
{
 _:b0 a eem:BrokenPedigreeChainException;
   ..same as the CONSTRUCT above..
   rdfs:label ''Broken pedigree chain exception''
WHERE
{  ?this a ped:Pedigree;
   ped:hasPedigreeStatus ped:IntermediatePedigree;
   ped:hasReceivedPedigree+ ?pedigree.
 FILTER NOT EXISTS {
        ped:hasPedigreeStatus ped:IntermediatePedigree;
        ped:hasReceivedPedigree+ ?pedigree.}
}
```

6.3   Constraint3: Pedigree Based Receiving and Shipping Event Correlation

For every pedigree, the set of events corresponding to the `hasTransactionInfo` relationship identify the shipping events. The set of receiving events recorded when the physical goods are received need to have a one-to-one correlation with the shipping events. This implies that the set of EPCs that are part of a receiving event(QueryR) have to be correlated with the set of EPCs in a specific shipping event.

```
#QueryR
SELECT ?epcisR ?epcR
WHERE
{
 ?epcisEventR a eem:EPCISEvent;
            eem:hasBusinessStepType cbv:Receiving;
            eem:associatedWithEPCList ?epcListR.
 ?epcListR    co:element ?epcR.
}
#QueryS
SELECT ?pedigree ?epcisEventS ?epcS
WHERE
{
 ?pedigree a ped:Pedigree;
        ped:hasTransactionInfo ?shippingEvents.
```

```
?shippingEvents a eem:SetOfEPCISEvents;
               co:element ?epcisEventS.
?epcisEventS a eem:EPCISEvent;
             eem:hasBusinessStepType cbv:Shipping;
             eem:associatedWithEPCList ?epcListS.
?epcListS    co:element ?epcS.
}
```

As noted further(cf. Section 7), the two SPARQL queries are independently executed and the results are combined in a dedicated storm bolt. If the validation fails, the bolt generates the triples for the `PedigreeCorrelationException`.

Validation queries for other constraints can be similarly specified using the various features available in SPIN.

7   Implementing the Validation Framework

Figure 5 illustrates the high level architecture that governs our implementation of the validation framework. Pedigrees generated by the upstream/downstream partner are stored in a repository (triple store) and accessed using a queue when a request is made through a Web service. We have used Apache ActiveMQ[26] as our messaging server for the implementation of the queues. A publish/subscribe mechanism is deployed to enable other downstream/upstream partners with relevant authorisation, access control and authentication privileges to subscribe to the pedigrees and dereference them when required. Our validation framework

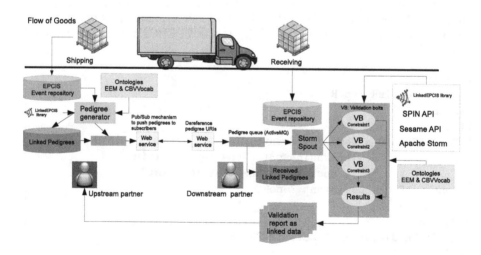

Fig. 5. High level architecture for the validation of pedigree constraints

---

[26] http://activemq.apache.org/

has been implemented using Apache Storm[27], a distributed realtime computation system for processing unbounded streams of data. A novel feature of our validation mechanism is the integration of Storm with external APIs and libraries for carrying out the validations. Specifically we integrate Storm with the SPIN API[28], the OpenRDF Sesame framework[29] and the LinkedEPCIS[30] library developed by us for encoding EPCIS events as linked data. The type hierarchy in LinkedEPCIS is based on the entities defined in the EEM and CBVVocab ontologies.

The validation workflow proceeds as follows: Linked pedigrees are generated using the algorithm and mechanism defined in [11]. When the goods are shipped, the shipping partner schedules the associated pedigrees to be retrieved by the subscribed partners. When the goods are received, the dereferenced pedigrees and the EPCIS receiving events are recorded and sent as streams of data to the validation framework, which has been implemented as an Apache Storm topology. Our Storm spout implementation receives the pedigrees through a queue while each of the bolts is assigned the task of validating a specific constraint. Bolts can execute SPARQL queries and carry out additional computation, e.g., the validation of constraint3 is carried out by first retrieving the results of the two SPARQL queries, performing a comparison between the results of queryR and queryS and generating the exception triples. Results from the validation are sent to the subscribing result bolt which is responsible for generating the aggregated validation results as linked data.

8   Evaluation

Our evaluation for the pharmaceutical scenario outlined in Section 2 focuses on the time taken for the validation of the various types of constraints identified in Section 6.

In order to estimate the volume and velocity of events generated in pharmaceutical event streams, we obtained a large representative sample of EPCIS event data from a well known pharmaceutical company[31], referred to grey literature and interviewed people closely involved in the pharmaceutical sector and EPCIS experts. We referred to a survey [8] that studied the cost benefit analysis of introducing EPCIS event-based pedigrees in the pharmaceutical supply chain. As per the survey, the average volume (number) of pallets, cases and items per month being shipped out of a typical manufacturing unit is 290, 5800 and 580,000 respectively. Interviews with experts corroborated the facts, however they also stated that for some large scale units, the number of items shipped could be as high as 100,000 per day.

---

[27] https://storm.incubator.apache.org/
[28] http://topbraid.org/spin/api/
[29] http://www.openrdf.org/
[30] https://github.com/nimonika/LinkedEPCIS
[31] Named withheld due to data confidentiality issues.

Assuming an average rate of production as 6 days per week and 10 hours per day, and using the sample data, we ran a simulation that replicated the volume and velocity of event generation. We generated the commissioning events based on the number of items ranging from 24,000 to 102,000 per day or approximately 40 to 170 per minute. As the number of items packed per case and the number of cases loaded per pallet could vary across manufacturing units, we generated aggregation and shipping events, considering aggregated items ranging from 100 to 500 (increments of 100) per case and number of cases per pallet ranging from 20 to 100 (increments of 20). We experimented with tumbling window sizes of 3, 5, 7 and 10 hours respectively and generated the linked pedigrees. Overall we ran a total of 400 combinations of commissioning, aggregation and shipping events to generate the pedigrees. For more information on evaluation of the algorithm for the generation of the pedigrees themselves the interested reader is referred to [11]. The event dataset dumps have been made available[32].

Next, for each of the 400 runs, we generated the receiving events using the same procedure as above. For every run, we observed the time taken by the respective storm bolts to validate each of the constraints formalised in 6. The evaluations were made on Mac OSX 10.9.2, 1.7GHz Intel core i5, 4GB 1333 MHz DDR3. The results from the evaluation are illustrated in Figure 6

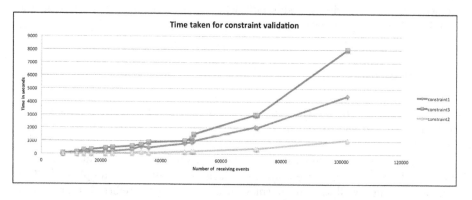

Fig. 6. Time taken for constraint evaluation for varying number of receiving events

As observed, constraint(1) and constraint(3) were computationally more time consuming. The time taken to validate the constraints increased linearly with the increase in the number of receiving events. Further, a major chunk of the validation of constraint(3) was done as part of the processing in the bolt after the query results were obtained, whereas validation of constraint(1) was only a result of the query execution. On the other hand, validation of constraint(2) took comparatively less time and did not vary significantly with the increase in the number of events.

---

[32] http://fispace.aston.ac.uk/pharma/eventDatasets

The differences in the time taken for the validation for each of the constraints, resulted in an overall increase in the validation time. The results show that in order to optimise the performance of the validation framework, a better approach would be to generate each pedigree with low-medium number of events. This would harmonise the time taken for the validation of the constraints and result in increased efficiency of the overall validation framework.

9   Conclusions

The sharing of traceability knowledge between partners greatly enhances their ability to track parts, components or products in transit from the manufacturer to their final destination. In the healthcare sector, visibility of datasets that encapsulate track and trace information is especially important in addressing the problems of drug counterfeiting.

In this paper we have shown how rule based frameworks such as SPIN, driven by Semantic Web standards and linked data libraries can be integrated with distributed realtime computation systems such as Apache Storm to process real time streams of supply chain data. We exploit this knowledge for the validation of constraints that are defined to ensure the quality, uniformity, consistency and completeness of datasets exchanged between supply chain partners. Our constraints are representative of the most commonly occurring scenarios in supply chain and it is worth noting that while we have chosen the healthcare sector as a case study, our approach is domain independent and can be widely applied to most scenarios of traceability.

There are several issues such as trust relationship between actors, access control mechanisms and performance optimisation of distributed storm topologies that need to be considered in supply chains, especially when commercially sensitive data is being shared among partners. In this paper we have abstracted from those issues. Our aim was to show the relevance of validating streaming supply chain event data to the problem of real time tracking and tracking in supply chains.

Much work still needs to be done, especially in making the visualisation of the validation reports intuitive to the partners. We are currently building a Linked pedigrees dashboard that would enable the visualisation of various aspects of linked pedigrees including the violation of constraints and the potential corrective actions taken.

Acknowledgements. The research described in this paper has been partially supported by the EU FP7 FI PPP projects, SmartAgriFood (http://smartagrifood.eu) and FISpace http://www.fispace.eu/

References

1. Anicic, D., et al.: EP-SPARQL: A Unified Language for Event Processing and Stream Reasoning. In: Proceedings of the 20th International Conference on World Wide Web, WWW 2011. ACM (2011)

2. Boley, H., Paschke, A., Shafiq, O.: RuleML 1.0: The overarching specification of web rules. In: Dean, M., Hall, J., Rotolo, A., Tabet, S. (eds.) RuleML 2010. LNCS, vol. 6403, pp. 162–178. Springer, Heidelberg (2010)

3. Eiter, T., Ianni, G., Krennwallner, T., Polleres, A.: Rules and ontologies for the semantic web. In: Baroglio, C., Bonatti, P.A., Małuszyński, J., Marchiori, M., Polleres, A., Schaffert, S. (eds.) Reasoning Web. LNCS, vol. 5224, pp. 1–53. Springer, Heidelberg (2008)

4. Främling, K., Parmar, S., Hinkka, V., Tätilä, J., Rodgers, D.: Assessment of EPCIS standard for interoperable tracking in the supply chain. In: Borangiu, T., Thomas, A., Trentesaux, D. (eds.) Service Orientation in Holonic and Multi agent, SCI, vol. 472, pp. 119–134. Springer, Heidelberg (2013)

5. Fürber, C., Hepp, M.: Using SPARQL and SPIN for data quality management on the semantic web. In: Abramowicz, W., Tolksdorf, R. (eds.) BIS 2010. LNBIP, vol. 47, pp. 35–46. Springer, Heidelberg (2010)

6. O'Riain, S., McCrae, J., Cimiano, P., Spohr, D.: Using spin to formalise accounting regulations on the semantic web. In: Proceedings of the First International Workshop on Finance and Economics on the Semantic Web (FEOSW 2012). CEUR Proceedings (2012)

7. Polleres, A.: From sparql to rules (and back). In: Proceedings of the 16th International Conference on World Wide Web, WWW 2007, ACM (2007)

8. Sinha, A.: Systems engineering perspective of e-pedigree system. Master's thesis, Systems Design and Management (SDM), MIT (2009)

9. Solanki, M., Brewster, C.: Consuming Linked data in Supply Chains: Enabling data visibility via Linked Pedigrees. In: Fourth International Workshop on Consuming Linked Data (COLD 2013) at ISWC. CEUR-WS.org proceedings, vol. 1034 (2013)

10. Solanki, M., Brewster, C.: Representing Supply Chain Events on the Web of Data. In: Workshop on Detection, Representation, and Exploitation of Events in the Semantic Web (DeRiVE) at ISWC. CEUR-WS.org proceedings (2013)

11. Solanki, M., Brewster, C.: EPCIS event based traceability in pharmaceutical supply chains via automated generation of linked pedigrees. In: Janowicz, K., et al. (eds.) ISWC 2014. LNCS, vol. 8796, pp. 82–97. Springer, Heidelberg (2014)

12. Solanki, M., Brewster, C.: Modelling and Linking Transformations in EPCIS Governing Supply Chain Business Processes. In: Hepp, M., Hoffner, Y. (eds.) EC-Web 2014. LNBIP, vol. 188, pp. 46–57. Springer, Heidelberg (2014)

13. Solanki, M., Brewster, C.: Monitoring EPCIS Exceptions in linked traceability streams across supply chain business processes. In: Proceedings of the 10th International Conference on Semantic Systems (SEMANTiCS). ACM-ICPS (2014)

Testing OWL Axioms against RDF Facts: A Possibilistic Approach

Andrea G.B. Tettamanzi[1], Catherine Faron-Zucker[1], and Fabien Gandon[2]

[1] Univ. Nice Sophia Antipolis, I3S, UMR 7271, Sophia Antipolis, France
{andrea.tettamanzi,faron}@unice.fr
[2] INRIA, Sophia Antipolis, France
fabien.gandon@inria.fr

Abstract. Automatic knowledge base enrichment methods rely critically on candidate axiom scoring. The most popular scoring heuristics proposed in the literature are based on statistical inference. We argue that such a probability-based framework is not always completely satisfactory and propose a novel, alternative scoring heuristics expressed in terms of possibility theory, whereby a candidate axiom receives a bipolar score consisting of a degree of possibility and a degree of necessity. We evaluate our proposal by applying it to the problem of testing SubClassOf axioms against the DBpedia RDF dataset.

Keywords: ontology learning, open-world assumption, possibility theory.

1 Introduction

A common approach to the semantic Web puts strong emphasis on a principled conceptual analysis of a domain of interest leading to the construction or reuse of ontologies as a prerequisite step for the organization of the Linked Open Data (LOD), much like a database schema must be designed before a database can be populated. However this approach has some limitations: it is aprioristic and dogmatic in the way knowledge should be organized; while it is quite successful when applied to specific domains, it does not scale well to more general settings; it does not lend itself to a collaborative effort; etc. That is why an alternative, bottom-up, *grass-roots* approach to ontology and knowledge base creation better suits many scenarii: instead of postulating an *a priori* conceptualization of reality (i.e., an ontology) and requiring that our knowledge about facts complies with it, one can start from RDF facts and learn OWL 2 axioms.

Recent contributions towards the automatic creation of OWL 2 ontologies from large repositories of RDF facts include FOIL-like algorithms for learning concept definitions [5], statistical schema induction via association rule mining [6], and light-weight schema enrichment methods based on the DL-Learner framework [9,2]. All these methods apply and extend techniques developed within inductive logic programming (ILP) [10].

On a related note, there exists a need for evaluating and validating ontologies, be they the result of an analysis effort or of a semi-automatic learning method.

K. Janowicz et al. (Eds.): EKAW 2014, LNAI 8876, pp. 519–530, 2014.

This need is witnessed by general methodological investigations [7,8] and surveys [13] and tools like OOPS! [11] for detecting pitfalls in ontologies.

Ontology learning and validation rely critically on (candidate) axiom scoring. In this paper, we will tackle the problem of testing a single, isolated axiom, which is anyway the first step to solve the problem of validating an entire ontology. Furthermore, to keep things reasonably simple, we will restrict our attention to subsumption axioms of the form SubClassOf(C D).

The most popular scoring heuristics proposed in the literature are based on statistical inference. We argue that such a probability-based framework is not always completely satisfactory. We will propose an axiom scoring heuristics based on a formalization in possibility theory of the notions of logical content of a theory and of falsification, loosely inspired by Karl Popper's approach to epistemology. Our research question is: "Can we apply a possibilistic approach to the task of testing candidate axioms for ontology learning?". In addition, "Could this be beneficial to ontology and knowledge base validation?".

The paper is organized as follows: Section 2 proposes a heuristics based on possibility theory, alternative to probability-based scoring heuristics. Its implementation is detailed in Section 3 and an evaluation is provided in Section 4. Section 5 draws some conclusions.

2   A Possibilistic Candidate Axiom Scoring Heuristics

Let ϕ be a candidate axiom and u_ϕ the support or sample size for ϕ, i.e., the cardinality of the set of its logical consequences that will be tested in the RDF repository. Notice that every formula which logically follows from an axiom is both a potential falsifier (if it is contradicted by facts) and a potential confirmation (if it is verified by facts) for that axiom.

Let u_ϕ^+ the number of such consequences which are true (confirmations), and u_ϕ^- the number of such consequences which are false (counterexamples). A few interesting properties of these three cardinalities are:

$$u_\phi^+ + u_\phi^- \leq u_\phi; \tag{1}$$

$$u_\phi^+ = u_{\neg\phi}^-, \quad u_\phi^- = u_{\neg\phi}^+, \quad u_\phi = u_{\neg\phi}. \tag{2}$$

A statistics-based heuristics for the scoring of candidate axioms used in the framework of knowledge base enrichment [2] may be regarded essentially as scoring an axiom by an estimate of the probability that one of its logical consequences is confirmed (or, alternatively, falsified) by the facts stored in the RDF repository. As Bühmann and Lehmann point out [2], estimating the probability of confirmation of axiom ϕ just by $\hat{p}_\phi = u_\phi^+/u_\phi$ would be too crude and would not take the magnitude of u_ϕ into account. That is why they base their probabilistic score on Agresti and Coull's binomial proportion confidence interval [1].

One problem with such approaches is that they only look for confirmations of ϕ and treat their absence as failures in the calculation of the confidence interval. This is like making an implicit closed-world assumption. An easy fix, in view of the open-world assumption, might be, for example, to use $\hat{p}^* = u_\phi^+/(u_\phi^+ + u_\phi^-)$ as the sample proportion instead of $\hat{p}$.

A more serious problem, however, is that these approaches rely on the assumption that it is possible to estimate the probability that an axiom ϕ is true given some evidence e, where $e =$ "ψ such that $\phi \models \psi$ is in the RDF repository", or $e =$ "ψ such that $\psi \models \neg\phi$ is in the RDF repository", or $e =$ "ψ such that $\phi \models \psi$ is *not* in the RDF repository", etc., which, by Bayes' formula, may be written as

$$\Pr(\phi \mid e) = \frac{\Pr(e \mid \phi)\Pr(e)}{\Pr(e \mid \phi)\Pr(e) + \Pr(e \mid \neg\phi)\Pr(\neg e)}. \tag{3}$$

Therefore, in order to compute (or estimate) such probability, one should be able to estimate the probabilities on the right-hand side of Equation 3. Now, this is possible only under the (strong) assumption that the data at hand are representative.

To capture the basic intuition behind the process of axiom discovery without making unwarranted assumptions, we propose an alternative axiom scoring heuristics based on possibility theory, which is weaker than probability theory.

2.1 Possibility Theory

Possibility theory [14] is a mathematical theory of epistemic uncertainty. Given a finite universe of discourse Ω, whose elements $\omega \in \Omega$ may be regarded as events, values of a variable, possible worlds, or states of affairs, a possibility distribution is a mapping $\pi : \Omega \to [0,1]$, which assigns to each ω a degree of possibility ranging from 0 (impossible, excluded) to 1 (completely possible, normal). A possibility distribution for which there exists a completely possible state of affairs ($\exists \omega^* : \pi(\omega^*) = 1$) is said to be *normalized*.

There is a similarity between possibility distribution and probability density. However, it must be stressed that $\pi(\omega) = 1$ just means that ω is a plausible (normal) situation and therefore should not be excluded. A degree of possibility can then be viewed as an upper bound of a degree of probability. Possibility theory is suitable to represent incomplete knowledge while probability is adapted to represent random and observed phenomena. We invite the reader to see [4] for more informations about the relationships between fuzzy sets, possibility, and probability degrees.

A possibility distribution π induces a *possibility measure* and its dual *necessity measure*, denoted by Π and N respectively. Both measures apply to a set $A \subseteq \Omega$ (or to a formula ϕ, by way of the set of its models, $A = \{\omega : \omega \models \phi\}$), and are defined as follows:

$$\Pi(A) = \max_{\omega \in A} \pi(\omega); \tag{4}$$

$$N(A) = 1 - \Pi(\bar{A}) = \min_{\omega \in \bar{A}}\{1 - \pi(\omega)\}. \tag{5}$$

A few properties of possibility and necessity measures induced by a normalized possibility distribution on a finite universe of discourse Ω are the following. For all subsets $A \subseteq \Omega$,

1. $\Pi(\emptyset) = N(\emptyset) = 0, \quad \Pi(\Omega) = N(\Omega) = 1;$
2. $\Pi(A) = 1 - N(\bar{A})$ (duality);
3. $N(A) > 0$ implies $\Pi(A) = 1, \quad \Pi(A) < 1$ implies $N(A) = 0.$

In case of complete ignorance on A, $\Pi(A) = \Pi(\bar{A}) = 1$.

2.2 Support of an Axiom

At the beginning of this section, we have introduced the notion of support or sample for a candidate axiom ϕ as the number of its logical consequences that will be tested in the RDF repository. We shall now define that notion more precisely.

Let BS be a finite set of *basic statements*, i.e., assertions, like the ones contained in an RDF repository, that may be tested by means of a SPARQL ASK query. We define the *content* of an axiom ϕ that we wish to evaluate as the set of its logical consequences, but we restrict it to basic statements, to ensure finiteness and testability:

$$\text{content}(\phi) = \{\psi : \phi \models \psi\} \cap \text{BS}. \tag{6}$$

The cardinality of content(ϕ) is finite, because BS is finite, and every formula $\psi \in \text{content}(\phi)$ may be tested, because it is a basic statement. Now we can define the support of ϕ as the cardinality of content(ϕ):

$$u_\phi = |\text{content}(\phi)|. \tag{7}$$

2.3 Possibility and Necessity of an Axiom

The basic principle for establishing the possibility of a formula ϕ should be that the absence of counterexamples to ϕ in the RDF repository means $\Pi(\phi) = 1$, i.e., that ϕ is completely possible.

A hypothesis should be regarded as all the more *necessary* as it is explicitly supported by facts and not contradicted by any fact; and all the more *possible* as it is not contradicted by facts. In other words, given hypothesis ϕ, $\Pi(\phi) = 1$ if no counterexamples are found; as the number of counterexamples increases, $\Pi(\phi) \to 0$ strictly monotonically; $N(\phi) = 0$ if no confirmations are found; as the number of confirmations increases and no counterexamples are found, $N(\phi) \to 1$ strictly monotonically. Notice that a confirmation of ϕ is a counterexample of $\neg\phi$ and that a counterexample of ϕ is a confirmation of $\neg\phi$. Furthermore, the first counterexamples found to an axiom should determine a sharper decrease of the degree to which we regard the axiom as possible than any further counterexamples, because these latter will only confirm our suspicions and, therefore, will provide less and less information and, similarly, in the absence of counterexamples, the first confirmations found to an axiom should determine a sharper increase of the degree to which we regard the axiom as necessary than any further confirmations, because these latter will only add up to our acceptance and, therefore, will provide less and less information.

A definition of Π and N which captures the above intuitions, but by no means the only possible one, is, for $u_\phi > 0$,

$$\Pi(\phi) = 1 - \sqrt{1 - \left(\frac{u_\phi - u_\phi^-}{u_\phi}\right)^2} \; ; \tag{8}$$

$$N(\phi) = \sqrt{1 - \left(\frac{u_\phi - u_\phi^+}{u_\phi}\right)^2} \quad \text{if } \Pi(\phi) = 1, 0 \text{ otherwise.} \tag{9}$$

Notice that this definition satisfies the duality of possibility and necessity, in that $N(\phi) = 1 - \Pi(\neg\phi)$ and $\Pi(\phi) = 1 - N(\neg\phi)$.

We combine the possibility and necessity of an axiom to define a single handy acceptance/rejection index (ARI) as follows:

$$\text{ARI}(\phi) = N(\phi) - N(\neg\phi) = N(\phi) + \Pi(\phi) - 1 \in [-1, 1]. \tag{10}$$

A negative $\text{ARI}(\phi)$ suggests rejection of ϕ ($\Pi(\phi) < 1$), whilst a positive $\text{ARI}(\phi)$ suggests its acceptance ($N(\phi) > 0$), with a strength proportional to its absolute value. A value close to zero reflects ignorance about the status of ϕ.

3   A Framework for Candidate Axiom Testing

We refer to the model-theoretic semantics of OWL 2 (as defined in [3]), which defines an interpretation $\mathcal{I}$ with a valuation function $\cdot^{\mathcal{I}}$ mapping OWL 2 expressions into elements and sets of elements of an interpretation domain $\Delta^{\mathcal{I}}$. We take the set of all the resources that occur in a given RDF store as $\Delta^{\mathcal{I}}$ and checking an axiom amounts to checking whether $\mathcal{I}$ is a model of the axiom. Also, calling linked data search engines like Sindice could virtually extend the interpretation domain to the whole LOD cloud.

However, unlike interpretation domains, RDF stores are incomplete and possibly noisy. The open-world hypothesis must be made; therefore, absence of supporting evidence does not necessarily contradict an axiom, and an axiom might hold even in the face of a few counterexamples (exceptions or possible mistakes). For example, out of 541 axioms of the form SubClassOf(C D) in the DBpedia ontology, 143 have an empty content (i.e., class C is empty) and 28 have at least one counterexample in DBpedia 3.9.[1]

A general algorithm for testing all the possible OWL 2 axioms in a given RDF store is beyond the scope of this paper. Here, we will restrict our attention to atomic class expressions and ObjectComplementOf expressions, needed to test SubClassOf axioms. The model-theoretic semantics of expressions of the form ObjectComplementOf(C) ($\neg C$ in description logics syntax), where C denotes a concept expression (called *class expression* in OWL 2) is $\Delta^{\mathcal{I}} \setminus C^{\mathcal{I}}$.

Now, let us define a mapping $Q(E, x)$ from OWL 2 expressions to SPARQL graph patterns, where E is an OWL 2 expression, x is a formal parameter which

---

[1] And one, namely SubClassOf(dbo:Person dbo:Agent), even has 76 counterexamples!

can be replaced by a SPARQL variable or an RDF term, such that the query
SELECT DISTINCT ?x WHERE { $Q(E,?x)$ } returns all the known instances of
class expression E, which we will denote by $[Q(E,x)]$, i.e., the equivalent of $E^{\mathcal{I}}$,
and the query ASK { $Q(E,a)$ } checks whether $E(a)$ is in the RDF base.

For an atomic concept A, $Q(A,?x) = ?x$ a A, where A is a valid IRI. For concept negation, things are slightly more complicated, for RDF does not support
negation. The obvious definition

$$Q(\neg C, ?x) = \{ \ ?x \ ?p \ ?o \ . \ \text{FILTER NOT EXISTS} \ Q(C, ?x) \ \}, \qquad (11)$$

has the problem of treating negation as failure, like in databases, where the
closed-world assumption is made. Since we want to get as close as possible to
an open-world semantics, $Q(\neg C, x)$ should be defined differently, as the union
of the concepts that are disjoint from C. One might try to express this as the
set of individuals x that are instances of a concept C' such that no individual
$z \in C^{\mathcal{I}}$ is an instance of C', yielding the query

$$\begin{aligned} Q(\neg C, ?x) = \{ \ &?x \ a \ ?dc \ . \qquad\qquad\qquad\qquad\qquad (12) \\ &\text{FILTER NOT EXISTS} \ \{ \ ?z \ a \ ?dc \ . \quad Q(C, ?z) \ \} \ \}, \end{aligned}$$

where ?z is a variable that does not occur anywhere else in the query. This
translation is conceptually more satisfactory than the one in Equation 11, but
it just pushes the problem one step further, because this way of testing whether
two concepts are disjoint is based on negation as failure too. The only way to be
certain that two classes are disjoint would be to find an axiom to this effect in
the ontology:

$$Q(\neg C, ?x) = \{ \ ?x \ a \ ?dc \ . \ ?dc \ \text{owl:disjointWith} \ C \ \}, \qquad (13)$$

otherwise, either we find an individual which is an instance of both classes, and
thus we know the two classes are not disjoint, or we don't, in which case the
two classes may or may not be disjoint. The fact is, very few DisjointClasses
axioms are currently found in existing ontologies. For example, in the DBpedia
ontology, the query SELECT ?x ?y { ?x owl:disjointWith ?y } executed on
November 22, 2013 returned 17 solutions only.

To compare these three alternative definitions of $Q(\neg C, ?x)$, we may refer
to the diagram in Figure 1. We wish to estimate the actual extent of $(\neg C)^{\mathcal{I}}$.
Clearly, $Q(C, ?x)$ (in dark grey) underestimates the real extent of $C^{\mathcal{I}}$ (in light
gray). Therefore, we may say that Equation 11 overestimates the real extent of
$(\neg C)^{\mathcal{I}}$, in the sense that it will regard as instances of $\neg C$ all individuals a for
which "a a C" is not found in the RDF repository.

Now, if b is such that "b a C" is not known, but "b a D'" is known for some
class D' and some instances of D are known to be also instances of C, then
it might well be that b is an instance of C as well. If, however, a is such that
"a a C" is not known and no instance of D is known that is also an instance of
C, then we are more likely to believe that a is not an instance of C. Therefore
Equation 12 regards as instances of $\neg C$ fewer individuals, those for which it is
highly likely that they do not belong in C.

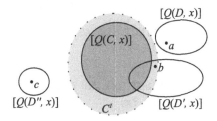

Fig. 1. A schematic illustration of the heuristics used to capture negation under the open world assumption. D'' is a concept which is declared to be disjoint with C in the RDF repository.

On the other hand, Equation 13 certainly underestimates $(\neg C)^{\mathcal{I}}$, to the point of considering it empty if "D'' `owl:disjointWith` C" is not declared in the RDF repository. Furthermore, an individual may be an instance of $\neg C$ even though it is not an instance of a class disjoint with C!

To sum up, Equation 11 is too optimistic, Equation 13 too pessimistic, and Equation 12 somewhere in the middle. Following the old adage "virtue stands in the middle", adopting Equation 12 looks like a sensible choice.

We will end this section by arguing that a suitable definition of confirmation to adopt in this framework is Scheffler and Goodman's *selective confirmation* [12], which characterizes a confirmation as a fact not simply satisfying an axiom, but, further, favoring the axiom rather than its contrary. For instance, the occurence of a black raven *selectively confirms* the axiom Raven $\sqsubseteq$ Black because it both confirms it and fails to confirm its negation, namely that there exist ravens that are not black. On the contrary, the observation of a green apple does not contradict Raven $\sqsubseteq$ Black, but it does not disconfirm Raven $\not\sqsubseteq$ Black either; therefore, it does not selectively confirm Raven $\sqsubseteq$ Black.

4   Evaluation on Subsumption Axiom Testing

The semantics of subsumption axioms of the form SubClassOf(C D) ($C \sqsubseteq D$ in description logic syntax) is $C^{\mathcal{I}} \subseteq D^{\mathcal{I}}$, which may also be written $x \in C^{\mathcal{I}} \Rightarrow x \in D^{\mathcal{I}}$. Therefore, content($C \sqsubseteq D$) = $\{D(a) : C(a)$ in the RDF store$\}$, because, if $C(a)$ holds, $C(a) \Rightarrow D(a) = \neg C(a) \vee D(a) = \top \vee D(a) = D(a)$. The support $u_{C \sqsubseteq D}$ of the axiom can thus be computed with the following SPARQL query:

$$\texttt{SELECT (count(DISTINCT ?x) AS ?u) WHERE } \{Q(C, \texttt{?x})\}. \qquad (14)$$

In order to compute $ARI(C \sqsubseteq D)$, we must provide a computational definition of $u_{C \sqsubseteq D}^{+}$ and $u_{C \sqsubseteq D}^{-}$. We start with the following statements:

- confirmations are individuals i such that $i \in [Q(C, x)]$ and $i \in [Q(D, x)]$;
- counterexamples are individuals i such that $i \in [Q(C, x)]$ and $i \in [Q(\neg D, x)]$.

This may be translated into SPARQL queries to compute $u^+_{C \sqsubseteq D}$ and $u^-_{C \sqsubseteq D}$:

$$\texttt{SELECT (count(DISTINCT ?x) AS ?numConfirmations)}$$
$$\texttt{WHERE \{ } Q(C, \texttt{?x}) \, Q(D, \texttt{?x}) \texttt{ \}} \tag{15}$$

and

$$\texttt{SELECT (count(DISTINCT ?x) AS ?numCounterexamples)}$$
$$\texttt{WHERE \{ } Q(C, \texttt{?x}) \, Q(\neg D, \texttt{?x}) \texttt{ \}} \tag{16}$$

respectively. Notice that an $i \in [Q(C, x)]$ such that $i \notin [Q(D, x)]$ does not contradict $C \sqsubseteq D$, because it might well be the case that the assertion "i a D" is just missing. Likewise, an $i \in [Q(\neg D, x)]$ such that $i \in [Q(\neg C, x)]$ will not be treated as a confirmation, based on our choice to regard as evidence in favor of a hypothesis only selective confirmations.

We evaluated the proposed scoring heuristics by performing tests of subsumption axioms using DBpedia 3.9 in English as the reference RDF fact repository. In particular, on April 27, 2014, we downloaded the DBpedia dumps of English version 3.9, generated in late March/early April 2013, along with the DBpedia ontology, version 3.9. This local dump of DBpedia, consisting of 812,546,748 RDF triples, has been bulk-loaded into Jena TDB and a prototype for performing axiom tests using the proposed method has been coded in Java, using Jena ARQ and TDB to access the RDF repository.

All experiments have been performed on a Fujitsu CELSIUS workstation equipped with twelve six-core Intel Xeon CPU E5-2630 v2 processors at 2.60GHz clock speed, with 15,360 KB cache each, 128 GB RAM, 4 TB of disk space with a 128 GB SSD cache, under the Ubuntu 12.04.4 LTS 64-bit operating system.

We performed two experiments of different type: an explorative test of systematically generated subsumption axioms and an exhaustive test of all subsumption axioms in the DBpedia ontology.[2]

For the former experiment, we systematically generated and tested subsumption axioms involving atomic classes only according the following protocol: for each of the 442 classes C referred to in the RDF repository, we construct all axioms of the form $C \sqsubseteq D$ such that C and D share at least one instance. Classes D are obtained with query $\texttt{SELECT DISTINCT ?D WHERE } \{Q(C, \texttt{?x}). \texttt{?x a ?D}\}$. Due to the sheer number of axioms thus generated, and to the long time it takes to test them,[3] this experiment could not complete at the time of writing and is still underway; however, a sufficient number of axioms was tested to allow gathering some statistics. Figure 2a shows the distribution of test time, while the plot of time vs. ARI of axioms in Figure 2b suggests that the time it takes to test an axiom is inversely proportional to its ARI. This is good news, because it suggests that putting a time-out on the test would be an acceptable heuristics to decide whether to accept or reject a candidate axiom, for an axiom which takes too long to test will likely end up having a very negative ARI.

By construction, all axioms generated in this experiment have at least one confirmation and, as a consequence, non-zero possibility (thus ARI > -1).

---

[2] Results available at URL http://www.i3s.unice.fr/~tettaman/RDFMining/

[3] Up to 27 hours for axiom SubClassOf(dbo:Eukaryote dbo:Artist)!

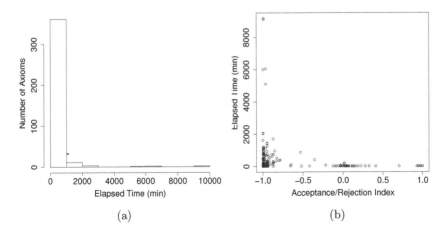

Fig. 2. A histogram showing the distribution of test time of systematically generated SubClassOf axioms (a), and a plot of the time taken for testing as a function of ARI

The ARI values of systematically generated axioms tend to cluster around the three values −1, 0, and 1 (see Figure 3a).

To assess the discriminatory ability of the proposed scoring heuristics, we have evaluated these results by sorting the 380 tested axioms by their ARI and by manually tagging each of them as either *true* or *false* based on common sense. Three out of the 78 axioms with an ARI of 1 are clearly false: SubClassOf(dbo:Eukaryote dbo:Species), SubClassOf(dbo:OrganisationMember dbo:SportsTeamMember), and SubClassOf(dbo:SportCompetitionResult dbo:OlympicResult). However, no scoring heuristics based on counting would be able to tell these 3 false positives from the true ones. Proceeding by decreasing ARI, the first false axiom encountered was SubClassOf(dbo:TennisLeague skos:Concept), with an ARI of 0.699854,[4] followed by the true axiom SubClassOf(dbo:Road gml:_Feature), with an ARI of 0.410399, followed by a large number of false axioms, starting with SubClassOf(schema:Product gml:_Feature) with an ARI of 0.326187. This positive ARI means no counterexamples were found; the 2,806 confirmations are all instances of classes dbo:Aircraft and dbo:Ship having, strangely enough, geographical coordinates.

A few seemingly true axioms are found with an ARI around zero. They are SubClassOf(schema:School schema:Place), SubClassOf(schema:School dbo:Place), with an ARI of 0.00830433, and SubClassOf(schema:School dbo:EducationalInstitution), SubClassOf(schema:School dbo:Organisation), SubClassOf(schema:School schema:EducationalOrganization), and SubClassOf(schema:School schema:Organization), with an ARI of −0.00830433.

---

[4] The confirmations of this and several other axioms of the form SubclassOf(C skos:Concept) with a much lower ARI are obvious mistakes: no individual should be a skos:Concept. This seems now to have been fixed in the live version of DBpedia.

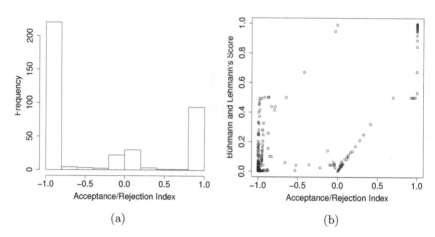

Fig. 3. A histogram showing the distribution of the acceptance/rejection index of systematically generated SubClassOf axioms (a), and the relationship between the acceptance/rejection index and the probability-based score used in [2] (b)

A dubious case is SubClassOf(schema:Museum dbo:Building), with an ARI of -0.031754, 3,957 confirmations and two counterexamples :Saint_Peter's_Basilica and :US_90. We tagged it as false, because one could imagine a museum hosted on a ship or an open-air museum, but we admit to our choice being debatable.

This distribution of true and false axioms suggests $\mathrm{ARI}(\phi) > 1/3$ as the optimal acceptance criterion for a candidate axiom ϕ. This would yield 4 false positives and 6 false negatives (corresponding to a 97.37% accuracy). However, it appears that the misclassification of the above axioms is to blame on mistakes in DBpedia. This highlights the potential for the proposed heuristics as a tool for RDF data validation: confirmations and counterexamples of axioms with ARI around zero is where the search for bugs should focus.

It is interesting to compare these results with those one would obtain by using a probability-based score. Figure 3b provides a comparison by plotting each axiom according to its ARI (X-axis) and its score computed as in [2] (Y-axis). First of all it is clear that both scores tend to agree in the extremes, with some notable exceptions, but behave quite differently in all other cases. The probabilistic score with the 0.7 threshold suggested by [2] gives 13 false negatives (7 more than the ARI) and 4 false positives (the three false axioms with ARI of 1, plus SubClassOf(schema:Museum dbo:Building), which we tagged as false). Among the false negatives, there are five axioms with an ARI of 1 which are rejected by the probabilistic score: they are all of the form SubClassOf(dbo:TennisLeague D). Then we find SubClassOf(schema:School schema:Place) and SubClassOf(schema:School dbo:Place), which were also rejected by the ARI, and six axioms of the form SubClassOf(C gml:_Feature), which have ARIs comprised between 0.41 and 0.997. Finally, most false axiom candidates get an ARI close to -1, whilst their probabilistic scores are almost evenly distributed between 0 and 0.5. We might say that, besides being more accurate, ARI gives clearer indications than the probabilistic score.

For the second, more validation-oriented experiment, we extracted an exhaustive list of SubClassOf axioms in the DBpedia ontology, in functional syntax, with the query

```
SELECT DISTINCT concat("SubClassOf(<",str(?x),"> <",str(?y),">)")
WHERE { ?x a owl:Class . ?x rdfs:subClassOf ?y }
```

thus obtaining 541 axioms. Testing them took "only" 1 h 23 min 31 s, due to the fact that most of these axioms have a positive ARI and can thus be tested relatively rapidly.

A large number of these axioms (143) turned out to have $u_\phi = 0$ (empty content) thus their ARI is 0. For 28 axioms, a negative ARI signals the presence of seemingly erroneous facts: the following table gives a few examples of axioms $C \sqsubseteq D$ with their conterexamples (instances of the subclass that also belong to a class disjoint with the superclass, i.e., a such that $C(a)$ and $E(a)$ with $E^{\mathcal{I}} \cap D^{\mathcal{I}} = \emptyset$: in this case, either $C(a)$ is wrong or $E(a)$ is).

Axiom	Counterexamples
SubClassOf(dbo:LaunchPad dbo:Infrastructure)	:USA
SubClassOf(dbo:Brain dbo:AnatomicalStructure)	:Brain [sic]
SubClassOf(dbo:Train dbo:MeanOfTransportation)	:New_Jersey_Transit_rail_operations, :ALWEG
SubClassOf(dbo:ProgrammingLanguage dbo:Software)	:Ajax
SubClassOf(dbo:PoliticalParty dbo:Organisation)	:Guelphs_and_Ghibellines, :-,[5] :New_People's_Army, :Syrian

5 Conclusion

We have proposed a candidate axiom scoring heuristics, based on possibility theory, to be used for automatic axiom induction from RDF data and, ultimately, to provide a solid basis for ontology learning. In addition, we have developed a framework based on the proposed heuristics, which uses the model-theoretic semantics of OWL 2 and SPARQL queries to test candidate axioms.

The results of experimental evaluation on the DBpedia dataset clearly indicate that the proposed heuristics is suitable for tasks such axiom induction and ontology learning and, furthermore, may be beneficial as a tool for ontology and knowledge-base validation.

One may object that, being based on possibility theory, our scoring heuristics is less objective than a probability-based scoring method. However, we have argued in Section 2 that scoring heuristics based on probability are doomed to be arbitrary and subjective or, in other words, *qualitative* and, therefore, hardly more rigorous or objective than the proposed approach. The experimental results corroborate this claim.

Future work includes extending the experimental evaluation to more general sets of candidate axioms and enlarging the test base by including additional RDF

---

[5] That is `<http://dbpedia.org/resource/->`. This IRI is dereferenced to the "hyphen-minus" resource.

datasets from the LOD. We also plan on improving the implementation of the framework by setting a time-out on query evaluation to reduce the computational overhead of axiom testing.

References

1. Agresti, A., Coull, B.A.: Approximate is better than "exact" for interval estimation of binomial proportions. The American Statistician 52(2) (May 1998)
2. Bühmann, L., Lehmann, J.: Universal OWL axiom enrichment for large knowledge bases. In: ten Teije, A., Völker, J., Handschuh, S., Stuckenschmidt, H., d'Acquin, M., Nikolov, A., Aussenac-Gilles, N., Hernandez, N. (eds.) EKAW 2012. LNCS, vol. 7603, pp. 57–71. Springer, Heidelberg (2012)
3. Cuenca Grau, B., Motik, B., Patel-Schneider, P.: OWL 2 web ontology language direct semantics (second edition). W3C recommendation, W3C (December 2012)
4. Dubois, D., Prade, H.: Fuzzy sets and probability: Misunderstandings, bridges and gaps. Fuzzy Sets and Systems 40(1), 143–202 (1991)
5. Fanizzi, N., d'Amato, C., Esposito, F.: DL-FOIL concept learning in description logics. In: Železný, F., Lavrač, N. (eds.) ILP 2008. LNCS (LNAI), vol. 5194, pp. 107–121. Springer, Heidelberg (2008)
6. Fleischhacker, D., Völker, J., Stuckenschmidt, H.: Mining RDF data for property axioms. In: Meersman, R., et al. (eds.) OTM 2012, Part II. LNCS, vol. 7566, pp. 718–735. Springer, Heidelberg (2012)
7. Gangemi, A., Catenacci, C., Ciaramita, M., Lehmann, J.: A theoretical framework for ontology evaluation and validation. In: SWAP (2005)
8. Gangemi, A., Catenacci, C., Ciaramita, M., Lehmann, J.: Modelling ontology evaluation and validation. In: Sure, Y., Domingue, J. (eds.) ESWC 2006. LNCS, vol. 4011, pp. 140–154. Springer, Heidelberg (2006)
9. Hellmann, S., Lehmann, J., Auer, S.: Learning of OWL class descriptions on very large knowledge bases. Int. J. Semantic Web Inf. Syst. 5(2), 25–48 (2009)
10. Muggleton, S., De Raedt, L., Poole, D., Bratko, I., Flach, P., Inoue, K., Srinivasan, A.: ILP turns 20: Biography and future challenges. Machine Learning 86, 3–23 (2012)
11. Poveda-Villalón, M., Suárez-Figueroa, M.C., Gómez-Pérez, A.: Validating ontologies with OOPS! In: ten Teije, A., Völker, J., Handschuh, S., Stuckenschmidt, H., d'Acquin, M., Nikolov, A., Aussenac-Gilles, N., Hernandez, N. (eds.) EKAW 2012. LNCS, vol. 7603, pp. 267–281. Springer, Heidelberg (2012)
12. Scheffler, I., Goodman, N.: Selective confirmation and the ravens: A reply to Foster. The Journal of Philosophy 69(3), 78–83 (1972)
13. Tartir, S., Budak Arpinar, I., Sheth, A.P.: Ontological evaluation and validation. In: Theory and Applications of Ontologies: Computer Applications. Springer (2010)
14. Zadeh, L.A.: Fuzzy sets as a basis for a theory of possibility. Fuzzy Sets and Systems 1, 3–28 (1978)

Quantifying the Bias in Data Links

Ilaria Tiddi, Mathieu d'Aquin, and Enrico Motta

Knowledge Media Institute
The Open University, United Kingdom
{ilaria.tiddi,mathieu.daquin,enrico.motta}@open.ac.uk

Abstract. The main idea behind Linked Data is to connect data from different sources together, in order to develop a hub of shared and publicly accessible knowledge. While the benefit of sharing knowledge is universally recognised, what is less visible is how much results can be affected when the knowledge in one dataset and in the connected ones are not equally distributed. This lack of balance in information, or bias, generally assumed a priori, can actually be quantified to improve the quality of the results of applications and analytics relying on such linked data. In this paper, we propose a process to measure how much bias one dataset contains when compared to another one, by identifying the most affected RDF properties and values within the set of entities that those datasets have in common (defined as the linkset). This process was ran on a wide range of linksets from Linked Data, and in the experiment section we present the results as well as measures of its performance.

Keywords: Linked Data, Datasets bias, Linksets Analysis.

1 Introduction

By using RDF links connecting one data source to another, the idea of Linked Data is to make applications able to discover additional knowledge using a *follow-your-nose* strategy [2]. This is summarised in the fourth Linked Data principle: *"include links to other related things (using their URIs) when publishing data on the Web"*[1].

Thanks to the efforts and guidelines provided by the Linked Data community, the process of aggregating knowledge distributed across sources of data is now well established. Such an aggregation takes the form of *linksets*, sets of RDF triples in which the subject is a URI entity from one data source, the predicate is an equivalence relation (typically, *owl:sameAs* or *skos:exactMatch*), and the object is a URI reference belonging to another external data source, from which it can in turn be *"dereferenced"*. Hundreds of millions of those equivalence triples have nowadays been published, which transformed the Web of (Linked) Data into a global data graph spanning data sources and enabling the discovery of new, unrevealed knowledge.

While the benefit of sharing knowledge is universally recognised, what is less visible is how much data analysis can be affected when the knowledge in one dataset and the corresponding knowledge in a connected dataset are not equally

---

[1] http://www.w3.org/DesignIssues/LinkedData.html

K. Janowicz et al. (Eds.): EKAW 2014, LNAI 8876, pp. 531–546, 2014.

distributed. This lack of balance in information, that we refer to as a *bias*, is generally assumed a priori when producing applications exploiting connected datasets. However, results can be highly affected by such biases, making patterns emerge that do not correspond to real phenomena. For instance, it is known that the Linked Movie Database (LMDB), whose instances are linked to DBpedia, is about movies. An application, such as a recommender system, might obtain different results when using DBpedia which includes a wide set of movies, compared to when using LMDB, which might be focused on (or "biased towards") a specific category of movies, e.g. English movies, black and white movies or movies from the '50s.

The motivation behind this work comes from this issue. When exploiting the equivalence statements into Dedalo [16], our graph search process to explain clusters using Linked Data, we had to face the fact that results were not as expected, as they were being affected by the bias introduced by external, interconnected information. Besides solving the issue, it became clear that being able to quantify a bias that an interconnected dataset introduces could help the deployment of more bias-aware Linked Data applications. What we propose is therefore a process to measure how much bias one dataset contains when compared to another one, by identifying the most affected RDF properties within the set of entities that those datasets have in common (defined by the linkset). To do this, we evaluate the distribution of the values of a property within the linkset, compared to the distribution of the same property in the entire dataset. We exploit the statistical t-tests to assess the significance of the difference between two distributions, and subsequently detect which values are the most affected by the bias. We ran the process on several linksets extracted from the Linked Data Cloud, and we evaluated its performance in terms of computation and quality of the detected bias.

2   Problem Definition

2.1   Background

In [16,17], we presented Dedalo, a framework to explain clusters of items using knowledge extracted from Linked Data. Dedalo is based on two main assumptions:

- if items are in the same cluster, there is an underlying common characteristics that makes them appearing together, and this goes beyond the clustering process;
- knowledge from Linked Data is a graph of URI entities connected through RDF properties, that can be blindly navigated in order to serendipitously discover new knowledge (possibly across different data sources), using link traversal and URI dereferencing, and thus they can be exploited to find common characteristics of the items of the cluster;

and two derived observations:

- some entities in a graph can have a common walk (expressed in the form of a chain of contiguous RDF properties) to a specific entity;
- if items of a cluster share the same walk to a specific entity in the Linked Data graph, this walk can be used as an explanation to their grouping.

Dedalo then applies an A* graph search strategy [17], aiming at finding the least-cost path from the set of initial nodes (the entities within the cluster) to a goal node, i.e. the entity they have in common somewhere in the Linked Data graph, and uses Entropy [16] to estimate this cost. Because Linked Data can be traversed by URI dereferencing, Dedalo explores the graph trying to improve the accuracy of the explanations, defined in terms of F-Measure, by iteratively deepening the exploration of the graph.

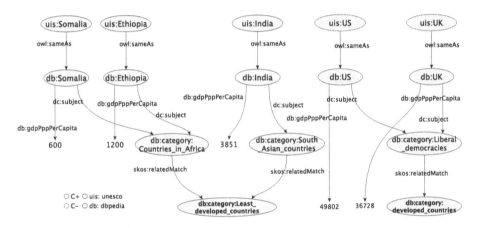

Fig. 1. Linked Data graph about countries

In a very short example, if we assume we have a cluster of 3 countries $C_1=$ {$uis:Somalia$, $uis:Ethiopia$, $uis:India$} and we want to understand why they have been put together when compared to a second cluster $C_2=${$uis:UK$, $uis:US$}, Dedalo[2] would iteratively build the graph in Figure 1 starting from the 5 initial nodes $C_1 \cup C_2$, by dereferencing them, exploring the (possibly external) values they point to and gradually detecting that the most interesting explanations for C_1 is that they are all nodes (a) labelled in DBpedia as "least developed countries" and (b) whose "GDP per capita is lower than 3,851\$ per year". This is expressed in the graph as walks of RDF properties and one final entity:

(a) ⟨$owl:sameAs$, $dc:subject$, $skos:relatedMatch.db:category:Least\_developed\_countries$⟩
(b) ⟨$owl:sameAs$, $db:gdpPppPerCapita.\leq.3,851\$$⟩.

2.2   Motivation

In a real-world scenario, we have a dataset of students clustered according to the UK district they come from. From the clustering, it turns out that in

---

[2] For a deeper analysis of how the search is held, please refer to [17].

certain regions, some faculties attract more students than others. Figure 2 shows two of those clusters: students enrolling to the Health and Social Care Faculty (left) are concentrated around specific places (e.g. in the Manchester area), while the Business and Law Faculty (right) attracts students from other places (e.g. districts around London). Our assumption is that there is an eco-demographic explanation to this, and that we can exploit Linked Data to obtain such information. To the best of our knowledge, this sort of socio-geographical information is contained in data sources such as DBpedia, Geonames or Freebase, and Dedalo, which relies on data links, should reach this information.

Health and Social Care.   Business and Law Faculty.

Fig. 2. Students enrolment dataset example

We introduced *owl:sameAs* links to each of the initial entities, so that Dedalo's search could go across external data sources, hopefully finding some useful explanations for those clusters. However, the best explanation obtained for the Health and Social Care cluster was as follows:

⟨*owl:sameAs, cyc:broaderTerm. cyc:TheNorthernHemisphere*⟩, F= 48,9%

Indeed, here more elements of the cluster appear to be located in the Northern Hemisphere, with an F-Measure of 48,9%. If we are talking about districts from the United Kingdom, what happened to the rest of the elements in the cluster? And how is it possible that such an explanation is the most representative for that one cluster, while other clusters also include only UK districts?

The hypothesis we can give is that if data were incomplete, the values would not be evenly distributed, creating a bias and, because of this, affecting the results. To prove this, we had to step back and look of the graph that Dedalo had discovered by following links between URIs. Did all the instances belonging to the dataset have a walk of RDF properties such as ⟨*owl:sameAs, cyc:broaderTerm*⟩?

The answer is that, out of the 380 graph sources (the UK districts), only 137 where connected to an entity e_i through the walk $\langle owl{:}sameAs, cyc{:}broaderTerm \rangle$, and, within the cluster, only 47 out of 66. This unequally distributed incompleteness (bias) is what affected recall and precision, and therefore, the final results.

2.3 Solution and Contribution

Finally, we had to adapt the F-Measure to our needs, introducing a weight to each walk, so to cancel out the effects of the bias. But adapting the accuracy score does not give any insight on how much bias is created when introducing knowledge from external data sources into our graph. If properties and their values are unevenly distributed along the dataset, then this constitutes a bias that can actually affect the results. If this is the case, one might want to identify it and adapt their applications accordingly.

For instance, the Linked Data Movie database is a dataset about movies, and some of its instances are linked to DBpedia, which is a dataset about multiple domains. As instances of LMDB are mostly movies, the entities in DBpedia that belong to the linkset LMDB-DBpedia will be only of type db:Movie, while DBpedia notably contains more types than this one. So, one can say that the LMDB has a bias towards movies. Similarly, LMDB could also be more focused on older movies, or on movies from Europe, while DBpedia, built as a Wikipedia extension, might be more focused on American movies. This uneven distribution of values is what we refer to as a bias here. This bias is usually assumed as a priori information, and its effects might remain hidden. Our objective is to quantify it, so to assess how influential it could be.

3   A Bias Detection Process

3.1   Finding a Bias: Problem Formalisation

Given two datasets A and B, assumed to be represented in RDF, we call E^A the set of entities belonging to A and E^B the set of entities belonging to B. A linkset $L^{AB} = \{(e_1^A, e_1^B), \ldots, (e_n^A, e_n^B)\}$ is a set of n equivalence relationships represented by pairs of entities (e_i^A, e_i^B) where $e_i^A \in E^A$ and $e_i^B \in E^B$. For example, with A=LMDB and B=DBpedia, a subset of L^{AB} might be $\{(lmdb{:}Stagecoach, dbres{:}Stagecoach), (lmdb{:}TheGreatDictator, dbres{:}TheGreatDictator), (lmdb{:}CityLights, dbres{:}CityLights)\}$ based on the triples:

```
<lmdb:Stagecoach owl:sameAs dbres:Stagecoach>.
<lmdb:TheGreatDictator owl:sameAs dbres:TheGreatDictator>.
<lmdb:CityLights owl:sameAs dbres:CityLights>.
```

We define as $S(D, L) \subseteq E^D$ the subset of the entities of the dataset D which are part of a relationship in the linkset L, i.e. $S(D,L)=\{e \in E^D | \exists (e,f) \in L \vee \exists (f,e) \in L\}$.

In order to measure the bias the dataset B has when compared to the dataset A considering the linkset L^{AB}, we compare the distribution of properties of entities of B with the distribution of properties of the subset $S(B, L^{AB})$.

We represent these distributions relatively to the types of the entities in consideration. We therefore call $classes(e, D)$ the set of entities connected to e through $rdf:type$ in the dataset D. We then call $properties(c, D)$ the set of properties that apply to instances of the class c in a dataset D. Finally, we call $values(r, E, D)$ the set of all possible values (entities or literals) of the property r in the set of entities E in the dataset D ($E \subseteq E^D$).

The idea here is therefore to compare the distributions of the values in $values(r, E^B, B)$ with the ones in $values(r, S(B, L^{AB}), B)$ for properties $r \in properties(c, B)$, with $c \in classes(e, B)$ for all $e \in S(B, L^{AB})$. These distributions are represented through the average and standard deviation for numerical values, and by a count of the entities that have each given values for all other types of values. The expectation is that, if B contains a bias when compared to A ($A{\to}B$), then some of these distributions will be significantly different between the entities E^B of B and the subset $S(B, L^{AB})$ considered in its linkset with A, showing for example different frequencies for the same values.

Figure 3 represents a simplified example of the comparison of LMDB (A) and DBpedia (B). Three DBpedia movies are linked to LMDB, i.e. $S(B, L^{AB}) = \{dbres:Stagecoach, dbres:TheGreatDictator, dbres:CityLights\}$, while E^B also includes others movies, i.e. $E^B = S(B, L^{AB}) \cup \{dbres:X\text{-}Men, dbres:Godzilla, dbres:CaptainAmerica\}$. As they are all movies, the only element in all the $classes(e, B)$ for $e \in S(B, L^{AB})$ is $db:Movie$, so we omitted it from the figure. We can see that all the entities of $S(B, L^{AB})$ are categorised as black and white movies, while the entities of E^B also include movies about superheroes. From comparing the distribution of $values(dc:subject, E^B, B) = \{db:BlackAndWhiteMovies, db:SuperHeroes\}$, with the one of $values(dc:subject, S(B, L^{AB}), B) = \{db:BlackAndWhiteMovies\}$, we can say that A is biased towards black and white movies, and therefore B will contain a bias when compared to A. Similarly, the average of the values of $dbp:released$ in E^B (i.e., $values(dbp:released, E^B, B) = \{1931, 1939, 1940, 2011, 2014\}$) is higher than the average in $values(dbp:released, S(B, L^{AB}), B) = \{1931, 1939, 1940\}$, so we could say, considering these datasets and this linkset, that LMDB is biased towards older movies.

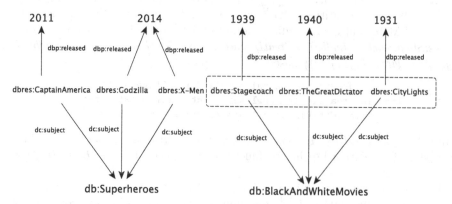

Fig. 3. Example bias between DBpedia and LMDB. The dashed line marks $S(B, L^{AB})$.

3.2   Approach

The process consists in five steps: (i) linkset extraction; (ii) subset's graph building, (iii) full set's graph building; (iv) bias calculation and (v) properties ranking.

Linkset Extraction. This step consists in building the linkset L^{AB}. Starting from two datasets A and B, we find in each of them entities that are related through an equivalence statement using one of the properties *owl:sameAs*, *skos:exactMatch*, *skos:relatedMatch* or *rdfs:seeAlso*. It remains out of our work's scope to argue about the quality of the equivalence: the aim here is to prove that there exists a bias between datasets when those are connected in Linked Data, whichever the declaration of equivalence can be.

Equivalent entities are retrieved using the SPARQL query `SELECT ?instance ?eq WHERE {?instance $equivalentProp ?eq}`, with `$equivalentProp` being one of the aforementioned properties. Entities in `?instance` are then kept in a set representing $S(A, L^{AB})$, while `?eq` entities are kept in a set representing $S(B, L^{AB})$.

Subset's Graph Building. This step consists in building the information related to the entities included in the linkset, from the target dataset B. More specifically:

1. the set of classes *classes*(e, B) the entities $e \in S(B, L^{AB})$ are *rdf:type* of, i.e. classes involved in the considered set of entities. As an RDF property might apply to several classes within a full set, and not all of them might be part of the properties that apply to the subset $S(B, L^{AB})$, we consider only the classes related to the instances of $S(B, L^{AB})$. For example, a property such as *dc:subject* applies to *db:Agent*, *db:Movie*, *db:Work*, *db:Organisation* and many others, but, as the entities of $S(B, L^{AB})$ are only of type *db:Movie*, we are only interested in values of movies.
2. the set of properties *properties*(c, B) for all classes c extracted in the previous step. For the three movies in $S(B, L^{AB})$ we obtain *dc:subject* and *dbp:released*.
3. the set of values *values*$(r, S(B, L^{AB}), B)$ for all properties r obtained in the previous step. This corresponds to entities or literals that are objects of triples involving the property r and an entity of $S(B, L^{AB})$ as subject. In our example, only *db:BlackAndWhiteMovies* is returned for *dc:subject*.

In order to extract those three components, we use a second SPARQL query: `SELECT ?type ?prop ?val WHERE {$i a ?type; ?prop ?val}` where `$i` is an entity from $S(B, L^{AB})$. To avoid high computational costs, we filter out classes with a low frequency, by setting a threshold $\delta_1 = 5\%$, i.e. for a class c to be considered, at least 5% of the entities in $S(B, L^{AB})$ should be of type c.

Full Set's Graph Building. Similarly to the three steps above, we can extract the information related to the entities E^B of the full set B. Using the set of classes obtained in step 1 and the set of properties obtained in step 2, we extract the set of values $values(r, E^B, B)$ for each extracted property r. This is achieved using a third SPARQL query: SELECT ?val WHERE {?x a $classType; $prop ?val} LIMIT 10000, with $prop being a property from step 2 above, and $classType being a class from step 1 above. As most of the data have been collected from large resources, we limited our population to 10,000 elements, considering this amount sufficient to demonstrate the bias. In our example, the result for *dc:subject* includes *dc:BlackAndWhiteMovies* and *db:Superheroes*, and the result for *dbp:released* includes *1931, 1939, 1940, 2011* and *2014*. Because the distributions of properties having a very large number of values (e.g. inverse-functional properties, titles of movies, IDs, labels, etc.) would not be comparable, we define a second threshold δ_2 such that properties whose number of possible values is above δ_2 are discarded. δ_2 has been set to the 90% of the number of entities in $S(B, L^{AB})$.

Bias Calculation. This step consists in comparing, for each considered property r, the two values sets $values(r, E^B, B)$ and $values(r, S(B, L^{AB}), B)$ in order to evaluate the bias that might be associated with r when comparing B to A. Because what we have obtained at this stage is two populations of a same observation (a specific RDF property r), and we aim to show a significant difference between their distributions, we use the *t-tests* from inferential statistics to demonstrate or deny the existence of a bias. T-tests are a form of hypotheses testing for real-valued populations, revealing whether a mean is significantly different than an expected value, or whether two means significantly differ from each other. "Significantly" here is intended to mean "showing statistical significance", i.e. that there is a low probability that the results are due to chance. This probability is defined as the p–value p. In a t-test, one states a hypothesis and, if p is below a certain threshold (generally $\delta = \{0.01, 0.05, 0.1\}$), then there is a p chance that this hypothesis is correct. If p is above the threshold, then the experimenter cannot reject the possibility that the stated hypothesis is wrong.

If we adapt this scenario to our context, we can summarise the process as follows:

1. *Develop a research hypothesis H to be tested mathematically.*
   $H =$ "the RDF property r is biased", i.e. there is a statistically significant difference between $values(r, E^B, B)$ and $values(r, S(B, L^{AB}), B)$.
2. *Formally state the null and alternate hypothesis h_0 and h_a.*
   $h_0 =$ "r is not biased"; $h_a =$ "r is biased".
3. *Decide an appropriate statistical test and calculate p.*
   There are different t-tests according to the one's needs. We chose the *independent samples t-test* when r had numerical values, so we could compare the average of the distributions, while we used a *dependent samples t-test* for the other RDF properties, and extracted the values whose frequency is the most different in the two sets.
4. *Make your decision based on the results.*
   If $p < \delta$, we can reject the null hypothesis (and therefore r is biased), else, we cannot reject the null hypothesis that there is no bias for r.

To make the information about the bias useful, i.e. not only indicate the presence of a bias but also show its most likely origin, once p is calculated for all considered r properties we extract the values that show the largest difference in the two sets. In the case of an independent t-test, these values are represented by the averages of $values(r, E^B, B)$ and $values(r, S(B, L^{AB}), B)$. In the case of a dependent t-test, we compare the normalised frequencies of each of the values in these two sets, and consider the ones with the largest absolute differences $|d|$ as the ones which best represent the bias. If $d < 0$, then A is biased towards the value in $values(r, E^B, B)$ of the property r, otherwise it is biased towards the value from $values(r, S(B, L^{AB}), B)$. In our example, A is biased towards black and white movies for the property dc:subject. As for the property dbp:released, we compare the two averages 1936 and 1976, to conclude that A is biased towards older movies.

Properties Ranking. Given the set of extracted properties and their bias estimated in terms of t-test, we rank them according to their (ascending) p-value. The most biased properties will be the ones in which the probability of "being biased by chance"(h_0) is lower than 1%, followed by the ones whose probability is below 5% and then below 10%. Properties above the threshold are discarded as considered non biased (we cannot discard the hypothesis h_0).

4   Experiments

To demonstrate the feasibility of the bias detection process presented in the previous section, we ran it on a wide range of linksets taken from the Linked Data Cloud. Datasets with associated linksets were selected from the Data Hub[3] and differed in sizes as well as in the domain they covered. When provided, we used the links between datasets, and the SPARQL endpoints (if active) to retrieve the property and value sets. When no SPARQL endpoint was available, we used the available data dump.

Our experiments have two main objectives: (i) estimating how computationally expensive it is to detect a bias, in terms of time, and (ii) analysing whether there is a significant bias between datasets, which kind of bias, and which kind of information we can derive from it.

Approach Performance. In Table 1 we show the performance of the process in terms of time taken to compute the property ranking. Experiments have been run on a 2.9 GHz Intel Core i7 machine with 8GB of RAM. We present the linkset size $|L^{AB}|$ in number of triples, the comparison direction $D_1 \rightarrow D_2$ and the time it has taken to run the full process described in Section 3. Results are sorted by time. For most of the linksets, it was possible to calculate the bias in both directions. In cases where no SPARQL endpoint nor data dump was available, we marked the dataset as D^{***} and performed only the bias computation in the available direction. Those results show that, generally, detecting the bias is not

---

[3] http://datahub.io/

an expensive task. This, of course, is highly dependent on the resources one has to deal with: for very big linksets (in number of linked entities) or rich graphs (in number of classes, properties and values), the computation is naturally slower. Typically, this is the case when we ran the process on DBpedia, for instance, and on large biomedical data sources.

Table 1. Computational costs in seconds

A	B	$|L^{AB}|$	time"
LinkedGeoData	Linked Food	38	0.04
data.open.ac.uk	Unistats	82	0.11
DBpedia	Finnish National Library	336	0.40
DBpedia	DBTune	882	0.65
DBpedia	Hungarian National Library	500	0.74
New York Times	Geonames	1,787	0.74
DBpedia	Food and Agriculture Org.	215	0.79
AGROVOC	Food and Agriculture Org.	256	0.84
DBpedia	Reading Experience Database	6,549	0.93
DBpedia	New York Times	9,123	1.33
Freebase	New York Times	10,302	1.45
VIAF***	Spanish National Library	3,000	1.45
LOD-Ecosystems***	UniProt	17,355	3.83
Linked Food	LinkedGeoData	38	8.35
EUROVOC***	Arbeitsrecht	247	9.43
DrugBank	DBpedia	1,481	9.65
Unistats	data.open.ac.uk	82	11.92
LOD-Ecosystem	GeoSpecies	2,814	13.00
DBpedia	Org. Economic Coop. and Dev.	223	17.97
Food and Agriculture Org.	AGROVOC	256	21.03
DBpedia	DrugBank	1,481	32.39
UniProt	DrugBank	4,168	44.44
Finnish National Library	DBpedia	336	65.66
Org. Economic Coop. and Dev.	DBpedia	223	71.22
Eurostats***	LinkedGeoData	1,558	125.55
UniProt	Bio2RDF	18,997	127.21
BioPAX	UniProt	58,398	144.91
Food and Agriculture Org.	DBpedia	256	146.90
Eurostats***	Org. Economic Coop. and Dev.	3,488	301.57
DBTune	DBpedia	882	305.69
DBpedia	SW Dog Food	461	321.79
SW Dog Food	DBpedia	461	346.89
Geonames	New York Times	1,787	366.37
Hungarian National Library	DBpedia	500	484.40
New York Times	DBpedia	9,123	575.75
DBpedia	Spanish National Library	36,431	613.68
AGROVOC	DBpedia	11,014	657.60
Reading Experience Database	DBpedia	6,549	682.11
LOD-Ecosystems***	DBpedia	43,452	751.82
Spanish National Library	DBpedia	36,431	827.21
Open Energy Info	DBpedia	10,069	830.39
DBpedia	Open Energy Info	10,069	834.12
Unesco	Org. Eco. Coop. and Dev.	17,338	1,143.42
DBpedia	AGROVOC	11,014	1,270.46
Org. Economic Coop. and Dev.	Unesco	17,338	1,565.79
DBpedia	Linked Movie Database	13,758	1,579.36
New York Times	Freebase	10,302	1,587.00
Linked Movie Database	DBpedia	13,758	1,908.11
GeoSpecies	LOD-Ecosystem	2,814	1,944.32
DrugBank	UniProt	4,168	4,606.75
BioPAX	Entrez Gene	36,006	5,253.63
Entrez Gene	BioPAX	36,006	58,752.77
Bio2RDF	UniProt	18,997	60,459.88
UniProt	BioPAX	58,398	67,405.53

Detected Bias. In the following tables we present some examples extracted from the results of the bias detection process. As many experiments were run and we could not present all of them, the whole collected and mentioned data as well as all the results are publicly provided online[4]. For a linkset L^{AB}, we show the most biased properties r (with the detected p–value), with the class and value the dataset is biased towards. Those are shown in average *avg* and standard deviation *stdev* (in case of numerical values), or as URIs towards which a given dataset is biased (for other types of values). We intentionally divided the results, first, to improve the readability and second, to highlight the (subjective) degree of surprise in the result.

As said, when having some background knowledge about the datasets, the bias is assumed a priori. Typically, there is an expected bias when dealing with geographical data, presented in Table 2: while the results are not especially surprising, we can detect the most biased information thanks to our process.

Table 2. Examples of expected biases in the geographical domain

BNFi→DBP

biased D	c	r	value	p
A	db:Place	dc:subject	db:CitiesAndTownsInFinland	$p <$1.00e-15
A	db:Place	dbp:province	db:WesternFinlandProvince	$p <$1.00e-15
A	db:Place	dbp:province	db:EasternFinlandProvince	$p <$1.00e-15
A	db:Place	dbp:longd	*avg*: 24.6, *stdev*: 0.78	$p <$1.00e-15
B	db:Place	dbp:longd	*avg*: 68.5, *stdev*: 23.81	$p <$1.00e-15
A	db:Place	dbp:latd	*avg*: 62.0, *stdev*: 0.62	$p <$1.00e-15
B	db:Place	dbp:latd	*avg*: 40.5, *stdev*: 2.82	$p <$1.00e-15

GN→NYT

biased D	c	r	value	p
B	gn:Feature	gn:parentFeature	gn:US	$p <$1.00e-15
A	gn:Feature	gn:parentFeature	gn:Africa	$p <$1.00e-15
A	gn:Feature	gn:parentFeature	gn:Asia	$p <$1.00e-15
B	skos:Concept	gn:inCountry	gn:US; gn:Mexico	$p <$ 3.34e-02
A	skos:Concept	gn:inCountry	gn:UnitedArabEmirates	$p <$ 3.34e-0

NYT→DBP

biased D	c	r	value	p
A	db:Agent	dbp:country	db:UnitedStates	$p <$ 3.87e-04
B	db:Agent	dbp:country	db:England	$p <$ 3.87e-04
B	db:Agent	dbp:country	db:Canada	$p <$ 3.87e-04

For instance, the Finnish National library (BNFi) is biased towards places in Finland, or the New York Times (NYT) is biased towards places in the US. In the first case, for A=BNFi and B=DBPedia (DBP), A is biased towards places whose subject is a DBpedia entity labelled as "Cities and Towns in Finland",

---

[4] http://linkedu.eu/dedalo/

i.e. for the class *db:Place* the property *dc:subject* is biased towards the value *db:CitiesAndTownsInFinland*. This is also confirmed by the latitude and longitude average values, corresponding to the (average) coordinates of Finland. In the second case, for A=Geonames (GN) and B=NYT, we can see that the full dataset B of the New York Times is biased towards places or concepts located in America or the US, i.e. for the class *gn:Feature* the property *gn:parentFeature* is biased towards *gn:US*, while the subset of Geonames entities for the same class and property has more distributed values, including *gn:Africa* and *gn:Asia*. This is also confirmed by the fact that NYT, when compared to DBpedia, is more focused on people from the US: for the class *db:Agent* the property *dbp:country* is biased towards *db:UnitedStates*.

Table 3 presents examples of datasets including a broader range of domains, in which one can expect some bias, but cannot detect which are the properties that

Table 3. Bias in the multi-domain linksets

Unistats→OU

biased D	c	r	value	p
A	ou:Degree	dc:subject	ou:SocialCare	$p <$1.13e-13
A	ou:Degree	dc:subject	ou:SocialScience	$p <$1.13e-13

OU→Unistats

biased D	c	r	value	p
A	kis:PartTimeCourse	dc:subject	kis:MedicalScience	$p <$6.80e-14
A	kis:PartTimeCourse	dc:subject	kis:Social Work	$p <$6.80e-14

RED→DBP

biased D	c	r	value	p
A	db:Scientist	db:almaMater	db:CambridgeUniversity	$p <$1.00e-15
A	db:Scientist	db:almaMater	db:UniversityOfEdinburgh	$p <$1.00e-15
A	db:Scientist	db:birthPlace	db:England	$p <$1.00e-15
A	db:Scientist	db:birthPlace	db:Scotland	$p <$1.00e-15
B	db:Scientist	db:birthPlace	db:UnitedStates	$p <$1.00e-15
A	db:Scientist	db:nationality	db:England	$p <$4.28e-03
B	db:Scientist	db:nationality	db:UnitedStates	$p <$4.28e-03
A	db:Writer	db:birthDate	*avg:* 1809, *stdev:* 96.21	$p <$1.00e-15
B	db:Writer	db:birthDate	*avg:* 1916, *stdev:* 40.43	$p <$1.00e-15
A	db:Writer	db:deathDate	*avg:* 1871, *stdev:* 99.19	$p <$1.00e-15
B	db:Writer	db:deathDate	*avg:* 1951, *stdev:*	$p <$1.00e-15

BNEs→DBP

biased D	c	r	value	p
B	db:MusicalArtist	dc:subject	db:AmericanSinger	$p <$1.00e-15
A	db:MusicalArtist	dbp:birthPlace	db:England	$p <$1.13e-13
A	db:MusicalArtist	dbp:birthPlace	db:Spain	$p <$1.13e-13
A	db:Writer	dbp:nationality	db:French	$p <$4.64e-03
A	db:Writer	dbp:nationality	db:Spanish	$p <$4.64e-03
B	db:Writer	dbp:nationality	db:UnitedStates	$p <$4.64e-03

are most affected. This is the case of the BNEs, the Spanish National Library, where data are related to Spain; the data.open.ac.uk (OU) and Unistats datasets, that include data about education in the UK, or the *Reading Experience Database* (RED), a research project about reading records of British subjects since the 15th century. While the most biased values could be expected, the process is useful in revealing the biased properties or classes: for instance, the BNEs is focused on artists and writers, while RED is focused on writers and scientists. Also, for A=RED and B=DBP, RED is focused on people born in England, i.e. for the class *db:Agent* the property *dbp:birthPlace* is biased towards *db:England*. In DBpedia, the same property is biased towards the value *db:UnitedStates*. RED is also biased towards people who attended universities in the UK, as the most biased values for the property *dbp:almaMater* demonstrate. Similarly, we identify that the OU dataset is more focused on Social Care and Social Science, while Unistats has more information about Medical Science.

Table 4. Biomedical bias examples

Bio2RDF→UP

biased D	c	r	value	p
A	up:Protein	up:isolatedFrom	uptissue:Brain	$p <$9.29e-04
A	up:Protein	up:isolatedFrom	uptissue:Cervical	$p <$9.29e-04
B	up:Protein	up:isolatedFrom	uptissue:Leucocyte	$p <$9.29e-04

BioPAX→UP

biased D	c	r	value	p
A	up:Protein	up:isolatedFrom	uptissue:Brain	$p <$6.79e-04
B	up:Protein	up:isolatedFrom	uptissue:Egg	$p <$6.79e-04
B	up:Protein	up:isolatedFrom	uptissue:OlfactoryMucosa	$p <$6.79e-04

DrugBank→UP

biased D	c	r	value	p
A	up:Protein	up:isolatedFrom	uptissue:Brain	$p <$1.33e-04
B	up:Protein	up:isolatedFrom	uptissue:Leucocyte	$p <$1.33e-04
B	up:Protein	up:isolatedFrom	uptissue:Erythrocyte	$p <$1.33e-04
A	up:Protein	up:organism	upspecies:HomoSapiens	$p <$ 1.49e-02
B	up:Protein	up:organism	upspecies:Campylobacter	$p <$ 1.49e-02
B	up:Protein	up:organism	upspecies:Myxococcus	$p <$ 1.49e-02

Another effect of the bias detection process is that it helps in understanding datasets we might not be familiar with. It is the case of datasets in biomedicine, that we show in Table 4. In a more restricted domain, datasets are likely to be more connected to each other[5] so we were able to compare whether results were consistent when dealing with the same dataset and different linksets. It is the case of UniProt (UP), for which we discovered that the bias introduced by connecting knowledge to other data sources is always towards cerebral tissues.

---

[5] See sources at http://linkedlifedata.com/sources.html

As a final discussion, Table 5 shows results with a high degree of surprise, i.e. when discovering unexpected bias. For instance, we unexpectedly discovered that the BNEs is focused on musical artists that are piano players, and on writers that write about fiction, while the RED dataset is focused on novelists and poets belonging to the 19th century literary movements (which is also consistent with the average age shown in Table 3) and who eventually committed suicide.

Table 5. Unexpected bias examples

BNEs→DBP

biased D	c	r	value	p
A	db:MusicalArtist	dbp:instrument	db:Piano	$p < 2.73e-04$
B	db:MusicalArtist	dbp:instrument	db:Guitar	$p < 2.73e-04$
B	db:MusicalArtist	dbp:instrument	db:Singing	$p < 2.73e-04$
A	db:Writer	db:genre	db:MisteryFiction	$p < 4.28e-11$
B	db:Writer	db:genre	db:DetectiveFiction	$p < 4.28e-11$
B	db:Writer	db:genre	db:Non-fiction	$p < 4.28e-11$

RED→DBP

biased D	c	r	value	p
A	db:Agent	db:genre	db:Novel	$p < 1.00e-15$
A	db:Agent	db:genre	db:Poetry	$p < 1.00e-15$
A	db:Agent	db:movement	db:Romantism	$p < 1.00e-15$
A	db:Agent	db:movement	db:Naturalism	$p < 1.00e-15$
A	db:Agent	db:deathCause	db:Suicide	$p < 1.00e-15$

5   Related Work

While works on data quality are common, to the best of our knowledge no work has addressed the question of how two datasets influence each other in the context of Linked Data.

The work of [15] presents some subjective and objective measures for assessing data quality in the context of databases, but this does not include how the quality can be influenced when introducing knowledge from external data sources. Some works in other fields have addressed the bias issue from their perspective. Authors in [3,5,7,8] focus on the publication bias, defined as a bias in which "the selection of studies for publication is made on the basis of the statistical significance of results, and/or on whether the results satisfy preconceived theoretical expectation". Those works use meta-analytics techniques to demonstrate the existence of the publication bias in different domains. Particularly, the approach presented in [8] makes use statistical significance tests to demonstrate the existence of such a bias in two major political science journals.

In the Linked Data context, some related work focuses on link production, link discovery or link quality evaluation. One example is SILK [18], a framework for the discovery of links in the Web of Data, relying on measures to assess the similarity of entities. The quality of interlinked data is argued in [9], which presents the framework LINK-QA for the assessment of mappings between Linked Data datasets using network metrics. Authors in [4] conduct a quantitative and qualitative analysis of the *sameAs network*, intended as the RDF graph of connected entities in the Linked Data Cloud. More statistical analysis on Linked Data [1,6] and metrics on the quality of Linked Data datasets are presented in [11,20].

A second wave of work in Linked Data has raised the discussion around the pragmatic use of equivalence statements: the trustability of the links, their ethical correctness, and the noise the linking introduces. In this we can include [10], focusing on the inaccurate usage of identity and similarity in Linked Data, that causes incorrect inferences; as well as [14], discussing the confusion of provenance and ground truth generated by *owl:sameAs* in bioinformatics. The authors of [12] identify a wrong use of *owl:sameAs* in the community and suggest an infrastructure to manage data co-references, while the ones of [13] scan the current status of Linked Data (showing its shortcomings and limitations), and try to propose some solutions to overcome those issues.

6   Conclusions and Future Work

This paper presents an experimental work to identify how much links between datasets introduce biases. The general idea is that the distribution of values in the subset of linked entities does not correspond to the ones in the full dataset, and this can affect the results of Linked Data-based applications, as we experienced when introducing equivalence statements into one of our use-cases. To prove the existence of such a bias we used the statistical inference tests, comparing the distribution of the values for a property within the set of linked entities, and the same property values within the full dataset. We created a process detecting the most biased properties, and showed not only that the process is simple and effective in terms of computational cost and time, but also that this process results in interesting information about the content of the datasets.

As future work, we will consider the extension of this work to include the bias parameter into Dedalo's explanations, by refining them on the basis of the bias, to see whether their quality can improve. A second line of research will be held on the discovery of incoming links, which are currently not considered into Dedalo's framework. Finally, we intend to improve the performance of the bias detection process.

References

1. Beck, N., Scheglmann, S., Gottron, T.: LinDA: A service infrastructure for linked data analysis and provision of data statistics. In: Cimiano, P., Fernández, M., Lopez, V., Schlobach, S., Völker, J. (eds.) ESWC 2013. LNCS, vol. 7955, pp. 225–230. Springer, Heidelberg (2013)
2. Heath, T., Bizer, C.: Linked data: Evolving the web into a global data space. Synthesis lectures on the semantic web: theory and technology 1(1), 1–136 (2011)
3. Begg, C., Berlin, J.: Publication Bias: A Problem in Interpreting Medical Data. Journal of the Royal Statistical Society 151(3), 419–463 (1988)

4. Ding, L., Shinavier, J., Shangguan, Z., McGuinness, D.L.: SameAs networks and beyond: Analyzing deployment status and implications of owl:sameAs in linked data. In: Patel-Schneider, P.F., Pan, Y., Hitzler, P., Mika, P., Zhang, L., Pan, J.Z., Horrocks, I., Glimm, B. (eds.) ISWC 2010, Part I. LNCS, vol. 6496, pp. 145–160. Springer, Heidelberg (2010)
5. Doucouliagos, H., Laroche, P., Stanley, T.D.: Publication bias in union-productivity research? Relations Industrielles/Industrial Relations, 320–347 (2005)
6. Ermilov, I., Martin, M., Lehmann, J., Auer, S.: Linked open data statistics: Collection and exploitation. In: Klinov, P., Mouromtsev, D. (eds.) KESW 2013. CCIS, vol. 394, pp. 242–249. Springer, Heidelberg (2013)
7. Gerber, A.S., Green, D.P., Nickerson, D.: Testing for publication bias in political science. Political Analysis 9(4), 385–392 (2001)
8. Gerber, A., Malhotra, N.: Can political science literatures be believed? A study of publication bias in the APSR and the AJPS. In: Annual Meeting of the Midwest Political Science Association, pp. 12–15 (2006)
9. Guéret, C., Groth, P., Stadler, C., Lehmann, J.: Assessing linked data mappings using network measures. In: Simperl, E., Cimiano, P., Polleres, A., Corcho, O., Presutti, V. (eds.) ESWC 2012. LNCS, vol. 7295, pp. 87–102. Springer, Heidelberg (2012)
10. Halpin, H., Hayes, P.J., McCusker, J.P., McGuinness, D.L., Thompson, H.S.: When owl:sameAs isn't the same: An analysis of identity in linked data. In: Patel-Schneider, P.F., Pan, Y., Hitzler, P., Mika, P., Zhang, L., Pan, J.Z., Horrocks, I., Glimm, B. (eds.) ISWC 2010, Part I. LNCS, vol. 6496, pp. 305–320. Springer, Heidelberg (2010)
11. Hogan, A., Umbrich, J., Harth, A., Cyganiak, R., Polleres, A., Decker, S.: An empirical survey of linked data conformance. Web Semantics: Science, Services and Agents on the World Wide Web 14, 14–44 (2012)
12. Jaffri, A., Glaser, H., Millard, I.: Uri disambiguation in the context of linked data (2008)
13. Jain, P., Hitzler, P., Yeh, P.Z., Verma, K., Sheth, A.P.: Linked Data Is Merely More Data. In: AAAI Spring Symposium: linked data meets artificial intelligence (March 2010)
14. McCusker, J., McGuinness, D.L.: owl:sameAs considered harmful to provenance. In: Proceedings of the ISCB Conference on Semantics in Healthcare and Life Sciences (2010)
15. Pipino, L.L., Lee, Y.W., Wang, R.Y.: Data quality assessment. Communications of the ACM 45(4), 211–218 (2002)
16. Tiddi, I., d'Aquin, M., Motta, E.: Dedalo: looking for Clusters Explanations in a Labyrinth of Linked Data. In: 11th Extended Semantic Web Conference, ESWC 2014 (2014)
17. Tiddi, I., d'Aquin, M., Motta, E.: Walking Linked Data: a graph traversal approach to explain clusters. In: Proceedings of the Fifth International Workshop on Consuming Linked Data, COLD 2014 (2014)
18. Volz, J., Bizer, C., Gaedke, M., Kobilarov, G.: Discovering and maintaining links on the web of data. In: Bernstein, A., Karger, D.R., Heath, T., Feigenbaum, L., Maynard, D., Motta, E., Thirunarayan, K. (eds.) ISWC 2009. LNCS, vol. 5823, pp. 650–665. Springer, Heidelberg (2009)
19. Zapilko, B., Harth, A., Mathiak, B.: Enriching and analysing statistics with linked open data. In: NTTS-Conference on New Techniques and Technologies for Statistics, Brussel (2011)
20. Zaveri, A., Rula, A., Maurino, A., Pietrobon, R., Lehmann, J., Auer, S., Hitzler, P.: Quality assessment methodologies for linked open data. Submitted to Semantic Web Journal (2013)

Using Neural Networks to Aggregate Linked Data Rules

Ilaria Tiddi, Mathieu d'Aquin, and Enrico Motta

Knowledge Media Institute
The Open University, United Kingdom
{ilaria.tiddi,mathieu.daquin,enrico.motta}@open.ac.uk

Abstract. Two typical problems are encountered after obtaining a set of rules from a data mining process: (i) their number can be extremely large and (ii) not all of them are interesting to be considered. Both manual and automatic strategies trying to overcome those problems have to deal with technical issues such as time costs and computational complexity. This work is an attempt to address the quantity and quality issues through using a Neural Network model for predicting the quality of Linked Data rules. Our motivation comes from our previous work, in which we obtained large sets of atomic rules through an inductive logic inspired process traversing Linked Data. Assuming a limited amount of resources, and therefore the impossibility of trying every possible combination to obtain a better rule representing a subset of items, the major issue becomes detecting the combinations that will produce the best rule in the shortest time. Therefore, we propose to use a Neural Network to learn directly from the rules how to recognise a promising aggregation. Our experiments show that including a Neural Network-based prediction model in a rule aggregation process significantly reduces the amount of resources (time and space) required to produce high-quality rules.

Keywords: Linked Data, Rules Aggregation, Neural Networks.

1 Introduction

When running a Knowledge Discovery (KD) process, the main ambition is to provide humans with useful, explicit information about the collected data. Such information, called *nugget* or *pattern*, is a statement describing an interesting relationship among a subset of the data [8]. Patterns are to be considered as any result of a data mining process, such as a series of clusters, a classification model, rules, etc. Two typical problems are encountered when producing patterns from a data mining process: (i) their number can be extremely large (data quantity problem) and (ii) not all of them are interesting to be considered (rule quality problem).

The typical strategy to overcome those problems is providing the patterns to human experts, whose role consists in analysing the results, discovering the interesting ones while explaining, pruning or refining the unclear ones. To cope

K. Janowicz et al. (Eds.): EKAW 2014, LNAI 8876, pp. 547–562, 2014.

with such a strenuous and time consuming process, many strategies to automatically assist the experts in the post-mining phase have been proposed in the past years, ranging from using interestingness measures for rules [10] to including the ontological knowledge [1,14,16,21]. However, technical problems are often to be encountered, such as time costs and scalability of the proposed processes.

In particular, those issues were encountered in our previous work, presented in [23], in which we described an Inductive Logic Programming-inspired framework to give Linked Data based explanations (rules applying to specific patterns – see Section 3), for clusters automatically obtained out a data mining process. While the obtained explanations resulted to be interesting and representative for each cluster, our major issue consisted in having to deal with a large amount of atomic rules (rules made of a single condition in the body) that need to be aggregated in a post-processing step in order to obtain a better representation of our clusters. When having to deal with such large amounts of rules, trying each possible aggregation requires too many resources. Most of the aggregations between rules might not be interesting, i.e. they would not produce any rule better representing the cluster, while the time and computational costs required by the process increase exponentially with the amount of rules to aggregate. To reduce such a process, what is required is a way to predict which rules are worth aggregating. However, in order to do so, it is first important to detect what knowledge about the rules is required to make a prediction.

In this work, we present a Neural Network-based approach to predict whether two rules, if combined, will lead to a better rule. We use statistical information about the rules (precision, recall and F-measure), as indicators for a prediction. Finally, we compare our process to other strategies for rules aggregation. The rest of the paper is articulated as follows. Section 2 presents the related work. Section 3 summarises the framework presented in [23] to produce Linked Data-based explanations, the motivation behind it and the unsolved questions that it left. Section 4 presents our problems, how we end up with proposing a Neural Network-based approach and the process we designed. Section 5 presents the experiments we ran, comparing our approach to some intuitive strategies for rules aggregation. The last section concerns future work and conclusion.

2   Related Work

No previous work seems to have been published in which Neural Networks are applied to Linked Data structures. Below we present some fields connecting to our research.

Association Rules Mining and Artificial Neural Networks. The problem of dealing with many rules and how to detect the interesting ones is a typical issue of Association Rule Mining (ARM). Many researchers have proposed methods for automatically detecting rules interestingness in the past. An extensive survey can be found in [10].

While Artificial Neural Networks (ANNs) have been largely considered in KDD subtasks such as clustering, classification and regression, few past works considered ANNs in the ARM context. In the latest years, ANNs have been reconsidered because of their ability of efficiently model data. Works in which ANNs are used as a predictive tool during the rule mining process have been appearing, such as [2,4,7,9,20]. Specific types of ANNs (SOM [2,4], ART [7], Hopfield [9] and BPNN [20]) are used to restrain the features space during the learning process to produce better, representative rules. None of those works seems to have taken into account the possibility of exploiting the Neural Network in the rule pruning phase.

Semantics for Rule Post-processing. Ontologies have been considered as a promising approach for patterns post-mining. The ontological knowledge is generally exploited during the post-processing phase to filter out meaningless rules and improve the computational efficiency. In the work of [1,14,21], domain ontology schemas are used to assist the user in the association rules interpretation process. Similarly, [17] uses taxonomies to prune uninteresting or redundant rules. While having detected and highlighted how KDD can leverage from the knowledge provided by ontological sources, those works lack in considering Linked Data as additional knowledge source for patterns post-processing. Such attempts are seen in the works of [6,18,24], interpreting data mining patterns using manually selected Linked Data, while only [23] reports an automatic approach to it.

Decision Rule Aggregation. Rule aggregation has recently been investigated by works dealing with decision rules. In [5], the authors use a process based on the Dempster–Shafer(DS) theory to aggregate linguistic decision rules in the context of multiple criterion-multiple participant sorting. Authors of [11] propose an algorithm to rules aggregation based on convex hulls (CHIRA). Other approaches concern decision rules joining algorithms [13,19,22], where rules are merged according to a predefined similarity (mostly defined on elementary conditions).

3   Dedalo: Getting Linked Data Explanations for Clusters

Motivation. The last step in a Knowledge Discovery process usually consists of the interpretation of the retrieved patterns, provided to and explained by experts with specific background knowledge. For someone without such expertise, results would hardly be understandable. Also, additional knowledge from domains that the expert might not be aware of could affect the quality of the interpretation.

For example, in one of our use-cases, we obtained a set of clusters $C = \{C_1, C_2, \ldots, C_n\}$ through a Network Partitioning algorithm, representing a set $\mathcal{R} = \{r_1, \ldots, r_n\}$ of academic researchers of the same department grouped according to their co-authorship. Someone not familiar with the research areas investigated in this department would find those clusters meaningless. However, someone familiar with such research areas would explain them pointing out the correspondence between each cluster and a group of people working on similar topics. More background knowledge, for instance from someone who worked in the department, would be needed to state that a cluster includes researchers having worked on projects led by the same person.

Such an interpretation process is then laborious, manual and time-consuming. With that said, the Web of Data naturally links datasets of different areas using RDF principles, making sources of knowledge accessible (and interpretable) by machines [3]. With the amount of information shared with Linked Data standards, it is possible to find common characteristics of subsets of items, such as the researchers in those clusters, that significantly distinguish them from others, therefore forming explanations for their grouping.

Background. Dedalo [23] is an Inductive Logic Programming (ILP) inspired approach to automatically produce explanations for clusters of items. In ILP, a set $\mathcal{H} = \{h_1, \ldots, h_n\}$ of first-order clausal theories (as in Logic Programming) is derived starting from a set of positive and negative examples $\mathcal{E} = \mathcal{E}^+ \cup \mathcal{E}^-$ (as in Machine Learning) [15]. To derive those theories, ILP applies reasoning upon some background knowledge $\mathcal{B}$ about both the examples, to derive a *complete* ($\mathcal{B} \cup \mathcal{H} \vDash \mathcal{E}^+$) and *consistent* ($\mathcal{B} \cup \mathcal{H} \nvDash \mathcal{E}^-$) explanation for $\mathcal{E}^+$.

In the same way, the information from Linked Data, expressed in RDF triples, is used as $\mathcal{B}$ to explain one specific cluster $\mathcal{C}^+ \in \mathcal{C}$, while the other clusters of $\mathcal{C} : \mathcal{C}^- = \mathcal{R} \backslash \mathcal{C}^+$ represent the negative examples to learn from. See Table 1 for a better understanding of the ILP framework.

Table 1. Our example described in ILP. $\mathcal{B}$ has been derived from Linked Data sources.

$\mathcal{E}$		$\mathcal{B}$
$e^+ \in \mathcal{E}^+$	`isInC`$^+$`('V.Lopez')`	`interestedIn('V.Lopez','Semantic Web')`
$e^+ \in \mathcal{E}^+$	`isInC`$^+$`('M.d'Aquin')`	`interestedIn('M.d'Aquin','Semantic Web')`
$e^- \in \mathcal{E}^-$	`isInC`$^+$`('H. Alani')`	`interestedIn('H.Alani','Social Web')`

$h_1 \in \mathcal{H}$:	`isInC`$^+$`(X)` $\Leftarrow$ `interestedIn('Semantic Web')`

Description. Dedalo has been designed as a graph-search process. Linked Data are represented as a graph of resources and properties (respectively nodes and edges) and traversed to collect information about items of $\mathcal{R}$, used as roots of the graph. Biased by the positive and negative examples, the rules explaining the cluster $\mathcal{C}^+$ that is being analysed are collected from the Linked Data background knowledge.

Given a subset of root items in the graph, there are paths (i.e. chains of property assertions, the edges) and an end value (a URI entity) that items have in common (see Figure 1 for a short example). When items in the same cluster, highlighted in red, share an path and an end URI value more commonly than items outside the cluster, then that couple <path,value> constitutes an explanation for it.

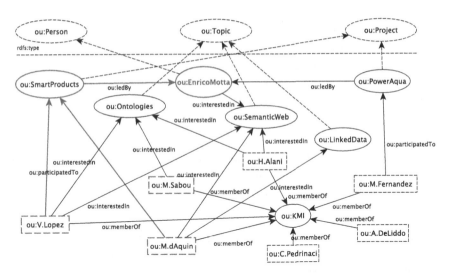

Fig. 1. Our running example. Items $r_i \in \mathcal{R}$ are highlighted in a dashed rectangle. The red colour highlights researchers in $\mathcal{C}^+$. A chain of edges and one end URI value shared by items is defined as an explanation (red-lined).

In our case, one of the best retrieved explanations for $\mathcal{C}^+$ is that items belonging to $\mathcal{C}^+$ are researchers who worked in a project led by the a person whose name is 'Enrico Motta', formalised as $h_1 = \langle$`participatedIn`$\rightarrow$`ledBy`.'`EnricoMotta`'$\rangle$. Dedalo's process consists in a Linked Data traversal based on an iterative discovery of new Linked Data entities, new edges and new explanations.[1]

Dedalo's Problem. For a given cluster $\mathcal{C}^+$, Dedalo produces a set of meaningful, but atomic explanations. Each explanation is scored according to the well known information retrieval F-measure[2], i.e. $fm(h_i)$. In our running example, the set of ranked explanations would consist of:

Rule	F-measure
$h_1 = \langle$ `participatedIn`$\rightarrow$`ledBy`.'`EnricoMotta`'$\rangle$	66.6%
$h_2 = \langle$ `participatedIn`$\rightarrow$`ledBy`$\rightarrow$`interestedIn`.'`Semantic Web`'$\rangle$	66.6%
$h_3 = \langle$ `interestedIn`.'`Semantic Web`'$\rangle$	66.6%
$h_4 = \langle$ `interestedIn`.'`Ontologies`'$\rangle$	66.6%
$h_5 = \langle$ `memberOf`.'`KMi`'$\rangle$	60%
$h_6 = \langle$ `interestedIn`.'`Linked Data`'$\rangle$	25%

Some observations about the explanations can be done here:

- some explanations, such as h_5, are frequent but not meaningful, as others items outside $\mathcal{C}^+$ share the same explanation;
- some explanations are redundant, such as h_1 and h_2 that share the same roots;

---

[1] Please refer to [23] for a detailed description of how the graph search is held.
[2] The next section provides a detailed discussion about the evaluation measures.

- some explanations, such as h_3 and h_4, if in a *disjunction*, would give a better explanation of the cluster, since the union of their root items (the dashed entities) is more representative of C^+ (someone is in C^+ if interested in Semantic Web or Ontologies, i.e. $fm(h_3 \vee h_4)= 85.7\%$);
- some, such as h_1 and h_3, if in a *conjunction*, would give a better explanation of the cluster, since the intersection of their root items is more representative of C^+ (someone is in C^+ if part of a project led by Enrico Motta and interested in Semantic Web, or $fm(h_1 \wedge h_3)=80\%$);

Dedalo's objective is to obtain the most representative explanation for a cluster. While in a trivial simplified example such as the one above, trying each possible combination it is not an issue, when dealing with thousands of rules extracted from many Linked Data sources, the time and scale of the process increase exponentially. Trying each rule conjunction or disjunction becomes a strenuous process. Therefore, we require a process detecting which aggregations are worth to do, or, in other words, a process predicting which couples of rules, that we will define as *pairs*, is worth aggregating and which ones can be filtered out. In this scenario, the second issue is what makes a good prediction. Which are the indicators for it? Are there information about the rules, that we can use to predict an aggregation?

To answer those questions, we propose an approach using Neural Networks to predict the interestingness of the conjunction and disjunction of two rules, using the statistical information we obtained from our initial data.

4   Proposed Approach

4.1   Evaluation Measures for Rules Ranking

Evaluation Measures. In typical KDD subfields such as Association Rule Mining, Frequent Itemset Mining or Sequential Pattern Mining, researchers constantly try to produce new, scalable approaches to post-mine the obtained patterns. Dedalo's produced explanations can be compared to such patterns.

Although numerous measures have been proposed to evaluate rules interestingness [10], there is no agreement on a formal definition of it. Standard measures include accuracy in classification-oriented predictive induction, precision and recall in Information Retrieval, sensitivity and specificity in medical data analysis, support and confidence in Association Rule learning. The first part of our work consisted in verifying whether the quality of Dedalo's explanations would be affected if using different measures. For this purpose, we tested some probability-based objective interestingness measures presented in the literature.

In our context, the results showed that the probability-based measures have common behaviours. Some measures are *"precision-like"* and favour rules applying in a high percentage of cases within a cluster (*rules reliability*); some others are *"recall-like"* and prefer the comprehensiveness of the rules, i.e., a rule covers a large subset of $\mathcal{R}$ (*rule generality*); finally, some of those are *"F-measure-like"*

Table 2. Summary of the tested rules evaluation measures and the best answer they would give according to our running example.

type	measure	best rule
reliability	Added Value, Confidence, Conviction, Information Gain, Leverage, Lift, Odd's Ratio, Precision, Prevalence, Yule's Q, Yule's Y, Two Way Support	⟨interestedIn.Linked Data'⟩
generality	Coverage, Relative Risk, Specificity, Support	⟨memberOf.KMi⟩
gen.-rel. trade-off	Accuracy, Correction, Cosine, Gini Index, Jaccard, Klosgen, Laplace, Linear Correlation Coefficient, Novelty, Weighted Relative Accuracy	⟨participatedTo→ ledBy.'EnricoMotta'⟩

and present a trade-off between generality and reliability. Table 2 presents a summary of the measures surveyed in [10] that we tested.

Our assumption is that Neural Networks can be trained to predict the interestingness of a pair to be predicted. Our goal is therefore to test whether the measures above can be used as features of a neural network for such a prediction.

Neural Networks to Predict Rules Combinations. The described measures can be used to train a Neural Network model, whose aim is to predict whether the disjunction or the conjunction of two rules will bring to a promising score improvement. Given a pair of two rules, statistically described by the aforementioned measures, the Neural Network can learn how to predict if their combination will bring to a score improvement (i.e., a new rule, with a better F-measure) or not.

Artificial Neural Networks (ANNs) are a well established Machine Learning approach, imitating the brain neurons learning process, to approximate real-valued, discrete-valued and vector-valued target functions [12]. With that said, ANNs fit our problem for the following reasons:

1. ANNs are a connection of units taking a set of input data and producing one single output. If we consider each measure as the input unit ("neuron"), the evaluation scores of each rules as the input data to learn from, the desired output can be defined as a boolean answer of whether the combination (conjunction or disjunction) of two given rules is worth it (1) or not (0).
2. ANNs can learn the dependencies of some given data (induction) in order to use such models for predicting outputs for future values (deduction). Therefore, we can easily detect which measures are important for a combination of two rules, and which ones are not.
3. ANNs data-driven self-adaptive methods adjusting to the input data. This means, ANN will iteratively use each rule description to gradually improve the prediction of a combination.

4.2   A Neural Network Approach for Rules Aggregation

Feature Selection for the Neural Network. The general idea is that there exists relationships between the features of a pair of rules, and those relationships can be the key to decide whether the combination is promising or not (what we define as a "good prediction"). To prove that, we experimented different measure combinations, with the aim of finding out the most efficient settings for the Neural Network training.

Coherently with the analysis provided in Section 4.1 (as well as in [10]), we finally detected the set of features presented in Table 3 as the most efficient one. Because each group of measures provided very similar results of rule (ranked) sets, we reduced each group to the well known information retrieval measures: Precision, Recall and F-measure.

Table 3. Neural Network features

Feat.	Description
P1	Precision rule 1
R1	Recall rule 1
F1	F-measure rule 1
P2	Precision rule 2
R2	Recall rule 2
F2	F-measure rule 2
|P1-P2|	Difference between P1 and P2
|R1-R2|	Difference between R1 and R2
|F1-F2|	Difference between F1 and F2

Neural Network Training and Test Sets. In order to train the Neural Network, we build the training set using the rules obtained from Dedalo's Linked Data traversal. We automatically created some rule combinations, representing the positive examples to learn from, calculated the F-measure of their disjunction and conjunction, and reported as a vector of a boolean answers whether the F-measure of the new pair improved (1) or not (0) with respect to the F-measures of the paired rules. As reported in the Experiments section, we relied on 6 use-cases and different sets of rules. Out of those, we created a training set of 30,000 combinations, randomly retrieved to be evenly partitioned in each possible output ([1,1],[1,0],[0,1],[0,0], where [1,1] means that both the disjunction and the conjunction are worth doing, while [0,0] means that none of them is worth). In the same way, we created a test set of 30,000 combinations to test the trained model.

Model Learning. Our Neural Network has been generated using the Neuroph[3] Java library. We trained different models to minimise the Mean Squared Error (MSE). Table 4 reports our model's technical characteristics.

Finally, the model has been tested on the test set, reporting a Mean Squared Error (MSE) rate of 0.24 and a Root-Mean-Squared Deviation (RMSE) of 0.49.

With such a level of accuracy we can confirm our insight that using the measures as indicators for predicting the result of a combination is, to a certain extent, feasible and, therefore, that the Neural Network model can be applicable to our purposes. The next section describes the Neural Network-based rules aggregation process we propose.

---

[3] http://neuroph.sourceforge.net

Table 4. Technical details about the trained Neural Network

NNet		Learning	
ANN model	Feedforward Multilayer Perceptron	MaxIterations	3000
Learning Rule	Resilient Backpropagation	Learning Rate	0.2
		Tuning set split	70%
Activation function	Sigmoid function	Validation set split	30%
Input, hidden, output neurons	[9, 12, 2]	Max Err.	0.1

4.3 Exploiting the Neural Network for Rules Aggregation

Once the trained Neural Network is obtained, our goal is to use it in a process for detecting, in a large set of rules, which ones are worth combining. We define a prediction value indicator p for a rule pair (r_1, r_2), taking into account the prediction returned by the Neural Network ($nnet(r_1, r_2)$) and combining it with the biggest F-measure in the pair under analysis ($max(fm(r_1), fm(r_2))$). In this manner, we favour pairs with a high probability of obtaining an improvement over a good F-measure rather than the ones with a low F-measure.

$$p = nnet(r_1, r_2) * max(fm(r_1), fm(r_2)) \tag{1}$$

As our objective is to obtain the best representation of our cluster in the shortest time, the rules aggregation process also uses the rule with the best F-measure ($top(H)$) to start predicting combinations. Given the set of rules ranked according to their F-measure ($list(H)$) and the best rule $top(H)$, $top(H)$ is paired with each rule $h_i \in H$ to produce the predictions p. If the prediction is positive ($p > 0$), we produce the conjunction or disjunction of the pair ($\langle top(H) \vee h_i \rangle$ or $\langle top(H) \wedge h_i \rangle$) and add them to H. The process is iteratively reproduced in order to improve the score, until the (user-defined) time is over. Algorithm 1 presents the detailed rules aggregation process we developed.

5 Experiments

5.1 Strategies and Data

Comparing Strategies for Rules Aggregation. To test our approach, we compared our Neural Network-based aggregation process to some strategies that might be adopted in common rule aggregation processes. We aim at analysing two characteristics in each of them: (i) the speed in reaching a new (better) F-measure and (i) accuracy of the score, intended as the level of improvement obtained compared to the previous best F-measure. We present them below.

RANDOM. Our baseline consists in the selection of a random rule to combine with top(H). While this is certainly a fast process, our assumption is that a new combination will not be very accurate.

Algorithm 1. Dedalo's rule aggregation process

---

time = 0
H ← list()   ▷ empty list of rules
while (time < stop) **do**
    H ← listRules()   ▷ rules currently discovered
    P ← list()   ▷ list of predictions
    topRule ← *top*(H)   ▷ the rule with the best score at the current cycle
    for h in H **do**   ▷ NNet prediction process
        newPair ← *pair*(topRule,h)   ▷ the best rule and one of the rules from R
        p ← *predict*(newPair)   ▷ actual NNet prediction
        if ($p > 0$) **then**
            add(pred, P)   ▷ Add the prediction if it is worth it
        end if
    end for
    for predicted in P **do**   ▷ Combining the filtered pairs
        newRule ← *combine*   ▷ Evaluate the score of the new combination
        add(newRule, H)   ▷ Add the new rule to the list
    end for
end while

ALLCOMB. The most naïve approach to rule aggregation is to try each and every possible combination in H, and then to detect the one with the highest score. This strategy should favour accuracy over speed.

TOP100. A naïve approach would also consider that the best score improvement is to be found in the top 100 rules of the list, therefore making every possible combination among them. While this strategy can be a good in avoiding redundant or useless combinations, the accuracy might not be guaranteed.

FIRST. This strategy naturally assumes that the first rule will provide the best improvements, when combined to one of the rules in H. Therefore, at each iteration $top(H)$ is combined to all the rules in H. Speed might not be guaranteed.

δ. Expecting computational and time problems, this strategy is refined upon the previous one. Meaningless combinations are here filtered out, by putting a threshold δ to the F-measure of the rules to aggregate. We set the threshold to the highest score (the F-measure of $top(H)$) at every iteration. In other words, we keep only combinations which improve over the current best score.

Besides those strategies, we chose two different settings for the Neural Network-integrated approach.

NNET-0. Given the positive prediction of a pair, this is combined a priori. While this strategy's accuracy is high, it might fall into speed issues.

NNET-50. Given the positive prediction of a pair, this is combined only if the prediction is higher than 50% of the highest score at the current iteration. This avoids creating meaningless combinations, favouring speed, but might result in a reduced accuracy.

Datasets. For our experiments we used three datasets, differing in size (small, medium, large) and topics (authors, papers and books). In detail, the initial datasets we used to run Dedalo's Linked Data traversal are presented below.

KMiA – The Knowledge Media Institute Co-authorship. A set of researchers clustered by a Network Partitioning algorithm according to the papers they have written together. We obtained of 6 clusters that an expert validated as consisting of people working on the same topics. Examples of the best rules found by Dedalo are:

KMiA1=⟨was part of project→led by.'ou:EnricoMotta'⟩ (71.1%)
KMiA2=⟨was part of project→led by.'ou:Peter Scott'⟩ (60.6%)

KMiP – The Knowledge Media Institute Publications. Research papers from the department clustered with K-Means according to the words that have been used in the abstract (TFIDF-weighted keywords). In this case, the expert explained that papers about the same topic have been clustered together. Rules examples are:

KMiP1=⟨creator→was part of project.'ou:SmartProducts'⟩ (54.9%)
KMiP2=⟨creator→was part of project.'ou:Sociallearn'⟩ (30.7%)

Hud – The Books Borrowing Observations. Books borrowed by university students have been clustered with XK-Means according to the faculty the students belong to. The expert explained that books of the same topics have been clustered together. Rules examples are:

Hud1=⟨has subject→is general topic of.'lcsh:CCTV'⟩ (20.2%)
Hud2=⟨has subject→is general topic of.'lcsh:Pulcinella'⟩ (13.2%)

Table 5. Experiment set-up informations. The $|H|$ and $top(H)$ are both the Linked Data traversal outputs and the rules aggregation inputs.

Test		Rules Aggregation				
		Input				Output
	$|C^+|/|\mathcal{R}|$	$|H|$	$top(H)$	max RAM	time (sec.)	$top(H)$
KMiA1	22/92	369	71.1%	4G	60"	86.3%
KMiA2	23/92	511	60.6%	4G	60"	63.9%
KMiP1	220/865	747	54.9%	4G	75"	63.9%
KMiP2	601/865	1796	30.6%	4G	160"	84.1%
Hud1	335/6969	11.937	20.2%	10G	2.500"	66.9%
Hud2	919/6969	11.151	13.3%	10G	3.000"	67.3%
	Input		Output			
	Linked Data traversal					

Table 5 presents information about our experiments. For the purpose of the readers' better understanding, we also provide information about the first part of the process, Dedalo's Linked Data search, out of which we obtained the Linked

Data rules. Secondly, we present information about the resulting sets of rules and the technical details of the aggregation process.[4]

5.2   Results and Discussion

As shown in Table 5, each test has been run for a limited amount of time. At each iteration, the best score amend the discovered rules and the time spent is logged. The results are summarised below, in Figures 2–4. The X axis is the time taken to find a new improved rule since the beginning of the process (the speed criterion), while the Y axis is the score of the best rule (the accuracy criterion). See Figure 3 for the strategy's legend.

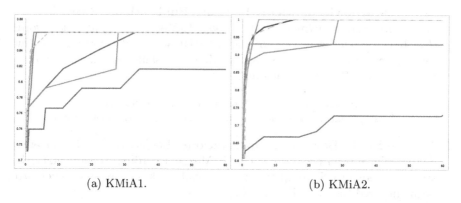

(a) KMiA1.   (b) KMiA2.

Fig. 2. KMiA results. Because of the small size of the rule sets, there is no need to use NNET-50.

In Figure 2a, FIRST, δ and TOP100 find the best score before the NNET-0 and the ALLCOMB approach, which can be explained by the small number of rules to combine. However, as soon as the number of rules increases, as shown in Figure 2b, their speed in finding the best score is highly reduced because they have to deal with a lot of redundant combinations that could be avoided. As expected, choosing random rules only brings F-measure improvements rarely, and by chance. Given the small size of the rule sets in the KMiA test, there is no need of a distinction between NNET-0 and NNET-50 in this example.

As the KMiP sets of rules are medium-sized, Figure 4a still presents a good performance in terms of time/accuracy of ALLCOMB, FIRST, δ

- nnet-50
- allComb
- nnet-0
- δ
- random
- top100
- first

Fig. 3.   Strategies legend

---

[4] Because our goal is to find the best score, we intentionally decided not to report the rules, but just their scores. Results are publicly available at http://linkedu.eu/dedalo/

and TOP100. From this example, however, it emerges that TOP100 is limited, as, after a certain number of combinations among the best rules, it is not possible to obtain any further score improvement. This demonstrates that the best score increases are not to be found with the combination of the top rules.

As soon as the number of combinations becomes more consistent (see Figure 4b), despite being fast and accurate in a first instance, neither ALLCOMB/FIRST nor δ are able to get to the end of the process, as they encounter computational problems (highlighted with a dot at the end of the lines). Meanwhile, the two Neural Network approaches do not show any issues and both reach the end of the process.

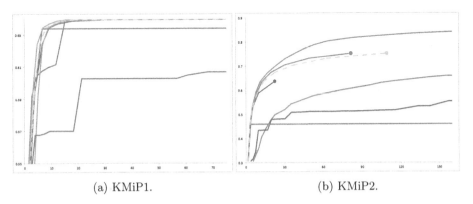

    (a) KMiP1.   (b) KMiP2.

Fig. 4. KMiP results. In (a), ALLCOMB/δ/FIRST are almost as fast as NNET-0 because the rules set size is still small enough. In (b), they cannot reach the end.

The benefits of the NNet-based approaches in terms of time consumption and rule accuracy are much more visible in Figure 5, where the number rules to be combined is higher. NNET-0 (orange line) and NNET-50 (blue line) are the strategies reaching a better score in the shortest time, without falling into memory issues. As in the previous examples, ALLCOMB/δ/FIRST present an initial fast improvement but cannot run until the end. This means that those strategies are indeed accurate, but their realisation is not conceivable without high computational efforts. As for the comparison between NNET-0 and NNET-50, in our settings, we did not experimented any computational issues. In general, NNET-0 is faster, probably because the filtering used in NNET-50 introduces an overhead at this scale. In the case of Figure 5b, the higher speed NNET-50 eventually reaches is probably to be attributed to the increasing amount of rules to be combined, making the filtering more useful.

In Table 6 we give a summary of the strategies characteristics: speed, rule accuracy and the computational efforts required, where [- -] corresponds to the absolute absence of the characteristics, while [++] is a high presence of it.

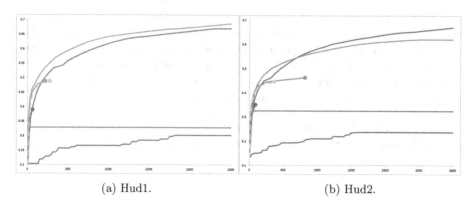

(a) Hud1.   (b) Hud2.

Fig. 5. Hud results. The memory issues of ALLCOMB/δ/FIRST are much more visible here, as well as the better performance of NNET-0/NNET-50.

Table 6. Strategies' characteristics summary on a range of $[--,++]$

	Speed	Accuracy	Scalability
RANDOM	++	−	++
ALLCOMB	+	++	− −
TOP100	+	− −	+
FIRST	+	− −	− −
δ	+	− −	− −
NNET-0	++	++	++
NNET-50	+	+	++

6   Conclusions and Future Work

This paper presents an approach combining Linked Data and Artificial Neural Networks for rules post-processing. While Linked Data knowledge is exploited to create high quality "atomic" rules, we use a trained Neural Network model to predict whether two rules, if combined, can lead to the creation of a new, improved rule. We compare the approach with some strategies that might be used for the same purpose, that usually fail in speed, scalability or accuracy. The results show that the NNet-based strategies significantly outperform the other strategies, with reduced time or computational efforts.

The first part of the future work will be focused on integrating the Neural Network in Dedalo's framework. As explained in Section 3, the Linked Data traversal issue relates to directing the search for a cluster explanation in an efficient way. A interesting work would be to test the Neural Network prediction each time a group of new rules is found, and therefore obtaining a better score in each of Dedalo's iteration, reducing the size of the discovered rules.

Other future work will be focusing on improving the Neural Network setup, trying new features and new models.

References

1. Anusha, P., Reddy, G.S.: Interactive Postmining of Association Rules by Validating Ontologies. International Journal of Electronics and Computer Science Engineering (2012)
2. Baez-Monroy, V., O'Keefe, S.: An Associative Memory for Association Rule Mining. In: International Joint Conference on Neural Networks, IJCNN 2007, pp. 2227–2232. IEEE (2007)
3. Bizer, C., Heath, T., Berners-Lee, T.: Linked data-the story so far. International Journal on Semantic Web and Information Systems 5(3), 1–22 (2009)
4. Changchien, S., Lu, T.C.: Mining association rules procedure to support on-line recommendation by customers and products fragmentation. Expert Systems with Applications 20(4), 325–335 (2001)
5. Chen, Y., Kilgour, D.M., Hipel, K.W.: A decision rule aggregation approach to multiple criteria-multiple participant sorting. Group Decision and Negotiation 21(5), 727–745 (2012)
6. d'Aquin, M., Jay, N.: Interpreting Data Mining Results with Linked Data for Learning Analytics: Motivation, Case Study and Direction. In: LAK 2013 (2013)
7. Eom, J.-H.: Neural feature association rule mining for protein interaction prediction. In: Wang, J., Yi, Z., Żurada, J.M., Lu, B.-L., Yin, H. (eds.) ISNN 2006. LNCS, vol. 3973, pp. 690–695. Springer, Heidelberg (2006)
8. Fayyad, U., Piatetsky-Shapiro, G., Smyth, P.: From data mining to knowledge discovery in databases. AI magazine 17(3), 37 (1996)
9. Gaber, K., Bahi, M.J., El-Ghazawi, T.: Parallel mining of association rules with a Hopfield type neural network. In: 12th IEEE International Conference on Tools with Artificial Intelligence, ICTAI 2000, pp. 90–93. IEEE (2000)
10. Geng, L., Hamilton, H.J.: Interestingness measures for data mining: A survey. ACM Computing Surveys (CSUR) 38(3), 9 (2006)
11. Gudys, A., Sikora, M.: An Algorithm for Decision Rules Aggregation. In: KDIR, pp. 216–225 (2010)
12. Kodratoff, Y., Michalski, R.S., Michalski, R.S., Carbonell, J.G., Mitchell, T.M. (eds.): Machine learning: an artificial intelligence approach. Morgan Kaufmann (1990)
13. Latkowski, R., Mikołajczyk, M.: Data decomposition and decision rule joining for classification of data with missing values. In: Tsumoto, S., Słowiński, R., Komorowski, J., Grzymała-Busse, J.W. (eds.) RSCTC 2004. LNCS (LNAI), vol. 3066, pp. 254–263. Springer, Heidelberg (2004)
14. Marinica, C., Guillet, F.: Knowledge-based interactive postmining of association rules using ontologies. IEEE Transactions on Knowledge and Data Engineering 22(6), 784–797 (2010)
15. Muggleton, S., De Raedt, L.: Inductive logic programming: Theory and methods. The Journal of Logic Programming 19, 629–679 (1994)
16. Nandhini, M., Janani, M., Sivanandham, S.N.: Association rule mining using swarm intelligence and domain ontology. In: 2012 International Conference on Recent Trends In Information Technology (ICRTIT), pp. 537–541. IEEE (2012)
17. Narmadha, D., Naveen Sundar, G., Geetha, S.: An Efficient Approach to Prune Mined Association Rules in Large Databases. International Journal of Computer Science Issues (IJCSI) 8(1) (2011)
18. Paulheim, H.: Exploiting Linked Open Data as Background Knowledge in Data Mining. In: CEUR workshop proceedings DMoLD 2013 collocated with ECMLP-KDD 2013, pp. 1–10. RWTH, Aachen (2013)

19. Pindur, R., Susmaga, R., Stefanowski, J.: Hyperplane aggregation of dominance decision rules. Fundamenta Informaticae 61(2), 117–137 (2004)
20. Rahman, S.M., Kabir, M.F., Siddiky, F.A.: Rules mining from multi-layered neural networks. International Journal of Computational Systems Engineering 1(1), 13–24 (2012)
21. Ramesh, C.R., Ramana, K.V.V., Rao, K.R., Sastry, C.V.: Interactive Post Mining Association Rules using Cost Complexity Pruning and Ontologies KDD
22. Sikora, M.: An algorithm for generalization of decision rules by joining. Foundations on Computating and Decision Science 30(3), 227–239 (2005)
23. Tiddi, I., d'Aquin, M., Motta, E.: Dedalo: Looking for clusters explanations in a labyrinth of linked data. In: Presutti, V., d'Amato, C., Gandon, F., d'Aquin, M., Staab, S., Tordai, A. (eds.) ESWC 2014. LNCS, vol. 8465, pp. 333–348. Springer, Heidelberg (2014)
24. Tiddi, I.: Explaining data patterns using background knowledge from Linked Data. In: ISWC 2013 Doctoral Consortium, Sydney, Australia (2013)

Temporal Semantics: Time-Varying Hashtag Sense Clustering

Giovanni Stilo and Paola Velardi

Dipartimento di Informatica
Via Salaria, 113 Roma
{Stilo,Velardi}@di.uniroma1.it

Abstract. Hashtags are creative labels used in micro-blogs to characterize the topic of a message/discussion. However, since hashtags are created in a spontaneous and highly dynamic way by users using multiple languages, the same topic can be associated to different hashtags and conversely, the same hashtag may imply different topics in different time spans. Contrary to common words, sense clustering for hashtags is complicated by the fact that no sense catalogues are available, like, e.g. Wikipedia or WordNet and furthermore, hashtag labels are often obscure. In this paper we propose a sense clustering algorithm based on temporal mining. First, hashtag time series are converted into strings of symbols using Symbolic Aggregate ApproXimation (SAX), then, hashtags are clustered based on string similarity and temporal co-occurrence. Evaluation is performed on two reference datasets of semantically tagged hashtags. We also perform a complexity evaluation of our algorithm, since efficiency is a crucial performance factor when processing large-scale data streams, such as Twitter.

1 Introduction

Hashtags are frequently, though not systematically, used by Twitter users to tag the content of their messages. Given the 140 character limits of messages, hashtags provide a natural way to better characterize the topics a message deals with. However, hashtags' popularity surge and decay, and furthermore, the same hashtag might have different meanings in different time periods. For example, recently Jawbone tried a *#knowyourself* campaign on Instagram[1], only to find that the hashtag was already being used generically by thousands of users in all sorts of different contexts.

In addition to polysemy, there is also a problem of synonymy: since new hashtags are freely and continuously introduced by users, different hashtags may share the same meaning, also as a consequence of multilinguality. These two problems reduce the effectiveness of hashtags both as a mean to trace users' interests in time (because of sense shifts), and to capture the worldwide impact of emergent topics (because of synonymy and multilinguality). On the other side, better methods to analyze the semantics of hashtags would be definitely needed, since hashtags are readily available,

---

[1] http://blog.bufferapp.com/a-scientific-guide-to-hashtags-which-ones-work-when-and-how-many

K. Janowicz et al. (Eds.): EKAW 2014, LNAI 8876, pp. 563–578, 2014.

while textual analysis techniques are limited both by complexity constraints, when applied on large and lengthy micro-blog streams, and by the very reduced dimension of micro-blog texts. Additionally, real-time detection of sense-related hashtags could be used to improve the task of hashtag recommendation, thus further facilitating the monitoring of on-line discussions.

In this paper we propose a methodology for hashtag sense clustering based on temporal co-occurrence and similarity of the related time series. We first convert temporal series into strings of symbols, to reduce complexity. Then, we cluster hashtags co-occurring in the same temporal window and with same, or similar, strings. The paper is organized as follows: in Section 2 we briefly summarize the state of the art on temporal clustering. Section 3 describes our technique to efficiently derive temporal clusters from large and lengthy micro-blog streams. Section 4 is dedicated to performance evaluation. Section 5 analyzes complexity, a relevant issue when dealing with very large data streams. Finally, Section 6 presents our concluding remarks.

2   Related Work

Hashtags have been used in literature to cluster tweets with similar topics. For example, in [1] hashtags are used as a pooling schema to improve LDA topics learned from Twitter. In [2] hashtags are manually associated to a set of 8 categories, plus an additional "catch-all" category. Tweets with hashtags in the same categories are conflated and a model is learned for each category; finally, the model is used for real-time clustering of new messages.

A number of papers deal with hashtag clustering, as we do. The standard technique adopted in literature is based on contextual similarity. In [3] the authors represent a hashtag h by the set of words in the messages including h, and then use K-means on map-reduce to create clusters. In [4] the authors cluster hashtags based on their contextual similarity and then use this information to expand context vectors associated to tweets including these hashtags. In [5] hashtags from different languages are clustered using a machine translation tool, MOSES. Finally, in [6] a combination of co-occurrence frequency, graph clustering and textual similarity is proposed.

As we motivated in the introduction, a better approach seems anchoring hashtag sense clusters to time. A number of works deal with the temporal aspects of hashtags and their persistence: [7] is concerned with the association of usage patterns and hashtag semantics, and [8] analyzes variations in the spread of hashtags. In [9] common shapes of Twitter hashtags are detected using K-Spectral Centroid clustering. Our objective in this paper is however different: rather than using a time-invariant measure of shape similarity to detect "generic" patterns of human attention, we cluster temporally co-occurring hashtags with a similar shape, to induce sense similarity. To the best of our knowledge, this is the first paper in which temporal similarity is used for hashtag sense clustering, however there are a several papers dealing with temporal mining for event detection in micro-blogs [10-17]. Among the most cited, in [10] a temporal analysis technique, named wavelet analysis or EDCoW, is used to discover events in Twitter streams. As a first step, signals are built for individual words by applying wavelet analysis on the frequency-based raw signals of the words. Autocorrelation is applied to measure the bursty energy of each word. Then, cross-correlation between each pair of bursty words is measured. Finally a cross-correlation table is used to build a graph, and graph-partitioning techniques are applied to discover relevant events. In [11] a technique named TopicSketch is proposed to achieve real-time detection of events in Twitter. Like for EDCoW, events are characterized as "bursty topics", i.e. a set of words showing a sudden surge of popularity followed by a decay. TopicSketch computes in real-time the acceleration (the second order derivative) of three quantities: a) the total Twitter stream; b) each word in the stream; c) each pairs of words in the stream. Given these (known) quantities, the distributions of words over a set of bursty topics $\{T_k\}$ is estimated by modeling the mixture of multiple heterogeneous processes of topics as a Poisson process, and then solving an optimization problem. Hashing techniques and process parallelization are used to keep the problem tractable in terms of memory cost and computational complexity. In fact, one of the main problems with temporal mining when applied to large and lengthy data streams is its computational cost. With respect to these two algorithms, we will show in Section 5 that our method is at least one order of magnitude more efficient.

3   Clustering Hashtag with Symbolic Aggregate ApproXimation (SAX)

In this Section we describe our algorithm, named SAX*, and its application to hashtag sense clustering. The underlying idea of SAX* is that hashtags (or words) with a similar temporal behavior are semantically related. The nature of this relatedness is either limited to a specific temporal slot, e.g. when hashtags describe a unique event (#pope,#habemuspapam), or is more systematic and repetitive, for example when hashtags refer to possibly recurrent, culturally related, issues (such as #followfriday,#thanksgodisfriday). SAX* consists of three steps: in step 1, temporal series of hashtags are sliced into sliding windows and converted into strings of symbols, using Symbolic Aggregate ApproXimation. Then, strings are matched against an automatically learned regular expression representing a generalized pattern of collective attention, in order to discard those hashtags that do not spread across the network. Finally, co-occurring hashtags with similar strings are clustered together.

To tune and evaluate our approach we collected 1% of Twitter traffic, the maximum freely allowed traffic stream, for one year from *June 2012* to *May 2013*, using the standard Twitter API[2]. Other datasets are available, e.g. the Twitter 2011 or 2013 datasets[3], the second being much larger than the first, but still spanning over only two months. A larger time span was indeed necessary to trace a sufficiently large variety of hashtags. Our dataset, hereafter referred to as the *1% Twitter stream*, is about 700 million tweets, with respect to 250 millions tweets of the Twitter 2013 collection, which is, to the best of our knowledge, the largest available collection used so far in micro-blog analysis.

---

[2] https://dev.twitter.com/docs/streaming-apis
[3] https://sites.google.com/site/microblogtrack/

In what follows, we first describe Symbolic Aggregate ApproXimation (SAX), the algorithm used to represent hashtag time series in a compact way, then, similarly to [9], we identify a class of temporal patterns indicating collective attention. Finally, we present the methodology to obtain SAX* clusters.

3.1   SAX Representation of Time Series

SAX is a technique to reduce a time series of arbitrary length W to a string of arbitrary length N, (typically $N \ll W$). Given a time series $S(t)$, this is first normalized through z-score[4] normalization and then discretized, using a well defined dimensionality reduction method called Piecewise Aggregate Approximation [17]. The PAA representation is as follows: given a (normalized) time series $S'(t)$ in a window W, this can be discretized into N partitions of equal length Δ (e.g. days, hours..). We denote with $\bar{s}_i$ (i=1...N, $N = \frac{W}{\Delta}$) the mean value of the function falling into each partition i. Then, the PAA representation is symbolized with a discrete string, using an alphabet $\Sigma : \{a, b, ..\}$ of n symbols. Since normalized time series have a highly Gaussian distribution, we can determine the breakpoints $\beta_1 .. \beta_{n-1}$ that produce $|\Sigma|$ equally sized areas under the Gaussian curve. Once the breakpoints have been established, the PAA representation is turned into a string of symbols in the following way:

$$\hat{s}_i = j, \qquad j \epsilon \Sigma, \qquad iff \ \beta_{j-1} < \bar{s}_i < \beta_j$$

Figure 1 shows the SAX string (with $\Sigma = 2$ and $\beta = 0$) associated with the normalized time series $S'(t)$ for the hashtag *Olympics*. The series refers to a 10 days window starting on July 25th, 2012, with a 1-day discretization (N=10, Δ= 1 day). The x axis represents the breakpoint and the dashed line shows the $\bar{s}_i$ values. Using the binary alphabet $\{a, b\}$, the correspondent SAX string for *Olympics* is aabbaaaa. Figures 2 and 3 illustrate the effect of z-normalization: Figure 2 shows the time series, in the same window as in Figure 1, for the hashtags: *Olympics, Olimpiadi2012, londra2012, London2012, Londres2012*, while Figure 3 shows the same series after normalization. Even though the five hashtags do not display identical behavior, especially before normalization, their correspondent SAX strings are the same or very similar, intuitively suggesting a correlation.

In our analysis, we are interested only in hashtags whose SAX representation denotes a pattern of collective attention. Rather than clustering time series as in [9], we selected manually a number of words from Wikipedia Events[5] 2011, we generated the SAX strings for these selected words and related hashtags on a previously acquired 1% stream[6], and we used the RPNI algorithm [19], available in the libalf[7] library, to generate compatible regular expressions. With an alphabet of 2 symbols, we finally learned the following regular expression:

---

[4] z-normalization is described in
http://code.google.com/p/jmotif/wiki/ZNormalization
[5] en.wikipedia.org/wiki/Event
[6] This stream had several holes, therefore we only used to analyze patterns of attention.
[7] libalf.informatik.rwth-aachen.de/index.php?page=home

$$(a + b?\,bb?\,a +)?\,(a + b?\,bba *)? \tag{1}$$

This regex captures all the series with one or two peaks and/or plateaus in the analyzed window, such as, for example, the sequences in Figures 1 and 3. Incidentally, we note that this regex turns out to be a generalization of 5 out of 6 shapes of attention learned by the algorithm described in [9][8]. The 6th shape has two major and one minor peak, which would require 3 symbols to be correctly represented.

3.2 SAX* Clustering

As suggested by the example in Figure 3, our aim is to cluster hashtags on the basis of the similarity of their time series. The SAX representation enables this similarity to be captured efficiently.

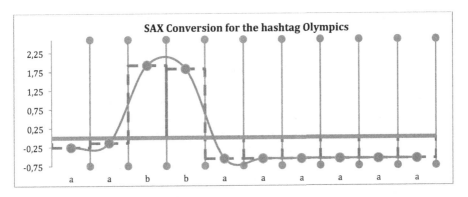

Fig. 1. Binary SAX representation ($|\Sigma| = 2$) of the hashtag Olympics

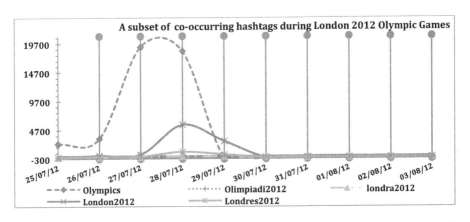

Fig. 2. Non-normalized time series for: Olympics,Olimpiadi2012,londra2012, London2012, Londres2012

---

[8] See Figure 8 of the mentioned paper, in which 6 shapes of attention of Twitter hashtags are shown.

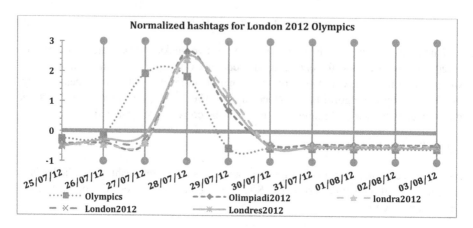

Fig. 3. Normalized time series for: Olympics, Olimpiadi2012, londra2012, London2012, Londres2012

To create clusters, we proceed as follows. In our 1% Twitter stream, we consider sliding windows W_i partitioned in 10 slots of one day each. Our slots are days, but a more fine-grained discretization could be adopted. At each execution of the clustering algorithm, the window is shifted by one day. Within each window, hashtags are converted into SAX binary strings. We also experimented different dimensions for the alphabet Σ (experiments are omitted for the sake of space) eventually finding that best results using our 1% Twitter stream are obtained with a binary alphabet. The parameters $W = 10, \Delta = 1day, |\Sigma| = 2$ perform at best on the 1% stream since this is not sufficiently dense, and only allows it to detect world-wide phenomena. Previous work (e.g. [11]) on a locally dense stream (Singapore tweets during few weeks) has shown that shorter slots (days or hours) should be used to mine geolocated streams.

Given the binary SAX representation of all the hashtags in our Tweet dataset, we consider only those matching the regex (1) in W_i, thereby greatly reducing the computational and memory requirements of the subsequent clustering phase (this will be discussed in more detail in Section 5). Let $L'(W_i)$ be the survived vocabulary of terms in W_i. Over these terms we apply a bottom-up hierarchical clustering algorithm with *complete linkage* [20]. In complete linkage, the algorithm starts with singleton clusters (e.g. each consisting of one term), and then progressively merges two clusters into larger ones, according to the aforementioned "smallest diameter" criterion, measured using a given distance function[9]. We stop hierarchical bottom-up clustering aggregation for a cluster $c_j^{W_i}$ when $SD(d(centroid, t_k)) < \delta$, where SD is the standard deviation of the distance between all terms t_k in $c_j^{W_i}$ and the cluster centroid. We further purge clusters smaller than f elements (f, δ are tunable parameters). Let $C^{W_i} = \{c_1^{W_i}, \ldots c_{ni}^{W_i}\}$ be the clustering result in W_i.

---

[9] We use the euclidean distance, but other measures, e.g. the edit distance, produce very similar results.

As an example, consider the 10-days window starting on July 27th 2012. In this window, we obtain the following multi-lingual hashtag cluster (the corresponding SAX* sequences are shown only for the cluster centroid):

```
[london2012, londres2012, ItaliansAreSoHot, JJOO, London2012, Londra2012, Londres2012,
Olimpiadi2012, Rai, london2012, londra2012,olimpadi2012, olimpiadi2012, tomorrowland,
London2012, Olympics,olympicceremony,JO2012, JJOO, JO, JO2012, JOLondres2012, Jo2012,
London2012, Londres, Londres2012, Olympics, jo, jo2012, joRTBF]

    [centroid: aaabbaaaaa,  SD: 0.17692605382612614]
```

We can observe that in this case the window perfectly includes the pattern of formula (1), as shown in Figures 2 and 3 (plotting some members of the above cluster), but this is not guaranteed in general. This is the reason for using sliding windows: sliding is better than slicing, since if a slice were to cut a pattern in two we wouldn't be able to detect the correspondent cluster. On the other hand, since consecutive windows overlap over 8 days, we may have many windows and many clusters that capture the same cluster or some of its subtopics. With reference to the previous cluster, the window W' obtained by sliding W one day to the right, would still generate more or less the same clusters, while sliding three days would miss it, since the correspondent sub-string does not match the regex (1). Therefore, a method is needed to capture the relevant events on a day-to-day basis. To this end, we proceed as follows: For every temporal slot Δ_j (Δ_j is one day in our case) consider the set $\mathbf{W}$ of all windows such that $\Delta_j C W_i$ ($|\mathbf{W}|=10$ in our case). For each $W_i \in \mathbf{W}$, select the subset of clusters $c_{\Delta_j}^{W_i}$ in W_i with a peak in Δ_j, e.g., if a binary alphabet is adopted, whose centroid has a "b" in Δ_j. Then, the set of clusters in Δ_j is: $C^{\Delta_j} = \left\{ c_{\Delta_j}^{W_i} \right\}$. Note that clustering is performed on 10-days sliding windows: day clusters are obtained in a post-processing step. Also note that in a day Δ_j there might be zero or more clusters with a peak.

4   Data Analysis and Evaluation

We extracted the hashtags from our 1% Twitter Stream, we removed hastags below a given (language dependent) frequency threshold[10] f in each W and we then run SAX* with $W=10$, $|\Sigma| = 2$, $\Delta = 1d, \delta = 0.35$ (see Section 3.1). These parameters were experimentally selected, but given the limited Twitter traffic available (1%), we observed that a more fine-grained analysis (larger alphabet and smaller Δ and W) produces less reliable results, as already remarked. Overall, we clustered a set H of 124.345 hashtags in 365 sliding windows. The average number of clusters per window was 33.24 (with standard deviation SD=6.76) and the average cluster dimension was 10.29 (SD=3.29). However, except for few examples (as the large *London 2012 Olympic Games* cluster shown in Section 3.2), hashtags are rather cryptic and extensive manual evaluation is almost impossible. To provide an objective evaluation, we designed two experiment: the first is a manual evaluation against two reference

---

[10] f depends on the language and has been set to 99 (English), 17 (Spanish) 4 (French) 3 (Italian), more or less proportional to the relative weight of Tweets in these languages.

classifications, the second provides internal validity measures of cluster cohesion. Both are standard validation approaches adopted in clustering literature and in previous works on hashtag sense clustering [1-5]. Finally, we also evaluate the complexity of SAX* and compare it with other temporal and topic clustering algorithms.

4.1   Experiment 1: Evaluation against Available Datasets

In order to evaluate the quality of extracted clusters, we used two resources:

i)   The hashtag classification presented in [2][11]: this dataset (named hereafter TSUR) includes 1000 highly frequent hashtags manually assigned to 9 categories: *Music, Movies, Celebrity, Technology, Games, Sports, Idioms, Political* and *Other.*

ii)   A user-populated hashtag taxonomy on the TWUBS on-line hashtag directory[12]: this taxonomy has three top categories (*Event, Organization* and *Topic*) and 32 sub-categories. For example, *Topic* has the following categories: *Art, Education, Entertainement, Gaming, Health&Beauty*, etc. Note that in TWUBS a hashtag may belong to more than one class. We crawled TWUBS and we downloaded about 40,000 hashtags with related classifications.

Both datasets use coarse categories, while our system captures more fine-grained senses, however, as already remarked, a manual evaluation is unfeasible, except for a number of very readable examples like the Olympic game cluster previously shown. The purpose of the evaluation is to show that SAX* clusters are "pure", e.g. most, or all of their members belong the same category. We also note that only a subset of the TSUR and TWUBS hashtags meet the conditions to exceed the threshold f and to match the regex (1) in at least one of the 364 windows W in our 1% Twitter stream. Overall, 243 hashtags from the TSUR dataset and 617 from the TWUBS dataset were also found in our set H of 124.345 hashtags. Let $H(W_i)$ be the set of "active" hastags in a window W_i and further let $C^{W_i} = \{c_1 .. c_N\}$[13] be the clustering generated by SAX* in W_i, and $C^T : [t_1, t_2 .. t_K]$ the correspondent "ground-truth" classification (either TSUR or TWUBS), such that each cluster t_m includes hashtags belonging to one category[14]. To assess the performance of our system we use the following measure of Precision: $P(C^{W_i}) = \frac{\sum tp_i}{\sum fp_i + \sum tp_i}$ were a true positive pair (tp_i) is a pair of hashtags such that: $h_k, h_j \in c_n$ in C^{W_t} $h_k, h_j \in t_n$ in C^T. Note that we do not use the popular Rand Index[15] since this index takes into account also the false negatives. However with SAX*, two hashtags that do not temporally co-occur are not clustered together, even though they could belong to the same semantic category. For this reason, we

---

[11] We thank the authors for providing the dataset.

[12] twubs.com/p/hashtag-directory/

[13] We here omit the apex denoting the window in which the cluster is generated, for the sake of simplicity.

[14] Note that K, the number of categories in W_i, is in general lower that the total number of available categories in the two classifications. Also note that TWUBS allows for multiple classifications, therefore some hashtag may belong to more than one t_m.

[15] http://en.wikipedia.org/wiki/Rand_index

cannot compare our results with those in [2]. It is further to be said that the method proposed in that paper, besides being based on contextual similarity rather than temporal similarity, is a trained method while SAX* is *untrained*. In addition to Precision, we also measure the Information Gain[16], defined as the difference between the entropy of the original distribution and that of the derived classification:

$$IG(C^T, C^{W_i}) = \sum_{j=1..K} \left(\frac{|t_k|}{\sum_{j=1..K} |t_j|} \right) log \left(\frac{|t_k|}{\sum_{j=1..K} |t_j|} \right) - \sum_{n=1..N} \left(\frac{|c_n|}{\sum_{j=1..N} |c_j|} \right) \sum_{k=1..K} \frac{|c_n \cap t_k|}{|c_n|} log \left(\frac{|c_n \cap t_k|}{|c_n|} \right)$$

In the formula, with reference to a clustering C^{W_i} of $H(W_i)$, bursty hashtags in window W_i, $K = |C^T|$ is the number of categories of the reference classification (either TSUR or TWUBS) having at least one member in $H(W_i)$, N is the number of clusters generated by SAX* in C^{W_i}, the minuend is the initial entropy of the set $H(W_i)$, i.e. the initial impurity of the examples, and the subtrahend is the weighted sum of entropies of each cluster $c_n \in C^{W_i}$. The IG then provides a measure of the improvement of SAX* over a *baseline classifier* assigning a category based on the a-priori probability distribution of the various categories in $H(W_t)$. We actually compute the normalized IG (NIG), since K may vary in each W_i. Table 1 shows average and standard deviation (SD) of NIG and Precision, over the 365 clusterings C^{W_i} derived in one year.

Table 1. Precision and Information Gain of SAX* in the hashtag clustering task

Golden Classifications:	TSUR (max K=9)	TWUBS (max K=32)
Average NIG	0.967	0.778
SD(NIG)	0.042	0.1002
Average Precision	0.88	0.77
SD(Precision)	0.127	0.128
Total # of evaluated hashtag pairs	5,678	10,206
Average # of clusters with $|c_i|>1$ in W_i	4.85	7.86

The Table shows that the quality of SAX*-induced clusters can be considered indeed very good. The average NIG is close to the maximum of one bit for TSUR and slightly lower for TWUBS, which also has a lower precision. This is coherent with the fact that the number of available categories is more than three times higher for TWUBS (32 against 9) and in addition, in TWUBS some hashtags have multiple classifications. In general, clusters are very pure (e.g. members belong to a unique category), as shown in the following two clustering examples, in which hashtags have been replaced by their semantic labels in TWUBS:

- On: <Jun   01,   2012>:   [[MOVIES]   [SPORTS,MOVIES,MOVIES]   [MOVIES,MOVIES] [SPORTS,SPORTS,SPORTS][SPORTS]   [TECHNOLOGY,TECHNOLOGY,GAMES,TECHNOLOGY,GAMES]] (NIG= 0.920]

---

[16] http://en.wikipedia.org/wiki/Information_gain_ratio

- On: <Jun 25, 2012>: [[SPORTS] [MOVIES,MOVIES] [MOVIES] [SPORTS,SPORTS]
  [IDIOMS,IDIOMS,IDIOMS,IDIOMS,IDIOMS] [POLITICAL,POLITICAL] [MOVIES,MOVIES]
  [IDIOMS,IDIOMS,IDIOMS,IDIOMS,IDIOMS]] (NIG=1.00)

We remark that numbers in Table 1 refer only to the set of hashtags in the two "golden" classifications that also appear in our clusters, since, as stated in the introduction of this Section, our clusters are much larger. As an example, we list some co-clustered pairs with a clear meaning: Giants-sfgiants, MyWeakness-factsaboutme, football-giants, Obama-healthcare, Obama-Obamacare, Dodgers-redsox, apple-iPhone, ff-followfriday, CNN-politics, HabemusPapam-Pope. The examples show that our sense clusters are indeed more fine grained than what captured by the reference classifications, however there is no practically feasible way to evaluate such senses manually. Another problem is that TWUBS and TSUR categories are fixed, and do not capture the temporal shift of hashtag meaning, which was one of the objectives of this paper. Next Section analyzes this issue.

4.2 Experiment 2: Internal Cluster Validity Measures

In this experiment we provide a measure of cluster quality based on the semantic similarity of messages including hashtags in clusters. Similarly to other papers [2,4], we represent each hashtag with a *tfidf* vector of the document D_h^i created by conflating all tweets including a given hashtag h, but we also add the constraint that tweets must co-occur in the same window W_i. We introduce three metrics: the first two are well known measures commonly used to evaluate the similarity of two items D_k^i, D_j^i belonging either to the same or to different clusters in a window W_i. The third one computes the similarity between the same two items D_i^1, D_j^2 when occurring in two different randomly chosen windows W_{i1}, W_{i2}. The objective of this third measure is to verify our hypothesis of a temporal shift of hashtag meaning. For each hashtag pair $h_k, h_j \in c_n$ and for all clusters $c_n \in C^{Wi}$ detected in window W_i we compute the average intra-clusters similarity $IntraSym(C^{Wi})$, based on the cosine similarity[17] $sym(D_k^t, D_j^t)$:

$$IntraSym(C^{Wi}) = \frac{1}{|C^{Wi}|} \sum_{c_n \in C^{Wi}} \left[\frac{1}{|c_n|(|c_n|+1)} \sum_{\substack{k,h_j \in c_n \\ k \neq j}} sym(D_k^i, D_j^i) \right]$$

Then, for each hashtag pair $h_k \in c_n, h_j \in c_{n'}$ and all clusters C^{Wi} detected in window W_i we compute the average inter-clusters similarity $InterSym(W_i)$ based on the cosine similarity $sym(D_k^i, D_j^i)$:

$$InterSym(C^{Wi}) = \frac{1}{|C^{Wi}|(|C^{Wi}|-1)} \sum_{\substack{c_n, c_{n'} \in C^{Wi} \\ n \neq n'}} \left[\frac{1}{|c_k||c_{k'}|} \sum_{h_k \in c_n, \ h_j \in c_{n'}} sym(D_k^i, D_j^i) \right]$$

Finally, for each hashtag pair $h_i, h_j \in c_n$ and all clusters C^{Wt} detected in window W_t we compute the average random clusters similarity $RandSym(C^{Wt})$ based on the

---

[17] en.wikipedia.org/wiki/**Cosine_similarity**

cosine similarity $sym(D_i^{t_1}, D_j^{t_2})$ when h_i, h_j occur in two non-overlapping randomly selected windows W_{i1}, W_{i2} where $i \neq i_1 \neq i_2$ and $i_1, i_2 \in random(W)$.

$$RandSym(W_i) = \frac{1}{|C^{Wi}|} \sum_{c_n \in C^{Wi}} \left[\frac{1}{|c_n|(|c_n|+1)} \sum_{\substack{h_k, h_j \in c_n \\ k \neq j, i \neq i1 \neq i2 \in random(W)}} sym(D_k^{i_1}, D_j^{i_2}) \right]$$

The main purpose of $RandSym(C^{Wi})$ is to compare the similarity of $D_k^{i_1}, D_j^{i_2}$ when the related tweets co-occur in a cluster in the same window ($i = i_1 = i_2$), and when, instead, they do not co-occur ($i \neq i_1 \neq i_2$). Inspired by the Information Gain, we compute the Similarity Gain by the following formula:

$$SymGain(W_i) = \frac{IntraSym(W_i) - RandSym(W_i)}{RandSym(W_i)}$$

Table 2 shows the values and SD of $IntraSym(W_i), InterSym(W_i)$ and $SymGain(W_i)$.

Table 2. Cluster similarity measures

	Intra	Inter	Rand	Gain
Average	0.2219	0.0083	0.0999	1.3331
St. Deviation	0.2504	0.0042	0.0434	1.6241

The Table shows that, as expected, $IntraSym(W_t) \gg InterSym(W_t)$ but also $IntraSym(W_t) \gg RandSym(W_t)$. This demonstrates the main point of our experiment: hashtag similarity is time-related. Consider for example two hastags, CNN and America, that co-occur in a cluster starting on October 22nd, 2012. Two examples of tweets in this window are (common words are underlined):

#America #CNN
Oct 23rd 2012: *Final presidential debate is tonight tune in #America!!!*
Oct 24th 2012: *Final Debate, Tune in on #CNN*

However, the same two hashtags may be used in very different contexts when found in separate temporal windows, as for example:

#CNN:
Oct 29th, 2012: *Might watch a bit of #CNN to follow #Sandy*
#America:
Dec 14th 2012: *Very sad day in #America. Pray for the families in Connecticut.*

A similar example is provided by the pair Obama, Obamacare:

#Obama,#ObamaCare:
Jun 29th, 2012: *@UserName01 What's your point of view on #OBAMA health care plan?*
Jun 28th, 2012: *#Obamacare Gives millions the opportunity to have health care plan.*

The hashtag Obama however may appear in quite different contexts, such as:

#Obama:

Oct 21st, 2012: *@UserName02 it is in the best interest of #Iran to help President   #Obama win. They will say anything to help in the next few weeks*

5   Complexity Analysis

In this Section we perform a complexity evaluation of SAX*, and we compare it with EDCoW [10] and TopicSketch [11]. For SAX*, the complexity analysis is based on [18] and on personal communication with the author; for EDCoW and TopicSketch our computation is based on the algorithm description presented in the respective papers, which we briefly summarize. We introduce the following parameters:

D	number of tweets in W	K	number of discovered events/topics (this is a manually defined parameter in TopicSketch)
t	average document (tweet) length		
L	vocabulary dimension (lexicon) in W		
L'	vocabulary dimension after pruning (when applicable)	H	number of hash functions in Topic-Sketch
Θ	re-sampling window in EDCoW		
W	window length	I	number of iteration of outer loop in TopicSketch
		i	number of iteration of Newton-Raphson method in TopicSketch

In what follows, in line with [10] and [11], we consider the problem of words temporal clustering rather than hashtags, however the nature of clustered items does not affect the complexity computation.

5.1   SAX* Complexity

The first step requires reading the documents, indexing the terms, and creating a temporal series for every term. Supposing an average length per document of t terms, this step takes *order of* (hereafter the big-o notation will be implicit) Dt. Then, we read the lexicon, pruning all terms below a given frequency, with cost L. Let L' be the pruned lexicon. Finally we remove all terms that do not match the regex (1), with a cost that is linear in the dimension of the window W: $L'W$. Let L'' be the final dimension of the lexicon. The worst case is when $L' = L''$ though in general $L' \gg L''$. The number of comparisons among symbolic strings during hierarchical clustering with complete linkage depends on the string length, which is $\frac{W}{\Delta} = W$ (since $\Delta = 1$) , therefore the worst-case cost is $(L' - 1)(W^2 L')$. After the clustering step, K clusters are generated. Finally, we apply cluster pruning – small clusters are removed - with a cost K. To summarize, the cost is: $Dt + L + L'W + (L' - 1)(W^2 L') + K$

5.2   EDCoW Complexity

A detailed description of the algorithm is found in [10] As for SAX*, the first step consists of the transformation of terms in documents into temporal series with cost Dt. In the first stage D_1 of the algorithm, every term-related signal s_i is converted into another signal s_i'; the new signal is obtained by applying Shannon Wavelet Entropy to sub-sequences of length Θ of the original signal s_i. In other terms a value s_i' is computed every Θ values of s_i. In stage D_2, two contiguous values s_i', s_{i+1}' are aggregated. The cost of the first stage operation is then: $L\left(\frac{W}{\Theta}(\Theta^3 + \Theta)\right)$. The second stage filters signals s_i' (of length $\frac{W}{\Theta}$) using the autocorrelation function; this part has a cost $L\left(\frac{W}{\Theta}\log\left(\frac{W}{\Theta}\right)\right)$ and produces a sub-lexicon L'. Next, EDCoW builds the cross-correlation matrix for all pairs of remaining terms. The cost needed to build the cross-correlation matrix is $(L')^2\frac{W^2}{\Theta}$. In the subsequent phase EDCoW detects events though modularity-based graph partitioning that is efficiently computed using *power iteration* at cost L'^2.

For each cluster $e \in E$ ($|E|=K$) the final cost is bounded by $K\,L'^2$. The final step consists of selecting the clusters on the basis of their related sub-graph and can be included in the previous phase without additional cost. The total cost of the algorithm is then summarized by the following formula:

$$Dt + L\left(\frac{W}{\Theta}(\Theta^3 + \Theta)\right) + L\left(\frac{W}{\Theta}\log\left(\frac{W}{\Theta}\right)\right) + (L')^2\frac{W^2}{\Theta} + K\,L'^2$$

5.3   TopicSketch Complexity

In [11] the authors present a detailed description of the algorithm, though they do not provide a complete complexity analysis. As for the other algorithms, the first step consists of reading the stream and collecting terms statistics with cost Dt. Then a dimension reduction is applied with cost $H(1 + L / L')$, where H are hash functions mapping words to bucket $[1...L']$[18] uniformly and independently. The cost of the subsequent phase is summarized by the computational cost of maintaining all the Ht^2 accelerations (this cost is provided by the authors). The last step is a topic inference algorithm, modeled as an optimization problem. The gradient-based method[19] to optimize the objective function f is based on the Newton-Raphson approach, whose complexity depends on the multiplication function[20]. Using a very conservative value of 32 bit precision the cost is at least: $I \cdot H \cdot K \cdot i \cdot L' \cdot \log(32)$. Though some minor costs are ignored for the sake of simplicity, the final complexity is order of: $Dt + H\left(1 + {}^{L}/_{L'}\right) + (Ht^2) + (I \cdot H \cdot K \cdot i \cdot L' \cdot \log(32))$

---

[18] [1...B] in the original paper [11].
[19] Table I of [11].
[20] http://en.wikipedia.org/wiki/Computational_complexity_of_
mathematical_operations

5.4   Complexity Estimates

Given the above formulas, we can now provide quantitative complexity estimates. We set the parameters as follows:

- the length t of documents is set to 9.4 words[21];
- the size of D grows from 100 to 10 million tweets, which is about the actual average size (9.163.437) of English tweets in a 10 days window in a 1% Twitter stream;
- the vocabulary L grows according to a Zipfian law with parameter $alfa = 1,127$ estimated on our Twitter stream. L' grows with the same law (starting from L), with an estimated parameter $alfa = 0,41456$.
- $\Theta = 3$ as reported in [10] the window W is 10 days, and $\Delta = 1$ day. Note that, in TopicSketch, W indirectly impacts on performance, since it limits to a manageable value the dimension L of the words to be traced, as the authors say. The impact of W and Δ is accounted by the cost of maintaining the accelerations, Ht^2.
- the number of clusters is set to 50
- according to [11] we set H to 6, I to 50 and i to 25.

Table 3 shows that SAX* is one order of magnitude less complex than ECDoW and TopicSketch, on a realistic stream of 10 million tweets. Note that, with respect to the empirical efficiency computation performed in [11], the complexity is here estimated on the theoretical ground and is henceforth independent from parameters, parallelization techniques and computing power. We note that ECDoW is mostly influenced by the first stage of signal transformation and TopicSketch is penalized by the Topic Inference algorithm. Furthermore, while SAX* and ECDoW are not influenced by the K parameter (the number of clusters), using TopicSketch on large Twitter streams with growing K becomes prohibitive, as shown by the complexity formula: in practice, the authors set K=5 in their paper but they do not analyze the effect of this parameter on performance.

Table 3. Complexity analysis as a function of the corpus dimension

D	t	L	L'	Θ	W	K	SAX*	EDCoW	TopicSketch
100	9.4	179	9	3	10	50	7,784	25,341	16,117,823
1K	9.4	2,401	25	3	10	50	73,086	306,630	47,259,589
10K	9.4	32,155	74	3	10	50	665,382	3,820,434	138,620,347
100K	9.4	430,593	217	3	10	50	6,042,708	48,659,378	407,068,448
1M	9.4	5,766,068	635	3	10	50	55,434,549	629,661,338	1,200,080,494
10M	9.4	77,213,473	1,862	3	10	50	**517,658,362**	**8,238,768.,557**	**3,584,819,505**

6   Concluding Remarks

In this paper we introduced a hashtag clustering algorithm based on the novel notion of temporal similarity. We presented SAX*, an algorithm to convert temporal series of hashtags into a sequence of symbols, and then to cluster hashtags with similar and co-occurring sequences. SAX* hashtag clusters, generated from a large and lengthy dataset of Tweets collected during one year, have been evaluated in three ways:

---

[21] In agreement with http://firstmonday.org/ojs/index.php/fm/article/view/4366/3654

- First, we evaluated the quality of clusters using two available datasets of semantically tagged hashtags, showing that SAX* is able to create almost "pure" clusters;
- Second, we used two standard cluster internal validity measures, inter and intra cluster similarity, along with a new measure, the similarity gain. We have shown that tweets including two hashtags h_i, h_j are more similar to each other when they co-occur in the same temporal window and same cluster, than when they occur in different temporal windows;
- Finally, we also conducted a complexity analysis of our algorithm, and compared it with two other temporal clustering methods presented in recent literature, showing that SAX* is one order of magnitude more efficient than the other compared methods.

References

1. Mehrota, R., Sanner, S.: Improving LDA Topic Models for Microblogs via Tweet Pooling and Automatic Labeling. In: SIGIR 2013, Dublin, July 28-August 1 (2013)
2. Tsur, O., Littman, A., Rappoport, A.: Efficient Clustering of Short Messages into General Domains. In: Proceedings of the 7th International AAAI Conference on Weblogs and Social Media, ICWSM 2013 (2013)
3. Muntean, C.I., Morar, G.A., Moldovan, D.: Exploring the meaning behind twitter hashtags through clustering. In: Abramowicz, W., Domingue, J., Węcel, K. (eds.) BIS Workshops 2012. LNBIP, vol. 127, pp. 231–242. Springer, Heidelberg (2012)
4. Ozdikis, O., Senkul, P., Oguztuzun, H.: Semantic Expansion of Hashtags for Enhanced Event Detection in Twitter. In: VLDB 2012 WOSS, Istanbul, Turkey, August 31 (2012)
5. Carter, S., Tsagkias, M., Weerkamp, W.: Twitter hashtags: Joint Translation and Clustering. In: 3rd International Conference on Web Science, WebSci (2011)
6. Modi, A., Tinkerhess, M., Antenucci, D., Handy, G.: Classification of Tweets via clustering of hashtags. EECS 545 Final Project (2011)
7. Posch, L., et al.: Meaning as collective use: predicting semantic hashtag categories on twitter. In: Proceedings of the 22nd International Conference on World Wide Web Companion. International World Wide Web Conferences (2013)
8. Romero, D.M., Meeder, B., Kleinberg, J.: Differences in the mechanics of information diffusion across topics: idioms, political hashtags, and complex contagion on twitter. In: Proceedings of the 20th International Conference Wide Web, ACM (2011)
9. Yang, J., Leskovec, J.: Patterns of temporal variation in online media. In: Proceedings of the fourth ACM International Conference on Web Search and Data Mining, pp. 177–186. ACM (2011)
10. Weng, J., Yao, Y., Leonardi, E., Lee, B.-S.: Event Detection in Twitter. In: ICWSM 2011 International AAAI Conference on Weblogs and Social Media (2011)
11. Xie, W., Zhu, F., Jang, J., Lim, E.-P., Wang, K.: TopicSketch: Real-time Bursty Topic Detection from Twitter. In: IEEE 13th International Conference on Data Mining, ICDM (2013)
12. Qin, Y., Zhang, Y., Zhang, M., Zheng, D.: Feature-Rich Segment-Based News Event Detection on Twitter. In: International Joint Conference on Natural Language Processing (2013)
13. Guzman, J., Poblete, B.: On-line Relevant Anomaly Detection in the Twitter Stream: An Efficient Bursty Keyword Detection Model. In: KDD 2013 (2013)

14. Osborne, M., Petrovic, S., McCreadie, R., Macdonald, C., Ounis, I.: Bieber no more: First Story Detection using Twitter and Wikipedia. In: TAIA 2012 (2012)
15. Diao, Q., Jiang, J., Zhu, F., Lim, E.-P.: Finding Bursty Topics from Microblogs. In: ACL (2012)
16. Naaman, M., Becker, H., Gravano, L.: Hips and Trendy: characterizing emerging trends on Twitter. JASIST (2011)
17. Petrović, S., Osborne, M., Lavrenko, V.: Streaming first story detection with application to Twitter. In: Human Language Technologies: The 2010 Annual Conference of the North American Chapter of the Association for Computational Linguistics (HLT 2010), pp. 181–189. Association for Computational Linguistics, Stroudsburg (2010)
18. Lin, J., Keogh, E., Li, W., Lonardi, S.: Experiencing SAX: A novel symbolic representation of time series. Data Mining and Knowledge Discovery 15(2), 107–144 (2007)
19. Oncina, J., Garcıa, P.: Inferring Regular Languages in Polynomial Updated Time. In: The 4th Spanish Symposium on Pattern Recognition and Image Analysis. MPAI, vol. 1, pp. 49–61. World Scientific (1992)
20. Jain, A.,, K.: Data clustering: 50 years beyond K –means. Pattern Recognition Letters 31, 651–666 (2010)

Using Ontologies

Understanding the User Experience

Paul Warren, Paul Mulholland, Trevor Collins, and Enrico Motta

Knowledge Media Institute, The Open University
Milton Keynes, Buckinghamshire, MK7 6AA, U.K.
paul.warren@cantab.net,
{paul.mulholland,trevor.collins,enrico.motta}@open.ac.uk

Abstract. Drawing on 118 responses to a survey of ontology use, this paper describes the experiences of those who create and use ontologies. Responses to questions about language and tool use illustrate the dominant position of OWL and provide information about the OWL profiles and particular Description Logic features used. The paper suggests that further research is required into the difficulties experienced with OWL constructs, and with modelling in OWL. The survey also reports on the use of ontology visualization software, finding that the importance of visualization to ontology users varies considerably. This is also an area which requires further investigation. The use of ontology patterns is examined, drawing on further input from a follow-up study devoted exclusively to this topic. Evidence suggests that pattern creation and use are frequently informal processes and there is a need for improved tools. A classification of ontology users into four groups is suggested. It is proposed that the categorisation of users and user behaviour should be taken into account when designing ontology tools and methodologies. This should enable rigorous, user-specific use cases.

Keywords: ontology use, ontology size, ontology visualization, ontology patterns, Description Logics, OWL profiles.

1   Introduction

In recent decades the use of ontologies has become widespread across a range of application areas. The Handbook on Ontologies (Staab & Studer, 2010) has chapters describing applications in bioinformatics, cultural heritage and recommender systems, besides knowledge management generally. As will be illustrated later, the use of Description Logics (DLs), specifically the variants of OWL, has become the dominant paradigm. With this has come an understanding of the computational properties of the various DLs and the development of efficient reasoners, e.g. see Möller and Haarslev (2009) and Motik (2009). This work has fed into tool development, e.g. the development of the Protégé ontology editor[1] and a variety of ontology visualization

---

[1] protégé.stanford.edu

K. Janowicz et al. (Eds.): EKAW 2014, LNAI 8876, pp. 579–590, 2014.

tools, e.g. see Katifori et al. (2007). During this time practitioners in particular domains have reported on their experience, e.g. Stevens et al. (2007). Others have undertaken relatively small scale studies of ontology users. For example, Vigo et al. (2014a) report on an interview study of 15 ontology authors and make a number of recommendations for improvement to ontology tool design. In follow-on work a Protégé plug-in has been used to harvest information about the authoring process and enable this process to be studied in detail, see Vigo et al. (2014b). This paper describes a survey which complements these kinds of studies by using a questionnaire to reach a large number of ontology users. The survey also complements the work of researchers who have analyzed actual ontologies. These include: Tempich and Volz (2003), whose goal was to create prototypical ontology corpora for bencharking; Power and Third (2010), who report on the usage of OWL language features; Khan and Blomqvist (2010), who were interested in the frequency of occurrence of content patterns from the ODP portal[2]; and Glimm et al. (2012), who investigated which OWL features were being used by the Linked Data community.

The remainder of this paper is organized as follows. Section 2 describes the survey, how it was conducted, and gives some information about the respondents. In section 3 we look at the various reasons for using ontologies. Section 4 discusses ontology languages and ontology tools. Section 5 discusses ontology size, using a variety of measures. Section 6 discusses the respondents' experiences with visualization tools and reports a range of attitudes to visualization. Section 7 discusses the use of ontology patterns and also reports on a subsequent survey specifically into pattern use. Section 8 then records some final comments from respondents, and section 9 draws some conclusions.

2   The Survey and the Respondents

The survey was conducted during the first three months of 2013 using the *Survey Expression*[3] tool. Responses were obtained using a number of contacts and relevant mailing lists. The latter included: the ontolog-forum[4], the U.K. Ontology Network[5], the Semantic Web for Life Sciences group and the Description Logic group on LinkedIn, lists maintained by the Open Knowledge Foundation[6], and the internal mailing list within the authors' university department. In all there were 118 respondents. In general, respondents only answered a subset of the questions. However, most questions resulted in several tens of responses. The survey aimed to improve the understanding of how ontology languages and tools are being used. The goal was to use this understanding to identify themes for future research into making ontology use more effective. In line with these aims and goal, the survey sought the respondents' views and experiences. In addition, factual information, e.g. about the size of ontologies, was sought in order to provide a context to help understand the other responses.

---

[2] http://ontologydesignpatterns.org/
[3] www.surveyexpression.com
[4] ontolog-forum@ontolog.cim3.net
[5] ontology-uk@googlegroups.com
[6] okfn-{en,Scotland,nl}@lists.okfn.org

Respondents were asked to categorize themselves by sector. 116 respondents provided this information, with the following distribution: academic (45%); from research institutes (25%); industrial (17%); and other (13%). They were also asked to give their primary application area. All 118 respondents provided this information and the distribution was: biomedical (31%), business (9%), engineering (19%), physical sciences (7%), social sciences (5%); and other (30%). The 'other' category included computer science and information technology and, to a lesser extent, humanities. 115 people responded to a question about the length of time they had worked with ontologies. 62% had over five years' experience and only 6% had less than one year. More detailed information is provided in Warren (2013).

3   Purposes

Respondents were asked for which purposes they used ontologies. There were eight options plus 'other'. Ignoring 'other', there were 332 responses from 72 respondents, representing an average of 4.6 responses per respondent. Table 1[7] shows the percentage breakdown and a two letter code which is used in the subsequent discussion.

Table 1. Purposes for using ontologies; percentages of 72 respondents

Code	Text in survey	percentages
CM	Conceptual modelling, e.g. formally defining a domain	72%
DI	Data integration, i.e. merging a number of databases	72%
SC	Defining knowledgebase schemas, e.g. as a means of storing and retrieving information	65%
LD	Linked data integration, e.g. linking data from different public knowledgebases	64%
KS	Knowledge sharing, e.g. between individuals in an organisation	56%
HD	Providing common access to heterogeneous data, i.e. providing a common schema for data access	56%
OS	Ontology-based search, i.e. using ontologies to refine search	50%
NL	Supporting natural language processing	26%

These categories were chosen to cover all likely purposes for which ontologies might be used, accepting that there would be some overlap between the categories. In fact, a correlation analysis revealed significant[8] positive correlations between all pairs from DI, KS, LD and SC, with two-sided p values ranging from 0.0006 for DI and SC to 0.0296 for DI and KS. The only other significant correlations were a positive correlation between DI and OS (p = 0.0356) and a negative correlation between HD and NL (p = 0.0496).

Maximal predictive clustering was also performed to categorize the 72 respondents to this question. This is a clustering technique suitable for binary data in which each cluster has a 'predictor' vector with components zero or one. The criterion to be

---

[7] Note that, because of the possibility of multiple responses, the percentages total to more than 100%. This is true of a number of other figures and tables in this paper.

[8] Throughout this paper 'significant' is taken to mean at the 95% level.

maximized is the total number of agreements between each group member and the group predictor. The criterion value was 432 for two clusters and stabilized at close to 500 for eight, nine and ten clusters[9]. A four group classification (criterion = 465) is discussed here because moving to five clusters only increased the criterion by four and led to a cluster with only five members.

The four categories of users were:

- *Conceptualizers:* 16 respondents with a predictor comprising only CM and with an average of 2.2 responses. Users in this category may be interested in using ontologies for modelling, rather than manipulating quantities of data. They might, e.g., be using reasoning to identify inconsistencies in a model.
- *Integrators:* 12 respondents with a predictor comprising DI, HD, LD, SC and with an average of 4.3 responses. These users may be more interested in integrating data from various sources, e.g. a variety of databases.
- *Searchers:* 11 respondents with a predictor comprising CM, LD, OS, SC and with an average of 3.9 responses. Like the integrators, this cluster's predictor includes LD and SC. However, whereas the integrators' predictor includes DI and HD, that for the searchers includes CM and OS. Searchers are more likely to be interested in ontological search, e.g. over the linked data cloud. None of the searchers expressed an interest in heterogeneous data.
- *Multipurpose Users:* 33 respondents with a predictor comprising all the response options except NL, and with an average number of responses of 6.2.

4   Languages and Tools

Of the 65 respondents to a question about which languages they used, 58 indicated OWL, 56 RDF and 45 RDFS. The other two predefined options, OIL and DAML+OIL received no responses. 11 indicated 'other', which included the Open Biological and Biomedical Ontology format[10], query languages, plus other more specialist languages.

The dominance of OWL was also indicated by the response to a question about which ontology editors are being used. Respondents were given a choice of 12 editors, plus 'other'. Multiple responses were permitted. 63 respondents replied to the question and figure 1 shows the tools for which there was more than one response, indicating the split between OWL and non-OWL. OBO-Edit and Neurolex were amongst the 'other' category; all the others shown were listed in the questionnaire.

When asked which OWL profiles were used, there were 133 responses from 56 respondents, indicating considerable multiple use of profiles. The range of responses is shown in figure 2. Respondents who used DLs were asked to indicate which DL features they used. The choice of features and the responses are shown in table 2. It is noteworthy that a number of people were using the more specialist features, e.g. the four object property characteristics at the bottom of the list (inverse functional, reflexive, asymmetric and irreflexive).

---

[9] When each point is in a cluster of one, then the maximum of 576 is achieved, i.e. eight responses x 72 respondents.

[10] http://www.obofoundry.org/

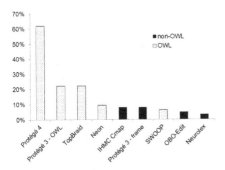

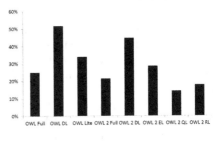

Fig. 1. Usage of ontology editors; percentage of 63 respondents

Fig. 2. Usage of OWL profiles; percentage of 56 respondents

Table 2. Usage of DL features; percentage of 47 respondents

object property domain	79%	hasValue restrictions	60%
object property range	77%	cardinality restrictions	51%
disjoint classes	74%	symmetric object property	51%
datatype properties	72%	functional datatype property	51%
intersection of classes	70%	datatype subproperties	49%
transitive object properties	68%	complement of a class	47%
object subproperties	68%	qualified cardinality restriction	43%
union of classes	66%	inverse functional object prop	36%
existential restrictions	66%	reflexive object property	30%
inverse object properties	64%	asymmetric object property	26%
functional object properties	64%	irreflexive object property	17%
universal restrictions	60%		

Respondents made a number of specific suggestions for language extensions. There were also general comments, e.g. the difficulty of design decisions such as classes versus individuals and classes versus properties; and the difficulty of grasping the implications of open world reasoning – one respondent commented that it would be "great if OWL semantics would (partially) support closed world reasoning". Another comment seemed to relate to the difficulty of rigorous modelling, stating that it was not always possible to characterize "strongly semantically".

Amongst the comments on the state of ontology editors were a number referring to the need for the kind of functionality normally found in other system development tools, e.g. auto-completion, version control, and distributed development features. One respondent noted the need for different tools for domain experts and for those "formalizing the ontology". Another commented that "Protégé is not suitable for working together with domain experts".

5   Ontologies and Ontology Sizes

Respondents were asked to list their most commonly used ontologies, to a maximum of five. 69 people responded and the most common responses were: Dublin Core (49% of respondents), FOAF (29%), Dbpedia (19%), the Gene Ontology (17%) and SKOS (16%). After this came a category comprising the respondents' own ontologies (14%).

For their most commonly used ontologies, they were then asked about the size of those parts of the ontologies with which they actually worked. Specifically, they were asked for the number of classes, individuals, properties, top-level classes and the depth of the hierarchy. This led to 125 responses from 40 respondents. Figure 3 illustrates the enormous range in the size of the ontologies with which respondents were working. Note that the distribution of the number of individuals has a particularly long tail, as to a lesser extent does that for the number of classes.

Many of the ontologies with a very large number of classes were in the biomedical domain. For example, the response in the range '1,000,001 to 3 million' represented the set of ontologies known as the Open Biomedical Ontologies (OBO)[11], which include the Gene Ontology. SNOMED-CT[12] was one of the responses in the range 300,001 to 1 million. Many of the ontologies of depth greater than ten were also in the biomedical domain. They include, for example, the OBO ontologies. Outside the biomedical domain, CYC[13] was an example of an ontology with depth more than ten.

Analysis indicated that the maximum depth of ontology[14] for the conceptualizers was significantly less than for the other three categories combined ($p = 0.020$, based on a Kruskal-Wallis one-way analysis of variance test). The maximum number of classes was also significantly fewer for the conceptualizers ($p = 0.040$). However, there was no significant difference for the maximum number of properties ($p = 0.083$), individuals ($p = 0.134$), and top-level classes ($p = 0.730$).

A Spearman's rank correlation applied to each pair from the dimensions: number of classes, properties, top-level classes and depth (i.e. excluding number of individuals) showed a high degree of positive correlation; the highest p-value was 0.007 (depth versus number of top classes). The number of individuals, on the other hand, was only significantly correlated with the number of properties ($p < 0.001$).

This suggests that the data can be represented by two dimensions; the number of individuals and some representative of the other four dimensions. Figure 4 shows a plot of the number of individuals versus the number of classes. The most striking feature of the plot is the empty area at the bottom right. The ontologies can be regarded as comprising two groups. In one group the number of individuals is greater than ten and in the majority of cases greater than the number of classes. In the other group the number of individuals is in the smallest category of zero to ten, whilst the number of classes occupies a wide range.

---

[11] http://www.obofoundry.org

[12] See http://www.ihtsdo.org/

[13] http://www.cyc.com/

[14] I.e. from the up to 5 ontologies which each respondent was able to describe.

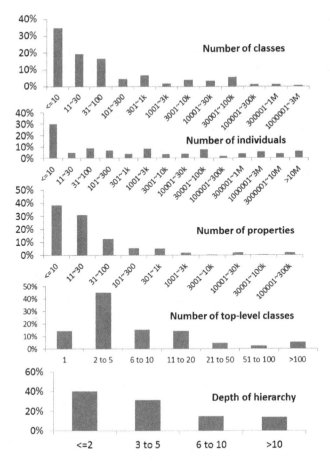

Fig. 3. Ontology size; showing percentage of responses in each size category

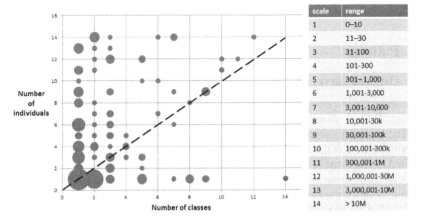

Fig. 4. Number of individuals versus number of classes; bubble size represents number of points; dashed line represents equal number of classes and individuals

6   Visualization

Respondents were asked which ontology visualization tools they used. Figure 5 shows all those tools for which there was more than one response and indicates which of these tools are incorporated into Protégé. Figure 6 gives the percentage break-down between the various alternative answers to the question 'how useful do you find visualization?', demonstrating a wide range of views. No significant relationship could be discerned between the perceived usefulness of visualization and the size of ontologies being used. However, the ability of each respondent to describe up to five ontologies makes this analysis difficult. A Kruskal-Wallis test revealed no signifi-cant difference in the attitudes of the four categories of users (p = 0.818).

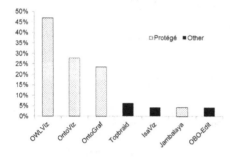

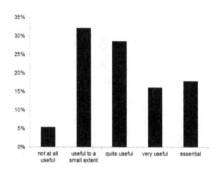

Fig. 5. Usage of ontology visualization tools; percentage of 47 respondents

Fig. 6. Perceived usefulness of visualization; percentage of 56 respondents

One respondent wanted to be able to visualize "schema with huge amounts of in-stance data in order to analyze the effects of changes in real time". Another respon-dent noted that "visualization is, especially for the end-user, really hard and not task-specific". This echoes comments in other fields, e.g. see Maletic et (2002) al. discuss-ing visualization in software engineering.

7   Patterns

7.1   Original Survey

There were 35 responses to a question asking from where ontology patterns were obtained. Table 3 shows the percentage of respondents indicating each of the catego-ries. The category 'other' included the OBO library, see section 5, and the W3C. One point of note is the bias in the biomedical community not to use the generic libra-ries cited or the Protégé wizard. Of the 14 responses from nine people in the biomedi-cal community, none were for the Protégé wizard and one each, from the same res-pondent, were for the two libraries. A Pearson χ^2 test revealed that this was significant (p = 0.039). One biomedical researcher noted "usually I do generate patterns myself". Respondents were also asked why they used patterns; table 4 shows the response to this question.

Table 3. Sources of ontology patterns; 35 respondents; 61 responses; %age respondents

Own mental models	46%	ODP public catalogue [15]	17%
Own or colleagues' collections	37%	Protege wizard	14%
ODP Portal (OntologyDesignPatterns.org)	34%	Other	26%

Table 4. Reasons for using patterns; 33 respondents; 113 responses; %age respondents

Enforce consistency	61%	Reduce modelling mistakes	52%
Make ontology development easier	61%	Speed up ontology development	42%
Encourage best practice	55%	Restrict language features	9%
Make more comprehensible	55%	Other	9%

Of the 32 respondents to a question about the use of tools for creating, editing and using patterns, 20 used no tools "other than standard ontology editing tools". Five of the respondents used the patterns plug-in to Protégé 4 and the remainder used a variety of tools, some specifically developed for ontologies, others generic. Respondents were also asked how they used patterns, specifically whether they imported patterns or recreated them, possibly modified. The great majority (20) indicated only the latter of these two options, five indicated only the former and four indicated both. There were five responses in the 'other' category, including "fully integrated into the tool" and the use of templates. The answers to these two questions indicate the informal way in which patterns are created and used.

Respondents were asked for general comments on their experience with using patterns. One respondent commented that the "best patterns are rather simple, not very complex, basic". A researcher in the biomedical domain expressed the view that there are "seldom some available patterns out there for us to use". This may be because the required patterns are frequently domain-specific rather than generic. Another respondent called for better tool support, stating that "tools should suggest suitable patterns". One comment was about the difficulty of understanding patterns: "initially hard to learn, but provide required functionalities"; this suggests the need for better ways of representing patterns in human-readable form.

7.2   Follow-On Patterns Survey

A smaller survey was subsequently undertaken specifically to investigate the use of ontology patterns. The survey was broadcast on the same mailing lists as the original survey, and also to some of the respondents to the original survey who expressed an interest in ontology patterns. 13 respondents provided information. A detailed report on the survey results is provided by Warren (2014).

Respondents were asked how they used patterns. Table 5 shows the options and the percentage of respondents indicating each option. Pattern tools being used were: Extreme Design (XD) Tools, see Presutti et al. (2009) and Blomqvist et al. (2010);

---

[15] http://www.gong.manchester.ac.uk/odp/html

Tawny OWL, see Lord (2013); Excel and XSLT; and an own unpublished tool. Respondents were asked how they identified the need for a pattern, with the options "by noticing repeated use of identical or similar structures" and "by systematically analyzing the ontologies I work with, e.g. using a tool". Of the 13 responses there were ten in the first category, two in the second and one who indicated both.

Table 5. Pattern usage; 13 respondents; 19 responses; %age respondents

Use patterns as examples and recreate modified	54%
Import patterns, e.g. as OWL files	46%
Use patterns as examples and recreate unmodified	31%
Generate with a tool specifically designed for pattern creation	31%

Table 6. Creating and storing patterns; 13 respondents; 21 responses

Diagrammatically	54%
Using an ontology editor and storing as, e.g. OWL files	31%
Not written down, from memory	23%
Using a formal language, e.g. MOS, in a text editor	15%
Using an informal language, e.g. English	15%
Other ("own UI to own DBMS", "XSLT source", "to application instance data")	23%

Table 6 shows the response to the question "how do you create and store patterns?" The most striking feature is that over half make use of diagrams. The two respondents from the biomedical domain both used formal languages, but no other technique, whilst none of the other eleven respondents used formal languages. Respondents were asked about the problems they experienced using patterns. Two noted the need for documentation and examples. Other comments included the difficulties of finding the right pattern, and of pattern generation and integration with existing ontologies. One respondent noted that when ontologies are imported, information about patterns is not available. Taken with another comment about the complexity of visualization when several patterns are used simultaneously, this suggests that it would be useful to have editor facilities for viewing patterns embedded in an ontology.

8   Final Comments from Respondents

At the end of the ontology user survey respondents were asked for any final comments on their experiences with using ontologies. A number of the resultant comments related to the difficulty of modeling with ontologies. One referred to the difficulty of designing classes, which had taken the respondent "many years of learning". Another, working in the biomedical domain, called for a more mature discipline of ontology design: "Ontologies should be built towards use cases and answering biological questions and this is not always the case. Engineering practices in the domain are rarely applied and immature." Related to the point already made about the need for different tools for ontology specialists and domain experts, one respondent noted "...tool support for non-experts working with ontologies / knowledgebases is generally poor". On the positive side, one respondent commented on the experience of using ontologies: "I couldn't build what I build without them".

9   Conclusions

The survey indicates a number of areas for research. The dominance of OWL suggests the importance of research to improve the understandability of OWL constructs. In a follow-up interview, one of the respondents noted that for the ontologist a significant problem is the difficulty of understanding the reason for incorrect entailments. For work on the understandability of OWL entailments see, e.g. Horridge et al. (2011), Nguyen et al. (2012) and Warren et al. (2014).

In the same follow-up interview, the respondent identified the major problem for domain specialists as that of searching and navigating the ontology. One approach to the latter is through visualization. It is clear from the data shown in figure 6 that there is a widely varying appreciation of visualization. Understanding when and for which users visualization works and doesn't work is another important research goal.

Some respondents found modelling difficult, e.g. because of the Open World Assumption. A better understanding of the difficulties could lead to the use of alternative language constructs, e.g. constructs which achieve closure, like the *onlysome* macro described in Horridge et al. (2006).

Section 7 suggested that there is a lack of appropriate methodology and tools for creating and using patterns. Research is needed into the current practices and requirements of users, particularly domain experts outside computing science.

In future research, and in tool development, there needs to be more awareness of the specific targeted end-users and of their goals in using ontologies. The importance of distinguishing between ontology specialists and domain experts has already been made. From the data in our survey we have also suggested a split into four categories of user. We do not propose this as the last word in user categorization. Indeed, it should be viewed as part of a tradition of user and application categorization, starting with the generic categorization of Uschold and Jasper (1999) and continuing with the categorizations specific to biology and medicine made by Shah and Musen (2009) and by Stevens and Lord (2009). Our point is that future developments need to be built on a better understanding of the specific requirements of different user groups. As part of this, precisely defined use cases need to be created. This will support development and lead to more precise criteria by which to evaluate tools and methodologies.

References

1. Blomqvist, E., Presutti, V., Daga, E., Gangemi, A.: Experimenting with eXtreme design. Knowledge Engineering and Management by the Masses, 120–134 (2010)
2. Glimm, B., Hogan, A., Krötzsch, M., Polleres, A.: OWL: Yet to arrive on the Web of Data? (2012)
3. Horridge, M., Bail, S., Parsia, B., Sattler, U.: The cognitive complexity of OWL justifications. In: Aroyo, L., Welty, C., Alani, H., Taylor, J., Bernstein, A., Kagal, L., Noy, N., Blomqvist, E. (eds.) ISWC 2011, Part I. LNCS, vol. 7031, pp. 241–256. Springer, Heidelberg (2011)

4. Horridge, M., Drummond, N., Goodwin, J., Rector, A., Stevens, R., Wang, H.H.: The manchester owl syntax. In: OWL: Experiences and Directions, pp. 10–11 (2006)

5. Katifori, A., Halatsis, C., Lepouras, G., Vassilakis, C., Giannopoulou, E.: Ontology visualization methods—a survey. ACM Computing Surveys (CSUR) 39(4), 10 (2007)

6. Khan, M.T., Blomqvist, E.: Ontology design pattern detection-initial method and usage scenarios. In: SEMAPRO 2010, The Fourth International Conference on Advances in Semantic Processing, pp. 19–24 (2010)

7. Lord, P.: The Semantic Web takes Wing: Programming Ontologies with Tawny-OWL. arXiv Preprint arXiv:1303.0213 (2013), http://arxiv.org/abs/1303.0213

8. Maletic, J.I., Marcus, A., Collard, M.L.: A task oriented view of software visualization. In: Proceedings of the First International Workshop on Visualizing Software for Understanding and Analysis, pp. 32–40. IEEE (2002)

9. Möller, R., Haarslev, V.: Tableau-based reasoning. In: Handbook on Ontologies, pp. 509–528. Springer (2009)

10. Motik, B.: Resolution-Based Reasoning for Ontologies. In: Handbook on Ontologies, pp. 529–550. Springer (2009)

11. Nguyen, Power, Piwek, Williams: Measuring the understandability of deduction rules for OWL. In: Presented at the First International Workshop on Debugging Ontologies and Ontology Mappings, Galway, Ireland (2012), http://oro.open.ac.uk/34591/

12. Power, R., Third, A.: Expressing OWL axioms by English sentences: dubious in theory, feasible in practice. In: Proceedings of the 23rd International Conference on Computational Linguistics: Posters, pp. 1006–1013 (2010)

13. Presutti, V., Daga, E., Gangemi, A., Blomqvist, E.: eXtreme design with content ontology design patterns. In: Proc. Workshop on Ontology Patterns, Washington, DC, USA (2009)

14. Shah, N., Musen, M.: Ontologies for formal representation of biological systems. In: Handbook on Ontologies, pp. 445–461. Springer (2009)

15. Staab, S., Studer, R.: Handbook on ontologies. Springer (2010)

16. Stevens, R., Egaña Aranguren, M., Wolstencroft, K., Sattler, U., Drummond, N., Horridge, M., Rector, A.: Using OWL to model biological knowledge. International Journal of Human-Computer Studies 65(7), 583–594 (2007)

17. Stevens, R., Lord, P.: Application of ontologies in bioinformatics. In: Handbook on Ontologies, pp. 735–756. Springer (2009)

18. Tempich, C., Volz, R.: Towards a benchmark for Semantic Web reasoners-an analysis of the DAML ontology library. In: EON, vol. 87 (2003)

19. Uschold, M., Jasper, R.: A framework for understanding and classifying ontology applications. In: Proceedings of the IJCAI-99 Workshop on Ontologies and Problem-Solving Methods (KRR5), Stockholm, Sweden (1999)

20. Vigo, M., Jay, C., Stevens, R.: Design insights for the next wave ontology authoring tools. Presented at the ACM SIGCHI Conference on Human Factors in Computing Systems, CHI 2014. ACM Press, Toronto (2014)

21. Vigo, M., Jay, C., Stevens, R.: Protege4US: harvesting ontology authoring data with Protege. In: HSWI 2014 - Human Semantic Web Interaction Workshop, Crete (2014)

22. Warren, P.: Ontology Users' Survey - Summary of Results (KMi Tech Report No. kmi-13-01) (2013), http://kmi.open.ac.uk/publications/pdf/kmi-13-01.pdf

23. Warren, P.: Ontology patterns: a survey into their use (KMi Tech Report No. kmi-14-02) (2014), http://kmi.open.ac.uk/publications/pdf/kmi-14-02.pdf

24. Warren, P., Mulholland, P., Collins, T., Motta, E.: The Usability of Description Logics. In: Presutti, V., d'Amato, C., Gandon, F., d'Aquin, M., Staab, S., Tordai, A. (eds.) ESWC 2014. LNCS, vol. 8465, pp. 550–564. Springer, Heidelberg (2014)

A Conceptual Model for Detecting Interactions among Medical Recommendations in Clinical Guidelines

A Case-Study on Multimorbidity

Veruska Zamborlini[1,2,*], Rinke Hoekstra[1,3], Marcos da Silveira[2],
Cédric Pruski[2], Annette ten Teije[1], and Frank van Harmelen[1]

[1] Dept. of Computer Science, VU University Amsterdam, The Netherlands
{v.carrettazamborlini,rinke.hoekstra,
a.c.m.ten.teije,f.a.h.van.harmelen}@vu.nl
[2] Public Research Centre Henri Tudor, Luxembourg
{marcos.dasilveira,cedric.pruski}@tudor.lu
[3] Faculty of Law, University of Amsterdam, The Netherlands

Abstract. Representation of clinical knowledge is still an open research topic. In particular, classical languages designed for representing clinical guidelines, which were meant for producing diagnostic and treatment plans, present limitations such as for re-using, combining, and reasoning over existing knowledge. In this paper, we address such limitations by proposing an extension of the TMR conceptual model to represent clinical guidelines that allows re-using and combining knowledge from several guidelines to be applied to patients with multimorbidities. We provide means to (semi)automatically detect interactions among recommendations that require some attention from experts, such as recommending more than once the same drug. We evaluate the model by applying it to a realistic case study involving 3 diseases (Osteoarthritis, Hypertension and Diabetes) and compare the results with two other existing methods.

Keywords: Clinical knowledge representation, Reasoning, Combining medical guidelines, Multimorbidity.

1 Introduction

Clinical guidelines (CGs) are documents that support health care professionals in patient diagnosis and treatment plan design. Computer Interpretable Guidelines (CIGs) are formal representations of CGs, intended to increase flexibility over paper based CGs, to minimize errors and to generalize the use of guidelines across institutions. CIGs are expressed in dedicated languages such as GLIF [1], Asbru [5] or PROforma [7]. They are mainly designed to promote the execution of

* Funded by CNPq (Brazilian National Council for Scientific and Technological Development) within the program Science without Borders.

K. Janowicz et al. (Eds.): EKAW 2014, LNAI 8876, pp. 591–606, 2014.

CIGs, i.e. to apply them to patient data for supporting diagnostics or treatment plans.

Unfortunately, these CIG languages are not flexible enough to support cases where (parts of) multiple guidelines need to be combined to handle situations where a patient suffers from several diseases, called *multimorbidity*. For instance, Aspirin is recommended as anti-platelets to patients diagnosed with Transient Ischemic Attack. On the other hand, Aspirin is not recommended (admonished) for Duodenal Ulcer patients to avoid increasing the risk of bleeding. Existing CIG-based approaches CIGs fail to detect such conflicts automatically [3,4].

In previous work [8], we introduced a conceptual model (TMR - Transition-based Medical Recommendations) that increases the reasoning capabilities of CIGs. The model relies on a refined definition of the notions of *recommendation*, *transition*, *care action type* and *situation type*. TMR paves the way towards an automatic identification of potential conflicts or interactions that can happen when merging guidelines, but it requires additional features to fully automatize the identification process. In this paper we provide an extension of the TMR model, called TMR4I, that allows automatic detection of *interactions* among recommendations that require some attention from experts, such as recommending more than once the same drug. We evaluate our model by applying it on a realistic case study that involves three guidelines concerning Osteoarthritis (OA), Hypertension (HT) and Diabetes (DB). We further show the added value of our model by comparing to existing approaches [3,4].

The remainder of this paper is structured as follows: Section 2 discusses related work. Section 3 introduces the preliminaries, including the concepts of the TMR model that underlie TMR4I. Section 4 presents the TMR4I extension. Section 5 describes our case study for multimorbidity. Section 6 discusses the results and outlines future work.

2   Related Work

Different CIG description languages were proposed to represent clinical knowledge (PROforma [7], GLIF [1], Asbru [5], etc.). Since the main focus of these languages was set on guideline execution, they have some limitations mainly related to the interoperability (CIG cannot be mixed), semantics (free text is often used to describe conditions and actions) and reasoning capabilities (e.g., the inference of new actions or restrictions is not supported) [2,6].

The increasing demand for clinical decision support systems (CDSS) that assist healthcare professional to define treatments for multimorbid patients highlights the limitations of classical CIG languages and indicates the necessity for new formalisms or for adapting existing ones. In [8], we have reviewed existing approaches for merging treatments plans or guidelines and we categorized them into: (i) guideline-level verification, (ii) on-prescription verification, (iii) after-prescription verification and (iv) on-treatment-execution verification. As re-usability is one of our major concerns, we focused on approaches of the first category. In this paper we are particularly interested in approaches addressing the multimorbidity problem which consists of combining recommendations regarding more than *two* diseases taken from their respective guidelines. In this context, the works done by Jafarpour [3] and Lopez-Vallverdu et.al [4] stand out.

Lopez-Vallverdu's approach [4] relies on *Rules* and *Actions* that regards administration of drugs, and adopts a standard terminology called ATC (Anatomical Therapeutic Chemical Classification System for drugs[1]). Therefore, using knowledge available in clinical guidelines, they manually built "knowledge units" for pairwise combination of three diseases: Hypertension, Diabetes Mellitus and Heart Failure. Those knowledge units regards the co-existence of incompatible drugs (drug-drug interaction), the existence of a drug incompatible to a disease (drug-disease interaction) and the absence of a drug necessary for a combination of diseases. Based on these units, they manually built a minimal set of combination rules in the format *pre-condition : condition → action*, where the first one regards the diseases, the second regards the presence or absence of drug recommendations for each disease, and the latter regards recommendations for adding, removing or replacing drugs. Although it is not clear from the knowledge format whether it is limited to two diseases, the strategy adopted by the authors for addressing the three aforementioned diseases is by pairwise combining them. Moreover, the manual identification of the interactions and their solutions is in itself a limiting factor for combining multiple diseases. Their approach is implemented in a proprietary system for combining treatments.

Jafarpour's approach [3] defines both (i) a OWL+SWRL based formalism for representing and executing CIGs (CPG-DKO) and (i) an OWL+SWRL based formalism for combining two CIGs. The latter defines *Constraints* (rules) as entities that relates pairs of interacting *Tasks* (actions). Therefore, for each pair of CIGs the potential conflicts or interactions are manually represented, together to their solution, by instantiating different types of constraints, for instance avoid repeating tasks, reusing test results, defining time-constraints or replacing tasks. This approach is then limited to pairwise combination of tasks within two CIGs, although several CIGs can be executed together. They apply their approach in a number of case studies, including one for combining OA+HT+DB. Section 5 presents more details about this approach.

Although both approaches introduce features for expressing the interactions and their solutions, both formalisms are still not expressive enough to support the automatic detection of inconsistencies like having "*administer insulin*" and "*avoid administering insulin*" since both rely on a textual expression of the care actions and the features linked to it. They assume that all potential inconsistencies are manually detected by domain experts and rules are created to deal with them, often introducing new recommendations to address the conflict. Moreover, the introduction of new recommendations requires further verification to check for eventual new conflicts that could arise. If all potential conflicts need to be solved by adding rules, it may lead to a combinatorial explosion of rules. This in turn, increases the complexity of detecting conflicting rules; especially if the verification is done manually by experts. Jafarpour defines SWRL rules that

---

[1] http://www.whocc.no/atc/

allow automatically detecting specific time/priority-related conflicts between pairs of the introduced constraints, but does not address other types of conflicts and does not find eventual conflicts with existing tasks. Finally, both approaches gather the knowledge they created for the pairwise combined CIGs in order to address the combination of more than two CIGs. For example, the constraints created between OA+HT, OA+DB and HT+DB are gathered to address the combination of the three CIGs OA+HT+DB. However, this strategy is limited since it does not cover for instance a constraint from OA+HT whose solution conflict with recommendations from DB. They cope with comorbidity but are problematic in case of multimorbidity.

As illustrated in this section, existing works are not tailored to our objective of increasing the reasoning capability of CIGs to handle multimorbidity. We aim to define a method that allows evaluating set of recommendations and deriving certain types of interactions requiring little or no human intervention (e.g. rules manually created). The TMR model (proposed in [8], overviewed in Sect 3), supports this goal by enriching the description of actions (with the pre-conditions and the potential consequences) and separating actions from recommendation statements (pursue or avoid an action). Section 6 presents a summarized comparison among the related works and our approach.

3   Overview of the TMR Model

This section briefly summarizes a slightly extended version of the TMR model, originally presented in [8] where we investigated the core concepts required for representing recommendations within CGs. Figure 1 shows a UML diagram of the TMR model. The concepts and relations presented as they were in the original version are depicted in gray shade to differ from the the new concepts and relations changed or introduced in this work. Those that have a slash sign before their names are further defined by FOL formulas (e.g. /similarTo). We consider the concepts as being atomic, since its compositionality is out of scope of this work.

- A **Guideline** is an aggregation of Recommendations, whilst the latter is **part of** one Guideline. It can be a **Single Disease Guideline**, or it can be a **Composed Guideline**, which is **derived from** the combination of two or more Guidelines.
- A **Recommendation** either **recommends to pursue** or **recommends to avoid** (originally *recommends* and *non-recommends*) one **Transition**.
- A **Transition** is **promoted by** a single **Care Action Type**, which in turn can promote one or more Transitions. A Transition can be **similar to** or **inverse to** another one (definition is further provided).
- **Situation Types** can be **Pre or Post-Situation Types** in the context of different Transitions.
- Every **Transition** have:
  - one **Transformable Situation Type** through the relation **has transformable situation**,

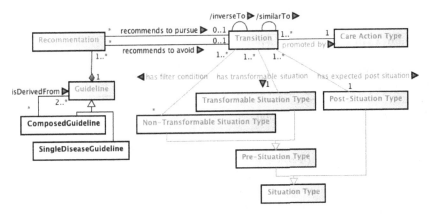

Fig. 1. UML class diagram for the TMR Model

- one expected Post-Situation Type through the relation **has expected post situation**, and
- zero or more **Non-Transformable Situation Types** through the relation **have as filter condition**.

For example, Table 1 presents the recommendation *"If the patient's temperature is over 37 degrees and he/she is over 10 years old then reduce the temperature by administering aspirin"* decomposed into the TMR concepts.

We introduce the binary relations /**similarTo** and /**inverseTo** between Transitions, which are required for detecting Interactions. In this work we consider a simple approach of comparing equality among Pre and Post-Situation Types, though these definitions would benefit from a richer definition of Situation Types and possible matches among them. Therefore, similar transitions (def. 1.1) are those whose Pre-Situation Types are the same, as well as the Post-Situation Types, but that are promoted by different Care Action Types (otherwise they are the same transition). Two transitions are inverse (def. 2.1) if the Pre-Situation Type of one is equal to the Post-Situation Type of the other. Both relations *similarTo* and *inverseTo* are symmetric (def. 1.2 and 2.2).

(1.1) $\forall t1, t2, sa, sb, ca1, ca2$ Transition(t1) $\wedge$ Transition(t2) $\wedge$ CareActionType(ca1)
$\wedge$ CareActionType(ca2) $\wedge$ promotedBy(t1,ca1) $\wedge$ promotedBy(t2,ca2)
$\wedge$ **ca1 $\neq$ ca2** $\wedge$ SituationType(sa) $\wedge$ SituationType(sb)
$\wedge$ hasTransformableSituation(t1,sa) $\wedge$ hasTransformableSituation(t2,sa)
$\wedge$ hasExpectedSituation(t1,sb) $\wedge$ hasExpectedSituation(t2,sb)
$\leftrightarrow$ **similarTo(t1,t2)**

(1.2) $\forall t1, t2$ similarTo(t1,t2) $\leftrightarrow$ similarTo(t2,t1)

(2.1) $\forall t1, t2, sa, sb$ Transition(t1) $\wedge$ Transition(t2)
$\wedge$ SituationType(sa) $\wedge$ SituationType(sb)
$\wedge$ hasTransformableSituation(t1,sa) $\wedge$ hasTransformableSituation(t2,sb)
$\wedge$ hasExpectedSituation(t1,sb) $\wedge$ hasExpectedSituation(t2,sa)
$\leftrightarrow$ **inverseTo(t1,t2)**

(2.2) $\forall t1, t2$ inverseTo(t1,t2) $\leftrightarrow$ inverseTo(t2,t1)

Table 1. TMR Concepts Summary

Situation Type	Represents a property and its admissible values	
Transformable Situation Type	Regards the situation that is expected to be changed	*Patient's temperature is over 37 degrees*
Non-Transformable Situation Type	Regards the situation that holds as filter condition	*Patient's age is over 10 years old*
Post-Situation Type	Regards the situation that is expected to be achieved	*Patient's temperature is below 37 degrees*
Care Action Type	Represents the action types that can be performed by health care agents in order to change a situation.	*Administer aspirin*
Transition	Represents the possibility of changing a situation regarding a patient by performing a care action type.	*Administering aspirin in patient over 10 years old reduces its temperature below 37 degrees*
Recommendation	Represents a suggestion to either pursue or avoid a transition promoted by a care action type **(in order to achieve a goal)**.	

In [8] we illustrated the applicability of TMR by describing the possible interactions among recommendations. These interactions can be *contradictory*, *optimizable* or reflect *alternative* recommendations (redefined in Sect. 4). We advocated that the TMR concepts favor the detection of such interactions, which may require some attention from experts when combining CGs due to comorbidity. Moreover, we considered not all interactions are unwelcome (e.g. the recommendations to inverse transitions may be desirable and the alternative ones are useful to avoid conflicts) although they could still require attention (e.g. defining which alternative recommendation is preferred). In the following section we extend the TMR model for the specific task of representing and detecting interactions among recommendations.

4   The TMR4I Model

The TMR4I (Transition-based Medical Recommendations for [detecting] Interactions) model is meant for detecting interactions among recommendations when addressing multimobidity cases. In this cases more than one disease, originally addressed in different CIGs, need to be taken into account. Therefore, the recommendations combined from the different CIGs may interact, e.g. presenting inconsistencies or being susceptible to optimization. The main concept in TMR4I is the *interaction*, which can be *internal*, among the recommendations themselves, or with some *external* knowledge base holding e.g. patient data (allergy information) or clinical knowledge (e.g. overdose). In this paper we focus on the internal interactions, as described in Table 2. Moreover, since the temporal/sequence aspects are still not addressed in this work, the interactions here defined are considered either time-independent or simultaneous.

Figure 2 illustrates in a graphical notation the interactions discussed in Table 2. We depict the three main types of Interactions, **Repetition, Contradiction** and **Alternative Interactions** as the initial letters followed by an exclamation mark connected to the interacting recommendations. An arrow that connects a Recommendation to a Transition means that the latter is recommended to be pursued, while an arrow ending with a cross means that the Transition is recommended to be avoided. Another dotted arrow connecting a Care Action Type to a Transition means that the latter is promoted by the former. Finally a Transition is connected to Pre and Post-Situation Types respectively at its left and right hand sides. For example, the third interaction (from top to bottom) is a Repetition Interaction among three recommendations for different Transitions promoted by *Administer Aspirin*.

Table 2. Interactions Summary

Contradiction Interactions	two recommendations that would lead to a conflict if recommended together (i.e. they cannot be both followed at the same time)
Opposed recommendations to the same care action	- *Do not administer aspirin to avoid increasing the risk of gastrointestinal bleeding* - *Administer aspirin to handle inflammation*
Opposed recommendations to similar transitions	- *Do not adm. beta-blockers to avoid lowering blood pressure* - *Administer ACE inhibitor to lower blood pressure*
Recommendations to inverse transitions	- *Administer ACE inhibitor to lower blood pressure* - *Administer midodrine to increase blood pressure*
Repetition Interactions	set of recommendations that are susceptible to optimization
Repeated recommendations to the same care action	- *Administer aspirin to reduce the risk of thrombus* - *Administer aspirin to relief pain* - *Administer aspirin to handle inflammation*
Alternative Interactions	set of recommendations that hold as alternatives.
Repeated recommendations to the similar transitions promoted by different care action	- *Administer aspirin to handle inflammation* - *Administer ibuprofen to handle inflammation* - *Administer naproxen to handle inflammation*
Non-recommended transition whose inverse transition is recommended	- *Do not administer aspirin to avoid increasing the risk of gastrointestinal bleeding* - *Adm PPI to decrease risk of gastrointestinal bleeding*

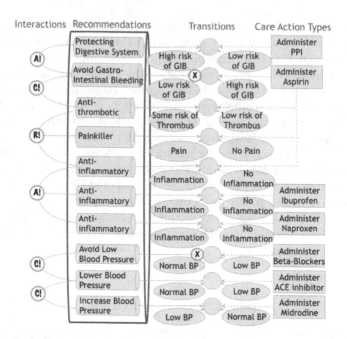

Fig. 2. Instance-schema for illustrating interactions among recommendations

Figure 3 presents an UML class diagram for the TMR4I model. Elements presented in a gray-shade mean they were previously introduced. The concept Recommendation is specialized into /**Internally Interacting Recommendation** (def. 3) to denote the ones that interacts with other recommendations.

(3) $\forall r, \exists i$ Recommendation(r) $\wedge$ InternalRecommendationInteraction(i)
    $\wedge$ relates(i,r) $\leftrightarrow$ **InternallyInteractingRecommendation(r)**

The interaction relation is reified as /**Internal Recommendation Interaction** and /**relates** two or more Recommendations in the context of a Guideline. The latter concept is specialized according to the classifications discussed in Table 2. They are further described and defined according FOL rules (def. 4 to 9).

Repetition due to Same Action: when Transitions promoted by a same Care Action Type are recommended to be pursued (def. 4.1). This interaction is cumulative within a CIG, i.e. if a recommendation is related to two interactions of this type, they are the same interaction (def. 4.2)

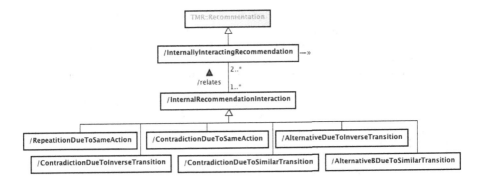

Fig. 3. UML class diagram for the TMR4I Model

(4.1) $\forall g, r1, r2, t1, t2, ca$ Guideline(g) $\wedge$ Recommendation(r1) $\wedge$ Recommendation(r2)
   $\wedge$ partOf(r1,g) $\wedge$ partOf(r2,g) $\wedge$ Transition(t1) $\wedge$ Transition(t2) $\wedge$ **r1 $\neq$ r2**
   $\wedge$ **recommendsToPursue(r1,t1)** $\wedge$ **recommendsToPursue(r2,t2)**
   $\wedge$ **CareActionType(ca)** $\wedge$ **promotedBy(t1,ca)** $\wedge$ **promotedBy(t2,ca)**
   $\rightarrow \exists i$ **RepetitionDueToSameAction(i)** $\wedge$ relates(i,r1) $\wedge$ relates(i,r2)

(4.2) $\forall i1, i2, r1, r2, r3$ **RepetitionDueToSameAction(i1)**
   $\wedge$ **RepetitionDueToSameAction(i2)** $\wedge$ Recommendation(r1)
   $\wedge$ Recommendation(r2) $\wedge$ Recommendation(r3) $\wedge$ r1 $\neq$ r3
   $\wedge$ relates(i1,r1) $\wedge$ relates(i1,r2) $\wedge$ relates(i2,r2) $\wedge$ relates(i2,r3)
   $\rightarrow$ **i1 = i2**

Contradiction due to Inverse Transitions: when two inverse Transitions are (simultaneously) recommended to be pursued (def. 5);

(5) $\forall g, r1, r2, t1, t2$ Guideline(g) $\wedge$ Recommendation(r1) $\wedge$ Recommendation(r2)
   $\wedge$ partOf(r1,g) $\wedge$ partOf(r2,g) $\wedge$ Transition(t1) $\wedge$ Transition(t2)
   $\wedge$ **recommendstoPursue(r1,t1)** $\wedge$ **recommendstoPursue(r2,t2)**
   $\wedge$ **inverseTo(t1, t2)**
   $\rightarrow \exists i$ **ContradictionDueToInverseTransition(i)** $\wedge$ relates(i,r1) $\wedge$ relates(i,r2)

Contradictory Interaction due to Same Action: when two Transitions promoted by the same Care Actions Type are are recommended to be pursued and the other recommended to be avoided (def. 6);

(6) $\forall g, r1, r2, t1, t2, ca$ Guideline(g) $\wedge$ Recommendation(r1) $\wedge$ Recommendation(r2)
   $\wedge$ partOf(r1,g) $\wedge$ partOf(r2,g) $\wedge$ Transition(t1) $\wedge$ Transition(t2) $\wedge$ **r1 $\neq$ r2**
   $\wedge$ **recommendsToPursue(r1,t1)** $\wedge$ **recommendsToAvoid(r2,t2)**
   $\wedge$ **CareActionType(ca)** $\wedge$ **promotedBy(t1,ca)** $\wedge$ **promotedBy(t2,ca)**
   $\rightarrow \exists i$ **ContradictionDueToSameAction(i)** $\wedge$ relates(i,r1) $\wedge$ relates(i,r2)

Contradictory Interaction due to Similar Transitions: when two similar Transitions are one recommended to be pursued and the other recommended to be avoided (def. 7);

(7) $\forall g, r1, r2, t1, t2$ Guideline(g) $\wedge$ Recommendation(r1) $\wedge$ Recommendation(r2)
  $\wedge$ partOf(r1,g) $\wedge$ partOf(r2,g) $\wedge$ Transition(t1) $\wedge$ Transition(t2)
  $\wedge$ **recommendsToPursue(r1,t1)** $\wedge$ **recommendsToAvoid(r2,t2)**
  $\wedge$ **similarTo(t1, t2)**
  $\rightarrow \exists i$ **ContradictionDueToSimilarTransition(i)** $\wedge$ relates(i,r1) $\wedge$ relates(i,r2)

Alternative Interaction due to Similar Transitions: when similar Transitions are recommended to be pursued (def. 8.1). This interaction is cumulative within a CIG, i.e. if a recommendation is related to two interactions of this type, they are the same interaction (def. 8.2)

(8.1) $\forall g, r1, r2, t1, t2$ Guideline(g) $\wedge$ Recommendation(r1) $\wedge$ Recommendation(r2)
  $\wedge$ partOf(r1,g) $\wedge$ partOf(r2,g) $\wedge$ Transition(t1) $\wedge$ Transition(t2)
  $\wedge$ **recommendsToPursue(r1,t1)** $\wedge$ **recommendsToPursue(r2,t2)**
  $\wedge$ **similarTo(t1, t2)**
  $\rightarrow \exists i$ **AlternativeDueToSimilarTransition(i)** $\wedge$ relates(i,r1) $\wedge$ relates(i,r2)

(8.2) $\forall i1, i2, r1, r2, r3$ **AlternativeDueToSimilarTransition(i1)**
  $\wedge$ **AlternativeDueToSimilarTransition(i2)** $\wedge$ Recommendation(r1)
  $\wedge$ Recommendation(r2) $\wedge$ Recommendation(r3) $\wedge r1 \neq r3$
  $\wedge$ relates(i1,r1) $\wedge$ relates(i1,r2) $\wedge$ relates(i2,r2) $\wedge$ relates(i2,r3)
  $\rightarrow$ **i1 = i2**

Alternative Interaction due to Inverse Transition: when two inverse Transitions are one recommended to be pursued and the other recommended to be avoided (def. 9);

(9) $\forall g, r1, r2, t1, t2$ Guideline(g) $\wedge$ Recommendation(r1) $\wedge$ Recommendation(r2)
  $\wedge$ partOf(r1,g) $\wedge$ partOf(r2,g) $\wedge$ Transition(t1) $\wedge$ Transition(t2)
  $\wedge$ **recommendsToPursue(r1,t1)** $\wedge$ **recommendsToAvoid(r2,t2)**
  $\wedge$ **inverseTo(t1, t2)**
  $\rightarrow \exists i$ **AlternativeDueToInverseTransition(i)** $\wedge$ relates(i,r1) $\wedge$ relates(i,r2)

Given the definitions of which and how internal interactions can be identified according to the TMR4I model, we present in the next section an approach of how to apply this model in a multimorbidity case study.

5 Evaluation on Multimorbidity Case Study

We evaluate the TMR4I model by applying it to a realistic (conceptual) experiment on combining 3 CIGs for Osteoarthritis[2] (OA), Hypertension[3] (HT) and Diabetes[4] (DB) taken from Jafarpour's thesis[3]. We make some simplification of the original case study both (i) representing only the recommendations that are relevant for studying the interactions and illustrating the approach and (ii) simplifying the features that are not yet addressed by the TMR model (e.g.

---

[2] www.nhstaysideadtc.scot.nhs.uk/TAPG%20html/Section%2010/
 osteoarthritis.htm
[3] pathways.nice.org.uk/pathways/hypertension
[4] pathways.nice.org.uk/pathways/diabetes

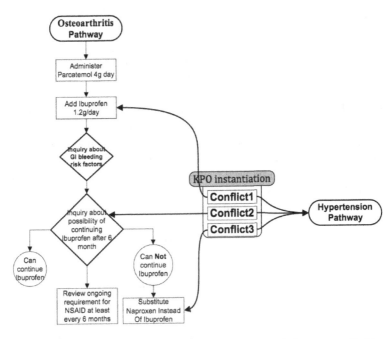

Fig. 4. The instantiation of the CPG-KPO and the parts of the osteoarthritis and hypertension pathways that participate in the merge [3]

quantities). We first introduce the experiment of [3] and then we discuss and compare with our approach.

Jafarpour (introduced in Section 2) creates constraints to resolve conflicts between tasks (recommendations) in *two* CIGs, as illustrated in Fig. 4. The three tasks regarding the administration of *Ibuprofen* or *Naproxen* are considered to be in conflict with the hypertension pathway, since these drugs may increase the blood pressure, according to experts. Then the constraints named *conflict 1, 2* and *3* are manually introduced suggesting the replacement of these drugs by *Tramadol* or similar. The role of those constraints is to interfere in the execution of the CIGs, i.e. when a task that is to be executed has one of these constraints associated, then instead of executing the task, the constraint instruction will be followed. In this example, the instructions are for substituting the task.

The goal in Jafarpour's approach is to produce a reusable *pairwise* combination of CIGs, such that several pairwised combined guidelines can be executed together to handle multi-morbidity. Besides the combination of OA+HT, the approach is applied to combine OA+DB and HT+DB such that the three of them can be executed together. As we discussed in Section 2, the interactions are not completely addressed by this approach. For instance, *Tramadol* is recommended many times in order to address the aforementioned conflicts and also to address another conflict between OA and DB recommendations, where *Tramadol* is recommended to replace *Aspirin* as anti-thrombotic. Since recommending the same drug more than once may lead to overdose, it requires attention from the experts. However, Jafarpour's approach does not detect the interaction we just mentioned.

In Fig. 5 we represent a (partial) merged CIG for OA+HT+DB and the identified interactions according to the TMR4I model. First, the effects that must be avoided for each disease, which are the reason for the conflicts, are explicitly represented as recommendations within each CIG (if this information is not yet available). E.g. for detecting the aforementioned conflict the recommendation *"Avoid High Blood Pressure promoted by Administering Aspirin"* is explicitly introduced in the HT CIG. Although this resembles the manual identification of the contradiction, it is actually not the case. Once this information is available as part of the CIG, it can be used to derive many interactions. The recommendations from the original CIG's are reused in order to create a merged CIG. Then, some interactions manually identified by Jafarpour can be derived (denoted as **C!** in the figure): (i) *Administer ibuprofen to relief pain* from OA contradicts *Do not adminster ibuprofen to avoid increase the blood pressure* from HT; (ii) *Administer thiazide to lower the blood pressure* from HT contradicts *Do not adminster thiazide to avoid increase the level of blood sugar* from DB; and (iii) *Administer aspirin to lower the risk of thrombus* from DB contradicts *Do not adminster aspirin to avoid increase the risk of gastro-intestinal bleeding* from OA.

Then, we manually introduce solutions proposed by Jarfapour, depicted in Figure 6 as the last two recommendations (one of the solutions regarding reducing the quantity is not addressed, since it is out of scope of this work). The resultant CIG is further verified by applying the same method and other interactions can be derived (denoted as **A!** and **R!** in the figure): (i) an alternative interaction is derived between recommendations for *Painkiller*, (ii) another

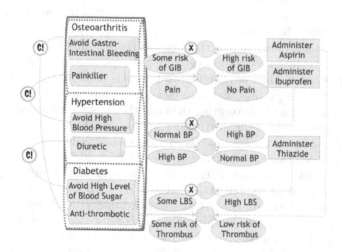

Fig. 5. Instance-schema illustrating the merged CIG for OA, HT and DB and the three contradictory interactions derived

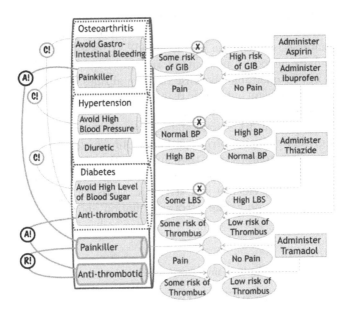

Fig. 6. Instance-schema illustrating new recommendations introduced into the merged CIG for OA, HT and DB and interactions identified

alternative interaction is derived between *Anti-thrombotic* recommendations and (iii) an repetition interaction is derived among the introduced recommendations for *Administering Tramadol*.

By performing this conceptual experiment we demonstrate that the TMR4I approach allows a more systematic detection of internal interactions both after combining CIGs and after introducing new recommendations in order to address the interactions. This approach favor the automatization of this task, in contrast with Jafarpour approach that requires ad-hoc interaction rules.

6   Discussion and Future Work

Our evaluation illustrates the improvements that can be achieved in addressing the multimorbidity task by applying TMR4I model, with respect to the studied approaches. By reusing and combining information, it improves the reasoning capabilities for deriving interactions among recommendations within several CIGs. Although there is still space for improvements in the current model (further mentioned in this section), we believe the benefits from a more detailed semantics for the CIG elements can already be observed.

While the related approaches [3,4] provide a pairwise identification of conflicts by manually introducing rule-constraints, we are able to provide the following improvements: (i) (semi)automatable identification of interactions among recommendations; (ii) detecting interactions among several recommendations within several CIGs (instead of only *pairwise* combinations); (iii) (semi) automatable verification of the resultant CIG containing new recommendations eventually introduced to address conflicts. We consider the identification of interactions to be semi-automatable (rather then autmomated): (i) "semi" because it can be needed to manually introduce implicit information required to identify the interaction and (ii) "automatable" because the formal rules we provide are simple enough to be executed by an automatic reasoner. Table 3 compares our approach to the two discussed in the related work.

As future work we plan to express and reason about hierarchies of Care Action Types (e.g. *Administer Aspirin* specializes *Administer NSAD*), as well as addressing sequencing, composition, time and quantities. Further improvements regard more detailed representation for situation types and recommendations, besides including goals, evidence and strength. Moreover, we believe that an external knowledge base providing extra information about the effects of care

Table 3. Comparison to related works

	Jafarpour[3]	Lopez-Vallverdu[4]	TMR4I Model
Core Concepts	Tasks (actions) & Constraints (rules)	Actions & Rules	TMR + Interactions
Representation of Action	Textual Not favor reasoning	Textual Not favor reasoning	Structured Favor reasoning
Language	OWL + SWRL	Proprietary Rule-based Notation	Conceptual model UML + FOL
Standard terminologies	No	Yes, ATC	Not yet
CIG knowledge acquisition	Manual	Manual	Manual
Reuse of CIG knowledge	Yes, associating rules to the original tasks	Yes, by reusing the standard terminology	Yes, copying recommendations, sharing actions/transitions
Interactions Identification	Manual Pairwise	Manual Pairwise	Semi-automatable Among several CIGs
Solutions Identification	Manual Introduced as text in SWRL constraints	Manual Introduced as standard text in a Rule	Manual Introduced as TMR recommendations
Outcome Verification	Automated by SWRL rules, limited applicability	Manual	Semi-automatable Verifiable by the same approach
Reuse of the Outcome for Combination	Yes, limited identification of conflicts among +2 CIGs	Yes, limited identification of conflicts among +2 CIGs	Yes
Implemented	Yes, allow executing together many pairwise combined CIGs	Yes, allow combining many treatments	Not yet

actions resulting from clinical trials can support both the identification of external conflicts (e.g. overdose or drug-drug interaction) as well as identification of solutions for conflicts (e.g. other drugs with same effect). Therefore we intend to reapply improved version of the model to new case studies. Finally, we are investigating the use of Semantic Web technologies to implement the TMR4I model. This will allow us to benefit from reusing medical knowledge and terminologies already available, as well as by providing reusable clinical knowledge.

7 Conclusion

With the ever aging of the population, multimorbidity is becoming a huge problem and require appropriate tools supporting the physicians to design adapted treatment plans. To this end, we have introduced in this paper the TMR4I as a conceptual model for detecting interactions among recommendations within several CIGs. We conceptually demonstrate that some improvements can be achieved in addressing multimorbidity, with respect to other studied approaches, by relying on a more detailed semantics for representing the recommendations and actions. Our approach favor combining several CIGs since it provide means for (semi) automatically identifying interactions among many recommendations within many CIGs, and effectively verifying the resultant combined CIG by reapplying the approach. In the future, we will work on the implementation of the proposed model and we will further extend the TMR4I model in order to address its limitations like the notion of temporality, besides evaluate the model on other use cases like guideline adaptation or re-use.

References

1. Boxwala, A.A., Peleg, M., Tu, S., Zeng, Q.T., Ogunyemi, O., Wang, D., Patel, V.L.: GLIF3: a representation format for sharable computer-interpretable clinical practice guidelines. Journal of Biomedical Informatics 37(3), 147–161 (2004)
2. Isern, D., Moreno, A.: Computer-based execution of clinical guidelines: a review. International journal of medical informatics 77(12), 787–808 (2008)
3. Jafarpour, B.: Ontology Merging using Semantically-defined Merge Criteria and OWL Reasoning Services: Towards Execution-time Merging of Multiple Clinical Workflows to Handle Comorbidity. Ph.D. thesis, Dalhousie University (2013)
4. López-Vallverdú, J.A., Riaño, D., Collado, A.: Rule-based combination of comorbid treatments for chronic diseases applied to hypertension, diabetes mellitus and heart failure. In: Lenz, R., Miksch, S., Peleg, M., Reichert, M., Riaño, D., ten Teije, A. (eds.) ProHealth 2012 and KR4HC 2012. LNCS, vol. 7738, pp. 30–41. Springer, Heidelberg (2013), http://www.scopus.com/inward/record.url?eid=2-s2.0-84893941704&partnerID=tZOtx3y1
5. Miksch, S., Shahar, Y., Johnson, P.: Asbru: a task-specific, intention-based, and time-oriented language for representing skeletal plans. In: 7th Workshop on Knowledge Engineering: Methods & Languages, pp. 1–25 (1997)
6. Peleg, M.: Computer-interpretable clinical guidelines: a methodological review. Journal of biomedical informatics 46(4), 744–763 (2013)

7. Sutton, D.R., Fox, J.: The Syntax and Semantics of the PROforma Guideline Modeling Language. Journal of the American Medical Informatics Association 10, 433–443 (2003)

8. Zamborlini, V., da Silveira, M., Pruski, C., ten Teije, A., van Harmelen, F.: Towards a Conceptual Model for Enhancing Reasoning about Clinical Guidelines: A case-study on Comorbidity. In: Knowledge Representation for Health-Care. LNCS, vol. 8903, Springer, Heidelberg (2014)

Learning with Partial Data for Semantic Table Interpretation

Ziqi Zhang

Department of Computer Science, University of Sheffield, UK
z.zhang@dcs.shef.ac.uk

Abstract. This work studies methods of annotating Web tables for semantic indexing and search - labeling table columns with semantic type information and linking content cells with named entities. Built on a state-of-the-art method, the focus is placed on developing and evaluating methods able to achieve the goals with *partial* content sampled from the table as opposed to using the entire table content as typical state-of-the-art methods would otherwise do. The method starts by annotating table columns using a *sample* automatically selected based on the data in the table, then using the type information to guide content cell disambiguation. Different methods of sample selection are introduced, and experiments show that they contribute to higher accuracy in cell disambiguation, comparable accuracy in column type annotation but with reduced computational overhead.

1 Introduction

The number of tables on the Web have grown to over hundreds of millions in recent years [1]. Efficiently accessing tabular data remains difficult for machines, an obstacle in automatic knowledge acquisition and towards the vision of the Semantic Web, as the classic indexing, search and Natural Language Processing (NLP) techniques fail to address the underlying semantics carried by tabular structures [4,5]. This has sparked increasing interest in research on semantic **Table Interpretation**, which deals with semantically annotating well-formed relational tables[1] such as shown in Figure 1. This work focuses specifically on annotating table columns that contain named entity mentions with semantic type information (*NE-column classification*), and linking content cells (or 'cells' for brevity) in these columns with named entities from knowledge bases (*content cell disambiguation*).

State-of-the-art methods of Table Interpretation relies exclusively on knowledge bases. A typical workflow involves 1) retrieving candidates matching table components (e.g., a column header) from the knowledge base, 2) constructing features of candidates and model semantic interdependence among candidates, and table components, and 3) applying inference to choose the best candidates. One key limitation is that they adopt an *exhaustive* strategy to build the candidate space for inference. In particular, annotating table columns depends on candidate entities from *all* cells in the column [4,7].

---

[1] Same as others, this work assumes availability of well-formed relational tables while methods of detecting them can be found in, e.g., [1]. A typical relational table is composed of regular rows and columns resembling those in traditional databases.

K. Janowicz et al. (Eds.): EKAW 2014, LNAI 8876, pp. 607–618, 2014.
© Springer International Publishing Switzerland 2014

However, for human cognition this is unnecessary. For example, one does not need to read the entire table shown in Figure 1 - which may contain over a hundred rows - to label the three columns. Being able to make such inference using *partial* (as opposed to the entire table) data can improve the efficiency of the task as the first two phases can cost up to 99% of computation time [4].

Using partial data for Table Interpretation opens up several challenges. The first is defining *partial* data - or a sample - with respect to each task. The second is determining the optimal size of the sample, as tables can vary in size and arbitrary thresholds may be ineffective. The third is choosing the optimal sample entries, since a representative sample is essential to ensure accuracy while a skewed sample may damage accuracy. Our previous work in [15] has proposed TableMiner to address the first two challenges. TableMiner starts with sample-driven NE-column classification, in which it gathers evidence for inference on a row-by-row basis in an iterative, incremental manner. The sample size is automatically determined by an entropy-based measure. It then uses column type information as constraints to guide disambiguation of cells in the column. A further 'double checking' phase follows to revise column type information and disambiguation results in a mutually recursive pattern until they become stabilized.

This work adapts TableMiner to explore the third challenge. A number of sample selection methods are introduced, based on the principles of promoting rich feature representation and reducing level of ambiguity in the sample data. Experiments are conducted on a large dataset. Results show that, compared against an 'exhaustive' baseline, using carefully selected sample data for Table Interpretation can improve learning accuracy by between 0.2 and 0.4 points in percentage depending on tasks, but significantly reducing computational overheads by up to 65% in the classification task and 48% in the disambiguation task.

The remainder of this paper is organized as follows. Section 2 discusses related work. Section 3 introduces the proposed methods. Section 4 discusses experiments and evaluation. Section 5 concludes this paper.

NE-column

Name	Area	Prefecture	
Trichonida	96,513	Aetolia-Acarnania	
Yliki	22,731	Boeotia	Content cell
Amvrakia	13,619	Aetolia-Acarnania	
Lysimachia	13,200	Aetolia-Acarnania	
...	...	...	

Fig. 1. Lakes in Central Greece (adapted from Wikipedia)

2   Related Work

An increasing number of work has been carried out in semantic Table Interpretation. Venetis et al. [11] propose a maximum likelihood model to annotate columns in a table with semantic concepts and identify relations between the subject column and other columns using a database mined with regular lexico-syntactic patterns such as the Hearst patterns [2]. A subject column typically contains named entities that the table is about, such as the first column in Figure 1. The database records co-occurrence statistics for each pair of values extracted, and the statistics are used as features in inference. Similarly, Wang et al. [12] first identify a subject column in the table, then based on subject entity mentions in the column and their corresponding values in other columns, associate a concept from the Probase knowledge base [13] that best describes the table schema. Properties of the concept are used to label the columns, and essentially this classifies table columns and identifies relations between the subject column and other columns. Probase is a probabilistic database built in the similar way as that in Venetis et al. [11], also contains co-occurrence statistics that are used by learning.

Limaye et al. [4] apply joint inference on a graphical model that represents the interdependencies among components. Table components are modeled as variables represented as nodes on the graph; then the interdependencies among variables and between a variable and its candidates formulated based on features derived from the knowledge base and the table. The task of inference amounts to searching for an assignment of values to the variables that maximizes the joint probability. Mulwad et al. [7] argue that computing the joint probability distribution in the model is very expensive. Built on their earlier work by [10,8,6], they use the same graphical model with a light weight semantic message passing algorithm for inference.

One limitation of existing Table Interpretation methods is that the construction of candidate space and their feature representation is *exhaustive*. For example, in the column classification task, they use features of all cells in a column in order to classify that column. It has been shown in Limaye et al. [4] that constructing candidate space and their feature representations is the major bottleneck in semantic Table Interpretation, while the actual inference algorithm consumes only 1% of computation time. This is further confirmed in Zhang [15]. Hence such tasks can benefit significantly from using only a small sample as opposed to complete data from a table. Further, as illustrated before, human cognition often prefers 'learning by example' as we are able to infer on partial data.

Sample based Table Interpretation opens up several questions. The *first* asks what makes an entry in a sample, since Table Interpretation deals with different tasks each requiring different types of input. The *second* asks how big a sample is optimal with respect to varying size of tables (number of rows and columns). The *third* asks which data elements in a table should be selected for a sample, as different sample entries may contribute to different learning accuracy. Though these questions connect with some challenges dealt by the research of active learning [9,3], the latter is a typical semi-supervised context where it focuses on interaction with human annotators to maximize the benefits of manually annotated training data. Table Interpretation methods however, are typically unsupervised due to the scope of tasks covered, and the uncertainty in data (e.g., number of domains) as well as their quantity.

Zwicklbauer et al. [16] is the first method that deals with semantic Table Interpretation using sample data. The goal is to annotate table columns using, as features, named entity disambiguation candidates for each cell in the column. A simple majority vote based method is used, where each candidate named entity for each cell from a sample of the column casts a vote to the concept it belongs to, and the one that receives most votes becomes the final concept label for the column. The sample has an arbitrary fixed size that is empirically decided, and the entries (i.e., cells in the column) are chosen in the order they appear in the column. Experiments show that comparable accuracy can be obtained by using the sample. The method however, does not disambiguate cells from their candidate named entities.

Our previous work in Zhang [15] introduced TableMiner that addresses the first two questions in sample based Table Interpretation. TableMiner starts by NE-column classification in an iterative, incremental algorithm using content cells in the column as input. An entropy based measure is used to automatically determine 'convergence' - a condition where additional cells are considered to add little evidence to learning. Effectively this allows TableMiner to use a sample from a column for classification, the size of which is automatically determined. Column type information is then used to guide disambiguation in the remaining cells of the column. A further 'double-checking' process follows to revise the results of the two tasks to enforce mutual dependence in a recursive manner. One question remains not answered in TableMiner is evaluating the 'goodness' of each sample entry and the effect of optimizing sample entries on learning, the goal that we aim to achieve in this work.

3   Methodology

This section firstly gives an overview of TableMiner, then describes the modifications of TableMiner for the goals set out in this work, followed by description of the sample selection methods.

3.1   TableMiner

TableMiner is previously described in [15]. It consists of two phases. The *forward learning* phase creates preliminary column concept annotations using a sample of data from the column. A sample in this task consists of a list of cells taken from the column. It is achieved by using an iterative, incremental algorithm shown in Algorithm 1. In each iteration, a cell $T_{i,j}$ taken from a column T_j is disambiguated (output $E_{i,j}$) independently, by comparing a bag-of-words feature representation of each candidate named entity whose name matches the text in the cell, against a bag-of-words representation of the *context* of the cell using certain similarity metrics. Candidate named entities are retrieved from the knowledge base, and context can be both *in-table* components such as cells on the same row of $T_{i,j}$ (to be called 'row context' in the following), or *out-table* Web page components such as table captions, Web page titles, and paragraphs surrounding the table. Then the concepts associated with the winning named entity are gathered to create a set of candidate concepts (C_j) for the column. Each candidate concept is then scored, also based on the comparison between the bag-of-words feature representation of the concept and its context. Note that concept scores can change at each iteration due to newly disambiguated cells adding new evidence. At the end of each iteration, C_j from the current iteration is compared with the previous. If scores of candidate concepts are little changed, the column classification is considered to be stable; the iterative algorithm ends and the highest scoring candidates are (C_j^+) chosen to annotate the column. The condition of 'little change' is evaluated using an entropy based measure to detect convergence in the candidate concepts' scores. Convergence essentially defines the sample size automatically.

The incremental, iterative learning algorithm with automatic stopping detection allows TableMiner to generate column concept annotations before processing data of an entire column, creating an equivalently sample-based column classification process. Empirically, it is found that TableMiner uses less than 50% of data in the majority of large tables (with more than 20 rows) in the *forward* phase.

The second *backward update* phase contains two sub-procedures. The first (Part I) uses the column concept annotations as additional feature in the disambiguation of the remaining cells. This is done by using the concept to limit candidate named entity space to those belonging to the concept only. As additional cells are disambiguated, C_j for the column is revised, either through newly added elements to C_j, or modified scores of existing ones. As a result, the winning concept for the column can change at the end of this disambiguation procedure. This triggers the second procedure (Part II), which repeats the disambiguation and classification operations on the entire column, while using the new C_j^+ as constraints to restrict candidate named entity space. This repeats until C_j^+ and the winning named entity in each cell stabilizes (i.e., no change). Effectively, this serves a 'double-checking' process to enforce the interdependency between the classification and disambiguation tasks, i.e., the disambiguated cells in a column should contain named entities with consistent semantic types.

Algorithm 1. Sample based classification

---

1. Input: T_j; $C_j \leftarrow \emptyset$
2. **for all** cell $T_{i,j}$ in T_j **do**
3. $prevC_j \leftarrow C_j$
4. $E_{i,j} \leftarrow$ disambiguate$(T_{i,j})$
5. $C_j \leftarrow$ updateclass$(C_j, E_{i,j})$
6.   **if** convergence$(C_j, prevC_j)$ **then**
7.   break
8.   **end if**
9. **end for**

3.2 Modified TableMiner – TM_{mod}

For the purpose of this study, TableMiner is modified (TM_{mod}) to contain only the *forward* phase and *part I* of the *update* phase. In other words, TM_{mod} firstly performs sample-based column classification on NE-columns then uses the concept of the column to guide disambiguation of the cells. By removing *part II* from the *update* phase,

TM_{mod} can become completely sample-based at column classification when convergence happens in the *forward* phase. The benefit compared to 'exhaustive' Table Interpretation methods could be two-fold. First, concerning column classification only, TM_{mod} can make significant efficiency improvement since it only processes a fraction of a table's data. Second, concerning disambiguation, TM_{mod} also makes savings in computation overhead by using column concept annotations as input to constrain cell disambiguation. This reduces candidate space for computation.

3.3   Sample Selection

As discussed before, TableMiner already addresses the first two issues concerning sample-based Table Interpretation. To address the issue of the 'goodness' of a sample, we propose several sample selection methods. Since column classification depends on the disambiguation of the cells in the sample, we hypothesize that a better sample should contain entries that are 'easier' to disambiguate, such that a higher disambiguation accuracy can be achieved. And we further hypothesize that a cell poses an 'easier' disambiguation target if 1) we can create richer feature representation of its candidate named entities, or its context, or both; and 2) the text content is less ambiguous hence fewer candidates are retrieved (i.e., if a name is used by one or very few named entities).

We introduce several methods to compute a score to represent the degree of preference of a cell to be selected for a sample. Given an NE-column, each cell is firstly given a preference score using one of such methods. Then the rows containing these cells are re-ranked based on these scores. In the context of Algorithm 1, the input column T_j will contain cells the order of which can be different from the original column. As a result, when convergence happens, a different sample could have been processed, possibly resulting in different classification results and then, disambiguation results.

Name length (nl) The first method gives preference to cells containing a longer sequence of tokens - potentially names of entities to be disambiguated, as the intuition is that in general, longer names are less likely to be ambiguous (e.g., 'Manchester United F.C.', 'Manchester') and therefore, easier to disambiguate. Hence the text content of a cell is tokenized and the numbers of tokens - to be called 'name length' - are compared. For example, in Table 1 'Aetolia-Acarnania' has two tokens and therefore receives higher preference over 'Boeotia'.

The next two methods evaluate the 'richness' of a cell's contextual feature representation, and in particular, focus on the use of row context. They are based on a **one-sense-per-discourse (ospd)** hypothesis. Given a relational table, if an NE-column is not the subject column of the table, then cells containing the same text content are extremely likely to express the same meaning. Note that one-sense-per-discourse is only assumed to be valid on non-subject columns, as subject columns do not always contain unique content at each cell, in which case they do however, express different meanings. A typical example is the Wikipedia article 'List of peaks named Bear Mountain'[2], which contains a disambiguation table listing different peaks sharing the same name 'Bear Mountain' (subject column). Methods of classifying subject/non-subject columns are not the focus of this paper, however, they can be found in [11,14]. The method in [14] is

---

[2] http://en.wikipedia.org/wiki/List_of_peaks_named_Bear_Mountain

used in this work. It is unsupervised, and utilizes features such as the relative position of a column to the leftmost NE-column in a table, duplicate cell content in a column, and frequency of occurrence of a column header's terms within the Web page.

The principle of *ospd* allows us to treat cells with duplicate content (from a non-subject column) as unity, to build a 'shared', larger and hence richer contextual feature representation by concatenating their row context. For example, to build a feature representation for the context of the cell at row 2 and column 3 in Table 1, we will use the context for the cells at row 4 and 5 in column 3 as well.

Method **duplicate cell content (dup)** re-arranges cells in a column and their corresponding rows by firstly grouping cells containing the same text content. Contextual features of each cell are built based on the *ospd* principle, essentially including the row context of all cells in the same group. Each cell then receives a score that is the number of cells in its group. Cells in the column and their corresponding rows are re-ranked based on this score. The combined effect with *ospd* is that top-ranked cells will have richer contextual feature representation as a larger number of row context is concatenated to create the shared contextual feature representation.

Method **feature representation size (reps)** begins in the same way as *dup* to re-arrange cells (and their corresponding rows) in a column and build contextual feature representations for each cell following the *ospd* principle. It however, defines 'richness' of a contextual feature representation by the number of tokens in the bag-of-words representation. The cells are then re-ranked by their *reps* score.

We also use a method (**ospd only**) that only applies the one-sense-per-discourse rule when building context feature representations, but preserves the original order of cells in a column. Figure 2 illustrates the transformational effects of each method on an original table.

4 Evaluation

4.1 Dataset

Two datasets, **LimayeAll** and **Limaye200** described in [14] are used. LimayeAll is a re-built dataset based on the original dataset in Limaye et al. [4]. The dataset contains over 6,300 random Web pages, most of which are Wikipedia articles. They cover multiple domains, such as film, music, games, location, organization, and events. A 'focus' table is extracted from each Web page as the target table in the experiment. The re-built version replaces the original Wikipedia pages and their focus tables by downloading the corresponding articles from the current Wikipedia website and extracting the matching tables, then annotating cells using named entities from Freebase[3]. This is done automatically by using the MediaWiki API[4] together with the Freebase MQL API[5] to map a Wikipedia article title to a Freebase topic id. It is shown in [14] that compared to the older Limaye et al. dataset, the re-built version is more balanced, and nearly doubles in size in terms of annotated named entity cells. Limaye200 contains a randomly selected

---

[3] http://www.freebase.com/
[4] http://www.mediawiki.org/wiki/API:Main_page
[5] https://www.freebase.com/query

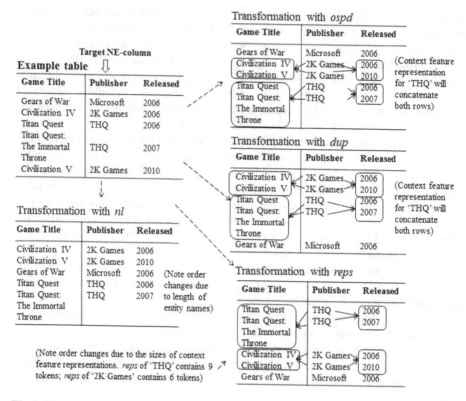

Fig. 2. Given a target NE-column, the sample selection methods re-rank the cells in the column as well as the rows containing those cells. They effectively transform the original table to a different representation.

Table 1. Experimental dataset statistics

Dataset	Task	Size
LimayeAll	Cell disambiguation	6,310 tables, 227,046 annotated cells
Limaye200	Column classification	200 tables, 615 annotated columns

200 tables from LimayeAll, and was manually annotated by concepts in Freebase for evaluating table column classification. Table 1 shows statistics of the two datasets.

4.2 Settings

We create a **baseline** TM_{bs} by modifying TableMiner to use *all* cells in a column for column classification, while leaving everything else unchanged. In the context of Algorithm 1 this means we drop the convergence check (statements 6, 7, 8). Therefore, TM_{bs} essentially represents an 'exhaustive' Table Interpretation method.

TM_{bs} is compared against five models. TM_{mod} represents the original TableMiner without the double checking procedure in the *backward update* phase, and also

Table 2. Column classificaiton results (F1) on the Limaye200 dataset and disambiguation results on the LimayeAll dataset

	TM_{bs}	TM_{mod}	TM_{mod}^{ospd}	TM_{mod}^{nl}	TM_{mod}^{dup}	TM_{mod}^{reps}
Classification	72.1	72.3	71.9	72.3	72.0	72.1
Disambiguation	80.9	80.9	81.2	81.3	81.22	81.24

without using sample selection methods. TM_{mod}^{ospd} applies the one-sense-per-discourse rule when building feature representations for cell context, but without using sample selection methods. TM_{mod}^{nl}, TM_{mod}^{dup} and TM_{mod}^{reps} each uses one of the three sample selection methods introduced above.

The standard Precision, Recall and F1 metrics are used to compute accuracy. For column classification in particular, we follow the standard practice as in [11,7,15] such that if a predicated type for a column does not match the ground truth but is a more general, related concept, it is counted as a 0.5 true positive. For example, the best semantic type for column 3 in the table of Figure 1 could be 'Greek prefecture'. If a model predicts 'Greek prefecture' it is counted as 1 correct; 'Location' as 0.5 correct; while 'Actor' as incorrect. Further, if a method predicts multiple winning candidates, each correct candidate receives only a fraction of its weight as $\frac{weight}{\#winning candidates}$ to penalize systems that cannot discriminate false positives.

4.3 Results and Discussion

As shown in Table 2, in the disambiguation task, the baseline is outperformed by any other settings but TM_{mod}, which in fact obtained no worse accuracy. This is very encouraging as it suggests that on the one hand we expect sample based Table Interpretation to reduce computation overhead in the task (to be discussed below), on the other hand it empirically results in comparable and even better learning accuracy. The three sample selection methods also added further benefits to TM_{mod}. In particular, the best performing method is TM_{mod}^{nl}. Comparing the other two methods TM_{mod}^{dup} and TM_{mod}^{reps} against TM_{mod}^{ospd}, it seems that the benefits are mainly due to the creation of a larger contextual feature representation based on the one-sense-per-discourse rule, as their improvement over TM_{mod}^{ospd} is small. Nevertheless, the consistent improvement suggests that they can make useful discriminative choices in the sample.

In the classification task, TM_{mod}^{nl} remains the best performing sample selection method, as it obtained the highest accuracy, outperforming the baseline but not TM_{mod}. However, there is little evidence of the benefits of the one-sense-per-discourse rule on this task, as none of the TM_{mod}^{ospd}, TM_{mod}^{dup} and TM_{mod}^{reps} can outperform the baseline. In fact, TM_{mod}^{ospd} slightly underperformed. While by adding the sample selection methods both TM_{mod}^{dup} and TM_{mod}^{reps} improved over TM_{mod}^{ospd}. Nonetheless, it is important to note that the sample selection methods obtained very competitive results, considering that their true benefits rest on computational savings.

To demonstrate the efficiency improvement due to sample based Table Interpretation, we study the convergence speed in the classification task. Table 3 shows the percentage of columns where convergence happened in the classification task, the average

Table 3. Analysis of convergence speed in the Limaye200 dataset. Convergence rate: the % of columns where convergence happens before all data the column are processed in the classification task; convergence speed: the average % of cells processed in these columns before convergence; Column size: the average total number of cells in these columns.

	TM_{mod}	TM_{mod}^{ospd}	TM_{mod}^{nl}	TM_{mod}^{dup}	TM_{mod}^{reps}
Convergence rate	52.7%	44.9%	53.6%	46.6%	45.3%
Convergence speed	36.4%	37.2%	36.3%	36.1%	35.3%
Column size	27.4	29.3	27.8	28.7	29.1

Table 4. Percentage of candidate named entities reduced in the disambiguation task compared to the exhaustive model

	TM_{mod}	TM_{mod}^{ospd}	TM_{mod}^{nl}	TM_{mod}^{dup}	TM_{mod}^{reps}
Reduction	34.0%	46.3%	32.4%	48.1%	46.8%

percentage of cells processed in these columns, and the average total number of cells in these columns. The advantage compared against an exhaustive method is significant: for around half of all the table columns processed in the data, less than 40% of their data were used in the classification task. Note that as shown before, the sample based Table Interpretation methods can still obtain comparable results to the exhaustive model, even if they are significantly disadvantaged in terms of the amount of input data. An average column where convergence happened contains around 30 rows, compared to an average of 11 in columns where the methods did not converge. We believe this is not a significant issue as these columns are very small.

Comparing the different sample selection methods, the best performing is again TM_{mod}^{nl} as it caused convergence in the largest number of columns and they generally converged very fast. Applying the onc-sense-per-discourse rule in fact reduced efficiency compared to TM_{mod}, as both convergence rate and convergence speed dropped. Both TM_{mod}^{dup} and TM_{mod}^{reps} build on TM_{mod}^{opsd}, and further improved efficiency.

Furthermore, we also analyzed the reduction of candidate named entity space in the disambiguation task. As Table 4 shows, through using column classification results as input to constrain candidate named entity space in the disambiguation task, all sample-based methods significantly reduced the total number of candidates to be processed by over 32%. By treating duplicate cell contents in non-subject columns as unity following the one-sense-per-discourse rule, methods TM_{mod}^{dup}, TM_{mod}^{reps} and TM_{mod}^{opsd} achieved the largest reduction. It is also clear that TM_{mod}^{dup} and TM_{mod}^{reps}, built on top of TM_{mod}^{opsd}, delivered further improvements.

It is expected that the significant reduction in the amount of data to be processed in both tasks translates to noticeable improvement in terms of CPU time. Empirically, it has been noted that over 90% of CPU time has been spent on retrieving candidate named entities for content cells from the knowledge base and building their feature representations. Computation of sample 'goodness' using any of the proposed methods consumes only less than 1% of CPU time. Overall, the results have shown clear benefits of sample based Table Interpretation methods over classic exhaustive models, as the sample based methods significantly reduce computational overhead, while in the meantime, achieve comparable and even higher accuracy. The sample selection methods appear to bring only marginal improvement in terms of accuracy, but add more notable benefits in terms of efficiency. The best performing sample selection method in accuracy is TM_{mod}^{nl}, and the best performing in efficiency is arguably TM_{mod}^{dup}, which largely benefits from the one-sense-per-discourse hypothesis.

There is, however, no correlation between the positive contribution to learning accuracy in the disambiguation task with the effect on the classification task. Manual inspection suggests that one possible reason could be the annotation system adopted in Freebase as well as its collaborative nature as a knowledge base. Freebase adopts a loose network of concepts instead of an ontology in the strict sense. A topic (e.g., a named entity) can be labeled with multiple concepts without a clear hierarchical definition. Since collaborative knowledge bases are largely driven by contributor's interest and popularity of topics, it is often the case that named entities belonging to the same semantic type are not necessarily annotated with the same group of concepts in Freebase ('Province of Quebec' has 3 associated concepts while 'Saskatchewan' has 10). This creates certain degree of 'randomness' that cannot be captured by the sample selection methods focused on the disambiguation of cells. A possible solution could be to prefer candidate named entities that have a larger group of annotated concepts. This will be explored in future.

5   Conclusion

This paper built on the idea of sample based semantic Table Interpretation, and proposed methods of making discriminative selection of sample data which can affect both learning accuracy and efficiency. Several sample selection methods have been proposed for the column classification task, primarily based on the principles of promoting richer feature representation or reducing ambiguity in the sample data. Experiments show that first of all, sample based Table Interpretation methods can significantly reduce computation cost of classic exhaustive methods, and also achieve equivalent or even better results. The selection methods are shown to further improve learning accuracy in the disambiguation task. No strong correlation is noted between the improvement in disambiguation accuracy and the classification, as they obtained only comparable accuracy in the latter task. However, these methods contributed notably in terms of efficiency. It is believed that the overall results are still encouraging, as they enable sample based Table Interpretation methods to perform equally well or even better, but with less data.

Future work will focus on several directions. First, we will address sample based interpretation in other tasks, such as cell disambiguation. Further, new sample selection methods will also be explored, and different knowledge bases other than Freebase will also be investigated.

Acknowledgement. Part of this work is carried out in the LODIE project (Linked Open Data Information Extraction), funded by EPSRC (EP/J019488/1).

References

1. Cafarella, M.J., Halevy, A., Wang, D.Z., Wu, E., Zhang, Y.: Webtables: exploring the power of tables on the web. Proceedings of VLDB Endowment 1(1), 538–549 (2008)
2. Hearst, M.A.: Automatic acquisition of hyponyms from large text corpora. In: Proceedings of the 14th Conference on Computational Linguistics, COLING 1992, vol. 2, pp. 539–545. Association for Computational Linguistics, Stroudsburg (1992)
3. Laws, F., Schätze, H.: Stopping criteria for active learning of named entity recognition. In: Proceedings of the 22nd International Conference on Computational Linguistics, COLING 2008, vol. 1, pp. 465–472. Association for Computational Linguistics, Stroudsburg (2008)
4. Limaye, G., Sarawagi, S., Chakrabarti, S.: Annotating and searching web tables using entities, types and relationships. Proceedings of the VLDB Endowment 3(1-2), 1338–1347 (2010)
5. Lu, C., Bing, L., Lam, W., Chan, K., Gu, Y.: Web entity detection for semi-structured text data records with unlabeled data. International Journal of Computational Linguistics and Applications (2013)
6. Mulwad, V., Finin, T., Joshi, A.: Automatically generating government linked data from tables. In: Working notes of AAAI Fall Symposium on Open Government Knowledge: AI Opportunities and Challenges (November 2011)
7. Mulwad, V., Finin, T., Joshi, A.: Semantic message passing for generating linked data from tables. In: Alani, H., et al. (eds.) ISWC 2013, Part I. LNCS, vol. 8218, pp. 363–378. Springer, Heidelberg (2013)
8. Mulwad, V., Finin, T., Syed, Z., Joshi, A.: T2ld: Interpreting and representing tables as linked data. In: Polleres, A., Chen, H. (eds.) ISWC Posters and Demos. CEUR Workshop Proceedings. CEUR-WS.org (2010)
9. Shen, D., Zhang, J., Su, J., Zhou, G., Tan, C.L.: Multi-criteria-based active learning for named entity recognition. In: Proceedings of the 42nd Annual Meeting on Association for Computational Linguistics, ACL 2004, Association for Computational Linguistics, Stroudsburg (2004)
10. Syed, Z., Finin, T., Mulwad, V., Joshi, A.: Exploiting a web of semantic data for interpreting tables. In: Proceedings of the Second Web Science Conference (April 2010)
11. Venetis, P., Halevy, A., Madhavan, J., Paşca, M., Shen, W., Wu, F., Miao, G., Wu, C.: Recovering semantics of tables on the web. Proceedings of VLDB Endowment 4(9), 528–538 (2011)
12. Wang, J., Wang, H., Wang, Z., Zhu, K.Q.: Understanding tables on the web. In: Atzeni, P., Cheung, D., Ram, S. (eds.) ER 2012 Main Conference 2012. LNCS, vol. 7532, pp. 141–155. Springer, Heidelberg (2012)
13. Wu, W., Li, H., Wang, H., Zhu, K.Q.: Probase: a probabilistic taxonomy for text understanding. In: Proceedings of the 2012 ACM SIGMOD International Conference on Management of Data. pp. 481–492. SIGMOD 2012, pp. 481–492. ACM, New York (2012)
14. Zhang, Z.: Start small, build complete: Effective and efficient semantic table interpretation using tableminer. In: Under transparent review: The Semantic Web Journal (2014), http://www.semantic-web-journal.net/content/start-small-build-complete-effective-and-efficient-semantic-table-interpretation-using
15. Zhang, Z.: Towards efficient and effective semantic table interpretation. In: Janowicz, K., et al. (eds.) ISWC 2014. LNCS, vol. 8796, pp. 487–502. Springer, Heidelberg (2014)
16. Zwicklbauer, S., Einsiedler, C., Granitzer, M., Seifert, C.: Towards disambiguating web tables. In: International Semantic Web Conference (Posters & Demos), pp. 205–208 (2013)

Author Index

Alec, Céline   1
Alsubait, Tahani   13
Aroyo, Lora   109
Augenstein, Isabelle   26

Bannour, Ines   413
Barker, Adam   385
Berdugo, Uriel   1
Biffl, Stefan   238
Brewster, Christopher   503
Bühmann, Lorenz   42

Cardillo, Elena   469
Champin, Pierre-Antoine   153
Chaudhri, Vinay K.   54, 66
Ciravegna, Fabio   26
Clark, Peter E.   54
Collins, Trevor   579
Consoli, Sergio   413
Cruz, Isabel F.   80
Cruz-Filipe, Luís   97

d'Amato, Claudia   304, 453
d'Aquin, Mathieu   531, 547
da Silveira, Marcos   591
Dijkshoorn, Chris   109
Dojchinovski, Milan   121
Donadello, Ivan   469
Dudáš, Marek   137
Dumont, Cyril   373

Ekaputra, Fajar J.   238
Ertl, Thomas   266
Esposito, Floriana   304, 453

Fanizzi, Nicola   304, 453
Faron-Zucker, Catherine   519
Fernández Breis, Jesualdo Tomás   288
Fleischhacker, Daniel   42

Gandon, Fabien   519
Gangemi, Aldo   413
Gaspar, Graça   97
Ginon, Blandine   153

Haag, Florian   266
Haller, Armin   485
Hammar, Karl   165
Hanika, Florian   181
Harth, Andreas   250
Hoekstra, Rinke   282, 441, 591

Ichise, Ryutaro   385
Imran, Ali Shariq   203

Jean-Daubias, Stéphanie   153
Jeschke, Sabina   197
Jongma, Lizzy   109

Kadlubek, Sabine   197
Kämpgen, Benedikt   250
Kastrati, Zenun   203
Katragadda, Rahul   66
Keet, C. Maria   209, 225
Khan, Zubeida Casmod   225
Kilfeather, Eoin   320
Klein, Ewan   385
Kovalenko, Olga   238

Lefevre, Marie   153
Lehmann, Jens   42
Lohmann, Steffen   266
Loprete, Francesco   80

Maynard, Diana   26
McCarthy, Evin   320
Melo, Andre   42
Meroño-Peñuela, Albert   282
Mikroyannidi, Eleni   288
Minervini, Pasquale   304
Motta, Enrico   339, 356, 531, 547, 579
Mulholland, Paul   320, 579

Negru, Stefan   266
Nickles, Matthias   333
Nunes, Isabel   97
Nuzzolese, Andrea Giovanni   413

Osborne, Francesco   339, 356
Overholtzer, Adam   54

Palmisano, Ignazio　288
Palmonari, Matteo　80
Papaleo, Laura　373
Pareti, Paolo　385
Parsia, Bijan　13
Payne, Terry R.　397
Pernelle, Nathalie　373
Presutti, Valentina　413
Pruski, Cédric　591

Quesada-Martínez, Manuel　288

Ratcliffe, David　429
Recupero, Diego Reforgiato　413
Reynaud-Delaître, Chantal　1
Richert, Anja　197
Rietveld, Laurens　441
Rizzo, Giuseppe　453
Rospocher, Marco　469

Sabou, Marta　181, 238
Safar, Brigitte　1
Sahar Butt, Anila　485
Saïs, Fatiha　373
Sattler, Uli　13
Scavo, Giuseppe　356
Schreiber, Guus　109
Schulte-Cörne, Stella　197
Sellami, Zied　1
Serafini, Luciano　469
Serral, Estefanía　238
Shrager, Jeff　66
Solanki, Monika　503
Spaulding, Aaron　54

Stadtmüller, Steffen　250
Stevens, Robert　288
Stilo, Giovanni　563
Stroe, Cosmin　80
Svátek, Vojtěch　137

Taheri, Aynaz　80
Tamma, Valentina　397
Taylor, Kerry　429
ten Teije, Annette　591
Testu, Benoit　385
Tettamanzi, Andrea G.B.　519
Tiddi, Ilaria　531, 547
Tsarkov, Dmitry　288

van Harmelen, Frank　591
Velardi, Paola　563
Vitvar, Tomas　121
Völker, Johanna　42

Warren, Paul　579
Welter, Florian　197
Wessel, Michael　66
Wielemaker, Jan　109
Winkler, Dietmar　238
Wohlgenannt, Gerhard　181
Wolff, Annika　320

Xie, Lexing　485

Zamazal, Ondřej　137
Zamborlini, Veruska　591
Zargayouna, Haïfa　413
Zhang, Ziqi　607